NET
OF
MAGIC

NET
OF
MAGIC

Wonders and Deceptions in India

LEE SIEGEL

The University of Chicago Press

Chicago and London

The University of Chicago Press, Chicago 60637
The University of Chicago Press, Ltd., London

© 1991 by The University of Chicago
All rights reserved. Published 1991
Printed in the United States of America

00 99 98 97 96 95 94 93 92 91   5 4 3 2 1

Library of Congress Cataloging in Publication Data
Siegel, Lee, 1945–
    Net of magic : wonders and deceptions in India / Lee Siegel.
      p.   cm.
    Includes bibliographical references.
    ISBN 0-226-75686-6. — ISBN 0-226-75687-4 (pbk.)
    1. Magic—India—History.   2. Conjuring—India—History.
    I. Title.
    BF1622.I5S54 1991
    133.4′3′0954—dc20   90-48328
                                                                        CIP

For Cheryl

who was willing to pick a card

Contents

ON THE STAGE THEN:
Bones and Earth
357

The Code:

Elements of Magic

"**M**ake obeisance to the feet of Indra, whose name is one with magic, and to the feet of Shambara, whose glory was firmly established in illusions." That is how the magic show begins. It is the invocatory stanza recited with uncanny laughter and the mannered flourish of a peacock-feather wand by the magician Sarvasiddhi as he appears in the court of the king of Kausambi in the *Ratnāvalī*, a Sanskrit romantic melodrama by Harshavardhana (seventh century). Asking the monarch what effect, trick, or illusion would be his pleasure to witness—"the moon on earth? a mountain in the sky? fire in water? darkness at noon?"—the magician boasts of a power to conjure up any world the king might wish to behold: "I shall cause Indra, the ruler of the gods, to be seen in the sky. You'll see the other gods too, headed by Brahma, Vishnu, and Shiva. And that's not all—you'll have a vision of heavenly magicians, celestial singers, and nymphs of paradise, all dancing around you" (Act 4).

My aspiration in writing this book has been to do a magic show like Sarvasiddhi's—like him to conjure up a world: the ancient and yet persistent realm of Indian magic. It is a world that I have toured in wonder both as a historian, searching and researching ancient India for the origins and history of magic, and as a traveler, searching and re-searching modern India for the remains of that magic, for the survivors—magicians now practicing the ancient art, conjurers on the street and illusionists on the stage. I'd like those earthly magicians, *jādūwālā*s and *indrajālin*s, past and present, to dance around you like the heavenly magicians around the king of Kausambi.

An inspiration in constructing this book as a magic show has been the nineteenth-century magician Robert-Houdin, who, in the overture to his *Confidences d'un prestidigitateur*, confided that in the act of writing he would be performing magic, "my audience shall be my reader, my stage this book." This book too is a set of tricks, illusions that are meant to represent realities, and realities meant to represent illusions. To accomplish these tricks I've used some of the academic methods of scholarship (in the "Historian's Notebooks"), some of the journalistic techniques of travelogue (in the "Traveler's Journals"), and some of the narrative conventions of fiction (in the "Scenes"). The "Traveler's Journals" (about India now) and "Historian's Notebooks" (about India's past) are both literally and figuratively "behind the scenes," realities behind illusions: eight scenes from the biography of an ethereal magician who incarnates and possesses again and again, then and now.

In his incarnation as the street conjurer, the ethereal *escamoteur* wanders, as he has done for centuries, from village to village, stopping here and there to lure a circle of people, hungry for diversion, with the curious call of his flute and damaru drum, hourglass-shaped like the one the god plays. The magic has hardly changed at all: a cloth ball, red or yellow, under this coconut-shell cup disappears only to reappear under that one; stones, one after another after another, larger and larger, appear from the magician's mouth, and then there are thorns and nettles, then meters of brightly colored thread, and then more dark and heavy stones; a borrowed shawl, visibly torn into shreds before the wide eyes of its dismayed owner, is suddenly, after the wave of a magic wand, a puff of magic breath, the muttering of magic words—*gilli-gilli-gilli* or *yantru-mantru-jālajāla-tantru*—made whole again before the even wider eyes of the amazed, laughing, or grimacing gathering; a mango seed, in a matter of miraculous moments, grows into a green, burgeoning bush that, to the astonishment of all, puts forth sweet, swollen fruit; a scruffy boy, the magician's son, is decapitated, or dismembered, or perhaps his tongue is cut from his mouth, and his blood, rich red with life, seeps into the earth they know, and then—how is it possible?—the child is healed, made whole, and there is genuine awe. Wonder-struck by the powers of the magician, the villagers, with their own secret hopes, fears, and desires, buy his rings and amulets, mementos of his magic, pieces of strange power. Two rupees, five rupees, eight rupees.

The villages, however, are but the camping places between the cities, where the real money is to be made, where the rings and amulets can be sold for ten, even twenty or thirty times what the magician himself has paid for them. On cluttered roadsides and street corners—horns honking, dogs barking, minds gyrating, senses throbbing, people shouting, grumbling, laughing, shoving, hawking, begging, fighting—in bazaars, markets, parks, almost anywhere, amidst any chaos, the vagrant conjurer, despite unrelenting police harassment, lays out his mat, squats down, poised and posed to begin beguiling the motley crowd. His son exhibits a dusty snake or makes a rupee vanish. "*Jādūgar! Jādūgar!*" someone calls out, "Magician! Magician! Come! Watch!" "*Jādū!*" they shout or whisper—"Magic! *Jādū!*" The Hindi word for that entertainment is tinged with the dark meanings of the Sanskrit term from which it comes: *yātu*, "sorcery, witchcraft, black magic, the powers and practices of evil spirits." The magician calmly capitalizes on the associations—a touch of fear might prod the astounded to reach into their pockets if there's money there.

There is a settlement, a Delhi slum, for these still (but less and less) itinerant street magicians; and it was there, in Shadipur Depot in June of 1987, that I first met these wonderful and outrageous characters whose world I've endeavored to conjure up in the first half of this book ("On the Street"). I claimed that I was a magician. Did they ever really believe me?

They are born to what they do. As blood members of a Muslim low caste, Maslets, bound together by a secret language and secrecy itself, they are trained in magic from infancy. The boys perform with their fathers until they are old enough to go out on their own, taking a little brother or cousin along—no one plays the magic show alone. The girls perform—handle the snakes, are stuffed into baskets, have swords passed through their necks—until they are women; then they are expected to bear new conjurers, nourish them, and teach them ancient secrets.

The magicians call other itinerant entertainers—Muslim bear handlers, monkey trainers, jugglers, and acrobats, as well as Hindu snake charmers, actors, and puppeteers—bhāi, "brother." Members of this raggle-taggle fraternity from all over India have begun to settle in Shadipur, making it not so much their home as the station from which they venture out into the world to perform. Collectively these entertainers are often called Madaris, a name that suggests an alliance with, or origin in, heterodox religious orders. And the magician cultivates the religious associations: performing near a mosque on Friday, the Islamic day of public worship, he'll whisper incantations that sound like the Arabic of the Qur'an or invoke the name of the Prophet, "Peace be upon Him"; in another part of town, near a temple later that day, he'll praise Shiva, Rama, or Krishna, and claim to have accrued his magic powers at the cremation grounds. The street conjurer is now, as he has always been, often a mock holy man; he knows there's money to be made in religion.

Likewise there are religious figures in India—priests and god-men, sadhus and gurus—who know there's money in magic, who, having learned the conjurers' sleights, pass off the effects as miraculous evidence of divine powers. In many ways such personae reenact an ancient show that was, once upon a time, set in a court and sponsored by a king. In that command performance, the ethereal magician played the priest, casting curses and binding spells, performing exorcisms and divinations, curing illnesses and warding off other evils, paralyzing enemy armies and entrancing women desired by the ruler. The later magician/entertainer played upon the performances of the magician/priest, imitating his language and gestures, evoking the mysterious mood of magic rite to enhance the sentiment of wonder that his own performance sought to inspire. Magic shows, apotropaic rituals transformed into amusing skits, became a fashionable courtly diversion in ancient India. While the magician/priest was reputed to effect changes in the world, to modulate reality, the magician/entertainer aspired to amaze and delight with that amazement, to modify not the world but our perception of it, to create illusions and a sense of wonderful wonderment. Thus the magician Sarvasiddhi typically bows, "Great king, lord of Kausambi, what illusion would you like to behold? Command, and I shall conjure it up."

In the second half of this book, the second act of the magic show ("On the Stage"), I've endeavored to conjure up the world of the stage illusionist, the realm of Sarvasiddhi, the court magician then, and now the world of the theatrical showman who, in his own mind at least, is the descendant (though more in spirit than in blood) of the courtly adept in the prestidigitatorial arts. Many of the stage magicians, to whom I was invariably introduced as a scholar, received me with hopes that my proposed book on Indian magic and conjuring might help them convince their government that they should not be taxed as entertainers, but exempted from taxation as traditional artists, guardians and perpetuators of the fine and ancient art of magic.

The modern stage magician, his court a theater, his patron anyone with a few rupees for a ticket, calls his magic *Māyā*, *Māyājāl*, or *Indrajāl*: "Illusion," "Illusion's Net," or "Indra's Net"—ancient terms for magic in India meant to distinguish it from the *jādū* of the streets. Out of the rude streets, on the unreal stage, from a burst of light and a cloud of smoke, the ethereal magician now appears most often as a maharaja. The curtains open on a dream of India's past, a moldering myth, exquisitely tawdry. In the glare and blare of it, greasepainted and electric-haloed, the modern Maharaja of Magic, to the crackle, fizzle, and blast of Indian and Western music, does a thousand tricks, Indian and Western, that he's done a thousand times before: pigeons, balls, and Campa-Cola bottles multiply or vanish; ladies are zigzagged or suspended in midair; there are flashing fountains of fire and endless streams of water gushing from a small bowl; escaping from his shackles or disappearing from a locked trunk, the magician returns to the stage, grandly bows, and, if the power does not go out, solemnly cuts a woman in two with an electric buzz saw. It's mystic kitsch and melancholy glitz. The Net of Magic now seems tattered in his hands. "Now people want to go to films or watch television," the magician sadly said to me. "We're something from the past." In him the past yearns to be present, glorious and potent. He remembers when the magician was a priest and magic a sacred rite. "The magician was a god on earth," the illusionist told me in his dressing room, "and God was a magician in heaven. That is what our scriptures say."

The wise Shvetashvatara told it to ascetics in a forest retreat: "A magician creates this world by magic. . . . Nature is an illusion and the Lord is the illusionist; the things of this world are but elements of him" (*Śvetāśvatara Upaniṣad* 4.9–10). That magician, whose magic show is this whole world, works with five elements—fire, air, water, earth, and pervading ether—combining them in a certain way so that things appear to appear, isolating them in another way so that things seem to vanish, remixing and reseparating them in still other ways to create endless metamorphoses, astonishing to behold.

ELEMENTS OF MAGIC

This book about magic is not really about magic. Magic, rather, is its method and a metaphor—a way of speaking about other things. This book is about a human need and longing to be deceived and about the pleasures of deception. India, past and present, is the setting and the set for the show. That land has always been a magic extravaganza for me, a perpetual and spectacular source of bewilderment and delight, astonishment and wonder.

As I leave the plane and make my way toward the counter—Indian Immigration and Customs—I sense that the magic show is about to begin, and I can hear the invocation: "Make obeisance to the feet of Indra, whose name is one with magic, and to the feet of Shambara, whose glory was firmly established in illusions."

ON THE STREET
NOW

_____

Birds and Fire

Scene One:

Diving Duck

The boy, soon to be sacrificed, followed the magician. He kept his eye on his father's red fez so as not to lose him in the crowd of souls who were pulled by invisible threads toward the park near the Old Fort that Sunday. The midmorning heat nagged every little affliction in the city and prodded every tired sense. The Indian sun—ancient god with flaming hair, his chariot coursing in a crisp, mythic sky—was the herald for a cloudless noon of gnawing aches and listless murmurs. Though it was not a day meant by any divinity or natural force for work, the magician, like the scavenging crow, counting on the flocks of people who sought refuge in the park, had his mind set on it. "It used to be cool here all year round. If this wasn't a paradise back then, would the Yamuna have chosen to flow by here? And why else would the Pandavas have built their palaces here, here at Indraprastha? If it wasn't once the loveliest site on earth, would Humayun have chosen this spot for his Purana Qila? The Yamuna has drifted away. The Pandavas have vanished like a dream, leaving not a trace. And Humayun's monuments are in ruins. Kali Yug! It gets hotter and hotter each year. Hotter and hotter, drier and drier, dustier and dustier. But what can we do? We have to earn a living despite it all. Never mind the heat. Never mind the dust. Never mind."

It was natural that the child should envy Adeel, his older brother, and the cousins and friends, Ayasan and the others, who, with the adult magicians, had gone to Kashmir, high in the mountains and closer to Paradise, to Srinagar, Gulmarg, Sonemarg, Pahalgam—names that conjured up fantastic images of ripe fruit and perfume-flowers, of wishing trees and wishing wells, of grassy hills and the abundant waters of freshly melted snows, trickling, dripping, flowing, gushing. He suspected that the seemingly luckier boys were eating fragrant, frost-cooled apples, drinking icy sherbets made from mangoes, tamarind, and even rose petals—every delicious thing his imagination could form and cling to. They were swimming in the bright blue currents of some wonderful lake; they rode in a painted boat. And he was left behind in the dusty heat and city chaos to be stripped to the waist and publicly slaughtered, drenched with blood as his neck was slit with the rusty dagger.

Ibrahim Pasha stayed in Delhi this summer because Kabir's mother was pregnant again, and the baby was expected any time now. Birth and death—little Kabir knew their specters. He had seen Kemal's birth and his brother's death and had himself died countless times. He had been reborn most often as a pigeon, but also as a stone, a lotus, a scorpion, a cobra, a mottled rabbit, even a small goat, but always, in the end, as himself. And today, in just a little while, his head would be offered to the dreadful goddess Kali, and once again he would retch and screech, tremble and convulse, before eager eyes.

The dry summer grass of the park was almost cool and almost soft beneath his bare feet after the miles of scorching dirt, strewn with rocks and clods, dung and garbage. The magician stopped beneath a great pipal tree. Its immense boughs must have ached as they reached and strained to hold their thirsty leaves toward heaven in such heat. "Here," Ibrahim Pasha smiled as he turned to his son, "the perfect spot, here in the shade, near the zoo, near the fort, and near the little mosque. We'll begin as soon as they're finished with prayer." Since he had lost his teeth, the magician tried not to smile with his mouth; now his pleasure and cheer would burst uncontrollably from his eyes. Toothlessness made him appear much older than he really was, and he was embarrassed by it, but the teeth that he had purchased at the bazaar blistered his gums.

Ibrahim Pasha combed his long, cinder-gray beard with his fingers and parted his darker moustache. He placed a bidi in his mouth, lit it, took a deep puff, and muttered the magic words: "God is great."

Kabir, setting down the ragged jute bag next to the baskets that the magician had arranged on the ground, squatted silently by his father as the man prepared. The boy whisked a fly away from his lips, yawned, and wiped the sweat and dust from his face with the hem of his shirt. He shut his eyes and waited. He wasn't nervous or in any way anxious about what they were going to do. He accepted it as he accepted the heat, as he submitted to everything in his life. He was resigned to suffer the noon, to play his part in the ordeal, and to endure the ritual slaying.

As soon as the first suppliants emerged from the mosque, Ibrahim Pasha began to rattle the damaru drum with one hand while holding the flute to his lips with the other. Standing and backing off, Kabir, holding the peacock feather in his hand, leaned against the tree and stood absolutely still. He knew that if he posed just like that, right there, he would, for the time being, be invisible to the gathering crowd. "It's a primary principle of magic," his grandfather said, "that any object becomes invisible when no one's looking at it." He had uttered the obvious with a tone of urgency and purpose that was only just recently becoming understandable to Kabir. The grandfather, who had taught his magic to Kabir's father, did not perform these days. Every day the aging magician was becoming more and more obsessed with prayer. He taught the boy to speak the words, and smiling gently, sometimes with tears in his eyes, he would ask him to recite: "You can say it, you can say it. God will help you learn these words: 'I take refuge in the Lord of the dawn from the evil of what he has created, from the evil of enveloping darkness, and from the evil of those who bind their spells.' "

The flute shrieked to startle sluggish passersby, to quicken dormant curiosity, to strangely lure and beckon. Then, softer and more tunefully, almost lugubriously, it called out, beseeched, and strained to entice and entrance. "Ho!" Ibrahim Pasha yelled; his henna-dyed curls, streaming wildly from beneath the clashing crimson fez, shook to the music as he played the drum faster and louder. "Ho! This is Mahadeo's drum! With this drum he started the universe going! And with this flute Krishna delighted the people of Mathura. He charmed heaven and earth with this very flute." As Ibrahim Pasha played his music, his soot-dark eyes, deep and dusky as the enchanting eyes of Krishna, laughed. He adjusted the fez, a hat he prized for the feeling it gave him that it made visible the dignity of his heart. Ready to begin, he rubbed his hands together. "Ho!"

A few men from the mosque, some loiterers from the street, several children from a tree that had offered itself for climbing, a lone family on the way to the zoo, and others—shadowy, tired people with nowhere to be and with no demands upon them beyond those that might rise up from within them at some unexpected moment, all loafing spirits with nothing more immediately asking for their attention—stood in the shade of the huge tree ready to be amused, amazed, or confused; to be, it seemed, distracted and diverted for just a moment from the other distractions and diversions of their lives. They came to be fooled. Some grinned, some grimaced, some looked blankly on.

Every crowd appeared practically identical to Kabir; it was as if the same phantoms of flesh and blood arrived to watch him die each time. There was no reason for him to care about any one of them. Those individual beings, like the balls of stuffed cloth that the magicians manipulated, could become indistinguishable from each other, completely interchangeable, if grouped and juxtaposed in a certain way; and though they did not know it, the magician, by the way he sat, by where he placed his props, by the direction in which he looked, and by innumerable other subtle sleights and unnoticed strategies, had indeed arranged his crowd.

Kabir wished his grandfather had come with them. The old man could manipulate the three cups and assorted cloth balls more boldly and dexterously than any other magician in Shadipur. A ball was placed under each cup; then all three were revealed to be under one of the cups; then they were back in their original positions; then they were gone; then they returned; then anything might happen—the three might merge into one larger ball or change color, material, or shape. There seemed to be infinite combinations to the trick and, through his grandfather's patter, each ball became some living being passing through realms of existence at the whim of the creator god, the primeval magician. "This man," the magician said with a great smile as he held up the red cloth ball, "is going to Kashmir." He then displayed a yellow ball: "And this man is going to Las Vegas, U.S.A." And then he held the blue ball in one hand as he pointed to it with the other. "And this fellow's going to Paradise. Watch him. He'll not come back."

The aging conjurer refused to perform now. Now, often to the annoyance of his family, he had become prone to philosophical reflection. "The magic show teaches us to believe something we shouldn't believe," he muttered with a laugh that mitigated the pomposity and arrogance implicit in the pontification. "In the performance, behind the illusion, beyond what seems marvelous, there's always something absolutely ordinary, some simple sleight or gimmick—a thread, a magnet, a bit of wax. What amazes is really not amazing at all. But in our lives, it's just the reverse. What seems ordinary is really extraordinary. Behind what seems simple to the eye is something very magical, absolutely amazing, and wholly marvelous."

Nissim Baba, who had the face of a bear, laughed at the old man: "Be quiet! What are you going on about? Magic doesn't teach anything. It simply amuses whatever crowds we can gather together. And that's our livelihood. Magic is how we eat. That's all."

Often their arguments would focus upon Kabir and the other children. Nissim Baba wanted to leave Shadipur, to return to the itinerant way of life. The bear face became ferocious: "A slum isn't a place for little ones." But the old man insisted that they stay for the sake of the children, so that they could attend school. "School will kill them," Nissim Baba, the lone voice for the old ways, insisted. "It will make them abandon magic. This isn't a good place. In the old days we stayed together. But now it's no good. The women, the old people, and the little children stay here, while the others go off to work in distant places. The family should be together. The government pretends they've given us something, but they're destroying us and our way of life. There won't be any more magicians in twenty years. What will happen to Kabir and Kemal, Ayasan and Salma, and the others? There won't be any more magic in the years to come."

Kabir stepped forward holding what appeared to be a rope, an old bicycle chain which Ibrahim Pasha had encased in a woven cotton tubing that was knotted at each end. He wiggled the device for all to see as his father, with English words, proudly announced the "Old Indian Rope Trick!" Kabir set the rope on the ground and waved his hands over it as he said the magic words, "*Gilli-gilli-gilli!*" And then he lifted it again, turning it and carefully holding it so that the links of the concealed bicycle chain stretched straight out, parallel to the ground. The rope, to the delight of the small crowd, seemed to defy the most basic laws of nature, as if to prove that the intractable force that pulls all things to earth could, if one only knew the secret, be overcome. Anything is possible for the conjurer. Death itself, if one only knew the right magic, might be outwitted.

DIVING DUCK

"How long have you been doing that trick?" the father asked his son with theatrical grandeur, and the seven-year-old boy recited the next line from the remembered script of the little play, an agon that had been performed in exactly the same way by Ibrahim Pasha and Kabir's grandfather years before, when Ibrahim Pasha was Kabir's age.

SON *(proudly):* Ten years!
FATHER *(laughing):* How's it possible? How old are you?
SON *(haughtily):* Twenty years old!
FATHER: Eh? If you're twenty years old, why are you so small?
SON: Because I've been worn down by all the walking my damn father made me do!
FATHER *(with mock anger):* Shut your mouth, you little liar!
SON *(sassily):* Then how will I eat?
FATHER: Through your ass!
SON *(laughing):* How's that possible, old man?
FATHER: Why shouldn't it be possible? After all, you have a hole there—I saw it.
I saw you shitting in the field this morning.

The crowd laughed, and their laughter seduced new onlookers into the group.

"Move along, little boy. These good people want to see real magic," Ibrahim Pasha said as he displayed the bamboo sticks which he himself had cut and fitted with the gimmick for the illusion, an apparatus worn and stained ashen brown by season after season of manipulation. Holding them with an end of each in one hand, his other hand was free to gesticulate and silently shout or whisper, to wave and weave wonders in the air. That soft and steady hand, so full of grace and miracles, directed all eyes to the ends of the sticks, which radiated away from each other. A distinction was clearly indicated: from the end of one stick a tasseled string dangled down, while from the end of the other there was no string visible, only the tassel which Ibrahim Pasha pulled slowly and with great purpose. As he tugged upon it, the tassel of the other cord rose up. Observing two actions, a pulling down and a simultaneous rising up, the not-yet-bewildered spectators, their minds as eager as all minds are to perceive connections in the world, saw a cause and saw an effect. But that was not what Kabir saw.

Pulling one tassel and then the other, again and again, creating the impression that the cord ran down one stick, across his palm, and up the other stick, Ibrahim Pasha was taking his time, hoping that in noticing the small group gathered around him, other strollers in the park might join them. "Although they might appear quite ordinary, these are magic sticks," the magician announced with a playful rolling of his head. "With these sticks Raja Bhoj performed for Akbar in this very spot, in the shade of this very tree. It's true. I swear it. God is my witness."

Kabir watched for the police. If they arrived, Ibrahim Pasha would have to make the quick choice, that difficult decision between moving along to find another crowd in a spot safe from the law, and staying put, which meant paying the police the customary bribe to let him finish his performance. It was all a question of balance: if the audience was rich and generous enough, something the magician was experienced at assessing, it was worth paying the bribe. The magician was not afraid of the police. And he was confident in his power to perform the teleportation, what his own father used to call "the only trick that counts": the magician transfers the money from the pockets of his spectators into his own purse before their open eyes. Wit is the gimmick, charm the gaff.

Ibrahim Pasha now had one bamboo stick under each arm and still, when he pulled down on the tassel of one, the tassel of the other rose. "You don't believe these are magic sticks? You think that there's a thread behind my back?" That was Kabir's cue. He ran up, grabbed one of the sticks, and jumped back, taking a position four or five meters away, making any real connection between the sticks impossible. "Give me that stick!" the magician shouted with convincing anger. "No!" the boy yelled with equally credible defiance. Ibrahim Pasha chuckled to give the fidgeting audience just a bit of the comfort and reassurance that it needed at this potentially awkward moment. Slowly he pulled down on the tassel of the stick in his hand. And slowly the tassel on Kabir's bamboo stick rose as the boy tilted the tip of that stick imperceptibly upward, allowing the weight concealed in it to slide slowly down.

A pair of emerald green parrots seemed to watch the performance from the tree above. Their heads turned. Their eyes blinked. Kabir held the inverted top of one of the magician's straw baskets up before each spectator to collect however many paise conscience or appreciation bade them give. Moving quickly from person to person, he stopped in front of a foreigner who had joined the crowd, a man with wire-rimmed glasses, dark curly hair, and fingers as pale as a leper's. The traveler smiled at the little boy, looked around a bit self-consciously and, as if in response to the judgment of the eyes upon him, he nervously rummaged his pockets for coins. Kabir waited patiently for him to find something. He had been taught that while foreigners are much more reluctant to pay than Indians, they will, if they pay at all, sometimes give more than Indians. The traveler put a rupee in the basket.

Ibrahim Pasha held up a cylinder of pleated cardboard. "Brahm himself taught this magic to me in a dream," he teased as he folded, bent, and twisted the cylinder into an umbrella, then a pot, then a top hat, then a pestle, then a fan, then some other recognizable thing—on and on, object after object appeared, disappeared, and reappeared transformed. The dirty cardboard, worn supple by the magician's handling, like the one sacred and absolute reality fancied in Hindu philosophy, assumed manifold, nameable forms, wholly recognizable through the magic power of imagination and perceptual superimposition.

DIVING DUCK

A crow, drawn by the snacks that several spectators were eating, watching the spectacle from above, turned its head sideways and opened its beak. The people saw the illusions, the crow saw the truth—a mere piece of cardboard. It squawked. Kabir threw a stone at the bird and waved his hands about to make it fly away, so that its rude, cacophonous cries would not distract his father's audience.

While the attention of the crowd was diverted, Kabir set up the rug and the bowl, rigging it with the long and undetectable horse-tail hair, for Ibrahim Pasha's next wonder. Even Kabir, who had seen his father do the trick a thousand times, could never catch him attaching or detaching that horsehair to or from the small wooden duck. The fine thread that had naturally been suspected to connect the bamboo sticks would be unsuspected here. The logic and perceptivity in which the audience would so naturally, so rashly and yet necessarily trust, would work together to deceive them.

Ibrahim Pasha was reciting a verse by the poet after whom his son had been named:

> The firebird built his nest
> Aloft, between earth and sky;
> His faith needs no place to rest—
> The firebird will never die.

Kabir put his hand in the water that would be used for the trick and wetted his lips with it and then his eyelids and his temples. He looked at the foreign traveler and wondered where he was from and why he was there. "Why are any of these people here on such a day?" He saw young Asad, the stooge, approach and nonchalantly take a place in the still growing crowd. No one would ever guess that he too was a player in the performance.

"Have you ever been married?" Ibrahim Pasha called out to the young mullah from the mosque who had come to investigate the commotion. "Yes," the man smiled. "And your father—was your father ever married?" Loud laughter, triggered by the magician's irreverent joke, drowned out the mullah's answer. Kabir laughed too. Laughter bound strangers into a group; later fear would reinforce the bond. Handing the man the small wooden duck, the magician asked him to tell the other spectators what it was. "A duck," the mullah said, and the magician laughed. "No, it's not a duck. A duck has feathers and is big. It's a piece of wood shaped like a duck. It's nothing but a painted toy. Ah, but you are a mullah, and mullahs surely don't lie. So if you're not lying, you must be stupid." The mullah, his clear eyes and the full cheeks above his pitch-black beard radiating good humor and a deep warmheartedness, laughed with the crowd that laughed at him. "I'll help you. I'll make the piece of wood come alive. With my marvelous magic I'll make the toy become a duck, a real duck, so that no one can call you a liar or a fool. I must blow on it to give it the power of breath. I must gaze at it to give it the power of the eye. I must rub it to give it the power of touch. I must mutter mantras on it—*yantru-tantru-jālajāla-mantru*—to give it the power of speech. All these powers I accumulated at the cremation grounds. If any of you don't believe what I'm saying, you're taking a grave risk. If you don't believe every word I utter you'll have bad luck for the rest of the year. It's certain. I'll show you my power." The magician held up a lime that appeared entirely ordinary to all who were present except Kabir and Asad. As he cut the small fruit in half, blood oozed from it. "Ho!" He squeezed the lime, and where the blood-juice dripped, right where Kabir had planted the sodium, smoke sputtered from viciously sparking, spitting fire. "This is the fire that burned Lanka!" The amusement of the crowd was tempered by an uneasy moment of a subtle fear that foreshadowed sharper and more palpitant terrors to come. Apprehension made them all the more vulnerable. Kabir wondered if they would dare to doubt him, or suspect that he did not have real powers, dark and dangerous. "These powers you can only get from the cremation ground. It's true. Don't doubt it. Doubt is from the devil. It doesn't matter whether you are rich or poor, man or woman, young or old, Mussulman or Hindu, pir baba or matted-hair baba—you can have these powers if you eat and sleep in the cremation grounds." Kabir disliked that part of his father's patter, because it made him imagine that the spectators would assume that he lived in the place of death amidst smoldering corpses with dogs and jackals, crows and vultures as his companions. He had seen the burning grounds of the Hindus, watched the white-wrapped corpses borne upon the bamboo stretchers to the pyre. Amidst prayers and lamentations, skulls were broken and death-fires blazed.

Ibrahim Pasha sliced another lime, squeezed it, and there was more blood, smoke, and fire. "Such limes with blood for juice grow in abundance in Kerala," a man, barely overheard by Kabir, whispered knowingly to his wife. "I have seen them with my own eyes. It is said—in one of the *Purāna*s I believe, though I am not absolutely certain which one—that wherever a human sacrifice was performed in ancient times, upon that very spot a tree would grow and produce fruit that would have human blood as its juice. And if you eat one of those limes, it will burn you up from the inside. This is the truth."

The brightly painted little wooden duck floated lifelessly on the dirty water. "What a stupid duck," Ibrahim Pasha laughed. "That's because it's a jungle duck, a tribal duck. But this duck loves music!" And as he started to play the gourd-flute and beat the drum, it seemed that the duck danced in time to the music, bobbed about upon the waters with the bewildering joy of finding itself suddenly animate, almost really alive, and shaking with real spirit to the gleeful tune. The line that separates the living from the dead, the real from the unreal, blurred and faded. And all of sudden, the moment Ibrahim Pasha stopped playing, the duck disappeared beneath the surface of the water. "Oh no! The duck is drowning," Ibrahim Pasha called out and reached into the bowl, pulling out the little toy that then seemed to jump out of his hand and into the crowd. When a spectator tossed it back, it lay lifeless at the magician's feet. "You've killed it," Ibrahim Pasha teased. "Who will pay for the cremation of the duck? Who will give something for the widow, for all the little ducklings? Whose heart here is not made of wood?" With appreciative laughter a few good sports tossed coins to Kabir. "But wait!" the magician smiled. "Is the duck really dead?" He quoted his own version of another verse by the poet Kabir:

> If I burn down my house, in fact I'll save it;
>   When I think I've kept it, in truth I gave it.
> I've seen a magic show performed within my head:
>   Death was tricked and fooled, swallowed up by someone dead!

Quoting Kabir, the magician believed, always informed the show with a certain urgency and power. It turned trivial tricks into sublime mysteries. The poet's words were seductive and full of authority; his very name, voiced loudly and with genuine respect, pleased Hindus and Muslims alike. And to please was one of the magician's primary objectives. "One who dies before his death, according to Kabir," the conjurer continued, pointing a finger of his right hand toward heaven to distract the eyes of his audience from what his left hand was doing, "becomes immortal in this Kali Yug!"

With a pass of the peacock-feather wand, the painted duck danced once more upon the water in the metal bowl, and Ibrahim Pasha played his pipe again to celebrate the little resurrection. "From life comes death. From death comes life," the magician observed as he set aside his flute. "That's magic." Kabir took the diminutive duck in his hand and held it up for the audience to see as he circled to collect their offerings. A few rupees were thrown into the magic circle, and as he gathered them up, Kabir prepared to vanish and to be transformed, automatically rehearsing in his heart each turn and step of the next trick.

Delhi was a furnace by noon, a great sacrificial pit that only appeared to be a city, and the lustral heat of it made it hurt to breathe deeply; the air would scorch the lungs and burn through the membranes there to incinerate the heart. And yet the crowd remained, perhaps for the shade of the great pipal tree, perhaps for the distraction provided by the show, for a refuge from reason and reality, or perhaps simply because the infernal temperature made it impossible to move away. Kabir wiped the sweat from his face with his sleeve. The fires of the early summer sun melted thought and stultified the will.

"There are women in Bengal who can turn men into goats and goats into men," Ibrahim Pasha joked. "It's true. I swear it. So why do we need an army? The government should just conscript a few Bengali women!" The audience laughed. "I could be of service to our government, for through my magic powers—secrets I learned from a Bengali woman—I can turn a man into a woman. I could turn the army of Pakistan into a band of females. Then our army could easily defeat them. I could do the same in China, in Sri Lanka, or anywhere else. Our army could take over the world. I could turn the men of the British cricket team into a bunch of English ladies." On cue Asad interrupted: "*Sālā!* Stop your boasting and get on with your tricks!" The crowd, their cheerful laughter abruptly silenced, turned to look at the audacious young man among them. "Go away, you fool," Kabir shouted as he was supposed to do, and Ibrahim Pasha scowled: "What? Do you doubt that I have the power to change a man into a woman?" Asad responded confidently: "Of course. No one can do such a thing." The magician invited his confederate to come forward out of the now nervous group. He moved his hands around in front of Asad's eyes as if to hypnotize him, to exert his magic power over the soul of a skeptic. "When I say the mystic words, my powerful mantra, this man will be a woman: *yantru-tantru-yantru-mantru!*" All at once Asad grabbed his testicles and screeched in a falsetto voice: "They're gone!" He stamped off in an exaggerated imitation of a woman's gait, and the crowd laughed once more.

Asad, who performed as the planted bystander for several of the Delhi conjurers, was what Kabir's family called *jāngaḍ*—he was an orphan who had been found by the magicians, saved by them from the perils of the streets, and raised among them as a Maslet. He knew their magic but, because he had not been born a Maslet, he would never—at least not in this lifetime—be able to marry into the caste, nor could he teach the magic to his own sons. But he was content to be a shill and absolutely good-humored about it. Asad was a natural actor and comedian, and Kabir was very fond of him. He could even joke about all the trouble he had had with the police. Asad had a way with both women and animals; he caught scorpions, snakes, and birds for the magicians to use. Sometimes Ibrahim Pasha or one of the other magicians would call him forward from the audience, pretend to hypnotize him, and then ask him to stick out his tongue. He would wiggle the goat's tongue he had concealed in his mouth so convincingly that no one ever suspected it was not his own. Then the magician, to the horror of his crowd, would cut off the tip of that tongue, shake the bleeding piece of flesh around before the eyes of the spectators and, as Asad rolled about on the ground gasping and spitting up blood, he would threaten: "If each of you gives me two rupees I'll restore his tongue. If not, this young fellow will never speak again! He'll never sing, he'll never pray! The money's for him, not for me. Be merciful!"

At Ibrahim Pasha's signal, Kabir jumped into the basket and stood there as the magician, with never a pause in his patter, placed the basket top on the boy's head and then draped the expansive, black blanket over him. Suddenly, at the moment indicated by a slap from his father, Kabir collapsed into the basket and, in preparation for the next stage of the trick, quickly untied the cord that secured the scruffy pigeon he had crammed into the load, the slender, hidden compartment in the basket. In the blanketed basket's darkness, womb-shaped and stifling, Kabir, clutching the pigeon close to him, squirmed into position, curling himself around the inside of the basket and pressing his back into the wicker. The pigeon—from terror, not from training—didn't move. But Kabir felt the furious pounding of the little heart beneath his fingers. Ibrahim Pasha jumped into the basket to convince the crowd that Kabir had truly disappeared. The boy pushed back to stabilize himself in a circle around his father's stamping feet. "Gone! Gone from this world! Completely gone!" Ibrahim Pasha yelled out, and Kabir felt the basket tipping one way and then the other as Ibrahim Pasha showed the audience that there were no escape hatches. In silence he endured the blows his father inflicted on the basket. Once Kabir was out of sight, the crow returned to the pipal tree, and the boy could hear its mocking squall.

While Ibrahim Pasha talked to the crowd of miracles and transformations, Kabir, to survive the heat, controlled his thoughts: he heard a rushing of the waters of the Yamuna; he pictured the icy peaks of the Himalayas; he smelled the apples of Kashmir. He imagined releasing the pigeon, seeing it soar and spire to cool heights, turning white as snow or cloud as it spread its wings to catch an ethereal current that would carry it into Paradise. He thought of disappearing, truly vanishing into a pleat in time, a fold in space, some hidden compartment in the universe. He tried to make the illusion real and, for a moment, the oblivion that his mind had conjured up gave him asylum.

When Ibrahim Pasha pulled the blanket away, light pierced the weave in the wicker, and the little boy readied himself. The first sword entered the basket from the top, straight down through the basket cover that concealed Kabir from sight, the cover he had used to collect offerings from the crowd. That sword, in no way endangering him, was the signal to move his legs slightly apart for the second sword to enter between them, the prompt, in turn, to move his arm so that the third sword could enter the basket between that arm and his side. Five swords pierced the basket and were removed. That proved, beyond all doubt, that the basket was empty. The blanket was replaced over the basket and it was dark again, as dark as if he had really been killed by the swords or vanished into the void.

Pretending to pluck a mosquito from the air and place it in the basket, the magician reached in to Kabir, who handed over the pigeon so that all would imagine that the captured insect had been turned into a bird. And then the bird, returned to the basket by Ibrahim Pasha and stuffed back into its load by Kabir, seemed to be suddenly transformed into the boy: when he jumped up and out of the basket, the crow took flight as the audience marveled at the miraculous metamorphoses. Once again Kabir passed in front of them with the basket top for a collection.

Ibrahim Pasha asked the mullah if he had any coins, and when the man produced one, the magician made a joke, teased the mullah, suggested that he had kept for his own what pious Muslims had given as charity for the poor. He had the man close his hand around the coin. When he opened his fist, there was dirt where the money had been. "Where's the coin?" the magician shouted. "Who's the thief?" he asked as he approached the foreigner. The magician opened the flabbergasted traveler's hand, and a coin fell out of it. Everyone, including the mullah, the traveler, and Kabir, laughed.

Ibrahim Pasha sat down on the ground and covered his lap with the blanket while Kabir moved the basket aside and prepared the props for the sacrifice. The magician sprinkled uncooked grains of rice into the blanket in his lap. "My legs form the stove," he said, beginning a list of correspondences worthy of those made by the Vedic priest at more solemn rituals. "My hand is the ladle, my tongue is the fire, my words its flames." And as he winnowed the rice, right before the eyes of the startled spectators, the rice was cooked. Kabir placed the puffed grain in the basket top and passed it around for tasting.

Kabir was ready to die now, "to die before his death," as the poet said. The young child knew what death was. He had seen his twin brother die, burned to death when the kerosene can had exploded the year before. He had heard the agonized weeping of his mother and father, his grandfather, and the other magicians. It was after that death that the grandfather had given up performing magic. "Your brother has gone to Paradise," the old man said with tears in his eyes. "And there he beholds the splendor of God as plainly as you and I see the radiance of the sun from here on earth."

"What tricks do the magicians perform in Paradise?" Kabir asked.

"There are no tricks in Paradise," the magician smiled. "No one needs magic there, just as no one needs sleep. Ah, but if you want to perform a trick in Paradise you may, and all the divine angels will surely extol you. But no one will be fooled by what you have done, for everyone in paradise understands everything completely and perfectly."

Kabir removed his shirt, and Ibrahim Pasha, ready to sacrifice his son, placed the dark, heavy blanket over him once more and menacingly waved a dagger about, the same knife he had used to slice the lime in half. "Kali appeared to me in the cremation ground. She will visit Mussulman, Hindu, Christian, or non-believer. She doesn't care. She spoke to me, her mouth dripping with blood. 'I hunger,' she said. 'Make a sacrifice to me,' she ordered." As the magician spoke in ghoulish, histrionic tones that penetrated the hearts of his spectators, Kabir drew the vial of what they called "magician's blood" from the pouch in the blanket, rubbed the crimson, clotted liquid on his throat and chest, positioned the trick dagger, and wiped his hands clean on the woolen blanket. When Ibrahim Pasha reached beneath the dark cover with the real knife, Kabir took it from his hand and placed it in the loop where the gimmicked dagger had been secured.

The little boy screamed and began to thrash wildly about under the blanket. "Do you dare to look?" Ibrahim Pasha shouted. "Women! Turn your eyes away!" The blanket was thrown back to reveal the small child with the knife penetrating his neck below one ear and emerging, bloodstained, underneath the other. As the father lifted his son by the knife, the boy waved his arms about and shook his knees spasmodically. The fragile body twitched and twisted as several of the spectators yelled out, "No! No!" And when the body slumped, the father lowered his son to the ground. The boy lay moaning softly, just loudly enough to suggest that the tenacious spirit of life still, though tenuously, resided in the blood-drenched flesh. It was that spirit that cried so piteously. "I must pull the knife all the way through so that I can take this head to Kali. She will add it to the garland of heads that decorates her breasts."

The foreign traveler, though he surely knew that it was a simple illusion, appeared disturbed, responsive to some dreadful reality latent within it. The ravening crow returned and this time watched in silence. The mullah glanced at his watch. The man who knew so much about the limes in Kerala reassured his wife that everything would be all right. A child grinned. An old woman looked away.

Ibrahim Pasha paused. The air was on fire and no one, not a single soul, moved. "Shall we spare the boy? There's a way! Kali will take a goat in place of the child. Ah, but that will cost hundreds of rupees and I'm not a rich man. You'll have to help me. If each of you gives me only two rupees I'll have enough to purchase an animal for the sacrifice. God, the merciful, the compassionate, the king of judgment, gave you your money. The least you can do is part with two rupees to save this little child."

As the people who had gathered around the spectacle began, solemnly and uneasily, to throw their money on the ground, Ibrahim Pasha carefully and gently covered his son with the blanket once more. Kabir switched the gimmicked knife for the real one and handed it to his father as soon as the man reached under the blanket. The magician wiped the blood from the dagger and slowly, somberly pulled the cover back. He kneeled down by his child and placed his head against the small chest and his fingers by the boy's nostrils. "The heart doesn't beat. The lungs don't breathe. What can we do? Can we revive him as we revived the little painted duck? That was a toy, made of wood! This is a real child, formed by God Almighty out of flesh and clots of blood." He whispered with tears gathering in his eyes, and the crowd was so still, so silent, that each and every whisper was as clearly audible as a scream. "We can trust God. God is merciful!"

The lies were bold but effective. It was surprising that Ibrahim Pasha would behave in this way and then even go so far as to paraphrase the Qur'an in the presence of the mullah: "When one of the children of the Prophet (peace be upon Him!) died, the Prophet (peace be upon Him!) spoke: 'Wash the child three times with water and lotus leaves and camphor.' I do this now to bring my son back to life. Ho!" the magician yelled. "Ho!" He sprinkled Kabir with water. "Ho!" He placed a leaf upon the boy's chest and a drop of oil upon his forehead. And Kabir opened his eyes. He sprang to his feet, smiled shyly, and Ibrahim Pasha smiled too. The magician himself applauded—"Ṣābāṣ! Ṣābāṣ!"—and grinned expansively, happily exposing his toothlessness, as Kabir collected the money that had been donated to redeem him from death.

"Praise be to God, the merciful, the compassionate!" the magician muttered, and some members of the crowd, relieved to see the boy alive, inspired by a vision of resurrection, or for whatever other reason, pushed forward to purchase the amulets that the magician now offered for sale. "Praise be to God to Whom all praises are due."

Asad, fully transformed back into a man, returned to help Ibrahim Pasha gather up his equipment. He brought a cool Campa-Cola for Kabir. The magician offered a bidi to Asad, lit one himself, and took a deep puff on it.

There were, as usual, stragglers after the performance. A man in Western clothes, someone that Kabir had not noticed in the crowd, took Ibrahim Pasha aside. Kabir listened as the man nervously explained that he had a son who was very confused. Confusion was making him weak, and weakness was making him wicked. The young man's marriage had been arranged, and a great dowry offered, but the insolent fellow was suddenly insisting that he had no intention of marrying and that he was going to go off to America. Ibrahim Pasha produced a lime and a nail from his bag. "You must take this lime. Write the name of your son upon it in black letters. Do you understand? Then, while your son is sleeping, you take this nail, only this nail, and with it you pierce the lime and you squeeze out one small drop of juice onto your son's forehead. Only one. Do you understand? The very next night you must do the very same thing. Pierce the lime in a different spot and squeeze out one more drop, only one, onto your sleeping son's forehead. Do you understand? You do this each night for ten nights, only ten, and then your own will will become the will of your son. What you desire he will desire. He will be a model of obedience." After the man had purchased the lime for twenty rupees and the nail for five, the magician warned him: "You must follow my instructions exactly. Otherwise something terrible might happen."

"What could happen?" the frightened man asked.

"Your son could die. Or he could become even more disobedient than he is now. Only God knows."

Then, while Kabir and Asad carefully packed the baskets and bags, Ibrahim Pasha spoke to the traveler. Because the man could not converse in their language, he spoke to the magician through another man, an Indian who, it turned out, claimed to be something of a magician himself.

On the bus bound for Shadipur Depot, Kabir climbed onto his father's lap to make room for Asad on the seat next to them. The *jāṅgaḍ* asked Ibrahim Pasha what the foreigner had wanted. "I'm not sure. He wants to visit Shadipur. He wants to see more magic and ask questions about it. He's writing some sort of book. He asked about the Indian Rope Trick. He loved our magic. Of course. No wonder. We were great today. When I looked at Kabir lying there on the ground, I actually almost started to weep. For an instant I imagined that he was dead. I was almost tricked by my own trick!" Kabir took the tiny painted duck out of his pocket, looked at it, and then closed his fingers around it.

DIVING DUCK

As the magicians were making their way home to Shadipur, the traveler was drinking a bottle of Golden Eagle beer in his room in Sunder Nagar. He tried to formulate some way of describing and explaining what he had witnessed: "The magician performed the Diving Duck routine, the Chinese Sticks, the Indian Basket Trick, and other conventional tricks including a bizarre and grotesque decapitation. He claimed that Kali wanted his son's head! The performance recapitulated Vedic sacrifice, in which the head of the Prajapati he-goat replaces the head of a human victim. But it recapitulated something more universal, more timeless, as well. The infanticidal impulse, perhaps dormant in every father, with its correspondent fear, perhaps latent in every son, was presented in the trick just as in the ancient rite. The myth in which Shiva beheads his son, Ganesha, was reenacted. A sinister fantasy was played out. What was the appeal of that? Why did everyone pay the magician (or the priest) for doing that? Did he diffuse or in any way resolve their anxieties? Our dread? Looking out at the performance, the audience, I suspect, saw into themselves. Ourselves. Myself. I was the magician. I was the child. That was the trick. . . ." Every sentence he wrote seemed lifeless, either tediously descriptive, ponderously analytic, or overladen with self-indulgences. The written words were devoid of magic. The traveler felt the pain and terror of language. Magic that was startling to see was drab in written description. He crumpled up the piece of paper and threw it into the wicker wastebasket.

Kabir, his head resting on his father's shoulder, rocked by the bus, let sleep begin to take him. He had just entered a dream—there was an owl, then a crow with a piece of smoldering meat in its beak, perched upon a basket in which there were dead falcons—when his father shook him slightly. He opened his eyes and looked around to remember where he was and what had happened—the bus, heat, hunger, home. . . .

"We're here. Come on," Ibrahim Pasha said as he eased his son from his lap. It was getting dark and Asad was gone. "Come on, let's go," he smiled as he handed Kabir the little duck that had fallen from the boy's grip. "Let's go home. Let's see how your mother is. Tomorrow we'll work on the Diving Duck Trick. You'll be doing it by yourself soon. Let's go," the magician said in the magicians' secret language.

Grandfather, meeting them as they approached their tent, made the announcement: Kabir's mother was at the Love and Mercy Medical Clinic. A magician had been born. *Bismillah!*

The moon and one star had appeared in the sky, and a falcon, a dark hawk in silhouette, circling high and then, as if finding some invisible rampart of air, coming still, to rest and watch, power-poised in some sultry current, floated in the infinite freedom of the plenitude above, way, way above, watching with the last light of dusk for its prey, some nocturnal animal urged by instinct to come out in the night.

And, some miles away, the traveler had started again: "The boy, soon to be sacrificed, followed the magician. . . ."

Traveler's Journal 1:

Delhi

The taxi driver could not understand why I wanted to go to Shadipur, that terrible and wonderful slum on the grimiest fringe of south Delhi, a murky realm of poverty and enchantment, of dilapidated hovels and smoky dreams. Shadipur is the eating, mating, and sleeping place, the birth and death place, of jugglers and acrobats, mimes and bards, painters and minstrels, puppeteers and pickpockets, snake charmers and monkey trainers, bear handlers and panhandlers, performers and players of every sort. And it is the sumptuously squalid home of the Delhi *jādūgars*—street conjurers, inheritors and preservers of an ancient tradition of magic. They are people with rich blood and baffling splendors in their eyes. With intractable hopes and urges, with schemes and dreams, plots and plans real and unreal, these souls have come from near and far, have extended intricate lineages from Uttar Pradesh and Rajasthan, from Maharashtra and Andhra.

This is the haunt and home of chickens and goats soon to be slaughtered, of ravenous crows and screeching mynahs, scratching dogs and sleepy cats, tethered mongooses and devenomed cobras, fearless rats and fantastic, primordial insects, all frenzied by the heat of the summer in which I made my first trip to Shadipur.

The hot and dusty breath of the earth, the pant and moan of it, and the hot and rude rub of the sky, the growl and grunt of it, were inescapable. The heat of the city at that time of year is always and exquisitely infernal. Reality melts away. We are in a cauldron of illusions. It's a mirage, persisting as if from some compulsive conviction to substantiate the ancient Indian philosophical axiom that the world is all appearance with no essence of its own, that what we perceive, like a city of cloud or the horn of a hare, like a vast, collective dream in which each dreamer dreams all others, is false: this world is *māyā*—it is a magic show. And the magician is known as God. "This *māyā*, this magic trick I do," the deity, as he reveals himself in the *Bhagavadgītā*, says, "conceals me. Not everyone can see me—the unborn and undying one."

25

Like Krishna, that magician-god, the ancient charioteer, blowing his conch as he drove the uncertain, uneasy Arjuna into battle, the taxi driver honked his horn to announce our invasion. The battleground, perhaps a field of dharma in those ancient days—grassless now as then, even weedless, strewn with stones, even bones, littered with broken pots, pieces of brick, wood, metal, glass, and paper, human scraps and refuse, discarded things and feelings—resisted the groaning vehicle, refused to be penetrated by the black-bodied, yellow-topped car. "This is not a place for the squeamish," the taxi driver warned.

When the automobile stalled, stuck fast in the rubble, people rushed to see who had come to them. They laughed at the surprising spectacle. Someone yelled out the only English words he knew: "Hello, Mister! One, two, three! Good-bye, Mister!" Others joined in: "Hello! How are you today?" "Where is your from?" "Good morning and good night!" "I don't speak English very well, thank you." "I love you!"

The battleground, after you emerge from the car, as you leave the world you assume you know behind, becomes a playground, a slipshod sideshow in some eternal carnival, a labyrinthine hall of dirty mirrors and cracked glass. The turbulent, accidental walkways reach this way and that, crisscross, zigzag, turn back on themselves, or suddenly end against some crumbling wall with dung patties slapped upon it, or against some splintered fence that separates nothing from nothing, that just stands there existing for its own sake. It is not a barrier or a marker. It's just wood, disintegrating and without purpose. Everything seems haphazard here—the paths, the hovels, life itself. When I returned six months later, dwellings existed where rubble had been, and trash remained where people had lived before and felt at home. And six months after that, it was different still, and I could not find my way. As in a kaleidoscope, the patterns shift endlessly, the images are fleeting.

The mud huts, some of them decorated, carved, or embossed with mud words or mud designs, some of them utterly uncared for and in mud-ruin, and planlessly, capriciously erected wherever some space in the dream, some neglected plot of chaos, yields itself up to be taken. The mud is dry. The roofs are skin: tarpaulin hides weighted down by broken bricks, rusted pipes, or any other heavy scrap. With sinews and ligaments of hemp and coir they are secured to decrepit wooden bones, the burdened beams and brittle braces so tenuously supporting this architectural phantasmagoria. Here and there are the tents of the newcomers among the occasional cement boxes in which the relatively more well-established dwell. And all around, as if belonging inside no particular cement, mud, or canvas dwelling, there are charpoys, beds made of carved wood and twisted thongs, and cots with deep sleepers and listless resters flopped and slumped upon them.

There is always some fire nearby for cooking, some earthen stove attended by a squatting woman, her head covered with bright cotton cloth. Perhaps she hums or even sings. Amidst metal pans, platters, and bowls, water pots, grain pots, broken pots, buckets and pails, kerosene cans and dried dung chips, wicker baskets and cardboard boxes, she pats the chapati dough. The variegated smears of gray and brown, the dirty wash of dust and smoke, are emblazoned by the vivid saris of the women of Shadipur—yellows, oranges, reds, greens, blues, in plaids and paisleys, in blocks and swirls—brilliant, primary colors, all full of energy and shimmering delight. The jingling of the silver anklets and glass bangles of these women is sumptuous music, a delicate and yet jubilant tintinnabulation woven into the roars and whispers of the slum: curses and jokes, howls of laughter and remorse, whistling and humming, the fizzle and crackle of an All-India Radio broadcast. The melodramatic torch song from a Hindi film approaches its crescendo, and from over the loudspeaker comes the call to prayer: "God is great." Four times all hear the blaring, electrified words of the muezzin: *"Allahu akbar."* Elsewhere there is the sound of Hindu devotion. *"Oṃ śrīśivāya namah,"* someone—a snake charmer perhaps—whispers with perfunctory solemnity and an offering of fragrant blossoms and incense. There might also be the faint sound of Christian prayer or peccavi in Shadipur. Everything but silence.

Children, with their giggles and cries, their taunts and teasings, are a chorus in this effusive dream, this improvisational comic opera. Their descant is the universal and eternal clamor of all childhoods. Children are everywhere, clinging and crawling, skipping and scampering, sucking to eat in the arms of mothers, squatting to shit on the ground, running to hide from us, peeking through a hole in a fence. Some have shaved heads, some dyed hair. They wear clothes too large or too small, garments just received from an older child or just ready to be given to a younger one. Nothing fits. But it doesn't matter. The children are ornamented with glass bangles and magical charms, strange protections against disease, vermin, snakes, bad luck, and despair. And myths shine in their eyes.

Odors overwhelm, taunt, and threaten the soul: the sweet smell of the jasmine worn in women's hair and the perfumed oils smeared upon their skin, the rancid scent of the urine of men and beasts, the sick aromas of puke and diarrhea, the hard and heady smells of kerosene and industry. And there is the consoling, spicy smell of cooking.

Everywhere in Shadipur revulsion and delight seem blended into each other. And everywhere in Shadipur, amidst the perpetual demolition, life seems mysteriously triumphant. That's the magic.

A woman swept the dirt. Why? What is all senselessness, cataclysm, and confusion for me seems intimately understood and accepted by them. They know the order in the chaos, the plan and form—the meaning perhaps—in all of this. They see the lines and markers that must remain invisible to me.

Little Salma recognized us. We had see her perform telepathic tricks from beneath a dark blanket; Chand Baba had vanished her in a wicker basket; Abdul had decapitated her. The little girl had screamed and begun to thrash wildly about under the dark blanket. "Do you dare to look?" Abdul shouted. "Women! Turn your eyes away!" The blanket was thrown back to reveal the small child with the knife penetrating her neck below one ear and emerging, bloodstained, underneath the other. As the magician lifted Salma by the knife, the girl waved her arms about and shook her knees spasmodically. The fragile body twitched and twisted as the magician spoke: "I must pull the knife all the way through so that I can take this head to Kali. She'll add it to the garland of heads that decorates her breasts. Of course, Kali would accept the head of a goat in place of the child's head. But I can't afford a goat. You could help me. Each of you could give a little something toward the purchase of a goat. Then I could spare the little girl."

Salma smiled here in a way that she did not smile at the performance. The lovely child, seemingly so fragile but in reality so hardy, was at home and safe.

Other children touched us, rubbed, and leaned against us without fear. This is a carnal place, but the carnality, the ache for pleasure, appears more alimentary than genital. All is mouth and anus, eating and defecating, taking in and releasing. Food is life and power.

The voluptuous heat of sex is here, but it is guarded and secret. Surely in the night, however, amidst the cries of babies, the snores of the elderly, the whispers of the sleepless, there are hushed convulsions of pain and pleasure, muted sighs of joy or relief, swellings and shivers, as fingernails dig into livid skin, as lips are bitten, as burning faces are buried in hair that is lush, loosened, and disheveled by desire.

Most of the magicians were in Kashmir for the summer months. But those who had stayed behind—Chand Baba and Chand Pasha, Iqbal and Kareem Baksh, Abdul and Apeez—greeted us and escorted us into Chand Pasha's one-room cement home. The taxi driver insisted upon waiting. "Otherwise you'll be stranded. You won't be able to find any taxis around here."

Chand Pasha smiled warmly as he rubbed his forefinger against his palm with a crystalline sparkle in his pleasantly wicked eyes. The gesture was a question: did I want hashish? His posture was thoroughly noble. The smile and glance were self-confident and proud; the laughter was resilient, self-assured, openhearted, and full of comfort.

This magician from Andhra had begun to do booked shows, to adapt street magic to the stage, and he was now being paid by the government to promote birth control. He would go into a village and, to draw a crowd around him, he would perform some of the standard tricks from the magician's repertoire—the Diving Duck, Chinese Sticks, Cups and Balls, the Egg Bag, whatever. Then, displaying a box, showing it to be absolutely empty, he would place a male doll and a female doll into it. The box was shaped like a village hut and lidded with a cardboard roof. Then Chand Pasha would replace the top of the box and shake the hut. "You know what Mama and Papa are doing?" The magician's patter, inevitably laced with obscene puns and juicy innuendoes, always prompts village laughter, expressions of delight at once vulgar and wonderful. And then Chand Pasha slowly opens the box; in addition to Mama and Papa there are six little plastic babies. The crowd is amazed and pleased to feel that amazement.

Repeating the trick, this time the magician drops a condom into the hut with Mama and Papa, and this time, after all the lewd shaking and steamy jokes, there are no baby dolls. "But the condom hasn't been used!" one villager observes, and the others laugh loudly. And Chand Pasha, laughing too, distributes condoms to the crowd and makes his way to the next village. The magician, unlike the usual government representative, can capture the attention of the crowd. But, Chand Pasha admits, there is something wrong about the trick, something ineffectual about the promotional strategy. Magic's connection with fertility rites is too strong. Magic celebrates tumescence and erection, fecundity and growth, attraction and breeding, birth and resurrection: a rope stiffens when enchanted by magic words, eggs are produced one after the other from an empty pouch that has been touched by a magic wand; after a few magic gestures, a womb-shaped pot flows with water again and again, seemingly unemptiable; that which is cut apart—cloth or paper, a woman or a child—is put back together. Magic reiterates the mystery of regeneration. It serves to remind us of the miraculousness of the creation's continuity.

Chand Pasha's brother, Chand Baba, who occasionally gets paid now to display the traditional Indian art of magic to young children in the elementary schools of Delhi, sat beneath a poster for the "Grand Magic Show of the Great K. Lal, World's Greatest Magician." Lal's eyes are stretched open wide and his hands spread majestically; his jeweled turban has a feather in it; cards and doves fill the air; and, beneath the magician, a lady, sawed in half, waits to be made whole again.

Chand Baba, more than any of the others, looks the part of a magician, with his unruly gray beard, his scrupulously gazing eyes, wide as a tiger's, his ironic grin and gesticulations. And the way he wears the clothes that typify the old way of life in Andhra Pradesh enhances the illusion of who the man is—an illusionist. He plays the part unceasingly and, in both senses of the phrase, "it becomes him." I had seen him perform in the park. Threading two ropes through the holes that had been bored in three wooden balls, he had tied the cords securely and handed the ends of them to two selected spectators. The spectacle was reminiscent of the image of the *sūtrātman*, the cord-spirit in Vedantic catechism that holds the three worlds together. "*Ek, do, tīn! Gilli-gilli-gilli! Yantru-tantru-jālajāla-mantru!*" The globes fell to earth, and the thongs remained in the hands of the astonished volunteers. Chand Baba smiled like the sage who sees through the illusion of the three worlds, he who knows the reality of the spirit, the secret of the cord.

I sat next to him on the charpoy, and while he stroked my arm now and then to reassure me that I was welcome, Iqbal, to my utter abashment, fanned me. He ignored all my gestures for him to stop. My embarrassment and my protestations were entirely inappropriate. Iqbal, with his fastidiously trimmed pasha's beard and his startlingly aristocratic equipoise, fanned me not out of any obsequiousness, but out of a certain human pity for a traveler so obviously unaccustomed to such weather, a person out of place in this part of Delhi, the vast, fuming, urban stew that was simmering in the persistent heat of the gradually disappearing afternoon. Iqbal informed me that one Naseeb Shah was coming down from Kashmir to meet with me. He would help me.

Abdul, the young and roguishly handsome conjurer who, with Iqbal, had performed an aerial suspension for me, proudly produced an album for me to see, squeezed in next to me on the charpoy and turned the pages one by one: there were letters of appreciation and commendation from various government officials, and photographs of the magicians with Zail Singh, Rajiv Gandhi, and the late Mrs. Gandhi; there were notes and the enthusiastic comments of foreigners, as well as magazine and newspaper clippings giving attention to street magic. The illiterate magicians smiled to watch me read them. And then I was asked to write something. Shankar, my friend and often my interpreter, translated: "Please mention how baffled you were to see a levitation performed. Explain that any stage magician can do this on a stage, but it's truly astounding to see it performed in the open air, completely surrounded by spectators. Only the street magicians are capable of this miracle."

Apeez brought me a Campa-Cola, a drink I detest but felt constrained to consume lest I seem ungrateful. No sooner had I finished it than another appeared as if by magic. The hospitality extended by the poor is always disarming. The setup entraps me, makes me the victim of generosity: if I finish the Campa-Cola, another one is brought to me; if I don't finish it, a magician asks, "You don't like Campa-Cola? Bring him Limca." I feel I'm a stooge in a routine, "Soft Drinks of India," a parody, intentional or not, of Waters of India, a standard number in the repertoire of Indian magicians, a trick made famous and conventional by P. C. Sorcar, the most renowned of modern Indian illusionists, in which seemingly endless waters flow from a lota bowl. The trick must have its origins in real magic, in a time when the magician's art engendered reality. If, in a season as hot as that summer in which I first visited Shadipur, he produced a flow of cool waters from a small, empty pitcher, the now so impersuadable sky would respond, would fill with clouds, break open and refructify the earth. The magician—the *indrajālin*, he who possesses Indra's Net—could move the ferocious heart of Indra then.

"Drink!" Kareem Baksh, whom I had seen several days earlier performing the Mango Tree Trick, grinned, and I obeyed. He offered me a bidi to smoke, and I responded by offering him a Deluxe Benson and Hedges International. He waved his hand in refusal and lit his own bidi. Kareem, his countenance dangerous, his skin a hide, hiding the intricacies of his thoughts and feelings, his hair hennaed, his fingers ringed and wrists braceleted, spoke, and I could not understand a word. I asked my friend, "Professor Shankar, Industrial Magician, Father of Junior Shankar, World's Youngest Magician," what he was saying. "It is too rude for translation." The other magicians laughed from their guts. Kareem's long moustache, waxed and curled upward against the downward curve of his ascetic lips, gave him an air of real power, an aura at once primeval and elegant that enhanced his show. His face was an actor's mask.

He had begun his performance by blowing smoke and flames from a flute. In ancient magic the magician accrued his power by austerities, by trances, meditations, and exercises that stored the heat within. And that inner fire was the mysterious energy of magic. The crowd gasped to see the fire from Kareem's lips. He used that energy to grow a mango tree from a seed before our very eyes. He groaned terribly and removed a stone from his mouth. "Dog egg," he said, and they laughed. Another groan, another sleight, another bit of misdirection, and another, larger stone appeared from his open mouth. "Horse egg!" Laughter was tinged with amazement. And there was another stone, and another, and finally an enormous one, an "elephant egg." Then he began to remove nettles from his mouth, handfuls, one after another, of sharp thorns. "A normal man would scream if he so much as stepped on one of these, but I, I have the power." His words were fire.

A few days later, when the magicians gathered in my room in Sunder Nagar, my friend Shalini argued with affectionate anger with Kareem Baksh about his attitude toward women. "Why don't you ever let your women perform? They know all the tricks," she challenged. Kareem shrugged his shoulders and entered the agon. "They have the knowledge, but not the courage."

"I have as much courage as you," Shalini laughed, and the magicians, six of them huddled together on my bed, laughed too. But Kareem scowled, "I'll teach you to take the thorns from your mouth, and we'll see if you can do it. We'll see how brave you are. To do this trick you'll need to fast for fourteen days." Shalini laughed again: "Never mind." She turned to me and spoke in the English they could not understand. "These guys are real bastards," she smiled affectionately, and the words seemed full of admiration.

"You see," Kareem shouted and jumped up with mock petulance, "Ram fasted for fourteen years in the forest because of just one wish of his stepmother, and you can't even fast for fourteen days." His understanding of drama, of creating effects on the spur of the moment—an understanding that is the real and essential genius of the street magicians—was perfect. As he finished his response to Shalini, he closed his eyes, paused, and made his exit. He walked into my bathroom. In a moment he called the other magicians to join him around the toilet. Kareem Baksh spit bright red betel juice into it and then flushed it. Each of them took their turn spitting and flushing, spitting and flushing, watching the magical whirlpool in the toilet bowl of miracles.

I asked to use the bathroom in Shadipur and the magicians laughed as I was led to a wall. Children gathered to watch me piss, and they giggled as if I did it differently than the men of the slum.

The women in Shadipur, the daughters, wives, and mothers of the magicians, all know all of the tricks, I was told. "They learn them when they're little girls like Salma. But when they grow up, they stop performing. Then it's their responsibility to teach their children magic."

Hearing the call to prayer, Chand Baba suddenly vanished. The rest of the magicians sat tight. I asked about religion, and Chand Pasha explained that all street magicians in India are Muslims. Shankar interpreted Abdul's conjecture: "Maybe there are a few Hindu magicians left in the south." Iqbal said it was possible but explained that of the more than one hundred magicians in and around Delhi, "all are Mussulman, all are Maslet. Well, all but old Guru Swami." Guru Swami is a one-trick magician—he has a trained animal, a "psychic bull," that appears to read the minds of the audience, guessing which man in the crowd is holding a certain object, or stamping the ground a certain number of times to indicate the age of another spectator. "Except for him, all are Maslet. And he's not really a magician." There is always a laugh—or at least a grin—when Guru Swami is spoken of. The magicians seem to look down on animal trainers and handlers in the way that fruit merchants look down upon vegetable vendors. "They're mainly Hindu, those snake charmers. But we're friends with them. We use snakes and other animals in our shows—we do some tricks with them, little things, like turning a stick into a snake, but it's only to draw the crowd. And some of them know a few tricks. But they're not really magicians."

Chand Pasha, who claimed to be able to trace his lineage back through nine generations of magicians, explained that his ancestors were all Hindus. "One day, maybe about two hundred years ago, I'm not sure, they were making a pilgrimage to the Ganga and, on the way, they stopped at Fatepur Sikri. There they met a certain pir who asked them where they were going, and when they told him, he laughed and pointed to the ground. Suddenly the earth cracked and out of the crack the Ganga began to flow. The Hindu magicians, amply impressed with the pir's magic, broke their *mālās* and immediately converted to Islam. The magicians of Delhi and the Jaipur Maslets descend from that one family group. At about the same time, a similar thing happened to a group of magicians from Pune and also to a group from Hyderabad. They're now Mussulman as well."

I repeatedly heard stories in which magic was used to gain converts to one religion or another. "The Nambudiri brahmins of Kerala," a South Indian amateur magician told me six months later, "after their bath, always throw the bathing water into the air as an offering to god. Saint Thomas pointed out to them that the offering always fell back to earth, that the ground was wet with that water. He did a trick for them. He threw water into the air and it didn't come down. I do this same trick in my own excellent stage show. That trick, in former times, so impressed the brahmins that many of them became Christians."

"While all the street magicians are Muslim," an aspiring stage magician, The Incredible Mayadhar, later explained to me, "all of the theatrical magicians are Hindu. Why is this, my darling man? Simple! Those of us who take to the theater tend to be from the upper crusts of society. We are cultured and proud of our position in society. But what about the lower crusts? Simple! In the nineteenth century many low-caste Hindu groups converted to Islam. Not only the magicians, but the mahouts—the elephant drivers—as well. The rationale is obvious. Islam does not have castes. It is egalitarian through and through. So the magicians converted in order to get rid of their low-caste status. Believe me, please."

"The explanation makes no sense," I argued, "because despite the conversion they remain low-caste. Their status in Hindu society doesn't change at all. The conversion might, in fact, lower their status. Islam in India, furthermore, seems to have its own caste hierarchy, a social stratification that, for all practical purposes, replicates the Hindu one. There are other problems with your explanation. Why, for example, did the snake charmers, who are lower on the social ladder than magicians, remain Hindu?"

The magician totally ignored my objections to his explanation. "Listen," he commanded excitedly, "I have a little magic routine on this topic. When I perform it for you, you will understand this whole complicated problem of caste in India. I do the standard color-changing silk routine that so many magicians do, but my patter, so full of humorous puns, is unique and of my own invention. The word in Hindi for caste and color is one and the same: *varn*. So I have four silks, each a different color, each representing a different caste. One changes into the other, back and forth, forth and back. 'Only a magician can change his caste,' I say. It's very humorous in Hindi. For the grand finale I tie them all together and roll them into a ball. I say the magic words, unroll the ball and there is only one large silk, and it is—can you believe it?—the glorious flag of India! What an effect! Believe me, please."

Dayanand, the secretary of the Indian Ring of the International Brotherhood of Magicians, offered me quite a different explanation of the conversion when I later visited him in Coimbatore: "The magicians were itinerant. Always traveling, traveling, traveling. That is why they converted to Islam. Islam, you see, allows a man to have four wives. The street magicians became Muslims so that they could have one wife in each place where they frequently performed."

Chand Baba's understanding of the conversion to Islam was the clearest: the magicians became Muslims simply and obviously because they realized the truth, that there is no god but God and Muhammad is His Prophet.

"What's the difference?" Kareem Baksh scowled: "One religion or another, it's all the same. The same truths, the same lies."

The magicians can quote with equal ease and feeling from the Qur'an, the *Rāmāyaṇa*, and the *Purāṇa*s, from Sufi saints and Hindu devotional poets. Religion is grist for the mills of their imaginations; their patter is spiced with sacred images, names, and notions. They use religion to tap into the fears and desires, the superstitions and deep beliefs, of the crowd. If their audience is Muslim, the patter might invoke Nizam-ud-din; for Hindus there might be quotes from Surdas. For both, Kabir would be recited:

> I am a spectator at god's uncanny magic show:
>> Playing his drum, he sets it up, performs,
> And spins the wheel!
>> The magic may be false
> (We do not know what we do know),
>> But the magician is true—
> He and he alone is real.

"I learned to perform this miracle from a pir from Samarkand," one magician will claim. "And this power," he'll add, "I acquired on the burning ghats of Varanasi."

Chand Pasha, seemingly bored by our discussion of religion and the past, handed me a horn for inspection, a sort of trumpet that appeared normal in all respects. Placing the mouthpiece against the side of his neck, he proceeded to play a tune, and the magicians themselves seemed to be amused by the trick or at least by my utter bafflement.

A crow, dusty and curious, appeared in the doorway, looked in, opened its beak, and turned its head to the side. Asad waved his hand menacingly, and the bird squawked insultingly and flew off. Asad commented on it, and all the magicians laughed. I asked for a translation of the joke. "Untranslatable," Shankar insisted.

Chand Pasha spoke readily about the life and world of the street magicians. "It's a good and free life. I can do what I want, go where I want. I don't need money or anything else. I can get off a train in any village or town without a paisa in my pocket. I just ask someone for a match to light a cigarette, and then I do a little trick with his matches. He'll laugh usually and ask if I'm a magician. Yes, I'll say and make my cigarette vanish. He offers me one to smoke, and I make it disappear in my mouth and reappear from my ear. At this point one or two other people have gathered by us. I borrow a handkerchief from one of them and give it to another." Chand Pasha asked me to tie a knot in my bandanna. He took it, tightened the knot, and handed it back to me. Following his instructions, I tied another knot, and another, and another, each one of which was tightened by the conjurer. He wrapped the knotted portion of the cloth up in the loose center and placed it in my hands. "*Gilli-gilli-gilli!*" he said as he passed his hands over mine, and then he asked me to open the bundle: the knots were gone; karma was undone.

Shankar continued his translation: "This trick brings a few more spectators, and then I do another trick or two, and I get a little money from these people, just enough for some food. Then I go to a hotel and order a meal. The restaurant is the perfect place to do some more tricks, to get some more money—every object on the table can be used in one trick or another. Often someone there will tell me he has seen a magician performing in the area. If so, I'll head for that place to make contact with him."

When the traveling magician finds the performing magician at work he greets him, "*Salaam aleichem!*" And then these men, though they may well be complete strangers to each other, from different parts of the land, can communicate in a secret language, a *jādūbhāsā*, a code parlance known only by the street magicians. In it they reveal, each to the other, that they are Maslets; in it they make plans: the new arrival can act as a confederate for the performer; in it they boast or joke, delineate their lineage, or confess their misfortunes. After the show, the performer will give the visiting magician half of his earnings and take him to wherever he is staying. Over a meal he informs his fellow magician where he might perform and suggests what kinds of tricks will pay off. Then the traveler goes on his way.

The magicians, who were until quite recently completely itinerant, as homeless as holy men, have, like so many urban Indians, a devout nostalgia for village life. "There are villages that still don't have television or films; magic is still entertaining there," Kareem Baksh explained. "You walk into the village, spread out your cloth, play the damaru, and then everyone in the village will gather around for the performance."

"And in the villages," Iqbal added with an ironic cheerfulness, "we don't have to pay off the cops."

"But even in the villages, magic is less and less popular," Abdul, picking up the thread of the patter, explained with a disgruntled shake of the head. "People don't pay like they used to. In the old days, in Gujarat, the villagers would give you their ornaments after the show. You could make a lot of money then. Magic used to pay well." Now, very often, the villagers pay the magicians with grain, which they sell to a local merchant after the performance.

The magicians are very poor by any standards that I know, but there is nothing impoverished or beggarly about their souls. Though they know the reality of hunger, they do not seem to experience any real fear of starvation, the penury of the eternal pariah, the dismal poverty of the farmer whose whole livelihood can, at any time, be decimated by some drought or flood, or the potential bankruptcy of the ever-nervous shopkeeper whose books are too delicately balanced. The magicians are not, like so many others in India, essentially victims. They are poor, but neither indigent nor anxious. They are streetwise. They have a sharp flash in their eyes and a crispness in their bearing that never grace the truly impoverished. Anytime or anywhere they need a little cash, they can perform and earn a few hundred rupees. And they share their take with the others. They laugh generously like courtiers, with carelessness and a majestic detachment, and that laughter is an inheritance, passed from generation to generation, to them from their ancestors, magicians who, before the priggish Aurangzeb zealously banished them from the court, were given lavish endowments by Moghul patrons or extravagant gifts of appreciation by grandiose maharajas. It is not the magicians who have fallen, but their patrons.

Priding themselves on having held their own, despite the difficulties of life in modern India, the *jādūgar*s refer to the plight of the vanishing *bājīgar*s, a cognate social group of itinerant acrobats and jugglers who also practice conjuring. Largely unable to survive in a changing India on what offerings they can collect by doing somersaults and rope walking, the acrobats have had to take up unskilled manual labor: in the countryside they have become migrant farm laborers; in the cities they have become rickshaw-*wālā*s or hustlers. Their claim that they were once Rajputs ("After Rajput Maharana Pratap took to the hills because of the assault of Akbar's army, the children of his nephew Jay became blacksmiths, while those of Vijay became acrobats") intensifies the humiliation and sense of loss. This is the Kali Yuga, the age of gloom and degradation.

It was beginning to get dark, and the taxi driver was anxious for us to leave. I wanted to stay. I was enchanted by Shadipur, charmed and dazzled by these extraordinary people, by their realness and ease in the world, their nonchalance and ruggedness. I asked when I would see Naseeb. "He said he'd come," Iqbal assured me. "He's coming from Kashmir for your sake. But he has had a few problems. Maybe he'll come today, maybe tomorrow, maybe next week. But he'll come for sure."

Naseeb's problems were later explained to me in confidence. He had had a brilliant idea. Increasing the number of his shows, borrowing, and pulling off a few shady little deals that were never quite clear to me, he had been able to amass nine thousand rupees to purchase two falcons. He had heard that if he could smuggle the hunting birds into Pakistan, he would be able to sell them to Arabs there, making ten rupees for every one he had invested: ninety thousand rupees. He would, by means of a simple and yet splendid magic trick, be a rich man. Taking the birds across the border would be no problem for the magician. He stuffed them into a load within the secret compartment in one of his magic baskets, a compartment in which pigeons were normally concealed for a variety of tricks. Several cobras were then placed in the separate, inspectable part of the basket. When Naseeb and his son Ayasan, walking across the border into Pakistan, were stopped by the officials there, they explained they were just going to do a performance in a nearby village. Naseeb amused the government customs men, the immigration and emigration officials, by multiplying and vanishing some coins. One of the officials opened the basket, but when the cobras raised their heads and fanned their hoods, the top of the basket was quickly replaced with a nervous laugh and a wave of the hand, a signal that Naseeb and his little boy could pass through.

Late at night in Pakistan the magician opened his basket, removed the cobras, and flipped the latch on the load. There was no movement. The falcons, which unlike pigeons cannot withstand restraints upon their freedom, were dead. Naseeb had lost everything.

"Please, it's time to go," the taxi driver insisted, and we followed him out, through the moldering and yet self-regenerating labyrinth of Shadipur, under the darkening, starless, moody sky of a hot twilight, accompanied by the graciously smiling magicians and by a wild herd of children. They waved good-bye as the day vanished and laughed as night was conjured up, and each took turns reaching into the taxi to shake hands. "Good-bye! Good-bye!" The children ran after the car shouting and waving as if there were some triumph in having the last good-bye.

I saw a falcon above Shadipur, a dark hawk in silhouette, circling high and then, as if finding some invisible rampart of sky, coming still, to rest and watch, power-poised in some sultry current, floating in the infinite freedom of the plenitude above, way, way above, watching with the last light of dusk for its prey, some nocturnal animal urged by instincts to come out in the heated night.

As the taxi swerved, jolted, bumped, banged, heaved, and honked its way, helter-skelter, through the clattering pandemonium of Delhi traffic, I felt a rush of wonder and a lunge of delight. I emerged from a spell of disillusionment with what for a while had seemed to me a helplessly and hopelessly desultory land, an India burdened by provincialism, bureaucracy, corruption, and a thousand unnameable woes, to enter the startling and marvelous world of the street conjurers, an exhilarative India of spirited traditions and infinite promise. It was impossible for me not to idealize and romanticize the magicians of Shadipur. They seemed so gracefully at home in the world, unruffled by the chaos around them, at ease in the uneasiest of places. Their skills were so fully embodied, their humor so vivid, their artfulness so natural. I had spent so much time over texts, struggling to decipher the recondite, black-inked words from an ancient language that continues to confound me even after so many years of study. Now my sources were alive— they moved, spoke, gestured. And they laughed. And these sources were as ancient as any of the books. I felt that if I had come to India with Alexander, Vasco da Gama, or Marco Polo, I might well have witnessed performances of the very tricks that I, with my own eyes, had seen Chand Baba, Kareem, Iqbal, and Abdul perform. They belonged to a hereditary brotherhood that linked them to a stunning past and protected them in the present, and for that privilege I envied them and attributed to them a completely unselfconscious happiness.

During my next trip to India, in winter, I realized that all was not what it had seemed. Behind the illusion of magicians that I cherished, there were the same rivalries, calumnies, jealousies, and feuds that most characterize any real community; there were the same angers, regrets, fears, and disappointments that must mark any real soul.

My subsequent visits to Shadipur aggravated problems there. There was gossip about what I was really doing. Some of the magicians felt and suggested to others that I was giving money to Naseeb that he was not sharing with them. Was he selling the secrets of the brotherhood, revealing the workings of their magic to me? There were rumors that I was going to take him to America, that he would be rich and leave the others behind. He would forget about his wife and children once he had a big house and an automobile, once he was doing stage shows in Las Vegas.

Shankar had initially presented me to the magicians as a magician. They were completely unimpressed by the tricks I could do, thoroughly unamazed by my ability to instantly locate the card that I asked them to freely choose and return to my deck. They could not distinguish the suits. When I multiplied cigarettes in a box, one of the unbaffled magicians remarked that it was not magic. "Anyone who purchases the gimmick can perform the trick. Magic requires skill. Each trick takes many years to learn and many generations to perfect." Shankar apologized for the words he translated.

When I returned to India in winter, I brought a trick with me that changed things. Sitting once again on the charpoy in Chand Pasha's one-room cement house in Shadipur, I held up a long needle for them to see. Chand Pasha, Chand Baba, Iqbal, Abdul, Apeez, Naseeb, and a few others, politely looking on, smiled patiently and even hospitably, but they were not prepared to be surprised. Slowly I inserted the needle into my arm. It entered the skin, crossed over the muscles, and reemerged. Or so it seemed. It appeared that the needle ran under my skin. What appeared to be blood oozed out of what appeared to be the punctures in my forearm. I removed the needle, turned it around and ran it through the wound again. There was more blood. Their gazes were wide and they looked back and forth at each other. I appeared to do what many Hindu renouncers and Muslim penitents really do, an act that might suggest some transcendence of the flesh, some fantastic ecstasy and power over oneself, a self-mastery and complete control. Shankar translated my patter: "This is not the trick. To stick a needle through your arm is not magic. You just have to be very brave. I took a vow at the mosque that I would practice celibacy for one full hour today. That's how I got this power." Removing the needle, I displayed the two bleeding holes in my arm for them to inspect in wonder. "Now for the trick. I shall heal those wounds. I must disinfect them first with some alcohol." I daubed the arm with cotton. "The power to heal is real magic. This power I obtained from Shiva." Passing my hand over my arm with a gesture I had seen them make many times, I intoned their own words: "*Gilli-gilli-gilli!*" They laughed nervously. When I displayed my arm, clearly showing that it was completely healed, they nodded in approval. This was their kind of trick—harrowing, menacing, distasteful, and evocative of religious associations. When I offered to show them how it was done, they insisted that several people leave the room. This was for family only.

Magicians are, of course, by nature and necessity, secretive and private. The ancient tradition of the *mantragupta* vow preserves and binds the group together. The way a trick works is a commodity, and the more people who know how it is done, the less its cash value. Secrets are the currency of intimacy and equality; secrecy is power, and it binds magicians together to form the confederacy of magic. With the Needle-through-Arm illusion, I had hoped to be admitted into the magic circle. When, several days later, I presented the needle and the rest of what was needed to perform the trick to Naseeb, he offered to initiate me, to let me be a stooge at one of his performances. No one would ever suspect that a poor street conjurer, an illiterate, vagrant rascal, could be in league with an apparent tourist, an obviously wealthy, privileged, and rather naive American.

Chand Pasha, I was told, tried to buy the trick from Naseeb for two thousand rupees, over five times what I myself had paid for it when I ordered it from Queen of Hearts Theatrical Supplies in Texas. But Naseeb refused to sell it. "Beautiful magic," he said, proudly pronouncing one of the few English phrases he knows, as he carefully opened the bottle of fake blood, smelled it, and grinned with delight. Taking a deep puff of the fragrant Kashmiri hashish, passing it then to me, and holding the smoke in his lungs, he dipped the needle into the plastic bottle of blood and filled it. Exhaling, he slowly inserted the shiny, gimmicked, surgical needle into his arm as I had shown him. Blood ran down his arm and dripped onto the floor. He smiled widely. "Beautiful magic! Beautiful!"

I prepared my arm for the trick, filled the needle, took a deep puff of the hashish, handed the needle to him, and let him perform the illusion on me. That's how we would do it in public. *"Atisundar jādū!"* I said, using one of the few Hindi phrases I knew. *"Atisundar!"*

I slept fitfully that December in Delhi. I had a fever, something in the lungs, and each night I shook with murky dreams. I understood those dreams as magic tricks performed by one aspect of myself for another. They had no meaning really—the illusions were for my beguilement and for a warning perhaps. One was recurrent. It always began realistically with my arrival in India. Customs. The officials reenacted what had actually happened when I had arrived awake and conscious—they let me pass through without opening my bags. But, in the dream, they suddenly called me back. Blood was dripping from my suitcase. Intensely conscious that the truth was sounding like a lie, I tried to tell them it was stage blood, not real blood, but fake blood for use in a magic trick. With mechanically obdurate gestures, they insisted that I open the bag. Within, under blood-soaked papers and notes, there were falcons, and they were dead. The beaks of the creatures of freedom were slightly open and twisted at unnatural angles, their eyes were gauzy and sunken, their wings closed and mashed against their bodies.

Their breasts were split open, and their beatless hearts exposed. It was their blood in my bag and on the floor. I tried in vain to explain that I did not know how they got there, that I had never seen them before. I swore it was true.

I was awakened by the telephone. "Professor Siegel, there is a man here to see you. He claims to know you."

"Send him up," I answered sleepily, grumpily, and yet automatically, as I searched the bedside table for my clock.

"No, this is not possible," the operator at the guesthouse explained. "You must come down to meet him."

I sat up. "No, send him up. I can't come down now, I'm not dressed."

"No," the operator insisted with a tone that was at once sternly officious and yet mildly cheerful. "We cannot have this fellow traipsing about this place so unaccompanied."

"Then bring him up. Have someone bring him up," I answered with obvious annoyance. "I can't come down now."

"No." She was firm. "Such a thing would not be appropriate. I do not believe that you will want this fellow in your room."

I gave up. But I tried, as I pulled on my pants, to figure out how I could have won, how I might have convinced her to do what I asked. With vengeance as my consolation, I decided to go down to the lobby shirtless and barefooted so that she would, in embarrassment, wish she had not made me come down.

My self-appointed guru was waiting in the garden. I had liked Naseeb the first time I saw him. Anyone would have done the same—it was easy to do. His smile, confident, abundantly friendly and yet tinged with ironies, welcomed me, and I welcomed him, in turn, with outstretched hands. "Lee Baba," he laughed, "America magic man!" We laughed together just as we would have done if we could have understood each other's language better, laughed as if we could have reminisced, joked, and bantered. Ayasan, Naseeb's seven-year-old son, was squatting on the ground. His stillness and utter expressionlessness were disconcerting. His hair, cropped close to the scalp, reminded me of the young monks, Buddhist children initiated into the order, whom I had seen in Ladakh. And like a monk, he kept his eyes cast gently down. His hands were as dirty as his bare feet, but the impenetrable face was clean. "Come up to my room, Naseeb." I pointed to the window as I tried out one of the Hindi phrases I had memorized for his sake, "*Merī prārthnā hai ki āp us meñ āiyī.*" Naseeb chuckled and said something to Ayasan, who then looked up at me for the first time and laughed just slightly. The boy, carrying the bags, followed us into the lobby of the guesthouse.

I stood shirtless before the perfunctorily demure operator behind the desk. "I want breakfast sent up to the room. Toast, juice, coffee." I asked Naseeb what he wanted, "Toast? juice? coffee?" He laughed: "Beer." I turned back to the operator: "Forget the toast, juice, coffee. Send up some beer. Three bottles of Kingfisher . . . No Kingfisher? Okay, three bottles of Golden Eagle."

DELHI

There are three classes of rooms in the guesthouse in Sunder Nagar where I stay: "Deluxe, Super Deluxe, and Extra-Super Deluxe." Naseeb and Ayasan followed me up the stairs to my Extra-Super Deluxe room to wait for the beer and for Shankar. We'd plan out our day. Naseeb would put on a performance in the park near the zoo, and he would astound the crowd by putting a needle through my arm.

We spoke as if we could understand each other. I wanted to know Naseeb, to know his knowing of things, to understand him and his understanding of magic and the world. More from lack of interest than secrecy, I believe, he was hesitant to talk about himself. With the help of a book and a friend, I had prepared a list of questions in Hindi. Still I could get only scraps of information, all of which seemed irrelevant and unimportant to him: he was about thirty years old and, yes, his father was still alive; he was fifty-eight years old and still performed. I asked if his father had taught his magic to him. No, he had learned it from watching his father. I wanted to know if, as a child, he liked doing magic. "No. It's not easy to do. I had to do it. For my family. For money."

He spoke too quickly and I was lost. He knew it, laughed, fell silent, and looked around my room. I read out another question: "*Āpkā ghar kahāñ hai?*" ("Where are you from?")

"India," he grinned.

"Yes, of course, but where in India? Are you from Andhra Pradesh, Rajasthan, Gujarat? What place?"

He said he was not from anywhere, that he was from everywhere, that while most people were either Bengalis, or Kashmiris, or Panjabis, or Tamils, only people like himself and his father, souls that had always been itinerant, could claim to be Indian. "All India," he laughed again, making a large circle in the air with his hand.

Every time during our acquaintance that I asked how many children he had, there was a different answer: ten, no seven, no four, actually six. I supposed it all depended on what "his children" referred to—how many did he support, how many were from his wife, how many were generated from his own seed, how many were in his elaborately extended family. Or maybe all of Naseeb's answers to my questions were just whatever he felt like saying at the moment, answers formed by whim rather than by any impulse to represent the truth.

I wanted to know what went on in his mind, his heart, and inside his bag of tricks. What were his fears, desires, aspirations, and passions? He had given me a package to deliver for him in America. It was addressed to a girl in New Orleans. I explained that that city was far from Honolulu, much, much farther than Madras was from Delhi, but that I would, upon my return home, mail it for him. With the assistance of someone who claimed to know English, Naseeb had written a letter to the girl: "Dear Miss, Where are you? I dream of you. I miss you. I never forget you. Why do you not come back to India? Why do you not send for me to come to your place? Why do you not write to me? Please remember me always. Love, Naseeb."

For fear that the package might contain hashish and that I might be arrested for bringing it into the United States, I opened it. There were bidis to smoke, bangles to wear, a perfumed oil called *Night Ranee,* a ring with a shiny black stone in it, and a photograph of Naseeb looking uncharacteristically melancholy.

Ayasan untied the rope around one of the bags and removed two snakes, "mama and baby," which he proudly displayed for me. He tied the baby snake into a knot and placed it on my coffee table with a proud smile. The boy who brought the beer was afraid to come into the room.

Ayasan was seven years old when I first met him, and his ten-year-old brother was, and still is, deeply envious of him. The brother is forced to go to school each day, to learn to read and write and do mathematics, utterly useless and nonremunerative skills, while Ayasan is free—he knows magic. He can, and does, go off, all by himself, taking a cobra, a set of cups and balls, an egg bag, a few coins with him, and the damaru, that hourglass rattling drum that announces a show; on the streets he can earn enough money, any time he wants, to take himself and a few other boys to see a film. "Give me money," little Ayasan says to his audience, "so I can learn some more magic." Grandly he can treat his fellow urchins to an ice cream at Gaylord's. Ayasan had another animal in a bag, something he called a *piju,* a creature that looked like a racoon to me. It looked like a mongoose to the people in the streets and, claiming that it was a mongoose, Ayasan would tell his audience that he had hypnotized it and the cobra and that, because of his magic power, those natural enemies had become friends. Ayasan held the baby snake, still in a knot, right up to the *piju*'s nose to demonstrate the animal's complete lack of interest in devouring the reptile.

Shankar, who is about Naseeb's age, arrived with his son, Shankar Junior, who is not much older than Ayasan. Shankar is an "industrial magician," employed by Syndicate Bank to go from village to village, places "where people ignorantly tend to keep their money buried or hidden under their beds rather than in the bank." He shows them a twenty-rupee note. Suddenly it vanishes. "Stolen, gone forever," he says. "Ah, but if I would have had a Syndicate Bank Traveller's Cheque like this one, and it would have been stolen (the displayed traveler's check is vanished in the same manner as the bill), ah, then I could simply go to Syndicate Bank, and they would replace it with cash." After making the twenty-rupee note reappear in his hands, Shankar proceeds to open accounts and take orders for traveler's checks from the villagers. Shankar Junior, who has inherited his father's beguilingly sweet and generous smile, his wide and delighting eyes, has been a stage and television magician since he was three. He was interested in Ayasan and spoke to him in genuinely friendly terms. But the poorer boy backed off and was cool. Naseeb was more comfortable with Shankar than his son was with Junior. Through Shankar we could speak. Through him I asked why he thought people liked magic—why did they gather around him? Did it invest their lives with some sense of mystery? Did they enjoy it because it was an art of the past, unlike television or films? "Magic is just entertainment, just like a film but better because you don't have to buy a ticket or plan to go. A film is just an expensive magic show where you see things that aren't really happening. Street magic is better because the actor is standing right in front of you."

Shankar recited a line that is most often attributed to Robert-Houdin: "The conjurer is simply an actor playing the part of a magician." His skills are used to create the illusion of magic powers. "Do people think that Naseeb has power," I wondered, "real, extraordinary powers?"

The street magician laughed over Shankar's long and complicated translation of my short and simple question. Naseeb lit a cigarette: "Of course, they're supposed to believe it. Those spectators who are just entertained may give a few rupees or nothing at all, but those who really believe pay a lot."

Shankar, under the burden of his morality, accused Naseeb of purposely misleading people.

"Of course, that's how I make my living," Naseeb responded happily. "Listen, I have no choice. After a performance, the spectators always ask how I did this trick or that trick. I can't tell them, of course, because then the trick would lose its fascination. But if I don't tell them, they get very angry with me; maybe they feel stupid for not understanding how it's done. So I tell them I perform my magic with powers that I've obtained at the cremation grounds. They accept that. They like that. They want to believe such a thing is possible, and they tell their friends about it. Sometimes someone will tell me his problems. He'll say he's afraid someone has done some magic against him. Or he has a problem with *bhūts*—malevolent ghosts. So he pays me to help him out. If he's a Hindu, I tell him I'll perform a magic *pūjā* at the Kali temple for three hundred rupees. If he is Mussulman, I charge three hundred and twenty-one rupees to perform a *pūjā* at the shrine of Pir Quaza Garib Navaj. Why should I feel bad? Their faith only increases their enjoyment of the show and their appreciation of life. And I benefit as well. Everyone is happy. That's what magic should do—it should make everyone happy."

"Are there people with real power?" I asked. "Is there real magic?" And both Shankar and Naseeb were eager to answer. Naseeb said no: "No, but I shouldn't ever say it. I earn a living only if people believe these things, only if they believe at least in the possibility of miracles. But there are no real miracles, and all the holy men and god-men, Sai Baba and Jesus and other men like them, are just doing tricks, tricks that I can do, that I can teach you to do, tricks that all the street magicians can do. Those miracles described in the Qur'an, the *Rāmāyana*, and the Bible—those were all just tricks."

"Yes, I'm afraid it is so," Shankar injected. "But in previous times maybe it was possible to perform real magic." The magicians discussed that one. Naseeb said he had heard that Raja Bhoj could do real magic but that he didn't do it so very often because it is so dangerous. Once Akbar asked him to perform such real magic for him. Raja Bhoj tied up his wife, Bhanumati, and made her levitate. He called out some magic words, and her head fell off. He called out again and again, and other parts of her body fell to the ground. Then he burnt all of those parts and said some mantras, and Bhanumati leaped out of the flames, whole again and smiling. "Maybe it's so."

I asked if he believed it.

"Naseeb says," Shankar said, "that when you ask people that question, they always answer, 'I'm not sure, but anything is possible.' They neither completely believe nor disbelieve. 'Anything's possible,' they think, and they take pride in being open-minded. That's gullibility." It became apparent that Naseeb's answer had faded into Shankar's: "Most people are gullible. Especially in India. People are easily duped by Tantric con men, bogus god-men, and corrupt priests. In my own village in Kerala I have seen Tantrics cheating people with a simple trick. The fake sadhu comes into the village with a rooster, digs a hole, and puts the rooster into it. He fills the hole with dirt and lights a fire on top of it. He is very clever at packing the dirt so loosely that the rooster can breathe, and the fire doesn't harm the bird because heat rises. The sadhu says some mantras, puts out the fire, and digs up the rooster. All are amazed to see that the bird is still alive. The magician then cuts off the rooster's head and uses the blood of the animal for the blessings, curses, or predictions that he sells. And if the rooster happens to die in the hole, the magician blames it on the presence of evil influences— someone in the crowd is wicked or lustful or some such thing. And the villagers look at each other and they believe it. There is another trick these fellows do. After putting a very sharp knife in the ground, the blade pointing upward, they will hold a chicken in their hands and say some prayers over it. When they set the chicken on the ground, it goes over to the knife and decapitates itself. The people are then afraid of the magician, afraid that he can exert the same power over them. So they will give him any amount of money. It's a simple trick. You can try it. Put itching powder on the neck of the chicken. The bird kills itself in attempting to scratch the itch on the knife blade. There are priests in temples throughout India who cheat people in the same way, using magic tricks in the name of religion. My friend Premanand has dedicated his life to exposing those rascal priests. You'll meet him in Coimbatore."

The things that troubled Shankar merely amused Naseeb. For the street magician, it seemed, it was only possible to deceive someone who wanted or deserved to be deceived. Shankar was more compassionate. He knew that anyone can be tricked, that the quicker and more intelligent a person is, the more easily he can be fooled. "It is easier to dupe a clever man than an ignorant one," Robert-Houdin noted in *Confidences d'un prestidigitateur:* "The more he is deceived the more he is pleased, for that is what he paid for."

One of the grandest functions of magic is that it demonstrates that all human beings are fools, that our faculties of perception and reasoning can and do so often lead us astray. Magic reminds us that we cannot trust that anything is so, real, or true. That reminder would be disturbing if it were not so entertaining. And magic, as Naseeb had said, is above all else, "just entertainment." Being a magician, I fancied, meant living a life in which the world, every delight and terror, every birth and death, every clash and caress, every moment and eon, was entertainment.

Whenever I asked Naseeb about religion, I suspected that his answers were contrived, improvised on the spur of the moment. But if Naseeb was indeed a liar, his lies were good-hearted and generous; he fabricated things rather graciously, just so that I would have something to write in my book. He told me he was a devotee and follower of Fakir Taj Uddin Baba. "He was in the military service under the British," Shankar translated. "He wanted to leave and become a fakir, but they would not grant him permission to do so. His mother also refused to give him her blessings for such a pursuit. But defiantly he ran away and meditated for twenty years. Then he returned to society. When he came to Nagpur, the people there threw stones at him. He accidentally stepped on a dead dog, and the dog immediately came to life. Then people started worshiping him. I don't believe the story about the dog, but I do believe he must have been a great man, or a great magician, or people wouldn't have made up the story about the dog."

We planned out the day. Naseeb and Ayasan left for the park, where we would meet them for the performance near the zoo. After I prepared my arm for the needle trick, Shankar, Shankar Junior, and I followed. Chand Baba, wearing a red fez and an American baseball jacket emblazoned with the logo of the Los Angeles Dodgers, was there with another child, a cousin named Kabir, who was holding the rig that is used for the Mango Tree Trick. He was about the age of Ayasan and Shankar Junior. Without any readable expressions on their faces, they were squatting amidst their bags and baskets on the sidewalk with Naseeb and Ayasan, as we approached. "No magic," Naseeb said with complete resignation, as he rose to greet us. The police had asked for two hundred rupees as a bribe to let them perform. I offered to pay it. "No, then another policeman will come, and he'll ask for the same or maybe even more, to see just how much you will pay. And then another will come. And then another." I invited them back to the guesthouse, but they declined. I invited them to Karim's for lunch. No, they wanted to return to Shadipur. "Tomorrow," Naseeb promised, "tomorrow at Khan Market." The two magicians with the two boys disappeared into the crowd.

I was invited that night to the home of K. D. Kapur, a Lieutenant Colonel of the Indian Army, whose father-in-law, a sweetly smiling and nearly deaf old man named Dr. Opal, was being honored by the Society of Indian Magicians. He, the oldest Indian member of the brotherhood, and I, the American professor who was writing a book about Indian magic and conjuring, were to be made honorary members of the Society of Indian Magicians. I sat next to him on the plush couch, lavishly upholstered with Chinese silk brocade, and as he took my hand in his in a gesture of warm hospitality and friendship, I could not help but think of sitting with Chand Baba on the charpoy just a few days earlier in Shadipur. "We are brothers," he smiled. "All magicians are brothers. Isn't it so?"

Shankar and I had decided that inviting Chand Pasha to join us might alleviate some of the tension between him and Naseeb that my attention to the latter seemed to be aggravating. I thought, furthermore, that Chand Pasha might benefit from meeting people from this level of the Indian social hierarchy, that they might be able to get police permits for him and the other magicians of Shadipur, and that they might be able to arrange paid shows for him. It was a mistake. Chand Pasha went to the bazaar that day and bought a suit—something he could hardly afford, and which he certainly did not need—for the grand occasion. He looked terribly uncomfortable in Western clothes. His neck, squeezed by the starched white collar of the brand-new shirt, seemed to itch like the necks of the suicidal chickens of which Shankar had spoken. He kept stretching and craning it and sticking his finger in between it and the collar. He smiled uncomfortably. The exuberant ease and innate self-assuredness that characterized him in Shadipur, where he was one of the most successful of all the struggling performers who lived there, had given way to a nervousness and self-consciousness that did not suit him any more than the new clothes.

The moment Chand Pasha entered the drawing room, his incongruous white sandals caught the olfactory attention of the Lieutenant Colonel's miniature Yorkshire terriers. He had, no doubt, in Shadipur, stepped in things of infinite appeal and interest to the dogs. His feet carried the delectable scents of the street, the balmy aromas of Shadipur lanes—excremental essences, the sexual vapor of canine urine, the pungent traces of discarded food, putrid and delicious to the ravenous noses of the pets that had been confined to the inodorous luxury of the government mansion. Though Chand Pasha kept kicking them, they could not hold their shiny wet, black noses back. As the other man who did not fit in there, I felt a certain sympathy for Chand Pasha. And with a suspicion that the Lieutenant Colonel would not like seeing his little pets kicked in the face, I tried to call the dogs, whistling and snapping my fingers to lure them away from the reeking feet of the magician. But it was to no avail.

Tiffin was served: cashews spiced with the seasonings that had drawn adventurous merchants and swashbucklers to India in the past, pakoras laced with chiles, lime, tumeric, and ginger, samosas filled with vegetables or lamb or paneer, cakes made with raisins, coconut, or banana, turnovers, popovers, and halvas, cookies, honey puffs, and sweet sweetmeats in sweeter syrups, so sweet that it hurt to eat them.

When the manservant, with a condescending nod and an expression that was half-smile and half-grimace, duly stopped with the tray before Chand Pasha, the magician, still kicking at the dogs, piled his small plate high, filled it beyond its apparent limits, and, holding that plate in one hand, he reached with the other to eat directly from the tray. He slurped the food down with a great gulp of tea into which he had stirred at least four full spoons of sugar. He belched, took a deep breath, and belched again. Then he smiled, rubbed his lips with the sleeve of his new suit, and signaled to the servant to bring him more. The hashish he had been smoking had, no doubt, made him hungry. It also gave him the courage necessary to attempt an entry into the demure conversation of the drawing room. Boldly he dove into the placid pool of polite prattle before him. I feared the splash. In a Hindi that was painfully vulgar and yet wonderfully brawny, the rich and intricate voice of the streets, Chand Pasha boasted that he had once shaken the hand of Rajiv Gandhi and that he had been taken to London for the Festival of India there. He suddenly tried to speak English, the appropriate language of the Delhi salon: "Guard changing, Buckingham Tower, Princess Di, her crown jewels, Piccadilly Circus—I see it all. I love it all. I perform all magic. All people love me. I am great." The servant rolled his eyes.

Each of us was asked to perform a trick for the venerable Dr. Opal. Placing a small mirror behind a coin on the table, Shankar Junior began. "Here is reality," he said, pointing to the coin before the mirror; and pointing into the mirror, he added, "and that is illusion. In magic, illusion becomes reality." He lifted the little hand mirror, and behind it was a real coin in the spot where the reflection of the coin had been seen. He lowered the mirror again to show two real coins and two illusions. Once more, as he lifted the mirror, the reflections became manifest in reality. Then he did the trick in reverse, changing reality back into illusion; the coins disappeared just as they had appeared, until there was only the one coin with which he had started. It was philosophy in gestures, a demonstration of the epistemological axioms of the Vedanta system: empirical existence, the cosmos, is but a reflection in *brahman,* the substratum of all phenomena, the absolute and only reality; the world has no more substance than the coin in the mirror, "than the reflection of a city," says Shankara in the *Vivekacūḍāmaṇi,* "in a looking-glass." The philosopher and the child magician both teach that we cannot trust our senses to reveal what is real, to know the truth. Every magic trick reiterates the metaphysic.

Shankar Senior vanished some silks. Ashok Bhandari, who promised to show me some ancient Indian manuscripts on magic, did card tricks in the European style, and The Incredible Mayadhar did his best with an egg bag. I performed the Needle-through-Arm, and people applauded politely. When everyone but Chand Pasha and Dr. Opal had been asked to perform, the president of the ring began to recite his concluding remarks. "Chand Pasha," I interrupted. "We haven't seen Chand Pasha's magic." They nodded uncomfortably as the street magician stepped forward with the dogs still excitedly sniffing his sandals.

Borrowing a handkerchief from Dr. Opal, Chand Pasha stood in the center of the room, his eye on the tray of sweets that the servant had not yet taken away.

He handed the handkerchief to the Lieutenant Colonel's daughter and asked her to tie a knot in it. He went around the room asking others to tie additional knots, five knots in all, as he made his way toward the tray. He asked a young girl to hold the knotted handkerchief. The misdirection was classical. With all eyes in the parlor upon the girl, the magician grabbed a last handful of food. Four cakes on the plate and five knots in the handkerchief suddenly disappeared and Chand Pasha kicked the little dogs once more. The refined audience did not appreciate the feat. The servant sneered at the empty plate and the full magician. Chand Pasha did not understand the etiquette appropriate to the drawing room; but then these people did not understand the manners of the street. That was the abyss. Hunger is the basis of a hierarchy which etiquette refines and polishes.

"Good night, Professor Siegel," Dr. Opal said as he shook my hand. "It has been most pleasant to have made your acquaintance. I do hope that you have a highly rewarding time in India and that your research on Indian magic and conjuring is most successful."

"How will Chand Pasha get back to Shadipur? It's late. Haven't the buses stopped running?" I asked. "These people know how to get along," I was told. "They have their ways." The street magician disappeared into the lugubrious darkness of the smoky Delhi night.

My fever persisted. There were chills, and it was getting difficult to breathe. Washing my face with cold water, I looked into the mirror that had a crack in it. The reflection appeared pale; the illusion of a face was drawn and sickly. "I have to fly to Coimbatore tomorrow," I told the doctor. "Will I be well enough to travel?" He shrugged his shoulders as he wrote out the prescription: "I'm not a magician."

I took my medicine, prepared my arm for the needle trick, and set out for Khan Market. Naseeb and Ayasan were already there when I arrived, and the *piju*, an animal that always seemed to arouse people's curiosity and draw them to the performance place, had been chained to a stake that Ayasan had pounded into the ground of the dirty, grassy clearing behind the shops. As I was to be a stooge in the performance, we did not acknowledge each other. Naseeb began to play the damaru with one hand and the flute with the other. The drumbeat was the pulse, the pipe song the life breath, of an invisible presence, the ghost of a magician from the past summoned up from death to see the persistence of his art. I felt Naseeb's clear, sharp, deadly dark eyes could see him, that tenuous spirit awakened by the tune, the shrill cry of the flute. I shut my eyes, and I could see him too. "My name is Muladeva," the magician said.

Overhead a falcon hawk, above the rude and ubiquitous crows, soared in circles, its wings stretched out into the swirled currents of the midday blue, floating in an infinitude it seemed, soaring in the song of the flute, watching the chained *piju* no doubt, eternally ready for the kill, and haunting my memory of the scene.

Naseeb's mat had been carefully laid out: there were the pictures of Rajiv Ghandi and Zail Singh with Naseeb, Chand Pasha, Chand Baba, and Kareem Baksh; there were the rings and amulets that he would sell; there were the implements of the trade—his wand, his cups, my needle, and bags unopened; there was his hand-thrown, gimmicked clay pot for pouring endless bowls of water; and the mat, a mandala, was graced with symbols—a monkey skull, the innards of some bird, the bones of a dog, a horseshoe and some shells, a jewel and a black Shiva-linga, the blood-filled limes, and the knives.

Removing the snakes from the stained jute bag, Ayasan carelessly threw them on the ground near the *piju*. The hawk circled lower and then rose once more. The snakes, dusty and lethargic, did not move. "Are those rubber snakes?" Naseeb asked his son. "No," the boy snapped back, "they're just tired because they went to a film last night and didn't get home until late." The people who had been drawn by the *piju*, the flute, the drum, or the sight of other onlookers, laughed. "If they're real snakes," the father asked his son, "why isn't your mongoose attacking them?" Ayasan grabbed the *piju*'s tail as he answered, "Because I've hypnotized him. I'm a magician." Naseeb laughed and challenged him to show the slowly gathering crowd some tricks. The boy yelled something back. "What did he say, Shankar?" I asked. My dear, kind, and completely good friend again insisted that it was "too rude for translation." I beseeched him to English it, but he was adamant: "It is far too obscene for your good ears." It was annoying—I wanted to understand everything. "Come on Shankar, I can handle it—fuck, shit, cunt, prick, piss—my ears can take it. Motherfucker! Cocksucker! What more can I say?" He smiled sweetly at me, cheerfully swiveled his head, and pointed to Naseeb, who, in response to taunting and challenges from Ayasan to perform some tricks himself, was doing coin magic. The sleights were sure and graceful. He held up his hand to show a one-rupee coin between his fingers and an identical coin in his palm. "I have only one coin here—this one is but a reflection of this one," he explained, and the two coins became one. All the while Ayasan's irreverent, disrespectful, and apparently obscene commentary was making the crowd laugh. And other onlookers were drawn to the show by that laughter.

Naseeb understands exactly how to control the crowd. With sleight of tongue, with words as well as gestures, he manipulates them as if they were coins in his hands. He always begins by playing dumb, then he's funny, then serious and adept, then terrifying and angry, and then, finally, as they pay up, he is humble and pious. He plays the fool, the clown, the conjurer, the sorcerer, and the holy man with equal ease and skill.

Borrowing a shawl from a rather dignified, elderly Brahmin in a fresh, clean dhoti, Naseeb, to the delight of the crowd, began to tear the cloth into pieces. "He is only really tearing a small portion of it," Shankar explained, "but he makes it appear that it is completely in shreds. The real skill here is in picking the right shawl, knowing which person will not object to losing a bit of the cloth. This man will not be angry. He'll consider it the price he has paid to enjoy the show. Naseeb won't restore it immediately. He'll set it aside and go on to another trick. That way he holds his crowd; they'll wait to see if he really can restore the shawl." And that is what he did. He began to remove marbles from his mouth, each one larger than the one preceding it, and then, still and constantly comically mocked by Ayasan, he plucked handfuls of sharp thorns from his mouth just as Kareem Baksh had done.

No sooner had he begun to pull meter after meter of colored cord from his mouth, than suddenly a policeman in an olive green uniform and a beige beret broke through the crowd waving his stick. He slapped the magician across the face, pushed him to the ground, and kicked the magic jar that would have flowed with endless waters. He crushed it under his feet and used his stick to scatter the amulets and rings. More policemen, these in blue and white, broke into the clearing as the constable struck Naseeb once more. I lunged forward yelling for them to stop. A soldier had his automatic rifle ready. Slumped on the ground, Naseeb endured it, kept his eyes down, contained the fury, and Ayasan kneeled next to him. At a gesture from his father, however, the boy jumped back up to gather the implements and put the snakes and *piju* back in their respective bags. People began to disperse, some backing up, some turning to walk away, some running. Others pushed in closer. The man whose torn shawl remained to be restored, handed Naseeb a ten-rupee note and vanished into the market. I tried to talk to the police. "Look, I have letters from the Ministry of Education. I'm here on a government grant to study Indian street magicians. I'm with the American Institute of Indian Studies. I'll take this up with the Minister of Education. I'll talk to a Lieutenant Colonel of the Indian Army—he has an interest in magic." The cop laughed and kicked over Naseeb's photographs. "Why talk to such lowly officials. Have the magician talk to his friend Rajiv Gandhi." I produced my wallet to indicate that I was prepared to pay a bribe and he laughed again. He shook his stick at Naseeb and shouted, "Get out of Khan Market. Never show your face here again. This is a VIP area."

While I continued my attempt to reason with the policeman, Shalini tugged at my sleeve. "Leave it alone. It's time to go. These cops can shoot on sight, and there are no questions asked. The crowd is angry. The people here detest the police, and they want a provocation. Let's go. Let's find Shankar and go. I can feel the tension in the air and the anger. The whole thing could explode at any minute. The police want the violence, they want the opportunity to flex their muscles, to show that they are in control."

Some of the audience that Naseeb had drawn together followed us to the car. A shoeshine boy stuck close to me. "That's Constable Kushi Ram," he said. "He's a *rākṣasa*. Everybody here hates him. The other day he beat up a beggar. A rich woman tried to stop him. She wanted to help the beggar, a crippled fellow, forlorn in every way and form. Kushi Ram threatened to beat her as well. She said she would inform her husband. Kushi Ram just laughed and said he's beat him up too and anyone else she cared to bring to Khan Market. By the way, your shoes need polishing." It was true—something that looked like bird shit was all over my shoes. The same stuff, I noticed, was on the shoes of others in the motley group that followed us to Shankar's automobile. The shoeshine boy, I was certain, understood quite well the workings of misdirection, the most basic principle of magic. He had slopped this stuff on our shoes while our attention was diverted. And like a magician, he would get paid for his deceit.

We went to Karim's for lunch. Naseeb and Ayasan spoke very little, and they hardly ate a thing. Assuming that his very apparent sadness was the result of having earned only ten rupees for his efforts, I tried to give him the 250 rupees he would surely have earned if Constable Kushi Ram had not broken up his show. But he refused it. Shankar insisted that I was responsible for Naseeb's despondency. "This sort of thing happens to him all the time, at least once a week. He's used to it. But he wanted to impress you, to put on a good show for you, and to give you the opportunity to perform the needle trick with him. If you had not been there, Naseeb would not be so sad." Shalini agreed.

I wanted to fix it, to have revenge, to use all the influence that I could muster to arrange for Naseeb to perform in Khan Market, to get the necessary permits to constrain Constable Kushi Ram so that he would have to watch Naseeb's magic show. I contacted Dr. Opal, and through him the Lieutenant Colonel of the Indian Army, as well as Dr. Pradeep Mehendiratta, the director of the American Institute of Indian Studies; I wrote letters to the Ministry of Education, the Delhi Police Department, and to acquaintances in the press. Armed with copies of these letters as well as copies of all the documents relating to my research fellowship, Shankar promised he would pursue the matter while I was in the south. "By the time you return to Delhi," he assured me with his eternally sanguine smile, "Naseeb will have the appropriate permit and papers to perform in Khan Market."

The violence of Delhi, the miserable turbulence and seething anger and anguish that could be sensed in the crowd at Naseeb's show, had become apparent on the first trip in May. As I sat in Shadipur talking to Naseeb, some Sikhs in another part of town drove slowly past a house where a young child's birthday was being celebrated. A magician, I was told, had been hired to perform for the party. Suddenly something broke through a window in the house, and there was an explosion. The innocents were torn to pieces. Blood was on the walls. Gleeful laughter turned either to hideous screams of survival or the horrible silence of death. There were roadblocks everywhere in the city. As we went from place to place, our taxi was stopped every kilometer or so. Police behind sandbag walls aimed their rifles at our heads, and if our taxi driver were a Sikh, he might be questioned or even searched. There was a curfew in Old Delhi. Hindus and

Muslims were murdering each other in the name of some ideal or other. Though the heat of summer had given way to the chill of December, the tension, the sense of a violence that could erupt at any moment, persisted. There was acrimony and rancor in people's eyes. And there was fear.

The newspapers were full of stories of innocent people accidentally killed by police. Maybe it was an accident. The victim said the wrong thing, made the wrong move, looked like the wrong sort of person.

Upon my return from the south, Shankar proudly showed me the police permits he had been able to secure for Naseeb's command performance at Khan Market. When we arrived there, Kushi Ram was nowhere in sight. A toothless old man with laughing eyes put his arms around me, "Thank you, thank, you, *Sāb*," he said, and his gratitude was explained. "They hate Kushi Ram. They hate the police. They're happy that you've helped the magician."

The *piju* and the cobras were on display; Ayasan was doing his own version of cups and balls, and Naseeb was smiling proudly over his challenge to the authority of Kushi Ram. In time, he draped a thick black blanket over Ayasan for a demonstration of telepathy. The child was able to tell how much money a certain man held in his hand, the color of a shawl at which Naseeb pointed, the number of fingers held up by another spectator. And then the child looked into the hearts and souls of members of the audience, revealing secrets that made them nod in wonder and approval: "You make money, but you can't save it. You want to do some work, but something is preventing it. You have many friends, but some of them have become enemies."

Just to make sure that I was ready to have my arm pierced by the needle, Naseeb casually glanced at me. The magician was about to restore a shawl that he had apparently torn into shreds when Kushi Ram, accompanied by two guards carrying automatic weapons, appeared. Standing before Naseeb, with the guards behind him, their faces blank, their hands ready, Kushi Ram, speaking quietly, carefully, precisely, ordered the street conjurer to leave. "This is a VIP area. No crowds here."

Shankar nervously, but with formal conviction, produced the permits and papers. Without reading them, Kushi Ram folded them up and put them in his pocket. "This is a VIP area. No crowds here," the policeman reiterated as he looked back at the gunmen. "No crowds," he repeated loudly for all to hear, and Naseeb's audience, grumbling but not really surprised, dispersed.

We tried again the very next day, this time out of the center of the city, at Vasant Vihar. Naseeb started the magic show near a movie theater about half an hour before the movie was scheduled to begin so that his crowd would be made up, at least partly, of people waiting to go to the movie. They would, he reckoned, if he could hook them soon enough, settle for the cheaper entertainment he provided. And hook them he did—with his cobras and *piju*, with his skulls and bones, his jokes and irreverent banter, with all the power of his art. At one point, just before the movie was to begin, as people started to leave the crowd around him and head toward the theater, Naseeb called out, "If anyone leaves this magic circle, my son will die." On cue Ayasan fell on the ground, retched, convulsed, and began to vomit blood. He lay there next to the cobras, their necks sinuously swaying, their hoods dangerously fanned open, and members of the audience called out to the moviegoers, "Come back, come back, you're killing the child." Some returned and Ayasan recovered.

Such terrors were alternated with comedy. A volunteer was asked to inspect an apparently empty container. "What edible would you like to be in this empty box?" the magician asked as he covered the container. "Ladu" the man said, and Naseeb asked him to blow on the magic box. "Don't spit on it," Naseeb chided the fellow jokingly. "Blow on it. Blow!" He opened the box, removed the requested sweet, and stuffed it into the volunteer's mouth. When he asked the man, whose mouth was too full to speak, his name, the crowd laughed over the incomprehensibility of the answer. "Did you say Thakkur Das by any chance?" Naseeb asked. His smile was cool and commanding. "Good. I've been looking for you for three years. Your wife wants you to come home." The crowd laughed again. Naseeb had them in the palm of his hand.

Cups and balls were manipulated; coins were vanished and made to reappear; stones and thorns were produced from Naseeb's mouth; a shawl was torn to pieces and restored; a lota bowl, emptied again and again, refilled itself each time with fresh water. "Holy water from the Ganga," Naseeb laughed.

A man from the crowd was decapitated beneath a blanket, and then his head was restored. Ayasan's tongue was cut off and then replaced.

When Naseeb walked toward me, I snapped a picture of him. "I want you to help me with a trick," he said in Hindi.

"What's he saying?" I asked aloud in English as if I had not the slightest clue as to what was about to transpire. An innocent bystander, an unknowing confederate from the crowd, translated. People laughed at me, the tourist who had no idea what he was getting into.

Naseeb help up the needle I had given him. "I'm going to put this needle through his arm."

"What's he saying?" I asked again with feigned innocence.

"Oh nothing," the bilingual volunteer commented, "he's just going to do some magic on you."

"It won't hurt me in any way, will it?"

And the audience laughed nervously when he answered, "No, surely not."

Holding up a ring for the audience to see, Naseeb announced that it, like all the rings on his mat, had great power. He placed the ring on my finger, and then, pulling my hand toward him to extend my arm, he gently pushed my coat sleeve up, then quickly inserted the needle as we had rehearsed. The shocked crowd audibly gasped.

"He feels nothing because of the power of the ring."

As he removed the needle and displayed the two bleeding puncture marks on my arm, I tried to act astonished.

"And now I'll heal the foreigner," Naseeb declared, and he began to recite the Qur'an. Wiping my arm with cotton and what was supposed to be a disinfectant, he made my wounds disappear, and all applauded in amazement.

The magician donned a skullcap, one just like those worn on the hallowed heads of people who have made a pilgrimage to Mecca, and announced that the rings, rings just like the one that had spared me of my pain and allowed me to be healed, could be purchased. These rings, which he had purchased in Chandni Chowk for fifty paise, were sold for five rupees each.

I held out my five rupees so that I could keep the ring upon my finger. Naseeb solemnly kissed it, waved a lime over it, and muttered a mysterious mantra. Other members of the crowd pushed and shoved, extending their money, anxious to buy one of the magic rings. Each sale came with more blessings, mantras, prayers, and promises of fortune.

While Naseeb continued to sell the rings as well as various amulets, some teenage boys started to tease Ayasan, to threaten and make fun of him. One of them pushed the child. But Ayasan was not afraid. When he pulled one of his snakes from the bag, the older boys shrieked and it was Ayasan's turn to laugh.

Shankar and I went to the car, which was parked far enough away so that no one who had been in the audience would see us leaving with Naseeb. Soon the magician and his son arrived with great smiles on their faces, utterly and deservedly proud of their wonderful performance.

The police suddenly appeared behind them and rushed to arrive at the car at the same time as Naseeb and Ayasan. One of them, his stick ready for action, snapped sternly at me in English. "You may not travel in this automobile with these people."

"That's what you think," I laughed. "These are my friends, and we are leaving here together."

"We will not permit it."

"Fuck off," I shouted, expressing the sentiments that I had wanted to convey to Kushi Ram. "This is my friend's car. You can't tell us who can or cannot ride in it. We haven't broken any laws."

With a startling shift in the tone of his voice and posture, the policeman shook his head rather sadly, and then softly, even beseechingly, with what seemed to be genuine concern and care in his voice, he insisted, "I'm very sorry, sir, but, despite your insults to us, it is our duty to protect you. You may not go with them."

"You aren't protecting me, you're annoying me. I'm perfectly safe. This magician is my friend. We've known each other since last May. He and I and the owner of the car, my friend Shankar, are going to get into the car and go to the guesthouse where I stay in Sunder Nagar."

"No, no, no," the policeman shook his head again. "It's not possible. He's not your friend, though you believe it. He has hypnotized you. All of the magicians have the power of hypnosis. They can even do mass hypnosis. He has hypnotized you so that you think he is your friend, so that you trust him. Now that he has your trust, now that you are under his control, he will steal all of your money. He may even kill you. If he had not hypnotized you, how could he have put a needle through your arm without causing pain to you?"

"He hasn't hypnotized me," I laughed. "The needle was a trick."

"It was not a trick," the cop insisted. "There was blood to prove it."

"Tell them, Shankar," I chuckled again over the ridiculousness of it all. "Explain it to them."

The policeman wouldn't listen to Shankar. "This fellow is in league with the magicians," he maintained. "He works for them. Because he speaks English, he's able to get foreigners for these people to cheat and rob. If they were not so successful with their criminal activities, they would not have been able to purchase such an automobile as this one. You may not go with them." The policeman, who seemed somewhat nervous, even frightened, dispatched one of his companions to fetch a taxi for me.

"I am saving your life," he said. "I shall even pay for your transportation out of my own humble pocket. I'm doing this for your own good, sir. You must trust me." The taxi pulled up.

Touched by the overworked and underpaid cop's gesture, by the odd mixture of officiousness and kindness, ignorance and innocence, I turned to Shankar. "Take Naseeb to the guesthouse. I'll meet you there. I'll take the taxi just so the cop can feel he's done a good deed and just so that he doesn't become disillusioned about the real power of Indian street magicians."

Back in Sunder Nagar, in my room, over bottles of Kingfisher beer, smoking bidis and Deluxe Benson and Hedges Internationals, we celebrated Naseeb's performance. Naseeb wanted to know how much the policeman had given the taxi driver. "Ten rupees," I said, and the magician laughed: "He cheated the driver—it's a twenty-rupee ride! But what could the driver do? Say no to the cop? That same cop charged me one hundred rupees as a bribe to put on my show."

The night I left India in January, Naseeb and I went to Shankar's for dinner. Shankar Junior performed with an egg bag for us, and Naseeb, in turn, showed the boy how to manipulate cups and balls like a real street magician, squatting on the ground. As Shankar Senior showed a videotape of the Las Vegas magical extravaganza of Siegfried and Roy, I wondered what Naseeb thought of the slick illusions, the lavish sets, scantily clad dancers, and the gaily garish and glitzy magicians who turned ladies into tigers and made elephants disappear. He seemed mildly amused.

When I pointed out to Naseeb that I was still wearing the ring I had bought from him in Vasant Vihar, he seemed mildly embarrassed. Pulling it from my finger and replacing it with the ring he always wore on his own, he confessed, and Shankar translated: "The ring that you were wearing doesn't really have any power. I was fooling the crowd. Wear my ring. It truly does have power. It is real magic."

We agreed that when I returned in May, one year after I had first met the magicians of Shadipur, I would travel with them in Kashmir.

"How will I find you?"

"Just come to India." He smiled as Shankar explained his words. "When you arrive you will know how to locate Naseeb."

"How?" I asked again.

"Magic!" Naseeb said in English with a laugh.

We shook hands and said good-bye.

With his ring upon my finger, the blood-red stone clutched in the clawlike setting, I watched him from the fifth-floor window of Shankar's walk-up apartment in Rajouri Gardens. The shawl hanging from his shoulders looked, in the silhouette created by the insect-swarmed street lamp, like wings, the pinions of some nocturnal bird resting before the reach for flight. I looked south, over the rooftops, through the smoky air of Delhi late at night in winter, toward Shadipur.

I stayed at the window and could picture the magicians sleeping in their hovels. In a small tent, Ayasan, Salma, Kabir, and several other children huddled together for warmth like baby animals under a thick, charcoal-colored, woolen blanket. An owl screeched, and the children heard it in their dreams.

Scene Two:

Soaring Pigeon

Owl screech and night scream, hoot and howl of desire or vision, yap and yowl of fear or warning: screech, scream—*Ullū! Ullū!*—and Kabir thought it was his mother who, since the death of his twin brother, had so often cried in the night. The birth of the baby had not, as Ibrahim Pasha had hoped it would, changed things. When others spoke of the woman's madness, whether with concern or derision, both shame and sympathy overwhelmed the child.

Kabir squirmed from under the thick woolen blanket, over his brother Adeel, in between Ayasan and Salma, out of the tent, while little Kemal, deeply sleeping, filled the space he had left behind. The night air was frosted and smoky, the sky starless. Its barrenness startled the heart and made it cower. Shivering, Kabir crawled on all fours over the ashes of the fire where the family had sought warmth earlier that evening, and, like an instinctively fearful young animal displaced from its lair in the night, he lowered his head between his shoulders and pushed into his father's tent. Burrowing under the blankets as into warm, sustaining earth, tunneling in between his parents, he gently took his mother's hand to pull her pliant, listless arm over his shoulder, across his chest, and to press it over his heart. Her other arm held the baby. Faintly, so faintly, she moaned in her dreams, and softly, so slightly, he rocked his body to lull and lower himself back into warm sleep. He did not like being awake while others slept, alone while not alone in the darkness.

When he woke up again, the tent was empty. Through the flaps he could see his mother, squatting by the fire, a dark shawl over her shoulders, clapping the dough between her hands for the chapatis. He could smell the daal cooking. And he could hear the baby crying and his grandmother, holding the infant, shaking him up and down, listing her complaints about the place, the world, the universe, about the day, the year, the age. Then, as she did almost every day, she described what had happened at Bhopal. "Disaster after disaster! It's an everyday occurrence. Did you hear about the fire in north Delhi the other day? Forty-seven people trapped. Most of them burned to death!" She told it to the baby.

Kabir crawled out of his rickety home. Wrapping himself in the thick blanket, cupping his hands for warmth around the scratched and dented metal tumbler of hot, sweet tea, he leaned against his father, fitting his body into the contours of Ibrahim Pasha's side. Removing the false teeth he had put in his mouth to eat breakfast, Ibrahim Pasha smoked his first bidi of the day. "God is great," he said as he took a deep puff and softly laughed. He spoke in the magician's language with Nissim Baba, declining the invitation to go along with him to Faridabad, to spend the week there performing in the villages of Haryana. And though he paid no attention to Kabir, the boy felt that his father was speaking that language for his sake, so that his son would hear it, know it and know in it, know how to see through it and feel with it.

"Don't leave today," Ibrahim Pasha said. "Put it off until tomorrow. Today we're going to see the M. T. Bannerji magic show. He's just arrived from Calcutta. Come with us."

"Why would I want to stay here just to see that fool?" Nissim Baba, always wanting some excuse to leave Shadipur, sneered. "He's no magician."

"Sure, it's true—he's not a *good* magician; but he is a magician. And he doesn't charge other magicians for tickets to his shows. And that's good. He invited us, all of us. It's good for the children to see some of his items, to get an idea of how stage magicians perform. Some of the illusions aren't too bad. I saw him last year in Lucknow. Professor M. T. Bannerji, " the street conjurer laughed and used the English phrase: "World's Greatest Magician." And Kabir repeated it aloud, mimicking the voice of a foreigner.

At the call to prayer, Kabir's grandfather appeared and, in pure Urdu, asked his son to accompany him to the little mosque in Shadipur. "No, no," Ibrahim smiled gently to his father. "No, I can't go right now, but please pray for me. Please." And Grandfather nodded his head in assent. That was enough to satisfy him.

Nissim Baba asked Ibrahim Pasha if he could take the cobras with him to Faridabad. As the men spoke of snakes and magic, Nissim Baba held a match under the hard, dark brown chunk of hashish, and Ibrahim Pasha, emptying half the tobacco out of one of Nissim Baba's Charminars, handed him a big pinch of it to mix with the now softened drug.

Crows, hungry for the remains of the magicians' breakfast, were hovering, squawking as if in argument, as they vied for the choicest perch on this tent, that tin roof, on this wire or that post. They chased off the mynahs and pigeons when they came too close. High above the other birds, displaying the detachment of the heavens, a lone brahmany kite circled once and again and then rose higher still and out of sight, spiraling into the smoke, through the haze, into the bright, blue clarity that was hidden above from the eyes of the earth.

Grandmother was still complaining and enumerating the atrocities of life. "Did you hear what these Hindus are doing? The mother and father get the dowry for marrying their son to some innocent girl. Then they pour kerosene on the girl and set her on fire. They report it as a cooking accident, and then they marry their son to another girl, get another dowry, and do the same thing again!" The old woman reminded Kabir of some kind of bird: her nose was the beak, her voice the squawk, and as she leaned forward on her cane, it looked as if she were perched on the stick, clinging to it with one talon. Ibrahim Pasha ignored her when she called out to him. He signaled to his wife to take care of her and relieve her of the crying baby.

While the men smoked, spoke, and joked, Kabir listened for the sumptuous resonances of his father's playful laughter. When Ibrahim Pasha placed his red fez on his boy's head, it came down over his ears, eyes, and nose, leaving only his mouth and the chin that rested on the black blanket visible. Kabir did not adjust it; by playing the part, he extended and expanded the magicians' laughter and delight.

"That foreigner is coming here again today," Ibrahim Pasha told his comrade, pausing to put his teeth back in so that he could chew some betel. "Did you meet him? He brought some gifts, some American gimmicks, pocket magic, not very useful, but amusing. He's writing a book and has so many questions. He's mostly interested in Naseeb, and Naseeb wants to go to the U.S.A. with him. But I don't think he'll take him. He's cheating Naseeb. Anyway, that's my opinion. He's taking up all of Naseeb's time. And what's he giving in return?"

Kabir's mother brought more tea for them. She licked her finger and with it wiped the ashes from her son's cheeks, the soot that remained there from when he had crawled into their tent in the night.

"Naseeb's no fool. We have to trust him, to believe that he knows what he's doing with this fellow."

"No, he's no fool, but all of us can be greedy. We're born greedy. Just look at the baby if you don't believe it. Listen to your baby! Cry, cry—feed me, feed me! And if Naseeb thinks this foreigner will take him to the U.S.A. and make him rich, well then, greed is making a fool of him."

Kabir flocked with the rest of the children to greet the foreigner. It was something different to do, and Kabir wanted the woman who came with the foreigner to photograph him as she had photographed the others.

Watching the foreigner as he asked questions of the magicians, watching him write things down in the notebook he carried, Kabir wanted to know what words he wrote. What language were they, what did they say, what did they mean? And did he write anything about Kabir? "What could he write about me anyway?" the boy asked himself sullenly. "He doesn't know me."

After the visitors were escorted into Chand Pasha's concrete house, the pride of the magicians' section of Shadipur, after the children were chased away, Kabir went to find his grandfather.

"*La ilaha illa'llah*," Grandfather would recite during those moods that seized him after going for prayer, "*muhammadun rasulu'llah*." And then, with his eyes closed, after a long and deliberate pause, he would paraphrase some part of the Qur'an, alternating shouts and whispers, tones of anger and contrition, modulating melancholy and bliss. "Death to man, to man who is thankless! Death to him! From what did God create him and why? From a drop of sperm He made man and set his life in order, made his path, and then from God comes the death of man and his burial. Then when God, the almighty, the merciful, the most high, wills, He brings man back to life again." Whenever he spoke that way his eyes would fill with tears. "This year I must go to Mecca. I must. I must go before I die, and I'll die next year," he'd laugh oddly. "Yes, I want to die when I am sixty-three. That must be the proper age to die. That was the age of the Prophet Muhammad—peace be upon Him—when he died."

The old man laughed, then kissed the boy, held his hand tightly in his own, and spoke of the Prophet. Just as Kabir endured his grandmother's complaints, so he indulged his grandfather's sermons, which inevitably culminated in a quote from the poet Kabir:

> "I'll never let go," the *cakor* vows all too soon,
>   Mistaking flames of the coals for sweet rays of the moon;
> That vow was the last one that bird ever did speak,
>   For by eating the coals, he burned his tongue and his
>   beak.

He laughed and kissed Kabir again. "Are you going to the Bannerji show today?" he asked, and the boy nodded nonchalantly.

"He's a Hindu. From Calcutta. The Hindus burn their dead. That's no good. I saw the father perform once in Lahore, before Partition. It was no good."

Kabir, his father and brother, Ayasan, Chand Baba, Apeez, Iqbal, and Asad squeezed out of the overcrowded, battered, fuming bus near the Kabari Bazaar to walk toward the great circus tent that had been erected near the Jama Masjid. Kabir could hear the call to prayer crackle over the loudspeakers. He liked to walk like that, among the men, to feel the jaunty rhythm and safety of the group. Birds circled in the sky and the boy, as he walked behind his father, stretched his steps to match Ibrahim Pasha's graceful gait and virile stride. The men were joking about Professor Bannerji.

"The father of this idiot, this ridiculous fool, was good."

"No, no—his father stole everything from Sorcar. Terrible, he was terrible. Just a bad version of all of Sorcar's items without anything new."

"And Bannerji Junior does a bad version of his father's bad version of Sorcar. Let's hope there's no Junior Bannerji Junior to carry on the tradition."

"There was a son, but not now. Bannerji—what a *cār-sau-bīs*—is in a lot of trouble. Did you hear? Suleiman Yusuf Shah told me. Remember him, the sword swallower, the Maslet from Ludhiana who joined Bannerji's troupe? He says that Bannerji got caught fucking his assistant. Her family wants money. His wife's family wants money. The wife left him, took the son. Problems! Problems!"

"This is nothing new for him. His entire show was run out of Madras when he was caught fucking the wife of the chief of police there."

"He's obviously no good at tricking people, whether it's in magic or in fucking."

When the magicians arrived at the great grayish green tent, the old man, Professor M. T. Bannerji Senior, dressed in a black Western suit, sitting at a small table of decaying wood by a fire that had been built in a metal refuse bin, rose to greet them with a cough and a smile. His yellowish waxen hands let go of the tickets and the string-tied packet of rupees to come together in a gesture of greeting. The blue-black dye with which he had tried to hide his gray hair had stained his temples and there were the remains of the sauce from his lunch on his graying white shirt.

It was out of a love for his own Bengali language that he had refused to ever speak a word of Hindi. Only Bengali and English. And so, though surely knowing that they could hardly understand a word of what he said, he addressed the street magicians in what he considered nonpartisan English: "I make humble obeisance to you! I, the great Professor M. T. Bannerji Senior, formerly loyal magician to His Excellency the Right Honorable Victor Alexander George Robert Bulwer-Lytton, am honored by your presence. My son, the great Professor M. T. Bannerji Junior, at this time the world's greatest magician, is likewise magnificently honored. My late, great, beloved father, official court magician to Her Majesty, Queen Victoria, Empress of India, great herself, would also be fulsomely honored. For you, he so often opined, the magicians of the street, you, you are the true masters of our prestidigitatorial art, the very true gurus of *Indrajāl*. It is true, and therefore cannot be denied, that we—my father, my humble self, and my magnificent son—can perform incomprehensible marvels, uncanny illusions, ineffable legerdemains, unexplainable mysteries, and breathtaking feats upon the stage. But it is you—and you alone—you who can perform fully surrounded." Enchanted by the mellifluence of his own voice, he went on and on: "And for your skill, I honor you! I hail you! You! I bloody worship you! As proof that this praise is not vacuous, I humbly offer a modest gesture of lofty honoring: a ticket to my son's magnificent performance for each and every one of you, absolutely free of charge. This is our *daksinā* to you. Do not so much as try to pay us even one measly paisa!"

Kabir clung to the few words he had understood: father, son, world, greatest, magic, magician, queen, guru, *Indrajāl*, illusion, street, stage, perform, skill, ticket, free, pay, paisa.

"Furthermore," the old man, now sitting as if exhausted by the labor of his speech, continued, much to the embarrassment of his cashier-assistant and to the mild amusement of the magicians, "I shall grant you the honor of giving my son the honor of meeting him backstage after the magnificent show. There and then he will be obliged to answer any questions you may have about his magic, and then and there also he will provide you with personally autographed posters, beautiful memorabilia, and very highly glossy photographs. What more can I say on this magnificent occasion, this auspicious confluence of magics. Today street magic meets stage magic here, right in this very spot, just as Ganga meets Yamuna at Allahabad."

As the magicians were escorted out of the cold and into the smoky warmth of the tent, toward the unfolded metal chairs that were being cordoned off for them, Kabir noticed the foreigner sitting in the front of the tent near the stage by the stove that had been lit for him and the woman photographer. They waved to the magicians.

Foreign music roared ferociously through the electrical crackle and static of the dented metal speakers to keep out blares of traffic, the stridor of crowds, calls to prayer and commerce, and all the other sonic atrocities of the Delhi streets. Glaring, flaring white lights were suddenly off, and out of an explosion on the nearly dark stage, a flash of golden hot light and white smoke, Professor M. T. Bannerji Junior, "the World's Greatest Magician," dressed in a black tuxedo, wearing a black top hat, a red satin cummerbund that had obviously been cut from the curtains behind him, and almost white gloves, stepped with a gaping grin and a flourishing bow.

The red satin curtains parted to reveal a backdrop painted with a swirl of images that were exotic to Kabir—dice and dominoes, a roulette wheel and a wheel of fortune, cards (aces, sevens, and the face cards), an American flag, and words that Kabir could not read: "Stardust Hotel and Casino of Magnificent Las Vegas, U.S.A."

The music choked, then changed to screech and gurgle more hectically and viciously than ever as the magician removed his hat, reached into it, pulled out a pigeon, and bowed again with a cloying and tawdry panache. There was a burst of trumpets and a drumroll and then a tango. Bannerji took off the gloves theatrically, tugging at each finger in time to the music, and, as he dropped them on the table before him, each one of them in turn turned into a dirty, gray pigeon. "The pigeons," Ibrahim Pasha leaned forward to explain to his son in whispers, "are supposed to be doves, white like the gloves." He muttered an English phrase: "Dove-to-glove."

As Professor Bannerji, his smile seemingly frozen or cast upon his pink-painted face, held up one of the dusty pigeons, an egg appeared to drop from it. And then another. And then another. The magician caught each egg and set them, one by one, on the table. A boy, no older than Kabir, dressed like a circus clown, brought out a dove pan from the wings of the stage and took the pigeons away with him. The magician, after bowing again and again, and after donning a wrinkled white apron and a soiled white European chef's hat, opened the metal pan and showed it to be empty. Once he had cracked each egg and emptied the whites and yolks into the pan, he made a great fuss of stirring it all up, adding salt and pepper, tasting it, adding more seasonings, and stirring it again, all the while nodding, rocking, and shaking his head to the music. The smile never changed. Then, although it did not make much sense, he added kerosene to the mixture, lit a match, and dropped it in. Extinguishing the burst of flames with the lid of the pan, he proudly bowed, and removed the lid again. Another motley pigeon, ruffling its wings, hopped, dazed, out of the pan where the fire had been. The magician bowed again. And again. And again. The audience applauded feebly.

Amidst a barrage of illusions and tricks performed in a variety of costumes, Professor M. T. Bannerji returned again and again to the production and disappearance of pigeons. He transformed a pigeon into a duck and the duck back into a pigeon. The only applause came from the assistants on the stage. When he turned one of the birds over in his hands, massaging its stomach gently with his finger, and setting it down on the table, it lay there perfectly still. As the magician gestured with his hands, fingers widespread, the pigeon, still on its back, rose slowly in the air, floated up in front of Professor Bannerji's blindingly livid smile. As the magician passed a shiny metal hoop over the hovering bird to show that there were no strings attached, Ibrahim Pasha explained to Kabir how the trick was done.

As he watched the show, Kabir decided that he would perform with pigeons the next day and he rehearsed each of the tricks in his mind. By hiding one pigeon in the load of a basket, he could turn an imaginary mosquito into a real bird, just as his father did. And another pigeon would be loaded into a dove pan to be produced from flames just as Professor Bannerji had done. Kabir would ask Iqbal for the pan and Asad for the birds, for it was Asad who captured the pigeons for many of the magicians. He liked birds and, always with an ironic laugh, called them angels. He claimed to understand their language. "Hear the baby *papiha's* call? 'Where's my papa?' it cries. 'Fly higher!' Father answers. 'Fly as high as you can! You won't get burned by the sun!'"

Asad explained that the prophet King Suleiman had also known the secret language of birds. "The Qur'an says so. He had an army of birds and used them as spies and messengers. Birds are sacred. The *Rāmāyan* says so too. Most magicians clip their wings so they cannot fly away," Asad told Kabir. "And they use the same pigeons for each performance. But my idea is that for each dove or pigeon trick, the magician should use a new bird, freshly caught, its wings uncut, still bearing the look of the heights. When it's released, it will spread its wings majestically and fly away, and for the audience it will be a wondrous image of freedom. Watching the pigeon soar, the people will feel themselves freed from all that binds them."

Asad knew the avian lore. He told Kabir stories of Garuda, "the great bird upon whose back Lord Vishnu rides, the enemy of serpents who stole the nectar of immortality from the gods." And he spoke of Jatayu: "When Ravan abducted Sita from the forest, Jatayu, hearing her piteous cries, attacked the demon just as a thunderbolt assaults a mountain. The enraged king of Lanka drew his sword, slit Jatayu's neck, and cut the wings from his body. The demon fled then with the beautiful Sita. It was through will and devotion to Lord Ram that the wingless bird was able to stay alive, to wait for Ram's return so that he could inform him of what Ravan had done. Tenderly Ram held the dying bird in his arms, and, beholding the beautiful face of God, Jatayu felt neither the pain of his wounds nor any fear of death. Once he had told Ram the whole story of the abduction of Sita, he could let go of his life, for his mission was complete. Ram and Lakshman performed the funeral rites for him, set the body of the vulture upon the pyre, lit the fire, and sang his praises. As the body of the vulture was consumed by the flames, the soul of Jatayu ascended in a chariot of fire to Paradise, where it was given a new form, a perfect body with great wings of pure gold. *Jay Rām! Jay jay Rām!*"

Professor Bannerji, dressed now as a maharaja, turbaned in pink satin, pink plumed and sashed, almost iridescent in his knee-length primrose jacket, dripping, even oozing, with what looked like diamonds, rubies, and pearls, still stretching his smile so that it would have been seen from the very last row if anyone had been sitting there, put another one of the scraggly pigeons in a brown paper bag, set the bag on fire, and scattered the ashes with a flourish. He blew up a yellow balloon, popped it with a pin, and the dove-gray, battered bird was resurrected. Foreign music gave way to Hindi film scores that were no less loud with electrical crackle and cackle.

Just as Ibrahim Pasha decapitated Kabir on the streets, so Professor Bannerji decapitated a maharani, the beautiful Miss Lakshmi. He introduced her onto the stage, put the stocks on her neck, displayed a sword as shiny as Ravana's, slapped it against the table to indicate that it was solid, and then forced it through the center of the stocks, straight through the lady's neck. "There should be blood," Kabir thought to himself. "Blood makes a trick better."

Just as Ibrahim Pasha would so often put Kabir into the basket, Professor Bannerji directed his lady to step into a four-legged box decorated with the image of a boy climbing a rope—the Old Indian Rope Trick. And just as Ibrahim Pasha would cover the wicker basket, Professor Bannerji locked down the lid of the box. One by one, swords, slapped against the table again, were thrust through the box from every direction, at every angle, and then a spear was inserted straight down from the top, down through the very center of the magic box. When the front flap of the box was removed, the container was empty except for the network of criss-crossing blades that reflected the bright spotlights aimed at the center of the stage.

The box was sealed again, the swords and spear removed, then opened again, and as the maharani took her bow to a scattered applause that was barely audible over the blare and blast of the tin speakers, Professor Bannerji disappeared.

SOARING PIGEON

The maharani danced to the clack and clamor of a scratched recording of "Tequila." As she finished, Professor Bannerji, dressed as a surgeon, all in dirty white, masked and rubber-gloved, returned to the stage to perform the operation. A table and electric saw were rolled out, and the magician sawed the lady in two.

When, after the performance, Kabir and the others went to Professor Bannerji's tent, they interrupted what seemed to be an argument between the magician and the beautiful Miss Lakshmi. As the maharani, who had been dismembered and made whole again no less than four times in the last two hours, made her exit with apparent anger, the flustered maharaja turned to the street magicians with hands together in a ceremonious greeting. The exaggerated smile of the stage persisted.

"I am honored by your presence! For while I am quite adept at the performance of marvelous illusions which prompt the sentiment of wonder in the hearts of one and all, it is you—the *jādūgars* of our streets, bazaars, and villages—who are the greatest artistes of all. You and you alone can perform fully surrounded and under any and all conditions. The lowest is the highest! That is a marvel in and of itself!"

He cupped his hands around Kabir's face and asked the boy his name. "The magic of the future, my little one, is in your hands. Preserve it, my child! Develop it! Enchant the world!"

He turned to the men and spoke with the same histrionic grandeur that informed his father's oratory. "I love children, all children. I love their innocence. I love their sense of wonder. All magicians are children at heart. It is the magician's mission and obligation to remind a world that is bleak and busy, rationalistic and moralistic, weary and woebegone, of the child within each adult's heart—isn't it so? For the child all is magic—everything is amazing, stupendous, and miraculous. 'Be as a child!' our beloved Ramakrishna taught, and Muhammad and Jesus concur. Adulthood is a loss. It is the death of a child! Magic is the promise of resurrection—isn't it so? And why not? Anything can happen in the Net of Magic."

The magician handed Kabir and each of the other children a rolled-up poster for the "Grand Magic Show of Professor M. T. Bannerji, World's Greatest Magician."

Kabir scrutinized it by the fire that night: Bannerji's eyes were stretched open wide, and his hands were spread majestically; his jeweled turban had a feather in it; cards and doves filled the air, and beneath the magician, a lady, sawed in half, waited to be made whole and alive again.

In the morning, in the cold, as he folded up the poster to pack it in the jute bag, Kabir told three-year-old Kemal what items they would be performing that Sunday afternoon near the Purana Qila, not far from the zoo, next to the little mosque where Kabir had died and been reborn from the wicker basket so many times. "Don't pick your nose at the performance. And keep an eye out for the cops," Kabir ordered as he began to take an inventory: the basket, dove pan and kerosene, the cups and cloth balls, the knife and limes, the sodium and stones, the damaru drum and gourd-flute, the peacock feathers, rug, gimmicked metal bowl, and the painted duck that his father had given him last summer, the Chinese Sticks that Nissim Baba had made, and the two mottled pigeons that Asad had captured just the day before and marked with lampblack so that the crowd would not be able to distinguish one from the other. "Perfect twins," Asad said proudly. "You can vanish one, produce the other from somewhere else, and everyone will think the pigeon has been transported through thin air."

Putting the borrowed snake in a cotton bag full of dirt, Kabir handed it to Kemal to carry. "No poison," he reassured the child.

The serpent, sluggish from the cold, carefully watched by the sparrows in the nearby tree, attracted a few spectators while Kabir played the drum: "With this damaru Mahadeo started the Universe, and this is Krishna's flute." As Kabir performed his cups and balls routine, Kemal watched his every move, sleight, and gesture carefully, with admiration and delight. The boy knew what he was doing.

The small circle of spectators inspired the curiosity of other passersby, and a crowd slowly began to gather around the two children. Kabir set out the autographed poster of Professor M. T. Bannerji, drew the magic circle with a stick, a branch from the nearby pipal tree, and then played the flute again.

A pair of emerald green parrots and a lone mynah watched the performance from the nearby tree. Three foreigners, a man and two women, had joined the still growing audience, and Kabir wondered what they were saying amidst their laughter: *"Il est si mignon, ce gamin, ce petit Robert-Houdin. Il a du culot, n'est-ce pas? Il faut avoir les photos."* Kabir liked it that they were snapping pictures of him. People might see him in the U.S.A., the U.S.S.R., Australia, France, Germany, Arabia, Great Britain, even Las Vegas, anywhere in the world. They threw some coins on the ground—two rupees and seventy paise in all—and Kemal, picking his little nose, gathered them up with his free hand.

As he manipulated the Chinese Sticks, Kabir recited his father's patter: "With these sticks Raja Bhoj performed for Akbar in this very spot. It's true, I swear it. God is my witness." He knew that God was not angered when magicians lied. "God is merciful," his grandfather always assured him.

The crowd, amused over the incongruity of a child acting like an adult, laughed over Kabir's performance, entertained but not, it seemed to Kabir, amazed as they were by his father. The boy wanted to stun, dazzle, and bewitch them no less than Ibrahim Pasha, Naseeb, Chand Baba, or any of the other men. He wanted to take power over them. And he wanted their money. He wanted to hand the money to his mother just as his father did and to see her smile as she counted it.

"What's your name?" Kabir asked a smartly dressed boy about his own age who had just joined the audience with an ice cream in his hand.

"Indrajit Sharma," the boy called out proudly, and Kabir invited him into the magic circle. His mother insistently wiped the ice cream from his chin before she would let him step forward. After asking the boy whether he was Hindu or Muslim, Kabir handed him the wooden duck and then requested him to inspect the object and tell the audience what it was.

"A duck," Indrajit Sharma replied, and Kabir laughed. "No it's not a duck. A duck has feathers and is big. It's a piece of wood shaped like a duck. It's nothing but a painted toy. So you're either a liar or a fool. And Hindus, I'm told, don't lie. So you must be a fool."

Everybody but Mother Sharma laughed. "I'll help you, Indrajit my friend, my Hindu brother, so that you don't have to be either a liar or a fool. I'll make the piece of wood come alive. With my marvelous magic I'll make the toy become a duck, a real duck, so that no one can call you a liar or a fool. Okay? I must blow on it to give it the power of breath. I must gaze at it to give it the power of the eye. I must rub it to give it the power of touch. I must mutter mantras on it—*yantru-tantru-jālajāla-mantru*—to give it the power of speech. All these powers I accumulated at the cremation grounds." The young magician's tightly huddled audience smiled and laughed quite comfortably over the patter. The afternoon sun, behind the haze, had made the air a bit warmer.

The brightly painted wooden duck floated lifelessly on the dirty water. "What a stupid duck," Kabir laughed. "That's because it's a jungle duck, a tribal duck. But this duck loves music!" And as he started to play the gourd-flute and beat the drum, it seemed that the duck danced in time to the music, bobbed about upon the water with the bewildering joy of finding itself suddenly alive. Then, in an instant, the moment Kabir stopped playing, the duck disappeared beneath the surface of the water. "Oh no, the duck is drowning," Kabir called out and reached into the bowl, pulling out the little toy that then seemed to jump from his hand into the crowd. When a spectator tossed it back it lay lifeless at the child's feet. "You've killed it," Kabir teased. "Who will pay for the cremation of the duck? Who will give something for the widow, for all the little ducklings? Whose heart here is not made of wood?" With appreciative laughter a few good sports, including Mr. Sharma, tossed coins to Kabir.

Kabir showed the dove pan to be empty. "Here we will cremate our duck. Is there some Brahmin here to recite the mantras? Indrajit, are you a brahmin? Yes? Okay, you recite the Veda for us." Again the crowd laughed with genuine delight, and Kabir and Indrajit laughed too. "No, that will take too long. Brahmins go on and on. I'll do it: *Dam māro dam, nitya jāī gam, bolo subah śyām, Hari Kṛṣṇa Hari Rām!*"

The young magician set the little toy in the dove pan and poured in the kerosene from the Campa-Cola bottle. As he lit the match and dropped it in, the bird disappeared in the flash of flames. Slapping the cover on the pan as quickly and deftly as Professor M. T. Bannerji, Kabir recited his father's words: "From life comes death. From death comes life." He played a few notes on the flute and repeated the words with a sudden solemnity. "From death comes life." And, as he removed the cover of the pan to reveal a real living pigeon where the burning wooden duck had been, he grabbed the bird before it could fly away and then held it by its legs so that it flapped its wings wildly and desperately for the audience. "*Şābāş*," people laughed and threw more coins into the magic circle.

It wasn't enough for the child. The trick had not had the power Kabir had hoped it would. It did not bring in the money he had expected. Nor had it turned amusement into awe. As little Kemal circled, once to pick up the coins that had been tossed in and once again with a hand outstretched in supplication for additional alms, an idea came to Kabir, an inspiration that made him tremble.

"You don't believe this is real magic, that I can make life from death?" the child-magician challenged. "This isn't child's play. These aren't magic tricks. This is real." As Kemal, smiling proudly, watched the spectacle, the older boy seemed like a real magician to him, fully grown up, a man. "Women and children must leave now," he announced. Indrajit Sharma struggled with his mother in an attempt to stay. "Go," Kabir shouted with what sounded like genuine fury, "Women and children go!" People laughed to hear a child telling children to go away, but the laughter was becoming uneasy and nervous. It was clear that something serious, even dangerous, was about to happen.

The pigeon, its wings now restrained, struggled to free itself from Kabir's grip. But the boy held the bird firmly in one hand as he squatted, reaching with the other into his bag for the little black pouch of colored stones which he emptied out on the ground. "These are magic gems," he said with conviction as he picked up each one of them, all twenty-one of them, and gently touched them to the bird's head. When he had set each stone down, a small circle was formed by them. He raised his father's knife and stabbed it into the earth right in the center of the circle of stones. Closing his eyes, he softly muttered what sounded like Arabic prayer. The crowd was silent as the child stood up, faced in the direction of Mecca as indicated to him by the position of the small mosque nearby, and spoke aloud: *"Bismillah!"*

Silently and with a certain reverence, he lowered the bird to the ground, stretched out its wings behind it and stepped on them to keep the pigeon in place. Turning the bird's head to the side, he stroked its neck with his fingers as if to hypnotize it. Grayish pink skin was exposed as he gently plucked some of the neck feathers. Within himself he asked God to forgive him for what he was about to do and then, still facing the holy city, he drew the knife out of the earth and slit the pigeon's throat.

The fragile body twitched and twisted as several of the spectators yelled out: "No! No!" Streams of blood squirted in rhythmic spurts from the severed vessels of the opened neck as Kabir continued to force the knife through the spine. "I must pull the knife all the way through so that I can take this head to Kali. She'll add it to the garland of heads that decorates her breasts."

He dropped the head on the ground and the beak opened as if it were about to screech or scream. The mynah in the branches of the tree above him took flight, and a pipal leaf fell. Kabir, his hands and face splattered with blood, cut the wings from the spasmodically struggling body of the headless pigeon. His gray kurta and baggy pajama pants were stained with the blood. It gurgled from the bird's throat. Kabir touched the bright, oozing blood with his finger and then wiped it on one of the stones in the circle. He repeated the gesture, again, and again, squeezing the blood from the bird like juice from a lime to mark each of the twenty-one stones with it. And then, before an audience that was transfixed with horror, he placed the sacrifice, still warm, still ever-so-slightly struggling, into the wicker basket.

"From death comes life," the child said again as he waved the wings of the bird over the basket. "That's what it says in the Qur'an. That's what it says in the *Rāmāyan*." He dropped the wings into the basket and then the head. "And that's what Kabir says too."

He reached into the basket to arrange things and then covered it. Kemal was motionless, his mouth hanging open, his eyes just as wide, as he watched Kabir strike the basket with a stick in the same way that Ibrahim Pasha struck the same basket when it was Kabir within it. "Ho!" he shouted and struck the basket again. "Ho!" he shouted as his father did. "Ho!" and then he removed the basket top. The crowd stood still. Kabir stepped back. And then, all of a sudden, a pigeon, appearing from inside of the basket, perched on the rim of it. Ruffling its feathers, fanning its wings, it glanced nervously around and then, seemingly startled by the gathering of men, it leapt skyward, opened its wings wide and flew up, higher, higher, ascending as the spirit of Jatayu must have done when it was freed from death and purified by the fires that Lord Ram had kindled for it. The bird circled higher and higher still, and Kabir and Kemal and each one of the men in the oval around them watched in awe and even envy. Catching a current, the pigeon, as if with the golden wings of the resurrected Jatayu, soared to disappear in the infinite expanses of heaven, into what appeared to be the unlimitedness of its freedom.

When the bird was out of sight, Kabir tilted the basket forward so that all could see that it was empty, and then he squatted by the circle of blood-stained stones. "These gems," the magician said, "have the power to protect you from death. If a man is in an automobile accident and he has one of these stones in his pocket, even if his head and his arms are cut off in the wreck, he will be made whole again. Through the magic power of these stones he will come back to life again."

From watching his father at work, Kabir knew how to set the price of the stones. They had to cost enough to suggest that they had real value, but not so much that the skeptical would not think it worthwhile to purchase one just in case it might have some, even just a little, power.

"Ten rupees," the magician said firmly, and the men pushed in close around him, shoving their money forward, anxious that there might not be enough of the magic gems to go around. Kabir sold all of the twenty-one blood-marked stones. An old man seemed very disappointed that there was not one left for him. "I'm going to see a film tomorrow at the Rivoli Cinema at Connaught Place. If you're there at one o'clock, I'll be able to provide you with one of the gems at that time, one that has even more power than the ones I sold here today."

"I'm going to take you to Karim's in a taxi, a big black-and-yellow taxi driven by a Sardarji. That's where foreigners and professional stage magicians and film stars and politicians eat. We'll have chicken or mutton, all you want," Kabir told Kemal as he watched the little boy pack up the basket and jute bag according to his instructions. "We'll have the driver wait for us while we eat. Then we'll have him drive us to Gaylord's so you can have some ice cream. And then maybe we'll go to a film if we feel like it."

Kabir held Kemal's hand to lead him along the Mathura Road in search of an empty and available taxi. The blood, still on his hands, face, and clothes, had dried and darkened.

They stopped at a pile of refuse that was being burned by the roadside to discard the head, wings, and body of the pigeon. It was getting dark. Kabir and Kemal, standing with the pariahs who had gathered by the fire to keep warm, saw the feathers ignite and watched the flames consume the remains of the bird. He saw Jatayu. Then there was the fleeting image of a child in the fire, the flash and flicker of a dream or memory, and he did not know if it was himself or his twin brother. Watching the flames, he felt free from all that had ever bound him.

One of the beggars, raggedly draped in a contaminated blanket, coughed as he stretched out his hand to Kabir. The magician reached into the pocket of his shirt to find a rupee for him.

As they walked, Kabir, still holding Kemal's hand, looked carefully at the faces of the people around him, looking at them as he had never looked before. He looked at them as if he knew them, recognizing something in everyone. He felt affection as he looked at some, anger as he looked at others, and pity as he looked at still others. Kabir felt that he knew things that he had not known before. He would not have been able to name or describe those things, to explain them to his mother or father, or to little Kemal, but that didn't matter. He was, at that moment, without worry or fear, care or need. And he laughed aloud.

"I'm going to Kashmir this summer," he told Kemal as they climbed into the back of the taxi. "Maybe I'll take you along. I'm going by airplane or maybe in a taxi. People will want to see me perform. I'm going to buy some doves with my money, beautiful white doves. I'm through performing with pigeons. I'll take the doves with me to Kashmir."

As the taxi stopped near Karim's, Kabir laughed again. "Everyone is going to want to see me. Everyone will come to the Grand Magic Show of Professor Kabir, the World's Greatest Magician. Yes, let's go to Kashmir."

Traveler's Journal 2:

Kashmir

The sudden soar of the flock, the harsh angle and dark pattern of the flight, would have seemed to warn of disasters, and the smoke, more lingering than rising over the morning fires, would have seemed to augur sadnesses, if, there in the graveyard, the vagrant children had not been laughing.

India had been blistered by the fires of summer, and street performers from all over the northern plains, seeking audiences in the cooler air of Kashmir, seeking refuge by its bracing waters and on its morning-frosted earth, had pitched their rough tents in the cemetery on the Baramullah Road, across from the Batmaloo bus station, and over the splintered, creaking planks that so precariously bridged the trickling rivulet of sewage. They came like birds of passage. And in that desultory camp of wanderers the children laughed.

They laughed to see us trying to keep our balance as we crossed the makeshift viaduct and, apparently entertained by the intrusion into their world, they surged to greet us with a disarming mirth, to touch our hands, grab our arms and legs, to rub, poke, or slap our backs.

"Naseeb," I said, holding out the photograph that had been taken a year earlier in Delhi, "Naseeb Shah—*jādūgar.*" The giggling children inspected the image: an Indian street magician showed a magic trick to a foreign traveler. An urchin's dirty hand, shoved through the cram and crush of the rag-clad, chattering crowd, snatched the picture and disappeared.

"Come back," I shouted and pushed, elbowing and kneeing a path, trying to jostle forward, after the running boy, toward the dark, tattered tents. A man with a crimson turban, his betel-stained teeth just as red, with the unclouded black eyes of a brahmany kite, walked slowly forward and then stood his ground to wave his hand in a gesture that anywhere in the world, at any time, is understood: "Come. No danger. Come here." The other hand held a stick that menaced the children with semaphores no less universal: "Get away. Stop that! Go!" While his welcome to us seemed genuine, his threat to the children apparently was not. They ignored the man and laughed all the more.

BIRDS AND FIRE

"Naseeb," I said, "Naseeb Shah—*jādūgar.*" And the man, now poking at the persistently thronging children with the stick and scolding them with ineffectual curses, turned and walked, glancing back just once to make sure that we were following him, between, around, and over the Muslim graves, deeper into the place of death where life surged and persevered.

Suddenly we saw him, the magician, dressed in a black kurta, standing by his tent in the graveyard camp, smiling, and then laughing with characteristic exuberance at the sight of us. "*Namaskār,* Guruji," I laughed with the amazement of having been able to actually find him. "*Salaam aleichem,* Naseeb." And he laughed too: "Lee Baba, hello. Hello, Lee Baba Madame." It was very good to see him again.

Before I left Hawaii, I had no idea how I would be able to locate Naseeb. The magician could be anywhere. But, trusting him when, in December, he had said that as soon as I arrived in India, I would know how to find him, I flew to Delhi and checked into the guesthouse in Sunder Nagar.

"Naseeb has informed me that he will be waiting for you," Shankar explained with the abundant cheerfulness that he always seemed to derive from being helpful to me or anyone else, "across from the Batmaloo bus station in Srinagar."

"But," Shalini warned with the ironic smile that inevitably shaded all that she said about any of the people of Shadipur, "you must get there as soon as possible. These folks keep moving. Naseeb can't stay put very long."

There was, as there always is in India when one urgently feels a necessity to get to a certain place at a certain time, a problem. Because it was 114 degrees in Delhi, everyone wanted to go to Kashmir; and so there were no tickets available on flights to Srinagar. Mehendiratta, whose very metier, as director of the American Institute of Indian Studies, is to be connected and have influence, to know everyone in the government, in the airlines, in every official institution, couldn't, I heard, get airline tickets for his own son. "Even the Lieutenant Colonel of the Indian Army has been unable to get tickets," Shankar said with the deep dolefulness that overwhelmed him whenever he was not able to be helpful. "Even bribes are useless at this point. All bribes have been taken. All seats are booked and sold."

The amateur magician with professional aspirations, that very small man with such enormous dreams, The Incredible Mayadhar, insisted that I would be able to go. "No problem at all, my darling man. We are magicians, isn't it? And what are magicians doing that other mere mortals are not doing? Simple! Among other items, they are always, contrary to the laws of nature, making objects, such objects as pigeons or doves, and—need I say more?—Indian Airlines tickets, appear from even the thinnest air. Manifestations!" He chipperly grinned, and then, with a keen sense of the dramatics of secrecy that magicians cultivate, he looked around, over one shoulder and then the other, as if he were about to reveal some important information that no one in the Dasaprakash restaurant could be permitted to overhear. I leaned forward. "Listen, please," he said in a lowered voice, "I know the minister of tourism. He is my personal friend. He can get any tickets for you. Believe me, please. If Rajiv Gandhi is going to Kashmir, and his own official airplane is on the blink, what then? What? Simple! Contact my fine friend, the minister of tourism! This man always has a certain number of tickets set aside for the most important VIPs and for his personal friends such as yours truly, The Incredible Mayadhar. Here is my plan. The minister of tourism likes magic very much. So much you will not believe! He is damn crazy about magic. Believe me, please. I will introduce you. You will do some tricks for him, and all the while he will be saying, 'I know that one. I know that one.' He is always saying that. But then you will do your Needle-through-Arm, thereby flabbergasting him through and through. On his very hands and knees he will be begging you, 'Teach me this item. Be my guru.' When he then, at that most crucial point in my brilliant plan, says that he will do anything to learn this trick, you then, and not before, pose your humble request for tickets to Kashmir. Simple! If no tickets are available, he will even go to such a limit as to provide you with your own airplane." The magician smiled again. "Believe me, please."

When, as a guest at a meeting of Indian magicians earlier that year in Delhi, I had met The Incredible Mayadhar, I had been assured by him that I was, as a member of the International Brotherhood of Magicians, his brother. "We are all brothers. You and I, Siegfried and Roy, Sorcar and Lal—we are all brothers, isn't it, my darling man? All magicians, no matter whether we are speaking of the lowly magician on the dingy streets of Old Delhi with his cups and balls or of the august illusionist on the gorgeous stages of Las Vegas turning alluring ladies into terrifying tigers, all are our kith and kin. In all times, past, present, and future, in all places, north, south, east, and west, whether we are speaking of Raja Bhoj or Chung Ling Soo, Blackstone or Okito, we are brothers." The catalogue of our brethren, including the famous as well as the obscure—Kellar, Dante, and Doug Henning, as well as Professor Bhagyanath in Madras, Miss Melinda in Las Vegas, Emil Kio in Moscow, B. N. Sarkar everywhere, and the host of the meeting in Delhi that night—was, no doubt, meant to convince me that he, The Incredible Mayadhar, really knew about magic and magicians. And when he learned that I was writing a history of Indian magic in particular and that I was interested in its connections with religion, he set out to convince me that he was the willing source for everything that I could possibly need to know. This was not, I am convinced, pretension or pedantry on his part; it was, rather, his way of being gracious. He sincerely wanted to assure me that my travels would not be in vain, that I could always turn to him for any information on anything connected with either India or magic. "Hinduism is the oldest religion in the world. Isn't it? Therefore it follows, if one is willing to be objective, that all other religions evolved, to use Professor Darwin's fine word, from Hinduism. Magic always evolves out of religion. Isn't it? Therefore it follows, by pure logic, whether we are using the logic of our Akshapada or that of your Aristotle—what difference?—that all magic, all over the world, evolved out of Indian magic. There it is—isn't it?—all that you need to know! Simple!"

Anxious to get to Kashmir, fearful that I might miss Naseeb, I appeared at the Mayadhar Photography Shop-cum-Studio in the morning, armed with the necessary props to perform the Needle-through-Arm illusion. "Why do you want to go to Kashmir, my darling man?" he asked me. "It is not a good idea. There are so many tourists now. And why do you want to go by airplane? It is not a good idea. There are so many terrorists now. Tourists and terrorists! It's no good at all. There is a much more excellent idea. You will take a video-bus to Simla! I know a travel agent. He is my personal friend. He likes magic very much. He will be arranging everything. Everything. Believe me," The Incredible Mayadhar said. "Believe me, please."

I insisted that I needed the plane tickets for Kashmir, that the only reason I had come to India at all that summer was to meet up with Naseeb. "I have to get to Srinagar as soon as possible. That's all there is to it. Let's telephone the minister of tourism now. No, better yet, let's go to the ministry. I'll perform the Needle-through-Arm for him. I must have the tickets."

The Incredible Mayadhar frowned. "No. Madame will be much happier in Simla. You must not take her to Kashmir. People are not honest there. You must not introduce her to lowly street magicians. They are Muslims of the meanest ilk and caste, isn't it? Well I know the social behavior and mental makeup of these people. Well I know the tricks in their sleeves. Believe me, please. I cannot be party to helping you to go to Kashmir for purposes of fraternizations with tricksters and Madaris. I would be unable to forgive myself if anything were to happen to Madame. Believe me, please." His painfully strained frown suddenly yielded to an unabashedly blithe smile: "You will be going to Simla by video-bus and staying in a five-star hotel. This is a beautiful idea, isn't it? Believe me, please. As far as your study of Indian magic, I will be a gold mind of information on that subject upon your return."

"Good-bye, Mr. Mayadhar," I sighed, and again he made the joke he cracked every time I addressed him: "You can call me Incredible."

Like a throng of vipers trying to wiggle their way into the tiny burrow of some retreating rodent, convulsive phalanxes of shoving, shouting, or groaning bodies converged in the choked doorway of the Indian Airlines office. Naively believing that they were in what was supposed to be a neat British queue, tourists hysterically uttered such ridiculous irrelevancies as "Excuse me, I was here first." The air-conditioning was broken. Of course. The computers were down. Of course. Near the door there was a small machine that distributed little pieces of paper with numbers on them, meaningless figures printed to create the illusion that one would ultimately be helped, served after people holding lower numbers and before people with higher numbers. But that machine, the symbol of fairness, order, and other such antiquated

British notions, was, in all senses of the phrase, out of order. Despite the greater heat and tumult within, despite the fact that once inside the office the best one could hope for was a reservation to Kashmir in no less than three weeks (and that only if and when the computers began to work again), people persisted in shoving and shimmying through the entrance. Many of the souls cramming their way into the bloated upheaval, as the servants of people who needed tickets, didn't really care if they got the tickets or not. It mattered that they tried (that was their job), not that they succeeded (that depended upon some higher power). And because they were unattached to the fruits of their actions, they could persist without feeling the futility of wanting to accomplish anything. But we could not.

Envying that detachment, utterly frustrated and defeated, we sat outside the airlines office on a pile of broken concrete slabs, discarded remnants of real deconstructionism, contemplating our options, and we decided the only thing we could do was to go to the Imperial Hotel for beer. Fighting our way through the beggars, hawkers, sellers, vendors, loiterers, fortune-tellers, and tourists that cluttered Janpath, I heard a voice that is familiar to any one who has ever walked around Connaught Place: "Change money?"

"No."

"Best rate. One dollar—sixteen rupees."

"No."

"Hashish?"

"No."

"Best hash. Kashmiri hash."

"No."

"Carpets?"

"No. Go away." I snapped, still walking, weaving, pushing forward.

"Best carpets. Kashmiri carpets."

"No," I muttered exhaustedly. "Good-bye."

"Airline tickets? Tickets for Kashmir? Houseboat in Kashmir? Best houseboat."

I stopped and turned. "Tickets to Kashmir?"

"Yes."

"When can we go?"

"Today. Tomorrow. Any day. Any day but yesterday or before. Follow me, Sāb."

The shadowy man, one of those vague entities whose success in life depends upon being wholly nondescript, the phantom we followed along Janpath, down the lane, up the alley, and around the corner, was dismissed once we were inside the cramped little room, the Delhi office of Mohammad Shah and Sons, Golden Phoenix Tours and Trekking. The man's function, like the snake or *piju* in Naseeb's performance, was to draw innocents into the ring. We had been lured into the net, and now the show began.

"Don't worry about anything, man. Life is too long to have worries," Habeeb Shah, clinging to my hand after shaking it, smiling the unctuous grin of a Hindi movie star, explained. "Tomorrow at this time you'll be having a drink on your very own houseboat on Dal Lake in Srinagar, Vale of Happiness, without a care, at peace with yourself in the most beautiful place in the world. Life is happiness; happiness is life—that's my philosophy. If you're not happy, I'm not happy. Okay? Don't worry about anything. I'm cool, I've been to the States. I'll take care of you, my brother. Trust me—I'm a philosopher." He turned the fan toward us.

Tossing a hundred-rupee note contemptuously down on the table, he summoned a man from the next room with a loud shout, "Tea!" The cowering old man nervously picked up the money that, because of the whirling, droning fan, seemed to quiver and tremble. "Tea! Bring tea for my American friends. Or scotch? Anything you want, my friends. Should I send him to my house—it is only ten kilometers or so from here—to get a bottle of Johnny Walker for you? Red Label or Black? Or Chivas Regal? Or do you just want tea for now?"

After I unfortunately suggested that tea would suffice, Habeeb asked us our names ("Hey, first names are enough—we're friends, aren't we?"), where we were from ("Oh yeah, I've got a lot of friends there; I've been all over the States"), whether or not we were married ("Don't worry, I'm cool—I don't care."), and our professions. "Magician," I said. "I'm a magician and Cheryl's my assistant."

"Like you saw her in half, right? I love that trick! Can you do that one? Tell me how it's done—come on, I'm cool, I won't tell anyone else. Hey, wait, do some magic tricks for my son," Habeeb said energetically as the disarmingly handsome boy entered the room, smiled, nodded at us, and seated himself to watch his father, to look and learn just as Ayasan did in the presence of Naseeb. "I love magicians because magicians make people happy. And I want everyone in the world to be happy," Habeeb, The Incredible Habeeb, announced exuberantly. "Yeah, I'm a magic man too—I can get tickets to Kashmir out of nowhere! I'm a magic man—I can read minds. I can look into your assistant's eyes and tell you what is on her mind and in her heart. She thinks I'm tricking you. Here, Shirley, do you know what this is? It's a hundred-dollar bill. One hundred smackerooos! Take it. Examine it. Hold it. And if you're not in Kashmir tomorrow, you can keep it. Money means nothing to me. Only happiness. I want everyone in the world to be happy. Happiness is life; life is happiness. I'm a magic man. I'm cool." He laughed proudly and with a certain incomparable effervescence. "Yeah, I may be the world's greatest magic man."

It was true. He was a magician, and he was cool, and we were in Kashmir the next day. It was a neat trick. In order to perform it one needs to be a member of one of the Kashmiri families that have banded together to buy up all the airline tickets for Srinagar. The set-up and secrecy are protected with bribes. The performer can then, adding a substantial commission on top of the price of the tickets, sell his precious commodity to people on the condition that they stay on his houseboat. In order to make sure that they keep their part of the bargain, that they do not go to another houseboat, that they pay him for all their meals, that they buy carpets, shawls, and papier-mâché from him, that they pay him for any tours, trips, or treks out of Srinagar, and that they tip him generously at the end, the magician does not—and this is most important—give them their return ticket to Delhi until the day of their departure. The trick involves all the traditional conjuring sleights and strategies: misdirection, magician's choice, and one-ahead.

Eight places on the plane were taken up by one man, a dead man. The seats had been removed so that the coffin could be set in place. "It was impossible for him to be placed in with the luggage," the stewardess explained. "He is after all such an important figure in the political and cultural life of Kashmir and all of India. Would you like more curd?" The important man, who apparently was not quite important enough to merit a private plane, was returning home for his funeral accompanied by his closest friends, by colleagues, and, though it seemed rather superfluous, by bodyguards. Occasionally people from the entourage would lean into the aisles or stand to look at the coffin as if checking on how the dead man was doing.

We flew with him over the burnt, brown, barren plains of the north, and directly above Amritsar where the police, preparing that day to open fire, had the Golden Temple surrounded, and then into the sudden and prodigal green valley of Kashmir, and there, at the airport, amidst all the mourners, soldiers, ubiquitous loiterers, and police, Ali Shah, the brother of Habeeb, was waiting for us.

Once we were in the car, Ali apologized for not being able to smile at the airport on account of the dead man. "Under normal conditions I would have greeted you with smiles and embraces, beautiful bouquets, and even a red Kashmiri carpet. But, don't worry, there will be plenty of time for that. First let's get to your home-boat in Kashmir. Most Kashmiris call them 'houseboats.' But I want you to think of my houseboat as your homeboat." He interrupted his English speech, spiced as it was with hyperboles and sugared with expressions of fraternity, to scold his driver in Kashmiri. Agilely he switched back and forth between the two languages, the two tones, attitudes, and audiences, all the way to Dal Lake, where we were loaded into a small, brightly canopied shikhara in which we were rowed across, past Nehru Park, to the floridly carved and garishly decorated boat, the New Golden Phoenix. A severe, unshaven old man, wearing the *pheran* coat that typifies Kashmir and the lacy white skullcap that often indicates a pilgrimage to Mecca, stood absolutely still on the porch of the boat watching our slow arrival.

"There must be no talk of money," Ali insisted with the same smile that Habeeb had shown us in Delhi. "No, first you must try Kashmiri tea. You must drink and make yourselves comfortable. No talk, my dear friends, of money until you are 1000 percent happy. Your comfort and happiness is all I want—not your money."

In the attempt to get comfortable and happy per Ali's instructions, I discovered that we did not, contrary to Habeeb's promises, have the houseboat to ourselves. Furthermore the large, light bedroom in the back of the boat, the room depicted in the photographs that Habeeb had shown us, was occupied. When, after being directed to our small, dark room, overcrowded with Kashmiri arts and crafts, I expressed my disappointment, Ali buried his head in his hands. "This hurts me so deeply. The pain I feel is unbearable. I cannot believe that my brother has made such promises. I will scold him personally." He looked towards heaven. "Nothing like this must ever happen again. It's my duty to keep my brother's promise. But what can I do? Would you have me throw these people off the boat? They are good people from London. I believe they are honest people. But, if you insist, I'll toss their belongings into the lake this instant. It's a matter of honor. I do not care about money. I care only about your happiness, my honor, and the honor of my family. What shall I do? My God, help me. Shall I throw these people off the boat?"

The old man watched me and listened carefully as I consented to take the smaller room for the duration of the British couple's stay. Two servant boys, Mir Deen, the scruffy one with bloodshot eyes set close together, and Deen Rather, the very young one with the large, dark eyes set far apart, carried our bags to the room and, despite our protestations, completely unpacked them for us. Mir Deen, smiling idiotically, handed me my toothbrush upon which he had squeezed some toothpaste, and pointed to the water that he had turned on for me. Deen Rather, frowning, held a towel for me.

After I had brushed my teeth under Mir Deen's strict supervision, we were summoned by Ali and asked to produce the contract that I had drawn up with Habeeb. The old man squatted on the floor smoking a hubble-bubble. "My God, I don't believe this. I can't believe that my brother has asked you for so little. Please, I beg of you as a friend, one man to another, do not tell anyone else on this homeboat how very little you are paying, or they will insist on paying that same rate, and my family will go hungry this winter. But I am an honest man, and I must honor the promise of my brother. You must be a very good friend of his, like a brother to him, and since you are like a brother to my brother, it follows that you are like a brother to me."

Ali was in the midst of explaining that, aside from all the other unexpected charges, the government of Kashmir required us to pay a 25 percent visitor's tax, when the old man at his feet interrupted him in Kashmiri. Their animated conversation, salted with sighs and peppered with grunts, was heated. It bubbled; it boiled over. With his hand over his heart and his eyes slightly closed, shaking his head ever so slightly, Ali explained. "I do not believe this. This is truly amazing. There must be something about you. Perhaps it is because you are a magician. You are much more intelligent than I, so perhaps you will understand it, even though I do not. This God-fearing old man, Mr. Mohammad Shah, loves you. He has begged with me, pleaded, and finally demanded, that I do not charge you the government's required 25 percent. No, he wants me to charge you only half of the tax. And I must comply, for this man, servant of the Almighty, is, yes it's true, my very own beloved father. He says that you are like a son to him. Thus once again, you are like a brother to me. He desires to personally pay the other half for you. This God-serving man, though he risks government chastisement and even penalty if you should ever tell anyone about this, wants the honor of having you, such a great magician, on our humble homeboat. Will you be so generous as to accept his awe-inspired and inspiring offer? Will you put your pride in a bay and accept this? Of course, I know that it must be difficult for Americans, wealthy as they are, to let a poor and humble Kashmiri man do such a thing. But, please, my brother—it means so much to him."

In order to tolerate being so outrageously cheated, I kept telling myself that the ridiculously large sum of money that I had to hand over to Ali was the price of a magic show. We pay to be deceived, and the better the deception, the more it's worth. Besides, it was the cost of the ticket to Kashmir, and I had to get there in order to find Naseeb.

"Naseeb," I said again, smiling with the utter astonishment of having actually been able to find him. I held up my hand to show him that I was still wearing the ring he had given me. He indicated that it was because of the power of that ring, the fire in the blood-red stone, that I was, against all odds, standing next to him again.

We were urged into the small tent, crammed and jammed in amidst the boxes, bundles, bags, and baskets of magic equipment, and the other paraphernalia necessary for survival. Touching the sack upon which I had almost sat, I felt something move within it and realized it was the snakes. "Where is the *piju?*" I asked.

Naseeb laughed, "Dead."

Reaching under myself to remove whatever it was that I was sitting so uncomfortably upon, I found a jaw bone. "Dog bone!" Naseeb smiled. "*For* a dog or *of* a dog?" I wondered.

Out of the throng of children that had packed themselves around, against, and over the tent, four of them, Naseeb's own, scrunched their way in. When Naseeb's wife, radiant with the prankish, knowing smile that epitomizes every member of the family, squeezed her way in, I asked her name. "Naseeb Madame." I asked the name of the baby she held, the infant magician garlanded with black strings and copper amulets, anointed with medicinal powders and balms, his upper lip encrusted with dry snot and the scar of his circumcision red and swollen with infection. "Naseeb Baby." I asked the name of the wizened, one-eyed man who had forced himself into the tent as well, the perspiring, seemingly febrile man who was apparently trying not to laugh because, when he did, it made him cough painfully. "Naseeb Father."

There was no room for Ayasan. He nevertheless wiggled his head under one side of the tent, and grinned mirthfully up at me, displaying his irrepressible dimples. "Decapitation," I said, and his head, all I had seen of him, instantaneously disappeared.

The walls of the tent rippled with the shapes of the children's bodies on the outside, and the man who had led us to Naseeb found a place in the top of the tent for the head that was turbanned with meter upon meter of crimson cotton. I asked if he was a magician. No, he was an itinerant umbrella repairman who spent his life keeping up with the rains. He squeezed his arm through the mass of bodies to hand me a bidi, and I squeezed back, turning and twisting my arm back through to reciprocate with a Benson and Hedges Deluxe International. With my legs scrunched against my body, with less room in the tent than any magician's assistant ever had in the performance of the Zig-Zag Lady, less room than a boy in a magician's basket or a pigeon in a load, I couldn't reach the matches in my pocket. Naseeb, who watches everything, handed me his. As I lifted my arms above my head to light the match, and craned my neck back to light the cigarette, a small child was forced by the crowd onto my lap. When he (or maybe she) removed my wire-rimmed glasses and put them on, Naseeb's wife giggled, "Gandhiji." Naseeb corrected her: "Dr. Ambedkar." Then Naseeb Father, sucking smoke from the chillum, had his suggestion; and then the umbrella repairman tried to outwit him with the name of yet another famous Indian who had worn glasses. And every proposal drew laughter and the laughter made the tent swell and bulge like a pregnant sow, overburdened but happy in a gross sort of way.

I could not succeed in grabbing the hand—Ayasan's I think—that kept reaching under the flap of the tent behind me to pinch me. Crammed in as we were, I could hardly answer affirmatively when Naseeb asked if our houseboat was crowded. I was embarrassed to confess to Naseeb, in the presence of the inhabitants of graveyard, how astonishingly much we were paying to stay on the houseboat. I lied. When we were invited to stay there in Naseeb's tent with his family, I explained that I would have much preferred that, or at least another tent or a modest hotel, except that paying in advance for the houseboat, food and all, had been the only way I could get to Kashmir. I invited Naseeb to visit.

On the way to the boat, in the scooter rickshaw, Naseeb told me he had performed the Needle-through-Arm illusion at a Maslet wedding in Ghaziabad. He laughed proudly as he informed me that the magicians had been completely fooled by the trick. Big weddings, he reflected, provided Maslets with the opportunity to come together, to see each other's routines, learn new tricks, and talk about important things: "This place, good place; this place, bad place; this place, police problem; this place, no police problem."

Once we boarded the shikhara, Naseeb couldn't talk anymore. Since he did not know how to swim, he was genuinely terrified that the boat might capsize.

"Diving Duck Routine," I joked. "Don't worry," I added, holding up my hand. "Nothing bad can happen—we're wearing our rings."

The old man, who had watched our approach from the roof of the houseboat, took me aside once we were on board. "Saighal, don't bring these peoples on houseboat. Dirty peoples. Not honest peoples." When Mohammad Shah spoke, his face usually took on the expression of someone who has just taken a bite out of a lemon. At other times, in his more mellow moments, it was the expression of someone who has just stepped in shit.

I introduced Naseeb to the English couple, Robert and Weleja, and asked the obsequious Mir Deen, who passed the order on to the ever-menaced Deen Rather, for Kashmiri tea. Four cups were brought. "No," I insisted, "a cup for the *jādūgar* too." Naseeb laughed, "*Ek Lipton-chāī.*"

At Naseeb's urging that I do some "Hawaii-*jādū*," I vanished a Benson and Hedges and made it reappear from behind my ear. Then Naseeb started. With the little metal cups that the tea strainers were set in and three balls spontaneously formed from the paper napkins, he did his cups and balls routine. "Tell Naseeb," Robert said, "that Weleja and I both thought that was very good, and we do so look forward to seeing him perform on the street tomorrow." Not understanding a word of what Robert had said, Naseeb looked at me quizzically. I translated his English into our Englishindi, a loosely inflected but syntactically precise language: "*Angrejī-sāb saying, atisundar, jādū good. Angrejī-madame liking too. Tomorrow-din, street program coming.*" Naseeb smiled at Robert with the universal happiness of feeling appreciated. All the while the ever-vigilant, vulture-like Mohammad Shah crouched nearby smoking his hubble-bubble. As Deen Rather was removing the tea, Mohammad Shah began to speak to Naseeb at some length in Urdu, and the magician, nodding his head occasionally, listened carefully. When I asked what they were talking about, Mohammad Shah snapped at me angrily. "Not Saighal business; Mr. Mohammad Shah business!"

Naseeb rose to follow Mohammad Shah out of the window of the New Golden Phoenix, along the boards that circled it to the little bit of land in the back where the servant boys slept, where the chickens were killed, the food prepared, and where Mrs. Mohammad Shah sat all day puffing on her hubble-bubble. The potbellied old woman, her eyes langorously opening and closing, wrapped her lips around the stem of the pipe and drooled.

"It's such a pleasure to meet Naseeb," sighed Weleja, a cellist for the BBC Radio Orchestra, a woman whose hair, complexion, and physiognomy, but not in any way her accent, posture, or demeanor, revealed Indian origins. "He's the first honest man we've met on this trip, the first Indian I feel I can trust." I suggested that of Naseeb's many charms and virtues, honesty did not seem to be one of the more salient ones.

Robert, a violinist for the BBC, explained the source of their distrust of India. "We had booked everything in London—tickets, houseboat, the lot—and we were at the airport in Delhi waiting for our connecting flight to Srinagar when this man—Habeeb—approached to ask if we needed a flight to Kashmir. 'No, thank you very much,' I said assuring him that we had everything we needed. 'Did we need a houseboat?' he asked. 'No,' Weleja told him. You were really rather curt with him, darling. Well, at any rate, as I looked at him talking to Weleja, it occurred to me that I had noticed him earlier in the airport, and I had thought that he was looking at us and pointing us out to another man. Of course, I didn't make anything of it at the time. He was pleasant enough. He struck up a bit of a conversation with us, told us he loved Britain, that he was sorry that we no longer ruled India, that he had been to London, that he had so many English friends who had been very good to him. He said that he hoped our respective paths would cross again. Then, as if the idea had suddenly struck, he asked us to meet his family in Kashmir. It would be an honor for them, he said, and an opportunity for us to get to know the real Kashmir—not the Kashmir of tourists. We could have an authentic Kashmiri meal with a true Kashmiri family. It sounded absolutely delightful of course, just the sort of thing one would hope for on one's holiday. Then he asked to see our houseboat reservation slip, explaining that he needed the name of the boat and its manager so that he could have his brother call on us there. Weleja looked for it in her purse. But it was gone. Everything was gone, stolen—our tickets to Kashmir, our tickets back to London, our money, Weleja's passport—everything. A pickpocket had made off with the lot. It was dreadful, really very terrifying to be in such a fix in a foreign country with no friends, with no one to turn to."

"No one," Weleja frowned, "but our dear, new friend Habeeb, Mr. Happiness himself. I actually fell into his arms in tears. 'My God,' he kept saying, 'how can such a thing happen! India has been like this ever since the British left. I will do anything in my power to help you.' "

Robert had to pick the story up again as Weleja just couldn't go on. "Habeeb told us not to worry about anything, that he would take care of everything. He would get new tickets for us and a boat. He kept assuring us that it was his pleasure to help us, that coming to our rescue was the only way he could compensate for the duplicity of his countrymen. He said he felt personally responsible."

"And he bloody well was!" Weleja broke in angrily. "A nasty piece of work, that Habeeb! He told us not to worry about the money. We could work that out later. He asked us to put our lives in his hands." Tears formed in the corners of her eyes. "And we did," she laughed painfully.

"Yes," Robert said with a classic British wistfulness. "I'm afraid we did."

Since Robert and Weleja had to go into town anyway to wire their bank in London for the money to pay Ali the exorbitant fee they had been informed they owed him for room, board, and for the carpet that they thought had been a gift, they decided to come along with us to see Naseeb's performance outside the tourist center near Lal Chowk.

The magician and his son were waiting for us there. "Police problem," he said, and refusing to let me try to deal with it, he took us by scooter rickshaw to a street corner several kilometers away, a bit of ground that seemed too small, too muddy, too random and unremarkable, to be a likely spot for gathering an audience and enchanting them with his illusions. But as Ayasan tossed out the snakes and began to play the plaintive gourd-flute and the damaru drum that Lord Shiva plays, a few Kashmiris straggled over from the nearby shops to join Robert, Weleja, Cheryl, and me.

No sooner had Naseeb, squatting on the ground, started doing some sleights with coins, the comic warm-up for his serious pitch, than the inevitable, stern, and officious policeman approached to put an end to it. This long-running allegory, in which the policeman represents regulation and reality, while the magician stands for frivolity and fantasy, has many variations—sometimes law prevails, sometimes pleasure.

"No crowds," the cop said flatly. Handing him the calling card of K. D. Kapur, Lieutenant Colonel of the Indian army, as well as my own and, in addition, my University of Hawaii Faculty Card, my International Brotherhood of Magicians and Society of American Magicians membership cards, an expired reader's card for the Bodleian Library, and, just for good measure, a Pan Am WorldPass Frequent Flyer identification card, I assured the policeman that this was no ordinary show of street magic. "This is official government business. I have been hired, under the auspices of the Ministry of Education, by Oxford University Press to write a volume on Madaris for their forthcoming series, *The Peoples of India.* I have been brought to India expressly for that purpose. If I am to fulfill my responsibility to the people of India, it is absolutely necessary that I be able to watch this gentleman perform in his natural setting. And, for that volume, this photographer must take some pictures of him on a typical Kashmiri street."

After looking at each of the cards, the cop calmly explained to me that it was his duty to protect the people of this particular area, under his jurisdiction as it was, from being cheated and robbed. "It is common knowledge, my good sir," he said, "that magic and pickpocketing go hand-in-hand. The magician distracts the crowd, and the pickpocket goes about his business."

I rashly insisted that I, as well as Lieutenant Colonel K. D. Kapur and Ravi Dayal, representing the Oxford University Press, would be personally responsible for Naseeb, that I (and if not I, then Kapur or Dayal) would personally reimburse anyone who was pickpocketed during the performance. After being photographed, at his own request, for *The Peoples of India,* and agreeing to let Naseeb perform "for one half hour only," he turned to walk away. He stopped, turned around again, and spoke: "By the way, my good sir, your library card has expired."

Naseeb did his show, and the policeman never came back.

I was pleased with myself, happy that I had been able to help the magician, until that illusion was dispelled when Naseeb, in the shikhara on the way back to the houseboat for lunch, explained that he had already bribed the policeman earlier that morning. His appearance, a symbolic demonstration for the general public of an official concern for law and order, was just part of the bigger show. "One can hardly tell where reality ends and illusion begins," Weleja uttered in amazement.

Naseeb, no longer afraid of riding in the shikhara, smiled to watch his son leaning out of the boat, dragging his hand through the water like a rudder and not noticing, in his little reverie, how wet his sleeve was. I asked Naseeb about the pickpockets, and speaking with great admiration for the skill that their ancient art requires, he admitted that pickpockets frequently asked if they could work with him. He had turned them down not out of any impulse to obey the law, but because they inevitably caused problems with the law, and he already had quite enough problems of his own with the police.

Once on the houseboat, Robert and Weleja ordered Mir Deen to bring tea; Mir Deen commanded Deen Rather to do it; I opened three bottles of Golden Eagle beer; Naseeb crumbled hashish into his palm and mixed it with the tobacco from one of my Benson and Hedges; Cheryl took Ayasan to the bathroom to wash. And Mohammad Shah watched it all.

A young woman with a cheerful smile crossed the plank that connected the New Golden Phoenix to the Old Golden Phoenix and, climbing in through the window, introduced herself as "Carrie from Australia." She happily explained that she had been given a free trip to Kashmir and a thousand dollars in return for marrying a Sikh who was in jail in Australia for forging immigration papers. "I mean, I didn't have to sleep with him or anything. The lawyer told his family that he might have a chance of gettin' out of jail if he were married to an Australian." She laughed and pointed through the window of the Old Golden Phoenix to the body on the bed. "And that's Grant. He's from Australia too. We don't see much of him. Ever since he found out you can buy Valium over the counter, he mostly just lies there. The shikhara guys bring it to him. He says he hopes to go to Goa one of these days, when it gets too cold here in Kashmir."

"Would you like to join us all for lunch?" I yelled over to Grant. "We're having roast chicken."

"Sure," he answered cheerfully, almost energetically. "Could you have it sent over? I'd like to eat in bed today."

After lunch, still at the table, I levitated a ten-rupee note. "*Śābās*, Lee Baba," Naseeb laughed and Ayasan, laughing too, imitated his father's expression—"*Śābās!*" By their laughter I could tell that, though the method I had used for the trick was not employed in India, they had immediately known how it was executed.

"I think I know how you did it," Weleja said excitedly. "You have little balls of helium which you stick up under the note and then, when you hand the bill around for inspection, you simply pop the ball and, since helium has no smell, the whole thing goes unnoticed." There is never really any point in trying to figure out how a decent trick is done. Reason always leads us astray. The answer is always simple. But reason overlooks the simple in its need to discern or make connections between causes and effects.

While we were sitting around the table, Naseeb and I taking turns at parlor tricks, Ayasan was searching our room, rummaging every suitcase, closet, and drawer. Cheryl, after making him surrender the cards (both the stripper-deck and the Svengali deck), the flashlight, the hat, the lighter, the photograph of his father, the postcard of the Purana Qila, and the small tape recorder (loaded with the cassette of "Black Magic Woman"), pushed back his still wet sleeve, strapped her watch on his wrist, and smiled. "You can have this. Gift."

The boy, extending his arm to display his new watch, smiling happily, gazed wide-eyed at himself in the full-length mirror. He made faces in the glass. He touched the finger of the boy in the mirror with his finger, kissed his lips, shook his finger at him as if to scold him, and then he boxed with the boy. He stopped, still staring at himself, and took a deep breath. He squatted on the floor, still looking in the mirror, and miming a performance of cups and balls, he laughed, "Naseeb Shah." Jumping up to grab a white face towel that was lying on the bed, he held it up under his nose like a beard, returned to the mirror, and laughed again: "Chand Baba." Then the beard became a turban: "P. C. Sorcar!" He dropped the towel on the floor and ran away to hide.

Meanwhile, Naseeb and I were making arrangements to meet early the next morning at the graveyard. For the next month we would spend each day with him, following him to wherever he decided to perform.

Although there are always modifications and improvisations, according to Naseeb's mood and whim, and depending on the temperament of the crowd as he perceives it, each of the performances ("programs" Naseeb calls them in English) has an essentially uniform structure. There is, when the shows go well, always the same movement, the same transformation of a mere curious skit into a slapstick comedy that turns into a grisly horror show that fades into a stunning miracle play that finally gives way to a solemn liturgical drama in which Naseeb is the priest and his audience, initially only inquisitive spectators of a bit of roadside conjuring, themselves become players in the play, celebrants in the rite. They are, in the end, the suppliants: they seek power; they are under the spell of magic. And in hopes that it might be real, they are willing to lay down a little money. That is how Naseeb, like his father and his father's fathers for innumerable generations, earns his living.

The prelude is performed by the boy who, dressed like his father in a kurta and pajama pants (his earth brown, the father's coal black), sets out the dusty, lethargic serpents and plays the snake charmer's gourd-flute to conjure up individual fears and collective memories: the serpent in Eden, intimating temptation, or the Naga King, Ananta, emblematizing eternity. The snakes both lure the people forward, close enough to see, and keep them at a distance, far enough away not to see too much. The natural balancing of curiosity and fear within those who happen to pass by establishes the perimeters of the stage. With a stick the boy then circles in front of them, engraving a line in the earth to make clear and explicit the demarcation between the two realities, the one in which the spectators live each day, and the magic one into which they are going to be given a glimpse. In that reality, with its own set of unnatural laws, within the mandala that the boy has drawn, the magician constructs his altar, arranges the bones and stones, limes and daggers, amulets and rings, and the tattered bundles of documents, the certificates and letters that prove that he is indeed the great magician Naseeb Shah.

He begins by letting them doubt that greatness, his skill and power, by briefly allowing them to think that their perceptions are valid and their reasoning is effective. In teaching me his cups and balls routine, Naseeb demonstrated how to make it look like I was concealing one of the balls under one of the cups. The move was subtle—it had to be done slowly enough to make sure the spectator saw it, and yet quickly and deftly enough so that the spectator would believe that he was not meant to see it, that another observer, someone not quite so sharp, would have missed it. This prepares the spectator for the revelation that the magician is always one step ahead of him, and for the realization that his perceptions are being controlled by the magician. But at first they must think they know, that they see through the magic: "You put it in the other hand! It's under your foot! It's in the fold in your pants!" And if they don't shout the words, Ayasan does their heckling for them, voices their thoughts and suspicions. Then, all at once, they are shown that what they saw did not happen, what they thought was untrue, and what they believed was unreal. There is then the surrender, the yielding to their need, our dark longing, to be deceived; the roadside crowd gathered around a vagrant con man and a scruffy little boy becomes the spellbound audience at a persistent play, a cosmological, social, domestic, and psychological drama, that everyone has at some time seen in some sacred sanctuary or darkened theater, in some room or dream.

The main characters in the drama are the father and son, personifications of all authorities and all spirits of rebellion, of all fathers and sons, rulers and subjects, priests and initiates, gods and mortals. The relationship between them is established in the agon. The child mocks the adult: "*Cār-sau-bīs!* You're no good at these tricks. *Sālā!* You're slow today—you must have gotten drunk last night." "*Baccā!*" the father answers, "You're too small for such big talk, like the puppy that barks at the tiger!" In the beginning youth presents its challenge, and the scenes, rich with vulgarities, prompt raucous laughter. But as the drama unfolds, the child is slaughtered, his head removed, or his tongue cut out. The magician, the sacrificer, establishes his authority by displaying the potency of his magic, the power to re-member what has been dismembered, to resurrect that which has been sacrificed. Once the child accepts the authority of the sacrificer, he shares in that power and demonstrates his access to it by reading minds and making prognostications, knowing inner thoughts and future events, seeing and hearing in what is darkness and silence to the uninitiated.

Once the themes are established, the secondary players—volunteers from the audience, each one of them representing all of the spectators—are introduced

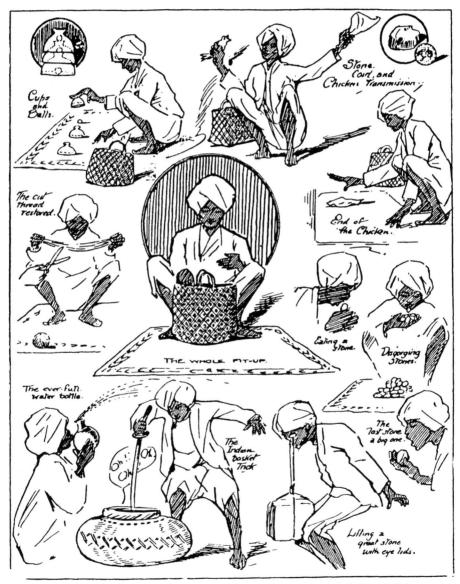

FIGURE 1 *Standard Tricks of the Street Magician.* From *The Magazine of Magic* (1916); courtesy of the Supreme Magic Company (Bideford, Devon, England).

into the mandala, and with them the images by which the themes are developed. It is at this point that the magician chooses several of many possible variants: the Chinese Sticks (in his routine, Naseeb says one stick is a Muslim and the other a Hindu), the lota bowl for Waters of India (which Naseeb says P. C. Sorcar learned from Naseeb's own grandfather), the Diving Duck (which Naseeb says no one can do better than Chand Baba), or perhaps the Egg Bag (which Naseeb says Western magicians stole from India). In that routine the egg, like all objects within the mandala or upon the stage, all theatrical or sacramental props, is at once an egg and much more than an egg, at once ordinary and extraordinary. It is a symbol with a history and a constancy, and as a symbol, it accrues power. It is a magic object. Naseeb vanishes the egg and then accuses his volunteer of having stolen it, of having consumed the symbol. "Open your mouth," he orders in Urdu and looks into the man's throat; then "Wider," he says in Kashmiri. In what he thinks is English, he then commands: "Single down, mister" (a phrase that is supposed to mean *bend over*). Holding the bag, clearly shown to be empty, under the indicted thief's mouth, Naseeb, the prosecutor, slaps the man's back and adjures him to cough. "Harder!" The egg does not appear. Stepping around the charged man and, unbeknownst to him, holding the egg bag under his buttocks, Naseeb again bids him to cough and the audience roars with laughter when they clearly see the egg drop into the bag. There are scatological jokes ("What kind of omelette will a turd-egg make?") and licentious ones ("What rooster was tall enough to fuck this hen?"). Within the symbol, waste and impurity are reconciled with nourishment and rebirth. Richly obscene, street-corner laughter echoes the apotropaic laughter of an ancient fertility rite. And the laughter assures the magician, Naseeb now or the priest then, that he has those who laugh under his control.

A shawl, borrowed from a member of the audience, is wrapped around a coin, borrowed from someone else, and the bundle is placed in the armpit of the man who laid the magic egg. "Clap your hands," Naseeb dictates and laughs. "Are you making chapatis?" The laughter of the audience is binding. When the cloth is unfolded, the coin seems to have vanished. Could it be in the cloth? Naseeb, much to the chagrin of the man whose shawl it is, appears to tear that cloth into pieces. "Don't worry, *Sāb*, I'm a magician—I can put together what has been taken apart—that's my specialty." But Naseeb makes us wait for that. First the egg-thief must be tried for the new offence: he is asked to clasp his hands together, interlocking his fingers in his grip, and then, after the magician has waved the damaru over the clutching hands and recited the mantra—*yantru-tantru-jālajāla-mantru*—the man, if he is guilty, will be unable to pull his hands apart. In this farce, this slapstick satire of legal institutions, the man is always guilty. Powerless to disengage his hands, he appears to be shackled by some hypnotic power, and despite the pitiful cries for release, Naseeb pushes him away. "Leave me alone," the magician shouts with mock severity, letting a slight laugh show through to put the audience at ease. "Just be quiet. We'll get to your sentencing soon. But first I have to put this gentleman's shawl back together." The forlorn man with his hands frozen together begs for mercy, shouts with anger, is silent with terror, and the audience laughs. But the laughter is nervous. Naseeb, taking his audience right up to the edge, to the line between amusement and fear, readies them for more serious magic. The transition will be made when they watch the pile of bones—the jaw bone of a dog or goat, the skull of a monkey, and bits of bone that we fear are human—spark, burst into flames, and issue dark, sulphurous smoke at a word and gesture from the magician. After the shawl has been restored (there is laughter when Naseeb momentarily makes it seem that he has made a mistake, that the trick has failed), and after the man's interdigitated hands are released (there is the laughter of relief), there is no more laughter. Comedy is but the seduction. It opens the soul wherein terrors will be confronted and mysteries explored. To establish himself as a guide into the labyrinth of mysteries, the magician shows his uncanny powers, his *siddhis*: just as Sai Baba and other god-men produce stone or metal lingas from their mouths, he draws stones from between his stretched lips, stone after stone, and metal balls, larger, larger, and larger still, and meter upon meter of colored cord—red, yellow, green, black—and handful after handful of sharply pointed thorns. The menacing barbs are placed in a pile amidst the stones, globes, and tangled cord. Perhaps one of the snakes will slither under the ominous pile. Urgent words, a voice of fire, commands the audience to be silent, to spread their hands apart. Blood oozes from a lime that the magician has pierced with his knife. "Clap your hands!" They obey. "Stop!" They acquiesce. Invisible threads are hooked into each soul and the magician, holding those threads in his hand, tugs the audience forward, eases up, gives them slack, then pulls them in again, closer still.

"Women leave the circle. Children, go!" Although those particular members of the audience are dismissed only because they do not have the money in their pockets that is Naseeb's object, their discharge gives the impression that what is about to happen is fraught with real danger and a terror from which the women and children must be protected.

"Mussulman?" Naseeb asks the man whose hands were locked together. "Hindu?" And with the answer, he utters a prayer that he attributes to the appropriate text—the Qur'an, the *Rāmāyaṇa*, or perhaps the poetry of Kabir. The man is seated, his head covered with the restored shawl, the cloth infected with magic, and the magician slowly lowers his body back, laying his head upon the ground in preparation for punishment, absolution, and resurrection. Holding the knife, sharp edge up, on his knee, Naseeb then fiercely slaps his hand down upon the blade. "*Bismillah,*" he screams and, with arcane ritual gestures and mumbled mantras, he magically transfers the slice across his palm to the neck of the covered man. Again he does it, and again, "*Bismillah! Bismillah!*" Three times to cut all the way through the neck. Then on his knees, as in prayer, he takes the head, clearly visible through the shawl, in his hands and moves it, turns and twists it, forces it to one side of the torso and then the other, to demonstrate that it has truly been severed. He pushes his foot into the stump of the man's neck and scans the faces of his audience, looking into the eyes of each man. Someone moves, crosses his arms, or speaks to the man next to him. The child magician falls on the ground, rolls in the dirt, convulsing and vomiting blood. His tongue twitches between his blood-stained lips and teeth. "Quiet! Be still!" the father warns the spectators as he forsakes the headless body, bends over the writhing form of his son, and cuts the boy's tongue out with the knife he had used to lacerate his own hand. As the boy moans piteously, rocking back and forth, digging his fingers into the dirt as if to clutch to life on earth, the magician, the knife dripping with gore still held in one hand, the quivering, bleeding piece of tongue in the other, circles the crowd.

"Two rupees, two rupees, two rupees," Naseeb announces. He needs two rupees from each of the men, not for himself, but as an offering to God, so that the man and child can be saved. "God gave you that money in the first place. Although you cling to it, it's not your money. It's His." Notes and coins are thrown into the circle, given not out of appreciation for a good performance or out of generosity for a poor itinerant performer, but offered out of a genuine fear for the headless man, the tongueless child, and, most of all, for themselves. The decapitated man, a volunteer from among them, is an effigy of them, a scapegoat sacrificed on their behalf, and they hope not only for his resurrection but that by throwing two rupees into the magic circle, they will share in the magic, gain in return even just a bit of power or, at least, a bit of luck.

Naseeb makes sure to see that all present witness that each man who has thrown in a five, ten, or twenty rupee note receives the exact amount of change due to him. It must be clear that Naseeb is not interested in personal gain, that his concern is with matters of life and death, with making whole what has been rent. And solemnly the magician displays his power to accomplish that.

The recapitated man seems dazed. The boy, his tongue restored, seems to have a new seriousness about him, to know things he did not know before. The sacrificial ritual has given him an omniscience that complements his father's omnipotence. The magician, after tightly wrapping the shawl around the child's head, circles the audience touching things and, as he does, the blindfolded child identifies each of them: "watch," "turban," "*pheran*," "cigarette," "belt," "beard," "shirt."

"What color is the shirt?"

"Red." the boy answers in the entranced and eerie voice of a medium or a shaman.

"P. C. Sorcar learned this magic from my grandfather." Naseeb says non-chalantly. "Sorcar rode blindfolded on a motorcycle. This boy could do that for you now, but I cannot afford a motorcycle. I'm a poor man. P. C. Sorcar was a rich man. That is because people would pay him twenty or thirty rupees each just for what you are seeing my child do without having to buy tickets. People gave Sorcar great sums to read their minds. This boy can do it and there's no charge."

The magician asks a man to come forward and "single down" so that the child can whisper in his ear: "You made some money but now it is gone. . . . You are very well liked, but some friend has turned against you. . . . There are some family squabbles . . ."

"Did the boy tell you the truth? Did he know? Yes? He did? Good! You, all of you, can know such things. You can do things that ordinary men cannot do. The power is in the stones in these rings, the rings the boy holds in his hands. These are powerful stones, lucky gems, magic rings. P. C. Sorcar used to sell rings, exactly like these, for one thousand rupees apiece. His son still does it."

"The rings," Naseeb announces, one hand holding up the silver box in which he keeps the magic rings as the other adjusts the skullcap that attests to his piety. "These rings work equally well for both Hindu and Muslim." He fingers the garland of *rudrākṣa* beads.

The men, arms extended, money in their hands, push into the mandala, crowd around the magician, anxious to purchase some morsel of power or luck. But Naseeb, knowing that he must not seem too anxious for their money, takes his time. He displays the photograph of him blessing the ring upon my finger, the one of him ceremoniously giving Cheryl's ring to her, and the photograph of Rajiv Gandhi, torn from some magazine—the arrow that Naseeb has drawn on it, pointing to Gandhi's ring, is meant to imply that the Prime Minister purchased or received the ring from Naseeb.

"If you doubt the power of the stones, just ask the foreigner to show you his ring. He has come all the way from Hawaii-America to buy these rings, which he'll sell for thousands of dollars there."

I was always prepared to do the trick. Showing my hands to be empty, I'd point to the ring, say "Ring-*śakti*," and then, using the standard Western method, take my lit cigarette, insert it into the hand that bore the magic ring, and squeezing that hand tightly closed, I'd ask someone to blow on the ring. With a *"gilli-gilli-gilli"* and an *"ek, do, tīn,"* I'd open my hand to show that the cigarette had vanished.

"But what if they try it Naseeb?" I asked, "What if, after buying the ring, they actually attempt to extinguish the cigarette in their hand?"

"No," he laughed and gave an explanation that was based on the assumption that the world is divided into cowards and fools. Many of the people who buy the rings, wanting to try the trick, will slowly, cautiously, move the cigarette toward their hand. But they'll be too frightened to actually push it into the skin. Those are the cowards, the majority of men. Of course, there are a few fools, Naseeb grinned, who will actually squeeze the cigarette and burn their hand. He laughed happily. Angrily they try to find Naseeb and if they do, he speaks to them: "What? You didn't hear my warning? Or you didn't believe it? You tried to use the ring without the mantra? Oh, dear God, no wonder you burned yourself!" When they then ask him for the mantra, he explains that it costs one hundred rupees. No one, absolutely no one, has ever given Naseeb the money for the magic words.

Naseeb served each man in turn, held each hand, solemnly placed a selected ring on each finger, blessing each stone with a solemn puff of his breath, a kiss, and a few whispered words of power. When all the rings were sold, he and Ayasan carefully rolled up the mat, packed their bags, and returned with us to the houseboat to count the money and have some lunch.

I tried to keep track of how much Naseeb was earning for each show—about two hundred rupees, maybe two hundred and fifty on a good day, it seemed to me. He had lied to Shankar, who in Delhi told me that Naseeb had boasted of taking in at least five hundred rupees per show in Kashmir and that he very often did two shows a day. "With the twenty thousand rupees a month minimum that he said he would make in Kashmir this summer," Shankar sighed, "Naseeb plans to buy an airplane ticket to visit you in Hawaii. He also hopes to stop over in Moscow, Las Vegas, and other such places. He dreams that he will make a lot of money on such world travels."

Shankar shook his head. "I'm truly worried about Naseeb. He squanders his money all over the place. I think he may be a drinking man. Did you hear about the albino bear? While traveling in the South, doing some magic programs there, Naseeb met a man on the street who had a white bear on a rope. The bear did not perform any tricks at all, and the man was not a bear trainer. He had merely fastened a cup to the bear's paw, hoping that with such an unusual begging bear he might, just sitting on the roadside, be able to collect some alms from charitable people for food for himself and the bear. He was not doing so well. So when Naseeb offered him a large sum of money for the animal, all that Naseeb had, the man accepted it at once. Naseeb was sure that he would be able to make a lot of money with that albino bear. He would sell it, at some great profit, to a Qalandar for training. Or, he told me, he would smuggle it into Pakistan and sell it to some Arabs there. He would tell them it was a polar bear. You see, he had it in his head that rich Arabs are all mad about the idea of owning a polar bear. He had other schemes in mind as well, but I'm not sure what they were.

"In any case, no one, no one with any money at all, was even mildly interested in buying the albino bear. Of course not. A Qalandar will not buy a grown bear that is not trained. And why would an Arab want a polar bear? So the animal lived in Naseeb's tent with him and his family and it cost him a small fortune to feed that extra mouth. The bear became ill, and Naseeb had to pay for medicines. Naseeb said that he was relieved and very happy when the bear finally died. But Ibrahim Pasha told me, I don't know if it is true, that Naseeb paid a large sum of money to a Qalandar to perform a funeral for the animal. The albino bear was bathed, blessed with rose water and such, wrapped in two meters of white funeral cloth, laid to rest on a charpoy, showered with flower petals, and shouldered away for burial. Can you believe it? What will ever become of Naseeb?

"And what of the boy, Ayasan? In order to teach Naseeb the basic principles of banking, I have opened an account for him at the Syndicate Bank. But despite my urgings that he put one half of everything he earns into that account, he has put not one paisa in the bank. My only recourse is to trick him. I will book some programs for him at some schools without telling him how much they will be paying for his efforts. Telling him that, as his agent, I am responsible for disbursing his money to him, I will give him only 50 percent of his earnings. The other half I will put into the Syndicate Bank. Like magic—I'll fool him for his own happiness. Then, one day, he will be informed that he has saved a bit of capital, and he will be happy."

Naseeb smiled as he counted the money in the shikhara. "Good program," he congratulated himself. "*Śābāś!*" When we arrived back at the houseboat for lunch, I was informed that a man named Mister Pintoo Master had come to see me. "No good man," Mohammad Shah sneered as he turned to order Mir Deen and Deen Rather to set out the lunch, and as the meal was served, he raised his hand threateningly to frighten Ayasan out of the place he had taken at the head of the table. "No, Maharaja Ayasan Shah sits there," I insisted, "only there."

Naseeb corrected me, "*Yuvrāj*"—the young prince, heir-apparent in the kingdom of the road, a solvent empire, ever fluctuating and slowly disintegrating. Naseeb spoke with Ayasan—joked? scolded? consoled? instructed?—in the secret language of the pretechnological, preindustrial, kingdom of magic. And the prince played the part, nonchalantly snapping his fingers to get the attention of Mir Deen and Deen Rather, then pointing to his plate to indicate a desire for more omelette, never condescending to speak to those people whom he considered so far beneath himself in the complex, all-pervasive, and absolutely fundamental hierarchy that is Indian society. The servants, though they in turn placed the child much lower than themselves in that netlike hierarchy, silently, on their hands and knees, cleaned up the mess that the boy, unaccustomed as he was to eating with utensils, was making on the Kashmiri carpet which, like everything else on the boat, was for sale.

"Eat Saighal!" Mohammad Shah ordered, spitting my name, hissing it, seeming to pull it painfully from his mouth in the manner that Naseeb and Kareem Baksh pulled thorns and nettles from theirs. The old man, who continuously insisted on his honesty, continuously cheated us. I confronted him when, after overcharging me for the purchase of twelve bottles of Golden Eagle beer, he announced that I needed another dozen—but, according to my careful count, only eight had been drunk. "What do you think, Saighal? Mr. Mohammad Shah took beer? No! I am Mussulman—never drinking—not one drop. No. I am no magic man. Not knowing to make beer disappear. You are magic man. I am honest man. Mussulman! Mr. Robert or Mr. *jādū*-man steal beer."

Mohammad Shah used many of the same techniques to control and deceive the people on his boat that Naseeb Shah used to dominate and beguile the people at his shows. While the people on Mohammad Shah's boat might imagine that they were guests, paying according to some established and reasonable rate, and while people in the crowds that might gather around Naseeb might assume that they were entertained spectators, free to make a donation or buy a ring, in fact, both Mohammad Shah's customers and Naseeb Shah's audience were prisoners. They were the prey caught in Indra's Net.

Though Mohammad Shah kept warning me to beware of Naseeb, he himself insisted on seeing the magician alone each day. Naseeb finally explained it to me: "Mohammad problem man—money problem, boat problem, wife problem, people problem, child problem, all problem." He laughed and repeated it in Hindi, adding a few more qualifying Hindi nouns, but keeping the English word *problem*. That Naseeb was selling amulets, which he had bought for less than five rupees, to Mohammad Shah for over a hundred rupees each, delighted us as well as Robert and Weleja who had just discovered they had paid three thousand rupees to the old man for a six-hundred-rupee carpet. And it pleased Carrie too. "Not that the arse-hole's actually cheatin' me," ever unchagrinned, she grinned. "I mean he's fuckin' over that husband of mine—who bloody well deserves it—sendin' the bills to his family. Now there's a pack of tricksters, that lot. One cheater cheatin' another. That's life, isn't it? I like it. It's the best entertainment in town. I mean talk about bloody magic shows!"

Carrie wanted to come along with us the next day to Harwan to watch Naseeb. When in the morning I yelled over to ask Grant if he too wished to join us, he slowly lifted his head from the pillow: "No thanks. I mean it sounds great and all, but I think I'd like to get some rest today."

Harwan is a village that has grown up around the road. While the branches of its great trees, oak and elm, maple and magnolia, gesture messages of persistence, the purling stream adjacent to the road whispers of transience. Mists, rolling down from snowy Himalayan peaks, rest on pine-green ridges, settle into stone-gray crevices, and rise slowly again to disappear into skies without color. Eagles, kites, and hawks circle in those descending, resting, rising mists.

When the itinerant magician and his son, followed by the three foreigners, entered Harwan, the villagers, as villagers all over India for over two thousand years have done with the same curiosity, set work aside to watch the play. Kashmiri women in their brilliantly colored scarves and *pheran*s, some carrying wood, freshly chopped and bundled, some toting babies, freshly adorned with jewels, lac, and lampblack, seemed more beautiful in the village than in the town, splendid against the muted greens of the leaves above, the soft browns of the earth below, the burnt and muffled reds of the Kashmiri brick house that was a backdrop for the show. A bald man, beckoned by the sound of the flute, peered through the embroidered curtains of the cracked window on the second story of that house to watch the boy set out the snakes and draw the magic circle. Children, some carrying magnolia blossoms or peony bouquets, some eating sweets or honey-buttered bread, some holding another's hand or the borders of a mother's *pheran*, gathered around the circle.

Women and children, Naseeb always insisted, are no good. They don't pay for their pleasures. And there was something wrong with the men of Harwan: perhaps there was not enough money in their pockets, not enough conviction in their minds that reason and perception are trustworthy, not enough fear or desire in their hearts, or not enough playfulness in their souls. The old man with the henna-dyed beard, from whom Naseeb tried to borrow a shawl, fought with the magician over it and would not let him take it. The young man with the bell-bottom pants whom Naseeb had pulled into the circle, panicking in the midst of his decapitation, jumped up and, before he had been officially recapitated, ran off revealing his head to be quite intact. The middle-aged man with the smell of whisky on his breath denied that any of it was true when Ayasan whispered in his ear: "You made some money but now it is gone. . . . You are very well liked, but some friend has turned against you. . . . There are some family squabbles . . . "

And other men, regardless of age, seemed too squeamish to watch the magician cut out his son's tongue without averting their eyes. Noticing, as Ayasan lay writhing on the ground, blood gurgling from his mouth, that he was no longer wearing Cheryl's watch, I assumed that he had sold it, that he needed money more than he needed to know the time.

Although Carrie, Cheryl, and I bought rings to encourage the hesitant crowd, it didn't seem to help. Pride prevented Naseeb from either displaying signs of discouragement over the flop of his show, or admitting that such failures are common in the villages. "Villages good," he insisted and enthusiastically described the fortunes we would see him take in Gulmarg, Sonemarg, Tanmarg, and Pahalgam. In the domain of magic, to say something will happen can cause it to happen. We'd go to all those villages and then, once the road was open, Naseeb announced, we'd go to Ladakh. The "Lambas" (his word for Buddhists), he assured me, because they were so superstitious, because they lived in a world of magic, were quick to buy his rings and amulets, his protections and prognostications. Lambas were the most gullible, then Hindus, then Muslims. I asked him about Christians, the followers of "Issa" (as Jesus is called by many North Indian Muslims), and he explained that they were even more credulous than Lambas; after all, Issa himself was a *jādūgar.* The miracle of the loaves and fishes was done with an egg bag; water was turned to wine with a lota bowl, gimmicked just as it is for Waters of India; Lazarus was a confederate; and the resurrection of Christ was done by the same method as the levitation I had seen in the park near the Purana Qila. Jesus, Naseeb announced, was also very good at cups and balls.

In the bus, on the way back to Srinagar, Naseeb decided that we'd stop to give a performance at Shalimar Garden. When the man who ran the tea stall next to which Naseeb had begun to set up tried to chase him off, Naseeb assured him that his magic show would be good for business, that after standing around watching magic, people would need some tea, a Campa-Cola or a Maaza, even something to eat. He said that magic was good for everyone.

With the Moghul gardens behind him, I could imagine Naseeb performing for Jahangir, who so loved Kashmir, especially at that time of year. I could see the great Moghul there, picture the flotilla of canopied boats moored by that very spot on the lake. Surrounded by an entourage of courtesans (voluptuous and obedient, adept in caresses and songs) and courtiers (skilled in hunting or statecraft, in telling a joke or revealing a plot), all of them to be enjoyed but none of them to be entirely trusted, the Moghul, reclining, drinking opiated wine and chewing opiated betel, would watch the magician manipulate the cups and balls, tear apart and restore a courtesan's silken shawl, perhaps decapitate and revive a courtier who volunteered in order to impress his emperor. Jahangir, persuaded by the entertaining reminder that one can never believe what one sees or hears, assumes or thinks, threw gold coins to the wandering conjurer and, amused, paid dearly for one of the magician's rings.

Naseeb did not fare as well. The tourists, arriving in buses from Srinagar, were on too rigorous a schedule to stop for more than a moment or two to see what the magician was doing, and the hawkers and vendors around the garden were too busy pursuing those hurried tourists. It was mostly children who were drawn to Naseeb, and they scattered when the schoolmaster, waving a stick, came running, shouting at them to get back into the classroom. Ayasan laughed at the children, whom he pitied for having to go to school.

On the way back to the boat, Naseeb told me that he needed two hundred rupees for his wife's brother to get back to Delhi because of some emergency that could not be explained in either the little English he could speak or in the little Hindi that I could understand. Knowing full well that I would not ask him to return it, he assured me that he would pay me back the very next day, right after his performance.

After we arrived back on the boat, I made a receipt for myself that could be presented, if needed, to the Internal Revenue Service: "Two hundred rupees ($15.38), research fee to Naseeb Shah (field informant). *NB:* Cannot provide receipt—informant illiterate."

Mohammad Shah, perched as always on the roof of the houseboat, watched for our arrival just as the Kashmiri kingfisher surveys the waters of the same lake for fish coming to the surface in need of food. He tried to convince me not to move into the large back room that had been occupied by Robert and Weleja, who had left Kashmir that morning while we were in Harwan—the room that had, of course, been promised to the new arrivals, two Englishmen, an older and a younger one who claimed to be uncle and nephew. It was obvious that they were not really related, but no one cared. Everything on the boat, after all, was a lie: Cheryl and I said we were married; Carrie, to keep the Kashmiri men at bay, said she was waiting for her beloved husband to join her there; Grant said he didn't know why he was so tired; Ali said we were paying less than the other guests; Mir Deen said he was my friend; and Mohammad Shah said that he was an honest man.

Andrew and Uncle Nigel, nervously pretending not to notice that Naseeb was smoking hashish or that Ayasan, with his perpetually filthy fingers, was doing sleights of hand with the sugar cubes in the bowl on the tray in front of them, sat drinking their tea as they waited to meet with Ali. Mir Deen, grinning, and Deen Rather, frowning, stared at them. "I can't begin to tell you," Nigel said, "how absolutely delighted Andrew and I are to be here. Almost didn't make it, you know—nasty bit of luck in Delhi. Ghastly place, frightfully hot, and—well, you'll never believe it—right there in the airport, under the very noses of the police, a pickpocket made off with everything—tickets, passports, money, the lot. Well, if that didn't throw a spanner in the works! I can't imagine what we would have done if we had not met that marvelous man, dear Mr. Habeeb. He just happened to be there in the airport, seeing some friends off. It was really serendipitous, it was. He saved our lives. We mustn't forget that, Andrew."

"If you think he's nice," Carrie, taking a deep puff of Naseeb's hashish, smiled, "you're goin' to love his brother Ali."

When Mohammad Shah's daughter appeared to inform Naseeb that her mother needed to see him, the magician, lighting one of my Benson and Hedges and leaning back to smoke it, told the young woman to have her mother wait, that he'd be there in a while. He knew not to move too quickly, to seem too eager. The victim, whether Mohammad Shah's wife smoking her hubble-bubble out back or Uncle Nigel sitting there sipping his tea, must be made to wait.

While Naseeb consulted with Mrs. Shah, reading her palm, foretelling her future, and selling her rings, Ayasan was taking pleasure in the exploration of our new room, in going through the new drawers and closet, jumping on the new bed, flushing the new toilet, making faces in the new mirror, and stealing an old deck of trick cards.

Before leaving the boat Naseeb, lent me the Needle-through-Arm trick that I had given him in December, suggesting that I use it to make Mohammad Shah afraid of me. Naseeb had already told him that I was a "Tantra-man." If he thought I had certain magical powers, he might not cheat me quite as completely as he otherwise would. Because of the relative complexity of the set-up, Naseeb didn't use the illusion for street shows, but he did use it on such occasions as school programs, and during one such performance, a teacher had fainted at the sight of it. He laughed as he told me that the teacher's head had hit the desk in the fall. The children had clapped their hands gleefully at the sight of the "real blood." Naseeb laughed again, "Not *jādū*-blood." Everyone loves the sight of blood, Naseeb assured me. Everyone is compelled by explorations of their aversions and fears.

BIRDS AND FIRE

When we arrived early the next morning at the Batmaloo bus station, Ayasan was wearing a wig that he had made out of an old piece of brown carpet. His hair had been shaved off in preparation for an interview that he and his father were going to have with a woman at the Kashmir television station. "Lamba," Naseeb teased Ayasan, who was embarrassed by his new baldness, as he handed me the calling card of the man who had arranged the television interview: "Mr. M. C. Pushpalal, B.Sc., Esq., Fabulous Plot Writer, High Calibre TV Artiste, Marvellous Party Planner, Announcer-cum-Magician, Stage Manager, Entre-Paner. Contact: Bazarr Batmaloo, Srinagar-Kashmir 190001, India. No-Telephone-As-Yet." Mr. Pushpalal, just as he had organized the interview (which, to the best of my knowledge, never materialized), was also going to book Naseeb to perform at schools, weddings, and meetings of the Indian Rotary Club. He was, furthermore, going to get a room for Naseeb and his family at the Jahangir Hotel. There would be room service, a bath and a toilet, a telephone and a television. But in the meantime Naseeb still had to earn enough for his family to eat; and so we boarded the bus to begin the four-hour ride to Gulmarg.

Like hawks descending upon their prey, the hawkers dove at us as we emerged from the bus. "Pony trekking? Coat renting?" they squawked in Hindi, English, French, German, and Italian. I insisted that we were not interested in the sights, that we were there to watch Naseeb, the magician who was rolling out his mat as the boy with the piece of carpet on his head played the drum and flute. "What is a point of looking at him? He is nothing. Only one good magician—God Almighty. Take ponies. See God-magic. Mountains, forest, sky, glacier. Real magic show. Rent my coats, cold up there. Don't rent other man's pony, other man's coat. Not honest men. I am only honest Kashmir man." The patter of the vendors in Kashmir, like that of the magicians, is always the same. And he kept it up as he followed us to where Naseeb was beginning to do some coin magic. "Magic nothing. Not real." As the hawk abandons the rat when it sees the rabbit, the renter of coats and ponies left us, mid-sentence, to descend upon the bodies that emerged from the just-arrived tourist bus.

After the long ride and almost an hour of performing, but before Naseeb was able to make his pitch and sell the rings, it started to rain. The spectators around the magician and his son, like the crows and eagles in the sky, vanished. Thunder echoed through the mountain passes like ominous moans of ancient gods. Then there was the four-hour bus ride back to Srinagar. On the way home, when Ayasan fell asleep with his head on his father's shoulder, Naseeb adjusted the little boy's carpet-wig and cradled him in his arm, resting a hand gently over his heart. Cutting the boy's tongue out, decapitating him, shouting at him, and chasing him around their street stage, externalized and perhaps disposed of all the real anger that might be felt by a father for his son. The violence was just play, even though that play was their work. Outside the mandala, beyond the show, the game, the job, the father displayed only tenderness toward his son. Ayasan made Naseeb laugh quite often, but Naseeb always took him seriously. He never once scolded the child who was quickly learning all that he knew, all that he had learned from his own now-so-frail father.

Through the dirty window of the bus I saw the sudden appearance of four eagles in the sky and, moments later, the rains let up. The birds knew it first. Fires burning in the mountains across the valley released great, white, spiraling pillars of smoke. Two crows chased one of the eagles, and it retreated. The golden eagles of Kashmir, no less than its people, have surrendered their grandeur. The hunters in the heights no longer watch for the longtailed marmot or the rock squirrel; like the calumnious crows, they feed now on human garbage.

As the bus neared the Batmaloo station, we passed a crowd that had gathered around some spectacle. "*Jādūgar?*" I asked. No, Naseeb answered, it was a Qalandar, a bear handler, and he knew it because the crowd was arranged in a circle. When a magician works, the audience forms an ellipse because the mandala has two centers, established by the father and the son respectively. The oval makes misdirection possible. Whenever the magician needs to divert the attention of his spectators so that he can take something from his bag, dispose of something, or load something into his mouth, he has only to suddenly throw something else to his son. I have seen it happen a hundred times, and it never fails. Every eye in the audience, fearing that it will miss some bit of trickery, follows the object through the air without remembering that it has done so. We are fooled exactly to the degree that we try not to be fooled, deceived to the degree that we want to know the truth, tangled all the more by trying to wiggle out of Indra's Net.

A circle forms around the Qalandar because he works alone, standing close to his bear, keeping the attention on the animal at all times. When I asked Naseeb about the albino bear, he pretended he didn't understand. And when I tried it in Hindi, he kept up the act, pretending not to understand anything except the word "*bhālū.*" He laughed, "*bhālū, bandar*—bear, monkey. *Bhālūwālā, bandarwālā*— Qalandar, bear-man, monkey-man."

Most of the time it was good not to have Shankar or Shalini or anyone else to translate our conversations; there was, I felt, a certain honesty that existed between us precisely because our verbal communication was now more limited than it had been in Delhi. Without the subtleties of language, it was not quite as easy for us to lie to each other. Words can distract from perceiving the look in the speaker's eyes, the gestures of his hands, the posture of his body, all those things that have the potential to belie the falsehood behind what is verbally sworn to be true. Out of necessity a language developed between us, a language with its own vocabulary (drawn from Hindi and English and including many synonyms, most of which were qualitative adjectives), its own grammar (with almost all verbs being present participles, and all nouns, despite an absence of prepositions, remaining uninflected), its own syntax (the verb following the direct object following the subject in short, clipped sentences), and its own ornaments, tones, and cadences. Soon it was possible to lie in this language too.

In our language Naseeb explained that while the Qalandars were not very good at sleight of hand or real magic, most of them could do a few tricks, enough conjuring to fool a crowd and sell some rings or lockets. Maslets and Qalandars are brothers, he said, and they greet each other as such: "*Salaam aleichem.*" He told me about a little trick that two of his Qalandar brothers performed in Bombay. One of them joins a small and carefully assessed group of people who are waiting for a bus. When the second Qalandar comes along, the first one acts surprised:

QALANDAR ONE: Hey, I know you! I saw you perform some magic once, real magic. It was in Lucknow, a few years ago. A man had a watch. You put it in a box and when you opened the box there were two watches. I'm sure it was you!

QALANDAR TWO (*pretending to be embarrassed, speaking in a lowered voice, but making sure that everyone can hear him*): Yes, that was me. Occasionally I do such things.

QALANDAR ONE (*impatiently, excitedly*): Do the trick for me now.

QALANDAR TWO (*lowering his voice more*): It's not exactly a trick, not something to be done frivolously, without a purpose. And besides I am in a hurry.

QALANDAR ONE: No, please just try it! There's enough time before the bus comes. Please, I'm a very poor man. Do you have the magic box with you? Let me put my money, such a little bit of money, in the box. If I could double my money I could afford to feed my family today.

QALANDAR TWO (*lowering his voice still more*): Since you are such a poor man, I suppose I should do this for you. God gave me this gift in order to help poor and unfortunate people. But let us step over there, away from all of these people. (*They move away from the people waiting for the bus but remain close enough to be observed by them; the second Qalandar gives some money to the first, who has produced a small wooden box from the bag over his shoulder*).

QALANDAR TWO (*just loudly enough so that his words will be heard by those among the people waiting for the bus who strain their ears*): Okay, turn around, take twenty-one steps. Slowly. Close your eyes. Repeat these words twenty-one times: '*La ilaha illa'llah*' ['*Oṃ śrīśivāya namaḥ*' if their target in the crowd is Hindu]. Slowly . . . slowly. . . . Okay, turn around. Come here.

QALANDAR ONE (*racing over*): A miracle! Thank you! My money has doubled. A miracle! A blessing! Thank you!

QALANDAR TWO: Do not thank me. Thank God.

The rest is inevitable. The shill runs happily off. The Qalandar rejoins the group waiting for the bus and, as he boards it, he makes sure to sit or stand next to one of the more well-to-do looking members of that group, someone he knows will question him about the magic he has witnessed and will slowly get around to asking if he can perform it again for him. "I'm not sure. You seem to be a man of means. God gave me this gift to help only those people who are desperately in need of money." When the man begs, explains that though he is not poverty-stricken, he is indeed in desperate need of money for some particular reason or another, the Qalandar hesitantly agrees to meet with him in some deserted place: "I can make no guarantees. The outcome is in God's hands. He is the magician."

After the man has put all of his money, usually his watch, and often some of his wife's most valuable jewelry into the box, after he has turned, walked twenty-one paces, closed his eyes, and while he is repeating the sacred words, "There is no God but God," the Qalandar runs off to meet with his friend and find another bus stand.

"Beautiful Magic!" Naseeb laughed, "Qalandar-*jādū!*" One of the Qalandars who was camped in the graveyard with Naseeb wanted to know if people in "Hawaii-America" enjoyed trained bears.

"Well, I'm not sure," I had to answer. "We don't really have any."

Several days later, Naseeb explained to me that the man was planning to save his money in order to bring his bear to Hawaii where he and the bear and Cheryl and I would become very rich by putting on street shows and selling amulets. When, later that month, we went to Shadipur to take a message from Naseeb to his mother, the Qalandar greeted us as old friends and excitedly introduced us to his bear. "Disco!" he shouted. "Disco!" and the bear, with the rope tied through the silver ring in its nose, danced for us with as much exuberance as was possible in the hellish swelter of Delhi. His three-year-old child, naked and head-shaven, wrestled a baby bear for us, and then the Qalandar took us to Naseeb's mother's tent where, with Shankar's help, I delivered the message that her son, because of police problems, had moved from Srinagar to Baramullah.

The old woman, her white hair discernible through the diaphanous blue shawl, the sparkle, as naughty as Naseeb's or Ayasan's, visible in her eye through the thick, scratched, and crooked glasses, smiled at us happily. Her arm was broken, and the filthy cast was supported by a rope around her neck. The Qalandar's explanation, at least as Shankar translated it, made no sense: "There was a terrible dust storm in Shadipur, making it impossible to see, and on top of that, there was a mad dog, a dog with rabies, running through the area, attacking people, even going into the tents to attack. A child died, a magician's child. The men were trying to catch the dog, to beat it to death with sticks. In the dust storm, violent as it was, Naseeb's mother was struck by accident. Someone mistook her for the rabid dog."

She asked Shankar if I could get a message to Naseeb: she wanted her husband and son to come home; she needed help; her brother had died a few days earlier; there were other problems too. Through Shankar, I had to tell her that I would not be seeing Naseeb again.

It had rained all night in the valley of Kashmir. And that ceaseless breaking of dark clouds had made it difficult to sleep, hard not to envision the tents in the graveyard: dark, wet mud, full of bones, turning swampy in the midnight deluge; dark, wet forms, clothes clinging to shivering flesh; dark, wet faces—Naseeb and his wife, his father and Ayasan, his baby and the other children, countless, clamoring children, the umbrella repairman, his wet turban a darker red, and the Qalandar, in the dark, trying to shelter his dancing bear. Rain, more rain. And all night, though muffled by the racket of rain, there had been the haunting din of human cries.

In the morning, a cloud, crawling langorously down the mountains, sliding gently across the silent, silky surface of the lake, veiled the huddles of shikharas against the banks and seemed to mute the cries of crows and croaking of frogs. Birds sheltered in the boughs of the trees along the shore and in the latticework— the leaves and flowers crudely carved—of the houseboats. I chased a crow from ours.

I was anxious for Naseeb to arrive. He had never been so late before. Waiting on the porch, sitting still, I watched for a boat that might be bringing him through the rain that fell upon the lake and through rising mists and vapors.

"Lousy weather we're havin'," Grant called out from his bed. "Not a very good day to do much of anything. I think I'll just stay in today." Carrie came over. "Did you hear all the commotion last night? I don't mean the storm. I mean the screamin' and cryin'. Do you know what it was? It was right outside my window, so I had a bloody ringside seat. Good old Mohammad Shah was beatin' the boy, Deen Rather. He was really givin' it to him. I thought he was goin' to knock his head off. And all the while Mir Deen—now there's a real shit-head for you—just sat there laughin' at the show."

The story was interrupted by the appearance of Nigel on the porch. "Andrew and I are leaving today, off on a Himalayan adventure. To Ladakh. Mr. Ali has most graciously arranged everything." Carrie laughed out loud.

I stayed on the porch, still waiting, now really worried about Naseeb. The same shikhara that took Andrew and Nigel to the shore soon brought their replacements back to the boat. As the rather urbane older gentleman and his wife climbed on board the New Golden Phoenix, I asked where they were from. "From?" the man frowned. "We are Palestinians. Palestine is our homeland. But because of the Americans and the Jews, we are forced to live in Kuwait."

When he discovered that he and his wife did not have the beautiful, back room that they had seen in the photographs in Habeeb's office in Delhi, the luxurious room that Habeeb had promised them, and that, in fact, the room was being occupied by an American Jew, he was, to say the least, disconsolate. "But it is my room!" he insisted. "I paid Mr. Habeeb precisely for that room." The Palestinians had no idea as yet just how bad their problem really was. While Habeeb in Delhi had been working his scam on them, Ali had his own sting operation underway in Srinagar. He had charged Andrew and Nigel for an excursion to Ladakh, a package that included a car (with Abdul, Mohammad Shah's youngest son, at the wheel), lodging, meals, and "expert religio-philosophical tours" of the Buddhist monasteries there (with Abdul as the guide), knowing full well that the road to Leh would not be open until sometime after the Englishmen were due in Delhi for their flight back to London. They put on the show: every day, just after dawn, Abdul would take the two of them on the four-hour drive to Sonemarg, where they would be told by a man (who was presumably being paid by Abdul) that the road was not open yet but that they should try again the very next day; and every day, just before dusk, Nigel would climb aboard the houseboat behind Andrew muttering, "Still no luck today!" Of course he couldn't get his money back—every document that every guest ever signed was always clearly emblazoned with the phrase, "No Refunds." Nigel always took a generous, fair—dare I say British?—view of the situation: "Well I mean it's not really Mr. Ali's fault that the road isn't open yet, that the snow on the passes hasn't quite been cleared away. I'm sure it will all work out in the end. We'll just have to be patient." Maybe it was because he adopted that liberal attitude that Ali offered to let him keep the room that he and Andrew checked out of each morning. All of this left the Palestinians without any room at all. While assuring them that they could have the bedroom as soon as the road to Ladakh was open, Ali informed them that he would provide two cots so that they could sleep in the living room. When they threatened to leave the houseboat and move to a hotel, Ali had to remind them that once they moved off of his boat, he no longer bore any responsibility for providing them with tickets back to Delhi.

It was when they realized that they had no toilet in the living room that the Palestinians entered into negotiations with us. It was, as Yasir Arafat would surely appreciate, a complex situation. I was sympathetic with them, but I liked having my own room.

Naseeb didn't show up until the next morning. It was the first time I had ever seen him either physically dirty or emotionally rattled. He told me the story. Two days earlier the police, as they did each week, had come to the cemetery to collect their bribe, the extortionate fee of fifty rupees per week for each of the thirty or forty tents that were pitched in the graveyard, for which the vagrants were permitted to camp there. Then, the very next day, the day Naseeb had not come to the houseboat, the police arrived at the cemetery, armed with lathis and automatic weapons, to inform the itinerants that they could not remain there any longer. They had to leave Srinagar.

I asked Naseeb about Mr. Pushpalal, the man who was supposed to get a room for him at the Jahangir Hotel. Naseeb shook his head. Mr. Pushpalal had explained to Naseeb that it was too dangerous for him to live at the hotel, that because he was a magician, he would be blamed for anything bad that happened at the hotel. "If there was a fire in the hotel," Mr. Pushpalal had said, "or even if someone were to slip and fall down the stairs, all would immediately come to the conclusion that some Tantric practices were the cause of the disaster. Naseeb would be arrested."

Assuring me that the situation was not troubling him, that he had put up with this sort of thing all of his life and that he was resigned to put up with it for whatever remained of that life, he suggested that the only thing that disturbed him was the inconvenience it was going to cause me. The only solution that he could come up with, the only way that we could continue to spend our days together, was if he and Ayasan would move into one of the many small hotels near Lal Chowk. I watched the trick; I listened to the patter: "I won't be able to be with my family, but that's okay—I'll do it for you. I'm not a rich man. I don't have the money for a hotel. I couldn't accept the money from you, because you're my friend. But maybe a loan. I could pay it back in a few days, after my programs in Sonemarg and at Hazrat Bal."

"Sonemarg. Tomorrow," he suddenly smiled and slapped my knee, putting all despondency behind him. "Sonemarg! Best magic place!" He forced out the words without letting go of the hashish smoke that he held deep within his lungs. Looking into my eyes and smiling, he suddenly released the smoke with a great and carefree laugh. I gave him the money.

When we met Naseeb and Ayasan early the next morning at the bus station, I asked where they had slept. The magician happily explained that they didn't have to move their tents after all. A conjurer from Andhra, camping there in the graveyard with the others, had died the night before, and because of his death the police had agreed to let the vagrants stay for another week or so, so that Islamic mourning rites could be performed and arrangements could be made for the disposal of the body. I wanted to know more about the magician who had died. "Was he sick?" I asked Naseeb. He shook his head, and his answer made me wonder if we ever understood each other at all: "No. Not Sikh. Mussulman."

On the bus, on the way up to Sonemarg along the Ladakh road, Naseeb proudly announced that Ayasan had done a program by himself the day before. He had cut his little sister's tongue out in front of the bus station and had earned thirty-two rupees. Then Naseeb talked about Mohammad Shah, laughing about the old man's problems, and I could not help but wonder if he laughed about me in the same way during his sessions with the Mohammad Shah family. He told me that Mohammad Shah, insisting that he could not afford the sixty rupees for an amulet to take care of a problem he was having with his wife, asked Naseeb to get the money from me. Mohammad Shah's family, Naseeb added, like the police in Vasant Vihar, believed that the magician had hypnotized me and that I would do whatever he commanded.

Andrew and Nigel were sitting with Abdul at a tea stall near where we got off the bus in Sonemarg. "We're still waiting to find out if the road is going to open," Nigel said with a sanguine smile. "It's awfully good of young Abdul here to be so patient. He's taking damn good care of us." As Uncle Nigel chattered, slowly and loudly in hopes that some of his English might be understood, Abdul Shah, son of Mohammad Shah, winked at me as if I were a confederate in his magic show.

After finding a spot near the shacks where coats and ponies are rented to tourists, Naseeb was having to deal with an angry competitor. The young man from Kabul with a patch over one eye, who sold medicines on the streets, magic cures for impotence, baldness, frigidity, flatulence, constipation, convulsions, diarrhea, migraine, and sometimes cancer, claimed that he had a right to the muddy clearing where Ayasan had set out the snakes. Salaaming him, offering him one of my Benson and Hedges, touching his shoulder, and calling him brother, Naseeb convinced the medicine seller that he would benefit from the crowd the magician drew. There would be all the more people to fool, all the more medicine to sell. Naseeb explained to me that the medicine was an old trick. The skin seems hot. One feels the heat and imagines that such mysterious fire cures.

The audience, in which the medicine seller had taken a place, was beginning to grow, and Naseeb was getting ready to tear a borrowed shawl when two men pushed their way into the crowd. One of the men held a rope, a leash that was tied to the network of chains that was draped over the other man. A garland of chains around his neck was connected by a chain that ran down his back to another set of shackles around his ankles. The manacled man, a derelict soul dressed in rags, holding a dirty piece of Kashmiri bread in his tethered hands, was shouting; the hideous ravings distracted Naseeb's audience. There was feral fire in his eyes and birds of madness screeching in the cage that was his heart. People who wanted to watch the magic show yelled at the madman, shooed him away, and the man who held the rope pulled him back with a jerk and a slap on the face. The madman cowered like a leashed dog, punished for forgetting to heel. When he whimpered, the man who held the lead petted him gently and caressed him.

The police, who had been called by some shopkeeper, a seller of trinkets or a renter of coats and ponies, to chase off the madman, were as anxious to break up the performance of magic as they were the display of madness. I tried to intervene, explaining to them that I was a writer for *National Geographic Magazine* and that Cheryl was a staff photographer. "We're working on a piece on Sonemarg called 'Heaven on Earth.' We don't want to show tourists, that wouldn't be good for tourism. Tourists don't like tourists. The magician's performance photographed against the splendor of the Himalayan peaks—that's the look we want, exotic and alluring."

We argued over the editorial policies of *National Geographic Magazine*, the policeman holding the position that all people wanted to see beautiful panoramas of mountains, forests, and rivers, "unspoilt by lowly folk," and I proposing that such pictures were hackneyed, that photographs of a magician would capture a traditional India. "As the mountains have not changed, so the magician looked like this over a thousand years ago, performed like this, probably in this very spot, for the caravans making their way through the mountain passes to join the traders along the silk route. Photographing him here, in this setting, will conjure up images of that in the minds of our readers. India is the land of magic. I want to use magic as a metaphor for social, philosophical, psychological, and aesthetic issues within Indian cultural history."

"I am not interesting!" he sneered.

"Do you mean 'interest*ed*?' " I asked, but got no answer. "Look, I've been given permission to do this work by the government of India, by the minister of tourism. He's my personal friend. He likes magic very much." I was appalled to hear The Incredible Mayadhar's words spontaneously coming out of my mouth. But they were to no avail. "Please, let me talk to your superior."

"I am superior!" the cop snapped with a petulant grimace and a flourish of his lathi. That was that.

We waited for the bus back to Srinagar at the same tea stall at which I had seen the Englishmen and Abdul, and Naseeb, doing his best not to appear discouraged, insisted on buying tea for us. Ayasan, who had disappeared, suddenly reappeared eating cherries from a newspaper wrapper. He spit the pits at my feet, a gesture that seemed aggressive; but then he mitigated the apparent hostility with a laughter that implied, "Just teasing, just kidding." He dropped the cherries in Cheryl's lap, pointed at them and then at her mouth. What seemed to be an expression of a boyish crush on her was also mitigated with laughter. He disappeared again.

The motor revved, black fumes were coughed out of the exhaust, and the shuddering bus started to roll forward. Amidst the shouting, shoving, and arguing that are absolutely essential to all travel in India, we pushed our way into the battered vehicle. Panicked because Ayasan was nowhere in sight, I shook Naseeb's shoulder to warn him that the boy was missing. The shoulder shrugged, and the magician laughed. If the eight-year-old child missed the bus, he'd find another way back to Srinagar, or he'd spend the night and do some magic to get enough money for a ticket on the following day. Still I was relieved to suddenly see the great grin and dimples, the rug that was a wig, and the bag of snakes tied to Ayasan's back appear in the open window of the unlatched door that was flapping back and forth as the bus gathered speed. Because his father was now far away, beyond the boxes and bundles, the cages of chickens and baskets of summer melons, and all the seatless passengers, Ayasan crawled in with us, over our laps, to squeeze in by the window.

We were startled to see, across the aisle from us, still in the chains, the madman. His tormented head was out of the open window, and, as a dog cannot help doing, he gulped at the swift moving air outside, cold, crisp mountain air that made his eyes stream with tears. The man who held the rope leash slumped forward, looking very tired and very sad.

The road was wet from the early summer melting of the snows, and as the bus skidded, swerving to miss the edge of the road, the drop into the deep abyss of rock in the mountainside, the madman pulled his head back into the bus, and over the blare and crackle of the taped torch songs from Hindi movies, he howled. People around him either laughed or yelled at him. A mountain man with a beard dyed henna-red poked the madman in the chest with his gnarled walking stick, and people laughed all the more. Swiveling around with the usual "You are from which place?" the passenger in front of us, over the screaming and raving of the lunatic, the music, and the laughter and taunting of the passengers, calmly told us his name and explained that he was a schoolteacher in Kangan. After asking us if we would visit his family and "stay some weeks in our home," he expressed his sadness that we would be unable to do so, but hoped that we would remember to send him postcards from Hawaii. "And there is one other thing that I would like for you to send."

"What's that?"

"An X-ray machine. My cousin is the village doctor, and he needs this machine."

"Oh, sure," I said. "What color would you like?"

"That is not so important. But if X-ray machines come in yellow, or some other cheerful color, that would be excellent."

"No problem. They come in every color. Say, excuse me, could you tell me what that madman across the aisle from us is screaming about?"

"You mean the one in the chains?"

"Yeah."

"Oh, it's just nothing. It's crazy talk. The man, I believe, is himself crazy."

"Yeah, but what's he saying. What is the crazy talk?"

"Mussulman! Mussulman!" The schoolteacher said, translating the agonized, delirious jeremiad of the madman with a cheerful expression and an amused tone. "Mussulman, Mussulman, you killed my mother. Mussulman, Mussulman, you killed my father. Mussulman, you are wicked. Shaitan is waiting for you. His mouth is open. He is waiting. Mussulman, you think you are tricking others. It is yourselves that you are fooling. And Shaitan is waiting. I know you, I know that you are mad. Mussulman, you did not fast for Ramadan. But you feasted for Id. You stuffed your guts. Who does the tricking? Who is tricked?"

People were laughing and teasing, laughing all the more when the man who held the leash, his clothes as ragged as the madman's, slapped the chained man's head. The madman stuck his head out of the window again and furiously, desperately, gulped for air.

"He is definitely crazy," the teacher smiled as he placed his hand on Ayasan's leg. "This other fellow is his brother. He says he is taking him to Kangan, that there is a certain pir there. He is a magician. He will cure the man of his madness.

The others are joking. They are saying, 'You don't need a magician, you need a psychiatrist.' Perhaps I will get my cousin to see this maniac."

Liquid, blood red, was dripping down the window, leaking from some package on the overburdened roof of the rickety, careening bus, and the wind was blowing it in, all over Ayasan's kurta. He licked it from his filthy sleeve, and his grubby smile suggested that it was sweet. The teacher invited the boy to climb over the seat and sit on his lap, but Ayasan stayed put.

The bus slowed down as we entered a village, and though it did not stop, people jumped off, others climbed on, and the madman, becoming madder than ever, stuck his screaming head out of the window again. The teacher, more amused than ever, now stroking Ayasan's leg, continued his translation: "Mussulman, Mussulman, I shall perform intercourse with your wife. Pardon my French, Mrs. Hawaii, but this is what the crazy man is saying. I shall perform intercourse with your mother. I shall perform intercourse with your daughter. I shall perform intercourse with your sister." The teacher listened and laughed. "Oh, now he is just listing other relatives and other similar things that he will do."

The howling head was jerked back through the window. The madman's brother slapped him, pulled the leash through the metal bar on the back of the seat, and tightened it so that the madman could not move. It reminded me of a trick I had seen Naseeb do the year before in Delhi, an escape, for which the magician was bound with ropes and chains much as the madman was tethered. Naseeb's eyes had flashed like the madman's, he breathed in gasps as the madman did, he groaned like that man, but, in the end, Naseeb was free and could smile. I could see Naseeb in the front of the bus, sharing his hashish with the driver.

At Kangan the madman and his brother, the mountainman and the schoolteacher, descended. "If they don't have yellow X-ray machines, never mind. Any color will suffice. My cousin is not a fussy fellow."

As we continued our way down the mountain road, I looked at Ayasan, who had fallen asleep, his head on Cheryl's breast, and I wondered what would happen to him. His future seemed cluttered with police and lies, littered with dead falcons, dead *pijus*, and dead albino bears. I saw his eyes moving beneath the closed lids, and I wondered what the child dreamed. Or, I wondered, was he really sleeping, or was he feigning it, just as he shammed his convulsions on the street, just to place his head there? Anything was possible, anything but certitude about what was real and what was false.

When the bus chugged into the Batmaloo station, I assumed that Naseeb and Ayasan, who surely must have been as tired as we were, would go to their tent in the graveyard, but Naseeb, needing beer as badly as I did, wanted to come to the boat.

Watched, as always, by Mohammad Shah, we climbed out of the little shikhara and onto the New Golden Phoenix, the Boat of Lies, on the Lake of Deceit, in the Vale of Fraud.

"Good magic, Saighal? Lots of money, Saighal?" Mohammad Shah asked with his customary glower.

"Yeah, great. We're richer than ever."

Mir Deen ordered Deen Rather to get three bottles of my beer. It was Kingfisher beer, not Golden Eagle; a trick, I mused, the conventional transformation of one bird into another, but I was too tired to worry about it or try to figure it out. As Deen Rather set the beer down, he whispered something under his breath that I hardly considered in need of pointing out: "Mr. Shah bad man. No good man."

Carrie came in to report the events of the day. "It's been a great day. The usual show. Grant hasn't moved. The Palestinians just went out after spendin' the entire day in your room, lyin' on your bed. I asked them if they had your permission. They said it was their right. I let them be—I didn't think Australia ought to get involved in the Middle East crisis. The queers went off in the car with Abdul again, actually took their bags with them—do they really believe that they're goin' to get to Ladakh? Mohammad Shah beat the boy again. I guess he said somethin' to the old man, talked back to him, or called him a name, because the old fart threatened to cut his tongue out. At least that's what the boy told me. Of course, who knows who's tellin' the truth around here? Mohammad Shah actually waved a knife at him. Unreal! I couldn't help but wish you were here. I mean, I thought you'd really appreciate that one, bein' as Naseeb does that tongue-cutting trick on the boy in his show and all. Don't you just love Kashmir?" She laughed and took a swig of beer. "Oh yeah, and some guy showed up, some character named Mister Pintoo Master. He said he needed to see you, that it was a matter of life and death. Isn't Kashmir great!"

I asked Naseeb, who was busily blending the hashish and the tobacco in his palm, if he had ever heard of someone named Mister Pintoo Master. He assented with a nod, a laugh, and an explanation that he was a "Kalakar-man," a sort of performer who, according to Naseeb, did some juggling and acrobatics, some singing and dancing, and, of course, some magic. Wondering what he could want with me, what could be "a matter of life and death," I asked Naseeb if he had any idea. "*Dhan*—money," Naseeb smiled as he poured the smoking mixture from his palm back into the Benson and Hedges from which the tobacco had been emptied.

Just as the shikhara and rickshaw drivers always asked Naseeb about it, so Carrie, while Naseeb was using our toilet, asked me how much I was paying the magician to spend his days with me. I insisted that I wasn't paying him anything. "We're friends," I said.

"That's nice," she smiled. "That's really nice."

When Naseeb returned from the bathroom, he wanted me to show him how my portable, battery-powered typewriter worked. "America magic machine," he laughed, as he looked with pleasure at the demonstration and at the results. He asked me to type out a certificate to add to his collection of legitimating documents. Affixing an adhesive sticker, the seal of the International Brotherhood of Magicians, to the University of Hawaii, Department of Religion stationery, which was ready in the typewriter, I began to write. Naseeb prompted me with Hindi and English phrases, including: "Naseeb Shah, World's Greatest Magician."

Just as Naseeb had his bundle of documents saying how great he was, so Mohammad Shah had a guest book in which he had asked people to write their comments about the houseboat. It had no doubt been out of a fear of not getting their return tickets to Delhi that people had written things like, "This has been the greatest experience of our lives. Mr. Mohammad has been like a father and Mr. Ali like a brother. Everything was wonderful." Some comments, like censored messages from hostages in other parts of the Islamic world, were ambiguous, imparting the impression that they were written under duress: "What a place! Unforgettable! I can't even begin to say what an incredible experience this has been. There are no words to express how I enjoyed staying here. These people are really unbelievable—they'll treat you as you've never been treated before."

Mohammad Shah had, upon our arrival, asked if I knew French. He wanted a translation of the comment written in the book by the Parisian couple whom we had replaced on the boat. I read the scribbled message: "*Cet enculé, le père Mohammad Shah, m'a roulé; j'ai casqué une fortune içi. J'en ai plein le cul de lui, cette conne. Il faut faire gaffe au père Mohammad Shah, ce vieux rappiat. Attention les amis! Ce n'est pas un 'houseboat'—c'est une taule. Dégagez!*" I assured Mohammad Shah that it simply said that he was wonderful and the boat was the "world's greatest houseboat." It was the only time I ever saw the man smile; faint and evanescent though it was, it was a real smile that shimmered slightly on the rancorous, unshaven face of the old Kashmiri *conne*.

Naseeb asked me for a favor: the next time I came to visit him, would I mind bringing a cassette tape player for his wife? He would pay me for it, of course, and he only wanted a small one because if he had a large model, the police would see it, confiscate it, assume that he had stolen it, and send him to jail. I had my own assumptions: even if Ayasan had not already told him about it, Naseeb, when he used our toilet, had surely seen the small cassette player in the bedroom, and he knew that if he pitched it right, if the patter was good, and if I had been well enough misdirected not to realize that he had been in our bedroom, I would certainly give him the tape recorder.

Watching him play with it, smiling as he listened to the tape of "Black Magic Woman," I felt a complete distrust of him. That was of course appropriate, since he is a magician, but I also felt things that were not so appropriate—an annoyance with him that was aggravated by his request, after Carrie had left the room, that I urge her to buy a ring from him for three hundred rupees. Handing the ring with the shiny black stone in it to me, he said that he was sure she would go for it if I told her it was a good buy. I would have no part of it. I insisted that she was a friend and that we don't cheat friends in America, that she didn't believe in ring power anyway, that the only reason she had bought a ring from him in Harwan was to encourage the villagers to do so, and that she had done so because she liked Naseeb, because she wanted to please him, wanted him to be her friend.

Startled by my sermon, Naseeb shook his head and, laughing rather oddly, assured me that that was no problem, that even though he had himself paid over two hundred rupees for the ring, he would give it to her as a gift. He would do it, he said, because he was my friend. And when he looked me in the eyes, I felt his annoyance. I guessed his thoughts: that I had lied to him when I met him a year earlier by telling him that I was a magician; that my friendship amounted to no more than my need to get information for some book that would make a lot money for me and none for him; that, once my book was done, he would never see me again; I would be luxuriating in Hawaii, while he was wallowing in Shadipur or in some graveyard.

Mohammad Shah took Naseeb out to the back, to the little bit of land where the chicken coop was, so that the magician could counsel the family and equip them with more rings and amulets. With the old man out of the way, Deen Rather came to me, trembling, looking over his shoulder again and again as he whispered to me: "Call father. Call brother. Say Mr. Shah bad man. Hitting Deen Rather. Help me." He started scribbling a message in Arabic script but, hearing footsteps and the creaking of the planks that circled the boat, he crumpled up the paper, hid it in his *pheran*, and carried out the tray with the empty beer bottles upon it.

Before leaving that night, Naseeb asked if I would arrange a magic show for the next morning, Sunday morning, on the houseboat, if I could invite the foreigners to attend. Sunday mornings were no good in town since every Indian would be watching the *Rāmāyaṇa* on television. We bickered over how Naseeb would be paid. I suggested that I would explain to each of the guests ahead of time that since the magician earned his living by performing magic, we should each chip in fifteen rupees for the show. Naseeb didn't like it. He'd pass a cup around at the end, and they would certainly be so impressed that they would give much more than fifteen rupees, and then, to top it off, they'd buy the rings. After seeing a needle forced through my arm, above the hand that bore the ring, after seeing me extinguish and vanish a cigarette in that same hand, and then, after hearing my testimonial, the story of how my arm was chopped off in an automobile accident but that, because of the ring on my finger, the arm was easily put back in place to instantaneously heal, the foreigners would surely pay dearly for his rings.

"No," I insisted. "I'm not going to be your shill. I'm not going to lie to the foreigners about the rings."

He laughed my objections aside and took the ring from his own finger. "This ring," he said, "*satya-śakti*, real power." He pointed to the moon-shaped mark in the stone. "*Candra-śakti*, moon power," he whispered as he put the ring on my left hand (the Tantric hand, he said). Then he touched the other ring he had given me, the one with the blood-red stone on my right hand. "*Sūrya*. Sun. Sun-stone, moon-stone—all power." He taught me how to do the magic, to extend my arm fully, to reach toward the moon with my left hand open wide, to slowly rotate the hand, to bring the fingers slowly together like a closing claw, to pull the tightly clenched fist slowly toward my mouth and to blow gently on the moon in the stone. If I did that, he assured me, I could have anything in the world I wanted.

What I wanted most of all was to watch the *Rāmāyaṇa* on Doordarshan television the next morning, the serial that had transformed the television set into India's new domestic shrine before which, each week, with incense burning, the devout, their hands reverentially together in worship, would wait with tear-filled eyes for a vision of Lord Ram. And this week Lakshman was going to decapitate the black magician Indrajit, something I especially wanted to see. But Mohammad Shah would not permit it. There was going to be rain, he said, and with rain there could be lightning, and if I had the television on, the lightning would be sure to strike the aerial on the roof, and the New Golden Phoenix would go up in flames.

I invited the tenants of the houseboat to come to the magic show, and each of them happily gave me fifteen rupees for Naseeb in advance. "I love a good conjuring show," Nigel said, "and we shall, it so happens, indeed be here for it today. I've decided that there really isn't time for Ladakh. Maybe next year. Mr. Ali has kindly arranged a tour of Shalimar Garden this afternoon. The roses are in bloom, and we're going to pack a lunch." Andrew, obviously sick of the older man's constant cheerfulness, rolled his eyes in boredom, if not disgust.

Carrie said she was going to get Grant out of bed for the occasion. And the Palestinians were in definite need of entertainment—wanting every opportunity to use our bathroom and lie on our bed, they had hardly ever been off the house-boat. Mohammad Shah, Mir Deen, Deen Rather, Abdul, Ali, and two shikhara men who sold chocolates, film, postcards, macaroons, hashish, opium, and any-thing that anyone might want them to procure, joined the audience in our living room, the Palestinian's bedroom. None of the Kashmiris, needless to say, chipped in anything for the show.

As I had given Naseeb one hundred fifty rupees before he began, I was annoyed when, after each trick, he passed around a cup among the members of the embarrassed audience, who looked to me for hints on the fiscal protocol for Indian magic shows.

Naseeb pointed to the moon-ring on my left hand as he gestured to me to come toward him. As he ran the needle through my arm, blood dripped onto the newspaper he had spread out on the floor. It soaked into the story of the battle between the police and Sikh militants at the Golden Temple.

"Ring power," the magician said in English as he removed the needle, pointed with it to the bleeding puncture marks in my arm, and then slowly reinserted it. Grant, who had dozed off while Naseeb was performing with the

Chinese Sticks, suddenly opened his eyes and looked at the needle in my forearm. "Magic," he smiled. "I love magic," he said, his voice trailing off as his eyes closed.

Mohammad Shah looked away. "Enough Saighal. Stop. No good."

As the old man got up and left the room, Deen Rather smiled happily over his squeamishness. The shikhara man's eyes were wide open in a titillation that was fed by both terror and wonder. After the performance, he insisted on examining my arm, touching it, rubbing his finger over it, and asking me repeatedly if it hurt. His utter amazement fed hopes that the magician could help him. He had a problem: he was just helping the man who owned the shikhara in which he had come to the magic show; he had a shikhara of his own, but it had been stolen. He asked Naseeb the big question: can your magic help me? Naseeb assured him that he could use his magic to find the thief. They would meet privately later that evening.

My guru revealed the timeless secret of the magic to me. He would show the man a piece of paper on which there was a name invisibly written in lime juice, a name that would become visible when the paper was held over a flame in a demonstration of the magic. Then, giving the man a blank piece of paper, selling him a locket, and instructing him to place the paper in the locket, Naseeb would inform the man that he must wear the locket for three days. At midnight on the third day, when he removed the paper, unfolded it, and held it over a flame, the name of the man who stole his shikhara would be clearly visible.

"But what happens when he does it, when he sees the paper is blank?"

Naseeb seemed surprised that his disciple was so slow in catching on, that I had learned so little about how Indian magic, the ancient as well as the modern, the hieratic as well as the folk, was done. After collecting the money for the locket, the magician would explain that if the man had any selfish thoughts, uttered any false words, or committed any malicious deeds during the three days that he wore the locket, the paper would be blank. If a man struck Naseeb as particularly honest or unusually virtuous, he would tell him to wear the locket for a week. Not a single person had ever asked Naseeb for a refund.

The shikhara man, in the meantime, bought a ring. Nigel purchased one for Andrew. Grant, awakened by Carrie, saying he wanted one too, left to go back to his room to get the money, but never returned. The Palestinian gentleman, asserting that, while he was not superstitious, neither was he parsimonious, gave Naseeb the money for the ring but refused to receive the goods. When Naseeb handed the ring with the shiny black stone in it to Carrie, she tried to pay him. But he wouldn't take her money. He looked over at me and laughed, "Friend."

With Mohammad Shah, who was apparently ill from seeing the needle penetrate my arm, out of the room, Deen Rather had the courage to squat on the floor at Naseeb's feet and tell the magician his woeful story. Mohammad Shah had given his father two hundred and fifty rupees, for which the boy owed

Mohammad Shah one month's work. The old man was abusing the boy, making him work seventeen or eighteen hours a day, and while Mohammad Shah slept, Mir Deen was ordered to supervise the boy's labor. "Why?" Deen Rather asked me. "Why he do this? Money? Why? When death, no money. No houseboat. When death only two meters cloth. That's all. So why he do this to me?"

Naseeb took a letter from the boy, gave it to a bus driver at the Batmaloo station with instructions to deliver it to the boy's father in a village beyond Anantnag. The boy tried to pay Naseeb, but the magician wouldn't take it. The next day, we were awakened by the shouting, the furious argument, between Mohammad Shah and Deen Rather's father. We never saw the boy again. The magician freed him from the boat, just as he had so often freed his own child from a basket pierced with swords.

Mohammad Shah was in an even more foul mood than ever that morning. When Nigel, shaking the old man's hand and smiling politely, was saying, "Well, Mr. Mohammad, thank you so very much for all of your hospitality. We'll be back next year, so that we can make that Ladakh . . . " Mohammad Shah cut him off: "No words, Mr. Uncle! Money! Tips for poor peoples!"

Nigel, quite flustered, insisted that Habeeb had led him to believe that service was included.

Mohammad Shah shook his fist at the departing shikhara. "No good peoples!"

The Palestinians were being misdirected with a "free" ride to Shalimar Gardens, a ploy to get them out of the houseboat so that the Englishmen's room could be given to the couple arriving from France. "French peoples, good peoples, honest peoples, money peoples," Mohammad Shah said in their presence, turning to surreptitiously wink at me as he proudly produced the guest book containing the comments in French that I had translated for him.

The Palestinians were quite hysterical when they discovered the French people and were told that they were still going to be sleeping in the living room. "This is the kind of thing that drives man to violence," the man said to me with a profoundly sorrowful look in his eyes. They did not heed my warning not to go to the police, my suggestion that the police were corrupt and probably on Ali's payroll; as a result, they ended up leaving Kashmir by second class bus even though they had paid, and paid handsomely, for an airplane ticket.

"Bad peoples," Mohammad Shah said as he watched them sadly waving good-bye to us from the shikhara that took them away.

Since Naseeb normally arrived in an unpainted, uncanopied little boat that had no pillows and was rowed by a scruffy boy, no older than Ayasan, I was surprised to see that it was him in the shikhara that was so ornately decorated in an attempt to fulfill any tourist's fantasy of Moghul elegance and Himalayan carefreeness. Seated next to Naseeb on the brightly upholstered pillows, dressed in a white shawl, covering her smile with her hand, was "Naseeb Madame." As she climbed out of the shikhara and onto the stairs up to our porch, Naseeb paid the toothless shikhara driver the ridiculous fee he asked and grandly, even demonstratively, added a tip.

As she handed Cheryl her gifts, the box of sweets and the samosas that she had wrapped in a sheet of newspaper, her stunning smile was exposed. On her extended arm I noticed the watch that Cheryl had given to Ayasan.

Pointing at my typewriter, her husband told her that it was on that very machine that I was writing the "*Naseeb-pustak*," his biography, the story of his trials and tribulations, his temptations and triumphs. Taking the piece of paper out of the typewriter, I showed it to her, running my finger along each line and stopping at each uppercase *N* to say "Naseeb . . . Naseeb . . . Naseeb." She saw one, pointed to it and laughed, "Naseeb." The laughter was as naughty as Ayasan's, as carefree, and it came as easily as his did, flowing bright and sweet like the golden honey of Kashmir. She laughed at the sight of Naseeb's rings on our fingers, at the sound of the Hindi-English language in which Naseeb and I spoke, at the taste of the stale but expensive English biscuits that we ate with tea. When she lowered her shawl to her shoulders, I could smell the jasmine in her hair.

Naseeb wanted to know if my book was good, if I was going to make a lot of money on it, if his picture was going to be in it, if his wife's photograph could be in it too. And he wanted to know the name of the book.

"*Indrajāla*," I said, *Indra's Net, Net of Magic*, which to Naseeb does not refer to magic in general, but to a particular trick: a magician directs his assistant to stand in a box, which is then closed, locked, sealed, circled with chains, and freely inspected; the magician, directing volunteers to unchain, unseal, unlock, and open the box, exits; when the box is opened, the assistant has vanished, and there, where the assistant should be, the magician stands.

When I asked Naseeb about his wife's brother, the one with the big problems who had suddenly had to go to Delhi for some emergency, he looked at me as though he had no idea what I was talking about and changed the subject, explaining that his wife thought we should move off the houseboat and into their tent with them, where the food and company were better.

After tea, while Naseeb was preparing the hashish, Cheryl took his wife to show her the bathroom, where she, like her son, made faces in the mirror. While we were alone together, Naseeb reminded me that I must frighten Mohammad Shah, that the old man, after seeing the needle trick, was ripe for it, and that the more I could convince him of my Tantric powers, the less I would be cheated when it came time to leave. He gave me some sodium wrapped in a pink card, Naseeb's appointment record for the "Love and Care Immunization Ward, Delhi," with instructions to place it on dry ground, to put a chicken head over it, and then, while muttering some Sanskrit mantras, to sprinkle it with water. The head would burst into flames. Naseeb laughed heartily over the thought of it, and we made our arrangements to meet the next day, Friday, at Hazrat Bal, right outside the great mosque.

Never was Naseeb as good as he was on Fridays, the holy day of Islamic communal prayer, when, near the mosque, dressed in fresh white, his white lace skullcap clean for the occasion, his magic words were the same as those that crackled from the enormous speakers: *"Allahu akbar!"* "God is great," he would cry as the blood dripped from the knife in his hand, as the severed tongue seemed to twitch in the other. *"La ilaha illa'llah Muhammadun rasulu'llah,"* he moaned, as the decapitated man waited to be healed. "There is no god but God, and Muhammad is His prophet," and the bright lustral fires of piety danced in his eyes.

On Fridays even the most cynical souls permitted themselves to believe things that cannot be proven, even the meanest spirits allowed themselves to be charitable, and even the most bitter hearts felt a little hope or a bit of gratitude. And to prey upon those people who came to pray there were the performers— jugglers, bear or monkey trainers, maybe a snake charmer, certainly a magician, and the fortune-tellers, palm readers as well as astrologers, the beggars, the maimed as well as the merely hungry, and the hawkers selling anything that anyone might ever want to buy. Watched at all times by the police, they lined the walkways to the mosque, seeped into any empty spaces in the bazaar, found places where there weren't any, and extending their hands or raising their voices, they made their pitches.

We joined the audience that had formed around a magician from Ludhiana. The three-year-old child, squatting by the basket of cobras in the circle, watched his father put the burning camphor in his mouth, run the flaming torch over his bared chest, swallow the blade of the knife, spit up the blood, cure himself, and then begin to sell the amulets. Naseeb promised to teach me sword swallowing. Easy. You simply swallow a lotus stalk, which prevents the sword from actually slicing into the esophagus. No problem. Anybody can do it.

Naseeb, accepting their hashish, spoke at length with them in the secret language of Maslets. He asked me to do the cigarette vanish for them, and as I did, he made a joke that prompted laughter. I wanted to perform the cups and balls routine he had taught me, but he wouldn't permit it. "No. More training!" he said in English, and they laughed again. Their wives were squatting in the rubble nearby, four beautiful women, one of them feeding a baby, a future magician. All the while they were pointing at us, joking and laughing too, sweet and dirty laughter.

The Ludhiana Maslets stayed for Naseeb's program, and throughout it the three-year-old magician never took his eyes off Ayasan, giggling when the boy mocked his father, falling silent, his eyes wide open, when Naseeb cut his son's tongue out. Even some of the beggars took time off from their work to watch Naseeb. A leper bought a ring. A blind child, smiling at the sound of the wondrous spectacle, held his hands together as if in prayer all during the show.

Naseeb's audacity never ceased to amaze me. On my last Friday in Srinagar, as he was performing the interlocking hands trick with a randomly chosen volunteer who was following all the whispered promptings perfectly, he elaborated the drama and improvised tricks in a way that seemed startling on such a holy day. When the volunteer begged Naseeb to free his hands, the magician opened the palms but left the fingers interlocked. To no avail the man tried to pry his hands apart with his knee. The magician then held the man's hands and, just when one expected him to separate them, reclosed them over the volunteer's crotch. The volunteer, his penis apparently caught in his locked grip, walking with difficulty, pleaded with Naseeb to release him and the crowd laughed uproariously. Finally Naseeb, agreeing to help him, pulled his hands away from his groin. "Oh no," Naseeb yelled out, "you've pulled your prick off!" And the volunteer, grabbing his crotch, spontaneously shrieked a falsetto "Gone!"

Naseeb, with the great mosque behind him, looked into the heavens: "Allah, the merciful, Allah the great, hear my supplication! Allah who made man from clots of blood, restore to this man what he has lost!" He reached toward the sky with the gesture he had taught me to use in getting power from the moon, shouted, "*Bismillah!*" and pointed between the victim's legs: "Touch!"

All eyes were upon the volunteer. His hands were loose. He reached down to feel his genitals. The crowd was silent. "It's the wrong one," the man cried out, "too small!" and the crowd broke into wild, irreverent laughter. They wept with wonderful laughter. The leper and the blind child laughed too.

Naseeb prayed to Allah, the maker of the world, almighty Lord of the universe, to give the man a bigger penis. And of course it worked. Allah is merciful.

As always the comedy merely prepared the crowd by making them vulnerable to the terrors that were to follow. The magician prompted them to utter the holy words, "*Allahu akbar!*" Three times they echoed him and threw not two but five rupees into the mandala to insure the healing of the headless man and tongueless boy. And, before going to pray in the mosque, they purchased rings from the magician in hopes that the stones in them might, like prostrations before God, in some strange, magical way, enhance their lives.

Later that day, the day before the day we were to leave, inspired by Naseeb's program, I decided to try the sodium-and-chicken-head trick for Mohammad Shah, setting it up by saying that I had never seen a chicken slaughtered and that I would very much like to do so. Insisting that it was much more exciting to see a goat killed, the old man offered to have Mir Deen, for a nominal fee, take me to the meat market in town. "We want to start slowly," I explained. "You know, start by seeing chickens get it, then we can move on to goats, sheep, and whatever."

"Saighal and Madame so many chicken eating! More money for chicken!" Mohammad Shah's ranting was cut short by the sight of Mir Deen taking the wrong chicken, the hen saved for her eggs, from the coop. He slapped the boy on the head and pointed to the one he wanted killed, and that provided me with the distraction, the misdirection, I needed to drop my piece of sodium on the ground

unnoticed. Mohammad Shah's wife, adorned with garlands of amulets and handfuls of rings, squatting nearby, swathed in the haze of smoke from her hubble-
bubble, didn't see what I had done.

Mir Deen, unfolding the wings of the chicken and forcing them together
behind the bird's back, faced Mecca and prayed out loud: "*Allahu akbar!*" Lowering the victim to the ground, he stood with one foot on the wings and the other
on the legs. The bird thrashed helplessly about and squirmed to no avail as Mir
Deen intoned the words: "*La ilaha illa'llah Muhammadun rasulu'llah.*" That
servant of both God and Mohammad Shah leaned forward, plucked the feathers
from the neck, then gently and tenderly stroked that neck, then deftly, quickly slit
the neck and whispered his prayers.

Blood was spurting out of the throat that was only cut part of the way through.
Mir Deen wiped the knife blade on the white down of the breast of the still
struggling and squirming, writhing and wriggling, bird.

"Isn't he going to cut the head all the way off?" I asked, still intent on doing
my trick.

"Stop Saighal. Not Mussulman way," Mohammad Shah shouted, shooing me
away with his hand as he stepped menacingly toward me. Though unaware of it,
he was standing on the sodium and forcing it into the mud. "Enough Saighal.
Go."

Suddenly he looked sad. "This not magic program, Saighal, this life. Life
and death. Not magic. Go."

Naseeb arrived by himself early on the day of our departure.

"Where's Ayasan?" I asked.

"Graveyard," Naseeb smiled. "Home."

He wanted to have more photographs taken of him blessing his rings on
foreign fingers. So Cheryl, Carrie, the French couple, I, and even a yawning
Grant, took turns posing with him for the pictures that he would show his
audiences as he declared to them that people had come from all over the world
to buy his magic rings.

In the midst of the shoot, I was called away to settle my account with Ali. "I
can't fool you, my brother," he said. "You are a great magician. I know that. So
I will be truthful with you. All I have cared about, this whole month, day in and
night out, is your happiness and the happiness of Madame. Not money. But you
have taken advantage of me. You have had these *jādūgars* on my homeboat. That
was wrong of you. I would not have allowed it if I did not love you as my own
brother. They are not good people. They have lice. My one worker, Deen
Rather—you remember that boy—he quit because he hated to serve these low
people. You see what trouble you have caused me? These magicians have eaten
our food. They have stolen some of our papier-mâché and other valuable Kashmiri crafts. Business has suffered because of them—they have frightened away
customers from our homeboat. I never said anything to you because, in my

concern for your happiness, I didn't want to trouble you. But now the time has come, my brother, for you to leave. Now the time has come for me to be paid. You are an honest man, you are a good man. I am an honest man and a good man. I must be compensated for all that I have lost because of these magicians." He said it all with a straight face. "The magicians are not like you and me. They are not honest people."

On the way to the airport Naseeb asked us to deliver a message to his mother in Shadipur, to tell her that because of police problems, he was moving his camp to Baramullah.

The taxi stopped at the fork in the road: to the right was Naseeb's path, the road to the graveyard across from the Batmaloo bus station; to the left, for me, there was the road to the Srinagar airport. We got out of the car. Cheryl embraced him, and he stood back, seemingly startled by it. He smiled just slightly and looked over at me. I wondered if I'd ever see him again, and as I looked at him, as if that might give me the answer, I saw that there were tears in his eyes. We shook hands, said good-bye, and I got into the taxi.

The tears had amazed me. I couldn't help but wonder about them. "Did you see the tears in his eyes?" I asked Cheryl. "Were they just like the fake blood? Is he that good a magician, that cool a con man, that he adds the tears, even though they're not really necessary, as the finishing touch to the magic show he's been performing for us? Just that last embellishment to make the illusion seem real, to make us believe what we'd like to believe? Or—and the very idea of this astounds me—is he actually a very sentimental man, utterly tender despite the harshness of his life?"

"Or both? Both—it's 'magician's choice.' "

I looked at Naseeb's rings on my fingers: at the blood-red stone clutched in the brass claws of the setting of the right-hand ring—the sun; and at the crescent in the dark stone in the left-hand ring—the moon. It was dusk, and closing my eyes, I could picture Naseeb, could vividly see the rakish smile and sharp eyes. He was in the countryside somewhere, standing beneath a great pipal tree, blowing upon his gourd-flute and then playing the damaru: "With this drum Mahadeo begins the world." Ayasan was setting out the snakes, and curious people were gathering.

The hawks that circled in the sky above them were the same as now, but the scene, it seemed to me, was taking place long, long ago. The magician, dressed as a sadhu, squatting as he always did to manipulate the cups and balls, began to speak: "My name is Muladeva, son of Shambaradasa . . . "

I did not wake up until we arrived at the airport.

ON THE STREET
THEN

Ropes and Air

Scene Three:

Knots

Long ago in the city of Ujjayini there was born a magician, Muladeva by name, son of Shambaradasa, adept at jugglery, accomplished in all the arts and sciences of deception—money-deceit, love-deceit, religion-deceit. Servant of no man, husband of no woman, worshipper of no god, Muladeva was tied to no one in the world. No one except his son, Indragopa.

The boy followed the magician, keeping his eye on his father's long, matted hair so as not to lose him as they made their way through the crowded streets of Kashi, down into the tangled net of pathways and alleys surrounding the temple of Vishvanatha, Lord of the Universe.

The rains had passed, but the streets were still wet, and Indragopa felt the mud ooze up through his toes as they walked. Catching the current of souls, some coming this way, others going that way, some trying to stop, some trying to climb out of it and into some shop or another (a flower shop, perhaps, selling ashoka garlands and blue lotuses, sinduvara and jasmine), others leaping back into the torrent of bodies out of the doorway of a dwelling, temple, or shrine, or out of another stall (a fruit shop, perhaps, selling melons and mangoes, pomegranates and jackfruit), the boy, lunging sideways so that the lumbering cow would not step on his foot, bumped into the man, coming from the other direction. The vendor dropped the brass pots, pans, and plates that he had been balancing like a juggler. Pushing forward to catch up with his father in the turbulence, Indragopa could not hear the curses of the man over the clatter of his wares, over the shouting of the hawkers ("Sweets!" "Betel, best betel for sale!" "Seeds, seeds!" "Cane! Cane—fresh juice of the cane!"), the prayers of priests and pilgrims' hymns of praise, the haggling of merchants and their customers, the laughter incessant. He wanted to stop at the stall that sold birds in cages (parrots and mynahs, pigeons and cuckoos) and at the shop that sold toys to buy one of the kites with images of the gods upon them (Indra and Shiva, Rama and Krishna, Kali and Skanda), but he was yanked forward as if an invisible rope tied him to his father. Through the thick aromas of camphor and sandalwood, and the heady stench of the rotting

123

refuse that even the crows and dogs had passed over, the smells of asafetida and sesame, roasting chickens and breads sizzling in oil made him hungry. But they never ate before a performance. "It's bad luck," Muladeva said.

Because they were dressed as sadhus, with ashes on their bodies, *rudrākṣa*-bead rosaries around their necks, and rough hides around their loins, they might have been mistaken, there amidst the hordes of devout renouncers who came to Kashi, for holy men, if the peacock feathers that the boy and his father carried had not indicated they were magicians. It was those feathers that caught and made sparkle the eyes of the three little ones, those children of the street, who cried out "Magicians! Magicians!" and jumped up to follow them out of the gully and to the square near the liquor shop.

Squatting down, elbows resting on his knees, Muladeva chewed the betel, savoring it, as he watched his son lay out the tiger-skin mat, put the wicker basket in place, and pose the monkey skull that Muladeva always swore was the skull of a child. The props were arranged: a muslin cloth with the thousand names of the goddess embroidered on it, the bamboo tripod that the boy himself had made, the five swords that Muladeva claimed were from the armory of the legendary King Vikramaditya, the *kamaṇḍalu* which Muladeva, in an exuberant mood, would claim had been Shiva's own waterpot, the human thigh bone that had been made into a flute upon which melancholy tunes were played. There was the box of rings and amulets which the magicians sold; and there were the magic ropes—cords of hemp and jute, leather thongs and metal chains, and strings of many colors. Muladeva spit red juice.

Indragopa's hair, recently shaved because of an incessant and finally unbearable infestation with lice, had grown just long enough to hold the dirt and ashes in it, those false signs of holy mendicancy. The corners of his lips were red from the pleasures of the vice into which his father had not long ago initiated him—betel, delicious betel, plain or spiced, sweet or bitter. Loosening the knot with his teeth, the child untied the cords of twisted coir around the cobra basket, nonchalantly pushed back the lid, reached in fearlessly, and tossed out a snake that was as long as the boy was tall. The startled serpent raised its head, darted tongue and eyes in every direction, and then lowered, cowered, and coiled. Indragopa stretched it out again and prodded it with his toe to exhibit the fearsome grace of its lithe and silent movement through the dirt. The snake, particularly valuable because the markings on its hood resembled the *Oṃ-kāra*, that sacred syllable upon which holy men meditated, had been won by Muladeva in a dice game. Uneasy about removing the fangs, the snake charmer had grumbled that it was a sin against the serpent god and that it would bring misfortune. But Muladeva had insisted. Still, just in case, the magician kept the fangs in the amulet that was tied around his left upper arm with a black cotton string.

Indragopa had to keep the fangless cobra alive by force, prying open its mouth with his fingers and stuffing the raw meat or fresh eggs down the gullet with a stick. "Eat, Ananta, or you'll die," Indragopa would murmur. The snake was trouble. Now mites were making it listless, and the boy had to try to pick them off one by one and crack them between his fingernails. "It's not easy keeping you alive." It was because of the mites that Indragopa kept Vasukija, the brown tree snake his grandfather had caught last year, in a separate basket.

Ananta, set out for all to see, and Vasukija, carefully hidden from every eye, were both in place. Everything was set. Muladeva folded another leaf and placed it in his mouth as Indragopa began to play the damaru: "This is Mahadeva's drum. With this drum he started the Universe going."

The drum beckoned a crowd from the passersby—servants on errands, students who had come to Kashi for Vedic study ambling toward the ghats, priests going to this temple or that, scribes on their way to something official, hawkers with baskets making their rounds, sadhus in saffron or ocher robes, in animal skins or naked, with matted hair or bald, renouncers going nowhere, staying nowhere. People joined the three little children who had followed Indragopa and Muladeva to the spot. More children and beggars, too many children and beggars without a cowrie shell to their name, took up places that could have been filled by wealthy merchants, even princes or kings. The drum diverted drinkers, laughing and desperate, out of the liquor shop, a barber out of his saloon, a soldier from his post. And it drew the old, the sick, the dying who lined the streets of Kashi; above all, the dying, people who had come to the holy city to expire on the banks of the Ganga in hopes that it would be their deliverance—"He who dies in Kashi goes straight to heaven, no matter what sins have been committed," Muladeva had explained to his son. "At least that's what they say. And the dying, people who know they're dying, need magic most of all."

"What's this?" a drunkard yelled out.

"Magic," Indragopa yelled back. "Watch me cast Indra's Net." Again he poked at Ananta with his toe as he shook the damaru ferociously. Crows circled above, dogs slunk by, cows chewed their cud, and Muladeva climbed up onto a wall that had dung patties freshly slapped against it. Perching there, he had a clear view of Indragopa beginning with the two coconut-shell cups and the three balls of sewn cloth. "This man is going to Anga," the child said. "And this man is going to Kashmir." And as he watched his son do the routine he had taught him, the routine he had learned from Shambaradasa, his own father, he smiled with a vivid memory of a moment, so fleeting and yet so persistent, at once trivial and yet somehow very important to him.

It was right after Indragopa's birth. When Mayeshvari handed her baby to Shambaradasa, the new grandfather laughed with tears in his eyes, and at the sight of his father holding his son, Muladeva had been overwhelmed by a strange feeling, a startling sense that he had disappeared like the child in the magic basket or the pigeon in the magic cloth, that he had been folded into some pleat in time and space. Although he had felt that his continuing in the world was an intrusion or that, at best, it made no difference at all, at the same time it was curiously exhilarating—it gave the magician a sense of liberation, of complete freedom from everyone and everything. Neither living nor dying, in that vivid moment, mattered at all. It made him laugh aloud.

And now he smiled to remember it, smiled as he watched Indragopa bewilder the crowd with the cups and balls, watched his son as he used to watch his father. Indragopa uttered the same words Shambaradasa used to intone. He was weaving the same magic, entrancing the crowd with the same wonder. Shambaradasa was unable to perform the sleights now. His fingers had been gnarled blue by disease and scarred red by the barbers' knives. "But at least they still hurt," the aging magician sighed. "It's when the pain goes away that you're in trouble." He stayed in Shittal village in Anga now, a refuge for those wandering performers—jugglers and acrobats, monkey trainers, snake charmers, and magicians among them— who no longer had the strength or need to wander or perform. Though Muladeva tried to visit there at least once a year, to take money to his mother, father, and grandfather, it was, sometimes, too difficult, just too far away. But whenever he heard that there was a camp of magicians near wherever it was that his wandering had taken him and his son, Muladeva would go there to ask if any of them were heading for Anga, and if they were, he would send some news of himself with them to his parents. Because he did not trust magicians, he never sent money with them. A life of magic had taught Muladeva to trust no one, not even himself, especially not himself—his own senses or his own intelligence, his own fears or his own desires. The magician had learned the lesson well—he trusted no one in the world except Indragopa. And the boy trusted him too.

Indragopa had finished the routine and collected the coins and cowrie shells that had been lost to him on bets as to under which coconut shell the ball of cloth would be found. Uncoiling his snake, he stroked its throat with his fingers to make it rise and fan its hood. "Show them, Ananta—show them. Do you see? On his hood is the *Om—aaaa, uuuu, mmmm*—Vishnu, Shiva, Brahma. And do you see these stones? These stones have been blessed by Ananta, rubbed against his hood for the power of the syllable. He who carries one of these stones will never be bitten by a snake. How can you obtain one? Only five panas, not more, and you will be safe from snakes, protected forever."

A barber, a scribe, a pilgrim, three students, and two priests, though teased by others in the crowd for doing so, each bought a magic stone from Indragopa. And, as soon as the money was collected, Muladeva jumped from the wall, pushed his way into the circle, squatted down, spit betel juice, and called out to the boy: "Is that your snake?"

"Yeah—what's it to you?"

"I have a snake that's bigger than yours," the magician began the routine, and, as always, the audience laughed at the innuendo. "My snake is named Vasuki. Have you heard of him? The gods twisted him around Mount Mandara, used him as a rope to churn the cosmic ocean, to create the world. Here, see him?" the magician asked as he held up the length of twisted hemp, then wiggled it on the ground, making the cord undulate in the dirt like a snake: "Vasuki!"

"You're drunk! That's not a snake," the child shouted. "That's not a snake, it's a rope. Why don't you go and hang yourself with it so that I can continue, so that these people can look at a real snake and see some real magic?" The audience, not only the drunkards and the students, but the priests and the dying as well, laughed at the child's mockery of the man and the man's mockery of the child.

"What do you mean, 'Not a snake?' What do you mean, 'Not real?' This is Vasuki, a real snake. You don't think so? Let's ask these people. They look like honest people to me—who could be more honest than a priest, a sadhu, a barber, or a scribe? Is this a real snake or not?"

"Real," several people playfully, in the mood of the show, shouted to tease the boy, and one of the fat Brahmins in the amused crowd preached to Indragopa: "Real or not, you better believe it is real. A boy should always believe his father. If your father says it's real, then it is real." There was more laughter, and Indragopa was quick to pick up the patter. "Father?" he snickered with mock scorn. "Why do you think he's my father? If anything, I could be his father. I'm not sure, but I do know his mother. So it could be. What is real is always hard to know; but it's even more difficult if we want to know who his real father is!"

Suddenly lunging forward, Muladeva grabbed one of the swords from the mat and brandished it menacingly as he chased his son around the circle, a ploy to widen and shape the area for the performance. Then, pretending to be out of breath, Muladeva squatted by the mat, set down the sword, and showed the rope once more: "I shouldn't be angry with the child. Anger is bad. That's what the *Gītā* says; it must be true because the *Gītā* is in the Sanskrit language."

Indragopa was squatting too, facing his father from the opposite side of their egg-shaped arena, listening to the patter: "Why should I be angry with one who is deluded, entangled in Indra's net of illusion. He needs not punishment, but enlightenment, freedom from the net. He mistakes this snake for a rope out of ignorance. I'll teach him discrimination. I'll show him reality." The audiences of Kashi, more than any others, relished these parodies of philosophical discourse.

Holding up the fine muslin that had been embroidered with the thousand names of the goddess, shaking and waving it, turning it this way and that way, Muladeva demonstrated that it was clearly ordinary and empty. "This cloth is like the veil of illusion," he said mimicking the pedantic rhetoric of the pandits on the ghats. Coiling the rope and wrapping it in the cloth, he continued: "Reality is enveloped in that veil. I, the teacher, will reveal it—reality, truth—to you, the student."

The audience became silent and still as they watched the magician pick up the monkey skull, in the eye sockets of which black rags had been stuffed: "*Om aim klim hrīm śrīm,*" the magician recited with a widened gaze: "Kahneshvari, Deluder, take away the illusions of those here who do not see reality. Reveal truth." He pulled the black cloth from the eye sockets of the skull. "Ho!" he shouted and blew hard into each empty eye once, twice, three times.

Slowly, purposefully setting down the skull, he reached for the bundle in which he had wrapped the rope and solemnly unwrapped it. The crowd gasped—"Amazing! Wonderful!"—as they watched the snake, the same size and color as the rope, slither forward from the cloth, darting its tongue, turning its head this way and that as if to survey the audience.

With every eye in the crowd on Vasuki, Indragopa had the moment he needed to switch the rope from the basket for the cobra that had been coiled up in front of him. And so, as their eyes shifted back to the boy, when Muladeva asked him, "Now, what do you think? Which snake is real? Which is a rope?" they gasped with amazement, wonder, and delight once more.

"You must be a very powerful magician," Indragopa conceded, and then, while his father told the story of how he had acquired his magic powers, the boy put his rope and Vasukija back in the snake basket to clear their stage for the next illusion.

"Years ago, when I was a child just about your age, my father sent me here to Kashi from our home in Anga, dispatched me to bring a jar of sacred water from the Ganga for him. As I was filling up that jar with due respect and solemnity, a Kapalika sitting by the river asked what I was doing, and when I told him, he laughed. 'Pots can be broken, holy water spilled. There is a way that you can have all of the holiness of the Ganga in a form that cannot be spilled, lost, or stolen. The *śakti* can be in you rather than in some pot or jar.' I asked him to be my guru, and he initiated me. With the money my father had given me for the mission, we bought flour from that stall just over there, rum from that liquor shop, and a goat from a stall that is no longer here. The Kapalika, muttering mantras that he was later to teach me, sacrificed the goat to Kali, mixed the flour with the rum and blood, and then, late at night, he cooked the dough over the fires that are fed with human flesh on the pyres by the river. Then we took the cakes to the shrine of Bhairava and smeared them with oil from the lamps burning before the terrible god. Half of the cakes he kept; the other half he gave to me with the instruction that in eating them I would gain the power of the god." As he finished the sentence, a transfixed audience watched him bite into a small cake and slowly chew it. "And so it was that I attained the power to reveal the reality veiled behind illusions."

"What else can you do?" Indragopa asked on cue. "Can you show us other realities?"

"What else can I do?" the magician laughed. "I have the power of the gods! I have the power of Brahma, Vishnu, and Shiva. I can create; I can change or preserve; I can destroy!"

"Then create!" the boy challenged.

"What would you have me create?"

"Create the world!"

"Everything, great or small, the world or a man, begins with a seed," the magician said showing his hands to be empty. "I can create a seed from which a world can be grown." He cupped his hands together, blew on them, muttered the mantra, "*Om aiṃ klīṃ hrīṃ śrīṃ* —ho!" and opened his hands. Resting on his palm there was a mango seed.

"*Bhoḥ!*" *the audience exclaimed with the pleasure of their wonder over the* spectacle as the magician continued: "And with this seed I can create a world. I have only to plant it here in the dirt like this, and then water it, like this." He poured all of the water, every drop, out of the *kamaṇḍalu.* "Now we must simply wait for it to grow, to bear flowers and fruit, for birds to perch in it, for lovers to come and lie down for shade beneath its branches, for . . ."

"I don't have that much time," Indragopa interrupted, and the laughter of the audience at that point—the tone and volume, the readiness and duration, of it—revealed to the magician what kind of crowd they were, how easy or difficult it would be to hold their attention, how readily and how generously they would pay; it told him what he needed to do to have power over them.

"You don't need much time. I have the power to speed up the universe or slow it down, the universe or anything within it. I have power over time," he said as he dug up the seed to show that it had already pushed forth roots and a small sprout. "See?" he smiled. "But we can make it faster still," he said, putting it back into the hole and covering it over again. Then, to the utter amazement of the people gathered around him, he poured a great gush of fresh water out of the *kamaṇḍalu* that, just moments before, they had all seen with their own eyes was completely empty.

Placing the tripod over the spot where the mango seed was planted and covering that with the muslin cloth in which the rope had turned into a snake, the magician muttered the mantras, pulled back the cloth, and all could plainly see the growth of the mango plant. It was already several fingers high. Again he poured water from what all knew to be the absolutely empty *kamaṇḍalu,* shaking it as if to make certain that this time not a drop of water remained in it. Again he covered the tripod and muttered the mantras. "Ho!" Muladeva cried and showed how much the mango plant had grown in those few moments.

"Amazing! *Bho bhoḥ!* Amazing! *Bhoḥ!*"

Indragopa watched the mango plant that, with each successive covering and uncovering, each watering from a pot that apparently could not be emptied, each recitation of incomprehensible syllables, seemed to grow and burgeon until it was too large to fit under the bamboo tripod.

Draping the magic cloth over the branches of the plant, Muladeva was able to produce a mango fruit and to pass it around for tasting. When he pulled back the cloth with the names of the goddess upon it for the last time, a pigeon, appearing in the branches of it, ruffled its feathers, fanned its wings, looked nervously around at the gathering of people, leapt skyward, flapped its wings and, by no magic, disappeared.

"Amazing! Wonderful!" the audience applauded.

"The leaves of this mango tree are very powerful—so much *śākti!* They can even bring the dead back to life."

"Nothing can do that!" Indragopa shouted out through the laughter and exuberant chatter of the crowd. "Yama isn't tricked by magic. Nothing, no one, can bring one who has died back from death."

The magician stood, removed the lid from the wicker basket, and the boy stepped into it when cued by the words: "No? I'll show you—I'll show you the reality behind the illusion of death just as I showed you the reality of the serpent behind the illusion of the rope."

Muladeva placed the basket top on his son's head, pushed on it, and the boy settled into the container, out of sight. He squirmed into position, curling himself around the inside of the basket and pressing himself into it. Tipping the basket to and fro, turning it around and around, Muladeva assured his audience that there were no escape hatches as the boy readied himself and broke the seal on the jar of what they called "magician's blood." Looking at their faces, into their eyes, he knew that they, every one of them, were ready to be deceived, that they wanted this illusion.

Indragopa screamed as the first sword entered the basket from the top. That sword was the signal to pour out the first portion of blood and to move his legs slightly apart for the second sword to enter between them, the prompt, in turn, to move his arm so that the third sword could enter the basket. He moaned piteously as he emptied the rest of the vial of blood. It oozed through the weave of the wicker and darkened the dirt. The three children who had followed the magicians covered their eyes and trembled. The five crisscrossed swords that penetrated the basket, now stained with blood, were removed. The magician announced the death of the boy to the terrified audience. A soldier in the crowd, assuring himself that this was only magic, resisted the impulse to draw his sword and take the murderer.

"With these leaves I can bring him back to life," Muladeva explained as, one by one, he tore the tough mango leaves from the tree that he had made to grow. When all of the leaves had been picked, he opened the basket to give his crowd a quick glimpse of the still, blood-drenched child. He covered the small corpse with the leaves. Replacing the lid of the basket, he sat on the ground with his legs crossed in the posture of a holy man, closed his eyes, and regulated his deep breathing. Not a soul in the crowd moved. They were as still and silent as the magician. The anxious moment persisted. Then, ever so slightly, the basket seemed to move. Another moment of stillness. The basket suddenly shook, and a human cry came from it. The lid flew off. The boy stood up and stepped out. The magician reached into the basket, removed a blood-stained mango leaf, and held it up for all to see: "Is there anyone here who would be interested in purchasing a magic leaf?"

Holding his breath, Indragopa immersed himself in the Ganga, rubbing and scraping his body hard with his hands to remove the dirt, ashes, and blood. Pushing off the bottom of the river, exhaling a stream of bubbles, then breaking through the surface, gasping for air, then submerging again, with breath held, the boy floated, still as a corpse but open-eyed in the water that was so murky with the scurf and scum of a million bathers, pious or desperate, and with their offerings and their debris—twigs and petals, bits of cloth and pieces of wood, string and ashes, traces of oil and powdery clouds of ointments and balms, things dead and alive, discarded and lost. Seeing his father's feet dangling there, he grabbed one of them with both hands and pulled with all his strength.

Muladeva struggled out of the water, crawled up the stone steps, slipping slightly, spitting dirty holy water, and coughing up curses. "Are you trying to kill me?"

"You just killed me, didn't you?" laughed the son, still in the water and splashing his father. "Revenge! And what if I did drown you? So what? I have a mango leaf to bring you back to life." He vanished beneath the surface of the water.

The pleasure the father felt over the amount they had earned with their show made it all the easier for him to laugh. And as he dried himself with the muslin of the goddess and bound and fixed his long matted hair with a strip of red cloth, Muladeva looked across the river, the illusion of a river, a goddess in reality, or the other way around, stared at the green fields on the other side, appeased by the recent rains, bright and empty. Not a soul, not a structure. A deep fear of something guarded the perfection of that emptiness. Muladeva's gaze rested in it.

With only his head above water, Indragopa looked up at his father, wondered if he himself looked like the magician or ever would. He let go of the image, let his eyes climb the steps, up through the vehement swarms of bathers, the herds of suppliants, over the stone stairs, strewn with clothes and the bodies to which the clothes belonged, steps wet and full of life, wet and brimming with death. There two fat Brahmins seemed to argue a point; over there three scraggly students dozed; here a deformed body, almost naked, joints raw, crawled lizard-like down to the bank; over here some women, eight of them, their wet, silken saris, their ornaments, their oiled hair bright and beautiful, laughed at him or at the misfortune that he had been cursed to represent; up there, way up there, two soldiers seemed to question a man who trembled in fear. Beyond them bodies began to merge, to lose all definition and melt into a monstrous, mottled body, wet, amorphous, fluctuating, hungry, with a thousand heads, a thousand eyes, a thousand hands, like the primordial being once sacrificed by the gods. And above that rush and squall of flesh, the temples of Kashi rose, as if arrogant over being made of stone, and waved their banners—red, blue, yellow, green—magic colors clutched, tugged, shaken by the hands of the wind. And higher still, above and behind the bright flags, a white kite, its string as invisible as the child clutching onto it somewhere in the distance, sailed in the company of black crows, dipped and rose, circled and danced with them in the sky. Above that were clouds, magic cities air-carved from gauzy mountains of mist and light. And above that there were only myths.

"I want a kite. I want a kite with Skanda on it," Indragopa said in an uncharacteristically childish voice as he splashed water at his father's legs.

"You can have it," the Muladeva answered at once, looking down at his son in the river. "You can have anything you want," he smiled, looking back across the river and seeing, amidst the boats of ferrymen, fishermen, and vendors, something floating there, slowly floating down river. "A very large tortoise?" he wondered. "The trunk of a small tree? Or the corpse of a holy man on its way from the Himalayas to the sea?"

Muladeva folded a betel leaf and put it in his mouth.

"Give me one too," Indragopa demanded as he climbed out of the water and grabbed the cloth from his father. Wisps of hair had begun to grow, as fast as the magic mango tree, it seemed to Muladeva, under the boy's arms and over his genitals. "Soon you'll be too big for the basket," the father laughed lightly. "What then? What will we do? It's okay. It looks to me like you're almost old enough to have a son of your own."

The boy covered his groin and turned away from his father who, nevertheless, continued to talk to him: "You should get busy. Find a girl. Get her pregnant. You know how to do that. Get a little boy for me. And for you too, of course. Let's have a little mother to serve her husband and look after her father-in-law. Did you notice that girl in our audience today—the one with leaf-shaped earrings?"

Indragopa looked at his father with disgust: "Stop it."

Muladeva laughed: "Get dressed, let's go. Anangasena's waiting for me."

And as he dressed, the son asked his father about his mother.

"Kali is your mother—your mother, my mother, my father's mother."

"No, my real mother, Mayeshvari. Tell me about her, tell me everything. Tell me the truth."

Muladeva had told him a thousand times about her, the daughter of the magician Vaitalaki and the courtesan Lilavati, about how she had left him to become a wife of a king in Kashmir named Amaruka. "He has sixty-four beautiful wives, one adept at each of the sixty-four arts. He took your mother because of her mastery of magic. She made the signet ring disappear from his finger, and when, in bewilderment, he asked her where it could be, she held up her hand to show him that it was there on her finger. That's all there is to tell."

"Not that," the son said impatiently. "I know all of that. Tell me the other things. Is she good? Is she kind?"

"I don't know," the father laughed. "How could I know? She's a magician, and, for that very reason, that's the only thing anyone can know about her. She's an even better magician than I am. Women are better than men at magic. We have to learn it, to practice it and train. But magic comes naturally to women. That's why magicians don't let their women perform on the streets. They're too good. Come on, let's go. Let's go to the pleasure district. Anangasena's waiting for me."

When the boy complained that he was hungry, the magician assured him there would be food in the pleasure district, and an egg for Ananta.

They climbed the steps, pushed their way through the crowd, and walked along the top of the ghats. The air was infused with scents of death, religion, and sex—corpses burning on sandalwood pyres, incense burning in the shrines, and men and women, perfumed with jasmine and camphor, burning with love. There was mourning, prayer, and laughter too.

The crowd thickened as they approached the ghat where the Nambudiri Brahmin, head shaved, devoid of sectarian markings, and wrapped in a sheet, was fanned by disciples beneath the great parasol. He looked like an overgrown baby surrounded by nursemaids as he delivered his commentary on the Veda. And Muladeva smiled at the sight of him: "Shankaracharya."

Whenever he spoke in public, he drew a great audience of Brahmins and wealthy people. "The rich, for some reason, love to hear about the meaningless of gold and the evil of attachment to it," Muladeva said to Indragopa. Though the magician found the speculations intolerably tedious, he appreciated the oratory, the metaphysical patter that so entranced the spectators and thus made it so easy for Muladeva, moving through the always large and pious crowd, to pick the purses there. It was as if they were working together. The magician, who had made so much money because of the Advaita-Vedanta school of Vedic interpretation, listened to the Brahmin recite a verse:

> The seed of the tree is ignorance;
>> the sprout comes from thinking one is
>> what one's body is;
> And the leaves, fresh and tender,
>> are attachments
>> to things of this world.
> The tree, the body its trunk, our senses its branches,
>> and objects of sense its flowers,
>> is watered with rituals.
> And all of the sorrows of life are its fruit;
>> the soul is a bird perched on that tree.
> That tree: this world.

Then he began his discourse on that tree of phenomenal existence: "It is like the mango tree that the lowly street conjurer grows for the amusement of an audience. It is an illusion, without substance—*māyā.*"

Indragopa, tutored since earliest childhood in picking purses, that art ancillary to sleight of hand, set down the snake baskets and the bags of magic to move toward the flock of devotees. He looked at them instinctually, like the cat that focuses all its being upon a flock of birds. The teacher, his father, restrained him, "No, no. Not now."

The boy pulled his arm back petulantly and shrugged his shoulders.

"Too dangerous now," his father whispered, pointing to the police and soldiers in the crowd. "I knew a boy once, a cousin of mine, in fact, who was caught picking purses here in Kashi. And then he lied by denying that he had done it. You know what they did to him? They cut out his tongue!"

"*Māyā* can be destroyed," the philosopher continued, "by realization of the pure and absolute *brahman,* the One, just as the false notion of a snake is removed by the discrimination of the rope."

Muladeva laughed softly into his son's ear: "They think he's wise, that he knows all about illusion and reality, and yet, listen to him, he has no idea how even the simplest trick is done. Come on, let's go. No purses today—we've worked hard enough already. Let's go. You can have something to eat. Let's go. Anangasena is waiting for me."

As Shankara the philosopher, surrounded by his disciples on the ghat, spoke of ultimate reality, Jihvika, the deep-voiced, white-haired bawd, surrounded by her girls in the brothel, gave the instructions for the evening, told the prostitutes to hurry up, to clean the walls and draw the designs on the floors, to fill the water coolers that hung in the windows and replenish the silver boxes with the camphor crystals, lozenges, and pills, to light the incense pots and oil lamps, and to prepare the betel and the wine. "Hurry up!"

After devouring an entire roasted chicken, Indragopa forced an unbroken egg down Ananta's gullet. "Let's go," Muladeva said impatiently. "Anangasena's waiting for me."

Shukradhara, the officer in charge of the brothel, nodded and welcomed the magician and his son with a betel-red smile, and Jihvika giggled obscenely, "This boy will be my lover tonight!" As she tried to push her blotched and bony fingers into his close-cropped hair, Indragopa ducked, dodged, and slipped away from the crone to follow his father to Anangasena's room.

Looking at herself in the hand mirror, she saw the magician's face appear in it, set the glass down, and turned around with a smile: "I heard about your performance today. The dance master told me. He saw it. So did Lakshmi. They said you turned a rope into a snake. Or was it a snake into a rope? Oh, I suppose that doesn't matter. They said you did something with a mango tree that was very wonderful. What was that?"

"I turned mango leaves into gold," the magician said as he picked up the woman's drinking cup and gulped down the mead that she had laced with mango oil. He spit out the lotus petal that she had floated in it.

"How did you manage it?" she asked, rather diffidently, as she concentrated on refilling the cup.

"The same way you turn your embraces into gold. Exactly the same way."

Tasting the mead, then handing the cup to his father, Indragopa picked up Anangasena's mirror and made a face at himself in it. His eyes were red from the heavy smoke in the room, the remaining vapors of the black *agaru* with which she had fumigated her robes. Setting the mirror down, the boy began to play with the prostitute's sandalwood fan, waving it before his eyes.

Anangasena trimmed her toenails and then painted her feet with lac as she spoke: "Do you think these feet are beautiful? I've earned a lot of money with them. I'd bet that I've earned more gold with this one little toe—do you think this toe is beautiful?—than you've earned with all your mango leaves. And I'm just beginning. I'm going to be a rich woman soon. I have a wealthy client who loves me with all his soul. He worships this beautiful little toe with more devotion than the priest, Shridasa, worships . . . "

Interrupting her with a forceful belch, Muladeva flatly told her that he wasn't interested in hearing about her customers. He poured another cup of mead for himself. But Anangasena insisted: "No, no, this little fellow will interest you very much. There is, thanks to me, gold in it for you too."

Muladeva listened.

"His name is Dhanamitra. He's the son of a wealthy merchant in Gujarat, a proud and therefore stupid father who, wanting nothing more in the world than that the heir to his fortune and perpetuator of his name be educated, sophisticated, and cultured from top to bottom, has sent him here to Kashi with a great allowance so that he can study the *śāstra*s, all of the arts, all of the sciences, and all of whatever else there is to study."

Taking the cup from Muladeva, she emptied it, laughed, and, relishing the magician's attention, continued: "He has hired me to . . . oh, *hired* is such a crude, vulgar word. He has *engaged* me to enlighten him in respect to the fine arts of love and the exact sciences of seduction. Under my tutelage he is to become a connoisseur of every sexual pleasure, human and divine, an expert in both theory and practice." She laughed as she loosened her bodice and displayed her breasts. "It won't come cheap; he has a lot to learn. Look here—look at how he has scratched and bitten them. All wrong! Obviously the work of a bumpkin from Gujarat. But he'll learn, in time and with money, he'll learn. I'll make a lover of him."

As she began to rub the sandal paste into the lacerations on her breasts, Muladeva, taking another cup of mead, asked her to hurry along with the story, to get to the part in which he became a beneficiary of the merchant's son. Indragopa, turning away from the spectacle of the woman's naked chest, rose and walked to the window in which the cage of pigeons was hanging. Sticking a finger through the reed bars of the cage and wiggling it at them, he tried to make the sound that pigeons make.

"Patience Muladeva! I'm getting to that now. The boy is not just studying love; he's studying everything—I already told you that. Right now, at this very minute, he's down at the ghats listening to some philosopher expound on the Veda. He's hired a flock of gurus, one for everything. There's the Sanskrit pandit and the wrestling teacher. There's the music professor who is instructing him to play the vina—Mother Kali, it's horrible! I hope you don't ever have to hear him play. Gomukha is teaching him how to cut silhouettes and stencils out of lotus leaves. There's room in this gold mine for you to do some excavating too. Our Dhanamitra wants to learn conjuring. He's mad about magic tricks. And do you know what I did for you, to fire his eagerness? I told that him no woman can resist a man who is accomplished at sleight of hand, that when a woman sees a man do magic with his hands, it inflames her imagination with unspeakable dreams of what other tricks those hands might accomplish. Not only that, I told him I knew a great magician, a conjurer named Muladeva, who just might, if funds were sufficient and if I spoke to him personally, instruct him in the arts of magic and conjuring. And believe me, I wouldn't have done all of this, if I didn't love you with all my heart."

Muladeva smiled and drank another cup of mead.

"And all I want," the prostitute smiled, "is half of the fee you get from him, only half, which won't leave much for me since I divide everything I earn with my mother; and, of course, there's Shukradhara. I'd ask you for more if I didn't love you so much."

They drank to consecrate the terms of the settlement, and then, when Jihvika called, went into the reception room where the other girls and the first customers of the evening were drinking. "Come on, Indragopa," Muladeva called to his son. "Come and enjoy yourself."

The magician was talking to the caravan driver from Kashmir when Dhanamitra, ornamented with gold amulets, coral talismans, heart-shaped earrings, and a mustard-seed *tilaka* on his forehead, his muslin robes stained yellow from the sandal paste that had been caked on his body, his lips and nails painted as bright red as his shoes, his eyes black and heavy with collyrium, entered the room, rushed to Anangasena, and caressed and kissed her suggestively despite the presence of the others. He recited words of praise: "You, whose breasts make the sinus lobes on the forehead of Indra's elephant seem paltry, are more dear to me than Earth to Varaha."

At a snap of Dhanamitra's fingers, his companion, a dwarf in clothes that suggested royalty, held out the silver tray of betel for him. Taking a leaf and methodically folding it into a triangle, he placed it into Anangasena's grinning mouth. He took another for himself, folded it into a square, opened his mouth wide and then, suddenly noticing Muladeva and Indragopa, dropped it on the floor. "You!" he squealed. "You and the boy! I recognize you even without the ashes, even with your clothes on! I'm a hard man to fool. I recognize you!" He prodded the dwarf. "Look Vamana, it's the magician and his son. I saw you today! I saw you make that mango tree grow. Amazing! Unbelievable! It took my breath away! Look here—see this amulet around my arm? Though I am not a superstitious man by nature, your performance was so sublime that I purchased one of your magic mango leaves! You are to Indra's Net what Kalidasa is to poetry! You are to conjuring what Panini is to grammar. You are to magic what Kautliya is to medicine. Need I add to my humble prolix? You are the world's greatest magician. I sincerely beg you to permit me as a connoisseur—though not as yet a practitioner—of the magical arts, to make obeisance to your foot, so like the five-petaled lotus in the number of its toes as well as in the way that it rises lotuslike above the waters of your craft that are so muddy with the efforts of other, less accomplished magicians."

Muladeva permitted it, Vamana praised the simile, and Anangasena made the introduction: "This is the magic guru of whom I spoke. And I have told him about you as well, explained to him your interests, and praised your eagerness, dedication, and diligence as a student."

"Anangasena, my ornament in the ocean of existence, though polishing the silver will not turn it into gold, it will, most certainly, make it shine. Thus I thank you for your praises. If I shine, it is because you have polished me so well. That is my goal—to become highly polished. Notice my use of the pun. But now, enough prolix. We must have a show! A performance of magic! Vamana, bring the blessed wine and betel of Gujarat. Bring whatever is wonderful and let Indra's Net be cast! Come Devamula, my guru, enchant us, bewilder us, inspire those among us who are men of taste to experience the aesthetic sentiment of wonder!"

As the magician fetched his bag and drew from it the props that he would need, the others—Shukradhara and Jihvika, the caravan driver and the conch blower, the bartender from the liquor shop and the old Shakta priest with hair dyed black, the son of a revenue officer and his nervous, acned friend from the south, and all of the women, of course—took their places. Indragopa, chewing betel from Dhanamitra's tray, stood in the corner to study it, not only his father's moves, but the reactions of the audience as well. Dhanamitra, with Vamana on one side and Anangasena on the other, seating himself directly in front of the magician, told the gathering that he wanted them to have a taste of the delicious wonder that he had himself experienced that day. "Pour the wine Vamana, wine for everyone, wine for me! I'm thirsty, thirsty! And on this, my thirst, I have composed a Sanskrit stanza—well not all of it, but most of it. Listen:

After sex had made me dry, I thought that I would try
   A little magic trick; so I began to lick
From her sweet lips a kiss—a taste of wine—a bliss!
   But that increased my thirst—my trick had tricked me
     first!"

As Vamana and Anangasena applauded his literary efforts, Muladeva told Dhanamitra that, although he himself was by no means learned in the Sanskrit language, he felt there was indeed something magical about his efforts.

"Exactly! Through the use of that trope known by the Sanskrit technical term *śleṣa*, what you in common vernacular parlance term *pun*, that is to say, playing on various meanings to words like *dry, trick,* and *taste,* I have done with words something akin to what you as a conjurer do. Does not a pun do with words what magic does with objects? But enough prolix on my part. The show! The spectacle! Amaze us! Weave your illusions! Oh, speaking of illusions, I listened to the discourse of Shankaracharya today on this very subject. And although I disagree with some of the details of his position on the nature of illusion, I find it generally convincing. But enough prolix on my part! On with the spectacle! Let us have illusions! Amaze us, O Devamula!"

After hesitating to make certain that the merchant's son was truly finished speaking, Muladeva displayed a peacock feather to the gathering, flipped it back and forth, turning it over, so it seemed, to show both sides of it. "This is a magic feather, unlike an ordinary peacock feather. Notice that it has an eye on not just one but both sides of it—two of the thousand magic eyes of Indra. Now watch! *Oṃ śrīndrāya namaḥ*, ho!" He recited the mantra, passing his fingertips over the feather, the two eyelike markings on it disappeared, or so it seemed, as he appeared to show both sides of it again. "The god has back the eyes with which he watches over magicians as they perform."

When the magician held up the length of rope, the same cord that he had turned into a snake that afternoon, Dhanamitra squealed, "Yes, yes—show us the famous Rope Trick! Can you do the Rope Trick? Do you know the secret?"

"Of course," the magician smiled, claiming that he had accomplished it, but explaining that it took a great deal of time to prepare and that it was very costly. The merchant's son insisted that he would do anything, pay anything, travel at any time to any place to see the famous Rope Trick. "Shankaracharya referred to it today in his discourse! He explained that. . . . Oh, there I go again. Prolix, prolix, prolix! It's just that I am learning so many things that it's hard to keep them all in—there's hardly room enough in my skull for all of this knowledge and wisdom. But now, back to illusions! Onward, O venerable Devamula!"

Muladeva appeared to cut the rope in two. "Short piece, long piece—father, son!" He smiled as he showed the two cords, wrapped them around his hand, and passed the peacock feather over them. "The son grows up to be as big as the father," he laughed, as he unwound the cords to show that they were now the same length.

As Dhanamitra applauded exuberantly, the magician tied the two pieces of cord together and displayed the knot. With a pass of the feather, a magic puff of breath, and a mantra muttered, the knot vanished. The whole was restored from its parts.

"I don't understand," Dhanamitra frowned. "Is it the father? Or is it the son? What does it mean?"

Anangasena assured him that it was "just a trick" and that he should not worry about its having any significance.

Signaling for Indragopa to come forward, Muladeva used the restored rope to tightly bind his son's hands. After the boy had circled the group so that each person could inspect the knots and be assured that the child was securely bound, he seated himself before his father. The magician covered the tethered hands with the cloth that had the names of the goddess upon it, and then, in an instant, with a wave of the peacock feather, the cloth was removed and not only were the boy's hands free, but the rope had vanished.

"Wonderful!" Dhanamitra screeched, nudging Vamana to do the same. "This trick is splendid! Is it coincidence that you should show this trick to me? I have written a Sanskrit stanza on the same subject. Listen:

> Tied tight's the knot of her sari, and yet
>   In my sight, by itself, it is unknotted!
> Is this her magic? Or is it Indra's Net?
>   Or wine? Or love? Or am I just besotted?"

"Wonderful!" Anangasena sighed for her patron, and the others, with irony or sympathy, to be polite or to enjoy the pleasure of mocking him, joined in that affirmation of the merchant's son's self-deceptions. Indragopa, seeing just how fragile his illusions were, pitied the young man.

Asking Dhanamitra for his cup, Muladeva, careful not to let it touch his lips, drank the wine and then showed that the vessel was completely empty. "Now that," he said, pointing to the wrapped betel that Vamana had prepared for his master, and the merchant's son handed it to the magician. Placing it on the mat in front of him, Muladeva turned the cup over and lowered it to cover the prepared *pān*. A wave of the eyeless peacock feather, a cry of "Ho!" and, when he lifted the cup, a scorpion darted out from beneath it. Everyone gasped. The dwarf leapt up, stepped on the scorpion, and ground it into the floor.

"I love that trick," Jihvika cackled.

Before Dhanamitra could think of a Sanskrit stanza on betel or wine cups, scorpions or death, Muladeva explained that he would finish, that Indra needed to watch over some other trickster. "But now he'll keep one eye and return only one to me," he said turning the feather over, back and forth, to show that it still had no eye-mark upon it. "Now watch! *Oṃ śrīndrāya namaḥ*, ho!" As he voiced the mantra, passing his fingertips over the feather once more, one of the eyelike markings returned, or so it seemed.

Dhanamitra was transported. "This indeed is that aesthetic sentiment of wonder upon which the aestheticians have expounded, the experience of which is akin to that experience of *brahman* which Shankaracharya, to the best of my understanding, posits as the highest of all experiences, so high even that it cannot be technically classified as an experience, not even in Sanskrit. Now an announcement: just as I wish to study the nature of that absolute *brahman* by listening to the discourses of Shri Shankaracharya, taking him as my guide on the path of knowledge; just as I have chosen the beautiful Anangasenacharya to enlighten me in terms of amorous consciousness and to initiate me into the study of the great tradition of erotics as codified and sanctified by the *sutras* of Vatsyayana; so, and I pray that you are not offended by my request, I wish for you to be my guru too, to teach me the science of conjuring, the art of magic. I too wish to cast Indra's Net of Magic. Accept me as your disciple, O venerable Devamula!"

The magician listened without any expression on his face. He remained silent for a moment, created suspense for the merchant's son, and then calmly he smiled as he handed the peacock feather to Dhanamitra: "This is for you. It is full of magic, full of *śākti*. It will be your wand and the emblem of your studentship as a magician."

With tears of gratitude and joy welling up in his eyes, suddenly spilling over his painted lashes and down his hairless cheeks, Dhanamitra, choking with emotion, offered to play the vina for the magician.

"No," Anangasena shrieked in panic, but upon seeing the devastated expression on her student's face, she covered her natural reaction with honeyed words: "No, not now, please. It's time to study the sweet tricks of love, to conjure pleasures. The teacher is anxious to teach. For in these lessons I feel that I, Anangasena, as if for the sake of the gods, am giving a body to Ananga, the bodiless god of love."

Thus flattered, Dhanamitra winked at all present and, with a blissful grin, escorted his preceptress to the classroom in which the bed was strewn with lotus petals.

While Anangasena was at work, Muladeva, despite his son's efforts to stop him from drinking any more, got drunk. He rested his head in his son's lap and told him not to be so serious. "You're acting more like my father than my son. Chew some betel."

When she had finished with Dhanamitra and sent him back to his guesthouse, Anangasena, herself quite drunk, came laughing to Muladeva. He asked her the cause of her laughter, but when she tried to tell it, it made her laugh all the more. She roared with laughter, moaned with it, gasped for breath through it, fell on the floor from laughing so hard, pounded that floor, giggled, sighed, and started laughing again. She couldn't, for the life of her, stop laughing.

"What's so funny?" Muladeva asked again and again, beginning to laugh himself, catching the bug of the laughter to which Indragopa seemed immune. The boy looked at the prostitute and his father with pity.

Anangasena was trying to explain it. Each time she started, "Dha, Dha, Dha, Dhana," the syllables turned into laughter: "Dha, Dha, ha, ha, ha, oh, Dha-hana, Dhana, ha, ha, ha . . ." With tears streaming down her face, she clutched herself to prevent her ribs from breaking, tried to put her hand over her mouth, called out to the goddess to help her control herself. She struggled with all her might to tell the story of how she had convinced Dhanamitra to sleep each night at his guest house, lying face down on a cot in which there was a hole. She had recited a passage in Vatsyayana's *sūtras* on *kāma* and explained it to him in detail: he was to tie a cord to his penis and then sleep with that organ dangling through the hole, pulled down by a weight tied to the other end of the cord. The weight of the weight was to be gradually augmented as the length and strength of the penis increased. It was impossible through the woman's wild laughter and his own drunkenness for Muladeva to follow the story.

Anangasena sighed, was quiet for a moment, and dried her eyes with the corner of her robe. "As soon as we got to the room," she moaned, "he showed it to me and, with the most sincere expression on his face that you can imagine, asked me if I thought the treatment was working." She started laughing again but more weakly now.

Muladeva gulped down another cup of mead. "Teach my son what you're teaching that idiot."

The prostitute, recovering from her seizure, let out a last, slight giggle as she looked at Indragopa. "He's a baby."

"No, no," the father mumbled. "He's ready to become a man. Go on, teach him. Teach my son."

Moving his father's head away, Indragopa stood and looked down at the man on the floor: his mouth was wet, his eyes red, his long hair disheveled. The boy left the room.

"I'm dying!" Muladeva moaned as he emerged from sleep. "My head's full of scorpions. My stomach's full of snakes. I'm dying. Where's the myrobalan, the balm, the balm? Where's the medicine?"

Anangasena, lying on her back, her legs spread indecorously, snoring loudly and smiling happily, was unwakeable and profoundly immovable.

"Where's my son?"

The magician lay back down, covered his head with his shawl, and slowly, painfully, tried to reconstruct the night. It was like putting a broken wine cup back together—a little piece here, another chunk there, so many pieces missing, this fitting with that, this fitting with nothing. When it started to take shape he sat up, cursed himself, then his son, then Indra and Shambara. He cursed wine and magic and love. He cursed the life magicians had to lead. And then he rose to search for his son.

"Indragopa!" he called out again and again, as loud as he could, as he made his way through the lanes of the quarter: lanes that last night had been fragrant with incense, flowers, and perfumes now reeked of sweat, urine, and vomit. Drunkards, asleep or dead, perhaps, in the mud, were sniffed by dogs. Their barking, not the songs, jokes, or the laughter of the night before, and Muladeva's desperate cry—"Indragopa! Indragopa!"—was all that could be heard in the pleasure district.

The father found his son by the river, at the place where they had bathed the day before. And because the boy's face was wet from bathing in the Ganga, Muladeva did not notice at first that he was weeping, that, on his cheeks, mixed with the holy water of the river, were tears. When he realized it, the father began to beg for the forgiveness of his son. "You're everything to me. The son is the life of the father. The son is . . . "

"No," the boy whispered. "It's not that. It's not that. Ananta is dead. I couldn't keep him alive." When he uttered it again—"Ananta is dead"—the tears gushed. Holding the child in his arms then, the father couldn't recollect when the boy had last wept. He couldn't remember him ever having cried, not since he was a baby. He had not even cried when his mother left for Kashmir.

Relieved that the snake and not himself was the cause of the tears, Muladeva attempted to console the boy: "We're going to make a lot of money off this merchant's son. You can buy ten cobras, ten Anantas, from the snake charmers. More than that. You can buy a monkey, a trained monkey."

The son dried his face. "You still haven't bought the kite for me. You promised me a kite, and instead of the kite you give me more promises. You never keep promises. You're a liar."

"Here," Muladeva laughed, and he gave the child the purse, all of the money that was left from what they had earned the day before with their magic. In the midst of counting it, the boy looked up: "A monkey?"

"Yes."

"Good. I'll teach it to do magic, to bring in more money."

"You can't teach a monkey to do magic," Muladeva smiled. "To do magic, you have to be able to lie. If an animal is hungry, or afraid, or angry, or happy, or tired, or whatever, it cannot help but show that. An animal cannot be taught to be false."

"But," Indragopa was quick to answer, "it can be taught to seem to lie. We can teach it to deceive even if it does not itself know it is doing so."

"Perhaps," Muladeva, unable in his current state to think anything through with clarity, mumbled as he stepped slowly into the Ganga to bathe.

Dhanamitra's first magic lesson was to take place in the guesthouse. Muladeva insisted that Vamana, the dwarf, who was sitting on the cot in the room, had to leave. "Everything I'm going to teach you is for you alone. No one else must see it. No one else must know. Secrecy is power. You must take the *mantragupta* vow. Never reveal anything."

When Vamana rose to depart, Muladeva noticed the hole in the cot over which the dwarf had been sitting. "I'm going to teach you eight amazing tricks that you can do. That's how we'll begin. You'll need to practice, practice, practice. Discipline and training are everything."

"Yes, O Devamula, I surrender to the guru."

"*Muladeva*—my name is Muladeva."

The disciple, after apologizing profusely for getting his guru's name wrong, asked the master if magic was a skill or a power.

"It's both," the magician said. "I'll teach you the skill; the power comes only from the gods."

"Do you, venerable one, my guru, have the power?"

"Indeed."

"How? Tell me how you got the power. I too want the power."

No sooner had the magician begun with the words "I was a renouncer," than the merchant's son interrupted him. "Oh, is this that story you told yesterday at your performance about the Kapalika who gave you the magic cakes?"

"No," Muladeva answered sternly. "You must be quiet. You must learn to be quiet, to listen and watch, if you are ever going to master the art of magic. That story was a lie. It was just patter, part of the act, the show. But this, this is true: I was a renouncer—the servant of no man and the husband of no woman, but the father of a son named Indragopa. You saw him yesterday and last night. He was the only cord that bound me to this world. In my wandering from place to place, followed by that child, I worshipped at the shrines of Kali, always seeking her blessings and her guidance. One night, I called out to her, sang her praises, and then announced my intentions: 'Because of my devotion to you, Mother, I now sacrifice this child, cut off his head as my offering to you, that you may add it to the garland of skulls that ornament your breasts, beautiful with the stain of human blood. In doing this holy thing, I sever all that binds me to the great round of birth and death. All knots are undone, all ties broken.' "

Clenching his fist as if holding a sword, Muladeva swiftly swept his arm through the air and hissed, and it conjured up the scene for Dhanamitra: the child's head fell from the body, rolled to the feet of the terrible goddess, and the merchant's son gasped in horror.

In an eerie whisper the magician revealed the words of the goddess: "Because, O Muladeva, of the perfection of your detachment from all things of this world and the perfection of your devotion to me, as proved by this act, a sacrifice surpassing all the sacrifices of the Vedic priests, I shall reward you with a divine gift. You shall, from this moment on, be capable of creating any illusion. You shall be a great magician. I give you my power, my *māyā!*"

Muladeva hesitated, then smiled. "All at once I used that power to perform my first magic trick—I restored the severed head of my son to his body. I brought him back to life!"

"You played a trick on Kali," Dhanamitra blurted out. "You got her magic, and you got your son back. 'You were able,' as my father would say, 'to keep both the goods you bought and the money you paid for them.' "

The magician laughed.

"Weren't you afraid?" the merchant's son cried out excitedly.

"No," the magician laughed again. "Kali, herself a magician, liked the trick. She was sufficiently well-pleased with my skill in fooling her, so impressed with the courage of my deception and my confidence that it would work, that she let me keep the power that she had given me as a fee well earned. She laughed so hard that her laughter, like lightning, broke open the clouds, and it rained for three nights and three days."

The mention of the fee that Kali had rendered made it follow quite naturally that teacher and student should discuss the financial details of tuition. Once that was done to the satisfaction of both, Muladeva taught Dhanamitra the simple sleights required to make it seem that he could cut a piece of rope in half, tie the halves together, vanish the knot, and restore the rope. After receiving the first payment in gold from the merchant's son, Muladeva gave Anangasena her share and the rest of the money to Indragopa. The boy purchased a monkey.

During his second lesson Dhanamitra learned how to draw a black *svāstika* on the back of his hand, wipe it off, turn his hand over, and show that the mark had mysteriously passed through his hand to the palm. "It's so easy!" he said, amazed at how unamazing the secrets of conjuring were turning out to be. "I'm afraid that once I learn all the secrets, nothing will amaze me, and I will lose all my sense of wonder."

"Don't worry," the teacher assured him, "the tricks in this world are endless, the surprises innumerable."

The monkey, tamed and named Vrishakapi by the hunter who had caught him and sold him to Indragopa, clung to the boy's neck. The hands of the animal, though small and black, seemed so human—the fingernails, the lines around the knuckles and on the palms, so like those on Indragopa's own hands. "Your hands and your eyes are like a person's," he said to the monkey as he broke off a piece of pomegranate for him and watched him pluck out and devour the small red seeds. "Not your sharp teeth, or your flat face, or your tail, or your feet, or anything else—that's all monkey. But your hands and eyes are human, and that's why you're going to be able to perform magic. It's all in the hands and the eyes."

The child magician taught the monkey to hold a cowrie shell, to show it in the palm of his hand, and then to place it in the other hand and close his fingers around it. Then, when Vrishakapi had it just right, he was taught to retain the shell in the first hand and make it look as if he were passing it into the other. And the monkey learned the sleight from Indragopa more quickly than Dhanamitra learned it from Muladeva.

"Too quick! It's not natural," Muladeva said. "Do it really—actually pass it from one hand to the other. Naturally! Do it naturally and observe your own naturalness. Naturalness is what will fool people. You have to learn to fake being natural. The deceit must be just like the truth, the illusion like reality, but more so."

"I know I'll get it right this time. Watch me Devamula!"

"Muladeva! My name is Muladeva! Muladeva!"

With the money his father earned from Dhanamitra, Indragopa had a basket woven, a small version of the one that he and his father used in their street performances. As soon as it was ready, the boy began to teach Vrishakapi the cues—to screech as soon as the first sword entered the basket from the top, to open the flask of magician's blood and empty it, to move his legs slightly apart for the second sword to enter between them, to move his arm at the right moment so that the third sword could enter the basket between that arm and his side. The only difficult part was teaching the monkey to be quiet and still until the signal to jump out of the basket.

Finally they performed the trick for Muladeva: "With these mango leaves I can bring him back to life," Indragopa said as he opened the basket, giving his father and Anangasena a glimpse of the still, blood-drenched monkey. He covered the small corpse with the leaves. Replacing the lid of the basket, the boy sat down on the ground with his legs crossed in the posture of a holy man, closed his eyes, and regulated his deep breathing. Anangasena anxiously clutched Muladeva's arm. Then, after another moment of silence and stillness, "Ho," the boy yelled, and the basket seemed to move just slightly. Then it shook. The lid flew off, and the monkey leapt out of it to scramble into Indragopa's lap for a piece of pomegranate.

"Wonderful! Wonderful!" Muladeva laughed with joy. "You're a great magician, my son. Wonderful! Wonderful!"

"Terrible! Terrible!" Muladeva frowned and shook his head, taking the peacock feather out of Dhanamitra's hand to show him yet again how to do the sleight, to turn the feather while flipping it over so that one side was shown as two. "You're never going to fool people unless you learn to do it naturally. You're trying too hard. You're too attached to the fruits of your actions. Don't try so hard. Try to stop trying. Here, take the coin and do the pass for me."

"The sleight of hand that I want you to teach me," said the merchant's son, accidentally dropping the coin, "is that special sleight used at the dice board."

"What?" Muladeva shouted angrily at the shuddering, cowering student. "What? Use the art of magic to cheat someone? Risk giving the conjurer's craft, our great and hallowed tradition, a bad name? Our knowledge of gambling sleights is never used for dishonest ends, but only to expose the deceits of other players. Can you ask for such a thing and still consider yourself worthy to be my student?"

With the collyrium from his eyes streaming down his cheeks in his tears, begging the magician not to end the lessons, Dhanamitra took a handful of gold coins from his purse and pushed them toward the feet of his guru.

"Stop crying," Muladeva snapped. As he looked at the gold, he was tempted first to announce that he could not, for any price, be bribed or bought, that money meant nothing to him, and then to claim that he would, however, take the money in order to help Dhanamitra appease his conscience. But the magician didn't try it—he silently picked up the gold. He knew the secret that separates ordinary liars from the professionals—he knew when not to lie.

"Stop crying," the Muladeva smiled gently. "We'll continue our lessons. I'll make a magician out of you. Anangasena will make you a lover. And Shankara will make you a philosopher. It's all one endeavor."

"I'll practice," Dhanamitra promised as he dried his eyes and apologized for his offense. "Practice! Discipline! Training! I will be as obedient and loyal as a son to you. I want to learn magic, how to perform it and what it is, what it really is. You are my guru! I make obeisance to you, O Devamula!"

Anangasena watched Muladeva count the gold and then took her share, reminding him that she would have to give a portion of it to Jihvika and Shukradhara.

"I'm no more greedy than you are," Muladeva said as he wrapped his arm tenderly around her shoulder. "I give half of all I earn to my father so that he can take care of himself and my mother. I'm sending my son to Shittal village where they're living. He'll take the gold to them for me, and I'll stay here with you until he comes back. Until then I just want to enjoy you and to rest. I want to rest—no tricks, no magic."

With Vrishakapi perched on his shoulder, carrying a basket in which there was magic, the snake Vasukija, and gold in one hand and the damaru in the other, Indragopa, walking east, toward Anga, began to shake the drum lightly and slowly as he went; and the sound of it made both him and the monkey want to perform.

"How's this for a trick," he said to Vrishakapi. "Just as my father earns his gold by fooling people, so I, the son, having learned everything I know from that great magician, can do the same. I am the same as he is. The trick is so easy. All I have to do is stop, not go to Anga. Then the gold is ours."

Laughing over the thought of tricking Muladeva, of deceiving the father whom he had learned to respect as one of the greatest deceivers in the world, he played the drum a bit louder, a bit faster, and it made Vrishakapi all the more restless. The monkey screeched.

"It's fine. It's fine. Don't be afraid," Indragopa whispered and stopped—stopped walking and stopped playing the drum. He stood still and was silent. He squatted down, put a betel leaf in his mouth and chewed it. He looked around, shook the drum, shook it harder, rose and then started back, back but northwards.

"We're not going to Anga. We're going to the mountains," he laughed. "We're going to Kashmir where my mother lives to perform magic there."

Faster and louder the young magician played the damaru, Mahadeva's drum, and he walked in perfect time to the rhythm of it.

PLATE 1. Diving Duck: Chand Baba. Photograph by Cheryl Wicker-Siegel (Delhi, 1987).

PLATE 2. Street Magic: Naseeb and Ayasan Shah. Photograph by
Cheryl Wicker-Siegel (Srinagar, 1988).

PLATE 3. Mango Tree Trick: Naseeb Shah and Kareem Baksh.
Photograph by Cheryl Wicker-Siegel (Delhi, 1987).

PLATE **4.**
Mango Tree Trick:
Street Magicians.
Photograph by
W. W. Hooper (Madras,
1880); courtesy of the
India Office Library
(London).

PLATE 5.
Decapitation of Salma.
Photograph by Cheryl
Wicker-Siegel (Delhi,
1987).

How Does He Do It?

... *Magicians Don't Believe It Can Be Done!*

1. Hindu uses ordinary rope to perform trick for German children, lets them examine it.

2. As the rope uncoils, the Hindu repeats supposedly magic words, rapidly.

3. An instant later the rope becomes rigid as if it had been hypnotized.

It's An Argument

Famous magicians Houdini and Thurston declared this trick impossible. Both spent months in India trying to learn it.

Neither found a person who had ever seen the trick! (The fellow pictured—where was he?)

The rope trick legend originated in China, has been told for 600 years.

The legendary rope trick is most complicated. After the rope is up, a little boy climbs it, disappears. The magician follows, brandishing a sharp sword, disappears, too.

Bloody pieces of the boy's body drop from the clouds.

The magician climbs down the rope, wiping off his bloody sword. He taps the rope, it falls.

Then he picks up the pieces of the boy, fits them together, and the boy lives again.

Magicians think the story of Jack and the Beanstalk comes from this legend.

Physicians and psychologists point out that the people of India are easy subjects for hypnotists. They suggest that the performer's hocus-pocus puts his audience into a trance in which they "see" whatever he tells them to.

$25,000 has been offered by the British Magic Circle, and $10,000 by American magicians to anyone who will perform the rope trick before them successfully. No one has claimed the prizes.

4. He permits a child to climb it. At the finish the rope falls at his feet.

PLATE 6. The Indian Rope Trick. *Look* Magazine; date and photographer unknown.

PLATE 7.
P. C. Sorcar
Senior.
Photograph by
Serge Lido (Paris,
n.d.), courtesy of
P. C. Sorcar Junior.

PLATE 8.
Muhammad
Masthan Thangal.
Photograph by Lee
Siegel (Trichur,
1987).

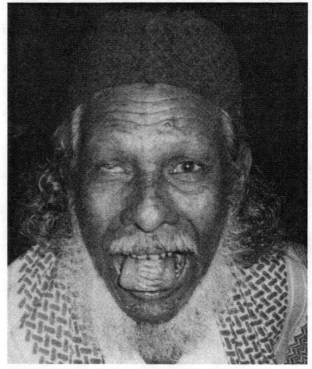

Historian's Notebook 1:

Wandering Magicians

"I could hear that damaru, Mahadeva's drum." The old stage magician who performed in the Western style closed his eyes as, with magic words, he conjured luminous specters out of the shadowy recesses of childhood memory: "I couldn't resist the call of the drum. It tugged me to the open window from where I could see them. Two magicians, a man and his son, carrying the flat cobra baskets and the bags of tricks. And I can still see them," he faintly smiled. "Still, right now, although it was almost seventy years ago, I see them walking in time to the rhythm of the drum. The boy's turban is red; his father's black. Naked to the waist, dark, lean and yet muscular, wearing only those ragged lungis, they perform their magic show in my dreams. I can hear the drum."

"*Jādūgar! Jādūgar!*" that child at the window years ago called out. "Please, *Mā*, please let the *gilli-gilli* man come in, please." Indulging the excitement, the mother promised the magician a few annas as servants and children gathered in the shade of the broad veranda to be amazed at the manipulations of the cups and balls, dazzled by the appearance and disappearance of an egg, frightened by a cobra or a scorpion, startled with the wonderful sight of a mango seed putting forth its shoots, then growing larger and larger into a bush and then a tree. "Reason, experience, knowledge—these mature faculties, damn them!—try to convince me that the mango plant was only half a meter high. But in the fields of memory there's a magnificent tree, as tall and broad as a house, its bright and leafy branches full of fruit, ripe and delicious. I can taste the mango from that magic tree. It's sweet," he laughed, and the sure magician's hands trembled, "so very sweet that it almost makes me weep to taste it."

"When I was a child . . ." I heard the wistful story again and again of the rat-tat-rat-tattoo of the damaru, the "dug-dug-dugee," and the wailing whine of the precatory pipe, an ancient anthem echoing in Indian memory, announcing the arrival of magicians who were inevitably invited into the courtyards of the grand homes of large and prosperous families to perform. "They were a regular feature of Indian life," the old man said with a certain sadness and a nostalgia not for tricks but for another magic, for a disappearing India of sweet mangoes, ropes rising in mystery, and small clay pots that seemed to hold rivers of clear, fresh water. It's an enchanted India that Kipling, at ease beneath a slowly waving palm-leaf punkah, knew or dreamed, found or made. "*Arré*, Brethren, here come I," one of his quick urchins of magic sang:

> Stripped to loin-cloth in the sun,
> Search me well and watch me close!
> Tell me how my tricks are done—
> Tell me how the mango grows!
> Give me a man who is not made
> To his trade
> Swords to fling and catch again,
> Coins to ring and snatch again,
> Men to harm and cure again,
> Snakes to charm and lure again—
> He'll be hurt by his own blade,
> By his serpents disobeyed,
> By his clumsiness betrayed,
> By the people laughed to scorn—
> So 'tis not with juggler born!
> Pinch of dust or withered flower,
> Chance-flung or borrowed staff,
> Serve his need and shore his power,
> Bind the spell or loose the laugh!

As the magician embodied the romance and mystery of India for some, he represented Oriental tawdriness and vulgarity to others. The Abbé Dubois, observing street magicians during his travels in India early in the nineteenth century, commented upon them with the sort of social judgments that are no longer fashionably confessed in print: "Among the degraded beings who form the dregs of society in India must be classed the jugglers, charlatans, mountebanks, conjurers, acrobats, rope-dancers, &c. There are two or three castes which practice these professions, travelling from country to country to find patrons or dupes. It is not surprising, with a people so credulous and endued with such a love of the marvellous as the Hindus, that such impostors should abound. They are regarded as magicians and sorcerers, as men versed in witchcraft and all the occult sciences, and are viewed with fear and distrust." The Abbé was himself, however, credulous enough, sufficiently baffled and tricked, to admit that the Indian conjurers did "perform really astonishing feats of legerdemain and agility. European jugglers would certainly have to lower their colours before them" (*Hindu Manners, Customs and Ceremonies*).

WANDERING MAGICIANS

Accounts of early travelers validate the old stage magician's claim that the street conjurer was indeed "a regular feature of Indian life," or that, in Dubois's terms, "such impostors did abound." Francisco Pelsaert, describing festivals in the streets of Agra in the early seventeenth century, mentions the performances of magicians, jugglers, dancers, and "other such rabble" (*Romanstrantie*). And a little later in that century John Fryer catalogued "*Bengal* Juglers, Montebanks, and Conjurers, as also the Dancing People" among the rabble of India. "They are Vagrants, that travel to delude the Mobile by their *Hocus Pocus* Tricks (living promiscuously like our Gypsies) . . . [these practitioners of] Slight of Hand pester every open place in great Cities and Publick Fairs, as they do in *Europe*." By classifying the itinerant conjurers "at the Heel" of "Jougies" and "Fakires," Fryer failed to make any methodological or functional distinction between such performances of sleight of hand as the Mango Trick and such displays of yogic prowess as "casting up one's Tripes by Mouth." One of these performers or ascetics, whichever the case may have been, "swallowed a Chain . . . and made it clink in his Stomach. Spectators (being mostly Ladies, for whose diversion he was brought)," were apparently not amused—"they [were] puking" (*A New Account of East India and Persia 1672–1681*).

Similarly, François Bernier, touring India in 1667, did not distinguish between "*Fakires*" or "*Jauguis*" and conjurers: "They almost continually perambulate the country, make light of everything, affect to live without care, and to be possessed of most important secrets. . . . When two of these good *Jauguis* meet, and can be excited to a spirit of emulation, they make such a display of the power

FIGURE 2. *Street Magician: Cups and Balls.* Watercolor (Panjab, 1860); courtesy of the India Office Library (London).

of *Jauguisism*, that it may well be doubted if *Simon Magus*, with all his sorceries, ever performed more surprising feats. They tell any person his thoughts, cause the branch of a tree to blossom and to bear fruit within an hour, hatch an egg in their bosom in less than fifteen minutes, producing whatever bird may be demanded, and make it fly about the room, and execute many other prodigies that need not be enumerated" *(Travels in the Mogul Empire 1656–1668).*

The confusion, Indian as well as European, of magician-entertainers with magician-yogis was natural and intentionally precipitated. Street performers earned their livelihood by capitalizing on the association, by imitating or impersonating those mendicant ascetics who, for over two thousand years in India, having renounced their domestic and social roles and having severed all attachments to the world to wander here and there in a penance for their birth, have been supported with the alms of pious members of society wanting, through their offerings, to have some redemptive share in the vagabond renouncer's holiness. Through ascetic practices, wandering sannyasis were (and are) believed to attain supernatural powers, the powers of Shiva, *siddhi*s, which, like every other aspect of life and death in India, have been systematically catalogued and normatively categorized: *aṇiman* (the power to become minute or, for the magician, disappearance) and *mahiman* (the power to become large); *laghiman* (the ability to become light, to levitate) and *gariman* (the power to become heavy); *prāpti* (the skill of obtaining things, effecting materializations, or, as explained by the traditional commentators on the *Yogasūtra*s of Patañjali [3.45], having the ability to touch the moon with one's fingertip); *prākāmya* (the power to will things so— telekinesis); *īśitva* (a power over the will of others—hypnosis) and *vaśitva* (a power to subdue one's own will—self-hypnosis). Demonstrations of any of these skills are proof of holy perfection and perfect holiness. The Buddha, that son of Maya, Queen Magic, is frequently referred to and depicted as a magician, a *māyāvin:* "Being one, he becomes many; or having become many, becomes one again; he becomes invisible or visible; unobstructed, he passes through a wall, hill, or some other such barrier as if it were made of air; and, as through the air, he moves through solid ground; he walks on water . . . and travels cross-legged through the sky" *(Sāmaññaphalasutta of the Dīgha Nikāya).* Returning to his home in Kapilavastu after his great awakening, the Buddha, in hopes of getting converts, staged a grand magic show: "After levitating, the Blessed One walked through the air as if on solid ground, then stopped in midair, first sat down, then lay down. He cut himself into many pieces and then he put himself back together. He walked on water as if it were land and then dove into land as if it were water. He produced water as if he were a cloud, and fire as if he were the sun" *(Saundarananda* of Ashvaghosha, 3.21–23).

I've seen versions of the same tricks performed by entertainers. The repertoires of the holy mendicant miracle worker and the not-so-holy itinerant conjurer overlap. The Buddha, like a child with a beginner's magic set, produces a piece of cloth—the conjurer's traditional foulard—from nowhere (*Cullakaseṭṭhi-Jātaka*), and he makes a solid cane hollow like a lotus stalk, by blowing on it like a *jādūgar* (*Naḷapāna-Jātaka*).

The *Bodhisattvabhūmi* of Asanga lists the *ṛddhi*s or magical proficiencies of bodhisattvas within a binary classification: *pāriṇāmikī*, the power of transformation (the bodhisattva changes the nature of an existing thing just as the magician turns a mosquito into a pigeon, the pigeon into a child); and *nairmāṇikī*, the power of creation (the conjurer, like the bodhisattva or a god, produces an egg from an empty bag, a lotus from an empty pond, plenum from void).

The magical potencies of the Buddha, *abhijñā*s and *ṛddhi*s—telepathy and telekinesis, clairvoyance, clairaudience, and clairsentience—were, it was postulated, acquired or realized in advanced meditation. Miraculous aptitudes, according to tradition, could also be attained through both devotional and Tantric ritual. A human being might achieve an identification with the god, not communion with the deity, but an actual incorporation of the divinity's essential energy. In devotional *pūjā* the officiating priest might identify himself with the god for the devotees, while in Tantric *pūjā*, the initiate himself could become the deity. Through such sacramental processes the human being was thought to assimilate the divine *māyā*.

Because there was money to be made, alms for ascetics and offerings for incarnate gods, money given in exchange for a participation in the holiness that supernatural feats were thought to express or represent, every street magician had a version of the *siddhi*s, *ṛddhi*s, and *abhijñā*s. As the wandering holy man seemed to be a magician, so the wandering magician seemed to be a holy man. And there was (and is) power, cash or esteem, in holiness. "The citizens of the town, gullible as they are, attribute divine powers to him—he's tricked them by means of his skill in the arts of deception" (*Daśakumāracarita* of Dandin, 2).

Perhaps it's because magic tricks that pass for miracles—producing holy ash, eggs, or Seiko watches from thin air, making a mango tree grow, turning a rope or staff into a snake, surviving a burial, reading the minds of others, levitating, and other popular items—are, if one only knows the trick, so very easy to do that the Buddha, at least as he is represented within one trend in Buddhist literature, censured or made light of thaumaturgical practices and displays of marvelous powers. "In order to underline the inadequacy of such attainments [as the abilities to become many, pass through walls, fly, walk on water and read minds] the Buddha recounted the story of a *bhikkhu* who possessed these magical powers, and how they served him nothing in his search for an escape from suffering" (*Dīgha Nikāya*). Apparently conscious of the close connection between tricks and miracles, the performances of jugglers and the activities of renouncers, the Buddha spoke of a magician who "upon the stage deceived people with his tricks." But, since death cannot be tricked, the Buddha explained, he himself, with nothing up his sleeve and nothing palmed, chose the holy path, the way of truth over the way of magic and deception (*Ayoghara-Jātaka*). He taught with an open hand.

ROPES AND AIR

Like the Buddhist arhat or bodhisattva, so the Hindu yogi, sadhu, or siddha and, more recently, the Muslim fakir or pir, have been customarily and popularly believed to possess magical resources. Magicians within each religion formed an extramural, syncretic, and complicitous caste of their own: "The caste which is particularly devoted to magic as a vocation is that of the Yogi, which is primarily Hindu but has Mohammadan elements affiliated to it. The Yogi claims to hold the material world in fee by the magical powers which he has acquired through the performances of religious austerities, but this claim soon degenerates into superstition of the worst type, and the Yogi in reality is little better than a common swindler, posing as a faqir" (H. A. Rose, "Magic [Indian]").

Since the magical powers of yogis were thought to have been attained through mortifications, self-crucifications, punishing the flesh for being flesh, spectacularly masochistic public demonstrations of painful austerities were in order: "At certain periods of the year, particularly in the month of April, many men of the lower castes observe temporarily the discipline of the ascetic sects, and may then be seen to cheerfully undergo self-inflicted tortures of a cruel kind, as, for example, passing thick metal skewers through the tongue, the cheeks, or the skin of the arms, the neck, and the sides, walking upon live charcoal, and rolling upon thorns. Amongst the motives most commonly ascribed to these temporary low-caste ascetics are the gratification of vanity and the desire for the pecuniary gain which their performance usually brings them; but there can be no doubt that many of them hope, and look for, other and less obvious rewards for their self-inflicted sufferings" (John Campbell Oman, *The Mystics, Ascetics, and Saints of India*).

The readiness of people to believe in the supernatural prowess of yogis, their anxiousness to be beguiled by magicians, is mocked in a seventeenth-century Sanskrit comedy, a monologue play in which the peripatetic narrator, describing the various people he encounters in the city, announces the approach of a street conjurer. Sarcastically laughing, he enumerates the abilities attributed to the predacious flimflam man: "He knows many kinds of magic—how to turn a single thing into many things, how to make insentient things sentient, and how to transform things into things which are not! He has an incomparable, superhuman power—he can keep rutting elephants at bay, make snakes lose their pride, and even subjugate the demons" (*Śāradātilaka* of Shankara, 182–183).

As the Indian court magician-entertainer represents a profanation over time of the Indian court magician-priest, one who imitated with tricks what the priest had been thought able to accomplish in reality, so the itinerant Indian street magician-entertainer represents an evolutionary banalization of the mendicant samana, siddha, yogi, sannyasi, or sadhu, simulating the powers attributed to them with an imitation that is either, depending on what you know or want, entertainment or fraud.

Prestidigitational techniques for close-up magic and parlor conjuring had been cultivated into skills by the time of the *Kāmasūtra* (c. third century c.e.), wherein various sorts of legerdemain are enumerated among the sixty-four arts that were de rigueur for sophisticated ladies and gentlemen in ancient India (1.3). Sleight of hand with dice, as well as the art of gimmicking the dice, became essential tricks of the gambler's trade: "Entering the casino to join the gamblers there, I witnessed their skill at the twenty-five gaming arts—at such tricks as loading the dice and moving a piece, unnoticed, from one place to another" (*Daśakumāracarita* of Dandin, 2). The conjurer was a swindler with bunko as his dharma. But trickery made him no less godlike than the sadhu or sannyasi, for the gods, after all, are and always have been tricksters themselves: like crooked gamblers, "the gods trick the demons out of their winnings, this world, the sacrifice" (*Śatapatha Brāhmaṇa* 1.2.5.10).

At some point the Hindu street magicians, protected by Indra and Shambara, Skanda and Vishnu, converted en masse to Islam, to faith in a god who is neither amused by jugglery nor tolerant of fraud. While it's difficult to determine either the period of or reason for that conversion, my suspicion is that the collective submission of the magicians' wills to the will of Allah occurred in the nineteenth century (much later than the conversion of such cognate groups as the bangle makers, who became Muslims in the thirteenth century): the magicians who performed in Jahangir's court in the seventeenth century were Hindus from Bengal; eighteenth- and nineteenth-century European travel accounts mention magicians with such Hindu names as "Covindsamy" (Govindaswami) and "Seshal" (Sushila); in a several-hundred-year-old series of visual depictions of Indian daily life, the magician, performing with cups and balls (using two cups and three balls just as in Naseeb's rendition of the ancient trick), is adorned with the sectarian markings that signal one who has renounced his own identity to emulate, and ultimately become, Shiva, lord of yoga, divine exemplar of the magic powers that are attained through austerities. The show's a con job (if the audience believes the methods for the effects are supernatural), or a parody (if the audience knows the methods are sleights), or a bit of both—in the shows I've seen there's always that ambivalence: to the degree that I know I'm seeing a magic trick, accomplished through human skill, I can't accuse the magician of fraud; but to the degree that I wonder if what I'm seeing might be real magic, a miracle accomplished through divine power, I'm tempted to buy a ring, amulet, or spell.

The stage magician Ashok Bhandari (who had promised to give me Sanksrit manuscripts on magic) gave me a pamphlet, the *Talismāt Nātak Kalān* (*Grand Drama of Magic*), published in Urdu in the nineteenth century by a Muslim bookseller and polemist named S. R. Malik, who claimed that the illustrated text contained "the teachings of Bhutanatha (Lord of Ghosts), king of imposters, nicknamed Mohasha, being the magnificent account of ancient adventures of spying, fraud, and deception as taken from old Sanskrit books and translated by Sahib Lal Ram Nath." The pious Muslim publisher announced his intentions in respect to the Hindu street magicians in a preface: "To save the public from their clutches, this servant of the nation, considering this a duty, wants to inform you of the tricks of these cheats and will, therefore, give detailed descriptions of all their tricks" (translated for me by Sam Mitchell).

Perhaps the conversion and simultaneous consolidation of street conjurers into a discreet group, the Maslets, a professional Muslim subcaste that identified themselves as entertainers, was meant to distinguish them, at least in the eyes of the law, from another group—the non-Muslim Jaduas, whose training in magic and conjuring was purely for the sake of criminal activities. A nineteenth-century account of their trade and strategems was given to government ethnographers by a superintendent of police in Patna: "They start out in parties of three or four and make inquiries for the whereabouts of some likely dupe, in the shape of an ignorant and superstitious person possessed of property. . . . When the victim has been selected, one of them proceeds to his village in the disguise of a Sadhu or anchorite, being usually accompanied by another as his chela, or disciple. Soon afterwards the others come, one of them perhaps posing as a considerable land-holder, and go about inquiring if a very holy Brahmin has been seen. They go to the house of their intended dupe, who naturally asks why they are seeking the Brahmin; they reply that they have come to do homage to him, as he had turned their silver and brass ornaments into gold. The dupe at once goes with them in search of the Brahmin, and is greatly impressed by seeing the landholder worship him with profound respect and make him presents of cloth, money, and cattle. He at once falls into the trap and says that he too has a quantity of silver which he would like to have turned into gold. The Brahmin pretends reluctance, but eventually yields to the dupe's entreaties and allows himself into the latter's house. . . . A variety of tricks are now resorted to, to impress the dupe with the magic powers of the swindlers." The mark hopefully hands over his silver to be turned into gold; and the magicians happily leave town (R. V. Russell and Hira Lal, *The Tribes and Castes of the Central Provinces*). *Śābāś!*

The first story I heard from the magicians about their conversion to Islam, Chand Pasha's rendition, had them dazzled by a pir while on a pilgrimage to the Ganga. Just as Naseeb had his own version of each of the standard tricks, so he had his own rendition of the legends: tales are, by nature, tricks; and tricks are enacted tales. The new revelation, heard six months later, stressed the magicians' shady origins and current honesty. They had been converted from the deceitful ways of Hinduism to the righteousness of Islam.

"Once upon a time, when Shah Pir was just a boy, no older than Ayasan, he was setting out upon a journey, taking a great offering of gold to the shrine of Pir Quaza Garib Navaj. It would, in accordance with al-Qur'an, be given to the poor. 'The countryside is full of scoundrels,' his mother warned him. She knew that the mind of a young boy would naturally be attracted by the spectacles which, in India in those days, he was sure to see everywhere on the roads—bear trainers and monkey handlers, acrobats and jugglers, snake charmers and, to be sure, magicians. Magicians everywhere! 'These *jādūgars* are swindlers,' the good mother told her boy. 'They dress as sadhus, but they are godless men. With their pretty tricks they attract the eye, but those tricks are but the bait to lure the prey into the net. After demonstrating how a coin can multiply or disappear, they'll ask to see a coin of yours, promising that they'll turn it into two. It's just a ploy to make you take out your purse so that they can have a look at it and, if it's large and heavy enough—they have the skill of knowing, with just one glance, to the anna, what a purse contains—they'll follow you and kill you for your wealth. Your money's all they want.' The woman sewed the family gold that the child was taking to the holy shrine into the hem of his shirt, so that it would not be detected by thieves and rogues. His purse contained only a few annas, just enough for tea to drink with the food she had prepared for him to take on his pilgrimage.

"He had been traveling for but a day when he came upon the Hindu magicians by the roadside. He heard the damaru and flute, saw the men and boys dressed as sadhus and yogis, and stopped to watch them perform with cups and balls. Delighted, he laughed when the ball of cloth disappeared from beneath the coconut shell, where he was so sure it was. Conjuring a coin from thin air with a snap of the fingers, one of the magicians handed the money to the boy, had him close his hand around it and, when the child opened his fist, two coins were there. 'Do you have a coin, my boy?' the magician asked. 'If you do, I'll double it for you!' Smiling happily, young Shah Pir spoke to the magicians: 'Since my blessed mother has explained to me that magicians want money so badly that they would even kill a child for it, I know that magicians must be very poor. I'm taking gold to a holy shrine so that it can be given to the poor in keeping with our most holy duty, charity. But now that I have met you, there's no need for such a journey. Holiness is not in any shrine but that eternal one within our heart. Holiness is in giving what we have to the poor.'

"As he spoke he tore open the hem of his shirt. The magicians saw the gold fall onto the dirt and watched with amazement as Shah Pir picked up the coins and then, still smiling, distributed the wealth equally among them. 'Multiply those coins and keep the profits if you wish for wealth in this world,' the child said. 'But give the coins to creatures poorer than yourself if you long for glory in Paradise. Remember the true meaning of "*faqīr.*" ' Overwhelmed by the boy's goodness, charity, and honesty, the magicians fell at his feet and took him as their teacher and guru. Thus we became Muslims. We used to be thieves, now we're honest. Because we're honest, we're still poor." Shankar tried to restrain the laugh that would accuse the magician of a lie.

Naseeb proudly calls himself a Madari, in popular usage the general name for various Muslim castes of street performers, including not only the Maslets, but also Kalakars, Qalandars, and others, names that suggest an alliance with, or origin in, Sufi orders. Ja'far Sharif's early nineteenth-century attempt to explain India to Europeans includes a discussion of Madaris: "The term is usually applied to any 'unattached' religious beggar who smokes drugs to excess. . . . They are by religion half Hindus and half Musalmans. . . . Some of them are jugglers. . . . [They] place an earthen pot without a bottom on their heads and put fire in it, on which they lay a frying-pan and cook cakes. They are one of the disreputable Orders of begging Faqirs" (*Islam in India*). Ja'far describes a performance by the Madari magician Angithi Shah during the Muharram festival of a trick that I saw Kareem Baksh do over one hundred fifty years later: "He walks about carrying a chafing dish, a fragment of an earthen pot held on the palm of his hand, containing live coals in which he heats one end of an iron chain while the other end, fixed on a rope, hangs by his side. . . . He holds up the chain by the rope, dips it in oil, which suddenly blazes up on the hot part, to the surprise of the onlookers who wonder that he is not burnt by carrying the fire. This he manages to do without danger by filling the bottom of the potsherd with a mixture of the pulp of aloes and cow dung covered with ashes, which remains cool and prevents the dish from burning his hand." In Gujarat in the seventeenth century, Jean-Baptiste Tavernier watched some jugglers perform the same trick, a version of a real religious austerity done as an entertainment for the English president of the district: "The first thing they did was to kindle a large fire, and heat iron chains to redness; these they wound around their bodies, making believe that they experienced some pain, but not really receiving any injury" (*Travels in India*).

A nineteenth-century survey of North Indian castes identified the Madaris as "one of the Beshara or unorthodox orders of Muhammadan Faqirs who take their name from the famous saint of Zinda Shah Madar of Makanpur. . . . The Madaris of Northern India have no real connection with the genuine Sufi sects. . . . The fact seems to be that the Indian Madaris were established in imitation of the Hindu Jogis and Sannyasis. . . . They seldom pray or keep fasts, and use *bhang* freely as a beverage." The earnest government ethnographer distinguished the itinerant performers from the religiously oriented caste: "Others, who are perhaps different from the true Madaris, go about with performing bears or monkeys or snakes and are jugglers and eaters of fire. They are wild looking people and rather resemble Nats and their vagrant brethren" (William Crooke, *Tribes and Castes of the North-Western Provinces and Oudh*).

As traditionally nonpastoral nomads (at least until the establishment of Shadipur), the Madari jugglers, acrobats, bear handlers, monkey trainers, and magicians pride themselves in having a richer, freer life than the more sedentary members of the lower castes within the Indian social hierarchy, who are ever vulnerable to the floods and droughts that continuously ravage India. Chand Baba explained that when he was a child, they—not only the magicians, but the puppeteers, bards, acrobats, and animal trainers as well—would follow the seasons:

"We'd show up in a village after a harvest or during the marriage season. Then there was plenty of work. Until recently the police left us alone in the cities. We used to make good money. When I was a child my father and I would walk through the streets of the residential districts, where the big houses were. I'd play the damaru and children, called to the windows by the drum, would see us. We'd be invited in to perform in the courtyards of the big homes. We'd do the Mango Trick and the mother would give us a lot of money."

The Maslets with whom I spoke distinguished themselves from the bear and monkey trainers who are seen, by themselves and others, as pariahs; they aligned themselves with the puppeteers and bards. "We're artists. We're actors. The magic show is a dramatic performance."

That drama, whether it is performed for aesthetic or criminal ends, was presumably once liturgical. The apotropaic function of the rite that the drama imitated gave way to a new social function—entertainment. And in the entertainment, the parody of a religious activity, enough of the images and actions of the rite have been maintained to create the ambivalence in the mind of the audience which, for the magician, is the source of that audience's willingness or eagerness to pay. Passing the hat or basket-top does not bring in the kind of money that is made by the sale of magic rings, amulets, and spells. So, while the conjurer-entertainer lampoons the magician-sorcerer (and so his audience laughs at the parody of the mantra recitation, "yantru-tantru-jālajāla-mantru"), he also makes sure the observers suspect the magic might be real (and so there is silence and terror when, with his son lying on the ground, tongueless and vomiting blood, the magician demands two rupees from each of the onlookers). The crucial suspicion is generated through symbols—the props of the magician, his costume, his language, and his tricks.

While previously, as attested by literary and pictorial sources, the magician dressed as a renouncer, a yogi or sadhu, and his son as the chela, now, since the conversion to Islam, the magicians wear kurta, pajama, or lungi. Now he disguises himself as a sorcerer who is disguising himself as an ordinary person. "Some of the people think," Naseeb laughed, "that, after the magic show, I change out of my clothes and into a loincloth, so that I can return to the cremation grounds. They suspect I'm a fakir-baba or yogi-baba and that I've put on these clothes so that I can mix unnoticed with everyday people." To maintain that suspicion, there is always some symbol present—the rosary of rudrākṣa beads around his neck or the ashes on his forehead for a Hindu audience, for his Muslim onlookers, the lace skullcap that implies that he has made the pilgrimage to Mecca.

The magician's peacock feathers, as carried by conjurers for centuries, are Skanda's, the patron deity of thieves and conjurers, associated with exorcisms and other magical practices; the flute that the magician plays is Krishna's; and the hourglass damaru with which, like the bear handlers, monkey trainers, and snake

FIGURE 3. *Street Magicians*. Reprinted from Milbourne Christopher's *Panorama of Magic* (New York, 1962); courtesy of Dover Publications.

charmers, he calls his crowd, is Shiva's. And because it's the magician's drum, Kabir says, Shiva plays it, "beats his drum to roll out the show," to show with that show that he, the god, is a magician, "duping gods and men and sages, baffling everyone in the house. . . . The magic is false, the magician true" (*Bijak*). Establishing the drum as a magic object, Naseeb moves it spellbindingly around a volunteer's clasped hands, and they can't be pulled apart, waves it ceremonially over a decapitated body to effect the recapitation, beats it liturgically before producing some startling, wonderful metamorphosis. "This is Mahadeo's drum!" The magic drum is an ancient image: "If you beat upon this side of the drum your enemies will run away from you; but if you strike the other side they will become your constant friends" (*Dadhivāhana-Jātaka*).

In the same *Jātaka* there is a magic gem that enables its owner to levitate, and just as the magic show always begins with the beating of the drum, so it always ends with the sale of such gems, blessed by the magician and set in rings or amulets. Attributing the restoration of a severed head to a body to the power of the jewel in the ring, the magician announces: "Ten rupees! Only ten rupees and it will keep all your troubles far away." The pitch works by playing upon a notion of a "ring-*śakti*" that is firmly established in that aspect of consciousness which is fashioned by tradition: a certain King Vinitamati was battling a Yaksha "and, when he was on the point of cutting off the Yaksha's head with his sword, the imperiled imp, speaking in a plaintive voice, begged for mercy. Once spared, the

Yaksha gave Vinitamati his own ring. The gem in it possessed the power of averting all calamities associated with the seasons—plague, drought, and flooding rains, rats, locusts, and foreigners" (*Kathāsaritsāgara* 12:72). A magician, a *vidyā-dhara*, gave a ring to the exiled lover-prince Avimarika: "Wear this ring upon your right ring-finger and you'll be invisible; wear it on the left and you'll be seen again" (*Avimārika* of Bhasa, act 4).

"This power," Naseeb and the other magicians say, "I gained at the cremation grounds." The macabre claim associates the magicians with the vanishing Aghoris and vanished Kapalikas, those Tantric ascetics reputedly versed in dark magic, in whose rites blood, alcohol, and flesh are necessary. The association and implied affinity is amplified by the use and presence of bones and skulls in any demonstration of street magic. The power of magic is a grace attained by one who knows death, who has confronted horror, and gone beyond terror and disgust by inverting those vulnerabilities into ecstasy and dispassion. Naseeb, his eyes like burning coals, his laugh full of an ecstatic scorn, anoints his monkey skull with blood, and when he squeezes a lime over it, the ground beneath the skull bursts into flames. The horror is exquisite misdirection, delectably grisly and gruesome, and it's a convention that was well established at the beginning of the century: "As a general rule the native conjurer begins his performance by introducing the monkey's skull. Taking this in his left hand and holding it close to the left ear, he calls on it to exercise the greatest care in guarding its secrets and in performing the tricks, for, be it noted, it is the monkey's skull which produces the effect, and not the performer!—at least, so the onlookers are given to understand" (Elbiquet, *Supplementary Magic*).

One of the magicians from Ludhiana, performing in Kashmir, had fixed a monkey skull on top of a pole that was planted in the ground both as a sign to attract an audience and a focal point around which to arrange that crowd. The image was redolent of the *khaṭvānga*, the skull-crested club or staff that is carried by Shiva, the Kapalika yogis who have emulated the god, and the sorcerers who claim to have the god's terrible power. The club or staff, like the damaru drum and water-bearing *kamaṇḍalu*, are religious accoutrements that have been profaned into the standard props of the magic show. The street conjurer uses the wand to turn over the cups in the traditional Cups and Balls routine, to secure and cover objects palmed in his hand, and to point at things and thereby misdirect the attention of his audience. The staff or wand traditionally held by the magician symbolizes, according to the *Kauśikasūtras* (47.12–22), the weapon of Indra, the prototypical magician—his *vajra*, or thunderbolt, the instrument that could be used to kill an enemy or bring the fecundating rains. Through symbolization, the earthly holy man and, in emulation of him, the performing conjurer absorb the divine power of the heavenly magician. Each time Naseeb touches his apparently empty clay pot with his wand, the reddish vessel miraculously pours out another gush of clear, fresh water. "Ganga water," the magician smiles.

It's an old trick accomplished with a gimmicked lota bowl and believed in through the association of the bowl with the renouncer's *kamaṇḍalu*. Bengali magicians performed it in the Moghul court for Jahangir: "They brought a large ewer, which in my presence they filled full of water. They reversed the ewer with its face downward, spilling the water to the last drop: they turned the vessel with its face upwards, and it appeared as full of water as at first. And this they could have repeated a hundred times over with the same effect; which I could not but consider equally curious and unaccountable" (*Tūzuk-i-Jahangīrī*). They performed a variant of the trick with empty jars which, when covered and then uncovered, each contained some eatable sweet or fruit—a trick that Naseeb does with a gimmicked tin can.

Reverend Hobart Caunter, a missionary in India in the mid-nineteenth century, saw the trick during a performance of Indian conjurers in the court of a maharaja, a spectacle arranged for both Indian nobles and European visitors: "One of the men, taking a larger earthen vessel, with a capricious mouth, filled it with water and turned it upside down, when all the water flowed out; but the moment it was placed with the mouth upwards, it always became full" (cited by Frost, *Lives of the Conjurers*).

P. C. Sorcar brought the trick to the stage, named it Waters of India, and innovated a now conventional patter that retrieved ancient associations. In his performance, each pour from the lota bowl was identified as the production of water from one of the sacred rivers of India, the six riparian manifestations of the goddess. Seeing it performed in the summer heat by Naseeb, with the threat of drought, I could feel the antiquity of it, of the roots of performance magic in endeavors to produce rain with sympathetic magic. By pouring water out of what is empty, the heavens are prompted to do the same. "Do as I do," is a stock phrase in magic, in both rite and show.

The antiquity of the Waters of India trick is suggested by a reference in the *Jātakas* to a magic pot: "If there's anything you want, just turn it over—a great river will pour out of it! The water from this lota bowl could flood a whole kingdom" (*Dadhivāhana-Jātaka*). The motif of the inexhaustible lota bowl, enacted in the magic, occurs throughout Indian folk literature: "Put your hand into the jug," a Yaksha tells an astounded human being, "and you'll obtain anything you want" (*Kathāsaritsāgara* 10.57). Two Asuras, sons of one named "Magic," fight over a magic wand and a vessel that has the wondrous quality of being immediately filled with whatever sort of food or drink its owner desired (*Kathāsaritsāgara* 1.3). This cornucopian vessel, whether heard about in a story or seen in a spectacle, has its psychological appeal in a fantasy, a recapitulation of infantile, magical perceptions of the world. The bowl is a metaphor for the maternal breast (just as the breast in Sanskrit poetry is inevitably a "jug") that, during a child's infancy, always refilled itself when emptied, as if in response to need, the thirst which is a will to live. Pleasure then was unlimited. The magic show intimates that early pleasure, retrieves it for a moment on the roadside, seems to promise that, despite the insistence of reality to the contrary, such regeneration and unqualified pleasure are possible. A magical reality supplants the nonmagical one; there is a momentary triumph of metaphors over what they represent and a transient suspension of the mature faculties. The child always has a role in Indian street magic—he is the sacrifice. Buy a ring from him, a souvenir. Only ten rupees. Wear it on your right ring-finger, and to the degree that it returns you to your own childhood, the magic shows and illusions of the past, you'll be invisible; wear it on the left, and you'll be seen, here and now, again.

Just as the magician's props are meant to suggest an apotheosis, so his language, incomprehensible and mysterious, establishes his esoteric power. *Omne obscurum pro magnifico.* With sounds the magician-performer further imitates, parodies, or poses as the real magician, that knower of the *mantra-śāstra*, the formulae, phrases, and syllables that people believe have a real power to effect or to attain things, worldly things or even liberation from the world. These utterances, devoid of all semantic meaning or power, are thought to have meaning and power to the degree to which they contain and activate the essence of the deity. The dynamic is understood in terms of a conviction that all correspondences in the cosmos are actual and ultimate, and that all phenomena represent merely the temporal and spatial manifestation within a particular of some more fundamental reality. A god can be a god or a person, an image or a sound. Magic in India involves the manipulation of these images and repetitions of these sounds. The magician-entertainer says *"gilli-gilli-gilli"* or *"yantru-mantru-jālajāla-tantru,"* both to invoke the mystique of *mantra-śāstra* and to parody the tradition, in the same way that the Western magician's "hocus-pocus," a profanation of *"hoc est corpus [meum],"* is both serious and not, simultaneously mocking the Eucharist and drawing upon its psychologically established powers. The word *jādū* can mean hocus-pocus or mumbo-jumbo: "Pray sir," asks a barber in the nineteenth-century *Panduranga Hari or Memoires of a Hindoo* of William Browne Hockley, "is that Sanscrit or what language?" And the narrator's reply is: "May be it is jadoo."

While *yantru-mantru-tantru* evokes a fear of Tantric forces, so *Bismillah,* the sound that begins all but one of the *suras* of the Qur'an ("In the name of God, the Merciful, the Compassionate"), shouted or whispered by the magician, provokes awe to no less a degree as it suggests the powers of *sīmiyā,* Islamic natural magic, a tradition that, despite condemnation by Islamic law, flourishes and includes both high, white magic and low, black magic—*jādū.* The Muslim magician in India is traditionally an exorcist and fortune-teller, a source for magic charms, amulets, and rings; he has the ability to detect a thief and retrieve stolen goods, to procure revenge on an enemy and influence decisions at court. Naseeb and the other magicians of Shadipur imply, with their props, amulets, and language, that they are real magicians. Naseeb will swear by any god that he has gleaned this knowledge from Muslim *murshids* and Tantric sadhus, gained his powers from both the tombs of Islamic saints and the burning grounds of the Hindus.

The power of the god that the magician has earned or stolen from the places of death to display in the streets and bazaars is essentially a cosmogonic power. Many of the traditional, conventional, and most ancient of the tricks in the street magician's repertoire recapitulate Indian cosmogonies. The world itself is created by magic: "The Magician creates the whole universe and by the same magic beings are captivated within it" (*Śvetāśvatara Upaniṣad* 4.9). The magician rec-reates images of what the Magician creates. Thus the dramaturgist Bharata explains that Brahma, the creator, is the deity who presides over the aesthetic sentiment of wonder, the *adbhuta-rasa.* "Wondrous indeed is the creation of the world," cries the voice in an anonymous stanza cited as an example of that sentiment: "This is so very bizarre! Amazing! . . . The creation of the world is out of this world!" (*Kāvyaprakaśa* of Manmatta, citation 43, after 4.29).

The production of an egg ex nihilo by sleight of hand reenacts one of the most ancient of Indian cosmogonies, the Vedic myth of the Hiranyagarba, the golden egg—nonbeing turned into being, which became an egg from which Brahma, the Creator, was hatched. I saw Chand Baba perform it in the park in Delhi in 1987, just as it was performed by Indian magicians, no doubt Chand Baba's forefathers, at the Franco-British exhibition of 1908. The Egg Bag, con-ventional in both Western and Indian magic, is a variant of the inexhaustible pitcher, the Waters of India, but, in addition to producing something from noth-ing, it also vanishes things back into the void and transforms one thing into another. In the show everything is a symbol. At once ever-full and ever-empty, the symbolic egg bag represents the matrix of creation, preservation, destruction, and recreation.

The Egg Bag Trick was shown to Jahangir: "They took a small bag, and having first shewn that it was entirely empty, one of them put his hand into the bag, and on withdrawing his hand again out came two game-cocks" (*Tūzuk-i-Jahangīrī*). After the cocks put on a fight for the great Moghul, they were covered with a sheet; when the sheet was removed, the cocks had turned into partridges; covered again, the partridges became black snakes; they were covered again, and when the sheet was removed, there was nothing.

Similarly a baffled Reverend Caunter, well over a hundred years ago, re-ported: "A large basket was produced under which was put a lean, hungry Pariah female dog; after a lapse of about a minute, the basket was removed, and she appeared with a litter of seven puppies. These were again covered, and, upon raising the magic basket, a goat was presented to our view; this was succeeded by a pig in the full vigour of existence, but which, after being covered the usual time, appeared with its throat cut; it was, however, shortly restored to life under the mystical shade of the wicker covering. What rendered these sudden changes so extraordinary was that no one stood near the basket but the juggler, who raised it and covered the animals with it. When he concluded, there was nothing to be seen under it; and what became of the different animals which had figured in this singular deception was a question that puzzled us all" (cited by Frost, *Lives of the Conjurers*).

Transformations in nature are the basis of magic, and magic the basis of those transformations. Plucking a mosquito out of the air, putting it in a basket where it turned into a pigeon, placing that bird back into that magic basket where it was metamorphosed into a little girl named Salma, Chand Baba performed his version of an old story: "Once upon a time there was a hermit who found a young mouse that had escaped from the claws of a kite. Out of pity for it and by the power of his asceticism he turned the mouse into a maiden," whom he then raised into womanhood (*Kathāsaritsāgara* 10:57).

An apprehension of the mystery of transformation, of appearance and disappearance, is the appeal of the Magic Album, an Indian trick that I first saw at the Hollywood Magic Shop when I bought a version of it for my son. "Look," said the boy, then about Ayasan's age, after only a few minutes of practice, "I've got a coloring book here." He flipped the pages to show me Mickey Mouse, Donald Duck, Goofy, Snow White, and other Walt Disney characters outlined in black, waiting to be colored in. "I like to color," he continued the patter, "but it takes a lot of time and I'm pretty busy, so I use magic to do my coloring quickly. See these crayons?" He showed a clear plastic box of Crayolas, did a magic pass, and the crayons disappeared from their container. "They're in the book," he said as he began to flip the pages once more, to show me that, yes indeed, the figures were all fully colored in.

When I saw Iqbal perform the same trick in the park, watched him, with a puff of breath, a pass of his magic ring, and a "*yantru-tantru-jālajāla-mantru*" for good measure, fill an empty notebook with writing, I assumed that it was a Western item, a gimmick that had found its way into the Indian repertoire in modern times. My supposition was undermined by an account in Jahangir's memoirs of the trick as performed for the Moghul court by a troupe of Bengali magicians over three hundred years earlier but not very far from where I myself witnessed it: "They produced a blank volume of the purest white paper, which was placed in my hands to shew that it contained neither figures nor coloured pages whatever, of which I satisfied myself and all around." And then, as magically as Mickey and Goofy were colored in, depictions of erotic postures appeared on the blank pages. "One of the men took the volume in hand, and the first opening exhibited a page of bright red, sprinkled with gold. . . . The next turn presented a leaf of beautiful azure, sprinkled in the same manner, and exhibiting on the margins numbers of men and women in various [sexual] attitudes." The great Moghul was dazzled. "In short, at every turn of the leaf a different colour, scene, and action was exhibited, such as was indeed most pleasing to behold. Of all the performances, this latter of the volume of paper was that which afforded

me the greatest delight, so many beautiful pictures and extraordinary changing
having been brought under view, that I must confess my utter inability to do
justice in this description. I can only add that although I had frequently in my
father's court witnessed such performances, never did I see or hear of any
execution so wonderfully strange as was exhibited with apparent facility by these
seven jugglers" (*Tūzuk-i-Jahangīrī*).

The same illusion was shown in reverse to Maksim Gorky by a Hindu that
he met in the Caucasus: "He asked me whether I would like to see pictures of
Indian cities. He gave me his album and looking at me said: 'Please look at these
pictures of Indian cities.' The album contained polished brass sheets on which
were reproduced beautiful views of different cities, temples and other views of
India. I looked over the entire album, alternately studying the pictures. Then I
closed the album and returned it to the Hindu. He smiled and said: 'Well, you
have seen views of India'; then he blew at the album and returned it into my hand
inviting me to look at it again. I opened it and to my surprise found only polished
plates without any pictures whatsoever. These Hindus are indeed a remarkable
people" (reminiscence of Maksim Gorky by Nicholas Roerich, quoted in P. C.
Sorcar, *Sorcar on Magic*). All that I have learned about the dynamics of magic
suggests to me that Gorky's recollection that he himself thumbed the pages of the
book is wrong. One of the methods of magic is the manipulation of memory. With
seemingly insignificant moves forgotten, as we try to reconstruct what we have
seen, we ourselves create the illusion; the magician merely encourages that.

"What's written in the notebook?" I asked Shankar, who, unable to decipher
the Arabic script, asked Iqbal. The magician smiled. It was selections from the
Qur'an. The miraculous appearance of the uncreated and everlasting word of
God in an empty book recapitulated the revelatory foundation of Islam. Religion
sanctified the trick, informed it with mystery, and invested it with power.

My assumption that Iqbal's trick had been Western in origin has been the
hypothesis of many Western magicians about Indian magic in general. While
questions of origin and influence are, in the case of magic, as in the case of so
many other aspects of folklore and Indology, difficult to answer with any real
certainty, I found it tempting to accept the explanation of The Incredible Mayadhar, a man who, living up to his chosen stage name, is generally not a very
reliable source of truth: "The Magic Album, purely Indian in origin, like the Egg
Bag and Waters of India, found its way to Europe with the gypsies. They performed these traditional Indian items to make people believe they had some
mystic knowledge, a belief, believe me please, upon which the gypsies capitalized
by charging for fortune-telling. Some of our tricks, like the Sands of India, are
only just now becoming popular in the West."

I ordered the Sands of India from Tannen's catalogue. In a box that was
decorated with a picture of a turbaned Hindu, there were three bags of colored
sand that could be stirred into a bowl of water. When a member of the audience

called out a color, the magician could reach into the bowl and produce a handful of sand of that color. And the sand was dry. The magician Kellar described witnessing the trick in the last century in India; Linga Singh, performing it in the early part of this century, stressed its Indianness; Doug Henning, the disciple of Maharishi Mahesh Yogi, performed it on national television. The magicians of Shadipur, who claim that their recipe for the preparation of the sands, the process for coating each grain with wax, has been handed down to them from antiquity, do a variant of the trick in which the magician, having eaten white, black, red, yellow, green, and blue sugar, spits out whatever color sugar is demanded by members of his audience.

The Sands of India, demonstrating the ordering of chaos in the retrieval of this sand or that out of the murky mixture, reiterates, before our very eyes, the primordial churning of the ocean by the gods and demons, the cosmogonic myth that celebrates the defeat of the demons and the coronation of Indra, tutelary deity of magic. The props of the magic show are there—the rope that is a snake, the staff that is a mountain, the wand and water gourd of the ascetic, the magic gem Kaustubha; and when the terrible poison Halahala is spewed from the heads of the serpent, Shiva, lord of siddhas, perfect exemplar of yogic powers, drinks that poison as if it were nectar. When the ambrosial drink of immortality is finally churned out of the ocean, Vishnu, by means of his skill at "deluding magic," vanishes it from sight (*Rāmāyaṇa* 1.45.15–44).

Among the many precious treasures that were churned from the cosmic ocean was the Parijata tree, a magical, wish-granting tree, first planted by Indra in his heaven and later stolen by Krishna, that could produce any requested fruit or flower on its boughs. The mythology of the Parijata tree was enacted by the Bengali magicians who appeared before Jahangir: "They stated that of any tree that should be named they would set the seed in the earth, and that I should immediately witness the extraordinary result." When one of the nobles named a mulberry and the magicians in various places "put some seeds in the ground, they recited among themselves in some cabalistic language unintelligible to standers-by ['*yantru-tantru-jālajāla-mantru*'?], when instantly a plant was seen springing from each of the ten places. . . . In the same manner they produced a mango, an apple tree, a cypress, a pineapple, a fig tree, an almond . . . " and Jahangir tasted the fruit of each of the trees which, delicious as each fruit was, "increased the astonishment already excited." They then made beautiful exotic birds appear in the foliage to sing wonderful songs to the emperor and then, at the end of the show, the trees withered as in autumn and returned to the earth. "I can only observe, that if the circumstances which I have now described had not happened in my own presence," the great Moghul says in wonder, "I could never have believed that they had any existence in reality" (*Tūzuk-i-Jahangīrī*).

The trick, conventionally performed with a mango seed, is one of the most ancient of all Indian illusions. One morning, while making his rounds, seeking alms and offering the teaching, the Buddha encountered a royal gardener who was taking a large and wonderful mango to the king, a fruit so big, luscious, and sweet that the devoted gardener, out of veneration for the sage, was prompted to give it to him, the Buddha, instead. Receiving it, the teacher seated himself and ate the delectable fruit, after which he called Ananda, his disciple, to his side and told him to give the stone of the mango back to the gardener to plant. And "when the gardener dug a hole in the ground, placed the seed in it and covered it over with earth, all at once the mango seed burst open—roots shot down into the ground, and a red stem immediately came out of the earth and rose high into the air. A crowd watched it grow hundreds and hundreds of feet—flowers burst into bloom and fruit ripened upon it. The wind began to blow so that the sweet, delicious fruit fell from the branches. And then the monks of the order came and they ate the wonderful fruit of the mango tree" (*Sarabhamiga-Jātaka*).

Ananda himself, the master-magician's apprentice, did his own version of the trick: "He placed a golden vessel on the ground, filled it with fragrant water and soil. A merchant dropped the seed of a bo tree into the vessel and, all at once, before the eyes of the gathered crowd, a sapling grew." There at the monastery of Jetavana, beneath the spreading branches of that tree, grown from the seed of the very tree under which the Buddha had his great awakening, disciples found solace and protection while the Buddha was away. This was the inauguration of the Bo Tree Festival (*Kāliṅgabodhi-Jātaka*).

Another performance of it is described in the fifth-century chronicle of Sri Lanka, the *Mahavaṃsa:* "When the Thera was seated the king gave him a mango fruit. When the Thera had eaten it he gave the kernel to the king to plant. The king himself planted it there and over it, that it might grow, the Thera washed his hands. In that same moment a shoot sprouted forth from the kernel and grew little by little to a tall tree bearing leaves and fruit" (15.41–44).

The Mango Tree Trick was among the most popular magical entertainments of the seventeenth century. The descriptions of it by many European travelers of that period indicate that the trick was most often presented as an act of real magic, a display of the magician's ability to modulate time. A group of magicians, as rendered by John Fryer, "presented a Mock-Creation of a Mango Tree, arising from the Stone in a short space (which they did Hugger-Mugger, being very careful to avoid being discovered) with Fruit Green and Ripe; so that a Man must stretch his Fancy, to imagine it Witchcraft; though the common sort think no less" (*A New Account of East India and Persia 1672–1681*).

A less skeptical John Ovington attributed the Mango Tree illusion to black magic because "a Gentleman who had pluckt one of the Mangoes, fell sick upon it, and was never well as long as he kept it 'til he consulted a *Bramin* for his Health, who prescrib'd his only Remedy would be the restoring of the Mango, by which he was restor'd to his Health again" (*Voyage to Suratt*).

Jean-Baptiste Tavernier, earlier in the same century, watched the Mango Trick performed by magicians "who travel from place to place with their wives and children," in Gujarat: "Having taken a small piece of stick, and planting it in the ground, they asked one of the company what fruit he wished to have. He replied that he desired mangoes, and then one of the conjurers, covering himself with a sheet, stooped to the ground five or six times. . . . He cut himself under his arm-pits with a razor, and anointed the piece of wood with his blood. At each time he raised himself, the stick increased under the eye, and at the third time it put forth branches and buds. At the fourth time the tree was covered with leaves, and at the fifth we saw the flowers themselves." An English chaplain who was present at the magic show, Tavernier explains, "protested that he was unable to consent that Christians should be present at such spectacles, and when he saw that from a piece of dry wood these people in less than half an hour had caused a tree of four or five feet in height, with leaves and flowers, as in springtime, to appear, insisted on breaking it, and proclaimed loudly that he would never administer the communion to any one who witnessed such things in the future" (*Travels in India*). The Episcopalian anger over the indulgence of native magic, the display of devilishly non-Christian powers, was no doubt justified in that the magicians themselves would hardly be the ones to excuse the spectacle with an admission that the magic was just a trick. When, in the last century, a fakir named "Covind-samy" performed a version of the Mango Tree Trick for Louis Jacolliot, using a papaw seed which the then chief justice in the French East Indies had himself chosen, the magician explained that it, like all magic, was performed by the *pitṛs*—those spirits of deceased ancestors who are honored in rites by the pious. Entering into communication with them, the magician prompts them to reveal their numenous power (*Occult Science in India*).

The Mango Tree Trick has been just as unimpressive to Westerners, particularly Western magicians, as it has been dazzling and amazing to others: "The Mango Tree Trick is one of the many disappointments that await those who expect from the Indian juggler something wonderful" (Elbiquet, *Supplementary Magic*); "Perhaps of all the Indian Tricks I saw, the Mango Tree was the real disappointment" (Will Ayling, *Oriental Conjuring and Magic*); "To my mind it is amazing what a spurious reputation the [Mango Tree] trick has gained. From a technical point of view, it is possibly the worst performance of the Indian conjuror" (Lionel Branson, *Indian Conjuring*).

The power and impact of the trick, and perhaps of all magic, is in the patter. There is the bewitching that the Western magicians could not enjoy. Kareem Baksh, taking his time, blending obscene jokes about the uterine mango with scatological ones about fertilizer, lacing that mixture with paraphrastic profundities from Kabir or Tulsi Das, spicing it with cynical jibes, offered up the allegorical brew, a burlesque epiphany, a seasonal drama, an ancient ritual enaction of a living mythology. To see him perform it was to see something done as and how it has been done, crudely and simply, slowly and with much ado, for literally thousands of years and figuratively more.

The Mango Tree Trick, a precursor to the illusions created by time-lapse photography, accelerates time to yield a supernatural view of a natural phenomenon. The magic is in nature. The miracle is the growth from the seed, the burgeoning of the plant, the flowering, and the giving of fruit. But, because the trick takes so long to happen naturally, we are not, without the help of the magician, struck with the appropriate wonder.

The inversion of the Mango Tree Trick, the deceleration of time, is the effect of the trick of being buried alive—the magician remains inhumed for days, months, even years, as if it were for moments, by slowing down or stopping his bodily processes.

By the end of the seventeenth century, through the popular accounts of so many travelers to India, the European reading public was well aware of Indian fakirs. One feat, whether it was accomplished by superhuman power or subterfuge, playing upon imagination's anxiousness to outwit death, particularly attracted attention—"Buried Alive!" In the mid-seventeenth century, there were reports from India that a group of workmen, digging outside the city of Amritsar, had uncovered the body of a holy man. "As they later told investigators, the corpse seemed remarkably well preserved and eventually showed signs of life. Though frightened, the workmen helped the holy man regain consciousness and, as soon as he could speak, asked for details of his experience. He replied that his name was Ramaswamy and he had been buried for more than a hundred years. A short time later, he was questioned by the guru, scholar, and historian, Arjun Singh, who discovered that Ramaswamy did indeed seem to have a remarkable knowledge of events that had occurred a century before" (recounted by Edward Claflin, *Street Magic*).

In the early eighteenth century a surveyor for the French government named Boileau, a scientist through and through, sent a wondrous story home of a fakir who had defied death: "The man is said, by long practice, to have acquired the art of holding his breath by shutting the mouth, and stopping the interior opening of the nostrils with his tongue; he also abstains from solid food for some days previous to his interment, so that he may not be inconvenienced by the contents of his stomach, while put up in his narrow grave; and, moreover, he is sewn up in a bag of cloth, and the cell is lined with masonry, and floored with cloth, that the white ants and other insects may not easily be able to molest him. The place in which he was buried at Jaisulmer is a small building about twelve feet by eight, built of stone; and in the floor was a hole about three feet long, two and a half feet wide, and the same depth, of perhaps a yard deep, in which he was placed in a sitting posture, sewed up in his shroud, with his feet turned inward towards the stomach, and his hands also pointed inward toward the chest. Two heavy slabs of stone, five or six feet long, several inches thick, and broad enough to cover the mouth of the grave, so that he could not escape, were then placed over him, and I believe a little earth was plastered over the whole, so as to make the surface of the grave smooth and compact." The inhumation resembles the burial of holy renouncers. While the feat, for the Indian spectators of it, represents the ideal of being dead-in-life, being a *jivan-mukta*, for the Western spectators, the same trick represents an opposite ideal—being alive-in-death. Boileau described the exhumation: "He was taken out in a perfectly senseless state, his eyes closed, his hands cramped and powerless, his stomach shrunk very much, and his teeth jammed so fast together that they were forced to open his mouth with an iron instrument to pour a little water down his throat. He gradually recovered his senses and the use of his limbs; and when we went to see him he was sitting up, supported by two men, and conversed with us in a low, gentle tone of voice, saying we might bury him again for a twelvemonth, if we pleased" (cited by Frost, *Lives of the Conjurers*).

Frost, in relaying the reports of Boileau and others, was quick to disavow any superhuman power involved in the trick: "One of these fellows boasted that he would appear at Amandabant, a town about two hundred miles away from Surat, within fifteen days after being buried, ten feet deep, at the latter place. The Governor of Surat resolved to test the fellow's powers, and had a grave dug, in which the fakeer placed himself, stipulating that a layer of reeds should be interposed between his body and superincumbent earth, with a space of two feet between his body and the reeds. This was done, and the grave was then filled up, and a guard of soldiers placed at the spot to prevent trickery. A large tree stood ten or twelve yards from the grave, and beneath its shade several fakeers were grouped around a large earthen jar, which was filled with water. The officer of the guard, suspecting that some trick was to be played, ordered the jar to be moved, and on this being done by the soldiers, after some opposition on the part of the dirty fellows assembled around it, a shaft was discovered, with a subterranean gallery from its bottom to within two feet of the grave. The impostor was thereupon made to ascend, and a riot ensued in which he and several other persons were slain" (*Lives of the Conjurers*).

Though amply impressed by the physical feats of yogis, the magician Dunninger, like Frost before him, recounts performances of the Buried Alive Trick only to expose its methods: "I have seen Hindoo magicians, or so-called *fakirs*, throw themselves into a cataleptic state. In this form of artificial death, they were placed in coffins, and buried deep below the ground. In this condition they would remain for days, after which they would be dug out again, and they resurrected themselves, to remain for a length of time further in this universe of the living." After divulging the Indian magician's reliance on a hidden breathing tube or a secret escape hatch, the Western magician added that "one cannot truly blame the Oriental for resorting to trickery, as in India this is his only form of livelihood" (*Complete Encyclopedia of Magic*).

FIGURE 4. *Buried Alive.* Reprinted from Samri Baldwin's *Secrets of Mahatma Land Explained* (New York, 1895).

The suspension of bodily processes, particularly the pulse and breath, is traditional and typical of yogic endeavors. That in India one is thought to gain merit and a share in the holy man's defiance of death by giving him money has made it a profitable trick for the magician to perform. But it's a dangerous way to make a living. So many magicians, holy men and conjurers alike, had apparently died while attempting it, that the Indian Government outlawed its performance in 1955.

"I would be performing it today if it were not illegal," the old stage magician who performed in the Western style said, and it led to a discussion of Houdini. "Death tried to trick him into trying to trick death and almost succeeded; but, no, Houdini backed off. That's the ultimate magic, the most perfect illusion—tricking death, the great escape—and, despite the law, I'll try it some day." The old man laughed. "When I was a child, when I saw those street magicians—the man and his son—I thought that they could accomplish anything. I would have bet that they could have played some sly tricks on death. That's when I decided to become a magician myself."

I was surprised when he disagreed with my conjecture that it was Houdini who first popularized the typically Indian Buried Alive Trick in the West. No, no, he shook his head, "It was another Western magician, another Jew in fact, a street magician, who made the illusion popular in the West. It was your very own Jesus Christ. He brought so many tricks back with him from his tour of India. But of all of them, that resurrection trick was the greatest, the one that has fooled the most people."

The magician stood, walked to the window, looked out into the streets for a moment, and then turned back to me. The silhouette spoke softly: "Jesus Christ had no son. That was the problem. He had no one to whom to teach his magic. Thus the real secret of the methods for the performance of the trick was lost in the West. That's the problem. The magician must have a son to carry on the tradition."

There was, I felt, a certain sadness in his voice, and I attributed it to the fact that he himself had no son.

Scene Four:

Cut-and-Restored

"I have no son," Muladeva said out loud. "I no longer have a son. You can't be a magician without a son. You can't perform. Without a son, I'm no one—I'm nothing. I'm dead."

Anangasena held the spittoon up to her mouth, spit the red betel juice, wiped her lips with the back of her hand, and smiled, "He'll be back."

"No, it's been a year," the magician answered, his words fading, so that finally only he could hear them. "He could have easily made it to Anga and back by now. He's not coming. I know it. He's left me. He's outgrown the basket. He's vanished."

"Help me," the prostitute said with a playful urgency she hoped would distract the magician. "Help me with my braid. Help me fix my hair. Help me to look beautiful."

"I no longer have a son," he said again. "Don't you understand what that means? He was supposed to go to my father. My father, my father! I haven't seen him for over two years. Is he still alive? Perhaps I have no father either."

Anangasena knelt before Muladeva and, pretending sulkiness, pouted: "You're not paying any attention to me. You're only thinking about yourself. What about me? I don't think you love me or that you ever have. You've been fooling me, playing little tricks on me. If you love me, you'll help me with my braid. Help me, please." She pushed a folded betel leaf between his lips and giggled.

Rising, he went to the window, looked at the pigeon in the cage there, poked his finger through the bars, and tried to make the sound that pigeons make while Anangasena fixed her braid herself.

Their silence was interrupted by the sudden commotion of Dhanamitra's excited entrance to the scene: "Unbelievable, amazing, my beloved—something unbelievable happened on the ghats today. Absolutely astounding. Listen. Shankaracharya was publicly challenged to a debate by the ritualist Mandana Mishra. The challenge was accepted, the debate begun and . . . oh, hello, Guruji! Hello Muladeva! I'm so happy to see you! As always to be sure! I've been looking for you. I want to show you some tricks. I've been practicing, practicing, practicing. Vamana couldn't guess in which hand I was holding the cowrie shell. I've made great progress since we last met. You'll see. I'm ready for a lesson tomorrow. I'm ready to learn that famous Rope Trick. Remember? You promised that someday you'd teach me the Rope Trick. I'm ready for it."

"You still have a lot to learn," Muladeva said in the appropriately stern manner of a guru, a tone that implied high standards tempered by great patience.

"I've already learned so many things," the perennial disciple answered with characteristically boyish enthusiasm, only to be interrupted by his teacher: "The only thing that you've learned in the last year is that my name is Muladeva, not Devamula."

The prostitute, sensing the cruelty of that blow to the heart of the merchant's son, tried to soften it: "Muladeva is teasing you. He was, just before you entered, in fact, speaking to me of the great progress you have made as a magician. I swear it's true."

Always hungry for such lies, Dhanamitra smiled. "Yes, I understand. Teachers, like fathers with their sons, must occasionally say rough things to test the dedication of their students. Hence Yajñavalkya was always taunting Shvetaketu. I'm honored by the praises, honored all the more because they were uttered behind my back and thus cannot be dismissed as mere flattery. I'll compose a Sanskrit stanza on that theme. Please come to my room tomorrow morning for our lesson. Please. Oh no, I'm sorry, not tomorrow. Don't come tomorrow. To-morrow is my vina lesson. Day after tomorrow. Come then. Will you come for sure? You missed our appointment last time."

Assuring the merchant's son that he would be there, the magician started to leave.

"No, no, don't go. You must stay. You must hear about what happened," Dhanamitra went on excitedly, turning back to Anangasena. "And you my be-loved, you who are to *Kāmaśastra* what Shankaracharya is to the *Upaniṣads*, you who are to sexual intercourse what Mandana Mishra is to Vedic sacrifice, you, to sustain this prolix for but a moment longer, who are to me what Indrani is to Indra, you, you in particular will be amazed and astounded, confounded or delighted, by what happened on the ghats today, for it has profound implications in terms of your own place in, and fulfillment of, the cosmic order of things. Listen, please listen, both of you. As I previously and in complete truthfulness explained, Mandana Mishra and Shankaracharya, the Mimamsaka and the Ve-dantin respectively, were about to enter into debate when the wife of Mandana Mishra suddenly appeared and laughed out loud, laughed at the great Shankaracharya—can you believe it?—and challenged him. And here, more or less, more less than more, is what she said: 'Because your knowledge of the world is incomplete, you are not worthy to debate my husband. Your perceptions are not valid inasmuch as you know nothing of the domain of *kāma*. You have no under-standing, rooted in either study of the *śāstra*s or in direct experience, of love or pleasure, desire or its fulfillment. Hence you cannot be considered wise, for wisdom is an omniscience of sorts, a knowledge not of parts but of a whole. Since, furthermore, *kāma* rules this world, and you, apparently and by your own admis-sion, are unaffected by *kāma*, that god or force, how can you presume to speak to beings in this world with any authority? You cannot speak about the renunciation of something of which you yourself have no experience, awareness, or knowledge.' She went on like that with greater philosophical eloquence than I myself, in all modesty and humility, can muster in this current state of intellectual ferment."

Dhanamitra turned to Muladeva: "Guruji, you who are to me what Ya-jñavalkya is to Shvetaketu, Kashyapa to Indra, and so forth, you will surely observe something of relevance to you and to magic, in this story—the woman has played a trick on the philosopher—a trick! Do you understand? Either Shan-karacharya has to admit that what she has said is true, leave it at that, and forfeit the debate; or, he must accept the challenge, in which case he is constrained to do just what I myself am doing in my own wonderful pursuit of fulfillment through education—to study the *Kāmaśāstra*, master the postures for sexual in-tercourse delineated therein with the same assiduousness that I myself have endeavored to learn them, an assiduousness no less than that which Patañjali applied to the mastery of all the postures of yoga."

The merchant's son turned back to Anangasena: "Perhaps he will select you to be his teacher! How wonderful that would be! Wonderful! You would be able to pass on to me metaphysical and epistemological insights gleaned during your amatory sessions with him! Oh, but I divert!"

He turned back to Muladeva: "The trick! Do you understand the trick? If he does this, if he indulges in sexual pleasures, even if he were to stringently practice holy semen retention, then he will no longer have the authority accorded to him on account of his purity and renunciation. His actions will contradict his philos-ophy or vice versa. Thus he will lose the debate. He will lose if he tries to win, no matter what he does!"

He looked back to Anangasena, then back to Muladeva, then back at the prostitute again, then back at the magician, then back at each one of them again, anxious for some reaction. Anangasena, finally realizing that he was finished, smiled. "That was a wonderful story! Bravo! And yes, I promise, yes I'll teach you every drop of wisdom that I am able to squeeze out of this Shankaracharya fellow if he comes to me to learn of love. And now, my beloved, you who are to me as the stallion to the mare, the bull to the cow, the bee to the flower . . ." She paused to look toward Muladeva and, with a slight tilt of the head and wink of the eye, signaled him to leave, then continued the patter that so amazed and enchanted her most generous client: "Now there are still things that I have to teach you on my own, so many things—techniques and truths, carnal mysteries more profound, I would say, and the wife of Mandana Mishra would certainly agree, than anything taught on the ghats by the Ganga."

Muladeva, leaving student and teacher alone, squatted on the floor in the gathering room next to Jihvika. The old bawd's naughty, wheezy laughter, scented with garlic, meat, and rum, turned into a fit of coughing. She tried to calm it with a gulp of the rum and then handed the jar to the magician: "Drink that. That stuff's magic, real magic, made by magic, and full of the magic power." She coughed again, spat, drooled, and cackled, "Let it work on you. Haha! You need it. You're tormented and I know why—you're in love with my daughter, and you can't stand it that she's in there with that boy, doing exactly what you imagine she's doing. Haha!" The wizened bawd, her swollen yellow eyes rolling in their sockets, laughed again, coughed again, gulped more rum, and drooled again.

"You're wrong," the magician defended himself. "I don't care what Anangasena does or whom she does it with."

"Listen," the shrew demanded, "I'm never wrong about anything. You see these lines on my face, my neck, my arms, all over my body? Haha! Each one of these lines is a notch to help me keep track, one line for each lover I've had. You couldn't count high enough to calculate the number of these wrinkles, deep or faint, long or short, depending on what kind of lover left it. And from each and every man—king or pariah, pandit or moron, priest or thug, poet or potter (the list would take a month to make)—I've learned at least one thing, most times more, many, many more. The lines on my body, the testimony that I'm no fool, form the script in which, upon the leaves of a book, parts of my body, there's a story written, a tale of lies and truth. I'm an expert on that—I know the truth, and the truth is what I tell."

She laughed at Muladeva and he at her as he took a swig of her black molasses rum.

"You can laugh at me," she snarled, "but that won't change the truth. I know about you. I can see what you're trying to conceal in your palm. I've looked into your bag of tricks. Haha! I know you. You used to be a magician. But now you're nothing but a parasite, just a common sycophant, like that nasty dwarf, like the vina teacher, like fat Gomukha, and the rest of those poverty-stricken parasites who hover around that little man from Gujarat with the big purse. Look at all the hungry flies buzzing around the steaming little piece of shit."

"Like your daughter," Muladeva taunted, "queen of the flies?"

"No, no," the old woman growled, and her head shook like the head of a jackal that shakes as it tries to wrench the meat from the bone. "My daughter continues to do what she did before she met that boy, and she'll persist after he's gone, gone and forgotten, leaving no more than a little wrinkle behind. She does what she was born to do and does it well. That merchant's son comes here to her, accommodates her, and obeys her every command. Haha! But you, you and the others, you go to him. It's easier to make a little money by showing him a few tricks than it is to perform on the streets, so you've given up what you were born to do, so that you can flatter him and even reveal the secrets of your tradition to him. Most pathetic of all, and on top of it all, you tolerate his making love to the woman with whom you are yourself in love. Haha!"

The magician shook his head in mockery of her, "Haha yourself, old witch. You're wrong. Give me another drink of rum."

"Do you like it?"

"Yes, I like it, I like what goes into your mouth better than what comes out of it."

"I like it too," the toothless hag smiled. "I like it and I need it. That's what keeps me alive. It's my magic potion. And it works. I've been alive for over a hundred years because of that magic rum, the decoction I've been drinking ever since I gave up the teat. Do you want to learn some magic? You're supposedly a magician and magicians can, so I hear, keep secrets, and so I'll give the secret recipe to you: I piss in the rum pot each morning."

Muladeva, suddenly tasting what he had been drinking, feeling it curdle in his gut, looked at her in shock and revulsion. "But of course my piss won't help you," she laughed again. "My piss, just a cup per day mixed with five of rum, will keep me alive. But you, if you want to live as long as I have, you'll have to drink your own piss in your own rum."

The magician had disappeared. The bawd coughed, took another gulp of her magic potion, laughed out loud, and clapped her hands with exquisite nastiness and vast delight.

When Muladeva arrived at the guest house at the appointed time on the appointed day, he found his disciple in despair. Falling at the magician's feet, Dhanamitra cried, "My father will kill me! My father will kill me! Help me, please help me. My father's going to kill me."

Since Vamana was sobbing too, Muladeva guessed that it must be serious and, more from politeness than concern, asked for an explanation.

"This is going to kill my father! Oh, it'll kill him for sure," the merchant's son now moaned. "It will kill him. And when it does I, his own flesh and blood, his pride and joy, his hope and glory, will be to blame. I will have killed my father!"

"Which is it?" Muladeva, still unconcerned, thought he ought to ask: "Which is it, your father is going to kill you, or you're going to kill your father?"

"Which is worse?" Dhanamitra sniveled, whimpering more to the heavens than to the magician, but the magician answered anyway: "It's definitely better to kill your father than to be killed by him, at least if you don't get caught, because then, at least, you're still alive. And that, to the best of my knowledge, is better than being dead."

"No! No!" Dhanamitra wailed, "I'd rather be dead. Let me die!"

"Fine," Muladeva, disgusted by his patron's histrionics, mumbled as he turned to leave. "I'll come back tomorrow, and if you're not dead, I'll teach you how to make the betel leaf turn into the scorpion under the wine cup."

"No," the student screeched, clutching his teacher's legs. "Don't leave me. You're my only hope. You've got to save me."

It was only when the magician finally heard his patron's explanation—"I have no money, not a single pana, not one cowrie shell, nothing"—that he felt the gravity of the situation and demanded the whole story. Dhanamitra had lost everything, the entire allowance for his education, in the liquor shop. At the dice board he had been cleaned out by a sharper named Dikpada, an itinerant entertainer like Muladeva—an acrobat and juggler who could swallow swords and balance himself on one foot atop a bamboo pole.

"You're my only hope, Guruji," the merchant's son continued to mewl. "You must save me. I know the man was cheating. I'm certain. He cleaned out everyone in the liquor shop, or at least everyone who was willing to play against him, which is to say Vamana, Gomukha, that old Shakta priest with the dyed hair, and, alas, my worthless self. Save me though I don't deserve it. Come with me tonight. He'll be waiting for me to bring him the rest of my gold, all of the money, not mine but my beloved, blessed father's as invested in me, his accursed son! I have betrayed Sarasvati and Kubera, my mother and my father, the merchant class and the people of Gujarat. You're my only hope. Remember? I do! You told me that you know the gambling sleights and that you use that knowledge to expose dishonest players. That's what you said. Remember? Please come—you must expose him, so that he'll have to return our money or go to jail. Or no, better yet, you could play him; use the sleights and fleece the rake. It's not cheating to cheat a cheater, not if you're cheating the cheater to get back what rightfully belongs to the cheated, to one who has not ever in his life cheated another man or woman, child or beast. Lies are not lies if they serve truth. That's what my beloved father, if not the blessed Manu himself, would say. Please."

"I'll do it," Muladeva nodded, feigning a certain righteousness, "for Anangasena. I know that the news of your poverty would break her heart."

"You're right! Oh, my beloved Anangasena!" Dhanamitra exclaimed as he dried his eyes and forced a smile into his mascara-stained cheeks. "I have dishonored her as well, she who is, I have no doubt about it, Savitri reborn, she who loves me no less than Sita loved Lord Rama. Because of this love she will no doubt feel my pain as her own. Her heart is made of gold."

"Yes," Muladeva couldn't help but laugh, "Her heart is made of gold!" And they prepared for the game of dice.

The magician dressed in Dhanamitra's clothes, the showy muslins of Gujarat, put the yellow mustard-seed tilaka on his forehead and the crimson lac on his lips. Because Dhanamitra had lost all of his gold, coral, and lapis lazuli ornaments to the acrobat, Muladeva had to wear green bracelets of braided creepers and a white flower garland around his neck. He fixed his black matted hair and fastened a blue lotus in the topknot with a multicolored cord. The magician looked at himself in the hand mirror and smiled at the made-up face.

"Anyone would mistake you for the son of a merchant from Gujarat," Vamana was happy to say and was correct at least in respect to the acrobat Dikpada. That tightrope walker, lean and naked to the waist, sharp-eyed, his thin lips as red with betel as his eyes were with sleeplessness and rum, accompanied by big-eyed, small-limbed twin boys, played with confidence against the man he thought was some mere country bumpkin. The children, each to the other like an image in a mirror, squatting behind the acrobat, one on each side of him, watched every bet and roll, every play and ploy.

The magician, starting the game with the last of the gold from Dhanamitra's purse, the money owed to the acrobat, let his opponent cheat to watch and know just how to outcheat him. "Fate controls the dice; our karma's in the roll," was the tavern keeper's observation, uttered like an invocation to begin a liturgy, a sacrifice, the game, and Muladeva smiled with the thought that if that were so, then he who had, as he had, mastered all the sleights, he who could throw any throw he wished to throw, was the master over fate, free from all effects of his or another's karma. Cheating was the path to liberation. Through deception, cool and subtle sleights of hand, no less than through austerities or devotion, one might be liberated from the bonds of fate. So even though it may have been Dikpada's destiny to win, Muladeva made him lose. The acrobat had no money left.

"My father will be pleased," Muladeva smiled. "The merchants of Gujarat, you must understand, don't hoard their gold like the misers of Kashi. We're not mean, greedy, without a certain grace. No, we appreciate the sparkle of the gold just as poets savor the sentiment of a well-turned verse; spectacles of gold's golden glistening moves our souls in the way that visions of the gods transport renouncers, the devout and holy ones I mean, the real ones."

Just as ascetics, when they discard all they have, are said to see the truth, Dikpada, in his sudden poverty, saw through the magician's lies: "You're no merchant's son, but a cunning scoundrel's heir, a trickster through and through—I recognize the sleights, the deceptions, and it brings the wicked Shakuni to my mind. You've cheated me as he cheated righteous Yudhishthira." Muladeva laughed. "You're Yudhishthira and I'm Shakuni! Bravo! I like the accusation. You flatter me, turning me, an innocent merchant's son, into a warrior, the great uncle of the Kauravas. Do you, by any chance, remember what Shakuni said to the prudish Pandava when that self-righteous prince of righteousness accused him of cheating with the dice? Let me refresh your memory: 'The scholar surpasses the nonscholar only through his tricks—it's but a trick that distinguishes the wise man from the fool.' "

"We'll see which one's the fool," Dikpada snapped. "Let's play once more."

Muladeva laughed again: "Why is it that a man who has lost everything always wants to play again? And the more he's lost, the more he wants to play. He drools for the dice as the hungry vulture drools for the sweet eyes of a guarded corpse. I'm sorry. The game's over, dear Yudhishthira. You have nothing left to gamble."

"Nothing?" Dikpada answered anxiously. "When Yudhishthira had nothing left, when he had lost his wealth, his palace, his kingship, his brothers, and even himself, he staked his wife. And Shakuni took the challenge. I have no wife now, but something better, far better than any Draupadi. I have these twins, named, if you'll excuse the change of stories, a change of epic proportions, Lakshmana and Shatrughna, sons of a prostitute in Ujjayini, not, in any way, ordinary children. No, they're worth far more than the son of a merchant could imagine. But a performer would, I assure you, know the value of these boys. I redeemed them when they were infants from the officer of the brothel for five thousand dinarakas each—that's ten thousand for the two—and have, since then, trained them well, so that now they're worth twenty thousand at least, probably much more. They can walk on a rope stretched between two poles, or balance on those poles. They can swing from one rope to another or, without a rope, turn themselves over and over in the air. It's as if their flesh was made of cloud."

When signaled by the acrobat, the small twins rose together, bowed at once, and simultaneously leapt up to somersault backwards in the air and land, at the same moment, upright on their feet. They bowed again and squatted, expressionless, behind the acrobat, their trainer, the desperate gambler.

"They are, furthermore, as you can see, obedient as well. Let them be my stake."

At these words Muladeva decided, tricked, and cried, "Won!" at Dikpada who, in a split second, had lost all that he had in the world. Gulping down the last of the rum in his cup, the acrobat rose to walk out the door and wander in the street alone. He slept that night in the open air, looking up through the fronds of a palm tree, into the heavens, gazing at the stars, aching with the immensity of that sky and weeping over the loss of the two little boys.

After the game, over the drinks and betel, happily sitting with laughing Anangasena in between him and his guru, the merchant's son applauded the magician's skill, promised to compose a Sanskrit panegyric to commemorate it, and then asked to have his money back.

"What money?" Muladeva frowned. "My money? The money I won at the dice board? You want me to give my money to you?"

"This is so awkward," Dhanamitra shook his head sadly. "I suspected this might arise but hoped it wouldn't, for you are, after all, my guru. And I must respect you. But the guru, to be respected, must respect the law, the truth. You must give all the gold to its rightful possessors. Money earned by cheating, by lies and deception, by any sleight of hand, does not belong to the one who has taken it. My father says that's what Manu says. The law is clear on that. But enough learned prolix on the subject of the legal *śāstra*s and down to particulars: in order to avoid prosecution, you must give, I must say, Vamana's money to Vamana, Gomukha's money to Gomukha, the Shakta priest's money to the Shakta priest, and my money to me. If you don't, the others—not I, of course, because you are my guru, but the others to be sure—will have you arrested. You'll be executed. Do you understand? You openly told them that you would cheat in the game. That's the problem. We have their testimony as to your own confession to the crime. The acrobat could not have been prosecuted on mere suspicion of deception, but you!—in your case there's a case. There's proof. Of course, out of sincere and real gratitude, not to mention justice, each of us will give you a fee for your efforts, the money you would have made had you been doing a performance of magic. For that is what it was. I spoke to them on your behalf before the game was even played. You'll be paid, for we are honest men both by choice and disposition. And, of course, it's your right to keep those boys. I'm sure they will have some value for you."

Muladeva had no choice, no option, and not a thing to say.

He let the boys sleep in his tent with him when he stayed in the camp of vagrant entertainers just outside the city, not far from the river; and Shukradhara agreed to let them sleep in the shed outside the brothel when Muladeva was with Anangasena. Under the tutelage of the acrobat they had learned to care for themselves and never pestered Muladeva. They seemed utterly unmoved, so unperturbed, by the prospect of never seeing Dikpada again, so completely un-affected by the fact that, in an instant, at the roll of the dice, one father had been replaced, as in a magic switch, by another. It was as if it had gone unnoticed, as if there were no difference in their minds between the acrobat and the magician. It startled Muladeva. Amazed to witness such detachment in children so young, it occurred to him, in trying to understand it, that though he had always assumed that attachment is natural and that one had to struggle toward detachment, as the sages said one ought to do, it was, perhaps, in fact, the other way around.

Each of them about half the age and half the weight of Indragopa, Laksh-mana and Shatrughna together became Muladeva's only son and, as a single son, the two as one, they were eager to learn magic. They mastered cups and balls, all the passes with coins and shells, all of the sleights of conjuring, the movements of the hands and eyes, quickly and with ease, as if skill at deception, at creating illusions, and at making things seem to be which in no way are was a most natural instinct. The new talent did not divert them from acrobatics, and Muladeva marveled at their agility, the ease with which they scaled walls or shimmied up any rope or cord, fearlessly walked along high and narrow ledges or tossed each other into spins and turns in mid-air. It was when he saw them one day pretending to be monkeys, calling out to Lord Rama as they swung from branch to branch in a great pipal tree, that the magician had the inspiration for the trick.

"I'm going to do it," Muladeva told Dhanamitra. "I'm going to perform the Rope Trick, that illustrious illusion, and you're going to have a part in it, an important part." As they walked together through the lanes of the pleasure district, the magician and the merchant's son laughed with delight over the prospects, Dhanamitra over the excitement of his first public performance of magic, Muladeva because it would be his first performance in over a year.

Anangasena was not dressed when the magician and the merchant came. In the lampless, flowerless room where no incense burned, huddled under the dark blanket as if it were cold, with no makeup on, no ornaments, no smile, she turned, saw them, and spoke almost in whispers: "Help me Muladeva, help me. Give me mango leaves, or feathers with the eyes of a god on them, or amulets, or stones. Help me. Jihvika is dead. Give me the magic to bring my mother back to life."

While Dhanamitra began to cry, Anangasena's eyes remained dry: "I need her. I'm nothing without my mother. I know you understand. I can't work without her. I can't survive. Bring her back, Muladeva, if you're my friend. Use magic."

"There is no magic like that," Muladeva revealed, as if she did not know it. "No one, no thing, can bring back someone who has died. Magic is illusion; death is real. It is most real. It is the one and only real."

"No, no, that's not true," she sighed, was silent, then spoke again softly with no feeling in her voice: "I know it's not. Death is—I know this now—the end of what is real."

The weakness that comes with grief prevented the prostitute from going with Dhanamitra, Muladeva, and Shukradhara when they took the corpse to the river. After bargaining with the priests over the price of the sandalwood, Dhanamitra paid for it and, with magical mantras muttered, the cadaver was set on fire. Muladeva broke open the skull of the woman on the pyre to release the old soul within it, and Anangasena, in a ritual performed by and for herself alone, released the pigeon from the cage that hung in her window. She watched the bird circle higher and higher. Catching a current, the liberated pigeon soared to disappear into the unlimited expanses of heaven.

As the three men sat there by the river, close to each other and silent at dusk, watching the flames devour the body, leaving, like a scavenger, only bones unconsumed, other corpses, tied with ropes to stretchers, propped upon the steps, were waiting with infinite patience for their turn to be burned and hallowed in the fire. Muladeva looked across the river, the watery body of the goddess, into the field on the other side, dark and empty, and he rested there.

Further down the river, just then, Shankaracharya spoke to the disciples gathered around him, explained to them how he would free himself from the net that Mandana Mishra's wife had so cleverly cast: "There is a king in Kashmir— Amaruka he is called—and he has sixty-four mistresses, one concubine for each of the amatory arts. Through powers gained by my austerities I have looked across time and space, seen through those illusions, seen him, far away, there and in the future. On the first day of the new year he will be out with his courtiers on a hunt, enjoying himself, and he will stumble, fall, and suddenly, unexpectedly, be dead. His magician, called immediately to his side, will mutter mantras, and the king will seem to rise. All will think that Amaruka lives, either that he has been returned to life or that he was never dead. It will not, however, be Amaruka in the body of that king, but I. And in his form I shall remain for sixty-four days to spend one night with each queen, to learn from them, each in turn, all the arts of love. In that way, without corruption of this chaste body, I can return to answer the challenge of the ritualist's wife. I shall be able to repeat, to say from experience, what I have always taught—that *brahman* alone is real. All else is illusory. Even the ideas of bondage and liberation are false notions conjured up by *māyā*. Tricks. The appearance, transformation, and disappearance of the snake do not abide in the rope. There is neither death nor birth, neither a rope that binds nor a soul that is bound, neither a seeker of liberation nor one who has found it. These are the tricks the mind plays upon the mind. I shall do this, and yet I shall not do this. It is all magic, not really done, but seemingly done so that others, enmeshed in the net, will think it done, see it done, and hear that revelation of the truth. With that truth the debate will be won for you."

As Shankara planned the illusion he would create for the sake of truth, Muladeva did the same. He thought about it. Late at night, with the children sleeping in his tent, it occurred to him, against his will not to think of it, that with these twins he could create an illusion that was almost real, a trick so perfect that it was, almost, no trick. He could slay one child, really kill the boy, cut him limb from limb, in the open, fully surrounded, close to the spectators, let the severed head be carefully inspected, and then, with the switching basket, bring what would seem to be, so undeniably, that same boy, back to life. He could see it done, the details making the illusion perfect, and the readiness of his imagination to put it together terrified him. "No," he had to say aloud to himself and stroked the head of the child—Lakshmana or Shatrughna, he wasn't sure. No, he wouldn't do it, not ever, that was certain. But could he do it?—he wondered. That would or could never be certain, and that uncertainty was a torment that would or could never go away. "No, I wouldn't harm either of these boys, like sons to me, not really, not ever. No. I'll get a monkey for the trick."

The hunter from whom he bought the animal said the monkey's name was Vrishakapi: "I name all my monkeys that. You have to name them something because no animal without a name can be tamed. So I name them all Vrishakapi. That's because they're wild when I catch them, wild like Indra's naughty son. He was so wild, Indra tried to cut off his head. That's what they say the Veda says."

Once he had the monkey, the magician began to prepare his assistants to play their parts in the illusion he was designing.

Instructions to Dhanamitra: "No one would ever believe that we're connected with each other. No one will suspect. After I say the words, 'No one must look into this bag,' a bag in which I will have put a snake, while I have my back turned, you step forward out of the crowd and, in defiance of my warning, open the bag and look into it. Then throw your hands over your eyes, fall on the ground, and scream, 'My eyes! My eyes are on fire! They burn! Help! Help! I can't see! Help me!' I'll get angry with you, shout that I warned you not to look into the bag. Don't listen to me. Just continue to cry out, 'I can't see! I can't see!' Vamana must then beg me to return your sight, to heal the wounds to your eyes. Do you understand? Practice. It must be natural. They must believe it. They must fear it. It's very important."

Instructions to Shatrughna: "You'll be in the basket. You'll lie still, still as a corpse. Without any movement at all you'll have to conceal the parts of the monkey in the load as I drop them into the basket. There must be complete stillness and silence until you're brought to life. After you jump out of the basket, circle the crowd slowly, again and again, getting close to them so that they are certain that it is you, the boy they saw before. Look into their eyes. Make certain they look at you."

Instructions to Lakshmana: "Early in the morning, before dawn, you'll come with me to the site. That night I'll have prepared the bag, sewn it with fresh leaves from the tree so that no one will notice it. We'll conceal it in the branches, in a place that you can reach. Before you go up the rope, circle the crowd again and again and slowly, getting close to them so that they'll remember your face. Look into their eyes. Make certain they look back at you. When your part is finished, after throwing down the last piece of the monkey's body, get out of the tree as quickly and quietly as you can. Go to Anangasena's room and wait for us there. Remember to take the bag with you—nothing must be left behind."

Instructions to himself: "All I have to do is kill the monkey."

When the magician took the monkey to the barber to have it shaved, it squirmed and screeched so violently during the procedure that they had to tie it up, bind its wrists and ankles with ropes, gag its mouth with cotton, and fix the cloth with the names of the goddess on it around its eyes. Looking at the monkey, hairless except on the top of its head, squirming in its bonds, and whimpering through its gag, Muladeva worried: "It's too small, too much smaller than the boy." But then he consoled himself: "No, it's alright. It'll do. The audience will be fooled—in their horror, everything will appear much larger and greater than it is."

The boy played the damaru there in the chosen site, near the great pipal tree, close enough to the King's Highway to attract unsuspecting souls to the spectacle, people on the road to the parks and royal gardens on the chosen day, on their way to the festivals of Indra that would be celebrated there. With the ashes on his body, the rosary of *rudrākṣa* beads around his neck, and the animal skin around his loins, with his *kamaṇḍalu*, bone flute, and monkey skull in place, and with the ropes, the swords, and wicker basket ready, the magician watched the boy. All that needed to be hidden had been hidden.

CUT-AND-RESTORED

The boy did as well as Indragopa would have done at that boy's age. He added somersaults to attract the crowd: courtiers and courtesans heading for the gardens, priests and pandits from the ghats, scribes and soldiers, barbers and merchants (Dhanamitra and the dwarf Vamana among them), vendors and pilgrims, travelers and farmers, a student, a renouncer, a caravan driver, and others too. The circle began to take shape. Watching the child move the cups and balls, the onlookers laughed with pleasure over the startling agility of the little hands.

"Which ball is under which cup?" the boy asked the crowd. "Where's the black one? Where's the white one? Are there any bets?" Their senses, a hundred wide eyes watching two small hands, and the logic that what one sees placed under a cup remains there unless it is moved would have told them that there was one ball under each of the two coconut-shell cups, the white one under the cup on the boy's right, the black one under the cup on his left. The last few moments of watching the boy's performance of sleight of hand, however, convinced them that there was no way they could know the answer to his question. They were sure only that they could not be sure of anything.

Muladeva pushed into the circle: "There is no ball, neither white nor black, no ball under either cup."

"You're wrong," the boy laughed. "There's one ball under each cup."

"I'm never wrong," the magician said with stern confidence and conviction. "Never."

"I'll show you," said the boy, with a confidence to match the man's, as he turned over the cups and then shammed surprise, faked fear, and leapt back and away from the two scorpions that darted out from under each of the cups. The audience gasped, astonished when they thought they could no longer be astonished.

When the magician gave him his cue by grinding the scorpions into the dirt with his bare foot, the boy recited his line: "You must be a very powerful magician."

"Yes, it's my curse."

"What do you mean?" the boy asked. "Tell us. How can that be a curse? Tell us who you are."

The magician delivered his monologue: "I, Muladeva of Ujjayini, son of Shambaradasa, servant of no man, husband of no woman, was, long ago, in a previous birth, in the days of Yajñavalkya, a Brahmin, a sage, Indradatta by name. Through study of the Veda, great austerities and perfect sacrifices, I had prepared myself for release from this great round of rebirth and redeath. Learned in all the *sastras*, a knower of *brahman*, my senses controlled through yogic practices, I was a teacher of teachers, a guru to gurus. The renowned courtesan Ambapali sought my instructions, blessings, and guidance. It was she who, so long ago, so many lives ago, took me to see the magician and his son, to watch them perform here, in this very spot. 'It's wonderful,' she said and pleaded with me to come with her, pleaded with such urgency that, though I had no interest in such idle illusions, I finally consented. The man began by throwing the end of a rope into the air; it rose higher and higher, into the heavens. The boy climbed the rope. Though the magician called out to the child, he did not return. Angered it seemed, the sorcerer pursued his son and killed him. The parts of the boy's body fell to earth. These the magician placed in a basket and, through his magic, the boy was made whole again, whole and alive. I couldn't understand how it could be done. I reasoned it through, but reason was to no avail. I consulted the Vedic texts; I contemplated it in deep meditational trances. I, who had believed that I knew all things, that I was wise and could not be fooled, couldn't understand how the magic had been accomplished. The clarity of my mind gave way to bewilderment and in that confusion I felt anger. I cursed that magician, cursed him to be strangled by that very rope with which he had made a fool of me, the Brahmin, the sage, the *jīvan-mukta*. The next day he was found with that rope around his neck, hanging in the branches of a great pipal tree. Some said that he had been robbed and murdered by thieves; others guessed that, in despair because the existence of a magician is so full of trouble, poverty, and sorrow, he had taken his own life. But I knew that it was my curse, so powerful because of the austerities I had performed, that killed the magician. And in a dream Indra appeared before my eyes to mete out my punishment: I, who had been on the verge of liberation, would be born again as a magician of the streets. Thirty-four times I would have that birth, and in that form would wander from place to place with my ropes, performing magic on the roadside. I would know the secrets of magic, of creating illusions, but I would be kept far from knowledge of the real truth, that knowledge which is liberation."

The crowd, wanting such a wonderful story to be true, listened to it with the same awe that fixed the attention of the crowd on the ghat that had gathered to hear the discourses of Shankaracharya.

"And so it is with ropes that I perform," the magician continued as, effortlessly and without comment, he vanished the knots from a rope that he held up for them to see. Wrapping the rope in his cloth, he transformed it with words and gestures, gaze and breath, into a snake—"Vasuki"—and placed the serpent in a ragged jute bag. "No one must look into that bag. Not ever!" he warned, as he rose, turned away from the bag, and walked forward to pick up the longer, larger rope that the boy had set in its proper place.

On cue, after weeks of diligent practice in preparation for his debut, Dhanamitra stepped out of the crowd, came toward the bag, and opened it. At once and with extraordinary, almost unbelievable naturalness, the merchant's son threw his hands over his eyes and fell on the ground, screaming, "My eyes! My eyes are on fire! They burn! Help, help, I can't see! Help me! Help!"

As the magician turned, angry with the realization of what the man, in defiance, had done, he shrieked, "I warned you! I warned you!" over the continued cries of Dhanamitra: "Help! Help me! I can't see. My eyes are on fire! I can't see!" A dwarf rushed into the circle, fell on his knees by the screaming victim of curiosity and pleaded with the magician, "Please help my friend. Help him! Return his vision. He'll never do it again. He's learned the lesson! Help him! I'll pay you anything, give you all my gold. Please, be merciful. Help him!"

The audience was stunned, overwhelmed by the suspense of the little drama, anxious to see if the magician would concede.

"This once, but not again," Muladeva finally declared. "Not again. My warnings must be followed." With mantras murmured into the eyes of the monkey skull, with mysterious hand gestures, and finally by touching each eyelid of the stricken son of a merchant, the magician cured him. In what seemed to be a mixture of joyous relief over his cure and a genuine terror of the one who cured him, the merchant's son dashed off, running so fast that the dwarf could hardly catch up with him. They went to wait in Anangasena's room, and there they laughed with the exquisite delight, tasted by them for the first time in their lives, of having deceived people.

The magician, standing in the middle of his open stage, holding the end of the long rope, began to twirl it and then threw it into the air. It fell back to earth. "Don't look at it," the magician shouted as he tossed the end of it up again, "or it will not stay in the sky." Once again the rope fell to earth and lay there lifelessly at the feet of the magician. "It will not rise if any eyes are following it," he announced as he turned, looked at each one in the audience, fixing his gaze for an instant in each set of eyes. "Don't look at it! Look down! I'm warning you," he screamed, "I'm warning you! Be careful. No one look up! There will be no cure this time. The power will burn through your eyes. The fire will consume the brain. I'm warning you. Look down!" When all eyes were cast at the ground, the magician threw the rope, weighted on the end, into the air where it engaged with the hook concealed in the overhanging branch of the tree.

"You! Boy! Take this jewel, my offering to Indra; take it," the magician ordered, handing Lakshmana the small pouch in which a rock was thought to be some precious stone. "Climb the rope, quickly. Go up the rope. Don't look up, but climb it, climb into Indra's heaven. Give him my offering; take what he gives you for me and return at once. But don't look up!"

The boy disappeared up the rope.

The magician spoke of the greatness of thousand-eyed Indra, patron of magicians, the god whose net is draped over this world. Reminding his audience not to tempt the violent power of Indra, to keep their eyes on him at all times, he spoke of illusions and reality, and they listened to every word.

"Where's the boy?" the magician, seemingly worried, upset, and anxious, asked. "Come back! Come back," he cried out, and because in his own heart he was (and he could not help but do so) really calling out to Indragopa, the audience sensed the sadness, fear, and pain. They knew that it was real.

Just as his rope had been turned into a snake, so his sorrow was transformed into anger: "Come back, my son! Come back!" He pushed the thought from his mind that he could climb the tree and really kill the boy.

The magician displayed the sword, brandished it, placed the blade across his leg, sharp edge up, slapped his hand down upon it, drew the blade across the palm, grimacing with pain, and then, with a gesture and a scream—"Ho!"—the slice was sent from his hand to seek the child's flesh. A small hand, drenched with blood, fell from the heavens onto the dirt near the feet of the magician and the crowd was too stunned to gasp or groan. The magician opened the wicker basket and dropped the severed hand into it. Again the sword was placed across his leg, slapped again, and another cut was, by magic, sent to search the sky. A little leg with bits of the cloth that had been last seen around the boy's waist, blood-stained, clinging to that limb, fell to earth. "Ho!" again, and there was an arm. And each piece of the child was dropped into the basket. Again, and the head, the face mutilated beyond recognition, rolled in the dirt. "Ho!" and the body bounced upon the ground, and then the end of the rope fell to earth. The magician deposited what remained of the boy into the basket and replaced the lid of it.

He hands drenched with blood, his face and ash-smeared chest splattered with it, the magician stood still, and the crowd could feel the change of his anger back into sorrow, real sorrow.

"With these pieces of rope I can bring him back to life," Muladeva explained as he cut the long rope into small pieces with the sword, enough of them for every member of his audience to have one, and opening the basket, he dropped the bits of rope into it over the dismembered child and replaced the lid. Sitting then upon the ground with his legs crossed, in the posture of a holy man, the magician closed his eyes and regulated his deep breathing. Not a soul in the crowd moved. They were as still and silent as the magician was. The anxious moment persisted. Then, ever so slightly, the basket seemed to move. Another moment of stillness. The basket suddenly shook, and a human cry came from it. The lid flew off. The boy stood up and stepped out. The magician reached into the basket, removed a blood-stained bit of rope, held it up for all to see and, as the resurrected child circled the crowd, asked, "Is there anyone here who would be interested in purchasing a piece of magic rope?"

As they walked toward the pleasure district, the magician placed his hand tenderly on the child's neck to tell him how well he had performed, what a fine child he was, and what a wondrous magician he would be some day. Muladeva thought it was Shatrughna but it was, in fact, Lakshmana—the boys had switched parts to trick the magician and Muladeva never knew. "We'll leave tonight, the three of us—you and I and Lakshmana—for Anga," he said. "We'll go to see my father there, to find out how he is. We'll see if my son is there."

But Indragopa was not in Anga— he was in Kashmir where, surrounded by a roadside crowd, he seemed to transform the snake Vasukija into a rope and to throw that rope into the air where it remained upright and stiff enough for the monkey Vrishakapi to climb it.

In a palace in Kashmir, a caravan driver showed a piece of rope to Amaruka. The man had brought many things to the king's court, things from Ujjayini and Anga, Pataliputra and Kashi, and so many other wonderful places. He brought delicacies for all of the senses—foods to be eaten, powders and oils to be smelled, jewels to sparkle for the eye, cloth so fine to the touch, and delectable tales for the ear. He told the story of the piece of rope to King Amaruka: "The magician said his name was Muladeva, though I am not sure, of all the things he said, what was true and what was not. But I am certain of what he did, of what I saw with my own eyes, and although you may not believe me, I swear that what I say is true. He seemed to be a holy man, a Kapalika. He had the markings and the wild hair, carried the skulls and recited their mantras. His power was great and terrible. He blinded a man in the crowd who annoyed him for some reason or another. He had a rope, Shiva's noose it seemed to me, the tether that binds us to the world, and after we had inspected it, he threw it up into the air. Instead of falling back to earth, it stayed there, erect, standing on end like a pole stuck in the ground. At a signal from the magician, to show us just how secure the rope was, an apprentice was directed to climb the rope. Muladeva called out to him to return, but there was no answer. The boy had disappeared. In apparent fury, the magician went after the child with his sword. The pieces of the boy's dismembered body fell to earth, and the rope became limp again and lay in a heap on the ground. After placing the parts of the child in a basket, the magician recited the sacred mantras and did other things, mysterious things that I do not remember, for I did not understand, magic things that made the boy whole and, before our very eyes, brought him back to life. That is the greatest magic, to make whole what has been rent, to bring to life that which has been taken up by death."

And as if it were a piece of evidence, proof that all of it was true, the caravan driver let the king inspect the bit of rope but said that he would not sell that piece of twisted hemp, bought from and blessed by the magician Muladeva, not for anything, not for any gold.

"Yes," the king said, "that's the magic—to be able to bring back one who has died, to bring the dead to life again." And he contemplated that magic, repeated the story to himself again and again. He thought about it as he lay on his stomach while two of his wives rubbed his body with ointments. The wife that had mastered the art of shampooing massaged his body with rollers. Lotus petals and jasmine floated on the surface of the waters of his bath. Amaruka stepped into the pool to sit on the stool that had been placed in it for his comfort. Tightening their breast bands and removing their gold bracelets, two other wives came into the tank to pour the pitchers of sandal-and-saffron-scented water over his head. With his eyes closed he could envision the performance of the magic trick vividly. He could see the child's head, and it made him shudder.

"Mayeshvari!" he cried out. "Send for Mayeshvari and the magician Vishvasiddhi. Send for them at once. I must see them," the king ordered and his orders were, as always, obeyed.

The magician and the courtesan arrived together and sat before their king. He spoke to them excitedly: "A caravan driver arrived a few days ago from Kashi to buy Chinese goods and sell wares from the south. I know him well and trust him, his gems and jewels are among the purest and finest in the world. And he's honest—well as honest as a merchant can be expected to be. He told me an extraordinary story. You, Vishvasiddhi, you Mayeshvari, the two of you, adept at magic and conjuring as you are, you must help me to understand it. He told me about the performance of a trick, a wonderful illusion that he witnessed himself with his very own eyes at Kashi.

"Out in the open, fully surrounded by spectators, on flat ground, far from any building, structure, tree, or anything like that, the magician displayed a rope— 'Shiva's noose,' he said—and, at his command, the end of the rope, like the head of a snake, rose in the air. It rose higher, continued to rise, and the caravan driver watched the end of it climb higher and higher still, until it was out of sight, piercing the clouds, going high into the heavens, connecting heaven and earth. And then a boy, the magician's son, suddenly, as if to escape from his father, climbed the rope, and he too disappeared from sight. The magician called to him, 'Come back, my son, come home!' But there was only silence. The magician then, holding the knife between his teeth, climbed the rope, and the astounded audience watched him also disappear into the heavens. Then, to the horror of one and all, parts of the boy's body—a hand, a leg, the head—fell to earth, and following that, the magician shimmied down the rope. He took the parts of the body and placed them in an empty basket. He recited the mantras, performed the ritual gestures, offered the prayers, and the boy was made whole again. He climbed out of the basket and embraced his father. A happy ending! Wonderful! Wonderful! That's the greatest magic, to make whole what has been rent, to return to life what has died, to have a happy ending. I must know how it's done. I must find a man who can perform it. A reward can be offered. The caravan driver said the magician's name was Muladeva—perhaps he can be found."

Mayeshvari, startled by the mention of the name, frowned, then smiled, shook her head, then laughed.

"Don't laugh, my beloved. This is important to me. I'm serious. I must see this trick and know how it's done. I need an explanation."

"There's the section of my *Indrajālasūtra*, my treatise and commentary on the tradition of magic and conjuring, which deals with this particular illusion," Vishvasiddhi smiled.

The king looked at him with suspicion despite his affection for the old magician. "There is a section on this in my *Indrajālasūtra*," he would always say whenever there was a discussion of, or question about, magic. And yet no one had ever seen the book or actually held the palm leaves in their hands. The king always wondered whether it was a trick, whether there was in fact any such book. Perhaps the magician simply fabricated it, improvised it on the spur of the moment to suit his purposes and create the illusion of the book's existence. Whenever the king asked to see it, Vishvasiddhi demurred: "Secret. The book is full of secrets. It cannot be shown." Amaruka reasoned that it didn't really matter whether it existed or not. The fact that Vishvasiddhi could, at any moment, make this or that part of it materialize in utterance, was sufficient. "Recite," the king ordered, "recite the parts of it which explain the Rope Trick. I want to understand it." He rested his head in Mayeshvari's lap. "And you tell me, my lovely one, if this old magician tries to trick me with his words. I want to know the truth."

"Of course," the old magician nodded, and he began: "The magician himself must believe it . . ."

Historian's Notebook 2

The Indian Rope Trick

The magician himself believed in the magic, swore that it could be done, that there was a man in Ghaziabad, really and truly, who performed the Indian Rope Trick. Definitely. And when I asked if the wonder worker was Maslet, "No, no," Naseeb laughed, "*kisān*" (farmer).

I wanted to go to the farm in Ghaziabad, not because I imagined I would actually see the Rope Trick, but because I have found while doing research in India that you unearth the most interesting things when you're trying to understand other things, that what you set out to discover is never as amazing as what is presented to you in place of what you thought you would like to see or learn. The country is a magic show.

But Naseeb insisted that he would go alone. And there he asked the farmer directly if he was indeed the person who performed the Rope Trick and, yes, the man said, oh yes, he had accomplished it. But when Naseeb explained that he wanted to arrange a demonstration of it for an American professor writing a book about Indian magic, the farmer demurred; much preparation would be needed, and it would be very costly. Never one to underestimate the American Institute of Indian Studies' capacity and eagerness to provide money for my field research, Naseeb assured the magic farmer that the professor would pay any amount to see it. "Well, it will take time. So much time!" the man frowned.

Naseeb declared that the professor would stay in India for it, no matter how long it took, or he'd return at any time, whenever the farmer was ready. There were, of course, other problems, so many problems; but no matter what excuses the farmer offered, Naseeb countered with avowals that I would do anything, pay anything, travel at any time to any place, to see the famous Indian Rope Trick.

Thus pressed and cornered, the farmer finally had to confess that he couldn't do the Rope Trick or any other trick for that matter. Pleading with Naseeb not to embarrass him by telling anyone, the farmer remorsefully revealed the history of the local legend, the mystery of the Ghaziabad Rope Trick: "Many years ago, just after Independence, someone who had come to my farm to buy some vegetables

193

noticed a rope on the ground and asked what it was for. 'The Rope Trick,' I joked, not thinking that he would take me seriously and boast to his friends that he knew someone who could perform the famous illusion. But he told everyone he met! And if people laughed at him for believing such a thing, the fool became angry and insisted that he had seen it with his own eyes. Soon people were saying, 'I have a friend who has seen the Rope Trick.' And I was named as the magician. Sometimes, if people said it was a friend who had seen it, the folks to whom they were telling the big news would doubt them; so, just to convince others that what they knew was true was true, they said that they themselves had seen it. So many people—so many people!—had seen me do the Rope Trick! And it was the most exciting thing to happen around here in a long time. The story spread. At first I tried to deny that I could do it; but they didn't believe me. 'You can't believe the words of a magician,' they said. They wanted to think it was so. I stopped denying it and a joke turned into a truth. Yes, it became true, and it was—let's be honest with ourselves—good advertising for the farm. More and more people wanted to buy vegetables from me just in case they might see the Rope Trick some day. And some of them said they saw me do it. Why not? Others had. I couldn't say my customers were liars—I had no choice but to admit that I could do the trick. The Rope Trick is not my lie, but someone else's. I'm a good man and basically honest. Why not bring the American here anyway? Maybe he'd like to buy some vegetables."

"What kind of vegetables does he sell?" I asked Naseeb, and the magician laughed: "Onions."

"Do you still believe it can be done?" I asked, and "Yes, yes," he said in English and laughed a laugh that was all irony and ambiguity. "Why not?" Understanding his answer, getting to the secret of the trick was, it occurred to me, like peeling that metaphorical vegetable, the onion.

"Yes," he smiled, "Rope Trick, oldest and greatest Indian magic."

I offered to give him the gimmicked rope, given to me by Tayade, that, if held in a certain way, would stand up by itself. But, no, Naseeb had a scorn for gaffs—they were, in his mind, just toys, props that hardly make the actor. With a certain condescension, he gave me some items that a Western magician, perhaps with a similar condescension of his own, had given him: a rope version of the Linking Rings Trick (one of the ropes gimmicked with magnets), a finger chopper, and a magical ball-point pen. The fantastic, amazing "Mystic Pen": the idea was to ask someone to think of a flower, any flower, hand them the innocent-looking pen, direct them to write the name of the flower on a piece of paper, and then ask them to smell the ink; through the peculiar dynamics of suggestion and the psychology of aromas, the word would have the fragrance of the flower that it indicated. It seemed to work on the boy who brought the beer to the room, but—rose, jasmine, lilac, hibiscus—all the words smelled the same to me.

THE INDIAN ROPE TRICK

After Naseeb had left, I took out my notebook and tried my new pen: "The Rope Trick. What does it mean, signify, represent? Represent, re-present, in India, about India, about us, in us?" I sniffed the words, wanting that indescribable smell that is India—spicy and fetid, dusty and musty, musky and excremental, funereal and sweet—that emphatic aroma that fills the nostrils the moment you step out of the airplane, the wild, cloying scent that coats the sinuses and that, after you are home, takes weeks, sometimes longer, to fade. I couldn't smell anything yet. I turned the page and tried again:

Historian's Notebook 2:

The Indian Rope Trick

The antiquity of the illusion, or at least the legend of it, it attested to by a reference in the *Jātaka*s, that collection of fabulous accounts of the incarnations of the Bodhisat, the Buddha before his birth as Gautama the sage of the Shakya clan. Among the myriad entertainers who try to make a young prince (a boy who has never in his entire life so much as smiled) laugh, there are two magicians who perform a trick, a combination of the Mango Tree Trick and the Rope Trick: "After causing a great mango tree to spontaneously grow in front of the palace, the conjurer threw a rope up into the air so that it caught on a branch of that tree. He climbed the rope. Some assistants followed him up into the tree, dismembered him, and threw the parts of his body down, onto the ground. The other conjurer put the pieces of his body together, doused the form with water, and the first magician, adorned with flowers, jumped up and happily danced a jig. Not even the sight of that moved the prince to laughter" (*Suruci-Jātaka*).

By the eighth century the trick was famous enough to exemplify the magician's art. Shankaracharya speaks of "the magician, the *māyāvin*, who throws a cord up into the air and, armed, climbs up it, beyond the range of sight, to enter into battle and be dismembered; after his bodily parts have fallen to the ground, he is seen to rise up again and there is no concern over thinking about the reality of the magic trick that has been performed" (commentary on *Gauḍapādīyakārikā* [on the *Māṇḍūkya Upaniṣad*] 1.7).

The classic account of the Indian Rope Trick, the version most often recounted, comes not from India but from China. The witness, Ibn Battuta, hardly a connoisseur of magic (it always increases his pulse and puts him on the verge of fainting), writing an account of his world travels in the fourteenth century, mentions a performance of the Rope Trick in Delhi and describes in some detail a presentation of it that took place at a banquet in the courtyard of the Khan's summer palace at Hangzhou. The conjurers could well have been Indians—Indian magicians, often Buddhist monks, seem to have frequently performed in the Chinese court. "All the arts of illusion came from the Western Regions, especially India," according to a tenth-century Chinese history. "When Han Wu Di opened [the silk route] to the West, illusionists began arriving in China [c. 128 B.C.E.]. During the reign of Emperor An Di [107–126 C.E.], Indian entertainers who could sever their arms and legs and open their bowels were gifted to the court; and from that time on every epoch had Indian illusionists" (*Chiu T'ang shu*, translated for me by Charlie Benn). Fo Tu Deng, court magician and chaplain in the empire of the Jie rulers (fourth century), who was known to have studied magic and conjuring in Kashmir, performing such standard tricks as the production of a lotus from an alms bowl and such typically Indian sleights as the pulling of his intestines from what appeared to be a hole in his chest, gained a reputation as a shaman; he was said to be able to predict the outcome of military operations, detect conspiracies, and cure diseases (E. Zürcher, *The Buddhist Conquest of China*; Arthur F. Wright, "Fo-t'u-teng").

In Hangzhou the magician observed by Ibn Battuta, commanded by the Khan to exhibit one of his marvels, tossed a wooden ball, in which there were little holes threaded with long cords, into the air, high into the sky and out of sight. The conjurer then ordered an assistant to climb the cord, and he too passed out of the range of the spectators' vision. Calling out to the boy three times but not getting an answer, the magician himself, in apparent anger, climbed the rope. Parts of the boy fell to earth—a hand, a foot, another hand, another foot, then the child's head, and finally the mutilated trunk. Descending, his robes stained with blood and gore, the magician made obeisance to the Khan and kissed the earth, and then, much to the amazement and relief of a horrified Ibn Battuta, put the boy back together. As the child rose up to take a bow, a Muslim dignitary seated next to the squeamish Maghrebian traveler leaned over to whisper in his ear: "It's all just a magic trick" (*Voyages*). The boy had not climbed the rope, the body had neither been dismembered nor reassembled and restored to life—it was, like so many things we believe have taken place, all an illusion.

Among the twenty-eight tricks that seven clever Bengali magicians performed for Jahangir in the seventeenth century, two, as chronicled in the Moghul emperor's paean to himself, if taken together, comprise a version of the Rope Trick: "They produced a chain of fifty cubits in length," the astounded Moghul who, it might be kept in mind, drank over twenty cups of wine a day, most of which were heavily laced with opium and other drugs, recounts, "and in my presence threw one end of it towards the sky, where it remained as if fastened to something in the air. A dog was then brought forward, and being placed at the lower end of the chain, immediately ran up, and reaching the other end, immediately disappeared in the air. In the same manner a hog, a panther, a lion, and a tiger were alternately sent up the chain and all equally disappeared at the upper end of the chain. At last they took down the chain and put it into a bag, no one ever discovering in what way the different animals were made to vanish in the mysterious manner above described. This, I may venture to affirm, was beyond measure strange and surprising. . . . [Later] they produced a man whom they divided limb from limb, actually severing his head from the body. They scattered these mutilated members along the ground, and in this state they lay for some time. They then extended a sheet or curtain over the spot, and one of the men putting himself under the sheet, in a few minutes came from below, followed by the individual supposed to have been cut into joints, in perfect health and condition, and one might have safely sworn that he had never received wound or injury whatever" (*Tūzuk-i-Jahangīrī*).

By the end of the nineteenth century, testimonials by travelers to India who claimed to have witnessed the Rope Trick were frequently, and much to the delight of the public, published in pamphlets and papers both in India and Europe. Credible witnesses like Sir Ralph Pearson, lieutenant governor of the North West Frontier Province, who, in the London *Morning Post* at the turn of the century, claimed to have seen the trick in the West Kandhesh district of Bombay Presidency, inspired cultural, scientific, and religious questions. There was considerable excitement in London in 1918, a year in which entertainments provided by Indian magicians were becoming popular in Britain, when a certain and very respectable Captain Holmes, just back from the colony, gave a lecture at Anderson's Hotel on Fleet Street on the Rope Trick, complete with photographs of its performance at Kirkee, a suburb of Pune. The Rope Trick was a sensational metaphor with which people talked about India, the mystic realm of fakirs and/or the corrupt land of fakers. The play on those words became a cliché.

For those with theosophical inclinations, the Rope Trick was a miracle, a reality that controverted all objective understandings of natural law; for others, more good-humored souls, it was a clever conjuring trick, an illusion that merely contradicted natural expectations of the effects of essentially incontrovertible natural laws; and for others, more hard-boiled chaps, it was a fantasy, if not a lie, that neither negated nor contradicted either their understanding of the world or their perception of it.

The interpretations of the Rope Trick that affirmed the phenomenal reality of the miracle were motivated by impulses both to establish empirical possibilities for miracles in general and, in particular, to mystify India, to perpetuate an idealized image of the supernatural domain of yogis, siddhas, and wonder-workers. Maksim Gorky, "kindled with an inner radiance" according to a reminiscence of him, spoke solemnly to friends at a gathering: "The Hindus are a great people. I will tell you of my personal experience. Once in the Caucasus I met a Hindu about whom many remarkable stories were circulating. At that time I was rather inclined to doubt. At last we met and I will tell you what I saw with my own eyes. He took a long thread and threw it up into the air. And to my surprise it remained hanging up in the air" (Nicholas Roerich on Gorky, quoted in P. C. Sorcar, *Sorcar on Magic*).

There's an occult and uncanny power in the world, an esoteric wellspring of mysteria to which ordinary beings do not have access but in which we, through some initiation, might share; India is a land particularly fertile with such power; it is a realm of miracles and real magic.

At the other end of the hermeneutic spectrum is a tougher view of magic and reality and, within it, a repugnant image of India—a debased land of superstition and ignorance, of scoundrels and liars: "The Great Rope Trick is a myth," Lieutenant Colonel R. H. Elliot, chairman of the Occult Committee of the London Magic Circle and formerly an officer in the Indian Medical Service, announced both in the *Listener* in 1934 and in his derogatory study of Indian magic, *The Myth of the Mystic East:* "It has never been performed and never will be. It sprang, Minerva-like, from the brain of an inventor of Jovian proportions and Goddess-like it has lived on far too long."

Investing enormous energy into debunking the Rope Trick, Elliot used it as one of many examples of the superstitiousness of a primitive land, "and primitive indeed it is despite its long civilisation. . . . If British rule were withdrawn, India would go back without hesitation to hook-swinging and to suttee" (117, 133). Just as the mystical, romantic interpretation of the legend as the record of a miracle had religious motives, the negative, realistic interpretation reflected political imperatives, a rationalization and justification of the British rule of India, of the appropriation of power by a rational people over irrational ones.

There is another interpretative trend, an aesthetic one, postulating that the legend tells a truth, that the trick was indeed performed, not as a miracle but as an artful illusion, a fine feat of the conjuring craft. The power displayed in the performance is the power of dramatic art. But Lieutenant Colonel R. H. Elliot's decree that the Rope Trick was mere fancy, that the testimonials of people who claimed to have seen it were utter rubbish, dismissed it both as a miracle and as a trick. That it had never, in any way, been done was the sober conclusion established at a meeting of the London Magic Circle held at the Oxford Theatre, presided over by Lord Ampthill, former governor of Madras and viceroy of India, and attended by politicians, scientists, hypnotists, magicians, socialites, and journalists, a meeting that was deemed necessary to bring reason to bear upon the conclusions people were apt to make in the flurry of accounts of the miracle or trick that were appearing in the press in the thirties, accounts inspired in part by a dramatic offer that had appeared in the *Times of India:* ten thousand rupees to anyone who could do the Indian Rope Trick in the open air. That not a single Indian magician came forward to claim the money proved that the Rope Trick could not be, and never had been, done. Proofs are, of course, proofs only when they substantiate what we suspect, want, or need to be true; proofs do not prove without complicity. Thus, Paul Dare, a fervent believer in the miraculous, tried to explain why the money was not earned with a public performance of the Rope Trick: holy men in India, those *"véritables saints hommes,"* who possess real and incontestable occult powers, never display them for money; furthermore they can't or don't read newspapers, certainly not English newspapers (*Magie Blanche et Magie Noire aux Indes*). Monsieur Dare, who himself claims to have witnessed a sadhu walk seventy meters in midair across a ravine, continues his dismissal of Lieutenant Colonel Elliot's dismissal of the Rope Trick with an insight that only a Frenchman could have: the English (*"race détastée au fond du coeur et non sans raison par les hindous"*) would be the last people to whom Indian holy men would want to show their occult powers. Lieutenant Colonel Elliot admits that when, after hearing of a "Biragi" who reputedly could perform the Rope Trick, or at least the levitational part of it, he had offered to pay to see the performance, the Indian acquaintance who had attested to the renouncer's abilities, explained: "Oh no, sir, you can't buy those things. You are known to be a sceptic, and these manifestations only come to believers."

Financial rewards offered for performances of the Rope Trick, still on occasion appearing in both English and vernacular newspapers in India, have been made both in hopes of seeing it and in order to prove that it cannot be seen. In 1875 Lord Northbrook, then viceroy, reflecting that the Rope Trick would make a smashing main attraction at a celebration he was planning for the visit to India of the Prince of Wales, Edward VII, advertised by proclamation throughout the Asian subcontinent an offer of ten thousand pounds sterling as a reward to any wonder-worker who could pull it off, an offer that suggests at least a hope, if not a belief, that it could, in fact, be done—if not as a miracle, at least as a spectacular bit of conjuring. Others—magicians such as John Booth, Will Ayling, Jack Gwynne—whether in wonder or doubt, have made the offer, to learn the techniques just in case they saw it done. "When traveling in India," a magician calling himself "Murray" announced in a magic magazine in 1934, "I actually interviewed a number of celebrated magicians, and offered them a considerable sum of money for the secret of the Rope Trick. Charles Bertram, J. N. Maskelyne, and Horace Goldin are others who expressed willingness to pay handsomely for the closely-guarded secret" (*"The Indian Rope Trick"*).

Many, however, certain of the impossibility of the Rope Trick, were confident that they were not gambling when announcing rewards of great sums of money to performers of the celebrated trick. Some magicians did so for the sake of publicity; certain British officials did it to demonstrate the fatuousness of local legends, the rampancy of the nonsense spread by the incorrigible fools and liars populating the colony. "A reward of a year's pay has been open to every Sepoy I have met who has seen the trick and can give me the name and residence of the performer," a man, known on the stage as the magician Lionel Cardac and in the barracks of the British Army in India as Major Lionel Branson, in the early part of this century wrote in *Indian Conjuring*, his treatise on the *jāduwālās* that he had occasion to see: "This for 23 years," he sneered, and "so far there have been no acceptances." With an imperial mixture of patronizing pity and scornful sarcasm,

Branson/Cardac wrote of the Indian Rope Trick with the insistence that not only are Indian magicians unable to perform that illustrious illusion, but that they were and are, furthermore, equally incapable of any other trick requiring any skill or any talent whatsoever. "It has always been a marvel to me how the Indian conjuror has gained his spurious reputation. I can only ascribe the fact to the idea that the audience starts with the impression, sub-conscious though it may be, of Mahatmaism, Jadoo or any other synonym by which Oriental Magic is designated. This allows them to watch with amazement tricks that are so simple that no English conjuror would dare to show them to his youngest child."

Discussions of the Rope Trick that dismiss reports of it as bunk state in doing so, implicitly or explicitly, that those who claim to have seen it are lying and that those who believe the lie are fools. The fame of the trick, for many commentators during the colonial period, simply validated the Western view of India as a land of liars and fools, of superstition, of religious gullibility in particular, of a people easily duped by magicians. "In their own native districts the fakirs are, it is true, the object of a certain reverence, which is fed by the abysmal ignorance, credulity, and superstition of the Oriental populace. Those critical travellers and explorers uninfected by mysticism report, after seeing the tricks of the fakirs on their own ground, that these gentry are an idle lot of swindlers, whose often most insane religious practices and other magical procedures secure them the name of holy men, and thus allow them to lead an existence free of material worry" (Ottokar Fischer, *Illustrated Magic*). "Like all ignorant people the Hindoos are very superstitious," the nineteenth-century American magician Harry Kellar unabashedly stated in his boast that it was thus that they could not understand that the "marvels he performed were within the power of a man who claims no assistance from the spirit world" (*A Magician's Tour*). The Hindu believes in the Rope Trick just as he believes in a lot of ridiculous things. And so Kellar dismissed the trick unequivocally: "The writers who declare that they have seen such impossible feats performed, as throwing up a ball of twine in the air to form a sort of Jack-and-the-bean-stalk, up which the juggler climbed out of sight, pulling the string after him, and the pistol shot of a companion conjurer brought the aerial climber to the earth in fragments, which, when brought together, became a living, uninjured man again, must have had their brains steeped in hasheesh." Kellar's sarcastic remark became the basis of an actual attempt to explain the trick, the theory that the magician who reputedly performed it was able to get his audience to see the illusion by burning hashish in a fire around which the spectators gathered: "*Les spectateurs sont sous l'effet de la musique assourdissante des tam-tams déchaînés,*" the self-proclaimed French fakir, Yvon Yva, postulated, "*mais surtout du haschich dont la propriété engourdissante et enivrante des vapeurs bien connue*" (*Les Fakirs et leurs secrets*).

Lord Frederic Hamilton, who confessed to have thought that he had seen the trick, theorized that the fakir had put not only hashish but also opium and other potent drugs unknown in the Occident into the brazier. Deep and rhythmic salaams, Lord Hamilton hypothesized, were the physical gestures that the cunning magician used to fully hypnotize his drugged audience (*Here, There, and Everywhere*). Such hallucinatory explanations, whether the fantastic vision is caused by drugs, hyperventilation, or mass hypnosis (the explanation given by Mandrake the Magician as I remember from one Sunday morning in my childhood), invests the Indian magician, ancient or modern, with a power over the minds of others that is at once enviable and dreadful. Alexander Cannon, a psychiatrist at the London County Council Mental Health Hospital, wrote a book on hypnotism, *The Invisible Influence* (extensively cited in *Sorcar on Magic*), in which, describing various orders of fakirs and yogis, he revealed that "one of the six orders is a sect that performs the lower kind of hypnotic work, namely the theatrical, where they hypnotize whole audiences collectively and exhibit the Rope Trick. The faquir stands on the stage or in their midst with a red rope in his hand and throws it about his head with the audible suggestions that he will climb it and disappear. This act has been seen and vouched for more than a thousand times. Photography is our own proof that the whole thing is a mere visual hallucination, because the camera records no such feat. It is an extremely difficult effect to produce in the West as in the hot climates the cortex of the brain is much more passive and the unconscious mind easier to deal with." Medical, quasi-scientific language promotes the idea both that Indians are at once more passive and suggestible (and therefore more gullible) than Westerners and, at the same time, that they are dangerous: Hindu Svengalis with a secret knowledge of hypnosis have the ability to control our minds if we let down our guard. A certain Sergeant Secrett reported that when he revealed to Earl Haig that his Lordship had not really seen the Rope Trick, but that he had been hypnotized by a wily juggler, the incensed fakir hypnotized a poisonous viper and sent it, unsuccessfully alas, to murder Sergeant Secrett (reported by Elliot).

"The Rope Trick and the mango trick," a superintendent of the Black Pagoda at Konarak explained to Francis Yeats-Brown, "are not supernatural, but due to collective suggestion" (*The Lives of a Bengal Lancer*). With a rather mystical awe, the magician Ormond McGill, after a visit to India in search of an explanation of the Rope Trick, proclaimed that "by directing his will, the magician causes his mental images to project themselves as real to the vision of his audience. In this way, he produces an illusion—a force which the Adepts call maya, whereby the senses of the observers report as fact things that have no real existence. In other words, the magician creates and projects a powerful concentrated thought form, which to the observers seems temporarily to exist as reality. Here, at last, is the real secret of the famous 'East Indian Rope Trick' " (*The Mysticism and Magic of India*).

All explanations, reasonable or unreasonable, absurd or sensible, are motivated. And just as it is not astounding to see imperialistic imperatives in the discussions of the Rope Trick that came out of Britain in the nineteenth and early twentieth centuries, it is no less surprising that more modern, Western explanations would not focus on a peculiarly Indian superstitiousness but would, rather, understand the story of the illusion as symptomatic of a more universal human need for particular kinds of fantasy. So, for example, the American magician and historian of magic, John Mulholland, with comparative references to the "Jack and the Beanstalk" tale of Europe and a story, "The Theft of the Peach," from Chinese folk traditions (contained in the seventeenth-century, early Qing Dynasty, *Liao zhai zhi yi* of Pu Songling), concluded that "the Indian Rope Trick is a pure fiction. But mankind has always had an instinctive urge to manufacture the myth that it exists. The idea of a stairway to heaven is a universal dream.... I am convinced now that the process by which people come to believe in the Indian Rope Trick is akin to brain-washing.... It's a towering legend, tough to chop down" ("The Great Rope Trick Mystery," *This Week* magazine [6 April 1958]). In support of his thesis Mulholland described an experiment which he conducted with the help of a psychology professor: during a lecture-demonstration on magic in the professor's class, the magician, while performing a variety of tricks, told the class about a particular illusion in which a coin traveled instantaneously from one spot in the classroom to another. Several weeks later, when the class was asked to recount what the magician had done, 80 percent of them stated that, among other tricks, he had made a coin travel instantaneously from one place to another. Mulholland's experiment, suggesting the ways in which the inevitable mistiness and mustiness of memory magnifies magic, insinuates another possible explanation for accounts of the Rope Trick. Sixteenth- and seventeenth-century travelers in India frequently witnessed roadside entertainments, the performances of conjurers, animal trainers, puppeteers, bards, and acrobats. "A young girl about 10 years old did first climb up a Bamboo 26 yards high & upon ye very top of all wch was not neare soe broade as ye palm of a hand hung" only to descend by a rope (Norris, *The Norris Embassy to Aurangzeb, 1669–1702*); and Peter Mundy, describing a similar acrobatic display, noted that a man sent a boy, his son, up a pole to dance on top of it, and then to walk upon a tightrope (*Travels*). That these rope dancers, *bājīgar*s, a group closely related to the *jādūgar*s, also performed sleight of hand makes it reasonable that stories of the Rope Trick might have emerged out the errancy of amazed travelers' recollections, out of fusing together elements from confused events to make a coherent and compelling tale—shake together a magic trick, a child on a rope, another on a pole, a story heard, a legend remembered, this oddity and that, and see what you get.

While this explanation, like Mulholland's, implies that the invention of the trick is unconscious and, to a degree, collective, there have also been assertions that it was purposefully and individually fabricated. The story of the trick is itself a trick played upon the public. Walter Gibson (the creator of the radio character "The Shadow") has, for example, suggested that the story of the Rope Trick was invented by the British military right after the Sepoy Rebellion of 1857 in order "to encourage enlistment in the British Army, because of the wonderful feats of Indian magic that new recruits would see there" (*Secrets of Magic*). And a certain Daddy Lyons, the manager of the magician Kellar's tour of India, himself claimed to have been the original author of the legend of the Rope Trick. He explained to the magician Dante that, while he was press secretary for the Davenport Brothers, those magicians one evening were telling some tall story to journalists about how an itinerant magician in Calcutta had passed a boy through a tree trunk. "Well," the old man laughed, "the devil was in me and I just had to 'top' that story: so I described how I had seen a fakir lead a crowd into the desert and perform *the* trick (the details of which you know so well). And I knew that I had them! The reporters tried to find explanations for such is their trade. They suggested trick ropes, blinding sun, mass hypnosis and people have been trying to explain it ever since! The Indian Rope Trick is now the world's greatest unexplained mystery! And yet, Harry, my friend, I swear to you that this legend, though seemingly hundreds of years old, is no more than a figment of my imagination. I invented the Indian Rope Trick!" (Val Andrews, *Goodnight Mr. Dante*).

During the last century and the first half of the present one, theatrical versions of that "world's greatest unexplained mystery" were popular. Publicity for stage shows that included theatrical renditions of the Indian Rope Trick (the reviews of, among others, Servais Le Roy, Howard Thurston, Harry Blackstone, Dante, Carl Hertz, Arnold De Biere, Horace Goldin, Kalanag, Nevil Maskelyne, David Devant, Chang, and Virgil, most claiming to be the innovator, all performing in Indian costume, with Indian music, and the perfunctory black boy to climb the rope) inevitably made statements that the magician had learned the secret of the trick from a yogi or fakir in India, implying that, even though it was being done on the stage, the magician could, if he wished, perform it in the traditional manner—out of doors, in daylight, and fully surrounded. Nevil Maskelyne explicitly claimed he could do it in the open air, but not in England—the Indian magician, he explained, made use of the much brighter Indian sun to blind his spectators. Horace Goldin, who also held the light-in-the-eyes theory of its method, professing to be "the only white man in the world to discover the secret," wrote a publicity booklet on it in which he described his adventures in the remote hills and jungles of India, "localities where white men had never been," and his heroic search for the secret of the Indian Rope Trick. Finally, in 1919, "I came across a yogi who made a practice of hanging head downwards from a tree for days on end. It came to my knowledge that this yogi was a master of the Indian Rope Trick which was performed as a sacred and secret religious rite. I went to see the yogi and spoke to him, but he made no reply. Immediately several disciples surrounded me. They produced daggers and made me understand that to speak to the yogi might mean death. I had to retreat gracefully, but I was determined to gain the secret. I got into conversation later with one of the yogi's disciples whom

I bribed with some money. He was reluctant to speak of the feat, but he inadvertently slipped a remark which gave me the original clue to the secret. Since that day I have been experimenting and at last I can perform the trick to my satisfaction" (cited in *Sorcar on Magic*).

Less famous magicians, aspiring to become more famous, imitated the tactics of Goldin, that master publicist, striving like him to appropriate some power or appeal from the Indian image. Among them, Arthur Claude Derby, using the Indianesque name Karachi, one of many respondents throughout the world to the challenge of the Occult Committee of the Magic Circle, published an advertisement for himself in the *Listener* of London (30 January 1935): "The secret of this trick I learnt many years ago from a Gurkha warrior whose life I had been the means of saving. On his death-bed, shortly after, he imparted to me the secret of this trick, at the same time adding his dying injunction that I should not perform it in public for profit except when driven to it by necessity. It is for this reason that the trick has not been performed for so many years, but now the time has come when I find it necessary to demonstrate its reality and convince a sceptical world that the secrets of the East have not entirely perished. I am not a rich man or I should not be driven to perform this trick of the Indian fakir" (cited in *Sorcar on Magic*).

The magician Rupert Slater, performing a stage version of the trick, had exotic patter, evocative of the mood of the Raj, in which he also claimed to have learned the secret of one of India's great mysteries from a native:

> I was only a private soldier sir,
> In eighteen eighty three
> A' trying to do my duty,
> At Bombay by the sea,
> And when I thinks of the Rope Trick
> I laughs to myself with glee.
> I shall never forget the day sir,
> Out on Barrack Square,
> The officers, men and the ladies
> Were all of 'em gathered there,
> When in the midst of the crowd sir,
> A rope went into the skies,
> And a boy climbed up the rope sire,
> Then vanished afore our eyes.
> So after the show was over,
> I spoke to the Magic Wallah,
> And he showed me how it was done sir,
> When I gives him half a dollar.
> (*Abbott's Encyclopedia of Rope Tricks*)

Such a reaffirmation of the Hindu's willingness to sell his most precious secrets for half a dollar must have been reassuring to British audiences.

Stage versions of the trick—those of Slater, Goldin, Maskelyne, or whomever—using dark curtains, wires, rigs, mirrors, and the like, are not very beguiling. The challenge to magicians to perform it outside, in the open air, is, in the context of the history of Indian magic, the challenge of the itinerant *jādūgar* to his more lavishly patronized theatrical counterpart both in India and the West. In an essay prepared for the Danish Society for Psychical Research, P. C. Sorcar claimed that he could and had done the trick out-of-doors, and that he had, furthermore, discovered the method for its performance in former times in India. Projecting onto the past what Western magicians have projected onto India in the present, Sorcar explained that "if we track back into history, we find that this trick was performed in India hundreds of years ago. At that time 'invisible thread,' electricity, etc. were not known. People were very much gullible" (*Sorcar on Magic*). Sorcar relates that the trick only took place in the mountains where the performers could wear long, heavy robes, as requisite for the trick, without suspicion. It was also necessary to perform in the hills in order to set the rigging: "They chose their site of performances by the side of two high hills or lofty places. The secret was a horizontal thread [made of human hair] stretching from one hill to another caught by two assistants at either ends. . . . Time selected was evening before dusk. After showing several tricks and thus killing a good length of time, placing the spectators in a magic mood already, and the dusk approaching, the magician started his Rope Trick. With the sound of weird Indian music associated with jaduwallahs, sound of tom-toms, dholok etc., the Rope Trick was started. The magician showed a coil of rope . . . the rope was about forty feet long and had a leaden weight with a knot at the extreme end. The magician threw the rope up several times unsuccessfully to create misdirection and then at a proper time threw the rope up in such a way that the end of the coil of rope engaged with the horizontal suspension. . . . Through the code of their weird music, the assistants from the two top rocky knolls started pulling their catgut rope-ends [attached to the wire of human hair] from either sides, just as we do for our "Floating Ball" or "Dancing Handkerchiefs" these days. The rope went up and up. When it reached about thirty feet or so, people thought it had gone up to the sky. . . . One very small boy climbed up the vertical rope, hand by hand and went to the top of the rope. . . . After a little by-play the magician would also climb up with the sharp knife between his teeth. Words of abuse, shouts, murmuring etc. were well-known by-plays of the Indian street magicians. They could easily misdirect their spectators through these. . . . When the magician went up and reached the boy, he threw parts of the boy's costumes (similar costumes) smeared with blood (blood-like colours) or some freshly butchered meat, which might be part of goat or monkey, one by one, to the ground. The assistants started picking them all up with very nice by-plays and acting—"where's the left arm, Ostad" and talks like that. The boy in the meantime took shelter underneath the flowing garments of the magician. . . . Amidst vigorous by-play and acting, the magician climbed down thoroughly exhausted. The assistants had in the meantime collected the seeming dismembered parts of the boy's body, including the missing parts that dropped here and there. The head was covered with the part of a boy's turban all smeared with fresh blood. The magician would then come near the basket into which the cut pieces of the boy were placed. More acting, more by-play and more misdirection—the boy slipped out and entered into the basket, just as they do in the traditional basket trick. . . . At command the boy jumped out of the basket quite hale and hearty to receive baksheesh (prizes) from his admiring spectators. . . . Sometimes the story of . . . Indra, the king of Heaven, and his fight with the demons was alleged to be told. Rightly at that time they did enough incense burning, bonfire in the name of Homa or Yajna and thus obscurity of vision was created by the smokes. . . . In those days very ordinary tricks of the street magicians and medicine men were regarded as big feats of magic. . . . So the great Indian Rope Trick is not a myth" (*Sorcar on Magic*).

A certain sadhu named Vadramakrishna, who seems to have read Sorcar's account, told the self-promoting American journalist, John Keel, who himself attempted a performance of the trick, that he had done it as a child. His method was the same as Sorcar's, except that he did it at night and blinded the spectators with bright torches that were fueled by hashish. The boy and fakir were tightrope walkers; the parts of the boy were monkey flesh.

"I've done the Rope Trick," P. C. Sorcar Junior, smiling playfully and proudly, manipulating a thimble, making it vanish, told me. "I don't mean on stage, but in an open field, surrounded by spectators. I can, at my magic command, make a rope appear to stand up without any visible support. I can even make a boy climb right to the top of it."

I asked if he chased the boy up the rope and dismembered him.

"No," he laughed and the thimble returned. "That was a barbaric trick. The magician actually killed the boy. It's true. Cutting him to pieces was no act, no illusion. He did not really put the pieces back together. No, the boy had a twin. For this reason, needing twins and having to kill one of them, the full trick was not performed very often. First the Rope Trick, just as I can do it, would be performed. Then the basket trick, which every *jādūwālā* still does. Seeing the two parts of the trick, the audience was satisfied that they had seen the whole."

The trick is, as Sorcar Junior suggests, a conglomeration (whether formed by the performing magician, the deforming memory of the spectator, or the reforming fancy of the tale teller) of two basic and conventional tricks traditionally and still performed by Indian street magicians: levitation and the cut-and-restored illusion. These are the two scenes in the allegorical drama of the Rope Trick, a divertissement that recapitulates a solemn ritual.

THE INDIAN ROPE TRICK

Having as a child seen the same levitation accomplished for a laugh by a circus clown, I was not, as I watched the performance of Iqbal and Abdul in the park near the Purana Qila, despite the skillful acrobatics and the artful concealment of the cleverly constructed iron gaff, nearly as mystified by the illusion as I was by the apparent mystification of the audience with whom I stood in a circle, the illusions of the illusion. "Amazing!" the man next to me exclaimed with all of the wonder of Jahangir. When I heard a description of what I myself had seen, a five-foot elevation had become one of twenty feet.

It was one of several versions of levitation and aerial suspension (both Aga levitations, using a gaff, and Asrah levitations, which utilize a substitute form for the person being levitated, a mannequin that is light enough to be lifted horizontally by fine wires) used by the *jādūgar*s, one that all the magicians of Shadipur insisted was an ancient one, passed down from father to son for hundreds, if not thousands, of years. Abdul excitedly shouted in Hindi that Iqbal was dead and then, looking straight at me, muttered the dark English word, a magic word: "Death." Watching Iqbal, floating horizontally beneath the thick woolen blankets, slowly descend to earth, I must have missed something. "Why is he dead?" I asked the man next to me, but he only put his finger to his lips to quiet me. "*Mṛtyu!*" the magician cried out again in Hindi, then in English, "Death!" then in some other Indian language, and then, preserving the resurrectory theme of the Rope Trick drama, he proclaimed that he had the power to return the corpse to life. The mantras were muttered, the gestures made, the blankets removed, and Iqbal suddenly opened his eyes, smiled, and leapt to his feet like the magician who danced for the prince who could not laugh, to sell the rings and amulets that had, moments before, been placed over his heart. The man next to me bought one.

It was a fine thought that five hundred years before me, Ibn Battuta, also a tourist in Delhi, had, not far from that very park, and on a summer day perhaps just as hot, witnessed the same trick performed by *jādūgar*s, perhaps ancestors of Iqbal or Abdul, Chand Baba or Naseeb. The sultan Muhammad bin Tughluk informed two yogis that the visitor had come from far away and that they should show him something the likes of which he would never have seen before. One of the magicians, seated on the ground before the sultan and traveler, began to rise from the earth, to ascend until he came to rest above them in midair. Ibn Battuta remarks that he was so astonished at the sight of the hovering yogi that he thought he was going to faint; the sultan had to procure a potion to bring him back to his senses. Removing one of his sandals, the other magician, as if in anger, began beating the ground with it, and then the sandal, as if animated by some magical power, rose up in the air and slapped the floating yogi on the neck, a signal that caused him to slowly descend back to earth. The sultan offered the traveler a display of much more amazing things, but the faint-hearted Ibn Battuta insisted that he had seen quite enough (*Voyages*).

In the five hundred years between Ibn Battuta's visit to India and my own, countless other travelers have been shown levitations and have written about them. In the early nineteenth century European newspapers were carrying reports of Sheshal, the South Indian "Brahmin of the air"; accounts of how, deep in a trance, he floated above the ground. "While the conjuring art seemed to be declining in Europe, Indian conjurors were exhibiting in their own land the marvels which have since attracted wondering crowds to the temples of magic which their imitators have set up in the capitals of the West. The aerial suspension was performed half a century ago [c. 1820] at Madras by an old Brahmin [Sheshal], with no better apparatus than a piece of plank, which, with four legs,

FIGURE 5. *Sheshal, The Floating Brahmin of Madras.*

he formed into an oblong stool; and upon which, in a little brass socket, he placed, in a perpendicular position, a hollow bamboo, from which projected a kind of crutch, covered with a piece of common hide. These properties he carried with him in a little bag, which was shown to those who went to see him exhibit. The servants of the house held a blanket before him, and when it was withdrawn he was discovered poised in the air, about four feet from the ground, in a sitting attitude, the outer edge of one hand merely touching the crutch, with the fingers deliberately counting beads, and the other hand and arm held up in an erect posture. The blanket was then held up before him, and the spectators heard a gurgling noise, like that occasioned by wind escaping from a bladder or tube, and when the screen was withdrawn he was again standing on the floor or ground. This performer died in 1830, without imparting to anyone the secret of this trick which was said, however, by a knowing native, to be effected by holding the breath, clearing the tubular organs, and a peculiar mode of respiration" (Frost, *Lives of the Conjurors*).

Within ten years Robert-Houdin, under the influence and inspiration of Oriental accounts, using the same method and gaff as Sheshal, floated his son Emile on a stage before the knowing natives of Paris, who firmly believed it was done with ether. And in London, at about the same time, a stage magician, Alfred Sylvester, billing himself as the "Fakir of Oolu," dressed as a maharaja, was also performing Sheshal's levitation. As could only be done on the stage, he embellished the suspension by removing the pole and supporting a floating maharani with his hand. Other Western magicians went to India to learn new methods of levitation. In 1875 Harry Kellar, in the company of the Prince of Wales and a throng of Indian dignitaries, watched a levitation in the maidan of Calcutta: "The old fakir took three swords with straight cross-barred hilts and buried them, hilt downward, about six inches in the ground. The points of these swords were very sharp, as I afterwards informed myself. A young fakir . . . at a gesture from his master, stretched himself out upon the ground at full length, with his feet together and his hands close to his sides, and, after a pass or two made by the hands of the old man, appeared to become rigid and lifeless. A third fakir now came forward, and, taking hold of the feet of his prostrate companion, whose head was lifted by the master, the two laid the stiffened body upon the points of the swords, which appeared to support it without penetrating the flesh." Two of the swords were removed and the child, in this performance of a trick that is still standard in the repertoire of most Indian stage magicians, remained suspended in the air. Jahangir witnessed the same suspension and, as the commander of an army, was intrigued as to how the magician was not injured by the sharp sword (*Tūzuk-i-Jahangīri*).

While Western conjurers during the colonial period sought, on the one hand, to expose Oriental miracles as mere magic tricks, to assert the immutability of Western laws of physics, they were also, on the other hand, motivated to maintain

FIGURE 6. *Levitation*. Reprinted from P. C. Sorcar's *History of Magic* (Calcutta, 1970); courtesy of P. C. Sorcar Junior.

the mystique of the mystic East, a mystique which would draw audiences to their own Indian-styled reviews. The Swedish magician Baron Hartwig Seeman performed a levitation, a trick he claimed to have seen and learned in 1872 in Banaras from an Indian magician he calls "Covindsamy." The Hindu floated a young girl in the air. Some days later, H. J. Burlingame explains in *Around the World with a Magician and a Juggler*, his biography of Seeman, the girl came to the European to take him to the swami, who showed him that his hand had been badly burned. It was the self-inflicted punishment for breaking the vow of his order never to demonstrate supernatural powers to foreigners.

It is very possible that Seeman's pious Covindsamy is the same Covindsamy described by Louis Jacolliot, at one time a chief justice in the French East Indies and at all times a confirmed believer in the extraordinary abilities of fakirs. His Covindsamy, claiming to be a holy man from Trivandrum, was encountered by the French diplomat in Banaras, where he showed him the extraordinary powers he had achieved through austerities and devotion: "Taking an ironwood cane which I had brought from Ceylon, he leaned heavily upon it, resting his right hand upon the handle, with his eyes fixed upon the ground. He then proceeded to utter the appropriate incantations. . . . Leaning upon the cane with one hand, the Fakir rose gradually about two feet from the ground. His legs were crossed beneath him, and he made no change in his position. . . . For more than twenty minutes I tried to see how Covindsamy could thus fly in the face and eyes of all the known laws of gravity; it was entirely beyond my comprehension" (*Occult Science in India*).

The same method of levitation used by Sheshal in Madras and by Covind-samy in Banaras has continued to be employed in this century. In 1936 a Mr. P. T. Plunkett published spectacular photographs of a South Indian levitation in the *Illustrated London News* (6 June), and similar photographs, taken in 1947 by Douglas Gordon, an Indian civil service official, widely published in Europe and America, convinced many readers that there were indeed Indian yogis who, through spiritual means, could defy known physical laws. The attitude was re-capitulated not very many years ago when Transcendental Meditation centers offered courses in which one could enroll to learn the techniques of levitation—not of performing the trick, but of experiencing the miracle. The trick, alas, is easier than the miracle—all the magicians of Shadipur can do it; but, it was explained to me, they rarely perform it because the gaff, the metal harness that must be worn, is cumbersome. There was a magician in the twenties, Azuri Yahya, I was told, who, in Calcutta, made a specialty of it. "It's a trick for one-trick magicians. It takes no skill, no patter," Naseeb explained with a certain scorn for that kind of magic. "You just sit or lie there with your eyes closed, hoping people think it's some kind of *samādhi*. You could do it. Easy. But it's okay—it fools a few people."

It seems to have fooled Jean Filliozat, to have brought the word *samādhi* (the yogic term for contemplative, beatific absorption) to the mind of that consummate professor, that conservative Indologist and medical doctor. In his scholarly dis-cussion of Plunkett's photographs, images which he was correctly assured were in no way faked or doctored, he states that the levitation is "*pour le moment com-plètement inexpliqué.*" The article clearly demonstrates the fundamental axiom of magic that the more one knows, the more easily one can be fooled. Filliozat's monumental erudition, his knowledge of Indian religious traditions, as well as his reliance on scientific modes of inquiry and analysis, leads him astray. He mistakes the *jādūgar* for a yogi and proceeds to project onto the trick all that he knows about yoga, Patañjali, and the tradition. Over the silent photographs, the profes-sor's Indological expertise functions as the magician's patter: "*Le yogin a accompli un exercice épuisant au cours duquel il s'est placé volontairement en état de rigidité musculaire complète,*" he explains, taking the apparent rigidity of the man in the photograph (actually a result of the metal harness the *jādūgar* is wearing) for a symptom of the exhaustion that supposedly results from the extraordinary exertion necessary for a yogi to display supranormal powers (*"Les limites des pouvoirs humains dans l'Inde"*).

Filliozat is tempted because levitation is, indeed, one of the conventionally enumerated powers often mentioned in yogic texts: through breath control, the body becomes light. Iqbal breathed heavily as he floated into the air, and the man next me, pointed as he whispered, *"prāṇāyāma."* Iqbal, to one who understood the trick as it was supposed to be understood, had not really been dead; he had merely suspended his respiratory and other bodily functions. You need knowledge in order to be fooled.

The magical, supranormal powers that are, according to Indian traditions, attained through penance or contemplation, austerities or devotion, are signs of transcendence. Thus the Buddha frequently taught the dharma while comfortably sitting or standing in the air, displaying a buoyancy that announced purity, a triumph over matter, earth and flesh, an immunity to the forces that tug upon us and keep us down. The Bodhisat possessed the power as an infant: "Seated cross-legged in mid-air, he revealed the truth to his father in sweet tones" (*Kaṭṭhahāri-Jātaka*). And later, after his great awakening from the dream in which we remain enmeshed, his release from Indra's net, the Buddha "seated cross-legged, passed through the air, over the Rohini River, much to the amazement of his relatives" (*Rukkhadhamma-Jātaka*). He had possessed this power, the ability to levitate, even in his former lives. In one incarnation he was an elephant, Ananda was the mahout, and Devadatta the king of Magadha. Upon a mountain precipice, the king argued with the mahout as to whether or not the elephant was well trained. "Show me," the king insisted, "make him stand on three feet." The mahout touched his elephant with the goad and called to him, "My beautiful one, stand on three feet!" And the elephant obeyed. When the king asked to see the elephant stand on two feet, the mahout issued the command and the elephant raised his back two feet. Then the wonderful elephant, on the very edge of the precipice, stood on one leg. "Now, if you can" the king scowled, "make him stand in the air!" "And the Great Being, endowed as he was with the magical powers that come with merit, immediately ascended into the air." And then, with the mahout upon his back, he flew to Banaras where he descended to earth and was installed as the royal elephant of the king there (*Dummedha-Jātaka*).

The power of the Buddha comes to his followers through their faith. In order to express his devotion to the Buddha, an elder bowed to his master: "The Blessed One is my teacher, and I am his disciple." As he spoke he rose into the air to the height of seven palm trees (*Mahānāradakassapa-Jātaka*). The same magical power can, however, in the context of later Tantric formulations, be attained through darker ritual practices. Antinomian rites take the initiate beyond norms and restrictions, beyond social and natural laws. Once upon a time the princess Kuvalayavali, startled by the extraordinary sight of some friends levitating, asked them how she too might accomplish it. "These are magic powers attained through a witch's spells and they can be exhibited only after eating human flesh—this magic is taught by the brahmin crone Kalaratri." The girl beseeched the witch to initiate her. "When, after bathing and worshipping Ganesha, I fell at her feet, she had me take off my clothes and then, standing in a circle, we acted out a horrible ceremony in honor of Shiva in his terrible form; after dousing me with water, she taught me some spells and then fed me on human flesh that had been sacrificially offered; after I had consumed the meat of a man's body, I was suddenly able to fly still naked into the heavens with my friends and to amuse myself there" (*Kathāsaritsāgara* 3:20).

It's impossible to know if such religious stories, the Buddhist tale of the power that comes with devotion or the Tantric tale of the power that comes with heterodox rites, result from people having seen magicians do the levitation trick, from their need to explain it, or if the trick is invented, its method worked out, by magicians who have heard the stories and realize that, because people believe such things as levitation are possible and a mark of merit or of ritual accomplishment, there is power to be had in the performance of them. In either case, the street magicians, of the present as well as of the past, try to elicit religious associations. They know the reward in that.

After the levitation had been done, Chand Baba showed the basket, tilted it this way and that way, slapped it with the sword, laughed, and signaled to Salma to come forward. Naked to the waist, ready to be sacrificed, she looked frightened, but was resigned to obey her grandfather's commands. Were her fears of the illusion or part of the illusion? She stood in the basket and we witnessed a spectacle that has been displayed for hundreds, probably thousands, of years on the streets of India. "Everyone who has been to the East," notes Lieutenant Colonel Elliot, "has seen the basket trick. It is an everyday performance." Early in the nineteenth century Reverend Hobart Caunter described just what we saw. His Chand Baba was a "stout ferocious-looking fellow," and his Salma was "a child about eight years old, an interesting little girl, habited in the only garb which nature had provided for her, perfect of frame and elastic of limb—a model for a cherub, and scarcely darker than a child of southern France. When she was perfectly secured, the man, with a lowering aspect, asked her some question, which she instantly answered and as the thing was done within a few feet from the spot on which we were seated, the voice appeared to come so distinctly from the basket, that I felt at once satisfied that there was no deception. They held a conversation for some moments, when the juggler, almost with a scream of passion, threatened to kill her. There was a stern reality in the whole scene which was perfectly dismaying; it was acted to the life, but terrible to see and hear. The child was heard to beg for mercy, when the juggler seized the sword, placed his foot upon the frail wicker covering under which his supposed victim was so piteously supplicating his forbearance, and to my absolute consternation and horror, plunged it through, withdrawing it several times, and repeating the plunge with all the blind ferocity of an excited demon. By this time his countenance exhibited an expression fearfully indicative of the most frantic of human passions. The shrieks of the child were so real and distracting that they almost curdled for a few moments the whole mass of my blood: my first impulse was to rush upon the monster, and fell him to the earth; but he was armed and I defenceless. I looked at my companions—they appeared to be pale and paralysed with terror; and yet these feelings were somewhat neutralised by the consciousness that the man would not dare to commit a deliberate murder in the broad eye of day, and before so many witnesses; still the whole thing was appalling. The blood ran in streams from the basket; the child was heard to struggle under it; her groan fell horribly upon the ear; her struggles smote painfully upon the heart. The former were gradually subdued into a faint moan, and the latter into a slight rustling sound; we seemed to hear the last convulsive gasp which was to set her innocent soul free from the gored body" (cited by Frost). "*Yantru-mantru-jālajāla-tantru,*" Chand Baba intoned as he stepped back from the basket, and slowly the cloth-covered lid rose as if of itself, higher and higher, eerie and mysterious, and the magician lunged forward to pull back the drape—Salma stood there, resurrected, reborn from the ancient womb-shaped basket. Perhaps the dried blood on her naked chest represented womanhood to some. The eyes of the child were dark, and her lips without a smile or frown. The expression on her face was that of one who in the darkness of the magic basket had gazed into death, eternal and real. When in the nineteenth century Harry Kellar watched the trick, he was stunned by the "agonizing cries and heart rending screams" of the boy in the basket. After it was over "Kellar paid the juggler two rupees (one dollar) and the secret of the trick was explained to him. He marveled at first that the man was willing to explain the mystery for so small a sum" (*A Magician's Tour Up and Down and Round About the Earth*).

Unbeknownst to Kellar, the reason that the juggler sold his secret for so little was that he, in fact, sold him nothing at all. He lied to Kellar when he revealed that he had concealed the boy in his garments. To trick the crowd, the magician did the trick; to trick the magician, he sold him a false method for the trick. Or if not Kellar, then I've been tricked, told the wrong method by Naseeb. Or both. In the world of magicians, there's no straight answer, no way of telling what is deception and what is truth; the truest truth always turns out to be but the cleverest deception. The *Talismāt Nātak Kalān*, the nineteenth-century Urdu pamphlet given to me by the magician Ashok Bhandari, purporting, after a pious prayer and an assertion that only Allah is responsible for anything miraculous, to reveal all the secrets of magic and conjuring, explains how to perform a levitation: "Hide a metal bar in the shirt of the one you are going to levitate; conceal a very large magnet in the ceiling. When positioned in the correct spot, the person will rise in the air."

Just as Naseeb never performed the aerial suspension, so too he never performed the basket trick and did not seem particularly impressed with it. The archetypal illusion, however, the act of putting back together that which has been taken apart, the display of a miraculous power to resurrect, recreate what has been destroyed, was, in the form of the cut-and-restored turban trick, an important part of his repertoire. He played it for laughs. It set the crowd up for the horror of his decapitation illusion and the trick of cutting off and then restoring his child's tongue, tricks that paid. Those two tricks are technically simple. But while they require almost no sleight of hand, it is in the performance of them that the magician displays his skill as an actor, the power that creates the illusion, terrifies the spectators and moves them to reach into their pockets for the money, at once alms and pay.

Whenever Naseeb performed the decapitation on a volunteer, he would ask, "Hindu? Mussulman?" as if that made some difference, and the question prompted the audience to supply the religious associations for what they saw, to weave the net of symbols in which they would find themselves caught. I myself did it, allowed thoughts of severed heads offered to the dreadful Kali to bring a false but powerful meaning to the tricks. Watching Naseeb decapitate a volunteer each day, then seeing the victim recapitated, I thought of a chilling story in the *Kathāsaritsāgara* in which Indivarasena, in battle with a *rākṣasa*, cuts off the demon's head again and again, and each time it immediately grows back (7:42). Naseeb, like all of the street magicians, in and with his magic, shows the audience a mythology that is embedded in their own consciousness, and that is the greater illusion, the trick of the tricks, the magic of magic.

If the audience was slow to pay after the decapitation, the magician would scold them angrily: "You'd give P. C. Sorcar twenty rupees to see the same thing; but when he does it, it's not as good as this—you're far away; it's on the stage. It's not real. This is real!" He'd play upon fear and guilt: "Only two rupees, that's all, and then this boy will be brought back to life. Have you no mercy for one of God's creatures?" By asking that question, even though it is all deceit, the magician performs an important social function. Society needs to have that question asked each day, and to have it asked on the streets where it is both most relevant and most easily ignored.

The audience tosses money into the circle. The magic words are uttered, the magic gestures made, and the child is resurrected. It's the finale of Naseeb's improvisational miracle play, just as it was the climactic scene in the legendary drama of the Indian Rope Trick.

Whether it is performed or said to be performed, whether in the world or the imagination, the drama takes place on the street (stage versions have usually had sets meant to conjure up the streets), out of doors, in the open, some clearing, no particular place, anywhere and thus everywhere, a space in which every object, person, and action is metaphorical. All magic tricks, in their defiance of the norms of possibility and causality, take place outside of ordinary space and time, an extraordinary context in which time can be modulated or reversed, in which objects can multiply, disappear, reappear, in which even, and perhaps especially, death, the fundamental reality, can be defied.

The Rope Trick, the play or story of the trick, begins with the agon. Just as in the beginning of each of Naseeb's shows, when Ayasan mocks him and is chased by him, scolded and menaced with a knife, so the child in the Rope Trick challenges the magician. This establishes the major theme of the trick: it is about the relationship between father and son as represented by magician and apprentice, and as representative of other relationships—guru and initiate, master and servant, god and human being perhaps, whatever hierarchical relationship any member of the audience associates with the spectacle.

The figure of authority demonstrates his power by making the rope rise in the air and remain erect. The rope, a prop and symbol still used in the performances of the *jādūgars*, is, in the Indian context, potentially suggestive of the *sūtrātman*, the soul or spirit that passes through the universe like a cord to hold all things together; it is possibly also and simultaneously evocative of both a negative binding, being tied to the wheel of transmigration and, as it reaches into the sky and out of sight, of a means of escape from the world. As animated to display the magician's power in this trick, the rope is, furthermore, specifically a symbol of sexual potency. It is not out of a facile and reductionist Freudianism that I make the observation that the risen rope invites phallic associations: I have three versions of the Rope Trick—one given to me by Tayade in Bombay, one purchased from Tannen's in New York, and one from the Hollywood Magic Shop that has a picture of Sorcar on the package in which it comes—and each and every time that I've shown the trick to someone, made the floppy rope stiff, there has been the inevitable racy joke and the happily dirty laugh. The association is irrepressible. The rope is a symbol of the sexual energy that the magician has and the boy does not have, the power that, as the trick unfolds, will be used to kill and resurrect, to initiate.

The power is shown to the boy. He is directed to test it, to climb the rope, to suspend himself there just as Sheshal or Covindsamy suspended themselves. The levitation, like the dismemberment and reintegration that follow, is metaphorical: the defiance of gravity, at once the literal force that holds us to the earth and the figurative spirit of gravity, of sorrow, is a consummately appealing trick—we adore the lie and find consolation in the illusion.

When the child, out of sight and tempted by the freedom gained in his distance from earth and the magician, defies the magician's order to return, when he exercises his own will and authority and expresses his own nascent sexuality, he is pursued by the magician, who wields a knife or sword, another symbol of his power, another main prop still and commonly used by Naseeb and the other street magicians, a symbol with which the child is symbolically decapitated, symbolically dismembered, and symbolically brought back to earth.

Naseeb used the knife with which he had drawn blood from limes and sliced off Ayasan's tongue to mark the ground with magic diagrams. The knife became a magic wand as it tempted spectators to see it as having a power independent of the magician. "Keep this sword," an Asura maiden says in the *Kathāsaritsāgara*. "It confers the power to fly through the air—it is full of magic" (9:56). Objects are magic objects to the degree that they are symbolic objects. The magician is he who knows the power of symbols and how to manipulate that power. All symbols, by their nature, are magical; Naseeb's rings and amulets are symbols for sale. That's why they work and why they don't.

The decapitation and dismemberment, like the cutting off of the tongue of the foul-mouthed Ayasan in Naseeb's performances, is a punishment for transgression against the father, a disregard of his sexual power. Ayasan's mockery of Naseeb is essentially obscene. The magic scene is evocative of the decapitation of Ganesha by Shiva, his father, the punishment inflicted when the child, promising to guard his mother from intruders while she was bathing, refused to let his father in. While the decapitation of demons is a conventional motif in Indian mythology, it is always, as in the myth of Shiva and Ganesha, a child, or a weaker, more helpless being (a little girl in the case of Chand Baba's basket trick, a young woman in the case of the stage magicians' sawing the lady in half, a dove in smaller versions of the trick) that is decapitated or dismembered in magic. It is crucial for the sake of the appeal of the trick and its inherent and implicit allegory that the observers of the magic show, like the suppliants at a ritual, identify with the victim, the object of the sacrifice, an affiliation that will allow them to find consolation in the resurrection to come.

The Rope Trick, like so many illusions in the Indian repertoire, recapitulates a cosmogony, the Vedic sacrifice of Purusha, the primal person, the performance of the "first religious rite in which, with sacrifice, the gods sacrificed to sacrifice" (*Rgveda* 10.90). The magic trick, like the hieratic ritual, demonstrates, on one level, the power of sacrifice as a mode of transforming the processes of destruction into sources of creation, of revealing promises of life within spectacles of death. "When the gods dismembered the person, how many parts did they divide him into? What happened to his head, his arms, his trunk, his feet?" From the sacrifice of the person, the world was created, "animals and birds, creatures of forests and villages, the Vedas, horses and cows, sheep and goats," and the four castes were constituted by his head, his arms, his trunk and his feet, the moon from his mind, the sun from his eye, the fire from his mouth, the wind from his breath, the sky from his head, the earth from his feet. Creation is accomplished through a dismemberment and re-memberment, a reintegration of the parts into a new whole.

In the Rope Trick—at once the acting out of the cosmogony, the death and rebirth that mark the seasons, the puberty rite, all of these mysterious transformations and more—the re-membering and revivication of the victim takes place in a womb-shaped basket. The child, curled up in a fetal position for the performance of the illusion, is, once the magician says the magic words and makes the magic gestures, reborn out of it. The horrid fear of the audience is transformed into pleasurable wonder, and magician and child, father and son, god and person, are reconciled. Sexual power, at first menacing, has become sanctified as the source of life and harmony. That sanctification is the trick. Knowing the secret, the son in time, utilizing the magic power, can produce a son of his own and then, as the magician, do the trick himself in turn, demonstrate the mystery, and perpetuate it. The members of the audience are, in some unspoken way, challenged or beckoned by their own wonder to perform a version of their own.

"What are you writing about now?" The Incredible Mayadhar asked me as he entered my room in Sunder Nagar, seated himself comfortably, and glanced over at the bottle of duty-free scotch.

"The Rope Trick," I said as I closed my notebook and handed him my magic pen. "Here, take this pen and write the name of any flower that comes to mind; write it here on this piece of paper."

"I know the trick. I have one of these pens myself," he smiled as he took the pen, wrote the word *rose* on the piece of paper, and smelled it. "Roses!" he said. "Wonderful trick. Even though I know that it is an illusion, believe me please, I always smell whatever flower-name I write. And, most extraordinary, the pen is bilingual—it does not matter whether I write *rose* or *gulāb!*" He set down the paper, picked up the rope that Tayade had given me, and examined it. "I have one of these ropes as well."

I offered him a scotch.

"Okay, but only four or five or six drops. What do you think, my darling man," The Incredible Mayadhar happily asked, "was the great Rope Trick ever performed?"

"Of course," I said to startle him.

"And the secret?" he smiled as he threw the rope up in the air and watched it stay there, erect. "What, please, is the secret?"

"Secret? Do you mean the method? There are, perhaps, methods of actually doing it. There's a farmer in Ghaziabad who has performed the Rope Trick, who did it just by having a piece of rope on the ground at the right time in the presence of the right observer, so that the story of a performance of it spread. If what a conjurer does is create the illusion that something is happening that is not happening, or that something has occurred that in reality has not occurred, then indeed the Rope Trick has been done. The illusion is reality, just like the magic pen. That the farmer can't repeat it, that one of many ways of doing it, is irrelevant."

THE INDIAN ROPE TRICK

The rope fell, the tumbler was empty, and The Incredible Mayadhar frowned. "There is a problem in your thinking, believe me please. I can explain the pen nonproblematically: the ink is scented with a melange of floral essences, and the nose naturally selects that perfume from the bouquet to which it has been directed through the autosuggestion of mental choosing as enhanced by writing. That is easy. But the Rope Trick! There wouldn't have been any stories about that farmer if people hadn't already heard the details of the trick. So when was that trick first performed? Where? By whom? What did the magician actually do? Or, more fundamentally speaking, did he do anything at all, something more than your farmer did—was the Rope Trick ever performed?"

Under the circumstances I had to concede that I did not know for sure.

"Of course it was," he smiled as he accepted the refill of his drink.

"And the secret?" I asked.

"Oh," he grinned all the more. "That I don't know! That is what you should research. Believe me please, my darling man. Maybe your research will lead to a solution. The greatest trick in the world! It is for the world's greatest magician to make that illustrious illusion reality for once and for all."

ON THE STAGE
NOW

Mirrors and Water

Scene Five:

East/Spring
The Reflections of Professor
M. T. Bannerji 1

"The greatest trick in the world, and I, the amazing and wonderful Professor M. T. Bannerji, world's greatest magician, he who is thoroughly me, *escamoteur extraordinaire*, shall perform it! Without a doubt, the illustrious illusion shall be reality for once and for all! The Indian Rope Trick!" The magician spoke out loud and in English to himself, the exuberant maharaja in the gilt-framed, full-length practice mirror: "And when I have accomplished it, out-of-doors and fully surrounded as in the more fabulous times of a more felicitous yore here in the sublime expanses of our beloved India, this *puṇya* place of magic, of miracles, marvels, and mysteries, then, yes then, it will be indisputable and absolutely incontrovertible that I, the magnificent *moi*, M. T. Bannerji, prophetic professor of prestidigitation, am indeed this wide world's greatest magician, greatest greatest of all the greatests."

Smiling over the thought, the maharaja adjusted the pink feather that flopped before his face as sadly as the willow branch that weeps in doggerel. In the red-satin, greasy-around-the-edges turban, that limp plume was secured by a large brooch that was inlaid with a rubylike piece of glass that did its very best to shimmer for him then. The magician snapped his fingers, and before his very eyes, a lit Gold Flake cigarette (the only brand he smoked, if he himself were the purchaser) appeared in his hand. "You are damn good, sir!" He smiled and winked at the princely figure in the antique looking-glass that had been used by his father before him. "Damn astonishing, to be sure." After one deep puff, he opened his mouth, inserted the cigarette lit end first and, as smoke curled out of his nostrils, closed his smiling lips around it ("Gone! Gone! Swallowed alive!"), shook his head, and removed the cigarette from his ear. "Damn spectacular, Professor M. T. Bannerji!"

Never taking his eyes off himself, he took another puff of the cigarette and then set it in that cherished ashtray, a gift from the peregrine Dr. Chatterji, a souvenir of sorts from the Stardust Hotel and Casino, Las Vegas, Nevada, U.S.A. Exhaling as he pushed back the sleeves of his majestic maharaja's brocade primrose coat, Bannerji flexed the agile magic fingers and reached for his mascara and the little brush.

"The eyes have it!" he whispered. "Just a touch of kohl there, a trace of indigo here, and a slight highlight in white, a whisper to accentuate the marvelous mesmeric power of the magician's eye!" For the last fifteen years or so, Professor Bannerji had been developing his hypnotic stare, the "electromagnific gaze," as he called it. Time was set aside each day for him to focus the eyes, stretched as widely open as possible, on a single spot, the center of the mystical Shri Yantra, and to stare intently at that magic diagram, restraining all natural impulses to blink, forcing the eyes to pierce the geometric image, to bore into it like a laser, to see through it, into the very core of the universe. And, indeed, after the years of practice, he could keep his eyes fixed like that for long periods of time without winking, squinting, or tearing.

"It makes you look crazy," his wife used to say. "Crazy and stupid. You look absolutely ridiculous. You are ridiculous."

Even as he shook his head, the eyes remained fixed on the single spot. "She will eat those words. One man's stupidity is another man's power, as our ancient rishis no doubt opined. Under this gaze, when fully developed, men will confess their deceits, women will be cured of fits of hysteria, and wild beasts will whimper at my feet."

Suddenly he heard the music from the adjacent circus tent—"That Old Black Magic"—the cue that he was to appear on the stage in exactly seven minutes, and though he had performed thousands of shows, the signal always made the heart shiver, the stomach tighten, the quick hands tremble just a bit, and the eyes close. Turning from the mirror and approaching the magic table, Professor Bannerji set the tumbler in place and filled it with water from the lota bowl. Flourishing the off-pink, silklike foulard, plucked with panache from his sash, and dropping it over the glass, with a wave of the peacock-feather wand to misdirect as the unwatched hand hit the gimmick's switch, he snatched the cloth back and smiled at the tumbler of scotch. "Just like Jesus Christ, that juggler of Jerusalem, conjuring at Cana," he laughed and vanished the whiskey into his mouth. There was a happy smack of the lips. "Five more minutes. Do I look suitably magnificent?"

Staring at the magician, who looked so like his father used to look in that mirror, he darkened the thin moustache, blotted the cheery cherry lipstick, and, with all his heart and soul, the showman smiled the resplendent magic grin, what he called his "magnoelectrific smile," the expression which, like the electromagnific gaze, he had practiced assiduously each day before the glass, so that now he was quite confident that he could smile longer than any man on earth. So assured was he of that, that he had written to the editors of the *Guinness Book of World Records:* "I, the great Professor M. T. Bannerji, world's longest smiling man, humbly challenge you to send your good representative to Calcutta, India, to empirically, under scientifically controlled, experimental conditions, time the astonishingly long duration of my radiant facial display of consummate happiness."

But now that the magician had decided to perform the Indian Rope Trick, he was relieved of the anxiety caused by waiting for a reply from the editors at Guinness. "The longest-lasting smile in the world is a mere trifling compared to the performance of the ancient Indian Rope Trick," he thought, still grinning at the effervescent maharaja in the time-tarnished mirror.

The music changed—*"Prem! Prem! Prem!"*—three minutes left. He took a deep breath and, to rest both the electromagnific eyes that would be battered by bright lights for the next three hours and the rosy, rouged cheeks that would have to bear the weight of the magnoelectrific smile for just as long, closed the eyes and let the cheeks droop. "Relax," the magician whispered to himself. "A little *prāṇāyāma*, if you please." And then, as happened so often, more and more all the time, when Professor M. T. Bannerji slackened the guard he kept on his sense of well-being, he felt the sorrow. When the gloom tightened its grip on his throat, the magician wanted to vanish, to hide, not to go on stage, but to take flight. "But where? Where?" The deflated maharaja felt like weeping, even screaming, under the ache of his existence in the present, degraded age, the Kali Yuga. The disobedience of women was a symptom of the age (his wife had abandoned him and gone to London, taking his only son with her and leaving him alone to care for his aged and infirm father, Professor M. T. Bannerji Senior); so too his financial problems could be attributed both to his birth on a Saturday, under the sign of Saturn, and to the depravities and debasement of the era ("People, preferring the fads of films to traditional performances of the ancient art of magic, would rather see the insipid Dharmendra on the silver screen than the great M. T. Bannerji on the golden stage!"). His wife did not answer his letters, and his current tour (Delhi, Srinagar, Calcutta, Madras, Coimbatore, Trichur, Cochin) had put the company on the brink of bankruptcy. "This," Bannerji reflected, "is surely that damn *duḥkha* of which the great Buddh, in his wisdom, was always speaking! Kali Yug through and through!"

The last change in the music signaled that there was one minute to showtime, just long enough for one last smoke and a big gulp of whiskey to brace the magician for the magic. With a flutter of the fingers and a wave of the hand, a paper rose appeared, and the maharaja offered the flower to the man in the mirror as he switched on the enormous smile and winked. "That's better, Bannerji!" he laughed. "Once we have performed the great Indian Rope Trick as it has not been seen for centuries, then, at last, we will have all that we want out of this life. Not much. Just four things, that's all: fame and fortune, the respect of men, and the love of women. Is that too much to ask for? Just four things! Is that too much?"

On the stage Bhutnath Dey, Professor Bannerji's Majordomo-and-Chief of Operations and Applications, attired in the black satinlike robe that Ratikanta

Tapadar, the production company's Deputy Manager-in-Charge of Tailoring, Costumes, and Hats, insisted was an exact replica of the "vestments donned by the learned doctors of Oxford University," tipped his black, tasseled mortarboard as he took his low, introductory bow. His son, the eight-year-old Sushil, wearing a dunce's cap, pushed out the six-foot-tall book onto the stage and positioned it so that the few members of the audience who were sitting near the front could read the title on the cover: *Net of Magic: Wonders in India.*

Wielding a pointer and watched by young Sushil, Bhutnath Dey opened the text and there, on the first page, was an ancient god, holding a rainbow in one hand and a fishing net in the other, a grinning deity whose iconography might have been unrecognized if not for the caption in Hindi, Bengali, Tamil, and English: "Indra, First Magician." Then the second page: "Indian Cave Man, First Mortal Magician." With each turn of the page, Bhutnath, bowing, smiling, and winking, pointed to the successive captions to each of the illustrations: "Dravidian Magician of Mohenjodaro," "Raja Bhoj, Ancient Indian Stage Magician," "Indragopa, Ancient Indian Street Magician," "Shri Patañjali, Real Magician," "Shri Shankaracharya, Philosopher of Magic," "Vishvasiddhi the Great, King Amaruka's Court Magician," "Birbal, Akbar's Court Magician," "Seshal, Flying Brahmin of Madras," "Ramo Samee of London Fame."

Sitting next to Sagar, the Deputy-Chief of Stage Technologies and Technicalities, on the raised platform from which the technician could see both the house and the stage and control the music and the lights, Professor M. T. Bannerji Senior surveyed the sparse audience. "Let there be light! More light!" he ordered Sagar. "Put on all the lights so that it will be more difficult for my wonderful Junior to see this audience. Blind him with the light! The less aware he is of how few people have shown up, given our current and temporary fiscal predicament, the better. When my son is conscious of a paltry and minimal house, he doesn't give it what we magicians call 'his all.' That, my good Sagar, is the difference between us—in my day, I could perform with complete enthusiasm even if no one showed up. That, my young friend, is greatness!"

The order was obeyed, and though it made Bhutnath and Sushil squint, it made it easier to read, on the remaining pages of the book, the names of magicians who had performed as maharajas: Carter, Kalanag, Gogia Pasha, Laxman Singh Gehlot, P. C. Sorcar Senior and then, finally, the last page. There was no picture on it, only a large black question mark under the caption, "World's Greatest Magician of the Twentieth Century." There was a pause as the tape changed—*"Dam Māro Dam"* gave way to Richard Strauss's *Also Sprach Zarathustra.* And, after turning up the volume all the way, Sagar readied himself to bang the cymbals together and positioned his toe on the button that would ignite the flashpot that Sushil had placed rather too visibly in front of the giant book.

Suddenly and finally, bursting through the question mark on the page, with a flash of light and a cloud of smoke, the great Professor M. T. Bannerji, World's

Greatest Magician, smiling his magnoelectrific smile and gazing into the blinding floodlights with his electromagnific eyes, costumed as a maharaja, took a cere-monious bow, raising his hand to his head as he did so in what looked like a gesture of obeisance but what was, in reality, a measure that prevented his turban from falling off.

Sagar put on a polka as Bhutnath and Sushil wheeled the great *Net of Magic* offstage and a backdrop depicting the Taj Mahal slowly descended behind the beaming maharaja, who snapped his fingers and produced a paper flower that he tossed into the audience. Another snap of the fingers and wave of the hand materialized a cigarette, which he extinguished in his mouth. Another manual flourish produced a pigeon from nowhere. Turning the bird over in his hands, the magician massaged its breast gently with his finger, and then, when he had set it down on the table which Sushil wheeled in, the bird lay perfectly still. As the conjurer gestured with his hands, fingers wide-spread, the pigeon, still on its back, rose slowly in the air, higher and higher. The maharaja of magic passed a shiny metal hoop over the hovering bird to show that there were no strings attached. With a wave of his hand, the bird slowly descended to the table again, from where it was picked up and placed in a brown paper bag. Professor Bannerji set the bag on fire, scattered the ashes with a flourish, blew up a yellow balloon, popped it with a pin, and the dove-gray pigeon was resurrected.

"*Śābāś!*" M. T. Bannerji Senior called out: "Bravo! *Jay Hind!*"

The magician always balanced his fire tricks with water illusions—Waters of India, Vanishing Vase, Fishbowl from Foulard, and Dr. Patañjali Patel as The Human Fountain.

The sound of the vina was the cue for Vimal, Deputy Director of Wings, Flats, and Curtains, to lower the backdrop depicting the Himalayan ashram, the prompt, in turn, for Dr. Patel to appear onstage for the demonstration that was timed to last just long enough for the great Bannerji to change out of his maharaja costume and into his black tuxedo.

Patañjali Patel, a yogi and retired mathematics teacher, appearing in a large white turban and a scant white loincloth, would swallow five enormous glass bowls of water, bow, and then forcibly regurgitate the entire volume of clear liquid, refilling each of the five bowls. Though not a trick or an illusion in any way but a real exhibition of yogic power cultivated for the sake of the purification of the body, this item, through the ingenuity of Professor M. T. Bannerji, had become quite a colorful bit of entertainment: the magician had convinced the yogi to place a live goldfish in each of the bowls and to spit them up, still quite alive, with the gush of water. The first time Dr. Patel had tried it, all of the fish ended up in the first bowl. But now, after months of diligent practice, he could some-times succeed in getting a single goldfish in each of the five bowls.

As the yogi took his bow, the classical Indian music yielded to the more vivace sounds of "Tequila," and the Himalayan ashram disappeared behind the whirlpool of images—dice and dominoes, cards, a roulette wheel and poker chips, the American and Indian flags—on the backdrop and, under a sign lowered from the flies ("Stardust Hotel and Casino of Magnificent Las Vegas, U.S.A."), Professor Bannerji, dressed in a black tuxedo and black top hat, a red cummerbund and white gloves, materialized a pigeon from nowhere and held it up so that the audience could behold the egg drop from its rear end. And then another egg appeared. And then another. After the magician purposely caught each of the eggs and set them, one by one, on the table, Sushil, dressed now as a circus clown, brought out a dove pan from the wings of the stage and took the pigeon away with him. The conjurer, after donning the white apron and full hat that Ratikanta Tapadar insisted was an exact copy of the uniform worn by the chef at "the famous Maxim's in Paris, France," opened the metal pan and showed it to be empty. Once he had cracked each egg, emptied the whites and yolks into the pan, stirred it all up, added salt and pepper, tasted it, added more seasonings, and stirred it again, all the while nodding, rocking, and shaking his head to the music, he added kerosene to the mixture, lit a match, and dropped it in. Extinguishing the spectacular burst of flames with the lid of the pan, he proudly bowed and removed the lid again. And there was the pigeon.

"*Śābāś!*" cried M. T. Bannerji Senior.

M. T. Bannerji Junior skipped offstage and over to Lakshmi, who was waiting in the wings to make her entrance, to perform the classical dance that she hoped might be her redemption from a world she considered tawdry, her deliverance into the beautiful world of films and television. "Perhaps some producer, agent, casting director, or the like, from Bombay will bring his children to see the magic show," she often thought to herself. "He will be bored by the stupid tricks, looking at his watch all the time, and then he will see the beautiful Lakshmi, me, dance like a pearl dangling before swine, enchanting the soul like Hema Malini or Parveen Babi. Some day I'll play the part of Mira Bai, and my performance will inspire people to be more spiritual. That will be my contribution to humanity."

"Go on my darling! Dance!" the magician said to the dreamer, discreetly patting her buttocks to propel her onto the stage. "Dance my beauty! Weave your magic spell upon our humble stage."

He turned to Dr. Patañjali Patel, "Look at her gambol, her sweet dance! Is she not an Apsaras? Does a more lovely *devī* dance in any *loka*? Is this not the real magic?"

"How I should know?" the yogi and mathematician, his shoulders slouched, answered despondently. "I am *brahmacārī*—such is my vow that women are of no attraction to any of my sense organs."

Professor Bannerji changed into his Chinese robes to perform his Ghost of Old Peking, Dragon's Dilemma, and Topsy-Turvy Pagoda, after which, when it was time for him to change again, Suleiman Yusuf Shah was scheduled to appear. But the fire eater and sword swallower, who had been a street performer before

Bannerji discovered him and introduced him into professional show business, was nowhere to be found. "He's drunk," Vimal said, "Whiskey and bhang! He started early this morning. He is almost entirely unconscious."

Desperate, panicked by the empty stage, Professor M. T. Bannerji frantically ordered Dr. Patel to return to the limelight and perform his water swallowing and spitting once more.

"But the audience just saw me do it not fifteen minutes ago," the yogi objected.

"Never mind," Bannerji insisted: "Do it again. It is a feat well worth seeing twice. And this time, endeavor to get the five fish in the five different bowls. Get out there now, please. And don't perform it too quickly. We need a few minutes for the set-up."

"But, I am sorry to say," Patañjali Patel confessed, "I have, just this minute, eaten a rasogoola that will surely come out with the water and the fish, thereby giving the audience a feeling of disgust."

"Never mind the details! Disgust is preferable to boredom; anything is better than nothing. The stage is empty. The audience is waiting. Get out there," Bannerji snapped with uncharacteristic anger.

Dr. Patañjali Patel obeyed despite his feelings of remorse (over having eaten the sweet) and embarrassment (over Suleiman Yusuf Shah's backdrop, the depiction of a circus tent filled with wild animals and bikini-clad trapeze artists, which it seemed to him was inappropriate for his exhibition of the ancient and holy yoga-*marga*).

Turning to Sagar, M. T. Bannerji Senior asked the question: "Tell me, my dear Sagar, ocean of truth that you are, did Dr. Patel already perform this very item only fifteen minutes ago? Or am I becoming senile? Tell me the truth."

"The truth is," Sagar answered, as he put on the tape of Hindi film scores, "that both are so."

As the magician backstage switched into the surgeon's costume, he signaled to Prem Guha, Deputy Manager-in-Charge of Properties and Sundry Acquisitions, for the table and electric saw to be readied. But when he opened the secret door in the gimmicked operating table for Lakshmi to take her concealed place within it, the temperamental dancer stamped her foot. "I'm not doing it!" she snapped. "I'm not hiding in that table again! I am not a mere chattel! Why do I always have to be the bottom part of the woman you saw in half? I deserve to be appreciated for my top parts!"

"Please," the surgeon pleaded. "Listen to me. It is because I adore you, both the top and the bottom of you, that I have arranged things in this way. After the sawing-lady-in-half comes, as you well know, decapitation. Because your head is so beautiful, it is you, you and only you, my beloved one, whom I wish to decapitate. If I were to both saw you in half and decapitate you, one right after the other, it would weaken both effects."

"No, I won't do it!" Lakshmi suddenly retorted. "It is a matter of my principles."

Professor Bannerji looked anxiously to Dolon Dey, Bhutnath's wife, who
refused to give up her role as the top half of the maharani. "Do you think I have
less principles than Lakshmi or that I am more of a chattel than she?"

"Kali Yug!" the magician cursed, shaking his fist in the air at the very
moment that Dr. Patel, leaving the stage empty again, arrived at his side to ask,
with a meek smile, if the performance had been satisfactory. Bannerji ordered
him to go back out: "Do it again. We're not ready yet. Go. Do your item again for
them."

"It is not a good plan," Dr. Patel pleaded. "It is not out of modesty or humility
that I say that the audience, most likely, has had enough of my regurgitations."

Grabbing a sword from the rack of props next to him, Bannerji pointed it at
Dr. Patel: "Get out there or die!"

The blare of the music spared Dr. Patel the sound of the groans of the sparse
audience when he returned.

"Sushil," Professor Bannerji called out. "Come on Sushil, take off your
chapals, roll up your trousers, put on these lady's anklets, and get in the table."
As the boy obeyed, his father, Bhutnath, warned the magician that he expected
extra pay for the extra item for his son. "Of course, of course," the flustered
conjurer answered, interrupting his own instructions to the boy, who was hidden
in the operating table. "You must slide your feet through the holes under the
sheet just at the right moment—I'll signal you. Then you wiggle them around so
that everyone thinks they are your mother's feet. You're a good boy, Sushil, and
I won't forget your service to me. You're going to be famous, because you're going
to be my partner when I perform the great Indian Rope Trick, not our stage
version, but the real thing, out-of-doors and fully surrounded."

M. T. Bannerji Senior put his hand on Sagar's knee with fatherly affection.
"You know," he said, "the more I see Dr. Patel vomit, the more I am coming to
enjoy it."

After M. T. Bannerji Junior appeared to saw Dolon Dey in half, separate the
parts, and put her back together, he exited to remove the surgeon's gown, under
which he wore the maharaja's primrose coat. As he adjusted the turban on his
head, Lakshmi danced once more upon the stage. Bhutnath, Prem Guha, Vimal,
and Ratikanta, dressed as dacoits, seized her and bound her with ropes. As they
put stocks on her neck, she did her best, just in case the producer from Bombay
was in the audience, to emote, using facial expressions alone, to express both
fright and fury, both vulnerability and dignity.

The maharaja swaggered onto the stage wearing a black mask and brandishing the shiny sword with which he had assaulted Dr. Patel, and after slapping the
saber against the table to indicate its solidity to the audience, he forced it through

the center of the stocks, straight through Lakshmi's neck. As he did so, he could not help but think to himself: "Although my Lakshmi has her moods and is prone to anger and pique, nevertheless, one must admit she is beautiful." He pulled the sword out of her neck, threw off his mask, released her from her stocks and bonds, smiled his exultant smile, and bowed to the audience, softly whispering words of affection to his beloved under his breath.

The maharaja directed the recapitated maharani to step into a four-legged box, decorated with the image of a boy climbing a rope, a picture that foreshadowed the climax of the magic show. The blare of *bhajans*, Sagar felt, gave the illusion a Puranic quality. Bannerji locked down the lid of the box and, one by one, eight swords were thrust through it from every direction, at every angle, and then a spear was inserted straight down from the top, down through the very center of the magic cabinet. When the front flap of the box was removed, the container, because of the undetected mirror installed within it, appeared to contain nothing but the network of crisscrossing blades that reflected the bright spotlights which were aimed at the center of the stage. The box was sealed again, the swords and spear removed, opened again, and the maharani took a bow. After a levitation, some small items (with silks and Chinese Sticks, the Egg Bag and a Bengal Net, large playing cards and Colored Sands), after another dance by Lakshmi, after four more costume changes, after two and a half hours of magic in all, it was time for the climax of the show.

Standing in the center of the stage, in the maharaja costume in which he had made his entrance, Professor M. T. Bannerji waved to Sagar, gesturing for the technician to turn down the music so that he could address the audience: "Ladies and gentlemen, you are about to witness my exhibition of the ancient Indian Rope Trick, the celebrated illusion that has likewise been performed on the stage for audiences by such magic luminaries as Blackstone, David Devant, Kalanag, Horace Goldin, and others of renown. What no mortal has seen for centuries, what no magician or sorcerer has performed for the same number of years, is this extraordinary magical feat out-of-doors and fully surrounded. Western and Indian scholars and magicians, seeking to know if such a thing is possible, have, many times in this century, offered rewards of crores and lakhs to anyone who can successfully accomplish it. To date no one has done so. It is, thus, with pride that I announce to you today, that I, the amazing and wonderful Professor M. T. Bannerji, *escamoteur extraordinaire*, World's Greatest Magician, shall perform it! The illustrious illusion shall be realized just as it was done for the great Jahangir, near the Purana Qila, in one month's time, on the occasion of the birthday of the great Buddh, who himself often performed the trick. Consult your newspaper for the exact time. As mass hypnosis will not be used, you may bring your cameras. If you attend, you will be amazed."

The magician bowed and signaled to Sagar to start the music again.

"If they come, I'll be amazed," Sagar said to the old magician. "Your son has lost his mind, and it's all Lakshmi's fault. Love makes men try to do things they are not, in reality, capable of doing."

Although the Senior Bannerji defended his son to Sagar, plainly stating that he was sure that if an M. T. Bannerji said he could do the Rope Trick out-of-doors, he could do it, in his heart he feared that his son had, indeed, made a fool of himself. And that was something that the retired magician had, in his own time, done more than once.

To the sound of Handel's *Messiah* Professor M. T. Bannerji tossed up the end of the sturdy rope that Bhutnath had set, coiled like a great snake, at his feet. It fell back to the stage. When he threw it higher, Vimal, perched in the flies, out of view of the audience, was able to catch it and secure it to the batten. Sushil, already rigged with the skeleton wire that would swing him out of sight at the right moment, climbed the rope to his position at the top of the stage. Still smiling the radiant smile, the maharaja of magic pulled a revolver from his silklike sash and with a flourish pointed it at the boy and fired, giving Sagar his cue to trigger the flashpot. When the smoke cleared, the boy was nowhere in sight. The props that were supposed to look like parts of his body—a leg, an arm, a hand, and a head—were gathered up by the magician and placed in the large wicker basket. After a grand magical gesture and the crash of cymbals, the lid of the basket flew off, and Sushil hopped out, smiling, to take a bow with the magician. They were joined on stage by the other members of the troupe, and Bannerji Senior applauded and shouted at the top of his feeble voice: "*Śābāś! Bravo! Śābāś! Bravissimo! Śābāśissimo!*" And while the audience began to straggle out of the tent to the sound of the Indian national anthem ("O Dispenser of India's Destiny, thou art the ruler of the minds of all people . . ."), the production company—Bannerji and Sushil, Lakshmi and Dolon, Bhutnath and Prem Guha, Patañjali Patel and Ratikanta Tapadar—continued to take bow after bow until it was silent. The tent was empty. Sagar turned off the lights, and Vimal slowly lowered the fire curtain.

Since Professor Bannerji had, just as he always did, given the street magicians free tickets to his show, they felt it was only polite to visit his dressing-room tent after the performance.

"I am honored by your presence," the maharaja of magic, still smiling as gloriously as ever, announced to the visitors. "For it is you—the *jādūgar*s of our streets, bazaars, and villages—you, itinerant like myself, who, everyday, perform fully surrounded and out-of-doors; you, and you alone, who have inspired the wonderful me to undertake my exposition of the old Indian Rope Trick!"

He leaned over, cupping his hands around the face of one of the magician's children: "What is your name?"

"Kabir."

"The magic of the future, my little one, is in your hands. Preserve it, my child! Develop it! Enchant the world! I have a son your age," he said and then turned to the men: "I love children. I love their innocence and sense of wonder. All magicians are children at heart. It is the magician's mission to remind a world that is bleak and busy, rationalistic and moralistic, weary and woebegone, of the child within each adult's heart—isn't it so? For the child, all is magic—everything is amazing, stupendous, and miraculous. Adulthood is the death of a child! Magic is the promise of resurrection—isn't it so? And why not? Anything can happen in Indra's Net."

As the magician handed Kabir and each of the other children a poster for the "Great Magic Show of Professor M. T. Bannerji," Bhutnath entered the tent with a foreigner who seemed, oddly enough, to be acquainted with the street magicians.

When Professor Bannerji took off his turban and placed it upon the head of Kabir, who was looking at himself in the gilt-framed, full-length practice mirror, everyone laughed. And Kabir waved his hands about in a parody of the stage magician.

"Like this," the maharaja said with a friendly wink, mistaking the mockery for an attempt at emulation, and waved his own hands, snapped his fingers, and produced a lit Gold Flake cigarette for himself to smoke.

When the street magicians made their exit, Bhutnath introduced the foreigner, from whom Professor Bannerji had previously received a letter regarding some plan to write a book about Indian magic. "For this book," the magician said, maintaining his magnoelectrific smile, "you will of course need to watch my performance of the Old Indian Rope Trick."

"I'd like that very much," the man, wearing an American baseball jacket with the insignia of the International Brotherhood of Magicians over his heart, smiled. "I've written a few things about it already. In fact, if it wouldn't be an inconvenience, I'd like to leave what I've written with you for your reactions."

"Certainly! Anything I can do for you, anything I can give you, anything I can tell you! Just ask." He presented the visitor with programs, publicity material, and a little flier, emblazoned with his name, entitled "Eight Amazing Magic Tricks You Can Do."

"For your study, you have come to the right place," the magician continued proudly. "I have dazzled audiences for the last seventy-three years."

"But how is that possible?" the surprised traveler interrupted. "You look so young. How old are you?"

"I, M. T. Bannerji personally, am only forty-three years old. When I say 'I have dazzled audiences,' I refer to myself not personally, but to Professor M. T. Bannerji, World's Greatest Magician, generally—he who, in the body of my father, began performing seventy-three years ago, when he was eight years old, and he who still performs, now in my body, as you just witnessed in the adjacent circus tent."

"And do you have a son?"

"Indeed—young M. T. Bannerji, and he shall grow up to play the part and perpetuate the noble lineage which we trace back to the great Vishvasiddhi, author of the *Indrajālasūtra*, King Amaruka of Kashmir's own court magician. My ancestor's feats are favorably noted in a *bhāsya* of Shankaracharya, World's Greatest Philosopher."

As the foreigner seemed interested in the relationship between magic and religion, between the performance of such tricks as levitation and actual yogic powers, Bannerji's discourse naturally turned to the subject of Dr. Patañjali Patel. "He has mastered so many *siddhi*s. This swallowing water and spitting out is mere child's play for the venerable yogi. He can suck water—not even to mention such other liquids as milk, honey, and mercury—up through the penile urethra and into the bladder. This purification process, completed by expulsion of the liquid, is surpassed by yet another, no less astonishing feat: Dr. Patel can, furthermore, suck water—or the other above named liquids—into his rectum through the anal aperture. Thus both bladder and rectum have been thoroughly purified and perfected through yoga. Dr. Patel is a great man, a genius I dare say. It is unfortunate that these items are not really suitable for the stage."

Relieved when the foreigner with his naive questions finally left, giving the magician an opportunity to stop smiling and have a drink of whiskey, Bannerji looked at himself in the practice mirror, at the mascara that ran down his cheeks like makeup from the forlorn eyes of a woman weeping with love. He leaned over the darker reflection of himself in the bowl of warm water that Rajah Rajahlingam, Deputy Chief-in-Charge of Travel and General Management, had, as he did after every performance, set out for his patron. He splashed the water on his face, then watched the face disappear in the chaos as the dark water dripped back into the bowl. "There's the idea for a trick in this," he thought as he dried his eyes.

Without changing out of his maharaja costume, he called for Sagar and Bhutnath and anxiously asked, "How much did we take in today?"

"Not very much," Sagar said. "But there is some good news. After the show a man approached me to request that you perform at his son's ninth birthday party. He's willing to pay handsomely because this child is the apple of his eye and heart. He introduced the kid to me as if he were presenting me with some VIP: 'This is the young gentleman, Shri Indrajit Sharma, an aficionado of magic in his own right, who will be honored on the day in question.' "

"My dear Sagar," the magician, more hurt than angry, responded. "I am not a clown, but an artiste. Would they ask Mr. Ravi Shankar to play the happy-birthday music for the child? Would they ask Mr. Satyajit Ray to make their home video of the party? I think not. Tell them Professor M. T. Bannerji, World's Greatest Magician, will be there only if Ravi Shankar and Satyajit Ray are also in attendance!"

"I think we need the money more than either Ravi Shankar or Satyajit Ray," Bhutnath Dey suggested.

"Money?" Bannerji laughed. "Once I have performed the Rope Trick, fully surrounded and in the open air, we will be rich from television engagements, command performances, and foreign tours to places like Las Vegas ('Vegas' as the natives call it), and Leningrad (I wonder if the natives call it 'Ingrad' or some such thing)." He laughed again. "That is what we must talk about right now."

Before revealing his method for accomplishing the illusion, Professor M. T. Bannerji made his colleagues repeat the oath that all members of his troupe had to recite whenever they became party to a new trick: "I (fill in name and title) do solemnly swear to protect and uphold at all times and in all places the sacred secrets of magic that have been entrusted to me, to conceal and never, not under any threat or offer, to reveal any of the methods used by the great Professor M. T. Bannerji to any being or even family member. If I break this sacred *mantragupta* vow, may I die a horrible death only to be reborn as a magician's rabbit to be pulled again and again from a black hat by my ears."

"The illusion will take place near the little mosque in the park by the entrance to the zoo on the Mathura Road. Vimal must obtain a police permit and, working at night while the place is forsaken, prepare the site, digging a hole there, constructing a secret underground hatch with a trap door over which the turf has been replaced in such a way that nothing unusual is suspected. This hatch need not be very big, just big enough for the boy. Since we'll be using the large wicker basket with the hinged bottom, the dimensions of the trap door should be such that movement back and forth from hatch to basket can take place unnoticed. Ratikanta must get busy on the costumes for myself and Sushil."

At the mention of his son, Bhutnath asked for assurance both that Sushil would in no way be endangered by the trick and that he would be paid extra for it.

"Of course," the magician, snapping his fingers to produce a lit cigarette, answered. "I'll ask the boy to lie down on the ground, right over the secret compartment, and then, with charcoal, I'll trace an outline of his body there, and then I'll ask him to stand up there upon his own image. Picture it my friends: I gaze at him with my hypnotic eyes; I demand silence from the crowd, warning them that any distraction could mean death for the child; throwing a large cloth, emblazoned with the holy appellations of the goddess, over the boy, I place my hands on the boy's head, holding on to the cloth of his turban through the drape."

The magician rose, closed his eyes, and conjured up the scene: "I am in deep concentration. A mystic trance! It is the *samādhi*! I am muttering mantras. I spread my hands and step back from the boy. Slowly, slowly the child begins to rise from the ground. Before the eyes and cameras of the spectators, he slowly ascends, higher still, the drape around his body wafting in the spring breezes.

Higher, higher the body floats, and necks bend as heads, mouths gaping in astonishment, tilt back to watch him rise higher still."

Bannerji opened his eyes and laughed: "At last the boy is out of sight, vanished into the heights! Everyone, baffled to say the least, looks at me in thorough bewilderment. Standing over the image of the boy on the ground, I take my sword and cut across the neck of the image—decapitation!—and then across the shoulders and thighs—dismemberment!—and while everyone stares, stunned, at what I am doing, suddenly (and there are gasps to be sure) a bundle wrapped in cloth that is emblazoned with the names of the goddess, stained with blood and appearing to contain bodily parts (we'll use the same props that we use for the stage version), falls on the ground near me. I carry that bundle over to the basket which is clearly shown to be empty, and I deposit it there. After pulling the basket over the image of the boy (which is to say, over the secret trap door), I focus my mystic stare, my illustrious electromagnific gaze, on the basket, intoning mantras and gesturing with mudras so as to create a Tantric mood. I break the sword in half (excellent touch!) and cry out: 'Rise!' There is a moment of silence. The top of the basket moves just slightly. There is a moment of stillness. Then, all at once, the lid flies off, and the boy jumps out with a smile on his face, the great grin of resurrection. Amazement becomes wonder, and wonder becomes awe. I bow and rest on my laurels as I am hailed, by one and all, as indisputably and absolutely the World's Greatest Magician."

Bannerji laughed aloud as he squeezed Bhutnath and then tousled Sagar's oily hair. "Great! Isn't it! And the method is straightforward enough. We must take Sushil's measurements and have a doll of his same size made out of inflatable plastic, like those toys and life-saving devices for the water. The two of you are in charge of the construction of the doll, which should begin immediately, as Sushil will need time to practice the switch, to rehearse dropping into the hatch and changing places with the inflatable boy. While holding on to the child's turban, keeping it still as he does the switch, I shall be sure that the cloth is draped loosely enough to conceal all movements within it. Simple, but it needs to be practiced. And the helium should be ordered at this time."

"Yes, we will order a tank," Bhutnath cut in. "What we don't use for the flying boy we can use in the future to blow up balloons and sell them at your shows. We can, furthermore, charge people a small amount for the opportunity to inhale the gas and then listen to themselves speaking in high tones and amusing voices. Everybody enjoys that. We'll make some money with this helium."

"Bhutnath, you fool," Bannerji smiled with affectionate anger. "First of all, we won't need money after I have performed the great Indian Rope Trick. Second of all, even if we did, we must never use helium for any other purpose—it would provide people with a hint through which they might come to suspect how I had done the trick. No one must ever know. I feel that I have everything worked out brilliantly, but we must all play our parts well if it is to be a success. While I have fixed everyone's attention on myself by slashing with my sword at the image of the boy, it will be your job, Bhutnath, to sneak up behind the bedazzled crowd with a bag in which you have the bundle of bodily parts and, at just the right moment, to throw that bundle into the air so that it lands in the proper place. A few confederates—Lakshmi, Dolon, Ratikanta, and Rajahlingam perhaps—should be in the audience to gasp and point skyward after the bundle has fallen, just enough gesturing to make others in the crowd think that, though they did not personally see the fall of the bundle from heaven, it did happen. Afterwards they will say they saw it, imagining it to be true even. People, because they believe the illusion was performed in ancient times, because they want to believe that, will naturally assume that I have discovered the ancient method for the magic. Thus, because they did not have helium in ancient times, no one will suspect that it has been used by me." Bannerji couldn't contain his glee. "It is great. It is brilliant. It is wonderful!"

Sagar frowned: "There is one problem."

"Problem?" Bannerji asked in disbelief. "What problem?"

"It is peculiar," Sagar said with a deep breath, "that no rope is being used in your performance of the ancient Indian Rope Trick."

"Minor problem," Bannerji laughed. "But I have thought of that and everything else. It is taken care of with my patter." The magician, his eyes glistening, his smile sparkling, picked up the red turban from the table, placed it on his head, spread his arms and rehearsed what he would say to the crowd: "Today, beholding a wonderful miracle, the amazing and celebrated Rope Trick, you shall know the power of the mind, the power of the gods, and the power of the magician to release those other powers. You'll witness things you thought were impossible: a child will ascend into the heavens, to be ruthlessly slaughtered by myself, sacrificed like Purusha, decapitated, his arms and legs severed from his body, and then, by me, M. T. Bannerji, World's Greatest Magician, he will be put back together again and returned to life. You'll know that death can be overcome. That is the promise of magic. That is the ancient secret of Indra's Net."

"There's still no rope in your Rope Trick," Sagar muttered despondently. "What is the Rope Trick without a rope?"

"I'm getting to that," Bannerji said with discernable annoyance over the pettiness of his employee. "I continue thus: 'In ancient times, because people were not as enlightened or intelligent as you are now, they could be fooled more easily than you. My scholarly research on the Rope Trick has revealed the following: in those former times most people had never seen a common kite before, and so they thought that the magician had thrown a rope into the heavens when, in reality, it was only the string of a kite. Because of your intelligence, I shall not bother with that part of the magic even though it has some symbolic value. The boy, in the traditional performance, appeared to climb the string of the kite, but he was not climbing at all. No. He was doing nothing, for he, himself, had no power or puissance. It was the magician who did everything, levitating the child with his great *śakti*, making him light—*laghimā*, we call it in Sanskrit—so light that he rose in the air, higher and higher, out of sight.' "

"Still," Sagar persisted, "I feel that to announce that you are going to do the Rope Trick and not to use a rope is false advertising. And, furthermore, I am confident that they had kites in ancient India."

"Okay, okay, what you are saying, though picayune and overly literal, is not total foolishness," Bannerji finally conceded. "I'll have some length of rope and make it stand up in the air using the standard *jāduwālā* method, telling my audience that to make rope stiff is nothing. Since so many other magicians have used this item—even Tayade is selling it from his shop—after doing it, I'll dismiss it as irrelevant to the real and powerful magic at hand."

Time for the Senior Bannerji's meal, at which the son was, as usual, expected, broke up the meeting. They arranged to reconvene in the morning.

When Bannerji Junior arrived at his father's tent, the old man was dressed in a maharaja costume, identical to the one his son was wearing. Sitting before the mirror, Bannerji Senior was putting the finishing touches on his makeup.

"What are you doing, Papaji?"

"Magic!" the old man laughed as he stood, waved his hands gracefully in the air, materialized a pack of cards, and fanned them with finesse. With one hand and one swift, smooth move, the cards were cut and spread. "Take one, my boy. This is not a force. You have your choice. Select any card you want. Very good. This is my version of cutting the boy apart. Tear the card you have chosen into pieces and put the pieces in the ashtray. We'll keep one piece out. This is a Vedic sacrifice—the slain boy, the torn card, like the soma, must be offered to the gods, burned in the fire, delivered into the heavens by Agni. Please ignite the pieces of the card, except the one piece which we have kept aside."

It was done, and then the old magician, smiling joyously, asked his son to spread the deck. When he did, there was one card that had a piece torn out of it, the Jack of Hearts, the card that had been selected, torn apart, and burned. And the piece fit perfectly.

"*Śabāś*, Papaji."

After the two men had eaten, the son helped his father out of the maharaja costume and makeup and assisted him in the simple task that in old age had become an arduous ordeal—getting ready for bed. And then, sitting on the edge of the cot, the magician held the old man's spotted hand, doing for his father what his father used to do for him when he was a child.

"You haven't asked me how I am going to perform the old Indian Rope Trick out-of-doors and fully surrounded," Bannerji Junior smiled. "And I'm not going to reveal my method to you, as I want to see if you, my guru, can figure it out for yourself. But I can tell you that you will be proud. The great Professor M. T. Bannerji, he who is both you and I, will triumph in glory. Through the Rope Trick the Bannerji name will be immortalized. It will be your immortality, Papaji."

Old Bannerji had fallen asleep, and as his son looked at him, he thought of his own son. He had mailed Sam Dalal's best magic set to the boy for his birthday, had sent both Christmas and Diwali greetings to him in Bengali, Hindi, and English, but there was only silence from London. He feared that the child was ashamed of him, that he believed all that his mother must have said.

Professor Bannerji, having forgiven Lakshmi for almost ruining the cutting-the-lady-in-half routine that afternoon, mounted his magnoelectrific smile as he snuck from his father's tent to that of the beautiful dancer.

"What are you grinning about?" the dancer asked.

"I smile, my beloved, because I am happy."

"Then you're a fool."

"Fool?" the magician laughed. "Fool? Could the ancient Indian Rope Trick be figured out and finally exhibited by a fool? I think not! Not 'fool,' but 'genius' is the word that you are looking for my beloved. Do you doubt that I, your great *moi*, shall perform it? Are you not happy and proud? Are you not anxious to behold it?"

She sneered, "The only trick I'd like to see you do is to make yourself disappear."

The sudden—and, he felt, unwarranted—assault hurt the magician deeply and, for some strange reason, made him want to take her in his arms by force and show his power to her, but he knew if he did so with that in mind, the power might not manifest, the trick might not work. It had to be, like all good magic, spontaneous and natural. "I adore you, my beautiful one," the magician said with a smile, a flourish of the hand, and a snap of the fingers that materialized a rose (though made of paper, a rose nonetheless), and as he turned to exit the scene, he tossed it playfully to her. "So much spunk my beloved Lakshmi has," he smiled to himself. "I like that in a woman."

Back in his tent, after a whiskey, Professor Bannerji picked up the manuscript the foreigner had left for him, the essay on the Indian Rope Trick, and he read the first lines: "The magician himself believed in the magic, swore that it could be done, that there was a man in Ghaziabad, really and truly, who performed the Indian Rope Trick. Definitely. . . ."

"What is this nonsense?" Bannerji asked himself. "This is not a scientific study of magic. This is some sort of fairy tale. This man must definitely come to my performance of the Rope Trick so that he can have fact rather than fancy for his book."

He threw the manuscript aside, lay his head back and, still dressed in his maharaja's primrose coat, with the light still burning, fell fast asleep and dreamed of a strange performance of the Rope Trick in which he was the boy, climbing the rope in terror of something, higher and higher and higher still.

Preparations for the real Rope Trick began the next day. Ratikanta Tapadar designed matching costumes for the boy and the magician, simplified maharaja outfits in ochre cotton, sewn without jewels or sequins, suggesting some sort of sadhu-maharaja, a holy prince, at once spiritual and elegant. "This, like the Nehru jacket some years ago, could well become the fashion in Paris, France," the tailor's wife thought to herself, "thereby making us rich and happy."

After a careful survey of the small park, Vimal began construction of the secret compartment. Prem Guha selected and cleaned the basket, rope, sword, drape, and bodily parts that would be used.

In a shop in Chandni Chowk, Bhutnath and Sagar found and purchased various inflatable toys and life-saving devices. They cut the laughing head off of the body of a clown who, when inflated, would bounce back up to a standing position whenever he was knocked over. "He looks like Bannerji," Sagar, punching the clown a few times, joked to Bhutnath behind the boss's back. They took apart a rubber raft that was formed of inflatable tubes and used the cylinders for the arms and legs. The abdomen was an inflatable pillow. They discovered that the material could be cut and then resealed with a hot iron. The nipples that were necessary for introducing the gas into the various bodily parts were melted into place. The construction of the boy in parts assured a flexibility that, through the deft handling of Professor Bannerji, would make one and all assume that it was indeed a living boy, the one the audience had just seen, under the drape that bore the names of the goddess.

The magician himself worked on the publicity for the event. He dictated a form letter and ordered that personally addressed copies of it be sent to Khushwant Singh at the *Hindustan Times* and Pritish Nandy at the *Illustrated Weekly,* to Mr. Som Benegal and others. "And the letter must be translated into all of the major Indian languages as well as French, Russian, Arabic, Esperanto, and the like. I want copies sent to *Pravda, Time* magazine, and the world-famous *Playboy.*"

He paced and smoked as he dictated to Mrs. Tapadar: "Attention! Flash! At sixteen hundred hours, on April 8, Birthday of the blessed Buddh, 1987, Professor M. T. Bannerji, World's Greatest Magician, of Calcutta, in the park near Purana Qila, will perform the Old Indian Rope Trick, in the open air and fully surrounded, exactly as it was done in ancient times in our beloved land. Thus our India will regain her former glory and fame as the World's Greatest Country of Magic, Miracles, and Mysteries."

After only a few days' work, Sagar and Bhutnath happily informed the magician that the boy was ready. Already dressed as a maharaja for the afternoon show, Bannerji hastened with his workers to his changing tent where the empty body lay on the table, like a dormant Adam waiting to be animated by the breath of God. After methodically, rather ceremoniously, opening each of the nipples on the six parts of the body, Sagar gently inserted the nozzle on the hose from the helium tank into the nipple on the side of the child's head and turned the valve.

Instantaneously the flat head became full and round and the clown face smiled happily as if with the great joy of discovering itself suddenly alive. Then the body proper, upon which Bhutnath had painted a red heart in the appropriate place, was filled. The buoyancy could already be observed and the magician, like a father watching the birth of his son, smiled proudly. Bhutnath put his hand on the boy's body to keep him down on the table as Sagar inflated the arms and then the legs.

As Sagar turned off the helium and stepped back anxiously, Bannerji's heart was pounding wildly, and his limbs were trembling with excitement. Bhutnath lifted his hand away from the boy's chest and took a step back.

Slowly the body rose an inch or so, seemed to hover a second or more, and then fell back to rest on the table, bouncing just slightly.

"Fly!" Bannerji cried out. "Fly up, high up, fly as high as you can!"

But the smiling child just lay there. Bhutnath stepped forward, inserted his hand under the child's back, and gave him a little boost. The boy floated up, rose several feet in the air.

"Yes, fly! Fly higher!" the magician shouted as if words would make it happen. "You won't get burned by the sun! Fly!"

But slowly the boy floated back to the table, and again he bounced, and again, and again, and then again he came to rest. He was still, and still he was smiling.

"I believe," Bhutnath said, "that we are having some sort of aerodynamic problem."

"No, no," Sagar insisted, "it is rather a gravopneumatic problem, one which I suspected might arise. By my calculations, given the weight of the boy's plastic skin, the turban, and the drape, in order to contain enough helium to float up in the air and out of sight, the child would have to be sixteen feet tall."

Professor M. T. Bannerji, gasping for breath, struggled to get out the words: "Out! Leave us alone!" The men did as they were told.

The magician, paralyzed with grief, stared at the motionless body on the table for a long time. Finally he sat down next to the child, buried his face in his hands, and, overwhelmed by pain and sorrow, feeling helpless and hopeless under the sign of Saturn, he wept as he had not wept for years.

By the time he lifted his head and opened his eyes, most of the helium had seeped out of the boy. Picking up the limp body, the conjurer held it on his lap, turning slightly in the chair, he could see the two of them in the gilt-framed, full-length practice mirror. The child's smile, though wrinkled by deflation, was still apparent, and perhaps because expressions of delight are contagious, Bannerji, though he was not sure how it was possible, smiled too, grinned back at the boy sitting on the lap of the maharaja in the mirror. "There is a purpose and a reason for everything that happens," he thought. "And if there is no purpose for something, there is a purpose in that. There is a reason for things to have no reason."

MIRRORS AND WATER

The magician cleared his throat to speak to the child. "Watch this, my son," he said, and as he snapped his fingers, a lit cigarette appeared. He took a puff. "I'm a magician, so what is the problem? Am I not a veritable Houdini, the first Indian magician to perform Houdini's famous death-defying escape from a galvanized iron can filled with water and secured with massive locks? If I can release myself from shackles, handcuffs, and bilboes, can there be any doubt that I, the great Professor M. T. Bannerji, can escape from this currently unfortunate state?"

The maharaja of magic mounted his electromagnific gaze and his magnoelectrific smile as he spoke to the boy out loud and in English: "I, the amazing and wonderful Professor M. T. Bannerji, he who is thoroughly me, illustrious illusionist, shall perform the magic." He laughed. "It is so obvious. I'll take my magic of India to Las Vegas, U.S.A., where I will enjoy fame and fortune, the love of women and the respect of men!"

Conscience was an obstacle. The man was concerned about his obligations and responsibilities to his father, Lakshmi, and the troupe—what would they do, and how would they manage without him?

"The great Buddh was troubled by the same sorts of attachments. But, for the sake of the nirvana, he left his kith and kin, departing at night without even informing them. Shankaracharya, and countless other sannyasis, did the same. Attachments must be overcome. Keeping these words of the *Gītā* in mind, I shall have the courage and strength to do so. Yes, I shall, without informing a soul, leave my beloved family, friends, troupe, and India, to go to Las Vegas where, after obtaining letters of introduction from my friend and supplier of magic, Mr. Jimmy Yoshida of Hawaii, I shall be graciously, if not royally, received by the many luminaries of magic—Siegfried and Roy, Miss Melinda, and their likes—who make their homes in that place."

Excitedly and happily jumping to his feet, the magician hugged the limp child to his heart, "Yes! I am going to Las Vegas—'Vegas' as the natives say!"

Traveler's Journal 3:

North/Summer

"The problem with the world today is that too many people put their personal and professional lives before their hobbies," Jimmy Yoshida said in explanation of why there hadn't been more people in attendance at the meeting of the Society of American Magicians that night at his house in Aiea, Hawaii. As a dealer in magic, he had, over the years, received orders from magicians in India, and he gave me a list of about thirty of them, including Bharucha and Tayade in Bombay, Sorcar and Lal in Calcutta, Shankar and Mayadhar in Delhi, and I wrote to each of them: "I was given your address by Mr. James Yoshida, the director of the local assembly of the Society of American Magicians (of which I have recently become a member; I am also a member of the International Brotherhood of Magicians). I am a professor of Indian Religions in the Department of Religion at the University of Hawaii, and I am beginning a book on Indian conjuring, a scholarly study of Indian magic—a history of its forms and functions. The research on the book has just begun; I am currently reading Sanskrit texts in which magicians appear as characters, and through those primary texts, I am trying to construct a history. I am also investigating the aesthetics of wonder and psychology of amazement as delineated in traditional Indian rhetorical texts. Ultimately, however, mere textual study will not be sufficient; I want to come to India and observe Indian magicians at work, both stage magicians and street conjurers. To that end, I plan to visit India in May or June of this year. I would like, at that time, to have the opportunity to meet with you. I must assure you that my interests are purely scholarly and academic, that I have no inclination to expose any secrets of magic."

Late at night, on the way from the airport into Bombay, I noticed, like the milky, faded skin sloughed by a snake, a poster peeling on a crumbling brick wall behind the still, dark figures that were huddled together for safety, sleeping close to one another despite the nocturnal heat of summer, amidst the brick and mud, the tarpaulin and corrugated metal. The remains of the poster showed a magician, his turban jeweled and feathered, his eyes wide open and full of stars, and his hands spread majestically as if with a sudden wave of them he would free those endreamed bodies from all gravity, make them slowly, gently rise into the air: "The Great K. Lal, World's Greatest Magician and his Great Mayajal."

Walking through the streets of Bombay in the morning, I was overwhelmed by sound (horns honking, people shouting, screaming, and laughing, machinery grinding and grunting, dogs barking and yapping, crows screeching, bicycle bells ringing), by color (bright Indian reds, oranges, and yellows, blazing greens and incandescent blues, and bleached, bright whites, all defiant of the dusty ochres and grays of the dirt from which all things come, the dirt that waits with infinite patience for our return), by feel (coarse, sultry air, polluted, heated, overbreathed, sticking to the skin), and by the voluptuous smell of summer (the olfactoragoria: pungent scents of bidis and masalas, traces of sweet hashish, almost rancid perfumes of summer melons—khira and kakdi—and cherries, mangoes and jackfruit, coconut and cane juice, and summer blossoms—mogra and chameli—flowers strung for the oiled hair of flushed women and laughing girls, the indiscreet, intimate aromas of shit, piss, and death, and the heady smells of dough bubbling in hot oil), and a thousand hawkers tried to sell me all of it, all of India: "Carpets? . . . Flowers? . . . Silk? Best Tailor! . . . Hashish? . . . Air tickets, tickets for Kashmir, with houseboat? . . . Antiquities? . . . Change money? . . . Mangoes? . . . Girl? Like Fucking? Boy? . . . Visiting Elephanta? . . . What you want? I have what you want . . ."

Tayade and Bharucha, looking like an Indian version of Abbott and Costello, waiting in the lobby of the hotel for my return, stood at attention by the desk. Tayade, the gaunt Abbott of the two, presented me with a gift (a little flier with the name of his shop printed on it, entitled "Eight Amazing Magic Tricks You Can Do") and informed me that they had been anxious for my arrival and that, as fellow members of the International Brotherhood of Magicians, it was their duty to help me in any way they could. "We will meet each day for one month for discussion, my brother," Tayade, dressed in an immaculate white Indian version of the Arrow shirt and neatly pressed Western pants, explained with a certain gravity and sense of mission. When I disclosed that I would only be in Bombay for a few days, that I had appointments in Delhi and Calcutta, he gave me permission to leave and a directive to collect notes and then to return: "At that time I shall explicate everything to you, giving you the real meaning of all that you know."

Rutton Bharucha, the shorter, more rotund Costello, smiled happily as the rather somber, almost dour, Tayade spoke: "I am not a magician; I am a dealer. Bharucha is the magician. Between the two of us you will thus be exposed to both theory and practice, means and ends. We will go to my shop now."

In the taxi on the way to Tayade's shop, where I was to be given a rope that seemed normal but became erect if held at a certain angle ("Now you too can do the famous Indian Rope Trick"), I asked Bharucha about his performances. "Onstage I wear beautiful Chinese robes. I call myself Wong Lee Foo, and my assistant is named Foo Ling Yoo—get it?" He giggled happily. Perhaps it was a guess that I was disappointed that he did not do something more traditionally Indian that prompted him to suddenly laugh again and say, "Frankly I was disappointed when I saw you. Getting a letter from a man in Hawaii named Professor Lee, I was hoping you were a Chinaman. I love the Chinese style. Onstage I imitate Chinese talking, and my audience gets a great laugh. Listen: 'Velly, velly nice to meet you Mistah Lee, velly, velly nice.' " He laughed proudly. "Everybody loves imitations of the way foreigners pronounce English—isn't it?— every audience finds it humorous. Velly, velly funny."

After visiting Tayade's shop, where I saw the cheap copies of Western magical apparatuses that were manufactured there, we went to a Chinese restaurant for lunch, over which Tayade delivered what seemed to be a prepared lecture on Indian magic: "When a baby is born everything is magic. Then, when he gets older, his parents confine him. 'Don't wet the bed,' they say. 'This is right and this is wrong.' And the magic is, thus, taken from his world. Through the power of the magician, we become children again. Do you or do you not agree with my first point?"

"Oh, I agree completely," I earnestly insisted. "In fact, it was through a child, my youngest son, that I got started on this project. He wanted to learn some tricks, so I bought him a volume of Tarbell's course on magic and, as I was helping him go through the book, I noticed how many of the tricks were attributed to 'ancient Hindu fakirs,' and I thought it would be interesting to look into it."

Tayade shook his head solemnly while Bharucha wobbled his cheerfully. "You can't trust what a magician says about magic—Tarbell made this business up," Tayade insisted. "The Indian magician is always just doing an imitation of Sorcar, and Sorcar was just doing an imitation of Western magicians who did Western magic in Indian costumes. Indian magic is just Western magic."

"Or Chinese," Bharucha said rather timidly but with persistent cheer.

"But what about the street magicians?" I asked, genuinely fearful that my visit to India might be in vain.

"They are just low-caste fellows who have picked up a few tricks to earn their daily bread. They are not artistes worthy of our study. But because of your interest, it is my duty to speak on the subject of them: they were always afraid that if literate and cultured people like ourselves came to know their secrets, we would do a much better job at magic than they ever could. Thus they used skulls and bones in their regalia to frighten us and keep us away. The bone of the street juggler was the first magic wand. That we owe to the street magician. Nothing more. Their tricks are really no good."

"But surely the magician was a figure in the ancient Indian court," I said as I finished off my fish masala chow mein. "There were Indian magicians—I've found references to them in Sanskrit literature. There was a purely Indian magic, even if it no longer exists."

"True! Correct!" Tayade said as if I had come up with the right answer on a quiz. "Birbal was court magician for Akbar, and Tenali Ramalinga was court magician for the King of Kerala. But their methods were not those of modern magic. They would simply burn hashish in a fire so that their audience, the king and sundry others, would have hallucinations. But there is no Indian magic in India today. You will find only Western magic in Delhi and Calcutta. Not only magic—everything. Every day India becomes less and less Indian."

I set out for Delhi full of hope however, and Shankar received me warmly with assurances that I would soon witness all there was to see and understand all there was to know about traditional Indian magic. "First, you will meet with Sanskrit scholars to discuss the history of Indian magic. Then we will go to Shadipur to meet with Indian street magicians. They will do a special show for you. One Mr. Naseeb is coming from Kashmir to see you. We will be seeing a tent performance of B. N. Sarkar, discussing magic with him after the show. You will attend meetings of local magicians' clubs, and both I and my son, Shankar Junior, world's youngest magician, will be teaching you how to perform Indian magic."

Shankar picked me up at the guest house in Sunder Nagar to take me to the meeting of Sanskrit pandits in Vani Vihar at the home of Professor Sukla of Delhi University. There was an antelope skin spread out upon a plastic-upholstered couch waiting for me to sit on it, and facing that empty seat, like sculpted disciples gathered around the invisible Buddha, the sober members of a Sanskrit club, mostly retired professors, sat on fold-out metal chairs to wait for the arrival of the American traveler who was doing research on Indian magic.

Professor Sukla greeted me with what I felt to be ironic reverence. Once seated on the antelope skin, I became the subject of the speech he delivered in Sanskrit. Looking at the scholar standing in front of the banner that was embroidered with the name of their club, I felt the fall of the *sabhā*, the ancient royal assembly where courtiers and courtesans gathered around their king to listen to the philosophical debates of erudite pandits or the elegant songs of poets, to watch a Sanskrit play about lovers, or to witness a display of wonderful magic. All has fallen, I felt, and I felt the fall, easing it only with the thought that perhaps the India I study never really existed at all, that life has always been just as it is now, that the history of Bharatavarsha is merely an illusion that I have been tricked into taking for reality.

While it was difficult for me to follow most of the drone of the Sanskrit, I understood all too well when Professor Sukla announced that I would, at that point, address the group in the holy language of the Veda. "*Sanskṛtam vaktum na śaknomi* (I can't speak Sanskrit)," I said quite automatically as I urgently searched the synaptic files of my culture-shocked brain for the first few *ślokas* of the *Nalopākhyāna* that are stored somewhere near the other lines of poetry that I have, at some time or other in my life, been forced to memorize ("If" by Rudyard Kipling, Polonius's speech to his son, and "The Midnight Ride of Paul Revere").

It was, however, enough that I could say that I couldn't speak Sanskrit. Speaking that language slowly for my benefit, he told the group that the fact that I could say that I couldn't speak it proved that I did speak it, and it was proof, furthermore, that Sanskrit is studied and known all over the world. Then he ordained that the remainder of the meeting would be conducted in English for the sake of Shankar, "who, though a South Indian Brahmin, is entirely ignorant of the language of the Veda."

He turned to me with solemnity: "We have prepared for your visit. First, I will expound on magic and mythology. Second, Professor Pathak will discourse on magic and philosophy. Third, it will be Professor Tripathi's turn to explain the place of magic in Vedic culture, with special reference to *Kauśikasūtra* and *Atharvaveda.* Unfortunately for one and all, Professor Tripathi has come down with influenza and so cannot be present. It will be our responsibility to imagine what he would have said. At that point there will be questions and answers. You will ask questions, and we will give answers. Then we will ask questions, and you will give answers. Following that there will be refreshments and entertainment."

Professor Sukla, setting a pile of wonderfully dusty and worm-eaten books in front of me, handed me a pen and a pad of newsprint with the command to take down all of the references that he had so assiduously compiled for me. Taking each book in turn and reverentially opening it, he gave the citation, read out the Sanskrit, and offered a paraphrase: "*Uttarapurāṇam* 1.24.65 . . . Kaikeyi knows magic—*māyājāla, indrajāla, pīḍā,* and *mantra.* In the story of Lord Rama you will find all you need to know about magic. Maricha is the tutelary deity of magicians, and Indrajit is their patron saint. *Padmapurāṇam* 1.52.7 and 1.64.96–104 . . . before our very eyes we see Rama using the veil of *māyā* and also in 3.58.221 and the verses which follow it we see God, as Lord Rama, assume his manifold forms. That is magic. And Hanuman practices *garimā* and *laghimā.* Thus the mythology of magic."

The philosopher recited an assortment of verses from works attributed to Shankaracharya and then explicated them. "Madame Magic, Maya, creates this entire empirico-phenomenal universe. She is *avidyā,* what you call *nescience.* She is neither the existent nor the nonexistent, nor is she not the existent nor not the nonexistent, nor does she partake of both, nor does she partake of neither—a matter of *neti neti* through and through! That is the problem. She can be destroyed only by the realization of pure *brahman.* For example, just as the mistaken idea of the perception of a snake is destroyed by the discrimination of a rope, so it is on the onto-psychological and religio-metaphysical levels. It is, in my humble opinion, not Madame Maya, her magic and illusions, that you should be studying, but rather the pure *brahman.* That alone is worthy of contemplation and dissertation."

Another professor who throughout the morning had been fidgeting about and trying to cut in, suddenly jumped to his feet. "Precisely! Why do you waste your time with trivial things? Magic is primitive superstition. For the pre-intelligent cave man perhaps it was religion. But in this day and age it has use only as entertainment for a child's birthday party. It is idle mumbo-jumbo and hocus-pocus."

"Let us be reasonable in this matter," an old man in a dhoti and, despite the torrid heat of the summer morning, a Western plaid jacket said from the back of the room as he stood, tapping his cane on the dreary green linoleum floor to get the attention of the others. "What some of you do not understand is that in America many Sanskrit scholars work on trivial themes. Think of the work of Professor Wendy O'Flaherty."

They argued heatedly until Professor Sukla insisted that it was time for the refreshments (a metal tumbler of some blood-red and excruciatingly sweet liquid) and the entertainment (Professor Sukla's chubby little son, his dimpled knees locked in nervousness, breathlessly reciting the eleventh chapter of the *Bhaga-vadgītā* at breakneck speed). After that, the pandits pretended to be unimpressed when the cheery Shankar folded up a piece of blank paper torn from my pad of newsprint and then unfolded it to reveal a ten-rupee note. Then, upon leaving, I was presented with a copy of Professor Sukla's book, a Sanskrit *kāvya* proclaiming the physical beauty, intellectual grandeur, and spiritual glory of India, and the persistence of her hallowed traditions in modern times.

One of the professors, following us out, spoke to me in nervous whispers: "What do my colleagues know? They are rational men with no sense of magic! But I am like you. Previously I wrote a very profound and important thesis on the subject of the *brāhmaṇa* caste in ancient India. It is an excellent book and received universal critical acclaim. In your own country even Professor Richard Salomon could not praise it highly enough. But now, like you, not to mention Professor Wendy O'Flaherty, I want to begin to do research on trivial things! Something like your 'Magic and Conjuring in India' idea. Trivial things—that is the future, that is what we must dedicate ourselves to!" When he asked me for suggestions as to some trivial topics upon which he could begin to do research, I had to confess that I couldn't think of any right off, but I promised him that, if anything really insignificant came to mind, I'd let him know.

B. N. Sarkar sent a car to Sunder Nagar to take us to where his tents were pitched near the Kabari Bazaar, in the shadows of the Red Fort, where magic was once performed for Akbar and Jahangir, where magicians from Bengal were seen to perform the Rope Trick, to pour seemingly endless waters from a small pot, and to produce birds, flowers, and silks from thin air, as hot then as it was now.

We were escorted into the enormous, greenish gray circus tent, led to a battered and threadbare couch in the very front, right under the stage, where a straining fan and overworked loudspeaker, both pointed right at me, blasted and shook me with hot air and a booming, crackling, belchy din that was supposed to be music—a jumble, in fluctuating rpm's, of "Tequila," the theme song from

"Petticoat Junction," Hindi film scores, the currently popular "*Ek, Do, Tīn,*" Bengali folk music, vaudeville ditties, and the scratching of a needle against the grooves of a worn-out record. It sounded as though the torrid heat of the Delhi summer was melting the vinyl of the records that were embedded with the manic cacophony that set the pace for the three-hour show in which B. N. Sarkar appeared as a maharaja, a pharaoh, a samurai warrior, a maharaja again, a Mandarin, a surgeon, a maharaja again, a cowboy, a tuxedo-clad Westernized Oriental gentleman, a lion trainer, and a maharaja again, and again, and again, faster even than Professor Sukla's son had recited the *Bhagavadgītā*. Flowers and flames, ducks and pigeons, bowls of water and bottles of milk and whiskey, clocks and eggs and scarves and cigarettes, women and children, balls and boxes, and a million other things were produced from thin air, then vanished or transformed into other things also destined to change or disappear. Death was defied. Women were cut in half, pierced with swords, beheaded, stretched across the stage, floated in the air. One lady, locked in a box, with a wave of the wand appeared instantaneously from the back of the tent. Rusty razor blades were swallowed and bright, billowing foulards regurgitated. From the most elaborate illusion to the cheapest trick, it was all tumult, a fevered, drunken, crazed, structureless display, and again I felt the fall.

"This is not B. N. Sarkar Senior, this is B. N. Sarkar Junior," Shankar whispered. "But they look alike, and the items are the same. There is really no difference except that one is older than the other."

"Which is the older one?" I asked jokingly.

"Senior, I believe," Shankar, always wanting to be helpful and always absolutely dedicated to taking both me and my research seriously, replied with a sunny smile.

After the pandemonius performance, we were led to Sarkar's tent. Behind the sickly gray-green canvas wall there was a surprising room furnished with Kashmiri carpets and plush, though stained and faded, silk cushions, an ornate sleeping-swing, a Japanese television and VCR machine, an air-conditioner and refrigerator powered by a groaning generator. And there was a large, full-length, standing practice mirror rimmed with an ornately carved wooden frame from which the gold-leaf was peeling. "All the comforts of home," the magician, still dressed as a maharaja, said merrily as, with a flourescent green silk scarf that I had seen him produce on stage from an empty cylinder, he tried to dab dry the sweat that was turning the thickly daubed cake make-up on his face into a dirty pink slime.

After ceremoniously presenting me with flower-*mālā* and a little flier imprinted with the name B. N. Sarkar and the title "Eight Amazing Magic Tricks You Can Do," he asked me to sit on the swing. "I travel with over a hundred people," he began to tell me what he thought I would like to know, and I could see him in the mirror. "We have, among our tents, a post office, bank, restaurant, tailor shop, laundry, hair-cutting saloon, power house—you name it—I am but an ancient Indian wandering magician who is equipped with all the amenities of modern life! I don't travel *to* a town, I travel *with* a town!"

"You don't have a bar by any chance in this town, do you?" I hinted with a joke.

"Snack bar only," he smiled, neither offended nor apologetic. "Liquor would be contrary to Indian purity and spirituality."

He gave me programs, pamphlets, and promotional materials on "The Great B. N. Sarkar," and there was, in those specimens, no use of the words *Junior* or *Senior*. In the photographs you could not tell the difference between the two men. The son and father had become one, an ageless maharaja, a holy ghost, "the World's Greatest Magician," more real than either man of flesh and blood. The father, I was informed, was ill, but "one of our tents, fortunately, is a hospital."

The son told me his father's story. "He was from a middle-class *kāyastha* family, destined to be a clerk rotting away in some office in Calcutta. Do you know Calcutta?"

"Yes, I'm going there in a few days. I really like Calcutta."

"It's a fine city. Best place to study magic. Best place for culture, for art, poetry, music, food—you name it. It is the Paris of India—just like Paris, exactly, except, of course, no Eiffel Tower. Yes, my place, my father's place. Best place. It was, in fact, in Calcutta that Goddess Maha Kali appeared to him with the message that she had chosen him to be the future world's greatest magician in India. His life is a romance. Mine as well."

A servant whispered something to him that made him stand, suddenly come toward me, and shake my hand in the Western style. "Good-bye. You must leave at once. My car will take you. In five minutes the curfew in Old Delhi begins. Then it is shoot-on-sight. They will shoot you for sure. If not the police, then the Muslims; if not the Muslims, then the Hindus; if not the Hindus, then the Sikhs." He laughed, "And even I, great magician that I am, will not be able to bring you back to life. So you must leave or die."

We chose to leave, and Sarkar's car found its place in the flood of people that gushed out of the old city, rushing as quickly through the chaos of the hot streets as Sarkar had moved amidst the chaos of his stage. There were police and soldiers carrying automatic weapons, and the parched air was full of dust, darkness, and a fear of death.

Shankar had arranged for the street magicians of Shadipur Depot—Chand Baba and Chand Pasha, Iqbal and Kareem Baksh, Abdul and Apeez, and maybe Naseeb Shah—to show me their repertoire; I was much more compelled by them than by the rather embarrassingly funky stage performers, but I was interested in the connections between the two figures, the modern equivalents of the ancient street juggler and court entertainer. I tried to make notes on it: "The street magicians are low-caste Muslims, the stage performers are middle-class Hindus; the street conjurers play themselves, the stage magicians play the parts of maharajas; the street magicians are tricksters, the stage magicians are illusionists; the street magicians have dignity . . ."

Shankar nodded as he read what I wrote. "But," he smiled, "there are other types of magicians as well. Myself for example—industrial magician." Shankar is employed by the Syndicate Bank to advertize their services in villages, where people still keep their money buried or hidden somewhere in their homes. He multiplies some coins as a way to explain interest. "I used to change a five-paise coin into a ten. People came with bags of the coins. So I started changing tens into fives. Now no one comes." Chand Pasha had a stipend to use magic to promote birth control in villages, and UNICEF had hired the magician B. Kamesh to promote breast feeding by showing a small vessel that could produce seemingly infinite amounts of milk. N. T. Rama Rao, the chief minister of Andhra Pradesh, has hired about sixty magicians to publicize himself and his programs—one of them, standing before a country crowd, drops a two-rupee note into a seemingly empty cylinder; "*Gilli-gilli-gilli,*" he says and empties a big pile of rice out of the cylinder with the words, "This is the government's gift to the poor." Shankar smiled: "The ancient art of magic is being used all over India for modern purposes. Magic keeps the past alive for the present."

Shankar accompanied me to the airport and wished me all the best of luck in Calcutta. "Some foreigners," he smiled, "seem to be troubled by Calcutta. They complain of what appears to be the poverty there."

"Oh," I responded, "I like Calcutta. The squalor there is no worse than in Watts, Harlem, or the South Side of Chicago."

"When you go to Calcutta," Rutton Bharucha had joked in Bombay, "you will find a Chatterji, a Bannerji, and a Mukherji, but you will not find any energy." He giggled happily, "Get it?"

"I like Calcutta," I had said. "It's an amazing city."

"Yes," he nodded. "It is the culture capital of India—it is the city of poets and singers, magicians and conjurers, of artistes and aesthetes of all sorts."

"Yes," I nodded along with him. "It's a fascinating city, a real theater-city. I really do like Calcutta."

I don't really know why I lied, why I always tell people I like Calcutta, when, in fact, I do not. Calcutta is, let's face it, a nightmarish, threatening place, a terrible demonstration of extremes. And yet all the foreigners and Indians I know always say they like it. And I inevitably nod and echo the hollow sentiment of appreciation. And I keep returning to Calcutta, in hopes, perhaps, that somehow the words will become true, that I'll overcome my fastidiousness, my distaste for corruption, filth, poverty, pestilence, and death, to suddenly and miraculously enjoy Calcutta. The moment will come, like the climax of the magic show, when one realizes that the boy's tongue has been restored, that the blood is not real, that the anguished screams are feigned, that everything, despite all appearances, is all right, that it is all just a show.

MIRRORS AND WATER

It is too evident to speak of Calcutta in terms of its overcrowding, penury, and squalor, too easy to detest that hideous, humid city of moldering English architecture, that funereal, ravenous city of putrid streets, the tenebrous labyrinth, sprawling bedlam in which the destitute are made to openly, nakedly, display their afflictions. The exits are few, and either it costs too much to pass through them or, if free, they lead to places more dreadful still. And, of course, it is too obvious, and a bit too self-pitying, to complain about the weather. It was one hundred thirteen degrees with the humidity at ninety-four percent on the day I arrived.

To say "I like Calcutta" is a perversity perhaps, or it is a way of suggesting that one has gone beyond the facade, that one has seen some order in the chaos, some light on the other side of the ravening black hole of Calcutta, or that one has, in some way or another, come to terms with the ubiquitous specters of human misery, the ravaging of human flesh, the rape and slaughter of innocents—lepers, deformities beyond imagination; beggars, for a few paise, making a spectacle of their vulnerability, their infancy, or their old age. For a few paise, a trembling dry hand is piteously extended, reaching for life as if from out of a worm-infested grave or smoldering, crow-and-jackal-watched pyre. But it is crass to talk of death. It is more agreeable to speak of the City of Joy, to resolve sickening thoughts and hopelessness in ironies and contemplations of the charities, however insufficient and ineffectual, of others. To say "I like Calcutta" is to say "I am hardy, strong-stomached, and courageous; I accept and appreciate India at her worst; I can embrace the world, life itself, at its worst." To say "I like Calcutta" is to pretend to some sort of enlightenment or to a pact with the dreadful goddess Kali. To say "I like Calcutta" is to lie.

I arrived at Dum Dum airport, the place after which the dumdum bullet, slashed across its point so that it expands when it hits its target, was named. And for me in the soul-sucking sprawl of Calcutta each sensation is such a bullet: every smell is fired up the nostrils to explode behind the protective bone at the base of the forehead; sounds, machine-gun-shot, puncture the eardrums, swell, bulge, and burst in the skull; sights, blunt or sharp and always hard, blast through the eyes, rip open tightening pupils, to shatter into fragments in the jellies of the brain; touch leaves splinters in the skin; the tongue burns with the taste of Calcutta. And the more delicious the food, always generously served in Calcutta, the more one is aware that each bite one takes deprives someone else. To eat in Calcutta is to plunder, to starve another.

I stepped out of the airport into the cruel fire of the Bengal summer like the condemned man stepping out in front of the firing squad—there was fear, curiosity, anxiousness, resignation, and a little hope, and, "No, no," I thought to myself, "I don't want the blindfold." I smoked a Benson and Hedges DeLuxe International, and taxi drivers swarmed around me like the jackals and vultures that come to pounce upon the cadaver of the executed man. I was swooped up by one, swallowed into the shuddering metal body, black and yellow, the colors of the Bengal tiger, and carried off.

"I like Calcutta," I told the taxi driver at dusk as we crossed the bridge over the parched river of filth, the English-engineered viaduct that was lined and littered, crammed and cluttered, with squalid hovels, contrived, not quite constructed, of discarded things—scraps of rusty, dusty sheet metal, rotten tatters of canvas, perhaps a warped wall woven of palm leaves, dark and dry with death, refuse refusing to be refuse—huts hardly held up by frayed ropes, or splintered sticks, or luck to uncertainly protect hapless, huddling, hungry, discarded people, shadow people. And "Best place!" the taximan grinned proudly, with uncanny delight. The cheerfulness of Calcutta startles me, fills me with admiration, confusion, and disbelief. The endurance, the ability of so many of the prisoners in this distressing city to ignore just how dreadful it is, to pretend that it is what it is not, is truly amazing.

The taxi driver, like Yama taking a corpse into the abyss of death, the darkest, most fetid bowels of a hideous hell, laughed. Happily he asked me perfunctory taxi-driver questions: "You are from? How long staying? For why you are coming Calcutta?"

"I'm an American *jādūgar*. I'm here to see K. Lal and P. C. Sorcar Junior."

Relishing sweet and rosy memories inspired by the names, he told me he had seen P. C. Sorcar Senior when he was a child. "Best *jādūwālā* you ever see, most number one." And I asked him about street magicians. "Not in Calcutta. Police—bastards!—chase them away. Go to Shittal village. *Jādū*-village."

All the way from Dum Dum airport to the American Institute of Indian Studies on Swinhoe Street, he honked his horn unceasingly to avoid collision with careening objects on every side of us—things mechanical and carnal; vulgar, hysterical intrusions upon an emptiness that beckons everything to return to it (speeding vehicles, zigzagging bicycles, lumbering cows, jostled pedestrians, limping beggars, sniffing dogs, crawling deformities, and so on, and so on, and so on). The honking of the horn is a battlecry—at once warning and supplication, a scream of both defiance and fear. And over that screaming of horns, his and all the others, the crazed caterwaul of the seething streets, it was difficult to follow his fond reminiscences of P. C. Sorcar Senior. But it had clearly been one of the most remarkable experiences of his life. Sorcar had taught the audience how to do a trick, how to make an *X* drawn with charcoal on the back of the hand pass through the hand and appear on the palm. The taximan cherished the secret. His English praises of Sorcar were punctuated with Bengali curses of all the battered vehicles—trucks, buses, vans—that almost hit us, and all the bicycles and motorcycles, rickshaws and scooters, animals and people, that we almost hit. Who hits whom is simply a question of speed and size—the larger, more swiftly moving body is always the hitter. But hitter or hit, the other is always guilty; one's self is always the victim in Calcutta.

While I can think of the nightlife in most of the cities I have visited, night in Calcutta, the streets lined with still, often silent, bodies, reminds me only of death—Calcutta nightdeath. There are the forays into hotel bars (the paintings on the wall in the cool Grand, not the scenes blazing on Chowringhee just outside, become my real India for a time), and then wonderful restaurants (Amber or the Blue Fox), or an evening in the gracious homes of friends (there is always talk of Tagore, Satyajit Ray, and Ramakrishna, and usually Indian classical music)—bright oases in which I have escaped from the nocturnal sidewalk truths. But outside there is a darkness waiting. And it moans. The darkness of Calcutta comes like no other darknesses I know, invading street and soul, gnawing its way down through an unclean sky, this febrile, famished darkness, pitiless and pestilential—there probably won't be street lights; the electricity will fail: "you will find a Chatterji, a Bannerji, and a Mukherji, but you will not find any energy." The energy will have been dissipated during the day; all power sources mercilessly drained by the desperate needings of too many people who have come from lands execrated by flood and famine in hopes of work or charity.

I could see no stars through the crude hot haze of the truculent night. It always seems to me, at night in Calcutta, that the day has suffered a humiliating defeat. The light has surrendered and publicly admitted its impotence.

There is no harmony here, no perspective, neither symmetry nor balance. No balance—and so people have to lie down. And they lie down everywhere in Calcutta, as if they have stumbled, fallen, or been bowled over, rudely shoved, pushed, kicked; and they cower and cringe. All is imbalance and negligence as far as I can see, and yet to say that would be to offend. And so "I like Calcutta," I said once more.

"Yes, best place, most number one!" The taximan smiled and announced "My Hoogly" as he proudly pointed into the darkness at one of the world's ugliest rivers, the abused, disgraced, and greedy river, wasted, stinking artery, corpse- and chemical-choked, a gagging estuary of acid in which dreadful blood-fed idols are washed and all the more grimy for their bath. Kali, gruesome mother, black magic woman, cutter of heads, smiled on the dashboard of the taxi. Camouflaged by darkness, she dances over Calcutta at night.

"Rain coming soon," the driver said, and like so many other words I have heard in Calcutta, I did not know whether it was a threat or a promise.

The taxi driver stopped me from getting out of the cab so that he could show me the trick he had learned from P. C. Sorcar in his childhood. Wiping the black cross from the back of his hand, he turned the hand over and the X appeared there, like the wound of a crucifixion, on his palm. He laughed gleefully as he apologized for not being able to tell me how it was done. "*Jādū*-secret!" he said like a pro, and I let him imagine that I did not know.

The driver, happily asking me to tell Sorcar Junior how much he had enjoyed his father's show, hesitated and then added that I should also tell the son that his *jādū* was good too. He admitted that he had never seen Junior perform, but he didn't want the son to feel inferior to his father. "I know the feeling," he said. For the sake of kindness, he explained to me, it is sometimes best to lie.

The child of the man and woman who cleaned the guest rooms at the American Institute of Indian Studies opened the door for me. After settling in my room, I showed the little boy how a black cross could pass from the back of my hand to my palm, how a coin, disappearing from my grip could reappear from behind his ear, and how I could remove and reattach the thumb of my left hand. His eyes were bright and his dimples deep, and he called me "*jādūgar.*" Because I could fool him, he was fond of me.

I telephoned K. Lal first thing in the morning. The magician had responded to my letter from Hawaii in March with a letter that was handwritten on stationery embossed and imprinted with no less than six colors of metallic ink, and adorned with images of the Indian Rope Trick and of the turbanned K. Lal himself, his hands separated in a grandly magical gesture. At the top of the paper the words were in a gold that stuck to the fingers: "World's Greatest Magician, The Great [in icy metallic blue] Great K. Lal [in an opalescent, candy-apple red] and his Great Mayajal [in shimmering silver]." At the bottom of the letter the words were printed in an austere black: "Warning: any Offer in this Letter does NOT Constitute a Contract." The letter, which contained a gracious invitation to visit him, explained: "I feel pleasure to understand that you are very much interested to write about the scholarly history of Indian magic. Yes, it is urgent that you boost the Indian magic history through your book so that every individual in the world should know the power and the influence and the greatness of our Indian magic. In this context please note that I am the biggest inventor of the history of magic since over forty years. Also I have discovered many delightful items with the wild animals. Hence I will be very useful to you in this regard. You will find me greatest. We can discuss more regarding magic tricks when you visit India."

No sooner had I telephoned him than he had sent his car for me, and I was received into a home consecrated to magic and full of people under the spell, souls old and young, bodies fat and thin—babies and children, brothers and sisters, aunts and uncles and cousins—a family hierarchy that was clearly ruled on the female side by Babi, the wife of K. Lal Junior, a woman beautiful enough to be disconcertingly conscious of her loveliness, and on the male side watched by the magician, the Great K. Lal Senior himself. I felt comfortable in the house—another oasis. The windows were closed to keep in the light coolness of the air-conditioning and to keep out the gross and grave sight of the streets. It was a home fragranced by the honeyed smoke of incense and the vigorously delicious aromas of Bengali cooking, a building with many floors and halls, rooms and rooms (rooms for eating and sleeping, cooking and talking, praying and practicing magic), crevices, crannies, and corners, echoing with shouts and reverberating with laughter, arguments, and teasing, doors slamming and kitchenware clanging;

there was sweet chaos, talking, joking, yelling, barking—there were dogs and cats throughout the house, and talk of Lal's tigers and elephants, lizards and snakes. The small, white dog that never left K. Lal's side obviously imagined that it was a human being, a chipper, shaggy, little person who did tricks even when no one was paying attention.

"And how do you like our Calcutta?" Lal asked with a great smile.

"Oh, it's a wonderful city. I really like Calcutta," I answered.

I asked him about Shittal, the village that the cab driver had told me about. "Maybe forty years ago there were magicians there. Now? Probably nothing. No need to go. I will give you what you need."

Lal showed me his library of books on magic (including early editions of Robert-Houdin's *Memoires* and Houdini's *Unmasking of Robert-Houdin,* Charles Bertram's *A Magician in Many Lands,* and Thomas Denton's *The Conjuror Unmasked*), his accumulation of conjuring magazines and journals *(Abracadabra, Phoenix, Genii, The Linking Ring, Mahatma . . .),* his collection of souvenirs (magic wands, top hats, decks of cards, crystal balls, trophies, ribbons, plaques . . .), and his photographs of himself. Posters of the face were everywhere: the Great K. Lal looked like every other Indian stage magician, which is to say that he looked basically like P. C. Sorcar Senior, slightly more virile perhaps, less puckish and playful, more decadent and more serious. A magician's success, in India, seems to depend on how much he looks like P. C. Sorcar Senior and the degree to which he performs as Sorcar performed, the degree to which he reincarnates him. Only minor modifications of the conventions are acceptable to the Indian audience, and innovation is unthinkable. I couldn't help but wonder if this axiom applied to political figures as well, to film stars, to religious leaders—if it represented some greater, deeply pervasive dynamic in Indian society.

"Here is a gift for you," he smiled as he handed me the little flier embossed in gold ink with his name and entitled "Eight Amazing Magic Tricks You Can Do."

Not only were Lal's looks predictable, so too all of the words were magical clichés, and every gesture was mannered. The body had been fashioned, the soul molded. The effect was that of being in the presence of an old actor who had been cast, hired—perhaps sentenced—as a youth to play the part of an Indian magician unceasingly and forever. He was an actor trapped in his role: the makeup had stained the face indelibly; the only expressions were those supplied parenthetically by the script. The part is that of the maharaja, an anachronistic, though thoroughly self-confident, aristocrat, an eidolon of grandeur in and for squalid times, a man whose function in the society is to supply people with wholesale fantasies, to sustain an illusion that India's glorious past persists and ought to persist in the certainly uncertain and tawdry present. *Ek, do, tīn, gilli-gilli-gilli,* and everything is beautiful; *yantru-mantru-jālajāla-tantru,* and clean waters flow easily and endlessly from a little lota bowl to cleanse the earth and make it fertile. What has come apart, what is broken, is in magic made whole once more. *Śābāś!*

Hyperboles, above all other tropes, oozed from the magician's mouth like molasses. Hyperbole is a way of life in India. Lips, a little too red, shaped the sounds, as eyebrows, a little too black, rose up to punctuate them. The Great K. Lal spoke histrionically, emoting with a mildewed majesty about the pageant of the magician's life, the great part that, through past karma, he had been born to play with unconditional dedication and wholehearted fervor. He spoke to me urgently about his life: to know him would be, in his mind, to discover everything of significance that there was to be understood about Indian magic. He was the avatar of wonder, a descent from another *loka* and another *yuga.* "Ask me any question. I will tell all. If I do not have the right words, the Great Junior will provide them."

The son, Lal Junior, a man about my own age, who looked, behaved, and sounded exactly like his father, who seemed to have surrendered his will completely to the patriarch, was the prince of the magical realm, heir apparent to the sadly ridiculous kingdom created in his father's mind, the brain that seemed to be a spinneret, an arachnoid organ secreting threads and filaments that spread out to form a net like Indra's over the house, the family, the servants, and the guests, myself included. The son, sitting at the right hand of the father, maintained his distance from me, looked at me mostly differentially, through his father's eyes. At times I sensed that he watched me with eyes of his own, and then I felt he did not like me—he sensed, I sensed, how attractive I thought Babi was. Of all the people in the house, her smile alone seemed natural, nontheatrical, a smile that was simply what it was—no more, no less.

When I asked Lal Senior if his own father had been a magician, if a lineage was being perpetuated, he admitted that, no, his father had been in the textile industry in Gujarat. "My grandfather was the Nagar Seth in . . ." Lal Junior explained that " 'Nagar Seth' means 'village chieftain.' " And then the father continued with his hand tenderly posed on his son's arm. "Naturally, whenever musicians, dancers, magicians, or any other entertainers came to the village to perform, they would take their meals at my grandfather's house. It was there that I first came to learn of magic and be enchanted by its spell. Though these magicians were mere wandering jugglers, poor men who dressed in the rags and carried little bags with them and performed simplest items for measly breads, I was fascinated by them and associated with them with the enthusiasm of the child. Recognizing that I was a naturally born magician, they taught me their tricks. Then my family moved to Calcutta. Of the whole world, India is home of magic: of the whole India, Bengal is home of magic. So it was that here in Calcutta I found my guru, the great Ganapati, who, by the by, was also the Sorcar's guru."

"Guru," the son felt constrained to explain, "means 'most venerable teacher'; Sorcar is another magician, dead now." And the father continued: "Ganapati also recognized my greatestness at once and consented to teach me all he knew, even knowing that someday I would surpass him. My parents thought I was in the school all day, when, in the actual fact, I was constantly with guru studying magic, practicing, training, becoming greater and greater. Because I did not go to the school, my English is not very great. Thus I have not, unfortunately for all concerned, been able to go to Great Britain, U.S.A., and Las Vegas. English is problem."

Lal Junior added the article: "English is *the* problem. English is the barrier. It is a language barrier."

"That is correct," Lal nodded. "The only reason the Sorcar had somewhat more Western audience than the Great K. Lal was that he was very good in English."

"Better at English," the son assured me, "not better at magic."

"When I was sixteen years old in age I attended All-India Magicians' Society meeting here in Calcutta. In those days magicians were sinister looking. In addition to being a bunch of half-starving creatures, they also took pains to make themselves appear particularly fierce and ugly. It was Tantric style ["Bad style," the son whispered]. The hair was unkempt and shaggy, not nice; the eyes were bloodshot from drink, and bhang [the son spoke over the father: "Bhang is a drug that low-type people smoke to forget their lives"], and opium; they flapped their dismal black robes like birds of prey, and they twisted their faces grotesque ["Grotesquely," corrected the son, and the father contorted his face to visually illustrate his statement]; upon their stage screens and toolboxes were invariably painted the skull and crossbones. It was small wonder that the ladies and the children never attended magic shows in those days. I addressed these magicians. I told them, 'Be professional!' I advised them to adopt the good taste and to become acceptable to public."

"He means 'acceptable in the public eye,' " the son explained—it seemed a subtle exegesis, but the son, to play his part, needed to say something, and beyond the misuse of articles, there was really very little to correct, since the father, who, I suspected, had delivered this very speech many times before in English, knew his lines. He continued: "Instead of cheered, I was jeered!" Lal Junior repeated the rhyme with a smile. "They said I didn't know what, why, or who I was talking about. I was a lad still wet behind my ear. Thus I scolded one and all: 'You should be more humble. You should be more modest. Remember the words that I am saying today. I am prophet of magic, saying both sooth and truth. The world will follow my suit as I produce magic show that is both beautiful and gorgeous. My audience will be weeping tears of joy. Then I will become president of this very society.' My prophecies were true. Now when I go to meetings of the Society, there is no jeering, only cheering, cheering for the Great K. Lal, World's Greatest Magician!"

The son nodded to indicate that it was all true, substantiating the assertion, I believe, as much for his father as for me.

Lal told me a story that was very significant to him, that for him contained the essential clues to the very meaning of his existence. After telling it, he gave me a newspaper clipping in which the story was reiterated almost word for word. He pointed to it, asking me to read "this great story," and to reread it, to understand it. "Someone whose name I shall not mention was jealousy ["Jealous," the son corrected] of my increasing popularity," he said, and the son nodded meaning-fully, almost angrily, as his lips shaped the name, "Sorcar." "This person paid ten thousand rupees to a member of my troupe to make a bungle of my greatest version of cutting-woman-in-half-with-electric-saw, a oft-copied item which I myself introduced to world." Lal explained that he was on the stage, ready to perform, that the girl was strapped to the table, and the electric motor was humming. As he uttered the phrase "tightly bound, seeming afraid, but trusting that I knew what I was doing," I sensed the sexual, sadomasochistic resonances in the conventional trick. The son became himself for a fleeting moment to say that he had been an eyewitness to the miracle. "I looked out into audience, and above heads of peoples gathered there, I saw luminous presence, something holy, not God, but what makes God a god, and I trembled with the premonition of what was to happen. I knew! That saw was like Vishnu's Sudarshana-Chakra ["Discus-weapon of God," the son injected], and if not for my vision, the girl would really have been cut in half, and the blade of saw would have flown into audience and killed peoples, cutting off heads and arms willy-nilly in its path, for the screws that hold blade in place had been removed. Never mind myself, and possibility of my death because of that saw—I am, everyday, ready to die for the magic." He paused, shook his head somberly. "But the show must go on," he said with conviction and purpose as if it had never been said before, and the son, to emphasize the point of the story reiterated the words: "The show must go on!"

"I put my fingers in the holes where screws were needed to keep blade in place and I dauntlessly proceeded with trick. The pain was excruciating but I knew that if I did not endure it, the young girl on table before me and countless members in my audience, people loving me, coming to me for dazzling and dazing with the wonderment, would die. Not to mention myself again. What else could I do? By the time I had finished, my fingers were bleeding, cut to the very bone, and I was drenched with the perspiration. It was something through and through! But the important matter was that trick was performed—the show went on. An act was accomplished with its usual complete, great success. It was gorgeous. Because of my greatest willpower, I was able to finish a show and thereby making everyone happy. But then, when it was over, I was exhausted ["Physically, emotionally, and spiritually," the son added], and I collapsed through and through and did not recover for a complete month. That girl and people in the audience never knew how close they had come to the death. Not to mention myself."

The story did sum up his life, but in different ways for me than it did for him. It represented something typical of all the stage magicians I had met, perhaps something characteristic of the street magicians too, and indicative of something in others as well, in myself perhaps—a need for grand archetypal melodramas, stories of life and death, heroism, sacrifice, and nobility, a hunger for epic illusions, a willingness to let them be real, a need to live with and in magnificent fictions, by them and for them, playing them out with conviction and commitment while completely ignoring the tawdriness of the sets, the silliness of the costumes, the absurdity of the script, the aimlessness and boredom of the audience. The real world outside Lal's doors, the streets of Calcutta, would be too terrible, too inexcusably painful, if not for the illusions that were brewing here and elsewhere for delivery to the masses. Imagination was salvation. Lal showed me an open letter from Jatin Chakravorty, minister of public works and housing of the government of West Bengal: "Life is becoming increasingly difficult for the common man particularly in Calcutta. K. Lal's magic show provides him with entertainments and helps him to divert his mind from reality. This is welcome." The show must go on.

Lal used the story to malign, by innuendo, his archrival, the late (but not, it seemed, late enough) P. C. Sorcar Senior, whose threat to Lal's "greatestness," was being perpetuated by Sorcar Junior. Rather desperately, Lal told me a long and circuitous story about a theatrical agent who, on the way to book "the Sorcar," saw Lal perform and hired him instead. Sorcar stories, references, and asides were episodes that constituted a subplot of the saga of Lal's life. While heroism and, through it, conquest—aesthetic, but also moral and social triumph—were the themes of the main plot in which he lived, jealousy, envy, and calumny were the themes of the subplot. Lal spoke of Bangalore in 1968 when, according to him, after he had booked a hall for his show, "the Sorcar" reserved another hall nearby and "it became a competition in art of magic." "Meaning," Lal Junior inserted, "not only who was best, but who was most beloved by people and everyday folk." Several days later, Sorcar Junior told me the same story, but in his version, of course, his father was victim and hero, the one who had booked the hall first, and Lal was the villain. One of Lal's written accounts of the competition explains that "as the human nature likes the charming personality, lovely physical structures, and effective actions like lightning, all public hailed the Great K. Lal as the World's Greatest Living Magician." Lal played the martyr. Suffering promotes the transubstantiation of the illusion into reality.

Lal seemed wounded by injustices: Sorcar was credited with the establishment of so many of the conventions of modern Indian magic which Lal insisted were really his innovations. He claimed to be the first magician ever to use music in a magic show, the first to have dressed his troupe in a variety of costumes, and the first to have used electric lights. "God is magician," Lal said with what seemed to be genuine piety. "Yes, God is magician. I am only and merely the world's greatest magician, but He and He alone is greatest magician in the universe. I believe we must be humble at all times. 'God uses light and darkness to perform His magic show,' I said to myself years ago, when just a young man, long before the Sorcar. 'Why not do same? What is good enough for God is good enough for the Great K. Lal.' So I copied God, and all other magicians in India, the Sorcar and others, started using the lights—they copied the Great K. Lal. Me! I am the Great K. Lal!" He said it with all the grandeur and purpose of the yogi who proclaims "I am Shiva! I am *brahman*! *So'ham!*"

Lal claimed, furthermore, that it was he, and not Sorcar as people usually suggested, who had first had the idea of wearing Indian clothes, of performing as a maharaja. It was the American magician John Booth, I had heard—and he himself intimated it to me in conversation—who first suggested that Sorcar discard the tuxedo in favor of the maharaja's robes. But Sorcar Junior denied that—it was completely his father's original idea. Less interested in who initiated the convention than in what it signified, I had looked at photographs of twentieth-century Indian magicians: before Independence the magicians (Manna the Great, A. C. Sorcar, Kamal Kumar Roy, Professor Nantu Goswami, and others), dressing for their British patrons, always wore tuxedos over-adorned with medals and ribbons. Did the transformation of the English aristocrat into a Hindu prince happen with Independence or before (suggesting some sort of political sentiment)? And why a maharaja? Why not a religious costume, to capitalize on the assumptions of inherent connections between Hinduism and magic—the robes of a sadhu, loincloth of a yogi, or the outlandish garb of a skull-bearing Kapalika? Or why not clothes that would appeal to democratic, egalitarian values—the simpler, folksy outfit of the street magicians?

Lal dismissed my questions with a declaration that the answers to all questions concerning magic lay in an understanding and appreciation of the genius and greatness of the great, great Great K. Lal. "Instead of the dreary tails and black hat that magicians all over the world were wearing like army uniforms, I wore a lovely churidar kurta ["Indian shirt," said the son] and a gorgeous jeweled turban ["Indian hat," said the son], looking more dazzling than the Maharaja of Mysore ["Indian prince," said the son]."

I looked at the framed pictures and posters of the magician on the wall, dressed in satin and silk frippery, jeweled brocades and rococo frills, and smiling, always smiling, a great theatrical smile that tried to tell the world that, despite hunger and death, pain and sorrow, "all is gorgeousness." "I am the World's Most Gorgeousest Magician!" He smiled proudly. And it was true—dressed as the maharaja of magic, he made Liberace look like a Buddhist monk.

The subject of costumes, through an association that was at first unclear to me, turned the discourse into an account of Lal's triumphal tours of Japan. "I am the rage of Japan."

His son corrected him: "I am *a* rage *in* Japan."

"Yes," Lal smiled proudly, emotionally, almost moved to tears, touched as he was by what he imagined to be a unanimous Japanese adoration, a Japanese acceptance of the myth for and in which he lived. Just as another Indian, Gautama the Buddha, was, according to Lal, more appreciated in Japan than in the place of his birth, so too the Great Lal had found his greatest following in Japan. "Yes, Japanese are mad over two Indian greats—the Great Buddh and the Great K. Lal. I am the household name in Japan."

"I am *a* household name," the son said, and though his father smiled gratefully at him, the smile faded into an impatient expression that seemed to convey instructions not to interrupt over every misused article.

"Not only have I shown Japanese people the magic, also I have taught Japanese people to lead the better lives and enhance a moral stature. Let me explain it for your book. When Japanese first contacted me, bowing and begging me to come to Tokyo, they wanted to see nude girls in my show. I didn't put up with the funny business. I emphasized that my assistant girls would at all times and all places maintain the Indian-style dignity. They would uphold the purity which is our Indian tradition. I delivered conditions: 'My ladies will never wear costumes of bikini or nude dresses which are meant to create the libido and are contrary to the Indian spiritual ideas. My women and girls come clothed or they don't come at all. Take them or leave them.' The Japanese apologized and said that I had inspired them to change their attitudes in matters of libido. I maintain a very strict discipline in my troupe: no liquor; no funny stuff with ladies. I must hoist a highest moral standard since I am the Indian ambassador to the world. Although the position is not yet established by government decree and post, it is by popular demand and in hearts of all people. When the world sees the Great K. Lal, they see India. This is the great responsibility. I am India. It was by realizing the same that I dropped the Kanti part from my full name, 'Kantilal.' " He paused so that his son could explain, " 'Lāl' means 'son.' "

"Precisely," the father continued, "I realized that, because of my calling, I was not merely Kantilal, son of Kanti, I was the son of India. I am India!" He smiled at me. But the illusion was fragile. Through the delicate fantasy, the translucent grandeur, a sorrow showed. There was gentle sadness in Lal's eyes at all times, and with it the sincere kindness with which certain sorrows sometimes grace us. He reminded me of Don Quixote. He was the Maharaja of the Sorrowful Countenance. His belief in art and beauty, in gorgeousness and greatestness, in morality and honor, and in his own destiny and onerous responsibility to keep magnificent illusions alive in a world that was degenerating around him, outside his door on the streets of Calcutta, made him at once completely ridiculous and yet, somehow, entirely likable, an ironic hero, an innocent champion of the absurd, magic's martyr.

When it was time for me to leave, Lal gave me a large set of the Great K. Lal memorabilia—booklets and pamphlets, posters and programs—all of which were dedicated to stating his "greatestness" in unequivocal terms: "He is, was, and ever will be the great Great K. Lal, Super-Magician, Most Greatest Magician of the Globe, wonder of the world, sitting on Himalayan Heights."

With the instructions that I was to study these materials, I was invited to return the next day with any questions that I might have on any of the testimonials, most of them autobiographical, to Lal's splendor. "Clarification," the son explained, "will be generously supplied." I was also instructed to bring my typewriter with me. "Though I have one of my self ["My own," the son interpreted], the alphabet of yours, as is evinced ["Evidenced," the son said] by your fan mail, is more gorgeous."

One of the beggars outside his door had elephantiasis. The testicles, swollen into a large, dark melon of flesh, hung painfully out of his loincloth and Lal's driver gave him something. As I got into the car, I addressed the small white dog therein with phatic phrases—"Good boy, good dog, nice dog"—that were meant to put the animal at ease and assure it that there was no need to bite me.

"Magic dog, Dante the Great, does not know English," the driver turned to tell me, "only Hindi and Bangla." And then, when he had spoken to the Great Dante in Bengali, translating what I had said, the dog looked at me as if pleased with my sentiments. The hot wind that came through the windows of the speeding automobile did little to lessen the hideous, wet heat of Calcutta. "Monsoon coming," the driver announced, and Dante's tongue dangled from his quick-panting mouth near my face.

"That will be nice; that will make it cooler."

"Nice for you. Not nice for others, not nice for the people who will drown. Not nice for them one bit. Today they are hot. Tomorrow they are not. Tomorrow dead."

Not wanting to engage what I felt was his aggression, I ignored him. Aggravated by that perhaps, and nagged by a need to show me the miseries of the streets, he drove slowly past a group of pariahs squatting in the gutter by a public tap that dripped dirty water. They splashed it on their faces to cool themselves. "Poor people," the driver said, stopping the car and looking at me in the rearview mirror. "Sick people. Sad people. Calcutta people."

Starting forward again, he asked me if I liked Calcutta. I said I did, and he grunted a sardonic laugh.

As we drove along, I looked at some of the materials Lal had given me, at the list of his many awards and honors (including things like "The Sheikh of Kuwait gave the Great K. Lal a Nobel Prize, highest award given by the State"), and the driver, warning me not to read while sitting in the back of the moving car, suggested that it would make me nauseated: "Keep your eyes on the road."

As he stopped the car at the gate of the American Institute of Indian Studies, he snapped an order: "Tomorrow eleven o'clock picking up. Bring typewriter for the Great."

As I emerged from the taxi, a gaunt, weedy young man with a briefcase in his hand, forced his grinning face forward toward me. "You are the great Doctor Professor Siegel?"

"Yes, sort of."

"Excellent. I am the great Shyamal Kumar, *jādūpradīp*, your devoted friend, brother, and humble servant. We meet at last. Every day I am waiting for your arrival. How are you liking my Calcutta?"

"I like Calcutta," I said. "It's such an amazing city." And the smiling young magician followed me into the door and up the stairs. "*Jādūgar!*" Ashok, the little boy in the guesthouse, squeaked with delight as we entered, and taking hold of my hand with wonder and affection, he inspected the palm and looked up the sleeve of my kurta to see if I was hiding anything.

"Can you show the boy some magic?" I asked Shyamal Kumar, and the aspiring magician cheerfully opened his briefcase, removed a mat, several decks of cards, a set of Chinese Sticks, assorted silks, an egg bag, and some other apparati, and proceeded to give a two-hour magic show for the boy and myself. The child tired of it after about fifteen minutes and left, but I had to endure it to the bitter end. "Good?" he asked after each trick; and "Good," I felt constrained to say.

After noticing my advertisement ("University Professor writing history of Indian magic seeking information and references . . .") in the American conjuring magazine *Genii,* Shyamal Kumar had written to me and, discovering that I was going to be visiting India, asked me to give him the dates of my arrival and departure so that he could cancel all other activities, both personal and professional, during that period to spend all waking hours with me "to discuss the history of Indian magic which will be helpful to establish our friendship forever." He had sent me photocopies of his publicity materials, of letters to him from other, more famous magicians, including both Lal and Sorcar, and of some of the tricks he had written up for various Indian magic magazines. All of the material was identical to the material I received and was to receive from all of the other aspiring stage magicians in India. The one thing that was unique was the line "Magician Shyamal Kumar is only Magician in India who does not claim to be the World's Greatest Magician." It undermined the humor, in my mind, to add, "But he promises to be soon."

He began to outline the program that he had painstakingly created for me: I was to spend that evening at his home watching him perform a full magic show for me (the one I had just witnessed, he explained, since it was not done in maharaja costume, did not convey the pure Indianness of his talent); then, the next morning, I would accompany him to the homes of all of his friends who were magicians, boys that he was teaching, and each of them, under his guidance, would do their routines for me; then, that evening . . . I had to cut him off, to explain that I had already made plans for the evening and that the next day I was going to visit K. Lal.

"You will take me with you. He will delight in my magic!"

I had to refuse, to insist that we had business, that it was rather personal and private, and that I really did have to go alone. In that case, he insisted, I would deliver all the promotional material which he had brought for me to K. Lal. He assured me that he would bring me a fresh batch of that material for my own keeping the next evening. "Oh, I almost forgot! I have a gift for you," he smiled proudly as he handed me the little flier, embossed with his name, and entitled "Eight Amazing Magic Tricks You Can Do."

I thanked him and said good-bye.

"What good-bye?" the young magician frowned. "We have business! I prepared a discussion of Indian magic for you!" I sat down, opened my notebook, and he began: "When a baby is born everything is magic. Then, when he is older, his parentfolk confine him. 'Don't wet the bed,' they say. 'This is right and this is wrong.' And the magic is, thus, taken from his world . . ."

That night, in the heat, under the straining fan and bare bulb, drinking warm Rosy Pelican beer, smoking Benson and Hedges, and sweating, I read through Lal's material: "The Great K. Lal's MAYAJAL is renowned the world over. Since centuries, India is known as Land of Magic. In ancient days the magicians were Rishis, Holy Mahatmas, Yogis and Madaries, and the art of magic was performed with supermental powers, mantras, and tantras. Now there is the Great K. Lal. Being illuminated by the mystic wisdom of great past, there glitters the brightest golden star in the heaven of the magic world, that is, the Great K. Lal, World's Greatest Magician. The Great K. Lal presents the gorgeous Show with soul stirring items, in amazing way that he brings down the heavenly world of joy and wonder, conspires in casting such an enchanting net on the stage that makes the spectators willing captives with great charm. During the performance, the spectators forget themselves and feel that they are really in some other wonderful and amazing world, Heaven on Earth."

Awakened by the sound of the damaru, I staggered to the window and watched the monkey trainer, who, suddenly seeing me, gestured for me to throw money. Retreating into the room, I dressed for breakfast. "*Jādūgar! jādūgar!*" the child cried out happily and affectionately as he joined me at the table to watch me drink coffee, smoke a cigarette, and read the newspaper. He did a version of my coin vanish for me, and "*Sābās,*" I said, "little *jādū*-boy." After going to my room to get one of my copies of the flier "Eight Amazing Magic Tricks You Can Do" for him, I returned to the paper and tore a column from it that had a quote from Rajiv Gandhi, a comment on some play that was being staged by the Left Front: "I am told that the play shows a magician conjure up a thousand crore rupees and then make them vanish into thin air. They are right: we have produced one thousand crore rupees for West Bengal, and it is the Left Front government which has made the sum disappear."

On one page of the newspaper there was an advertisement for a Dayaram's Shop on Jamunalal Bazaar Street in Calcutta: "If there is any land on this earth that can lay claim to be the blessed Punya-Bhumi, the land of miracles and magic to which every soul that is wending its way Godward strives, the great land where humanity has attained its highest in gentleness, purity, calmness, introspection, and spirituality, it is India." And on the very same page there was a story of a human sacrifice, *narbali*: district police had discovered the body of a young boy whose right eye had been removed and whose fingertips had been perforated. The paper glibly, repeatedly using the phrase *Tantric magic*, explained that the blood drained from those perforations had been, according to reports from local residents, sprinkled on unmilled rice from the fields around the village to insure a good harvest and keep cobras away. Nails, purportedly immersed in the blood and then dried, had been sold to villagers, who put them in water and then washed their domestic idols with the magic liquid.

Packing up my battery-powered typewriter, then descending into the street to wait for Lal's driver, I leaned against the wall, pushed into the bit of shadow on the bright, blazing-hot street. In an instinctual attempt to cool its mange-gnawed flesh, a mottled gray dog slumped into the gutter, rolled over in the sluggish flow of the dark water, the heady decoction of spit, piss, and gasoline. Her stretched, leathery nipples were flecked with red, raw sores, infected bites inflicted by her or some other bitch's pups. Rising, turning, she collapsed back into the sewage. I considered using my cigarette to burn off the blood-engorged ticks that circled the dog's eyes. But there seemed no point to it, I thought to myself, using that same line of reasoning that prevents us, survivors of the miseries of being, from giving even just a little bit of something to the destitute droves of sick and hungry human bodies who, despite what anyone says, still people the streets of Calcutta: "There are a hundred ticks and a thousand mites just waiting to take the place of each one I remove. There is no end to the misery."

I felt pity for the dog, and it fed a solemn, sentimental revery that is just part of any visit to Calcutta, something you have to get out of the way at some point so you can start telling people how much you like Calcutta. The horn honked as the car pulled up. I opened the door and spoke to the dog within: "*Namaskār* Dante!"

Dressed in a clean white kurta and spotless white pants, his bare feet white-powdered, Lal greeted me excitedly. "Let's get down to your business," he smiled exuberantly. "I could barely sleep all the night through, tossing and turning with my great thoughts on your research. With the pen in the hand, or the typewriter under fingers, whichever you prefer, take down my words and publish them in your book to win praises and prizes."

I looked at the son, expecting some corrections, emendations, or clarifications as I took out my pen and my notebook. But there were none—just a polite smile and wobble of the head.

"When the baby is born everything is magic. Then, when he gets older, his parents confine him. 'Don't wet bed,' they say. 'This is right and this is wrong.' And the magic is, thus, taken from his world." I was startled to hear him utter the exact same words that Tayade had used in Bombay, that Shyamal Kumar had used the day before, and I wondered who got them from whom. "To watch a child is to see magic; to watch magic is be a child [the son repeated the aphorism without any discernable correction]. Well, so much for evolution of magic in a individual person. Now, evolution of magic in the society. This is greatest. A thousand years ago and more ["*Or* more," said the son], it was king against king—they were cruel, raping the women and killing the children, and this sort of funny business and evil. They thought that they were all all-powerful, and they abused the power. Only power that they were afraid of was the magic power, and so the *dharma-guru* said he had that *śakti*. This self-made magician used ventriloquy to get *mūrti* to speak, and he had underground passages to get water or fire to come out of *mūrti* as he commanded. You have every word I speak? Good. Okay, he had the servants down underground to work his apparatus. These slaves were angry. They said to the *dharma-guru*, 'Hey, you damn guy, bloody *dharma-guru*, give us the freedom, or we are telling everybody how you do your tricks. We'll tell about secret passages, about voice-throwing, hidden wires, and secret mirrors.' The court magician gave the freedom to the slaves, making them promise not to divulge secrets. They kept their word, and they became the first street magicians. These are wandering *jādūwālās*. You have every word, the word for the word?"

When I assured him that I did, he asked me to read out what I had written. And the son, despite my assertions that I had studied Sanskrit and understood the technical terms, supplied translations of them: " *'Dharma-guru'* is king's teacher; *'śakti'* is god-power; *'mūrti'* is idol."

"But this is not a whole story," the Great K. Lal sighed. "For that we need to go back to paleolithic times ["Prehistoric times," the Junior inserted]. The cave man used a stick to kill the animals or dig grounds for the food. That *daṇḍa* was first magic wand because the people thought it did the killing. Understand? They were more ignorant than you and I. They thought that the stick had some power even when it was not being used. The man who was responsible for the stick was magician. Out of that stick, in due time, *brahmāstra* was developed in ancient India."

The son translated: "Atomic bomb."

"The atomic bomb?" I asked, and they simultaneously nodded in assent.

"Yes," the magician continued. "That is clearly stated in *Mahābhārat*, *Rāmāyan*, *Purāṇam*s and the like. But that should not concern us, except to say that while now it is the scientists who make atomic bomb, it was in ancient India the magicians who made these weapons. Magic in the old ["olden," according to the son] days was always used for war and for the killing. What is the *indrajālam*?—it is Indra's weapon: nuclear missile! Magic! And still magic is used for the bad purposes. There are three magicians ["Types of," inserted the son] in India: the street magician, as described above; the gorgeous stage magician, like the Great K. Lal; and the Tantric magician, practioner of Bhanumati-*khel*. The Tantric magician still uses magic for the killing and killing for the magic. He gets power by taking the head of boy, a Brahmin boy or own son, or he cuts out the tongue of boy—blood from this tongue is very powerful for magic. Or they get the blood by putting some holes in the fingers."

I suspected that he had read the newspaper that morning. The father patiently waited while the son explained that Tantra was "black magic" and that Queen Bhanumati was a sort of patron saint of that magic, and then he continued: "Before the Great K. Lal, when people thought of magic, they thought only of lowly *jāḍūwālās* and Tantrics. It was K. Lal, the great me, who made magic suitable to the stage and gorgeous through and through." Once again, and in the exact same words that he had used the day before, he told me that it was the Great K. Lal who introduced music, lights, and colorful costumes to Indian stage magic. Then he recounted other descriptions of his greatestness, word for word, phrase for phrase, out of the publicity materials that I had read the night before, a discourse that suggested once again that Lal is a man who lives by a script, who speaks in memorized words and practiced gestures. Conversation with him was a one-man show. In mid-sentence, during that particular meeting, he materialized a deck of cards, fanned it, doubled the deck, and then tripled it with extraordinary grace. But I marveled less over his manual dexterity than over his belief in the importance of what he did, his whole-hearted, whole-minded, and full-bodied conviction of the significance of insignificant entertainment. It was as though he believed everything that had been written by himself or by his son in those pamphlets. He believed in the grandeur of his art and of himself as the supreme artist. "And I am not merely an artist. Greatest magician must also be a psychologist. In all modesty, I must inform you that I am a greatest psychologist. I know how minds of people and animals work. That is merely fundamental to becoming a greatest hypnotist. I mastered the *mohana-vidyā* ["Mesmerism, hypnotism, or autosuggestion," was the son's translation] many years ago, but I don't use it in my shows. No. Never. I have heard that there are the magicians abroad who use the hypnotism to lure young girls to them for the funny business and so on. But this is contrary to Indian tradition of purity and spirituality. Now we'll eat."

As Babi set my food in front of me, I asked her husband if he ever sawed her in half. She laughed, and he shook his head in an ambiguous wobble that left the answer unclear to me. "Our wives are not performing on stage," Lal Senior answered sternly for his son. "They are too busy dealing with reality of the life in the home to be taking a part in our performance of the illusion."

After lunch Lal escorted me back into his den. "This morning we studied history and psychology of magic. This afternoon we deal with theory, and then we take care of business, and then you will go home for the rest, and then tomorrow driver will pick you up very early so that you have an entire day to watch videotapes of the Great K. Lal and his Great Mayajal. Breakfast, lunch, tea, and dinner will all be served to you as you watch. You will have time to observe the tapes carefully, to reverse and watch again and again in slow or regular motion any great parts which are particularly important to your research."

Lal's "theory of magic" consisted of an explanation that "there are in whole world only six tricks, three doubles: one—creation and destruction, *sambhava* and *pralaya;* two—exchange, change one way and other, sea into mountain, mountain into sea; three—cut apart and restore." These tricks, he said, were the "*mahāmāyā* of Mahadeva ["Great magic of great god," Junior said], and the earth magician only performs the little versions of great show." He smiled, sighed, and went on. "That is my job, to be on this earth what the god is in the universe. If you could have a video of this whole cycle of *saṃsār* ["Creation to destruction, destruction to creation," said the son] in fastest motion, you would realize it is only magic show through and through. Since such a video is not available, it is my duty as magician to remind all people of the miracle of the life, to help them to remember. Life is the magic show. We should feel the amazement each day. We should be amazed all the time. Read that last part to me again. It is Indian philosophy. It is great! Were you very capable of following the finest points?"

After I read out what I had written, he smiled. "Excellent. Now the business." After ordering the servant to bring my typewriter and briefcase, he asked me to put a sheet of University of Hawaii, Department of Religion stationery in the machine and stood over me dictating: "This letter is to be addressed to Sushil Kumar Sindhi, Minister for Finance, Planning, Industries, and Law and Judiciary, Government of Maharashtra, Mantralaya, Bombay. Dear Sir: I am the greatest and famous professor of America."

I interrupted: "I can't really say that, I mean that isn't *how* I'd say it."

"Please," Lal said looking at me impatiently. "You don't know how minds of the Indian bureaucrats work. I know. Write what I tell you. Begin: 'I am the greatest and famous professor of America. I write to you on the behalf of American people. It angers us in U.S.A. when we hear the great magicians like K. Lal must pay entertainment tax in Maharashtra.'" Lal smiled. "That's good, isn't it. It will be effective. Continue: 'What? Entertainment? You fools!'" He hesitated. "Maybe it is too emotional, too strong; we don't want to put them off. This is better: 'What? Entertainment? Nay!'"

"Nay?" I asked.

"Yes, nay—it is more formal, more suitable to the great and famous professor than a mere no. Continue: 'Nay! Magic is the art. This art of *Indrajāl* is the art par excellence of India. In America when people think of the magic, they think only of India; when they think of India, they think only of the magic. Magic is the greatest art, and Indian magic is the greatest magic. Magic is oldest art, and Indian magic is the oldest of the oldest, being the supreme art of Vedic era, not even to mention the previous times. Some magic items even have been excavated at Mohenjo Daro.'"

"Is that true?" I asked, and he stared at me utterly startled by my interruption. Realizing that I should know better than to ask a magician to tell me what is true and what is not, what is real and what is not, I continued to type.

"Letter writing now and discussion later, Professor Dr. Siegel. Where were you?"

"I was telling the Indian government about the discovery of conjuring apparatus at Mohenjo Daro."

"Excellent. Say it was Cups and Balls. They certainly had that. Then continue: 'Thus it is that I have come to India to study the great art of Indian magic with such luminaries of our magical universe as the Great K. Lal . . .' "

He went on and on, prompted occasionally with English words by his son, stopping every once in a while either to tell me to feel free to correct his use of articles ("the *a* and the *the* always are confusion? or *a* confusion? or *the* confusion?—I don't know"), or to ask me if I was keeping up with him, and I kept typing, figuring that I wouldn't have to send the letter, that I could tell him I needed to retype it; and then I could privately produce my own modified and at least slightly sane version.

On the second page he got to the point. "Magicians in America like Doug Henning and Siegfried and Roy, all of them aspiring to performing in the great and grand way of the illustrious magicians of India, such magicians as Gogia Pasha, Ganapati Chakraborty, and the magnificent Great K. Lal, never, nay, never pay the entertainment tax. They are considered artistes of highest caliber. Thus their artistic performances are tax-exempt in every state. Why do you not follow the suit? Why do you continue to levy the entertainment tax on the magicians in State of Maharashtra as if they were the mere entertainers? Mark my words, most honorable sir, the eyes of America are upon you. Think it over!" Lal smiled proudly. "I like the way the letter ends and, best of all, the way in which you are giving him the opportunity to decide for himself. He'll appreciate that very much. You've done the fine job. In the postscript you must regale him. Tell him from which places you have received your many prestigious degrees. Perhaps there is some other thing about you that is impressive. If so, add it at this time."

I pulled the sheet of stationery out of the typewriter and began to fold it. "No, no, you have forgotten to sign it."

"That's because it's not very well typed—it's full of errors. I'll work on it, retype it very neatly later this evening, sign it, and then mail it tomorrow morning."

"No, no," Lal said snatching the letter from my hand. "I do not want to take up any more of your precious time."

"I really don't mind; after all, you've been so hospitable."

"No," he insisted. "No, absolutely no. In India we expect the errors in every letter. It is not so important in India. The meaning is what is important, and meaning is there in the letter as is. Sign it."

Against my will and better judgment, feeling no choice in the matter, I yielded and signed the ridiculous letter. When I returned to Hawaii there was a response, dated 29 June 1987, waiting for me from the Office of the Minister for Finance, Planning, Industries, and Law and Judiciary, Government of Maharashtra: "Dear Dr. Siegel, I am directed to acknowledge the receipt of your letter dated 15th June, 1987. You have wrongly named my minister in your above referred letter. The correct name is Sushilkumar Shinde, and not 'Sushil Kumar Sindhi'. This may please be noted for your future guidance. Thanking you, Yours faithfully, [signed] V. S. Dhongade, Private Secretary."

When I arrived back at the guest house on Swinhoe street, Shyamal Kumar was, once again, waiting in front, and Ashok was smiling in the window.

"Did you give my material to K. Lal?"

"Yes," I lied.

"What did he say?"

"He said you are great."

Shyamal Kumar smiled happily, with tears of joy forming in his wide and anxious eyes. "You are going to see him again?"

"Yes, tomorrow."

"You will take me."

I explained that it was not possible, that Lal wanted to see me alone. He was disappointed but in no way discouraged. After doing another magic show for me, he resumed the lecture on magic that he had started the day before: "When man was born, because he was mortal, he had no desire to live. Because he knew he would die, there was no reason to do anything. Every endeavor seemed futile. So Indra, to save mankind, created *Indrajāl*. It is only because of magic illusions that man is willing to continue . . ."

The next day I was made to watch videotapes of Lal's show. The father, son, and Dante the dog watched with me, watched themselves with joy and wonder as if they had never seen the tapes before, as if they were amazed and did not know how the tricks were done. "In all modesty, I have performed over twelve thousand shows," Lal said. "Each of them is over three hours. That makes over thirty-six thousand hours, which equals fifteen hundred days. Do you know what that means? Dividing that by three hundred sixty-five, you come to realize that, had I performed continuously, without the breaks, that one show would have lasted for four years and two months! Imagine that!"

Lal's show, Mayajal, was performed against constantly changing backdrops that were meant to create an apparition of traditional India, an illusion of an illusion—the Taj Mahal, the ghats of Banaras, Hindu temples, expurgated representations of sculptures from Konarak. On one backdrop Shiva danced; on another Kali, her neck garlanded with human heads, her tongue dripping with blood, waved her sword. But the backdrop most often lowered was decorated with an expansive painting of Lal's own smiling face. Surrounded by clouds and floral swirls, stars and doves, cards and dice, and question marks, the maharaja smiled. His show was as gaudy as a Bengali sweet is sweet. In jeweled silks and sequined brocades, glistening golds and shimmering silvers he performed, and as I watched the television, the living Lal next to me spoke: "Gorgeous. My shows are gorgeous. Nothing ordinary to be seen. Pure magic!" He smiled happily. "Just like Las Vegas. I am gorgeous." Gorgeous indeed, gorgeous and glittering with an opalescent opulence. "Poor people see this show and forget unhappiness."

The routines were conventional, typical of early twentieth-century Western magic: ladies were sawed in half or stretched apart, their bodily parts rearranged; Lal manipulated Chinese Rings and Chinese Sticks, handled ropes and silks, cards and vessels of water; he produced animals—doves and ducks, cats and dogs (including the great Dante), snakes and lizards, and then they disappeared; a lady became a tiger, a tiger a lady ("Just like a dream," he commented with a great and gorgeous smile); an elephant vanished ("who but the Great K. Lal can do the feat?"); a traditional Indian philosophic metaphor was enacted (a rope became a snake, and then the snake became a rope); and then he did the Semitic version (a staff became a serpent—"The Great K. Lal is a Moses through and through"); there were mental mysteries and levitations, transpositions and apparitions. In one episode in his show he appeared as a sadhu and gave a sermon on morality. A group of Indian youths, dressed in Western clothes ("Hippies," explained Lal Junior) staggered onto the stage carrying large bottles adorned with the words *Vat 69*. Whiskey was changed to milk, and the youths vanished in a box marked "Moral Reform" and reappeared from the back of the auditorium sober and clean. Senior sawed a girl in half while Junior sawed a boy in half ("watch this carefully Dr. Professor"), and the bottom halves of the boxes in which the subjects were lying were transposed so that, once put back together, the girl was a boy, in pants, from the middle down, and the boy was a girl, in a sari, from waist to foot ("Not trick photography, honestly").

Over the noise and chaos, Lal smiled, "My shows are India." He held my hand in his. Again, at the door leading out of his house and into the steamy streets, he held my hand. The smile broadened as he said good-bye. "I am India," he said softly, a little sadly. "Look at me, think of the magic, and see the glory of India. I hope we meet again."

It was the last time I saw K. Lal. When I returned the following year, I tried unsuccessfully to contact him. Shankar with genuine sympathy explained that he wasn't meeting with anyone. "He had plastic surgery to make his face young. Something went wrong in the operation, and now one half of his face is paralyzed." It was a terrible image: one half of the face frozen in an eternal smile, the smile of youth, of magic, of entertainment, of the show, the gorgeous illusion; the other half of the face free, frowning in misery and despair over the split, the terrible reality of reality, the failure to capture eternity. The face of division and contradiction told a truth. I could still hear his words: "I am India."

When I arrived back at the guesthouse, I was amazed that Shyamal Kumar was not waiting for me. The child was, and I helped him practice some of the "Eight Amazing Magic Tricks," beginning with making a cross on the back of the hand pass through to the palm. The effect was about to take place when there was a knock on the door. It was Shyamal Kumar.

There was more magic; another lecture; a warning that I must move from Swinhoe Street, that when the monsoon came I would be trapped; an offer to move into his house, where his mother and his brother's wife would treat me like a maharaja; and a request: he had written some slogans and wanted my opinion; since I was a native English speaker and writer, he would take any suggestions I had. He watched nervously and anxiously as I read the flier: "Go North, South, East, or West and you find Shyamal Kumar's magic are always the best. Magician Shyamal Kumar is on tops for his props. Shows are a dream with Shyamal Kumar on the team. If your last show was tragic try Shyamal Kumar's magic."

"These are great," I told him. "I like them a lot. They capture the feeling and spirit of Indian stage magic and of your performances in particular."

He smiled proudly and asked me if there was any English word other than *tragic* that rhymed with *magic*. I couldn't think of one offhand.

I took him to the Blue Fox for dinner. As soon as we were seated, watched by the French couple in the middle of their meal at the table next to us, he began a magic trick by pushing a headless penny nail into his eye and closing his eyelid, a trick Robert-Houdin performed in Algeria to convince the natives of his supernatural powers. The magician appeared to force the nail down, manipulating it with his long, bony fingers, moving it under the skin, pushing it across his cheekbone, to finally remove it from his mouth. He smiled proudly and then repeated the trick in reverse, shoving the nail up under his lip, pushing it again, slowly, painfully working it back across the cheekbone and into the eye socket, from which he then happily produced it.

"*Hein! Régardes ce mec,*" I heard the woman say. "*C'est absolument dégueulasse, tu trouves pas?*"

"*Non,*" her companion assured her. "*C'est normal en Inde. C'est la religion—il est un yogi, un fakir.*"

"*Non, pas du tout—il n'a pas les vêtements d'un ascète—la bande-cullote!*"

"*Peut-être que c'est un fakir bourgeois.*"

"*De toutes façons, c'est débectant!*"

The maître d' asked me if anything was wrong, a question that seemed to imply that he would throw my dinner guest out if I so wished. When I explained that we were magicians, the obsequious man, reverentially fetching a book in which honored guests had signed their names and given their comments, opened to a page bearing the signature of P. C. Sorcar Junior, and I read the comment: "I may be the world's greatest magician on the stage, but you are the greatest in the kitchen. The meal was pure magic!"

MIRRORS AND WATER

Obviously excited, Shyamal Kumar announced that he would only eat what Sorcar had eaten—Tandoori fish. I ordered the same, and while we waited for the food to come, I rashly told the young magician that I had an appointment with Sorcar the next day. "You will take me to see him!" he cried out, and, no, I had to explain that I couldn't do that, but, yes, I falsely promised, I would take all of Shyamal Kumar's promotional material to Sorcar and tell him that of all the magicians I had seen perform so far in India, Shyamal Kumar was the greatest.

When the fish was served, the waiter warned me to watch out for the bones, that they were "difficult to swallow." The phrase struck me as funny—so many things in India are hard to swallow, I mused, not only figuratively but literally as well; I thought about the street magicians, Kareem Baksh and others, swallowing thorns, and B. N. Sarkar, and other stage magicians, swallowing razor blades, and then, all of a sudden, I laughed and yelled out: "That's it! 'difficulty in swallowing'—'dysphagia!' That's it, there's the rhyme, the word that rhymes with magic—'dysphagic!' " Shyamal Kumar, pleased with the rhyme, happily repeated it.

Over dinner he spoke of his admiration for P. C. Sorcar Junior, in whom, he said, the glory of the father lived on. "In my humble opinion P. C. Sorcar Senior was the greatest Indian of all times, greater than Gandhi even, doing more for an image of India than any other man in history."

I was about eight years old—about the age of the boy at the guesthouse, the age of Ayasan, about the age of my own son when he got his first magic set—when I saw my first Indian magician. It was, I am sure, P. C. Sorcar. It was on television, the Ed Sullivan show I think: a man in a long coat, with a large medallion sparkling over his heart, wearing earrings, and a jeweled, feathered turban, cut a woman in half with an electric saw. The next day my father took me to the Hollywood magic shop and bought me, among other gimmicks, a little guillotine with which I could make it seem that I had cut my finger off. And then what was severed could be restored. And there was pleasure in playing out such fantasies, the uncanny delight of magic. The same toy was in my son's first magic set.

As I look at the picture of P. C. Sorcar now—the satin turban, pinned with a jeweled brooch and festooned with a pink feather, the round, glistening eyes, the painted face with the mole on the right cheek and the thinly-trimmed moustache, the gaudy earrings, the high Nehru collar, and the theatrical smile, I know that it was P. C. Sorcar whom I saw as a child, and the image of him cutting that woman—exotic and mysterious, dangerous and flamboyant, terrible and comedic, violent and erotic—has haunted my involvement with India, each of my visits, and all of my research.

Of modern Indian magicians, P. C. Sorcar Senior, who called himself the Maharaja of Indrajal, is surely the most famous both in India and the West. All other Indian magicians simply reenact his show: they each play the part of P. C. Sorcar playing the part of a maharaja playing the part of a magician.

I visited the son, P. C. Sorcar Junior, who has, in every sense of the phrase, taken his father's place, reiterated and reanimated his life. He looks like his father, acts like his father, speaks like his father, lives in his father's house. Climbing the stairs of that grand Calcutta residence in the Indrajal Building on P. C. Sorcar Street in Ballyganj, I entered the foyer where a dusty rope stood erect as if by some miraculous power. A sign rested at the base of it: "Do Not Touch." I was on a set. I had entered a show, exited the drama of the Calcutta streets—at once horror show, sentimental melodrama, black comedy, a terrible farce, epic and satiric—to enter a magic show: I was greeted by a dwarf. He salaamed me ceremoniously and seated me with instructions to wait, that the magician, his master, would see me momentarily. A television camera suspended from the ceiling was pointed at the chair in which I was seated, and the dwarf, who had, like the beggars of Calcutta, made a commodity of deformity as a performer in Sorcar's show, seated himself across from me and stared at me as motionlessly as that camera. I smiled at him self-consciously during the painful silence, which I finally broke with the words: "It's wonderful to be here. I really like Calcutta."

A rueful grin belied disbelief, and the silence returned.

An extraordinarily tall man, who would, I later learned, be pounded on the head with a gigantic hammer in the magic show until he turned into the dwarf, entered to announce that the great Sorcar would receive me. Scene two began. The backdrop of the set for it was an enormous portrait of Sorcar Senior. Or was it the son? No, the mole was the one clue that it was the father. Sorcar, a man about the same age as Lal Junior and myself, appropriately princely, sprite and sparkling with an affable grin, rose from the large leather chair behind his desk to greet me with clasped hands, and the grin became the same great smile that was magnified by at least ten in the gigantic portrait behind him. In one of the five video monitors next to his desk, I could see the now-empty chair in which I had been sitting in the foyer. After I had expressed my fondness for Calcutta and my gratitude to him for receiving me, P. C. Sorcar Junior got down to business, explaining that it was very good that I was writing a book about magic, that everyone in the world needed to know about India's glorious heritage, her rich and wonderful cultural traditions as exemplified by magic and conjuring. He explained to me that I would demonstrate to the world that the gypsies took magic from India to the West, where, after it had declined in India, it flourished, only to be retrieved by P. C. Sorcar Senior, whose very destiny it had been to bring magic, Indra's Net, back to its true and rightful home in India and, more particularly, in Bengal.

"You are very fortunate to have been able to find me here at home in Calcutta," Sorcar smiled cheerfully. "I'm so busy, always traveling, traveling, traveling. I'm leaving in a few days to take my show to the Soviet Union and Mongolia, where I am especially loved and adored. But, of course, [giggling] I'm loved and adored wherever I go. The greatest Urdu poet in India has just completed an epic poem on my life! My artistic self is overwhelmed! I am, in all modesty, the great one! Ask me whatever you like."

"What is magic?" I asked, adopting an earnest, scholarly posture. "What is its appeal? What is its place in Indian cultural traditions? I have so many questions."

Ever smiling, Sorcar played with a thimble, making it disappear and reappear as he talked: "When a baby is born everything is magic. Then, when he gets older, his parents confine him. 'Don't wet the bed,' they say. 'This is right and this is wrong.' And the magic is, thus, taken from his world. The magician takes us back to our childhood, allows us to know the wonder of wonder once more. That's the point—to be astonished, utterly amazed, to live a life of wonderment is enlightenment. That's what our ancient seers taught in the Upanishads. Magic gives us a little taste of *mokṣa*."

"Then it is, in its essence," I interrupted, "connected with religion, even when it's just entertainment?"

Discarding the thimble, switching to a coin and rolling it across his fingers, making it change denominations, vanish, appear, and vanish again, Sorcar sighed: "Yes, religion is magic, magic is religion. Everywhere. In India too. Here the *Atharvaveda* is the source of Tantra, and Tantra is the source of magic. Here, as in the West, there is both white magic and black magic. Magic is neutral—the power can be used for either good or evil. This is the theme of the film that I've just finished. What a wonderful film! It is called *Gili Gili Gay*, and it's about good and evil. A great actor plays the dashing, swashbuckling hero, a white magician."

I asked who the actor was.

Laughing and switching the coin for the thimble again, my host answered: "Yours truly! And, in all modesty, I must add that the actor who plays the part of the villain, the black magician, is no less great. Do you know who that is?"

I feigned innocence: "You?"

And the magician, pushing the thimble aside and pulling a deck of cards out of the air, continued: "Yes! Yes! The magician is the greatest of all artists. Let me illustrate. When an artist is truly great we say, 'Your song was magic,' 'Your dance was magic,' 'Your painting (or whatever) was magic.' This shows that magic is the essence of all the arts. Some speak of magic aspiring to be art, but it is really art that aspires to be magic. Magic is the highest art, pure art, art's ultimate accomplishment. In ancient India it was classified into thirteen *rasas*: production, evaporation, transformation, transportation, penetration, flotation, restoration after destruction, acceleration or retardation of nature's speed, animation, escape, spectral demonstration of ESP, and ventriloquism. I have mastered all of these, but the mechanics of magic are not important—anyone can learn the mechanics. The great magician is a psychologist as well as an artist. I hold a degree with honors in psychology from Calcutta University."

He asked me what other magicians I had seen, and no sooner had I begun to list them than, pushing the cards, coins, and thimbles aside, Sorcar frowned a frown that stopped me. "You went to see this B. N. Sarkar? This is not magic. His father used to work for my father. So he took our name. He was a cook or something in the house, some kind of servant. I don't know. Who else have you seen?"

"K. Lal on videotape and . . ."

A laugh broke through the persistent frown: "It's sad—those Lals—eaten up with jealousy over the great Sorcars. Consumed with envy. It's pathetic. The problem is that none of these people have real magic in their blood. They are all newcomers to *Indrajāl*. My family, on the other hand, is a family of magicians, back into time immemorial, Vedic times, although I can only trace the specific lineage, the *guruparamparā*, back for eight generations to the court of Jahangir. When my ancestor Krishna Chandra Dev performed for the great Moghul, the emperor was so delighted that he gave the magician a village, Sutigram, near Dacca. Thus the title Sarkar—landlord—became part of our family name. My father adjusted the spelling to suggest the English *sorcery*. If you read Jahangir's diary, which you must do for your study, you'll see his comments about my ancestor. I quote from memory: 'The Bengali magicians really thrilled and impressed all of us with the Rope Trick, an unending flow of water from a small pot, as well as the production of birds and other living things out of thin air.' You see, I continue to perform just as my ancestor did. The theater is the modern court. Royal patronage ended when Aurangzeb banished magic to the streets, where it fell into the dirty hands of mere indigent roadside prestidigitators, fakirs, gypsies, and other low-caste people. At that time, another of my ancestors, Atma Ram Sarkar—he has become famous in the folk literature of Bengal—began creating extraordinary illusions—ghosts and dancing phantoms that screamed—and people believed that they were real. Some of his rivals, envious magicians like the Lals, jealous of greatness, came into his house while he was praying. They killed him and said it was the ghosts—that he had lost control over those *bhūt*s."

I asked if his father had trouble with rivals.

"No, everybody loved my father. Publicly, onstage, and with friends, he was warm and affable. He was not always that way with the family—he could be cold, even calculating. For example, he never encouraged me. Never. He refused to accept the idea that I would become a magician. He forbid it, in fact. I had to study magic secretly, and finally, to prove that I was indeed capable of being a magician, I had myself bound, placed in a bag that was secured with ropes and put into a box that was then wrapped with steel straps, locked, air-lifted by a helicopter, and dropped from over one hundred feet into the ocean." There was a sober, protracted silence and then suddenly a laugh as he continued: "I was out in forty seconds. My father was furious that I had risked my life, but on the other hand, I proved to him that I was a magician. The magician must be willing to die for magic, for the show, to give up his life for the illusion. That is what makes him an artist."

I didn't believe a word of what Sorcar said; you are not meant, after all, to believe that the soliloquies of the actor on the stage reveal more about the actor than about the character being portrayed. Sorcar smiled as he recited the old line: "I am an actor playing the part of a magician."

The story of the lineage was, at least according to Lal, Sorcar's contemporary, fellow student, and one-time friend, completely fabricated: the Sorcar family had been landlords in East Pakistan with no connections with magic until P. C. Senior. And the tale about Senior not wanting Junior to be a magician simply reiterated a story that the father himself always recounted about his own father's resistance to his own wish to become a magician. And Lal told the same legend. Rather than biographical fact, it was an episode in the archetypal life of the magician, revealing not trivial details about an individual, but significant insights into the nature of the magician-hero of a drama.

At the heart of the production, connecting each player of the part to a successor, allowing for the persistence and recapitulation of the illusion, was the mythology of the transmission. The Sorcar version takes place in Japan in 1971. The father collapses on the stage and utters his last words: "The show must go on." The son, the *yuvarāja*, quickly changes into his father's costume, dons the turban of the maharaja, and stands on the stage waiting for the curtain to rise again. "There was an apparition before my eyes. There was my father with that wicked smile on his lips. 'Let me see what you can do.' The curtain went up, and I finished the performance. I sawed the lady in half, the climax of the show. It was a runaway success, and I have never looked back since." None of it, as far as I could find out, was factual: Sorcar Junior was not in Tokyo during the last performance—he came there to take his father's body back to Calcutta for cremation. But he affirmed the splendid illusion: "While the flames of the funeral pyre consumed my father's body, I was performing on stage. And people cried out 'The Great Sorcar lives on!'" In one dramatic variant of the myth, reported in *The Illustrated Weekly of India* (3 August 1986), the father interrupts his show to inform his audience that in a few moments the curtain will descend. "And I shall never perform again. The minute the curtain goes down, I'll be dead. My assistants will pick me up and take my body out through one wing, but from the other wing I shall emerge again. The show will continue to live." Life is remolded into something that can be interpreted and invested with meaning. Individual being takes on that meaning only to the degree that it participates in the large and profound myth. The last trick, performed with a switching of look-alikes (an old, standard method) is a resurrection, and the people are reassured. Rebirth is through the son. The death of the father is the glory of the son. The show must go on.

Before seeing me out, Sorcar Junior gave me a great stack of books, pamphlets, and promotional materials in both English and Bengali. And, of course, he gave me a little flier embossed with his name and entitled "Eight Amazing Magic Tricks You Can Do." He invited me to return, to come to his country home, where I could spend my time quietly, "fishing, meditating, studying, and writing the story of the great Sorcars, a story that will inspire people all over the world."

The dwarf and the giant escorted me down the stairs, into the other set, the other drama, the streets of Calcutta, where I found Shyamal Kumar pacing back and forth, anxiously awaiting my emergence from the mansion of magic.

"When will he see me?" he asked abruptly, becoming angry when I said I wasn't sure. He wanted to know what my package contained, and when I told him, he demanded that I give him the books. My refusal made him sulk. I was surprised, slightly, sadly sorry, but quite happily relieved, when, agitated and frustrated, he left me alone.

I studied the books, the texts establishing and perpetuating the myth, creating the Indian magician, the Great Sorcar, obliterating the man and then conjuring up the ghost as if at a seance, books by and about him, written in an Indian-English that had been fashioned and styled into what reads like a bad translation of traditional Sanskrit panegyrics, a rhetoric that, no less than the Sorcar show, has been imitated by all the other magicians in India. One of the books, *TW'sGM: The Great Sorcar*, a photographic monograph, begins with an encomium by Madhab Choudhuri, former secretary of the All India Magic Circle, that compares Sorcar to Alexander the Great and Cromwell and hails him as a great Indian philosopher and "Master Artist—the Redeemer of Indian Magic. Magic is in his blood and faith in beauty and sublimity of magic is his creed. The magic genius of India found in this juvenile magic blood her future knight who would in his bloom of life reclaim her from wayside filths and debrises sported with by gypsies and jaduwalas. She threw her mantle upon the puerile enthusiast who with devoted assiduity began darning the vestment in his own fashion with intuitive beauty and richness of mind. Though torn by rough and vagrant use, sullied by preposterous neglect, the mantle to him was a vestige of pristine glory—a history of India's past. . . . From humdrum alleys and rabble-walked footpaths he has taken magic into recognition by the lights and ranks of the World as well as by the Government of the states and the nations. . . . He attends the daily worship of his tutelary deity and the weekly Rotary Club with the zeal and fervour that the situation demands."

Following Choudhuri's praises there is a little piece by "N. B." on "India's Glory—Her Three M's—Miracles, Marvels and Magic," that situates Sorcar in the current of Indian religious traditions: "Saint Kavir was dead. His Hindoo followers wanted a fitting funeral and Muslim disciples claimed a decent burial. Both were uncompromising. Heat and passion broke into broils. When the pall was drawn there was a bunch of laughing flowers instead of the dead body. Can it be accounted for any cogent reason or wit or knowledge? . . . Without any aid of scientific equipment Trailanga Swami remained in the depth of the Ganges for days and weeks unseen and untraced. On the day of his mother's 'Sradh' Bamakhyapa drew a circle to protect the place of 'Sradh' against gale and downpour that was certain in the sky. The surrounding contiguous places were ravaged and inundated but the area in the circle had not a drop of rain. . . . India is proud of these marvels and miracles. She is the land of mystery and magic that have been superbly woven into the fabric of glorious tradition. . . . India's magic is as old as her civilization. We have its references from prehistoric sources. Historical sources are also not very scant. Still it continues to be so." And that's where Sorcar comes in: he is the perpetuator of the past, the perpetuator of Indian culture, redeeming an Indian art from oblivion and offering it to future generations. Sorcar always stressed this about himself: "I started doing research on Indian magic. I wanted to discover some of the original feats of Indian magic which would prove to be a challenge and wonder to the modern world of magic. . . . I took the help of Sanskrit pandits of Nabadwip, Bengal. I sought help from my veteran professor of Sanskrit (Professor Shastri), ransacked the Imperial Library of Calcutta and discovered clues to several exclusive secrets. I must gratefully acknowledge that I got several secrets from Indian mendicants, yogis, fakirs, sadhus and even the street jaduwallahs" (*Sorcar on Magic*).

I wondered about the relationship between the stage and the street, both now and then. Sorcar Junior had said: "My father saw the tricks of the *jādūwālā*s and fakirs. He took those tricks and polished them, transforming them as he presented them in the grand style to the civilized world." And that was true. Sorcar Senior frequently did the same tongue-cutting trick that I was to see Naseeb perform again and again. Sorcar, unlike Naseeb, would joke: "This assistant talks too much. Shall we cut off his tongue?" Naseeb and other street magicians repeatedly and proudly told me that Sorcar always spoke of the *jādūgar*s as his teachers: "Sorcar pointed out that we could do tricks fully surrounded that he could only do on a stage. He acknowledged that the street magician is greater than the theater magician."

Sorcar, however, saw himself as the savior of the sullied art, one chosen to lift magic out of the gutter, out of the hands of those itinerant street magicians, to clean it up and return it to the court, a new court, an international theater: the television. Appearing live on the David Dimbleby show on the BBC, he sawed a seventeen-year-old Bengali girl named Dipty Dey in half, separated the body, and then, because he dragged the trick out, before he had time to put sweet Dipty Dey back together, the cameras had to be switched to another studio for the next scheduled show to begin transmission on time. The telephone switchboard at the BBC was jammed with terrified callers asking, "Is she all right?" Sorcar Junior laughed over the story: "His timing was perfect; he knew the time was running

FIGURE 7. *Sorcar's Version of Tongue-Cutting.* Reprinted from *Filmindia* (Bombay, 1951); courtesy of P. C. Sorcar Junior.

out. It was, like everything else he ever did, a publicity stunt." The next day, 10 April 1956, the Indian magician was on the front page of the *London Daily Mirror,* as well as the *Daily Telegraph, Daily Herald,* and *Daily Express:* "SHOCK ON TV—GIRL SAWN IN HALF BEFORE VIEWERS' EYES." Political cartoonists used the image: in one cartoon Sorcar cut the world in half for Eisenhower and Bulganin; in another he divided Germany into East and West.

Thirty-five years after being amazed by Sorcar on television, as I looked at the pictures, books, pamphlets, and fliers that I had collected—the Sorcar, Lal, and Shyamal Kumar material from Calcutta, as well as the assortment of the same material (with different names inserted) supplied to me by Shankar in Delhi, each of the pieces an echo and imitation of the others—I wondered about the meaning of the persona, the figure of the smiling, painted, gorgeous, and tawdry maharaja of magic, the part that each of the magicians I met or heard or read about—Sorcar and Lal with conviction, Shankar with hope, Shyamal Kumar with desperation—played or aspired to play: avatar of kitsch, epiphany of the absurd, incarnation of a cosmic silliness. The figure is an icon through which the past is worshiped, both India's past, its imaginary history, and the individual's past, his or her imaginary childhood. The fetish allows for regression out of the land of floods and droughts, famine and corruption, malaria and cholera, political violence and human sacrifices, into the sweet, bright land of milk and honey that never is but always was. Indra's Net is a weapon against reality, used to keep terrible truths at bay. And in the kingdom represented on the stage in each long, long Indian magic show, reality is obliterated: the blaring music is an assault on silence, the glaring lights an assault on darkness, and the pace of the manic, hyperkinetic performance is an attack on time. Backdrops rise and fall—there is the Taj Mahal, the pyramids, the Great Wall—and space loses its structure and rigidity. There is, in every sense of the word, no gravity. This is *Māyājāl, Indrajāl*, the Net of Magic in which all wishes are, at least for the moment, fulfilled.

So Shankar, dressed as the maharaja, doing his version of the one and only part, onstage in an industrial park one hot night in Delhi, produced currency from an empty bag. "Money, money, money," he smiled, tossing the notes into the air, "money, money, sweeter than honey." The eyes of the needy widened. It is a dream or, if not that, a madness, related to the ritual of the street performance, but different. On the street the father slays and resurrects the son. On the stage the man slays and resurrects the woman. She appears as a temptress to be tamed—put in a box, cut apart, and then restored. The eyes of desire widen. The magician is he who has control over the passions. He tames wild animals, mines gold from air, defies all limitations on the self. And in paying to see the show, there is participation in his amazing power.

When I was with the street magicians, everything seemed important, every detail suggested something significant. "They represent a way of life," I thought, said, and wrote, "that is utterly traditional, the itinerant life by the road, and it, with all its clues to the essential nature of Indian civilization, is vanishing." When I was with the stage magicians, listening to them speak of their mission, their greatness, and their magnificent art, nothing seemed important; every grandiose claim seemed insignificant. And yet they, as much as the street magicians, represent a way of life, an attitude and posture, that is traditional and endangered. "What moves me about the theatrical magicians," I thought, said, and wrote in my notebook, "is their boundless exuberance and enthusiasm, the depth of their commitment to the trivial, the meaningless, the absurd."

I had to set the notebook aside. Shyamal Kumar had entered without knocking. He had obviously forgiven me, for he was smiling happily. "Listen," he grinned: "If other magicians' tricks make you dysphagic, you should have a taste of Shymal Kumar's magic!" He laughed happily. "It's great. Thank you! Thank you! You gave me this great idea. Thank you! How can I repay you?"

"There is, in fact, something you can do. A street magician in Delhi told me how I could contact some of the street magicians in Calcutta. Two of them in particular, one named Ramjan and another named Suleiman Gafoor, supposedly hang out in the evenings on Tilajal Road, Park Circus, bridge number four. I'd like to go. Can you take me there?"

Shyamal Kumar said he could and would. He lied. Under ominously thick, dark clouds, he led me through Kalighat, along the terrible, dark lanes, shoving his way and mine through the crowded bazaar, to a dilapidated, several-storied building, before the entrance to which a woman, wrapped in dark and dusty cloth, was lying on the broken sidewalk. Her face was covered, but her breast was bare and clutched by a screaming infant, held but not sucked, and a passing, slinking, mangy dog, its tail curled between the almost hairless hind legs, sniffed the bodies fearfully, and then bolted at our approach. When Shyamal Kumar made her move out of the way so that we could enter the building, I challenged him, asked him how he could do that, how he could be so insensitive to her misery. He smiled cheerfully, explaining to me that she was really the lucky one, that his own house was rather small, while her house, wall-less as it was, was enormous—it was all of Calcutta. It was the whole world. "She is free," he said as if he believed it, and beckoned me into the building. "We are not." Distant thunder announced the coming of the rains.

"Where are we?" I asked, and he said it was a surprise, his gift to me, his closest friend.

"But I want to go to Tilajal Road!"

He insisted that would come later, but first, as a special treat for me, another friend of his, a photographer, was going to take our picture—a portrait of the great Indian magician and his American disciple and biographer.

Following him up the narrow staircase into a small, dimly lit and dirty room that was in total disarray, a room full of old cameras and camera parts, sundry photography equipment and bottles of chemicals, stacks of pictures and papers and magazines, I didn't answer when he told me that he promised to visit me in Hawaii. Switching from English to Bengali, Shyamal Kumar spoke to the old man who sat in the midst of the clutter, posed and proud, a king of the chaos. Listening, stroking the rough white stubble on his chin, head wobbling, he grunted what seemed to be agreement to what sounded like a request from Shyamal Kumar. Suddenly (but, since we were in Calcutta, not unexpectedly) the electricity went out. It was pitch dark. I could feel the steady slowing down of the whirling, creaking fan above my head. "For other photographers this would be a problem! But not for my friend!" Shyamal Kumar explained that the old photographer was blind, that we merely needed to make a noise and, expertly judging just where we were and how far away, he'd be able to point the camera directly at us, focus it, and snap the picture. I could hear the old man shuffling around in the darkness as he spoke to the magician.

"He wants to know if and how you like Calcutta."

"Tell him I like Calcutta."

"Smile!" Shyamal Kumar ordered. "Let your smile show how much you like Calcutta!" he said, and the flash went off.

"Again," he commanded, and I smiled as best I could, and there was the bright circle in my eyes, the remains of the flash, as I reached for the magician to hold on to him and be led out of the room.

When, after feeling our way down the stairs, we emerged, the woman, madonna of misery, our lady of sorrows, was gone. "Okay," I said, "let's look for the magicians. Let's go to Tilajal Road. Okay?"

"Yes," he lied again. He had another surprise in store for me—an evening of food and magic at his home.

I was led through back streets, dirty, sad, dark lanes full of the shadows of children and dogs, goats and bicycles, and unrecognizable things, silhouettes of broken walls and leaning architecture, passing figures, and what might have been ghosts. There was more thunder, and the heated air seemed sore and ready to burst. But it held back. I was pulled into another rundown building, Shyamal Kumar's home, and I stood still in darkness while he searched for a kerosene lamp, and then, by the light of it, he led me to a gloomy room that was empty except for the old, mottled, full-length mirror, rough around the edges, and not quite straight on the wall. "Sit down," he ordered, and I complied. Setting the lamp next to me on the cracked concrete floor, he left me alone, and I could hear words in the darkness, women's ghostly voices, Shyamal Kumar giving orders, and an argument of some sort. The young magician returned to me with a plate that was piled high with rice and what might have been some sort of fish. Handing me a small bowl of daal, an almost empty bottle of lime pickle, and a metal tumbler of water, he ordered me to eat and left me alone there again. I crunched down on what seemed to be little bits of rock in the rice and wished I knew the trick of turning the water into wine. The large and arrogant cockroaches on the cracked and peeling, streaked and stained green wall, unperturbed by the light or me, waved their antennae about as if begging for a chunk of my dinner. Suddenly there was music, a crackling rendition of the Indian national anthem ("*Jan gan man . . .*") getting louder, coming closer, and entering the room. Shyamal Kumar, wearing earrings and a turban that was fixed in front with a large jewel from which a pink feather limply waved, dressed in a long, shoddy brocade Indian coat and tight, dirty white, patched pantaloons entered carrying the tape recorder from which the music was fizzling. Without a word he set the music down and with a flourish produced a large silk scarf, holding it up to show both that it was empty and that it was emblazoned with a portrait of the magician and the words "Shyamal Kumar and his Indra Jal" in both Roman and Bengali scripts. He whisked the foulard around in the air a few times and then, pulling a deck of cards from its empty center, he dropped the scarf and fanned the cards. The cockroaches scattered.

The music stopped, and he sat down in front of me. "Great?"

"Great," I assured him.

"Food and magic both great?"

"Everything is great," I smiled, and he smiled in return.

Pointing to the mirror, he told me that it was in front of it that he trained. Each day he would rise before dawn to dress as the maharaja and stand before that mirror to practice his sleights and moves, spending sometimes twelve or thirteen hours in front of it. He told me that when he was training, when he could see himself there, dressed like that, performing for himself, he would sometimes amaze himself with his own tricks, fill himself with wonder, as if that was not him in the mirror, but actually some great maharaja, some marvelous magician from India's glorious past. In such moments he said, he was completely and absolutely happy.

After showing me some pictures that the blind photographer had taken of his show, he put on more music—the hysterical score from some Hindi movie—and performed for me with Chinese Sticks, linking rings, an egg bag, cups and balls, a dancing cane, and cards. At one point he produced a sticky Bengali sweet from an empty, rusty tin can and commanded me to eat it.

There was more thunder, and then it started—the rain. Pent up waters from scalded skies, bursting open, fell with fury upon the dirty city and gave me an excuse to leave.

He said the show was not over.

"But I really do have to go. I have to pack. I'm leaving tomorrow. And the streets are going to be really muddy. Thank you for a wonderful evening, but I really do have to go. Really."

"I'm sad you're leaving."

"I'm sorry. I really must go."

"Okay," he smiled with sudden cheerfulness. "But you know what they say—the show must go on! Correct?"

"Right," I insisted, "but it will have to go on without me."

"Right, so I will finish the show even alone, finish in front of my mirror! Then I am happy."

Ruthlessly it rained all night, and there was rattling thunder, the clamorous skies cracked by lightning—madly laughing Indra's ancient weapon—and as I tried to get to sleep, I kept picturing Shyamal Kumar in the sad, small room, dressed as a maharaja, the world's greatest magician performing for himself before the mirror by the light of the kerosene lamp. And in that mildewed mirror there was no sadness, there was no time nor any limitation on the human spirit. Within the looking glass there was neither loneliness, nor hunger, nor disease, nor death—no human misery or disappointment of any sort. Life was reversed into something easy and playful. Everything there was soft, smooth, and light. Within the magic mirror there was only sweet amazement and infinite wonder.

In the morning, sitting on the steps, waiting for Lal's car to take me to Dum Dum airport, I looked out through the door at the rain, at the great, gray puddle in front that was growing as if reaching out to join the other expanding puddles, to merge with them and then, with them, to converge with others and others and others, to become larger and larger. The puddle seemed to aspire to be a deluge, to wash the city, inundate the land, even cover the earth. And each heavy droplet of rain seemed to me a soul losing itself in the swelling puddle. Hitting the surface of the water, each drop bounced up once as if gasping for one last breath before sinking down, giving itself, its fragile boundaries, up to the waters, the expansion, the coming floods, and leaving behind it a ripple, a perfect circle amidst the imperfections of the street, an inviolate circle radiating outward from the center, where the droplet vanished and the circle appeared, to overlap the other radiating ripples, circles within circles, crossing circles within circles within circles, perfections which from a distance would look like chaos. And the sky rippled with percussive thunder, and the sound of the rain drowned out any plaintive cries of sorrow or muted murmurs of despair that there might have been in Calcutta. A small boy, trying to jump that puddle, was up to his ankles in water, and an older boy teased him. The flourish of laughter, in counterpoint to the bass notes of the rain, was a melody to lull the heart, to beckon it to beat in time.

The servant at the guesthouse, standing on the steps behind me to say good-bye and watch his small son lean against my back and put his arms around my neck, spoke. "Ashok has told his mother that he wants to be a magician," the man laughed. "He made a mark on the back of his hand pass through his palm. We don't know how he did such a thing. You see the effect you have had! Maybe he'll be the next P. C. Sorcar. Maybe he'll be the world's greatest magician."

"Why not?" I laughed, "Everybody else is."

"Come back to Calcutta and see us. See Ashok. See if he is doing magic and becoming great."

"I'll do that."

"Truly?"

"Of course I'll come back," I said, "I like Calcutta. I really do." And as I heard the words come out of my mouth, I was startled, utterly amazed, because, for some strange reason that I could not comprehend, I felt that the words were true.

"Yes," I laughed, "I like Calcutta."

Scene Six:

West/Fall
The Reflections of Professor
M. T. Bannerji 2

"I don't like Calcutta. No, it's Vegas for me, world's greatest place, number one, my wondrous Vegas, magicians' Mecca, conjuring's capitol—sweetest sweet paradise," Professor M. T. Bannerji said out loud and in English to the magician in the full-length mirror in the room at the Stardust Hotel and Casino, the wandering wizard from Calcutta, who adjusted the satin lapels of the travel-rumpled tuxedo, smiling the beaming magnoelectrific smile, staring the mesmeric electromagnific gaze, and snapping his nimble fingers to produce a duty-free Deluxe Benson and Hedges International from what seemed to be thin air.

"O my astonishing Vegas—most blessed city on earth! The holiness of our Varanasi, once Kashi, City of Light, having become all darkest night in this dread Kali Yug, manifests now—O irony of the *kalpas*—in this, my Vegas, this Navakashi, new city of illumination. O eternity of light—yes, oh yes, oh ever on, every second of every minute of every hour of every day of every year, *et cetera, ad infinitum, ad gloriam, ad* everything! My Vegas, most brilliantly beaming jewel adorning this earth—O Vegas, *param dhāmam*, now that sacred city of *brahman* of which our ancient *ṛṣis* spoke." He laughed with a curious joy that verged on an ecstasy. "Thus to this wholly holy place, I, Great M. T. Bannerji, World's Greatest Magician, number one, have, through birth after birth in this damn dark ocean of *saṃsār*, slowly and surely working my way toward the *mokṣa*, finally come. *Ecce homo* and *Oṃ śrī-Lāsa-Vegase namaḥ* to boot!"

Contemplating the name of his tutelary goddess, his *iṣṭa-devatā*, Lasa-Vegas ("The momentum of the dance," the impetus, source, and energy of the great *rāsa*-dance cotillion of existence), he could not help but laugh aloud all the more, an epiphanous laugh and a rapturous "I am here! The great *moi!* I have arrived! Without a doubt!" And as he winked at the magician, the signal of a shared knowledge of deep mysteries, that sorcerer in the mirror suddenly materialized two paper roses, one for each of them, one on each side of the glass. "You're damn good, Professor. You are a star-spangled Bannerji! You are showbiz and amazement tip to bottom!"

He had been like that constantly during the almost twenty-four hours that he had been in Las Vegas, a day that seemed at once an instant and an eternity, a day of transcendence, of absorption into and identification with a supreme and splendid, absolute and ineffable reality. Reality: there was certitude and clarity, a bliss and a peace, an indescribable experience that some, needing names to contain it, would term *beatitude*, others *samādhi*, and still others *jet lag*.

"No, no, this is something profound, a Ramakrishna kind of thing, I am sure of it, most definitely that peace which passeth all understanding, world's greatest peace, that supreme *sat-cit-ananda*," he had thought to himself as he stared, transfixed, at the roulette wheel and saw in it all of existence. He was the ball and the wheel, the bettor and bet, all and nothing, everywhere and nowhere. "Shankara was correct on every point," he smiled more intensely and gazed more deeply into the mirror. "I have, it seems, left dualities behind and passed on into that *brahman*-consciousness of which that world's greatest philosopher was always speaking. Hence no more pains or problems for me, M. T. Bannerji!"

Standing, struck with wonder, in the great betting hall of Caesar's Palace, "the sanctum sanctorum of the temple of *dharma*," as he thought of it, beholding the myriad screens that wrapped around him, he could see, all at once and live, a tennis match in Paris, a golf tournament in Sydney, a basketball game in Los Angeles, a hockey match in Montreal, a soccer game in Rio de Janeiro, cricket in Jamaica, and horse races in England and New York. Space, or what those desperate beings still enmeshed in Indra's net, still deluded by empirical, phenomenal existence, call *space*, was dissolved in the realization of the mysterious truth: "Everywhere is here! Yes! Here! Here in Caesar's Palace, Las Vegas, Nevada, U.S.A., planet Earth."

And as space was realized to be but an illusion, so too was the mental construct that the unenlightened call *time*. In the casinos, where the light is always the same, where the games, "the little *līlā*s in the great *līlā*," as Bannerji understood them, are played twenty-four hours a day, noon was the same as midnight, six in the morning the same as six in the evening; it was clear, so clear, that time is an unreality, a spurious concept that generates endless fears and desires. "It is because of these false notions of time and space, this *māyā*, that man is burdened with problems. It is so obvious! Why did I not realize it before? Why does everyone not see the truth? If only man would give up these illusions, these ideas of time and space!"

In the exquisite euphoria, everything had meaning and yet nothing had significance. "*Tattvam asmi*," Bannerji whispered to the mirror, "That I am! Yes, oh yes, and if this is not what our *Upaniṣads* were always talking about, I don't know what is. I am that *brahman*, the knower and the known. My intellect has been overcome! I have attained that great mindlessness of which the sages speak! *Oṃ śantiḥ Oṃ!*"

Professor M. T. Bannerji asked himself the question: "Should I wear this beautiful tuxedo? Or should I change into my equally beautiful maharaja's suit?" Because it did not matter, because he had gone beyond the trivialities of existence, because, after having transcended dualities, all was One, it was very difficult to decide what to wear. "Because, to the man of true holiness, the *jīvan-mukta*, all things are the same, he behaves not for himself, but for the sake of those other beings who are still trapped in Indra's net. Thus the goodness of the man of true realization. Thus saintliness. I shall dress not for myself but for them, the netted ones! They, the customers and employees at the Taj Mahal Motel and Casino, given the name of the establishment, will certainly prefer the maharaja garb." As Bannerji, like Gautama stealing out of the palace of Shuddhodana, had left India secretly, at night, without telling Lakshmi or his father, Bhutnath or Sagar, not a soul, not even Dr. Patañjali Patel, who surely would have understood, he had, wearing his tuxedo, taken only a plastic shopping bag with him in which there was room only for his maharaja outfit, some magic items and toiletries.

After carefully hanging the tuxedo in the closet, Professor M. T. Bannerji stood naked before the mirror. He showed his hands to be empty and clean, waved them gracefully in the air, and, snapping his fingers, produced the lit Benson and Hedges. "You are indeed the world's greatest magician, Bannerji," he smiled. "How many prestidigitators do you know who can perform as naked as a Jain, thereby insuring the public that there is nothing up their sleeves or up their anywhere else? Your *samādhi* has in no way hampered your skill. That is the beauty of it. To others, to those who do not know, nothing appears to have changed. To others, I, this naked apparition in the mirror, might seem to be an ordinary man."

He went to the telephone and dialed 736–0240, the number of the Aladdin Hotel and Casino: "Baghdad Showroom. Hello, this is the great Professor M. T. Bannerji, World's Greatest Magician, telephoning once again for Mr. Kirby Van Burch, Prince of Magic. . . . No, no, of course. I realize that. I know that he would contact me at his earliest convenience. I am telephoning simply to say that I am about to leave for the evening, that he should not worry, and that, if he wishes, he may try to contact me at the Taj Mahal Motel and Casino where I will be an honored guest at the magic extravaganza of Mr. Charlie Chuckles. Thank you."

He then telephoned Miss Melinda, First Lady of Magic, at the Landmark Hotel and Casino to leave the same message. "Is she, the beautiful-buttocked one," he wondered, "named for the wise King Milinda of Buddhist fame?" And he telephoned Siegfried and Roy as well. "Tell them they, or either one of them individually, can telephone me at any time. Time does not matter to Professor M. T. Bannerji, World's Greatest Magician."

Because he always provided other magicians with free tickets to his performances, he thought it rather small-spirited of Siegfried, Roy, Melinda, and Van

Burch not to do the same; but, in his magnanimousness, he forgave the magicians for their lack of courtesy and was pleased that everything had worked out so well. Everything had a purpose. If they had not charged, or if he had not lost all of his money, he might have been going to one of their shows that evening rather than to the spectacle of Charlie Chuckles at the providentially named Taj Mahal Motel and Casino. The whole strange chain of events was surely more than serendipity; the fruits of karma were, he felt, about to be harvested; destiny was about to have a denouement.

As he changed into his maharaja's clothes, he thought about what had happened in the last twenty-four hours, about the transformation of his understanding of himself and the world. He had arrived thinking of Las Vegas as a manifestation of the Goddess. And as in ancient India, in Indraprastha, so now, in Las Vegas, gambling was the ritual test in which karma was revealed, in which truth and righteousness were established. Bannerji had come with the thought that Devi lured the mean and greedy to the dice tables in order to take their money from them and distribute it to the great and good at heart, whom she also beckoned to the tables. One could tell, he had previously imagined, the righteous from the unrighteous by who won and who lost at the gaming tables. Not knowing that he, like Yudhishthira, the very prince of *dharma*, had a chance of losing, confident in his goodness and purity of heart, he had, dressed in his tuxedo, taken all of the money he had (the four hundred twenty-seven dollars left out of the five hundred dollars in foreign currency he had been allowed to take out of India), bought twenty twenty-dollar chips, and walked, with all the courage of Nala in ancient times, forward to the dice table in the Oasis hotel, the beautiful smooth field of lush green with the red and white numbers on it like flowers in bloom. "It is a miniature Moghul garden," he thought, and then reconsidered the spectacle: "No, no, not at all. It is the Vedic altar. Exactly! This man with the stick, pulling in these symbolical chips—the offerings—is the priest; the thrower of the dice, the *yajamāna;* and listen to the chants, the incantations and invocations ('Come on seven, come on . . . baby needs a new pair of shoes, yeah, come on—be sweet to Papa!'); and behold, Bannerji, this most beautiful woman in the world bringing you the soma—scotch on the rocks!" She smiled when he tried to pay her: "It's free. As long as you play, you can drink all you want." The gift, or rather the sentiments behind it, were moving to the traveler from Calcutta: "It is just like something from *Bhāgavata-Purāṇam.*"

Certain that it didn't matter either where he put his chips or that he did not have the slightest idea about how the game they called *craps* was played, utterly confident that he would win, Bannerji set all four hundred dollars—the twenty chips in two stacks of ten each—on the square closest to him, a beautiful red square adorned with the white lettering "BIG 8."

The *yajamāna* cast the dice: seven. Bannerji's chips were scooped up by the priest, who did not hear Bannerji's words over the chanting of the suppliants:

"There must be some mistake." There was no mistake—he had, in a split second, lost everything.

Snatching up the scotch with a hand that was quicker than the eye, vanishing it in one gulp, desperately forcing on the magnoelectrific smile, M. T. Bannerji, searching his soul for some explanation for the loss, turned from the table to walk toward the door, all the while trying to explain to himself out loud and in Bengali why he should not go up to his eighth-floor room and leap to his death.

With his hands over his painfully pounding heart, he gasped to suck breath out of the night air and fell back, dizzy, against the towering neon palm tree that flashed on the threshold of the Oasis. "Why," the man asked himself, "has the Goddess done this to the great M. T. Bannerji? Why? Why? Why? Is it because I was born on a Saturday, under the sign of Saturn, that malefic Shani?" He took another deep breath and closed his eyes. "Relax Bannerji, just a little *prāṇāyāma*, if you please. There is a reason and purpose for everything in the world. There must be or else . . . or else . . . I don't know." He opened his eyes to look above him, through the blazing neon fronds of the tree and into the heavens, to gaze at the stars, infinite in the desert night, and he ached with the immensity of it.

"*Buenas noches, amigo,*" a man dressed as a cowboy said to Bannerji, leaning into him with a smile almost as electromagnific as Bannerji's own.

"What?" the forlorn magician asked.

"I said '*buenas noches,*' you know, 'good evenin,'—you are Mexican aren't you?"

"No, of course not—I am Indian."

"Damn," the cowboy laughed as he slapped Bannerji heartily on the back. "I mean if that ain't something, hiring an Injun as the doorman! Well, whatever. Anyway, Chief, could you tell me . . ."

Bannerji cut him off. "I am not a lowly doorman. I am the great Professor M. T. Bannerji, World's Greatest Magician."

"Well, I beg your pardon, Great Eagle—but, hey, no need to go on the warpath over a little mistake. The tuxedo had me fooled. Do you play in a band here at the Oasis?"

"*Sālā*! Not musician—magician!"

"Calm down, pal. How was I to know what you are? Hey, where's your hat? Did the rabbit run off with it?" The man shook with laughter over his own joke and then pushed past Bannerji to enter the Oasis: "I'm headed for the crap tables, Chief. Lady Luck and I have a hot date tonight. If you wanna see some real magic, come with me. I'll buy you a drink."

"This bloody *cār-sau-bīs*, this miserable dog of a man, even a maggot in the defecation of that dog, and the like, will no doubt win some fortune, while I, the great glorious me, must suffer defeat. Why is it? How can it be so?" he asked himself, and like Gautama, who resolved to sit beneath the bodhi tree until he understood why there was suffering and what it meant, M. T. Bannerji felt he would be unable to budge from his place beneath the neon palm tree until he knew the answer to his own profound question. "Everything happens for a purpose. Perhaps the Goddess intended for me to lose in order to teach me for once and for all this *niṣkāma-karman*—to be unattached to the fruits of my actions, to see winning and losing as one and the same. It was to teach me just what Lord Krishna taught Arjuna on the battlefield. It was to teach me not to be attached to wealth, to overestimate the importance of gold . . ."

His quest for an understanding of the dynamics of fate was interrupted by a girl, beautiful like Sujata, the dairymaid who interrupted the austerities of the meditating Gautama with an offering of milk. She handed him the packet of papers with a smile and sweet words, "A gift for you." He looked at the offering, a booklet full of coupons which, if he understood correctly, could be redeemed for a myriad of wonderful things: an eighteen-ounce porterhouse steak dinner ("it's about time I tasted cow"), a shrimp cocktail, a movie rental, an eye examination, and a ticket ("drink not included") to "The Charlie Chuckles Wacky Review, The Magic of Laughter" in the Mirage Show Room and Cocktail Lounge at the Taj Mahal Motel and Casino, "just a little out of town, but worth the detour." Bannerji stared at the coupon in wonder. "This is it! 'Worth the detour!' Yes, yes, this was the purpose of my loss at dice. It was all so that I would receive this ticket, that I would be guided to this show. To lose in order to win. Topsy-turvy indeed is this existence of ours! It is fate that this Mr. Charlie Chuckles and I should meet, destiny that Chuckles and Bannerji—oh, I feel it—are meant in the great scheme of things to join forces, to bring the magic of India, with all its mystery and its spiritual basis, together with the magic of the West, with all its technical advances. It was important for me to lose my money so that I was not sidetracked by going to the show of Siegfried and Roy, or Mr. Kirby Van Burch, or the beautiful-buttocked Miss Melinda. It's so clear." He laughed out loud and looked through the rest of the coupons, mostly discounts on jewelry, automobile rentals, as well as various tours, meals, and shows, including one that was redeemable for a free entrance into Ripley's Believe It Or Not Museum at the Four Queens Hotel and Casino. He read it carefully: "Need a shrink?—see an authentic shrunken head and discover the Jivaro Indian secret used to shrink it! In a bind?—examine a pair of handcuffs actually escaped from by the great Houdini! On pins and needles?—see a Hindu holy man who has stayed on a bed of nails for eighteen years!"

He put the coupons in his pocket and, feeling better, lighter for his loss of money, returned to the casino; and it was there that his dark night of the soul yielded to an illumination. Money no longer mattered to him. He contemplated the spectacle: all was changed, and yet nothing had changed—the faces around the dice table where he had played were different, but the game was constant. The men who played the priest and *yajamāna* and the woman who served the soma were different, but the parts persisted—the priest, sacrifice, and libation-bearer were the same. The *līlā* itself was eternal, and, Bannerji realized, by taking part in it, we participate in a larger, transcendent and perpetual rhythm; our lives are meaningful to the degree that we feel our individual meaninglessness, to the degree that we are swept away by that eternal cadence. Then all sorrows lose significance and palpability, and as they do, paradise unfolds itself and is offered up to the awakened soul. He saw that wondrous *loka* before him: restaurants, eternally open, featuring "All you can eat"; drinks freely flowing as long as one continued to play; machines in which, with a pull of the handle, endless fruit—cherries, plums, bananas, oranges—spun before the eyes; women—gopis, houris, apsarases—danced in every hall; each temple had its *tīrtha*, a sacred bathing pool where, regardless of caste, one could be purified; and the bodies by those holy tanks were anointed with precious oils. And in that paradise Bannerji saw the man in the cowboy suit, the person he had scorned just moments before; but now, as he watched the man play, he felt only compassion for him, knowing that it did not matter if he won or lost, that, though he himself was unaware of it, he was in Paradise, swept up by the rhythm of Lord Shiva's cosmic dance. But that Paradise too was ephemeral, a precious illusion that led consciousness on to higher realizations still.

And so it was, in surrendering to the tug of truth, that Bannerji later—it could have been minutes, hours, eons as far as he knew—found himself in the great hall at Ceasar's Palace where, as for Yashoda gazing into the mouth of Krishna, all of time and space were presented to him. He gazed beyond the *māyā* that intractably veils this world. Then, in his own Stardust Hotel, he had looked at the slowly spinning and brightly burning orb of mirrors, high above him in the lobby, and each little mirror contained the entire room and all the forms within it; round and round it turned, and as he gazed up at the globe of mirrors rotating above him, breathing in and exuding infinite light, Bannerji's mind was illuminated by it, and he could hear the words that he had been made to memorize as a child, the speech of Arjuna from the blessed *Gītā:* "I behold your many faces and eyes, the manifold arms and trunks, form without limits—no beginning, middle or end—you, lord of all, appearing as the all . . . a conflagration, flames everywhere, radiant as an infinitely enormous sun, eternal, final resting place of all of existence . . . timeless being! O eternity!" And, as tears of wonder began to stream from his eyes, the magician heard the words of the god: "This *māyā*, the magic I perform, conceals me. Not everyone can see me—the unborn and undying one."

Under the magnificent spell of the theophany he felt ashamed of the greed that had brought him to Las Vegas: "Despite the admonitions of our Ramakrishna, world's greatest holy man, I was motivated by women and gold!" Before leaving India, justifying his secret flight, his escape from responsibilities, standing in his changing tent, before the gilt-framed, full-length practice mirror, he had had thoughts that he now understood as symptomatic of delusion and ignorance: "Westerners come to India in search of some guru—Sai Baba, Maharishi, and the like—renouncing their Western materialism for our Indian spirituality. I am precisely the reverse, as in a mirror. I, the great Professor M. T. Bannerji, hereby renounce my Indian spirituality for a great pilgrimage to Vegas in search of Western materialism and physicality. I want fame and fortune, the love of women and the respect of men. Is that too much to ask for? Or not enough? I want one million dollars minimum and carnal intercourse with beautiful women with golden hair, women with big breasts who wear bikini bathing suits and high-heeled shoes, wanton Western women who smoke and laugh in public, who drink scotch on the rocks and dance all night. If it's all a delusion, if all of these things are meaningless, that's okay with me, *sahaja*-sort-of-fellow that I am—I'll be quite content to make such delusion my reality. All of that meaninglessness will be meaningful to me. If all that debauchery and material comfort makes me miserable, as our philosophers (not having tasted it themselves) always say, well, then, okay, that misery will be happiness to me, the great Professor M. T. Bannerji, World's Greatest Magician!"

The magician had dreamed of opening a show in Las Vegas: *Net of Magic: Wonders from India*, a magic extravaganza in eight scenes, the biggest Indian magic spectacular mounted since P. C. Sorcar's Indrajal, a show that would present the most astonishing feats of Indian magic, past and present, featuring not only the traditional Indian stage items, but also the tricks performed by the itinerant street magicians of India. Sets would include the Moghul courts, the streets of Delhi and Calcutta, the gardens of Kashmir. Professor Bannerji would play the parts of Vishvasiddhi and Muladeva, of Gogia Pasha and a modern *jādūgar*, of an Indian holy man and of himself. The dream remained, but now, after his powerful, transformative experience of the All-as-the-One, the motives were different: he would do this not for himself, for material gain, but for all mankind. He would join forces with Shri Charlie Chuckles to create a universal magic show, the best of Indian magic made even better through the excellence of Western technology, an extravaganza which, through the presentation of the most exquisite illusions, would bring people to see reality more clearly, to see the world as he saw it now. Audiences would be immersed in a sea of *rasa* as natural amazement would intensify into the sentiment of wonder, a transcendental transport in which they would taste the nectar of *sat-cit-ananda*. And this reverie led him to yet another, even greater one, a realization of why he had been born: "I am an Indian gentleman, through and through, and so I must return to my beloved homeland, my India. With the inevitable profits of my magical triumph here, my conjuring *dig-vijaya*, I shall go to the desert of Rajasthan, the Nevada of India, and there I shall build a great and holy place, a city of magic, where people, regardless of caste or creed, will come to taste the *rasa* of wonderment and will thereby be delivered from ignorance. Illusions will lead people from delusion to *brahman*-consciousness. This place will be called 'Las Vedas, Nevaga.' "

It was in that revery that he had fallen asleep, and slept deeply, dreamlessly, and blissfully, awaking to realize that it was time (meaningless concept though it be) to rise and dress to attend the magic performance at the Taj Mahal Motel and Casino.

As he adjusted the turban, it occurred to him that it was just as well that the pink feather had been crushed in the plastic bag during his flight. "It was not subtle enough for this place," he nodded. "You look damn sharp, Bannerji," he said as he snapped his fingers and produced yet another Benson and Hedges.

The magician felt immediately at home and comfortable in the Mirage Show Room and Cocktail Lounge at the Taj Mahal Motel and Casino, not only because his maharaja suit matched the decor, but also because, as he was led to his table by a man in a tuxedo, they were playing "Tequila," that wonderful music he used in his own magic show. And on the table before him was a card with a picture of the familiar Taj Mahal. He read the advertisement for that special drink of the house: "The Taj Mahal Potion of Love, A Magical Old Indian Recipe Straight from the Kama Sutra: Champagne, Brandy, Triple Sec, Drambuie, Tropical Juices, and a Secret Ingredient that our Bar-Tending Magician just won't give away—a Drink fit for a Maharajah or a Maharanee. And you can keep the Glass!" When he ordered one, the waitress, the most beautiful woman he had ever seen, more beautiful than the woman who had brought him the drink in the Oasis, explained the two-drink minimum: "Order one, you still get two." Bannerji, contemplating the philosophical implications of that ("This is basically the position of Ramanuja on the nature of reality, I believe, at once monistic and dualistic"), was already finishing the second drink when the room went dark except for the spotlight on the black curtain. A voice, as velvety as that dark drape, announced: "Ladies and Gentlemen, the management of the amazing Mirage Show Room and Cocktail Lounge of the wonderful Taj Mahal Motel and Casino is very proud to present our very own wild and wacky man of mystery, the bad boy of magic himself, Charlie Chuckles and his outrageous review—'The Magic of Laughter.' Let's hear it for Charlie! And let's hear it for magic!"

As the sparse audience feebly applauded, Bannerji attributed their half-heartedness to an ignorance of the amazement that lay in store for them. "As in India, the fine art of magic has been all too supplanted by such vulgar and popular entertainments as films, television, and other symptoms of this Kali Yug." The magician smiled proudly as his Western counterpart and fellow conjurer, a man about Bannerji's own age, similar in stature to him but fairer, emerged through the curtains with a wry grin. "I'll help him enhance that smile into something more electrifying," thought Bannerji, now fundamentally motivated by compassionate impulses. "Under my tutelage he will become Professor Charles Chuckleji, World's Greatest Magician of America."

"Hey gang, how are ya? Everybody havin' a good time here at the Taj Mahal? I know I am. Hey, I've got some rope here—any of you losers at the gaming tables wanna hang yourselves?"

As he performed with the cord, cutting and restoring it, knotting it and vanishing the knots, cutting it again into three pieces of different sizes and then showing the three lengths to be equal, those and other tricks that Bannerji himself did, the Indian magician felt that the American should not be joking while doing those tricks. It was not that the jokes were so obscene that troubled Bannerji; it was that they were a distraction from the essential wonderment. "Laughter makes the body heavy, thereby hindering true spiritual and aesthetic transport. I will explain these workings of *rasa* to my brother after the show," Bannerji smiled to himself. He was wonderfully pleased and startled, however, when the magician asked his audience if they had ever heard of the famous old Indian Rope Trick. "You know, a guy throws a rope up in the air and it becomes stiff. Let's try it." The rope fell, floppy and lose. "I don't know why it didn't work. Here lady," Charlie Chuckles said, leaning into the front row, "blow on it for me." And when she did so, the rope became stiff and stood straight up in the air.

"Some reference to the *prāṇa* would make this patter more sublime and, therefore, effective," Bannerji felt.

"Hey, who's that big guy next to you, lady?" the magician asked the woman who had blown on the rope, and when she answered that it was her husband, the rope suddenly fell, loose and floppy again, and the audience, except for Bannerji, laughed a bit.

"Okay gang, now for the famous old Polish Rope Trick . . ."

As the magician continued, Bannerji could see he had much to learn. "I will be the guru; he will be the *śiṣya*. He has the talent and technical skill, but he needs my guidance for a greater understanding of the philosophy and psychology of the magic. He will read the blessed and pithy *Gītā* and, following the great success of my Net of Magic Extravaganza, I will take him back to India with me for continued study."

Plucking a handkerchief from his pocket, the Western magician blew his nose with it, waved it about, and then, with a flourish, the white cloth became a dove and the audience duly applauded, but as they did, he suddenly laughed, said "Watch this," and pulled the dove's head off with his bare hands. The audience groaned with disgust over the unexpected decapitation.

"Hey, come on, give me a break. What's the big deal? You eat turkey on Thanksgiving don't you? Yeah, yeah, I know you're all heart, you're worried about the bird. Don't worry, he's okay. Here, I'll give you the bird," he laughed, extending his arm and pointing his middle finger into the air. He covered his hand with another handkerchief (only Bannerji knew it was the same one), and then, when he removed the white cloth, the resurrected dove ruffled its feathers for all to see.

"You like that? Okay, let's try it with a human being," he said, giving the cue to the woman in the wings to bring out the sword and the neck stocks. Dressed in a pink satin bikini and red high-heel shoes, she was the most beautiful woman Bannerji had ever seen, more beautiful than the women who had brought him the drinks, more beautiful than the woman with the coupons. And as she entered, the rope that the magician held became stiff again, rose in the air once more, and several members of the audience chortled.

"Thanks, Suzanne. Hey guys, let's have a big hand for sexy Suzanne. She and I have a lot in common—we both do tricks! For the next item, I need a volunteer, somebody willing to stick his neck out."

While several people in the audience raised their hands, Bannerji spontaneously leapt up and ran up onto the stage.

"Well, if it isn't the Maharishi! Did the motel give you a bed of nails to sleep on? Hey, seriously, where are you from, Mahatma?"

"I am from Calcutta, India," Bannerji said proudly.

"And what do you do over there in Calcutta?"

"I am a magician. I am Professor M. T. Bannerji, World's Greatest Magician in India," he said, clicking on his electromagnific smile and magnoelectrific gaze, snapping his fingers to produce a cigarette, and offering it to Charlie Chuckles.

"No thanks, I've given up smoking," the American magician said out loud and then whispered under his breath: "Cool it, asshole, I do the magic around here." And then, loudly again so that all could hear, he told a joke: "What a coincidence! A couple from Calcutta, India, checked into the motel the other day, and, well, the wife had never used a Western toilet before, so she didn't know to put the seat down before she sat on it. So she got stuck. 'Hey Sabu,' she called out to her husband, 'get me out of here!' Hubby pulled and pulled, but he couldn't budge her. Finally he called the desk, and they said they'd send the maintenance man right up. So the Indian guy told his wife not to worry, that help was on its way. But the wife started whining, 'Oh no, Sabu, he'll see my whatcha-macallit. Quick, give me your turban.' So he handed her his turban—just like that one you're wearing—and she put it over her crotch. The maintenance man came in, looked at the situation, and said, 'I think I can get your wife out, but we may have trouble saving the guru.'"

The comedian chuckled mightily over his own joke, and as he did, Bannerji turned to the audience, pointed to his slowly opening mouth, from which an egg was emerging. Removing the egg and breaking it open, he displayed the silk that was within it, a banner emblazoned with the words "M. T. Bannerji, World's Greatest Magician."

And again the Western magician whispered to his volunteer: "Look, schmuck, what the fuck do you think you're doing?—I do the magic in this show. Get off the stage and back to your seat or out the door, or I'll call the cops." And then he spoke louder for the audience: "Hey, gang, let's have a big round of applause for the guru."

Bannerji, always enchanted by the sound of applause, meager as it was, made his way back to his seat, snapping his fingers as he went to produce paper roses for those women in the audience whom he thought were beautiful in any way, shape, or form. Everybody assumed that he was part of the show.

Charlie Chuckles selected a plump and giggly female volunteer and put her head in the stocks; as he forced the sword through her neck, it made Bannerji think of his beloved Lakshmi, long to hold her in his arms and put his sword through her neck. "Such is the *viraha*," he thought to himself, "that profound love-in-separation of which our great Indian *kavis* were always singing."

After the show was over, the waitress presented Professor Bannerji with a bill for forty dollars for the two drinks. When he offered the coupon to her, she explained that it did not include drinks. He tried to bargain with her, to give her sixteen dollars, all the money he had left.

"There's a joker in every pack," she groaned as she signaled for the man in the tuxedo to deal with Bannerji. "I am a colleague and confrere of Mr. Chuckles," the magician, trying to mesmerize the man with his gaze, said imperiously. "Did you not see me performing on your very stage? Your star will, no doubt, deal with this trivial matter of the lucre for the beverages."

The Western magician, informed of the situation, sent for the maharaja, and then stood to shout at him as he entered the dressing room: "Hey, fuckhead, what were you trying to do out there, upstage me? Don't you have any sense of ethics? I ought to shove a magic wand up your ass. What's with you? Answer me, what's with you?"

"Fine thank you," Bannerji answered. "And what is with yourself, my brother?"

"Hey, man, what's your problem? What do you want?"

Pleased that he had asked, Bannerji explained that he was the "World's Greatest Magician from India," that he had come as a pilgrim of magic to Las Vegas to mount the Net of Magic Extravaganza and that, in his dream of bridging East and West, he wanted to work with Charlie Chuckles. "I have selected you over Siegfried and Roy, Mr. Kirby Van Burch, or Miss Melinda, as my partner. I will instruct you in the performance of purely Indian items, including some that date back to the Veda."

"I don't know what the fuck it is you really want," the magician, shaking his head, said with what Bannerji believed was an illusory brusqueness adopted to conceal a heart of gold. "But if you're hoping to work Vegas, you're out of luck. You gotta have a green card, you gotta be in the union, you gotta know what the fuck you're doing. And you strike out on all counts, pal. Take a tip from me—get your ass back to Bombay or wherever the fuck it's from."

"Listen, my brother . . ."

"Hey, you're not my brother, man."

"All magicians—north, south, east, and west, in all times and in all places—are brothers," Bannerji said with a proud and sanguine smile.

"Shit. North, south, east, and west—most magicians are faggots and nerds. Gimme a break, man—pay for the drinks and get out of here."

"I am not able to pay," Bannerji confessed with a sudden plaintiveness. "You see, we are permitted only to take five hundred dollars in foreign currency out of India; I lost four hundred at gambling, and I have spent all the rest but sixteen dollars. You see, that is the immediate reason why I must perform soon."

"You're unreal, man, fuckin' unreal. I'll tell you what—I'll pay for the drinks. My treat, pal, really. But get outta here. Believe me, you're never goin' to work here, even if you had papers and were in the union. Magicians are a dime a fuckin' dozen here. Let me explain reality to you. Fuckin' God couldn't get a job as a magician here. It's not easy to survive, man. Face reality man! Do you think I'm ridin' on top of the world? I've been here for eight years, and just to make ends meet, I gotta work here nights and do fuckin' day gigs too. Do you believe it?—I have to play church groups, to do fuckin' Gospel magic for them. I show the people some tricks and then tell them only the Lord can do the big stuff. They eat that shit up. Church groups and fuckin' bar mitzvahs—yids love magic. Hey man, really, you're in over your head here. You're outta luck. Face reality. Just get your ass back to Bombay. Go do some yoga or something. I'll take care of the drinks."

"But . . . ," Bannerji started.

"But nothin', man, get out of here, or I'll throw your ass out. Count your fuckin' blessings as the Bible says—I'm going to take care of your drinks."

"Do I get to keep the glasses as promised?" Bannerji could not help but ask.

"Jesus fuckin' Christ!" Charlie Chuckles groaned as he pushed Bannerji out of the door of his dressing room.

The Indian magician couldn't understand the games that fate, the gods or God, his own karma, or whatever or whoever were playing with him, the tricks that were being played on him. Why, he wondered, when everything had fallen into place so beautifully—the gambling, the coupons, everything—did Mr. Chuckles resist the partnership that they both so obviously needed and were meant for. On the verge of that pain again, that abyss he carried around with him, it suddenly dawned on him: "I was attracted by the wrong coupon! I was not meant to see the magic show of Mr. Charlie Chuckles! No. Of course! What a fool I have been! I am meant to go see the Hindu holy man who has been on a bed of nails for eighteen years. It is clearly more than serendipity that he is here. Irony of ironies, that's it! It is extraordinary to be sure, that I should have to leave India, to come all the way to Vegas, to meet my guru, my teacher, to have *darśan* and caress his lotus feet, to shampoo those feet and drink the holy water from that washing, to receive his blessings and his guidance. I had to go away to come home, to leave my India to find her, to go out of myself to discover my inner being!"

But the old pain, the grip of gloom on the throat, was felt when Bannerji, after walking the several miles to the Ripley's Believe It Or Not Museum, discovered that the Hindu holy man was a wax model. Dressed like Dr. Patañjali Patel in a white loincloth and matching turban, arms crossed, legs extended, his gray beard falling lightly on his chest, the holy man, like all perfect sages, was still and silent, focused and at ease, utterly detached from all things in and of this world.

"Is that some buddy of yours?" someone behind Bannerji joked, but the magician did not acknowledge it. He turned, exited, and walked back to the Stardust Hotel and Casino, his face splashed with reflections from the flashing of lights, his ears stormed by the honking of horns and the laughter and senseless jabber of the throngs of strange people around him. He missed the greater calm, order, and sense of Chowringhee, the Strip of Calcutta.

With one last hope, a desperate attempt to believe the platitude that the best things happen when one is most down and out, that the heights are accessed through the depths, M. T. Bannerji went straight to the desk of the Stardust to ask whether Mr. Siegfried or Mr. Roy, Mr. Van Burch or the beautiful-buttocked Miss Melinda had telephoned him yet.

"No, but there is a message from the assistant manager. Could you step around here, please? I'll see you to his office."

Having registered at the hotel as "the World's Greatest Magician," Bannerji naturally supposed it was to discuss the possibility of his performing at the Stardust's Starlite Lounge, and so, as he entered the office with a magnoelectrific smile, he produced a lit cigarette for the assistant manager to smoke.

"No thank you, Mr. Mannerji, I don't smoke."

"That is Bannerji," the magician grinned, "Professor M. T. Bannerji, World's Greatest Magician!"

"Yes, of course, Mr. Bannerji. Let me get straight to the point. Since, Mr. Bannerji, you do not have a major credit card, we will need a cash advance on your room. You already owe us seventy dollars for the first night, plus twelve dollars for the breakfast, and five dollars, TV cable charge, for the porno movie."

"False advertising!" the magician interrupted. "Since Las Vegas is known all over the world as the universal capital of magic, I naturally assumed that a film entitled *Pandora's Magic Box* would be about conjuring. I was personally taken aback by what I witnessed on the television in my room—Pandora was no prestidigitator!"

"That's fine Mr. Bannerji. I'll subtract the five dollars from your bill, but you still owe us eighty-two dollars. You can stay as long as you like, Mr. Bannerji, but we must get that matter taken care of, and we must, I am sure you understand, stay one day ahead in our payments on the room."

Clicking on his electromagnific smile, Bannerji blurted out an exuberant, "No problem, my good man, I am this world's greatest magician, a VIP in entertainment circles. I can come up with anything you like."

"I'm very pleased to hear that, Mr. Bannerji," the assistant manager smiled politely. "When will you be able to bring the money to me?"

"In less than one hour. I merely need to see some of my colleagues from the International Brotherhood of Magicians to procure an advance on the salary which I shall be receiving for the staging of my wonderful extravaganza, *Net of Magic: Wonders from India* and then I shall not only give you the money, my friend, but free passes to my show to boot."

"Thank you, Mr. Bannerji," the assistant manager smiled soberly, "I appreciate that."

"And thank you, sir," Bannerji said with an exuberant bow as he rose, left the office, felt the weakness in his knees, stumbled into the lobby, and slumped in terror and confusion into a red, leatherlike chair that clashed with his primrose maharaja suit. There was the ache and nausea again, the raw grief and difficulty in breathing. He missed Lakshmi, his father in Calcutta, and his child in London; he missed Bengali sweets, the smell of sandalwood incense, the sight of women in saris, the cajolery of friends—Bhutnath, Sagar, Prem Guha, Vimal, and Dr. Patel. "I will go to jail. Just like Gandhiji and Pandit Nehru. Many greatest people go to jail, it's true, because of their commitment to a cause. I am, alas, the martyr of magic. It's not that I mind the suffering so much, but I want to be free so that I can enchant the world, entertain mankind, spreading wonder hither and thither with my magic. What can I do? I could telephone the professor in Honolulu, Hawaii, who is writing the book on Indian magic. I have his card. I helped him in India; he could help me here, now, could wire the money to me. I could then pay my bill and go back to India, to my beloved Calcutta. I like Calcutta; I do not like this Las Vegas, this U.S.A. It is not a spiritual place." The misery paralyzed him. Disjointed thoughts trickled in his brain like water from a rusty faucet. The beatitude had given way to real despair, not the kind of pain that makes one weep, but that desolation that leaves the heart empty and the face expressionless.

But on that face it was not pain that the young woman saw. She mistook the emptiness for an expression of peace, for that renowned Indian *śantiḥ, śantiḥ, śantiḥ.* And it so moved and compelled her that she approached the magician who sat frozen in the lobby of the Stardust Hotel and Casino dressed as a maharaja.

"You're from India," she smiled.

Bannerji looked up at the most beautiful woman he had ever seen, more beautiful than Lakshmi or Pandora, more beautiful than the women who had brought him drinks or the one who had given him the coupons, more beautiful than Sexy Suzanne or Miss Melinda, but, because the anguish choked him, he could not reply. "I'm sorry, I don't mean to interrupt you. But that expression on your face," she smiled softly. "I know what it means."

Bannerji nodded.

"I know all about India. I'm taking a course at the University of Las Vegas in Eastern philosophy. It's a great class. Shankara is my favorite philosopher. I really like Vedanta—I mean that's how I think of it, you know—everything is an illusion. Right? I mean right now I'm just imagining you, and you're just imagining me. We're not real. Well, I mean, we're kinda real, but we're not really real."

As she rambled on epistemologically and metaphysically, Bannerji looked at the young face, the golden hair, the eyes heavy with mascara, the lips glistening with fiery reds, and he wanted to fall into her arms, to be held by her and weep, to let her dissolve his woes in her embraces.

"But I know, of course," she laughed, "that that's just the intellectual level. And that isn't what India's really about. It's the spiritual level that counts. That's where you encounter reality. That's why I joined the Center, the Sathya Sai Baba Center, here. I guess you've probably heard of him in India. It's great, it's really good for me; it balances me, helps me with my problems. We sing songs and meditate and talk about Baba. If you'd like to attend one of our meetings, you'd be welcome. A couple of the people in the group have actually met Baba."

The very name of the holy man sparked the magician's mind, awakened it, and like a dog aroused by the hunter's whistle, it began to sniff at the words, to frantically follow the scent of them in pursuit of a way out of his predicament. "Is this not the answer to your problems, clearly more than serendipity, sir?" Bannerji asked himself, as a plan began to form and, as it did so, push back the pain that cluttered his soul. "Am I not a veritable Indo-Houdini, first in Asia to escape from a galvanized can filled with water and secured with massive locks? If I can release myself from shackles, handcuffs, and bilboes, can there be any doubt that I, the great M. T. Bannerji, can escape from a currently unfortunate state?"

"What's your name?" the girl asked.

Bannerji, his mind still reeling, racing, and jumping, didn't answer.

"I'm Alice," the girl said, extending her hand to shake his, "you know, like *in Wonderland* and *Through The Looking Glass*, like Alice Cramden in the *Honeymooners*."

Bannerji, placing his hands together in the traditional Indian greeting, whispered, "I know, Miss Alice. I know your name. I know." The magician smiled as he spoke, "Baba knows," and with a snap of the fingers produced a rose for her—paper perhaps, but a rose nonetheless, a miraculous rose plucked from the void.

"I have to make sure it is you, that it is really and truly you, the one true Miss Alice," the magician said as he reached into his pockets to find a piece of paper upon which he wrote: "She who comes in the name of the guru will pick the number on the other side of this piece of paper."

"Huh? What's this all about?" Alice asked with a sudden uneasiness. "I've got to get to work soon."

Producing another piece of paper from his pocket and setting it on the low table by the red chair, he asked her to pick any one of the sixteen numbers on it:

```
              FIRE

        1     2     3     4
                               E
  A     5     6     7     8    A
  I                            R
  R     9    10    11    12    T
                               H
       13    14    15    16

              WATER
```

Prompted by curiosity, she selected the number thirteen, and the magician drew a circle around that number and arrows from it to the borders where four elements were indicated. The fifth, ether, he said, beginning his interpretation, permeated the whole: "Yes, thirteen, close to air and water, far from fire and earth—this is your basic being, your essence. You are a cool and aerial person, up in the clouds, fundamentally spiritual and detached from the fire of passions and from the earthy flesh."

"Wow," Alice said with a nervous smile. "That's true, really true, and it's amazing that you say that, because nobody would ever think that about me; it's not the way I appear to others, but it's true, that's me, deep inside of myself."

"Of course, Miss Alice, that is why you picked the number, but please say no more, just concentrate. Pick another number, one that remains." She selected the number seven, and as he made the marks on the square, he spoke to the earnest girl.

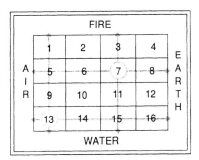

"You are seeking balance—seven balances thirteen, the lucky balances the unlucky. This is your external self, the person you present to the world, close to earth and fire, a woman of the passions, but that appearance contradicts your essential, innermost thirteen. Inner and outer determine the numbers that remain. To which number does your heart guide you? Do not let the mind confuse you. Let your soul chose—two, four, ten, twelve?" "Two," she said, and he smiled, nodded meaningfully, muttered a soft "Of course" to himself, and continued the explanation of the deep mystery of the numbers. "That is your future, close to fire, but not so close to earth. It suggests passion, but the passion is more spiritual than physical. Through it, once discovered and fulfilled, there will be release."

"That's right," Alice nodded incredulously. "I mean, that's what I'd like to find. That's why I joined the Sathya Sai Baba Center, and that's why I . . ."

"Please," the magician interrupted. "Do not tell me things about yourself—I know you well, deep within my consciousness. Only one number remains, number twelve, like the months and the signs of the zodiac, the number which suggests wholeness and completeness, that which will be experienced by you if you find that spiritual passion indicated by the number two."

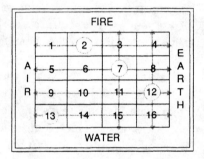

"Now, to determine your signature number, you must add up the numbers that you have freely, following the impulses of your inner being, selected: two, seven, twelve, and thirteen. Do so and then turn over the piece of paper before you."

"Thirty-three. No, that's not right. Thirty-four! Yes, thirty-four!" she said anxiously, nervously, now wanting it to be so, to convince herself and this mysterious man from India that it was indeed she who had been chosen for something unclear, but something important to be sure. And "Thirty-four," she said again (the sum that would have resulted no matter which numbers she had chosen in the old and easy, self-working force), and slowly she turned over the piece of paper, and there was the number thirty-four, proving beyond a shadow of doubt that Alice, though she had not known it before, had a mission in this life and a spiritual path to follow.

"God," she sighed. "What does it mean? I mean, what's going on? Who are you, and what's this all about?"

"You mean you really don't know yet?" the magician gently laughed. "You do know, yes, you do, but your intellect is, once again, clouding your consciousness. Within yourself you know. You know that Baba has chosen Las Vegas as the spiritual center of the twenty-first century. We have only thirteen years—thirteen, the number you selected first—to prepare."

"God, I don't believe this is happening," the girl laughed with slight discomfort. "Is this some sort of crazy joke?"

"Everything has a purpose," the magician said, looking deeply into her eyes. "When you first came to Las Vegas, though you did not know it and thought it was for other reasons, it was to take the class on Indian philosophy and to join Baba's center. The heights, as the Veda notes, are accessed through the depths. All has been but preparation for this moment."

"This moment!" she gasped, looking at her watch. "Oh God, I've got to get to work right now. I'm late. I've got to go—it's after one o'clock—there's a customer waiting for me upstairs. I'm a personal exotic dancer for Sinbad's Harem, and . . ."

"I know, Miss Alice," Bannerji said, putting a finger to her beautiful lips. "Baba knows. Go to work. I'll wait for you."

"Okay I'll only be an hour. We don't allow the guys more than an hour. I'll be down just after two. I'll meet you right here."

In order to avoid the assistant manager, Bannerji said that they should rendezvous beneath the great neon palm tree in front of the Oasis. He was sorry to have to leave his tuxedo and toiletries behind, but they played no part in this, his newest and greatest conjuring act yet. He had his passport, return ticket, and enough pocket magic on him (a Yoshida thumb-tip, a nail-writer, a Himber wallet, some "invisible thread," magician's wax, and a gimmicked pad for billet reading) to perform the magic, weave the mystery, create the illusion that he was some manifestation of the perfect guru or uncanny aspect of god. And there would be money in that.

"That I have no belongings with me will be a powerful and convincing touch," Bannerji said to himself as, waiting beneath the palm tree for his initiate, he smoked what he vowed would be his last cigarette for a while: "I must not smoke, drink alcoholic beverages, or eat meat in front of her. That will further substantiate my holiness."

"God, I left my flower in that guy's room. I'm so spaced out," Alice moaned as, at 2:15 in the morning, the magician opened the door to her red Thunderbird. "All of this is happening so fast, and I'm not sure what it means." Snapping his fingers to produce another rose for her, Professor Bannerji, by that simple trick, made her laugh happily. Though she was not sure what it meant, she was sure it meant something.

"Where should we go?" the girl asked, "I mean, I can't take you to my place. Fancy—he's my manager, sorta my agent—would kill you. He doesn't let me bring guys home. He's not a very spiritual person."

"Look within your heart, Miss Alice. Baba has put the answers there."

MIRRORS AND WATER

"Okay, first thing in the morning we'll go to Howard's apartment," she said after a silent moment of contemplation. "That's Dr. Rosenbloom, Howard Rosenbloom. He teaches the Indian philosophy class I'm taking; he's the one who started the Sai Baba group here. That's how I got into it. He's great. He's not just my teacher, he's my friend too. He's been to India and he's met Baba. He'll know what to do."

"Professors are often subject to skepticism and cynicism, to doubts that prevent them from seeing the truth. He may not understand."

"No, I'm sure Howard will understand. He's not like most professors—he's really open. He's always explaining that we have to find the courage to let go of logic and reason, to transcend the 'cerebral dimension of being,' as he calls it, if we are going to encounter the miraculous."

"He is correct on that point," the magician asserted with a solemn head-wobble.

"Okay," Alice smiled happily, "we'll get something to eat, take a drive, and then, in the morning, we'll go see Howard."

"I do not need food, Miss Alice," the famished Bannerji insisted, and even though, as they sat on a rock together beneath the enormous desert sky, he wanted to take a bite of the hamburger she had purchased from the drive-through window of the restaurant, he restrained desire for the sake of illusion.

"I like coming here, out to where it's quiet, with nobody around. I don't like Las Vegas. But I like the desert." As she spoke, she looked beautiful in the starlight: "Even though I picked those numbers, I still can't believe it. I can't imagine why I'm part of Baba's plan. I mean, you do know what I am, what I do, don't you—you do know?"

"Baba knows all," Bannerji, now comfortable in the part and at ease with the patter, whispered. "It was your destiny, Miss Alice, determined by the karma of your past lives. All has led up to this. You did not choose this role in life; it chose you, my Alice. Do you remember your past lives? No? Listen, please. I will tell you, and you will remember. Give me your hand."

He held her hand, palm upward, as he revealed to her the pageant of her transmigration through the great round of existence, sometimes looking into the delicate hand, at other times gazing into the star-filled eyes. Moonlight from the crest in Shiva's hair danced in reflection on the luscious gloss upon her lower lip, the shimmering red so perfectly matched by her glistening nails.

"Your first earthly incarnation was in Vesali thousands of years ago—a mysterious birth indeed. Do you not remember? You were discovered by a humble gardener in the grove, at the foot of a mango tree. He named you Ambapali and raised you. Oh yes, you grew into a beautiful girl, as brilliant and graceful as you were fair, accomplished in all of the sixty-four arts, gentle and yet strong, world's greatest woman! And all men who so much as saw you wanted to marry you: kings would have been willing to give up their kingdoms, merchants their fortunes, and holy men their vows, for your hand. The gardener, your guardian, installed you as a courtesan in the holy Kashi, City of Light, for if you were to be possessed by one man only, rivalry and jealousy between men would certainly arise. There would be wars fought for your sake. So you were to belong to all men. It is like God who, as the highest object of devotion, can be loved by all people precisely because he cannot be possessed by any individual alone. As Ambapali, like God, while you gave your love to all or any man, you were attached to none. You were proficient in all the arts—you even learned the art of magic from a sorcerer named Indradatta. But there was one being only for whom you felt a special devotion—Lord Buddh. When you heard that he was to speak in Kotigama, you went, together with your great retinue of exquisite beauties of the courtesan kind, to see him, and descending from your golden chariot to approach him humbly on foot, you bowed and seated yourself near the enlightened one to listen to his nectarous words. After the sermon you invited Lord Buddh and all of his monks to dine at your splendid mansion. This part of the story everyone knows. But what they do not know is that when he came for that renowned dinner, he instructed you, explaining that it was your dharma to keep the birth of a courtesan for century after century, thirty-four times—the number you freely chose. And this, dear Ambapali, dear Alice, is your thirty-fourth and last birth. After this life you will be a courtesan no more. You will be free. Lord Buddh promised it. You will be free. I promise it."

There were tears in Alice's eyes and sidereal reflections in those tears as she leaned against the conjurer, and he wrapped his arm around her tenderly as he continued to speak to her, to explain to her that it was destined for her to serve God in the form of a courtesan, that she had, as Mary Magdalene, served God in his incarnation as Lord Jesus, that she had, as a courtesan in the court of King Amaruka of Kashmir, served God in his incarnation as Shankaracharya. She was known as Mayeshvari then. In her last life she was a *devadāsī* at the temple of Lord Jagannath in Puri. "You have always served God with love and in return, though you have not always been aware of it, God has loved you and watched over you. Even now he protects you."

She had fallen asleep with his arm around her, and as he held her close to him, the smell of her hair, the feel of her satin blouse, the curve of her stockinged leg in the starlight filled him with desire. But he resolved to restrain his longing for her, the hunger for her kiss, knowing that if he did not, he was just a man, and that as a man he owed the hotel money, that as a man he was a failure, but that if he did restrain desire, he was a god, and that as a god he owed no one anything, that as a god he could succeed at anything. But the restraint was for her sake too: as a man he could do nothing for her—she knew lots of men; but as a god he could do the greatest things for her—he could make her feel loved with a sacred love that transcended any individual longing. It was all an illusion of course, but illusions were, after all, his specialty. There in the desert, in the cold night, he held her in his arms to keep her warm until dawn; and he was as silent and still, as restrained and calm as the Hindu holy man on his bed of nails at the Ripley's Believe It Or Not Museum.

When she awakened with a garland of paper roses around her neck, she called out, "Baba, Baba!" anxiously, afraid he might have vanished or that the whole encounter might have been an illusion, and the mysterious holy man appeared from behind her car, where he had been squatting to prepare for the magic of the day—smoking cigarette after cigarette to get the ashes he would need and setting in order the billets and pocket indices for displays of mentalism.

Alice left Bannerji in the car while she went into the apartment building to talk to Professor Rosenbloom alone. When, after nearly a quarter of an hour, she appeared, followed by a man about Bannerji's age, a man whom Bannerji thought would look rather like Charlie Chuckles if not for the beard and glasses, the magician leapt from the car and rushed toward him as if he recognized him, staring his electromagnific gaze and calling out: "Is it you? Is the rose in bloom? Is it you? Are you Rosenbloom?"

"How did you know my name?" the man asked with a professorial tone. "Did you tell him my name, Alice?"

"I don't know, I can't remember. I don't think so."

"Please, let me know for certain what I need to know," the magician said as he handed the pen and gimmicked pad of paper to the professor. "Please, write one word on this piece of paper. Don't think about it, don't let intellect cloud consciousness, just write the word that comes of itself. Tear off the piece of paper on which you have written the word, fold it up, and return the pad and pen to me."

When he had done what was asked of him, Professor Rosenbloom, grinning incredulously, watched the odd man in the maharaja outfit do as he had done. Giving his folded billet to Alice, the magician asked the girl to read out what was written on both pieces of paper. "Miracles," she said as she opened the first billet, and "Miracles," she said again as she looked at the second, and "Wow!" she added, "Wow! What's really amazing is that on both pieces of paper the word *maya* is written at the top and then crossed out!"

Before the professor had time to react to the first test and miracle, Bannerji had asked him the year of his birth "just to make sure it's you," and then, quickly jotting down a few numbers, he showed him the magic square that had the words "Rose-in-Bloom" at the top and the year of his birth at the bottom:

ROSE-IN-BLOOM			
8	11	25	1
24	2	7	12
3	27	9	6
10	5	4	26

'45

"Yes of course, forty-five, the magic number—please Rose-in-Bloom," the magician said with a warm smile, "show Miss Alice the perfection of the square. Add each of the horizontal lines—each adds up to forty-five; add each of the vertical lines—each adds up to forty-five; now add the two diagonal lines, and it is the same—forty-five; add up the four corner squares and add the four squares in the center—both equal forty-five." He continued to show them the many combinations of numbers that proved something or other, something unclear but significant and consequential to be sure. And then, with a magnoelectrific smile, the conjurer began to wave his hand about in a circular motion, palm downward, just as the famous Sai Baba did, and then it happened just as it happened when Professor Howard Rosenbloom had seen Sai Baba in Puttaparthi—from nowhere, ashes, holy *vibhūti*, flowed from the magician's hand. But, unlike Sathya Sai Baba, who always distributed the ashes to his devotees, Bannerji Baba was careful to cast his ashes to the wind so that the professor would not discover from the smell of them that they were the ashes of cigarettes, duty-free Benson and Hedges Deluxe Internationals.

Putting his hands together reverentially, the stunned devotee, choked with emotion, greeted the guru: "*Namaste* Baba, *namaste!*"

"*Namaskār,* my Rose-in-Bloom," the magician whispered as, snapping his magic fingers, he produced a paper rose for the man.

"You know who this is, Alice, don't you?" the devotee asked.

"He's a friend of Sai Baba, some kind of disciple," the girl, his student, responded with manifest sincerity.

Professor Rosenbloom and Professor Bannerji smiled meaningfully at each other, amused over the girl's innocence.

"No, Alice. It's him," Rosenbloom beamed. "Incredible as it may seem, as contrary as it is to our Western way of perceiving and thinking, it's Baba. He's taken on another form to come to us. It is his *līlā* that, through his *māyā*, he takes on many forms. I knew you'd come Baba, I knew you could feel my love, the love of all of us here. I've been waiting for you. It's him Alice. The mind tries to lead us astray, to tell us it can't be so, but I can feel it. I can feel the same energy, the *śakti,* I felt when I was with him in Puttaparthi. Look, Baba, I've still got the *vibhūti* you gave me." Pulling out his wallet, he produced a little pink envelope from it that had Sai Baba's picture on it and handed it to Bannerji, who immediately vanished it with cryptic words, "You have no more need of that."

As Howard Rosenbloom, at once smiling and weeping with the bliss that comes when the intellect is transcended, when the mind is suffused with supreme emptiness, muttered words of gratitude, M. T. Bannerji, dressed as a maharaja, his classic gaze and smile displayed for the occasion, produced another stream of ashes from his palm.

The magic show was a triumph. "*Śabāś!*" Bannerji said to himself. Indra's Net had been so perfectly cast, with such finesse, that the prey, the ardent devotee, insisted that Baba stay at his apartment, an arrangement which was convenient for the magician in that, among other things, it gave him the opportunity during the days, while the professor was at the University, to peruse the books there on Sai Baba and Indian philosophy, texts from which Bannerji could extract bits of wisdom, material for the patter in his new and amazing magic extravaganza. Also in the apartment he found the ingredients to make the vibhūti—blending ashes from sandalwood incense with a bit of talcum powder, a dash of flour, and a pinch of powdered sugar, he formed the pellets that were to be concealed in the fold of flesh between the thumb and the index finger, loaded there one at a time during what would appear to be a mere wiping away of the previously manifested symbolic ashes from his palm. And he produced the holy ashes for each of the members of the Las Vegas branch of the Sathya Sai Baba Center who came to hear his first sermon that autumn night. They sat around him with open minds and anxious hearts, with ashes smeared on their foreheads and expressions of bliss smeared on their lips.

Placing a small mirror behind a coin on the coffee table in front of him, the magician began his show: "Here is reality," he said, pointing to the coin before the mirror; and pointing into the mirror, he added, "and that is illusion. What is the difference?" He lifted the little hand mirror, and behind it was a real coin in the spot where the reflection had been seen. He lowered the mirror again to show two real coins and two illusions. Once more, as he lifted the mirror, the reflections became manifest in reality. Then he did the trick in reverse, changing reality back into illusion; the coins disappeared just as they had appeared until there was only the one coin with which he had started. Uttering clichés from the Indian philosophical traditions as gleaned from Rosenbloom's library, he explained that empirical existence is but a reflection in brahman, the absolute and only reality: "The world has no more substance than the coin in the mirror, than the reflection of a city in a looking glass, as Shankara so correctly opines. Life is magic, and magic is life. It is magic that the sun comes up and that a baby is born. But man, in this Kali Yug, has lost his sense of miraculousness. When a baby is born, everything is magic. Then, when he gets older, his parents confine him. 'Don't wet the bed,' they say. 'This is right and this is wrong.' And the magic is, thus, taken from his world. God with his miracles, if only we can overcome reason and logic, if only we can believe with all our hearts, takes us back to our childhood, allows us to know the wonder of wonder once more. That's the point—to be astonished, utterly amazed, to live a life of wonderment is enlightenment. It is the world's greatest state of consciousness."

Occasionally he would lapse into Bengali, adding a vowel to every word ending in a consonant, and telling them it was a Sanskrit quotation from the blessed Veda. "These words are untranslatable. The purport, however, is basically that 'reality is the greatest illusion, truth the most powerful deception.' " Any mention of, or quote from, the Gītā, he discovered, was especially effective, and so, as he turned a pearl necklace that a devotee from Reno (she was beautiful he thought, "very beautiful, but not as beautiful as Alice, Pandora, Melinda, Suzanne, the women with the drinks, or the woman with the coupons, not even as beautiful as Lakshmi, but beautiful nevertheless") offered him into a garland of paper roses, he announced with closed eyes: "This *māyā*, the magic I perform, conceals me. Not everyone can see me—the unborn and undying one." It was especially authoritative when he connected the *Gītā* with the Gospels, saying, for example, that it was in that statement from the *Gītā* that Jesus explained his transformation of water into wine at Cana. "The Qur'an," he would always add, "reveals the same." And it was more powerful still when, later in the sermon, he turned a simple string back into the woman's pearls and cast those pearls before them, saying "we must be detached from riches and wealth." When the woman begged Baba to keep the pearls, pleading that she wanted him to accept the gift as a gesture of her devotion, he still refused them, adamantly explaining that he had neither need nor desire for any earthly, material thing. That was proof to one and all that he must indeed be God. Because he wanted nothing, they were willing to give him all.

When they asked their guru how they should address him, he smiled. "It does not matter. Call me your own name, if you like, for I am you. Yes, it's true—look in the mirror, deep into your eyes, through your eyes into your soul, and you will see me there. I can be addressed," the magician continued, paraphrasing words that he had read that afternoon in Rosenbloom's copy of *Sai Baba, Man of Miracles*, "by any name that tastes sweet to the tongue, pictured in any form that appears sweet to the eye, that fills one with wonder and awe—Sai Baba, Jesus, Buddh, Krishna, Ram, Shiv, Allah, all the same! It makes no difference at all."

"I heard him utter the same words at Puttaparthi," Rosenbloom whispered to Alice, "the same thing, said with that same impish smile that beckons us toward enlightenment. He's like Krishna. He plays tricks on us to get us to see the truth."

Learning the moves as he went along, Bannerji found that the more abstract his words were the better, and that the devotees smiled and nodded with understanding when he said things that he himself did not understand, paradoxical things like "God, though formless, has many forms." In fact, he discovered, in whatever he said, no matter how stupid or meaningless, they found wisdom and significance. They loved absurdities and trivialities, things like "The goal is to become who you truly are."

"It is incredibly easy," Bannerji thought to himself one night as he lay comfortably in bed after a fine sermon, "being God. So much easier than being a man! The only hard part of being God is not being able to smoke. I like being God, it suits me. Certainly Lakshmi, my father, my son, and others, especially Dr. Patañjali Patel, would be proud to know that I, M. T. Bannerji, have become God. *So'ham! So'ham!*"

"If only you will realize the *ātman*, you become God yourself," he told his disciples. "Each one of you here can become God by simply merging your individual souls into the ocean of the universal *ātman*. Why is that difficult? Because your souls are now in solitary confinement. That is both the crime and the punishment."

"How do we do it, Baba?" the woman with the pearls asked in all earnestness. "How do we become one with the universal?" As he did whenever anyone asked about methods of realization, Baba merely smiled meaningfully and said the magic word: "Love." That mysterious word, the sound no one dared to say they did not understand, was more powerful still when Bannerji uttered it in Sanskrit: "*Prema—prema*, not the lowly *kāma*, but the sublime *prema*." The sound made them smile. Whenever he uttered it, he would glance over at Alice. She haunted his thoughts, inspired him with both sublime *prema* and lowly *kāma*. The smell of her perfume, the sweet tone of her laughter, the sight of her sitting at his feet, overwhelmed him with a desire to possess her and to give himself, all of himself, to her, to confess everything to her, to tell and show her the truth. But he knew that was impossible, that for him as God there was no going back, that he would have her love only as long as she believed in the illusion that she had allowed him to spin. And besides, he had not yet done what he had set out to do, what the *jādūgar* on the street or the magician on the stage, what all men of miracles, do—to get paid for his magic performance.

He began his seventh sermon by telling them of the ancient Indian Rope Trick. "I will use some topical, Las Vegas way of illustrating it for you. My Rose-in-Bloom, do you have cards?"

And the professor brought the cards from the desk, the cards that Bannerji, unbeknownst to him, had found there earlier that day, the cards that the magician then asked the professor to cut and spread. He directed Alice to chose one. "Don't let reason get in the way, pick the one to which your heart guides you. Very good. The jack of hearts. Tear the card into pieces and put the pieces in the ashtray. We'll keep one piece out. This is a Vedic sacrifice: the slain boy, the torn card, like the soma, must be offered to the gods, burned in the fire, delivered into the heavens by Agni. Please ignite the pieces of the card, except the one piece which we have kept aside."

It was done, and then the magician, after explaining that what he was doing could help his devotees understand the mystery of resurrection in a noncognitive, noncerebral, way, requested Alice to spread the deck, and when she did, there was one card that had a piece torn out of it, the jack of hearts. And the unburned piece fit perfectly.

When, thoroughly amazed, the devotees asked him for other miracles, he would chastise them: "These things are nothing, of no importance at all. It is my message that is important." They loved being chastised, he discovered, as much as they loved being fooled. Behind their guru's back they interpreted his words and gestures, debated the subtleties of his message, and some claimed that they had seen him levitate, others that he had materialized gold ornaments. When

Rosenbloom announced that he had received a letter from a friend in India who had just seen Sai Baba, Bannerji feared the game was over; but the apprehension was groundless—the letter merely proved that Baba was capable of being in two places at one time. The devout longed for miracles.

"There are no miracles. And yet all is miraculous. All is magical, and yet there is no magic," the magician explained to them. "I shall explain it. If, one hundred years ago, a man said that he could fly from Las Vegas to Calcutta, everyone would have said he was a liar. If he did it, everyone would say it was magic, some great miracle. And yet now, we are not surprised or amazed because we know about airplanes, about aerodynamics and gravimetrics. So the miracle has become an everyday event. The miracles I do for you will be commonplace in the twenty-first century, when Baba's love is established on earth. That is what we must prepare for. *Prema* is the preparation."

Frequently after the sermons Bannerji Baba would receive devotees privately to give them counsel. Although his own life had been, he felt, overburdened with "problems, problems, problems," he found it absolutely easy to solve other people's problems for them.

"I've got a lot of things to work on," the woman with the pearls confessed. "Family troubles mostly, but work problems too. Life's been pretty tough for me lately."

"Life is only a problem if you take it personally," the guru said, and though he wasn't himself quite sure what it meant, it seemed to help her. She insisted she understood, tearfully thanked him, and tried to give him the pearls once more. "No, you must not give me anything other than love."

Guru Bannerji waited until he was certain that all of the disciples were fully convinced that he wanted nothing of material value from them before he performed his last trick, the climax of his magical extravaganza: "I must endeavor to help you. Such is my mission. I must try to help you to be clean. You may come to me, bringing with you any lucre which you have acquired by theft or gambling, by the sale of stolen goods or drugs, by prostitution or pandering, or bringing any money that has been acquired out of greed. The choice is your own. If you bring these lucres to me, I have the power, the *prema-śakti*, to clean them for you. I shall purify your money and your selves, your *jīva*s. Only you, each one of you, in your own heart of hearts, knows if you are ready to be pure."

One by one, almost all of them came to him in the private meetings he called "*niṣkāma-karman* sessions," and each set a pile of currency before him. "It is not important that you tell me how you acquired this filthy lucre; it is only important that you want it to be cleansed, that you yourself want to be cleansed and unburdened," he said as he picked up each bill or coin, rubbed it with his fingers, chanting a mantra, "*Om yantru-tantru-jālajāla-mantru Om*." And each profane piece of paper and metal was magically transmuted into holy *vibhūti* with which the guru anointed the disciple's neck. And not a single devotee, much to Bannerji's own astonishment, asked for the money back. They believed, it seemed, that the cash was gone, truly transformed into the sacred ashes that they were instructed to wear "as a symbol of your detachment from worldly things." They understood the Vedic axiom that purity is not possible without sacrifice.

When Alice came to him, he refused to touch her money. "No," he smiled. "Nothing of yours is unclean or unholy. You are the chosen one. Remember it was your destiny, your divine mission to earn your money as you have acquired it in this life." As he snapped his fingers, a little pink envelope with a picture of Sai Baba appeared. Following the instructions of her guru, she opened it, looked at the mysterious words in the Indian script, and then read the English translation: "For the Greatest Beautiful Beloved of God that She may know that through Love, after the trials of this life, She will find Peace."

Explaining to her that he was leaving, that he would vanish suddenly just as he had appeared and that she must not speak of it until he was gone, he told her to close her eyes. "My beautiful Ambapali, remember me always. And remember that above all of the rest, I love you." As he said it, he leaned forward and softly, gently, closing his own eyes, kissed her forehead. Joy radiated throughout her body and filled her soul. She felt cleansed by the kiss of God, and she believed in the freedom and peace that he had promised her.

On the airplane, high above the world, flying from Las Vegas to Calcutta, looking down upon the earth, the realm in which fear and desire so ceaselessly weave delusion, Professor M. T. Bannerji, with thousands of dollars in his pocket and a happy grin on his face, decided that he should write a book. "Countless Western magicians—Harry Kellar, Samri Baldwin, John Booth, Charles Bertram, Howard Thurston; the list, like life itself, goes on and on—have come to India and then written their memoirs. Not one Indian magician has, to date, done likewise. Once again M. T. Bannerji will be the first and greatest. I am confident that I can do it. What is the difference, after all, between writing a book and doing a magic show? I shall call my book *Net of Magic: An Autobiography of God,*" he said to himself, and then, looking out the window at the city of clouds sprawling below, he thought about it: "For the sake of modesty, I shall write it in the third person."

Thoroughly inspired, the conjurer took out his pen and billet pad and scribbled the first lines of his story: "The greatest trick in the world, and I, the amazing and wonderful Professor M. T. Bannerji, world's greatest magician, he who is thoroughly me, *escamoteur extraordinaire,* shall perform it! Without a doubt, the illustrious illusion shall be reality for once and for all!"

Traveler's Journal 4:

South/Winter

Midnight. The telephone was ringing, and I stumbled through the darkness, dreading that the call would be bad news. There was a woman's voice on the line: "Hello, my name is Susan Shapiro. Is the swami there? I'm sorry to be calling so late, but I need to talk to him. Is he awake? I hope I'm not disturbing anyone."

"No, don't worry about it," I said, relieved that both my morbid fears and prurient assumptions about who might be telephoning and why were unwarranted. "The swami never sleeps. Just hold on a second." She seemed nervous: "He's not busy or anything is he?"

Although I assured her that he was "just meditating," she said she could call back. But I insisted that I would get him: "He told me he was expecting a call. He really doesn't mind coming out of *samādhi* for the phone. Just hold on, I'll get him." Setting the telephone receiver down on my desk, I yelled out, "Hey Swami, the phone's for you. . . . Yeah Guruji, that's right—it's an American woman's voice."

After pouring a shot of scotch for myself and lighting a cigarette, I returned to the phone. "Good ebening Madame, dhis is Svami Bannerji. I hab been vaiting phor your telephone calling. Phor dhe last halph hour eben I hab so strongly been pheeling dhe toughts ov vone anxious phor dhe speaking vid me." I did a parody of Peter Sellers' undeniably offensive parody of an Indian accent. And despite the blatancy of the racism inherent in such mockery, I would maintain that the lampoon is really rather benign; it's the voice that many Westerners who do research in India try to master in an attempt to keep themselves laughing, sane, and aloof in the face of the discomforts and frustrations of their work. And for me it was a routine, a show; it was patter. Like Hitler's favorite magician, Helmut Ewald Schreiber, who called himself Kalanag and dressed as a maharaja to perform the Indian Rope Trick and other exotic illusions from the mystic East, like so many Western magicians—Isaiah Hughes ("The Fakir of Ava") and Alfred Sylvester ("The Fakir of Oolu"), Yamadeva (Louis Guter) and Kar-mi (Joseph

317

Hallworth), Rajah Raboid and the White Mahatma—I was playing the part of a Hindu conjurer, an Indian mentalist: "I am so glad you habe teleponed, Madame Susan."

Though she had heard that the swami had the power to read minds, she was, nevertheless, dazzled when she heard him utter her name. How did he know? What did he know? She yearned for more, craved to be truly amazed, hungered for illusions; like all of us, she wanted to be fooled. Slowly and clearly explaining that she was thinking of a certain card, she asked the swami if he could guess which one it was.

"Guess?" the swami laughed. "No, dhis is not dhe guessing, dhis is dhe knowing. I am able to receibe dhe toughts probided dhose toughts are clearly sent and probided dhe sendar is habing vone excellent power of concentration and telepatijhation. Please, Madame, concentrate."

"I'm concentrating," the voice said with utter sincerity. "I'm concentrating."

"Yes, yes Madame," I continued. "I am beginning to see vone card. Ov dhe two colors, dhe red, vhat ve are calling dhe *rakta* in our belobed Sanskritam language, and dhe black, vhat ve are calling dhe *kāla*, I am dephinitely seeing dhe *rakta*—dhe red."

"Yes! yes!" she squealed with apparent excitement. "That's it—red!"

"Ov course," the swami said. "Ov dhe *rakta* cards, dhere are two categories, dhe adamantine diamond, vhat ve are calling dhe *vajra*, and dhe passionate heart, vhat we are calling dhe *hṛdaya*. Dhe image I am seeing is dhe image of lobe."

"Lub?" Susan Shapiro asked.

"Yes, lobe, as in 'Eberybody is lobing a lober.' "

"Oh, 'love,' yes, love," she said the magic word. "Love—hearts, yes, you're right! This is amazing!"

The swami spoke in mystic whispers: "I am seeing vone maharaja's phace—not dhe fadher but dhe son, vone *yuvarāja*, vone *hṛdaya-yuvarāja*, vhat you are calling dhe jack of hearts!"

The woman was ecstatic: "Incredible! I don't believe it. This is amazing! You're amazing, really amazing."

"No, no my phine Madame Susan," I said in all modesty. "It is you who are most amajhing. I am but dhe humble receibar; it is none odher than your good selph dhat is dhe most powerphul transmittar."

"Yes, you're right," Susan Shapiro confessed. "I've always felt I had certain powers, kind of like intuitions—I get hunches about things, and sometimes they turn out to be right."

The swami agreed with her: "Yes, I am dephinately pheeling dhat you are having dhe mental giphts. You are vone spiritual person, most dephinitely."

And she agreed with him: "Yes, that's right! This is wonderful! Can we try something else? Is that alright? I'm thinking of an object. I'm really concentrating. Are you receiving? Are you receiving me, Swami?"

There was a meaningful pause. Then came the voice out of the mysterious East: "I am seeing some sort of begetation."

"Oh god! Yes, yes!" she exclaimed. "This is unbelievable!"

"And dhe roots—I am seeing dhe roots hanging down phrom dhe branches."

"Yes! Yes! I don't believe it!" she said, but she did believe it.

"Dhis is vhat you are calling vone banyan tree. Is dhat correct, Madame Susan?"

"My god! This is wonderful. This is incredible! What else can you tell me, Swami? Tell me something, tell me anything."

The swami told her that she was a very perceptive and sensitive person with so much "lobe" in her heart, and, yes, she said, yes, that was true, and the swami indicated that there was one particular person, a man, who did not realize the vastness of that love. And, yes, that too was true. Using the art of the *māyāvin*, the science of the *indrajālin*, and all the craft of the *jādūgar*, Swami Gautama Bannerji had looked deeply into the soul of Susan Shapiro and unveiled mysteries there.

Now the secret of Swamiji's omniscience: how the trick was done. In the afternoon of the day on which the woman had telephoned at midnight, Neil Boisen, a magician and friend, had come into my office at the University. "Lee, I was really sorry you weren't home last night because I was at a party, doing some magic tricks, and there was a woman there who wondered if I had ever met anyone who could do 'real magic.' I told her about the swami and asked her to think of a card, any card. She said she didn't really like cards, that she'd rather think of an object, that, as banyan trees had been on her mind ever since she'd arrived in Hawaii, she wanted to think of a banyan tree. I explained to her that you can't ask a medium or mind reader for something so specific out of an infinite number of possibilities, that, just for the sake of the experiment, she should think of a card. She said she was thinking of the jack of hearts, so I told her to call Swami Gautama Bannerji, writing his name and your number on a piece of paper for her. The set-up was perfect. It would have been great. How am I supposed to impress women if you go out every night?" The first letter of the last name would have indicated the suit of the card to me (A = ♠, B = ♥, C = ♦, D–Z = ♣) while, through a simple mnemonic code ("Fakirs knew God"), the first letter of the first name would have revealed the face value of the card (F = 1, A = 2, K = 3, I = 4, R = 5, S = 6; K = 7, N = 8, E = 9, W = 10; G = J, O = Q, D = K). But I didn't need the code of course; the tip-off was better.

He came to my office again the next day: "She called last night—it must have been one in the morning—really worked up over her talk with the swami. She said that never in her entire life had she heard a voice that was so powerful, so full of wisdom, understanding, compassion, love, and blah, blah, blah. What I can't figure out is how the swami knew her boyfriend's name."

"She told it to him."

"Well, she thought he had known it all along, known that and every other detail of her life. It's sort of sad in a way, isn't it? And think of the implications for religious studies—I mean, who knows what Jesus and the Buddha really knew or said or did? We hear what we want or need to hear, see what we want or need to see." Neil and I laughed about it.

Late that night the phone rang again, and Susan Shapiro's voice was full of urgency, longing, and awe. Realizing that if I didn't do something about it, I'd have to talk to her every night, I told her that the swami had gone back to India that very morning. Upset by the news and anxious to contact him, she asked me for his address. "Address?" I laughed. "He doesn't have an address. The guy's a swami—he lives in a cave somewhere in the Himalayas."

She was disconsolate and full of a need to talk about the man of wisdom with whom she had been fortunate enough to have even a brief encounter over the telephone. She said she could see his face vividly, his beautiful brown eyes, his clean white beard, the serene smile, the beautiful hands, and asked me to tell her all I knew about him.

I conjured up his spirit for her, created an illusion which she saw vividly. Out of thin air, and without the use of wires, mirrors, or any other gimmick, a man of flesh and blood came to life before her very eyes. Perhaps it was cruel to continue the magic show, but the thought of telling her that she had been tricked seemed even more unkind. While everyone wants to be fooled, no one ever wants to discover that he or she has, unknowingly and without consent, been deceived.

She wanted me to tell her how I had met the venerable Swami Gautama Bannerji, the Himalayan Mahatma, the Enlightened One. "I'm a professor at the University here, in the Religion Department. I teach courses on India, and I try to write books about it. I'm working now on a study of Indian magic, and so I've gone to India to do research for it. Someone there introduced me to the swami. I can honestly say that I've learned a lot about magic from him."

"Oh, I'm sure you have," she sighed. "I'm sure you learned many things about life, about yourself, about everything. You're really lucky to have been able to spend time with him, to have had him staying with you. I'd give anything if I could be with him for awhile, close to him. I'd like to feel his presence. I'd like to learn from him."

Despite the fact that she was talking about me, that his great wisdom was really my own, I was beginning to find it rather sickening, and I suddenly felt an intense dislike for the swami. I could read his mind—I knew the prurient thoughts that the holy man was having about Susan Shapiro. I could picture him, and the image was the seed of a story.

"It's actually not much fun having a mind reader stay in your home," I told her. "I mean, you say to yourself, 'I wonder how long the swami's going to hang around,' and the guy immediately tells you that he knows you're anxious for him to leave. I didn't have any privacy while he was here. I couldn't think anything petty, or selfish, or dirty, the kind of thoughts—let's admit it—that we all have, without him grinning at me and announcing out loud what those fleeting thoughts had been. Frankly, I was happy to see him go. All that wisdom can get on your nerves."

"I can't believe you're saying that," she snapped, and I could feel the graze of the teeth through the earpiece of the telephone receiver.

"These Indian mystics and holy men," I laughed, "aren't really all they're cracked up to be."

She hung up on me.

Neil came to my office again the next day to inform me that the woman who had said that never in her entire life, before talking to me (the swami, the Indian holy man, the great magician), had she heard a voice that was so powerful, so full of wisdom, understanding, compassion, and love, had telephoned him to say that never in her entire life, before talking to me (the professor, the teacher of Indian religion, the writer about magic), had she heard a voice that was so petty and insensitive, so full of ignorance, cynicism, and jealousy. Although there was something rather poignant about the mystical bond of understanding between Susan Shapiro and Swami Gautama Bannerji, Neil and I, out of a dedication and commitment to the spirit of magic I suppose, laughed about it.

Neil helped me put together a bag of tricks to take to India that December, something to impress the magicians of Shadipur who had been so disinterested in the card tricks I had tried to perform for them earlier that year. I took the Needle-through-Arm, some mouth-coils, a spool of invisible thread, an assortment of Jimmy Yoshida thumb-tips, and, as a gift for Shankar Junior, a gesture of gratitude to his father, who was so tirelessly helping me with my research, a Pom-Pom Pole, a slickly constructed Japanese version of Chinese Sticks.

Shankar had written to inform me that he had been busy making plans for my study of Indian magic, that beyond seeing Naseeb and the street magicians of Shadipur and attending performances of stage magicians in Delhi, I would be doing other things that he had arranged: "Meeting in Puttaparthi with Sathya Sai Baba for studying him. Meeting with Premanand and Dayanand in Tamil Nadu for Firewalking and Standing-on-Sharp-Swords. Visiting Kerala for witnessing Miraculous Acts. Seeing Famous Indian Rope Trick in Ghaziabad with Naseeb. Other sightseeing visits and leisure activities in India as time permits and Mind wills."

The cold air of the Delhi night on which I arrived, exhausted, was infused with the smoke of industry and of the million little roadside fires around which homeless people, mostly men wrapped in coal-dark woolen shawls who had come to the city with big hopes of earning a little money, gathered, huddled, squatting, rubbing their hands together and then turning their palms outward toward the bright flames for warmth. Dark and cold were conditions of the soul.

The taxi was stopped four times on the way from Indira Gandhi airport to the guesthouse in Sunder Nagar, and each time an automatic weapon from behind a pile of sandbags and a flashlight from just outside the window of the cab were pointed through sharp black shadows at my face, and "Welcome home," the desk clerk said with a tireless smile. He asked if I was still studying magic. "Then you will be happy to know that your room is equipped with a television, so that you can watch *Rāmāyan* each and every Sunday. There has been so much magic in *Rāmāyan*—each week all of us here are saying, 'If only Dr. Siegel were here to see this trick and that trick.' You have missed quite a lot of magic in your absence. Especially the tricks of that demon Marich, Ravan's court magician. It is clearly established that he was the inventor of ventriloquy. Ventriloquy is magic, isn't it? Do you know how to ventriloquize? I have been practicing it myself. Marich could really throw his voice." With the energy of the itinerant bard who gains spiritual merit for the recitation of the holy story of the acts of Rama, the clerk, before letting me go up to my "Extra Super-Deluxe" room, recounted all of the episodes I had missed. Only when Hanuman finally got to Lanka was I able to go upstairs.

The mirror in the bathroom was still cracked. The sudden sight of it, the familiarity of the forgotten detail, made me feel at home. And as I looked at myself in that mirror, I felt as if a part of me had not left India but had remained there in the mirror, dormant behind the cracked looking-glass, silently waiting for the rest of itself, the aspect that gave it substance and mobility, to return.

Shankar woke me up. When I asked him how he had been and what had happened since I had seen him last, I heard the story of the *Rāmāyaṇa* once again. And then Shankar got down to business: "We will be going to Shadipur. I have made arrangements for your trip to the south, but I am still awaiting confirmation from the other side in regards to your visit with Sathya Sai Baba."

As he drove me to Shadipur, Shankar talked about the American magician Doug Henning, who was in India, working in Noida on the design and construction of Maharishi Mahesh Yogi's Vedaland, a spiritual amusement park, a Hindu Disneyland. As Disneyland had the Matterhorn, Vedaland would have the Kailasa ride; and there would be the monkey ride to Lanka, the chariot ride through Kurukshetra, and, of course, a levitation ride; instead of Disney's Seven Dwarfs there would be the Seven Rishis; Ganesha and the rat that accompanies that god would be their Dumbo and Mickey, Garuda their Donald Duck.

Magicians in both India and the West were gossiping as to whether the great illusionist Doug Henning had really given up magic. "He has definitely renounced it," Shankar said sadly. "I know that for a fact. He even gave his magic wand, the very symbol of our profession, to Shankar Junior. He is disposing of all of his equipment because Maharishi has told him that at this stage in his *sādhana*, he must stop performing magic in order to devote himself on a full-time and wholehearted basis to attaining enlightenment and working on Vedaland. In the end, the guru always asks the disciple to give up what is most important to him. I really don't understand Doug Henning. He is such a brilliant illusionist, the world's greatest magician in my opinion—so why would he want to give up the finest of all the performing arts for the sake of enlightenment? Magic makes other people happy, many people. Enlightenment makes only one person happy."

Shankar was puzzled that Doug Henning could believe in such things as levitation, teleportation, materialization, and mind reading. "It's very unusual to find a magician who believes in magic."

His head rocked and wobbled in a traditional Indian gesture of understanding as I told him about the mental miracles of Swami Gautama Bannerji. "What difference is there between that Swami of yours and Sai Baba or Maharishi?" Shankar asked wistfully, and answered "None whatsoever. I know that anyone can be fooled, but still I don't understand Doug Henning. As magicians, we ought to know that there are no miracles. There are only tricks."

"Is that a disconcerting revelation?" I asked him. "Does that bother you? I mean, do you wish there were miracles?"

"No! No! No!" he exclaimed happily. "Not at all—I love tricks. Magic is wonderful. It delights people, and I prefer delightenment to enlightenment. What I don't like is miracles, magic that does not admit that it is only magic. This you can discuss with Sathya Sai Baba."

In Shadipur, sitting once again on the charpoy in Chand Pasha's one-room cement house, I held up the long needle for them to see. Slowly I pushed on it, and it seemed to enter the skin, cross over the muscles, and reemerge, and the magicians seemed to believe the magic, seemed to be tricked. Only by being able to show them that I could fool them was I able to gain their trust.

Still enervated from my flight, and feeling the beginnings of a cold, I was anxious to get back to Sunder Nagar for a nap. I told the guesthouse clerk, still on the desk from the night before, not to awaken me. "Please, I'm going to try to get some sleep. Don't put any calls through unless they're long-distance; just get the message."

"Please Dr. Siegel, please be kind enough to offer me your opinion. I have been practicing my ventriloquy day in and day out," the desk clerk said in great earnest. "Please, let me show you and then give me your honest opinion as a magician. Your opinion means very much to me. Listen and watch my mouth carefully. I will make my voice come out of the cash register." Even though I could see his Adam's apple bobbing up and down and his jaw shifting about within his cheeks, it was at least true that his lips were not moving at all.

"Well, Dr. Siegel," he asked anxiously, "was it excellent?"

"It was amazing," I assured him. "Was it because the voice was coming out of the cash register that I couldn't understand any of the words?"

"Of course not. You could not understand the words because I was ventriloquizing in Malayalam. I cannot yet do so in English, since it is not my mother tongue. That will take time. If only you understood Malayalam, you would have been even more impressed than you were. I can assure you of that fact. I was saying a popular proverb from Kerala, my home, chosen especially for you, Dr.

Siegel. It says something to the effect that the magician himself is tricked when he believes that the people he tricks are tricked by his trick. It cannot be translated because it is all puns."

I thanked him for the demonstration and repeated my request not to be disturbed. No sooner had I gone up to my room and lain down on the bed than the phone rang again.

"Dr. Lee, my darling man! It is I, The Incredible Mayadhar, at your fine service! Welcome back to Bharatavarsha, eternal home of magic and mystery! Did you bring the magical items and apparati which I requested of you upon the occasion of your last sojourn?"

I had to admit that I had not.

"That is no problem, my darling man. Not at all—*pas de deux*, as the French say. It is, in fact, just as well, inasmuch as I have an entirely revised and updated list of equipment which I want you to bring from your U.S.A. I shall deliver the list over to your residence this very minute in order not to inconvenience you with an out-of-the-way type of visit to my own humble photography shop-cum-studio."

He had hung up before I could say no. Rather than knocking on the door, he stood outside of it shouting, "Open sesame!" And when I opened it, he laughed, "Magic words! Working every time! One hundred and one *svāgatam*s to you Dr. Lee, my brother! One thousand and one *praṇām*s! Let us not beat a bush! Here is my list of items. *Nota bene* that they are all Indian-styled items—Bengal Net, Sands of India, Slippery Swami, and *et cetera*—and yet (do you believe it?) they are unavailable in India. What has this life in the ocean of *saṃsār* come to? Kali Yug through and through! But I am not here for my own end. I am here for your service. Believe me, please. We are, after all, brothers, fellow members in good standing of the International Brotherhood of Magicians, isn't it? So, simply tell me what you need to know, and I will explain everything to you."

Fatigued as I was, without either the energy to resist him or the strength to throw him out, I told him that I was still interested in exploring the connections between Indian religion and magic.

"Simple, my darling man! God is a Magician—capital *M*. Man, through devotion to God or ascetic practices, can become godlike, that is to say he can become a magician—small *m*. Isn't it? A conjurer—small *c*—is someone who, through practice, study, and the purchase of magical equipment, can play the part of magician—small *m* only. Now one important question remains: what is a Conjurer, capital *C*? That is the question. What is the answer?" I didn't know.

"Simple! The Demoniac!"

"Huh?" I asked, with all the eloquence that conversations with The Incredible Mayadhar inspired. "Yes, the Demoniac is a Conjurer, someone who uses magic to give the impression that he is God. Believe me, please. Someone like Indrajit in *Rāmāyaṇ*, or like Sai Baba in modern times. It is our duty as members in good standing of the International Brotherhood of Magicians to expose the immoral uses of magic. It is our charge to show that God is God and man is man. Capital is capital and small is small. Isn't it?"

As we were still standing by the door, The Incredible Mayadhar told me to sit down and make myself comfortable. "I am so happy to see you again. Whenever I'm around you, I get that devil-may-care attitude. For example, normally I never touch drinks, not one single drop, not even half of a single drop. But whenever I meet with you, my darling man, I feel like living it up. You are good for me! Let's order beer and have a damn good time. Let us have one helluva ball! Where's Madame?"

I ordered the beer for him and explained to him that "Madame" would be arriving in a few days. I wondered how he, Shankar, and the people who worked at the guesthouse would respond to her arrival. When B. N. Sarkar put a lady in a box, vanished her, and another instantaneously appeared from the back of the tent, dressed in an identical sari, everyone seemed to accept the two women as being one person. I wondered if I had the patter and panache to pull the trick off as well.

Feeling guilty that I had made no effort to bring any of the magic equipment that he had requested of me, I gave him one of my Jimmy Yoshida thumb-tips. He demonstrated some coin sleights for me while we drank the beer, and then, suddenly, in mid-sentence, in yet another display of his total lack of any sense of timing or propriety, he rose to leave. "All play and no work will make The Incredible Mayadhar a dull boy," he said, ever proud of his command of English idioms, and vanished with the promise to return "in order to convey my humble *svāgatam*s to Madame."

A few moments after lying down on the bed and closing my eyes, a smiling Shankar arrived and said he hoped that I had enjoyed a good rest, because we had a long evening ahead of us at his apartment in Rajouri Gardens: first we would have a South Indian meal of masala dosas; then Shankar Junior would show me how quickly he had mastered the Pom-Pom Pole that I had brought for him; and then each of us would perform our latest trick; and finally we'd settle down for a night of magic on videotape, including his tapes of Doug Henning and those of himself and Junior. "And," he smiled, "I have a special surprise for you."

The surprise was that he drove the car from Sunder Nagar to Rajouri Gardens blindfolded. He was proud of the item, a black hood that could be inspected before it was placed over his head and closed with a rope around his neck. As the blindfolded magician told me that he still had not received any word about my proposed meeting with Sai Baba in the south, I wondered how the police would react if we were stopped at one of the numerous roadblocks in the city.

The fact that the bag was concealing his face made it easier for me to break the news to him that the soon-to-arrive "Madame Siegel" was a different "Madame Siegel" than the one he knew. Hoping that this kind man and his sweet family would not judge me too harshly, I explained that I was not really married to either one of them. The voice within the black hood assured me that I should not worry, that as far as he was concerned, good behavior was simply appropriate behavior, and bad behavior was only behavior that was inappropriate. It would be inappropriate, and therefore bad, if he had two wives or a lover, but for me, since I was an American, it was absolutely fine and good. He explained, furthermore, that, because he was a stage magician, he was in no way shocked by promiscuity. "In all times and places, theater people and entertainers, including magicians, are a bit looser in their morals, norms, and mores than run-of-the-mill folks. Stage magicians all over India have assistants, young females to cut in half and decapitate, attractive women who naturally bring charm to any production. And, of course, the ladies who will take such a job are not always of the highest breeding and moral caliber. And then, of course, there is, in any good magic show, a lot of costume changing backstage, and in so many places in India, the theater facilities are not so extensive, and, well, I think you understand this dimension of magic. My wife's parents were concerned about this before our marriage."

As he talked, I wished I could see the expression on his face. A Sikh on a motorcycle, his wife riding side-saddle on the back with a child on her lap and another child crammed in between them, stayed next to Shankar so they could look at the blindfolded driver. "This is great," I laughed, "you're the blindfolded one, and he's going to be the one who gets in the wreck."

Shankar was still thinking about sex. "In respect to love and related matters, the magicians in the theater are not, perhaps, so different from the magicians on the street. Freud, Vatsyayana, Kinsey, and others, were, in my personal opinion, on the right track: sex is indeed an important factor in this life. But it should not be abused. And that is precisely what these so-called god-men, priests, and sadhus are so often doing. They use some magic tricks to get women under their spell. Then, and excuse me for saying so, they have sexual intercourse with them."

"Can you teach me a few of those tricks?" I joked, but no laughter came through the black hood.

When late that night I returned to Sunder Nagar, the desk clerk handed me my key and wished me a good night without moving his lips.

After sleeping for fourteen hours and waking up late for an appointment with Mehendiratta at the American Institute of Indian Studies, I hurriedly dressed, dashed out, and asked the taxi driver who was parked in front of the guesthouse to take me to Defence Colony.

"You are *jādū*-man—correct?" he asked as I got into the taxi, and then he laughed: "I am correct! I am mind reader! Correct?" Once I admitted that he was right, he confessed the secret of the trick, a variant of the great magic of Swami Gautama Bannerji—he remembered me from the previous summer. He had driven us to Shadipur. "How is your wife?" he asked.

"She's changed a lot," I said and left it at that.

On the way to Defence Colony I saw, gathered in the small area that was formed by a rotary, in the midst of the violent bedlam of Delhi traffic, a group of motley sadhus in ragged orange robes, their hair wild, matted, and dirty. They had set up a shrine, some tents, and a stove; bright banners decorated the lone banyan tree that seemed to be withering from the toxic smoke, dying from the virulent fumes of that street, that overseasoned, bubbling stew of cars and carts, trucks, cycles, and buses, of refuse and litter, of cows, dogs, birds, and human flesh. "Gorakh Nath yogis," the taxi driver informed me. "From the Panjab. Magicians, real magicians. Powerful magic." I made him stop at once.

As I walked toward them, followed by my driver, with my hands together in a gesture of greeting, they beckoned me closer and motioned for me to be seated. Since I am not supple enough to sit in a yogic posture, my feet were in front of me, pointing at one of the holy men. The sadhu next to him, an emaciated man whose robes were soiled and torn, whose gray and thickly-matted beard reached almost to his waist, angrily jumped up, and the Panjabi-speaking taxi driver translated the shouting: "It's inauspicious to point feet at a yogi. It's wicked. It's a curse. It will bring trouble to my brother and trouble to you."

I apologized profusely and pulled my feet up under me. But then they were pointing at the sadhu behind me. Wherever I aimed my feet there were holy men. I stood up. The man at whom my feet were first directed laughed and signaled for me to sit once more. "Sit. Sit and point your feet at me," he laughed again, took a deep puff on the chillum, and passed it to me. "Smoke. You haven't done anything bad," he reassured me as he shifted his words to the group. "It's indeed very inauspicious if a Hindu points his feet at a sadhu. But if a foreigner points his feet at you, it's very, very auspicious. It's a blessing. It will bring boons to the sadhu and constant good fortune to the traveler himself." The man who had been so offended asked if it was true. "Yes, it's true." All of the holy men then wanted me to point my feet at them, and I duly complied.

Explaining that they were meeting there for a celebration of the birthday of their guru, that Gorakh Nath yogis would be arriving from all over India, they invited me to stay and enjoy the festivities, the meditations and prayers, the food and drugs.

"And Gorakh Nath yogis are magicians?" I asked.

"We obtain supernatural powers through our discipline."

"What powers?" I questioned, and he enumerated the eight traditional sid-dhis: vanishing, or the power to become minute and to become immense; levitation, or the power to become light and to become heavy and immovable; materialization, or the power to obtain things, and telekinesis, or the power to will things to be so; hypnosis, or power over the will of others and the same mesmeric power over oneself. I asked for a demonstration: "Can you levitate yourself?"

The yogi explained the problem to me. "Every day I practice *prāṇāyāma*, the control of the breath. In ancient times, in the days of Guru Gorakh, through *prāṇāyāma* one could become very light and float right up into the air. No problem. But now, because of air pollution, by practicing *prāṇāyāma* one only becomes heavier and heavier. Such is the Kali Yuga." Taking another deep drag on the chillum, he held the sweet smoke deep within his lungs as he continued to speak: "Guru Gorakh was the greatest magician of all times. On the occasion of initiating one of his students, he befuddled and bedazzled all of the holy people gathered around him by taking the seed of a banyan tree, placing it in the ground, and inspiring that tree to grow to its fullest height in but a few hours." He exhaled with a great smile. "Then, under the shade of that banyan, he served a meal of rice which he cooked in his bare hands without the aid of fire." As I had seen Kareem Baksh perform a version of the former trick and Chand Baba, with a blanket in his lap, apparently cook rice by merely winnowing it, I thought I understood how Guru Gorakh had accomplished his miracles. The holy man himself dismissed such performances as trivial. "There is really only one power for which we strive, only one act of magic that matters. We play a trick on Kala [Time] and on Yama [Death]. The goal is to become *jīvan-mukta* [liberated while living], to perfect the body, to purify it with the fire of yoga so that it is without limitations. That's the real magic."

Despite the increasing congestion in my lungs caused by both my incipient cold and the almost viscous, fumy air of the Delhi winter, I lit up a Deluxe Benson and Hedges International and offered one to the yogi. Taking the pack, he removed two and passed the rest of them to the other holy men. All of us were smoking at once as the man launched back into his discourse: "You see here, on this cigarette package there is a warning. We have the same in India." The sadhu handed the empty package to the taxi driver for an exact translation of the English into Panjabi. "Quitting Smoking Now Greatly Reduces Serious Risks to Your Health." The rascally yogi loudly, defiantly, and courageously laughed. "Ha! Smoking will harm *your* health, but not ours. *You* shouldn't smoke. See, you are coughing. But we are perfecting our bodies so that nothing can harm us. There is no disease, no degeneration, no death for the body perfected by yoga. He who truly perfects himself does not need to quit smoking. You try not to cough, but you cough anyway—you cannot control your body. But *we* have control of our bodies. Do you need a guru? You are looking for one? It can be arranged. Not very expensive."

I couldn't resist performing a trick that Shankar had taught me. "No, I'm already practicing American yoga, and through it I have mastered control of my body. At will, I can stop my heart from beating."

The sadhu did not believe me. Having casually reached into my coat to set it up, I had taken the film container from my inner pocket and secretly jammed it into my armpit. Extending my arm, I asked the holy man to hold my wrist and find my pulse. Once he could feel the beat of my heart, quicker than usual because of my fever, I muttered a mantra—"*Baruch atoh adonai eloheynu melech haolam*"—

and squeezed down on the film canister to cut off the circulation in my arm. My pulse stopped. The holy man laughed with amazement as he told the others that I was dead. After a few moments, I eased up on the canister, and my pulse could be felt once more. And again the holy man laughed as he told the others that I had been resurrected. He was amply impressed and certain that I had indeed mastered one of the *siddhi*s. He asked me the name of my guru.

"Guru Groucho Nath." I said, and he repeated the name and then offered to teach me hatha-yoga if I would teach him American-yoga, Groucho-yoga. As I agreed and promised to return, I knew that they knew that I would never see them again; but it was only polite to pretend. As a good-bye gesture, I again pointed my feet at each one of them in turn. They waved cheerfully as my taxi sped off toward Defence Colony.

My cold got worse. Curled up beneath the woolen blankets, I'd tremble with chills and then begin to burn, and kick the covers off. I had to call the room boy to change the sweat-soaked sheets every few hours, and in a delirium, I imagined the sweat was tears, that my whole body wept. Depression was a symptom of the sickness, and I could not imagine that it would ever go away. Remorse fueled the fever. But I kept telling myself that as soon as Catherine arrived, I had to go to the south. I had two nonrefundable tickets, and besides, Premanand and Dayanand would be waiting for us at the airport in Coimbatore.

The rationale for the trip to Tamil Nadu and Kerala was to find out if indeed all the street magicians in India were Muslims; if they were all Maslets as the Delhi magicians had insisted; if Naseeb was, as a performer, in any way typical and representative of a national street magic; if the repertoire in the south was, in fact, the same as that of the conjurers in the north. It appeared to be so. Dayanand was to show me a videotape of a performer in Karnataka who squatted on the ground to do the standard tricks—Cups and Balls, the Egg Bag, and Chinese Sticks. He also charmed snakes, read fortunes, sold medicines, manipulated puppets, and had a monkey that was dressed as a new bride and was trained to act out an obscene joke. The tape of the monkey was followed by one of Sathya Sai Baba. So many of the magicians I had met thought it was important for me, as a religion professor writing about magic, to go to the south for an audience with Sai Baba, the man who, by performing the simplest sleights of hand, was being venerated and adored as a living avatar of the eternal God.

And there was another, more enticing, reason for the journey south. Shankar had told me that Premanand and Dayanand would take me to a temple in Kerala where the priests were magicians, Tantric adepts who would show me miracles at midnight. A priest would remove his head, and that head would speak to me. I'd see levitations, materializations, and the transformation of water into wine, or of a man into goat. Things would vanish; things would appear. Indra's Net would be cast. The dead might even speak to me.

When I asked the doctor if I'd be well enough to make the trip, he shrugged his shoulders: "How should I know? I'm a physician, not a magician!" But as he made out the prescription, he assured me that it would be good to go to the south, suggesting that the polluted winter air of Delhi, so full of smoke and illness, was the cause of my influenza. "Don't you think there is some connection between medicine and magic," I asked the doctor, "some relationship between the physician and the magician?" He shrugged his shoulders once more. "How should I know? I am a physician, not a professor. You're the professor—you answer the question."

I thought about it, and after the doctor had left, I made some notes in my notebook: "Magic and medicine. It's not enough to look at the two endeavors and their practitioners in evolutionary terms; to see, as others have done, magic as primitive medicine. . . ."

I set the notebook on the bedside table, pulled the dark and heavy blankets up around my neck, and closed my eyes, and it occurred to me that India was making me quite crazy and that the viral infection in my lungs was enhancing it. I wished I believed in the power of the striped frog and colored threads, or at least in the efficacy of vitamin C and antibiotics. "I wished I believed"—the phrase seemed to me the clue to why there is magic, ancient magic, miracles, tricks that work, as well as conjuring, tricks that entertain. The longing to see existence as more than random and coincidental, to imagine that it is informed by some sense, that there are meaningful connections, that what happens, whether good or bad, painful or pleasurable, occurs for a reason and in accordance with some principle, force, or will—that longing is the source of magic. I pushed the blankets off and sat up on the edge of the bed. That winter was a season of longing for me, a period of loss and leaving, of severing connections and letting go. The study of magic was my diversion, and it provided me with metaphors with which to speak of unspeakable things.

"Pick a card, any card," I said to Catherine shortly after her arrival, and she was aware that, no matter which card she selected, I would know it; that what seemed like a free choice was not free at all. My attempts at magic seemed to sadden her.

The next day I said good-bye to Naseeb and Ayasan, to Chand Baba and Chand Pasha, to The Incredible Mayadhar and Shalini. On the way to the airport, Shankar informed me that there was still no confirmation of my meeting with Sai Baba. We left for Madras.

We checked into the Connemara Hotel, where I wanted to stay because it was there, just outside the gates of that hotel, almost fifteen years earlier, during my first trip to India, that I had seen my first performance of Indian magic. Bear trainers and monkey handlers, snake charmers and magicians, drug dealers and beggars, itinerants from all over the south would gather hopefully near the hotel, offering visitors to Madras some show, deal, or product, some opportunity to be fooled, to be entertained, or to be charitable. As I emerged from the hotel, I was drawn by curiosity toward a crowd that had formed around a man and a boy. And since at that time I could not distinguish between magicians and holy men, I thought it was a sadhu and his chela. Pushing for a place in the crowd, I watched the spectacle and listened, although I could not understand a word of the Tamil patter of the man who held the snake in his hand. Invigorated by the steamy southern heat of Madras, the striped serpent wiggled and writhed. There was a bucket of water in front of the showman with a metal tumbler floating in it. The man talked on and on, spit and spewed wild words, pointed dramatically to the snake, and circumambulated in the same rigorous and purposeful way that I was to see Naseeb circle his crowd and entice them years later. A man next to me nudged me, smiled happily, even proudly, and pointed at the spectacle: "Poisonous snake. Deadly snake. You will enjoy."

Suddenly the magician, the holy man in my mind, stopped, leaned his head back, took the head of the serpent in his free hand, and placed it in his widely open mouth. The boy squatted on the ground to watch his father. Quickly, the man used both hands to force the snake down his throat, and then he circled again with his mouth stretched open to show us all that it was empty, that the snake had indeed been consumed. And then he drank a tumbler full of the water. As it was my first time in India, I was as amazed to see someone drink Indian water as I was to see someone swallow a living snake.

My perception then was that the man was performing some sort of vow to gain transcendence of this world, wandering throughout the land in emulation of the ascetic Shiva, beyond revulsion and care. The snake was then a symbol. My recollection of him now, after my experience with the Maslets, is transformed. He was performing a magic trick to earn his living in this world, to survive, wandering throughout the land to tap into people's awe, their fear and love of god. The myth is but his patter. The snake is now a prop, but a symbol nonetheless.

The trick was not over. "Two rupees, two rupees, two rupees," the magician, probably a Kalakar, shouted, pointing to each member of the audience, and then, when we had thrown our money into the circle, he drank several more glasses of water, leaned his head back, and opened his mouth wide again. Having turned around in the magician's stomach, the serpent emerged from his throat, wiggled into the man's grip, and squirmed spectacularly for the crowd once more. Dazzled by the feat, the audience threw coins. I was ready to sign a traveler's check.

It's an old trick—a Bengali magician performed a version of it, producing eight snakes from his mouth, according to the *Tūzuk-i-Jahāngīrī*, for Jahangir over three hundred fifty years earlier in Delhi.

I asked the doorman at the Connemara, a ghost of the Raj, quaintly handsome in his lavish turban, long coat, and bright cummerbund, if he had ever seen anyone perform that trick outside the hotel. "Years ago these people, jugglers and snake charmers and the like, were always outside the hotel. But now you don't see them here. The police have chased them off, as this is not the image of India that the government is favoring these days. It's a pity. People like yourself who stay at the hotel always enjoy this sort of thing—snake charming and swallowing, cobra and mongoose fighting, bears and monkeys dancing, acrobats and magicians making things appear or disappear, sadhu-babas sitting on thorns and eating glass. There is a man here in Madras who has eaten an entire automobile! I'm not joking. He ate one whole Ambassador automobile. Of course he had to do that slowly, bit by bit, a little piece every day, but finally the entire automobile was consumed. There is a man to be admired. There is a man destined for the *Guiness Book of World Records!*" The doorman suggested that if I wanted to find that kind of entertainment, I should go down to the Marina Beach on Sunday afternoon.

In the meantime I called on Professor Bhagyanath, a professional stage magician, a man who, in costume, looked like Sorcar Senior and Junior, like Sarkar Senior or Junior, like Lal Senior or Junior, which is to say he looked like a doorman at an expensive Indian hotel or like Don Ameche in an old Hollywood extravaganza about Moghul India. Out of costume and almost out of makeup, his dark, dyed and oiled hair combed straight back, his moustache trimmed into what looked like an extra eyebrow on his lip, he had the bearing of a classical actor, the thespian sureness of gesture and manners, the suave smile and emotive eyes of performers from a more opulent Indian past. The magician's hands were steady as they greeted me with an old-fashioned graciousness and propriety. He explained that his days were idle, as he was awaiting the arrival of the papers necessary to take his show to the United Arab Republic. "Muslims love magic," he noted with a wry, detached smile as he showed me into his home, "and the Arabs have the money to pay for it. They really enjoy a good magic show, but they have to import it, because Muslims themselves are not permitted to perform magic. It is forbidden in the Qur'an."

"How is it then," I asked with genuine, academic curiosity, "that all of the magicians—I mean the street magicians—in India are Muslim? That's what I heard in the north."

Smiling kindly, though a bit indulgently, he spoke slowly and purposefully: "Let me explain things to you. A journey to India is like a visit to a magic show. You believe in the reality of what you are beholding. Ah, that's fine, fine indeed, if you are a tourist, a spectator at our all-India performance of magic. It's through a misunderstanding of how things work that the tourist-spectator is delighted and satisfied. His ignorance is bliss. But you, Professor, have aspirations to knowledge. You want to understand India, so you say, and you want to know about magic. And as a magician and an Indian I can, perhaps, tell you about a few things that occur behind the scenes. You say that all of the street magicians in India are Muslim. That is the appearance, the superficial view. In reality their religion, their Islam, is really a form of Hinduism. We have a trinity in Hinduism—Brahma, Vishnu, and Shiva: Creator, Preserver, and Destroyer—and, accordingly, there are three major sects, the worshipers of Shiva, the worshipers of Vishnu, and the Muslims—they worship Brahma, the Creator, calling him by his Arabic name, Allah. The street magicians perform *pūjā*s for him, recite mantras, bathe in our holy rivers, and observe Hindu rites."

I asked Professor Bhagyanath if he knew where I could see street magicians performing in the south. "They are," he assured me, "still performing in the villages, but not in our towns. The police won't permit it, and in any case, city folk don't have time any more for such sidewalk divertissements. The magicians are in the countryside, but it is impossible to know where they are at any given time; it's only through luck or fate that you will encounter them. When I was child, they were always a feature on the streets of Madras. Whenever I heard the damaru outside the house, I'd run excitedly to the window, and if it was indeed a magician passing by, I'd beg my father, who was always one to appreciate a good magic show, to invite him in. He'd give the magician a few rupees and then the '*gilli-gilli*-man' (as we called him then), always accompanied by a boy, his son, would perform for our family—Cups and Balls, Mango Tree Trick, Diving Duck, Bunder Boat, Rice Bowl, Basket Trick—all of the traditional items of Indian magic. I loved each show—I'd laugh, I'd cry, I'd shiver with wonderment. I believe that no one can really appreciate magic who has not felt its enchantment in childhood. Magic is, if it's good, a return to childhood. So that's how I decided to become a magician. I wanted to live that kind of life, wandering like that at my father's side, carefree, going into people's homes, enthralling them with wonderful magic. The street magicians were my inspiration. The same is true of all of the great stage magicians of India—Professor Vazhakkunnam and Gogia Pasha, Sorcar and Lal, all of us. But I'm sorry to tell you, what we do is really Western. Come, come to my workshop, look at my magic. I'll show you. You'll recognize everything. It's Western magic decorated with Indian designs. Each piece is a tragic symbol of the history of India, a symbol of conquest by foreigners."

Standing by the table on which he had, thousands of times, sawed a lady in half, and holding the saw in his hands, he invited me to lunch, with the apology that it would be a vegetarian meal in keeping with South Indian custom.

Over the lunch he talked lugubriously about the death of magic. He personified it, made a woman—Queen Maya—of it, and spoke of her as if she were a cancer-stricken lover, dying a painfully slow death. "I'm not mourning for her. We have to accept the passing and fading of things. But each time I perform, I can feel it. I sense the closeness of death. I can see it in the faces of my audience. The laughter and the applause become slightly, ever so slightly, more faint each time. Now people have television sets. They have no more use for magicians or acrobats or puppeteers, whether they are wandering on the streets of India, from village to village, or whether, like myself, they are wandering on a larger scale, taking big productions from city to city and country to country. All magicians are wandering performers. And the wanderers' days are numbered."

When Professor Bhagyanath asked me to show him a trick, "any little item," I vanished my cigarette, and it made him laugh sweetly. I gave him a Jimmy Yoshida thumb-tip, and he tried it on and softly laughed again. "It's good. Look at the Indian thumb-tip. You see, it's no good. The American one is good."

As I explained that it wasn't American, but Japanese, he frowned. "A lot of magicians, Lal and the others, are going to Japan to perform there, but I personally have no interest in it, because the Japanese are destroying magic. In every department store and toy shop in Japan, magic tricks, well-made items that use the principles of the most sophisticated stage illusions, are openly and indiscriminately sold. The problem is, then, that every Japanese child knows the essential secrets of magic. They know how I saw my lady in half, levitate her, and make her vanish. And now the Japanese are exporting these items. Soon there will be no secrets, and when there are no secrets, there is no magic. Secrecy is everything. In ancient times in India, the great truths were all secret, guarded by the holy sages in the forests. The secrets of life and death were only revealed to people who were ready to know the truth, qualified to pass beyond the world of illusions. In time, these secrets were written down and called the Upanishads. Now anybody can get their hands on these secrets, just as anybody can go into a Japanese department store and purchase any trick. Once the truths of the Veda became openly available to one and all, those truths were no longer true. The truth has to be secret, mysterious." He hesitated. "And it has to be a bit terrifying." He laughed, fell silent, and then spoke in a whisper. "Yes, the truth, by its very nature, is full of terror."

We moved to his office, and he sat with his back to the window, so that his face was obscured by shadow. He handled the thumb-tip, put it on, took it off, put it on again, practiced the moves, as he questioned me about my itinerary. I told him that Shankar had been working on setting up some sort of meeting with Sai Baba.

"Why do you want to see him? He's no good."

"I'm not really very interested in him, but he is, I suppose, an important figure for my book, for a taxonomy of Indian magicians—I see him as the modern version of the court magician who, in traditional India, was consulted by the king and other members of the court. Sai Baba seems to have that kind of power, real political influence, just as the court magician must have had; a power and influence derived from doing a few tricks, materializing gold and *vibhūti.*"

Professor Bhagyanath laughed. "Sai Baba's uncle was a street magician. Young Sai Baba—he was known as Satyanarayana Raju in those days—began by doing little magic tricks, but since he wasn't very good, it wasn't likely that he would have much success on the stage. That's why he became a god-man. It's easier to be a god-man than a stage magician. And certainly the income is better. You know, there was a story in the newspaper recently about an Indian god-man, some guru who had been in the United States. He was stopped at customs—they caught him with a bag full of gimmicks and magical effects from Louis Tannen's magic shop in New York! These swamis and gurus all have quite a few tricks up their sleeves, tricks that are always really quite simple. A sadhu, for example, will soak his loin cloth in milk and then let it dry out; he'll do that a few times to thoroughly inundate the cloth with powdered milk. Then, in the presence of devout people, he takes a bath in some tank or holy river, emerges from the water, removes his loin cloth, wrings it out, and passes the liquid from it for tasting— instant milk! Everyone is amazed with the miracle. The sadhu collects his *dakṣiṇā* and goes on his way. The trick requires even less skill than your cigarette vanish. When I was a young man, the hypocrisy and trickery of the god-men, their abuse of the art of magic, infuriated me. I personally exposed a priest in Trichur. He had rigged a shrine with a hook and a thread that was fine enough to be invisible in the shadows of the shrine. When he placed a garland before the Shiva-linga, closed the doors of the shrine, and reopened them again, the thread, attached to the doors, lifted the garland over the linga. And everyone thought it was a miracle, and they gave money—so much money—to the priest. I can perform magic that's much more astounding than that, and yet I make much less money than that priest did. It's the same old story: the more honest you are, the poorer you'll be. While the entertainer takes the credit for his tricks and collects money for his own talents, the holy man credits God and collects money for God. God can, of course, charge much more per show than any mortal. And he doesn't have to pay the entertainment tax. Religion is really just a magic show."

I told Bhagyanath about the temple I was supposed to visit in Kerala where the priests, according to Shankar, would perform wondrous magic tricks— decapitations, levitations, and resurrections—for me. "Yes, Kerala," Professor Bhagyanath nodded. "Kerala is the place of black magic. It's the home of Kuttichathan. Do you know about him, about the tricks he plays? He tries to prevent people from performing penances, since it is through such practices that you can gain control over Kuttichathan, that you can become a real magician. Let us say, for example, that you, in hopes of acquiring magic powers, stand neck-deep in the waters of some tank, river, or lake. That is when Kuttichathan takes the shape of a crocodile and comes for you. One minute a crocodile, the next a striped snake or a dog, a crow or an eagle, a goat or a pig! If you are afraid, your fear will make the illusion real, and then the crocodile will devour you. But if you are without fear, the magic can't work, and Kuttichathan is foiled. The priests of Kuttichathan are all magicians. And they worship him at midnight. If you make an offering to him, an offering of flesh and blood, you might entice him. He has, you know, one weakness—he has no thumbs. Yes, no thumbs, and so he cannot undo knots! And

MIRRORS AND WATER

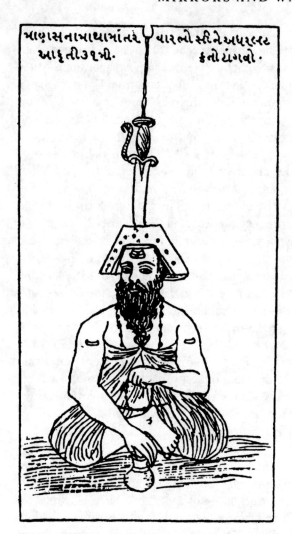

so if you can tie him up, he can't get away. Then he'll bargain; he'll offer you magic powers in return for his release. But be careful! Never trust a magician!"

Calmly, with the light behind him fading, Bhagyanath told me terrible stories of black magicians, and as he spoke of dreadful rites, of hexes, spells, and incantations, I thought of Naseeb and Ayasan: "The magician must kill his son, cut off the boy's head and offer the blood to the goddess. Then he must take the skull and place the tail of a striped lizard in it and burn it there. The black ash from the fire in the skull is powerful, full of magic."

"Do you believe it?"

"I believe that people have done these things for many centuries and that they still do them. And I believe that a man who kills his son, takes the skull of his child in his hands at night and lights a fire in it, crosses over into a world which neither you nor I understand. I believe that that man, from living in that other world, may have some power, may know some magic. When, on the stage, I saw a woman in half, I am aware that each person in the audience gets a glimpse of that other world. But I bring them home when I put the woman back together, when I show them that the magic was an illusion. The other magician's magic is not the magic of illusions. He is the real magician. He can be met in this world, but he lives there, over there."

It was dusk and time to leave. The magician gave me a flier with his name on it: "Eight Amazing Magic Trucks You Can Do." Assuring Professor Bhagyanath that I would return after my trip to Coimbatore and Kerala to tell him what I had discovered, I left the house and, haunted by his stories, walked up the narrow, unpaved pathway toward the main road to find a taxi. There was a dog. It growled as I approached in the twilight. "Kuttichathan," I whispered to myself. "Don't be afraid or he'll attack. Don't be afraid, keep walking." The dog cowered and crawled into the darkness.

There were dogs on the beach that Sunday when we went to the marina in search of magicians—trotting dogs, panting and sniffing, scavenging the littered shore. Boys were renting out their ponies, whip-scarred, hungry horses with ribs rubbed by old saddles, and foamy mouths rasped by rope and chain. "Good horse riding, master?" they cried and joked with mockeries: "Like U.S.A. cowboy!" And all along the walkways, set up for Sundays, were the stalls, their tarpaulin walls, shaken like salt-rotted sails, torn by winter sea squalls, set up for sales: glass bangles and plastic toys, crude amulets and cheap utensils for impoverished homes, all kinds of sweets, sweeter than sweet, and drinks—cane juice, coconut milk, and Campa-Cola. "Best you ever drink, Master! Campa-Cola? Limca? Maaza? Boiled water? Not problem water!" And there was a merry-go-round with four seats turned by a hand-crank, faster and faster, and the one child in it screamed, reached out with frantic arms for a mother who spun in and out of sight. In the coarse, dirty sand, strewn with coconut shells and cans, paper, glass, and wood debris, the excrement of dogs, ponies, and children, broken and busted things, boats with moldering hulls, like carcasses of sea monsters, were beached, tilted in the sand, awkward on land, their bones bared; and nets, still wet, and piles of rope and cord, with weights and floats, tangled and untangled, were tended, mended, unwound, and rewound by dark, wet fishermen. Indra's net could have been there, frayed and disintegrating on the beach. One of the fishermen was drunk, sick, and nagged by an angry, baby-pestered woman. To this dirty, deathly beach, salacious and discordant, noisy crowds flocked with crows and the gulls, dogs and ponies, aggressive vendors and buskers, on Sunday after watching the *Rāmāyaṇa* on television: families, mothers walking behind fathers, begged by children for sweets, and children alone, larcenous and desperate, and students with their sex stifled, petulantly pitiful derelicts, officious policeman armed with guns or sticks, Indian tourists from the north—a thousand faces, worried or sanguine, laughing or frowning, and yet only one face, impassive, expressionless, inured to the terrors of being. They came like Rama's army of bears and monkeys to the shore, put the city behind them to look out and in to sea. Everyone watched the swelling ocean. And it seemed to me that all of them were castaways on that beach, survivors of a terrible storm. The wreckages were inland; the typhoons were in the heart and soul.

Waves were like white gashes in the flesh of the insolent ocean, and clouds hung low and dull upon the water, their undersides bruised by clammy, salt-scented winds. The ocean seemed full of putrid things; of chemicals, acid and lye; and waste, human and industrial; of crematory ashes and inhuman shadows. No one swam in the dark gray sea that seemed to groan under the burden of its immensity.

"Good horse riding, Master?" the grinning boys still pestered us.

"This is Waikiki Beach of India," one man proudly told me.

There were no magicians on the beach, and yet it was so clearly a magic show, a carnival of illusions; and in the midst of it, on the walkway, there was a sideshow, a small tent, in front of which a sign was propped up in the sand, a peeling painting on dented, battered sheet metal of a snake with the head of woman. "One rupee. See snake-woman, Master. One rupee." And when we entered, a single-stringed instrument screeched, cried, and moaned for us, or her, or for one and all. On the table was the heavy, torpid, scaled body of a serpent, a large python, as dark gray as the sea, and where its head would have naturally been the head of a little girl (coming up through a hole in the table I presume) twisted and turned to stare at us. It was as if that being, half child, half reptile, lived in that other world of which Professor Bhagyanath had spoken, Kuttichathan's dark realm of terrible magic. Her eyes were gloomy hollows, caves in the rock face from which desolate cries seemed to echo; her lips were curled back to expose stained teeth, her oily hair, since there was no hand to brush it back, dangled here and there over the face. When the man, the barker for the show, her father I supposed, poked the body with a cane to make the serpent writhe, the girl winced as if she herself had been jabbed. That was the trick. And the man followed us out of the tent. "Snake woman good show? One rupee more, sir, for snake-woman feeding! Snake-woman always hungry!"

"Good horse riding, Master? . . . Campa-Cola? Limca? . . . Merry-go-round ride? . . . Bangles for Madame? . . . No mama, no papa, bakshish, Master! . . . Good horse! . . . Change money? . . . See snake-woman again? Half-price this time! . . . Water? What do you want?"

I was feeling feverish again and wanted to go back to the hotel to rest. On the way, from inside the motor rickshaw, I saw ahead of us a man walking with a staff and carrying baskets and bundles followed by a small boy with a bag over his shoulder, and it looked like Naseeb and Ayasan. As we passed by them, I turned to look and saw that the child's face was painted, made up to look like some sort of demon: a shiny black moustache curled ornately on his red cheeks; yellow teeth, tipped in red and outlined in black, protruded down his chin; the whites of his eyes were elongated almost to his unpainted ears; and an elaborate sectarian mark covered the boy's entire forehead. "Stop," I cried out to the speeding rickshaw driver, "Stop! *Bas! Bas!*" Certain that they were itinerant magicians, I ran back toward them, and they seemed startled by my quick approach. I stopped in front of them and smiled. "Magic? Maslet? Madari? *Jādū? Indrajāla?*" But none of the words were understood. The man wrinkled his face in dismay, and the child-demon trembled and looked up at his father as if for protection from me. Not knowing the Tamil word for magic, I searched for utterances that they might understand: "*Gilli-gilli-gilli-gilli? Yantru-tantru-jālajāla-mantru?* Magic?" Deciding to show them what I was trying to say, I offered the man a cigarette (which he turned down with a jittery shake of the hand), took one myself, lit it, puffed on it, and then, as they stared at me nervously, vanished it in my clenched fist. The man turned and, with his son close behind him, ran from me. Perhaps they feared that I was Kuttichathan and that I wanted their souls.

Back in our room at the Connemara, when I shuffled a deck of cards and asked Catherine to select one, she pulled the entire deck out of my hand and said she wanted to talk to me, to find out why I had become so interested in magic.

"Okay," I laughed, "I asked you to freely choose a card, and you tried to outwit me by taking a bunch of them. But to show you that I am really good at magic, I'll name all of the fifty-two cards that you picked. You selected thirteen spades, thirteen hearts, thirteen . . ."

"When does the magic show end?" she asked carefully, clearly exasperated but gently smiling as if to reassure me that she understood.

The fever reasserted itself, chills alternated with a sense of being on fire, and at midnight I slipped out of the sweat-drenched sheets to stumble into the bathroom. I washed my face and looked into the mirror at the pale, drawn, and sickly reflection. There was a delirium, one of those states of mind in which trivial ideas and obvious insights seem momentous and profound: "Every glimpse of this face, of myself, that I have ever had has been in a mirror! Photographs don't count because they're from the past. I can only see myself in reflections of the self, reduced and reversed, changed and always to some degree warped." I pictured a magician in the mirror, a stage magician wearing a silk turban that was adorned with a feather and jeweled brooch. "Professor M. T. Bannerji," I said in my parody of an Indian accent, and laughed. "At your service. I am you, but you reversed, reality inverted into illusion in order to become known. Isn't it?"

I didn't want to wake up, did not have the strength to struggle out of the net of dreams, but Catherine was shaking me, "We've got to go." Dreams, it occurred to me, are but another symptom of our fundamental instinct and essential impulse to deceive ourselves, to create false worlds in which to live. Magic is about dreams. "You've got to wake up. We've got to check out. Wake up."

I was dreading the trip to Coimbatore, fearful that I was going to be packed off from there to Puttaparthi to see Sai Baba, that I would be thrown into the crowd of Westerners who sat cross-legged, bliss-blessed, with epicene smiles on pale, pulpy faces; mellow, serene, sidereal souls; vegetarians who liked eating whole grains and taking enemas, who preferred herb tea to malt whisky; non-smokers who believe that all is one, that eternity is now, that there is some truth that can't be expressed in words, and that the intellect stands in the way of true understanding; docile, sensitive, pantheistic, creative, mystical, and sharing and caring people who think that Jesus and the Buddha said the same things in different words, that *brahman* is but a different name for the *tao*, that various religions are different paths up the same mountain, and—most egregiously of all—that India is a spiritual land. They'd insist that I eat *vibhūti* to cure my cold.

But Premanand, who was waiting for us at the airport, immediately assured me that I would not be seeing Sai Baba. Premanand, the puckishly smiling crusader whose life was wholeheartedly dedicated to exposing the hypocrisies of god-men, to demonstrating the ways in which they use magic to deceive people, to secure authority, power, and wealth, looked, with his long gray beard and locks, like a god-man himself, a comedic caricature of a holy man. Much to my relief, he explained that the miracle monger of Puttaparthi would not receive me, that through an intelligence network that included police and government officials, he had apparently heard that I would not be a suitably sincere devotee. My associ-ation with magicians had, presumably, caused me to be blacklisted. "No one," I was told, "who knows any magic is permitted to have an audience with him. Anyone familiar with the basic principles of conjuring would all too easily see through his facile tricks. He likes scholars, psychologists, scientists—people who vainly and foolishly trust their perceptions and their abilities to judge the causes of the phenomena that they witness. To the degree that they think they cannot be fooled, they are the easiest ones to dupe."

Earlier that year, in Calcutta, P. C. Sorcar Junior had told me, with a char-acteristically and radiantly boastful smile, how he had personally flummoxed Sai Baba: "Posing as an ordinary devotee, giving my name as Jahar, I took my place in line to receive the *prasād* that he was distributing. He'd wave his hand in front of each follower before producing a sweet for them. When he came to me, my outstretched hand was empty. And then, as he waved his about to materialize a sweet, I waved my own hand in the same gesture, saying, 'No thanks, I prefer rasogoolas' and I materialized a sweet of my own. That I was immediately grabbed by his henchmen and thrown out of his ashram shows that they them-selves don't believe in materializations. Otherwise, they would have seen the appearance of my rasogoola as a miracle caused by love for the guru."

K. Lal also insisted that he had exposed Sai Baba. All of the magicians I met seemed to have a grudge against the god-man. His tricks were so simple, so easily per-formed, and yet he was so wealthy from doing them. "It's his patter," Shankar reasoned.

Shortly before I had left for India, a man about my own age, a man who seemed rather effeminate despite his stocky, muscular build and full, peppery beard, had come into my office at the University of Hawaii, saying that he had heard I was writing something about magic. He asked if I believed in magic.

Seemingly relieved by my assurances that I did, he slowly and purposefully removed a photograph of Sathya Sai Baba from his wallet and handed it to me. Scrutinizing the familiar face of the popular, charismatic guru—the eccentric frizzy hairdo, the rather bloated, almost degenerate, cheeks, the ambiguous eyes—I wondered why and how he had become so powerful.

"Do you know who that is?" my visitor asked.

"I think I recognize him." I nodded. "Yes, I'm sure it's him."

"Yes," he whispered. "It is him."

"I thought so," I said.

"Yes, it's him—it is God," he said absolutely unabashedly, smiling that inflated, vapid ecosmile, that gooey metasmile, dripping with beatitude, that typifies the Western devotees of Eastern gurus.

"Yeah, I knew that," I assured him with that sardonic, incredulous smile that surely, in his mind, typifies Western academics who do research on Eastern religions. "Yep," I said, "I could tell it was God by the way he wears his hair."

Smiles vanished. The man asked if I had ever been to India, if in India I had ever had *darśan* of Baba, if I had ever felt his vibration.

"No, I didn't even know he had a vibrator, but . . ."

The offended man cut me off and began to chastise me, to tell me that my intellect was keeping me from finding the truth, from experiencing the love that is Baba; that cynicism was preventing me from beholding the magic that is everywhere around us. Baba, he explained, shows us miracles to awaken us, "to open us." As he put the picture back in his wallet, exchanging it for a pink piece of paper with Baba's face printed on it, a piece of paper that had been folded into a small envelope, I couldn't resist the opportunity that this diversion of his attention afforded me.

He slowly opened the little pink envelope to show me the ashes that it contained. "This *vibhūti* was materialized in my presence, before my very eyes, for me. Baba gave me these ashes. For me, they are a symbol of his *līlā.*"

"Aren't ashes a symbol of death?"

"That's what the Western compartmentalizing mind can't understand," he explained. "It's only through death that life can flow on, through destruction that there can be creation, real creativity. Creation and destruction—that's the *līlā,* that's the mystery."

I asked my deeply sincere and profoundly wimpy visitor to show me the hand gesture that God had used to produce the ashes, and he extended his hand, palm down, and moved it in a circle.

"Like this?" I asked, imitating the gesture.

"Yes," he answered, and when he did, I closed my hand, opened it again, and sprinkled a great pinch of ashes, a bit more than he had in the little pink envelope, from my hand into his.

The man was clearly insulted and angered by what he supposed to be a mockery of his god. He said he knew that I had not performed a miracle because my ashes were coarse. "Baba's ashes are soft and fragrant," he said almost tearfully. And I felt sorry for him and even a little embarrassed by my cheap shot. I confessed that my ashes had come from the ash tray.

He produced a book, *Sai Baba, Man of Miracles* by Howard Murphet, from the backpack he carried like a purse, told me to read it, and said that, despite my behavior, he would return to discuss the text with me. "You don't need to be so defensive. Baba's love won't hurt you. I'll help you, despite your cynicism, because I know that's what Baba would want me to do. You're a professor of religion; don't you think it's your responsibility to keep an open mind?" he asked, and then left, and I wondered about that, wondered, in light of what I had learned about the dynamics of magic, if an open mind is not simply a mind that is all the more easily deceived. I also wondered if my visitor knew Susan Shapiro.

Premanand liked the story. When he asked what method I had used to produce the ashes, I showed him my Jimmy Yoshida thumb-tip, and Premanand, as he examined it, told me that, formerly, Sai Baba had also used thumb-tips, "but ever since the gimmick was noticed by a child in his presence, he has given it up in favor of a much simpler version of the production, concealing the *vibhūti* in the fold of skin between his thumb and forefinger, and reloading his hand after each materialization under the pretext of wiping his ash-besmirched hand clean." He described another item performed by the holy conjurer: "He distributes photographs of himself, framed under sheets of glass that have been painted, over his forehead, with a clear, invisible, chemical—hydrochloric acid—that reacts with the smoke of the incense that his devotees inevitably burn in front of the image. The reaction leaves a residue of ammonium chloride, making it seem that *vibhūti* has miraculously materialized on the photograph."

As Dayanand set up the VCR machine to show me the videotape of both the street magician in Karnataka with his dancing monkey, and of Sai Baba appearing at the wedding of a government official's daughter, Premanand told me that he himself, when he was young, had believed in God and miracles, and that he had wanted to acquire miraculous powers. "I left home in search of God and miracles. I returned with the realization that we create God and perform a miracle when we do a good deed, a kind deed, for another human being." Premanand runs and supports both a home for mentally retarded children in Shrishaila and a hospital across from his house in Podanur where anyone can receive free medical care. I was treated there for my cold.

"Sai Baba doesn't allow himself to be taped of course," Dayanand explained gleefully, laughing naughtily. "It's too easy to see what he's up to on the video. But he made a surprise appearance at this wedding, and a man was taping the proceedings for the family. This cameraman, being no devotee of the god-man, secretly provided us with this tape." We watched the production of *vibhūti* again and again, forward and backward, in revealing slow motion and farcical fast motion, again and again, watched as the bride noticed God loading the *vibhūti*, already molded with rice water into pellets, some of which contained little medallions embossed with images of Kali. "My *vibhūti* is purchased from the very shop where Sai Baba gets his," Premanand laughed happily.

Mr. Pai, another magician, had joined us and, after the showing of the tape, told me that his late brother, formerly a government minister, had been a devotee of Sai Baba. "They were quite close. But then my brother lost an election, and this so-called god-man would have nothing more to do with him. My brother became disillusioned. He died in a state of utter disenchantment and despair." Mr. Pai had joined Premanand and Dayanand in the crusade against Sai Baba in hopes of some revenge against the living god who had caused his deceased brother such deep sadness. "One of my relatives, a member of my brother's immediate family—can you believe it?—told me I should not criticize Sai Baba," Mr. Pai said quite angrily. "She said that I had no right to criticize him, since I myself had no experience of him, that he had, after all, built some schools and hospitals, and that he had brought peace of mind to some people. So I asked her if she thought smoking cigarettes and drinking liquor are good. Of course, she had to say no, this pious Tamil lady who has had no personal experience of either tobacco or alcohol." He smiled proudly over his dialectical triumph. " 'You should not criticize smoking and drinking if you yourself have not tried them,' I told her. 'Furthermore the tax revenues that are collected because of these practices have gone into the building of hospitals and schools. Furthermore many people will tell you that they have gained peace of mind from smoking and drinking. In fact more people have been smoking and drinking than have been followers of Sai Baba. Many great scientists, artists, writers, and philosophers have been smokers and/or drinkers. Let us turn to smoking and/or drinking for peace of mind and enlightenment.' "

"Here, here!" I laughed and coughed: "I'll drink to that."

"Or," he zealously continued, "let us require Sai Baba to have the following words printed on the robes he wears: 'Quitting Devotion to the Guru Now Greatly Reduces Serious Risks to Your Mental Health.' "

Mr. Pai was an ardent soldier in the army that Premanand had enlisted in his tireless battle against Sai Baba. The courtroom was Premanand's current battlefield. He gave me a copy of his declaration of war, a Writ Petition against Sathya Sai Baba, accusing the god of breaking the law, of contravening the Government of India Gold Control Act of 1968—section 8 (dealing with regulations regarding the acquisition, possession, and disposal of gold), section 11 (prohibiting the manufacture of gold articles and ornaments), section 14 (requiring the submission of monthly accounts), and section 16 (necessitating the declaration of all gold articles and ornaments in one's possession). Premanand's legal argument goes something like this: Sai Baba must possess the gold that he distributes, and yet he has never declared possession of any of the gold ornaments that he has given to devotees; or, if he has not been in possession of those ornaments, he has illegally manufactured them. In any case he should be prosecuted. But, in the Andhra Pradesh High Court in 1986, Court Justice Anjaneyulu dismissed the case, decreeing that the materialization of gold by divine means was different than manufacturing it, and that the fact that the gold ornaments were spiritually manifested meant that the good Baba did not have them in his possession prior to the moment of materialization. Since the government of India officially and legally accepts the materialization of objects through spiritual powers as an empirical possibility and regular occurrence, Premanand argues, one can arrive from abroad and, at the customs counter at the airport, announce, "I have nothing to declare. I have brought nothing into the country. But, at this moment, in this suitcase, with the help of God and the blessings of Sai Baba, I shall materialize a VCR machine and some other dutiable foreign articles, and no duty can be charged." Premanand laughed as he spoke, but the laughter was informed with frustration and a sadness over the futility of dealing with the Indian courts. Sai Baba is too powerful an adversary. K. N. Balgopal, a Supreme Court advocate, Premanand's representative in Delhi, told me that the god-man's followers "include five cabinet ministers, thirty-six judges, in both the Supreme Court and in many High Courts, three chief ministers—well, at least 25 percent of the bureaucrats in the country. These are the people that interest the holy man. He materializes gold ornaments for them and *vibhūti* for the poor. There's a good return on his investment—he has one thousand crores in fixed assets [$10 million]. He's very powerful. And such power is dangerous, really dangerous."

Mr. Pai brought up the issue of a Seiko watch that Sai Baba had apparently materialized for some influential devotee. "Possibility number one: Sai Baba had the watch, which had never been registered with customs, in his possession prior to presenting it; in that case he must be prosecuted for smuggling or, at the very minimum, for the possession of smuggled articles. Possibility number two: if the watch was not illegally brought into the country, if it was produced (manufactured or even materialized!), Sai Baba must be prosecuted for infringement of the trademark laws for using the logo of the Seiko watch company. The god-man must also be charged for counterfeiting, since he has materialized gold coins for various devotees."

Premanand, who has dedicated his life to trying to rescue people from their blind entanglement in Indra's Net, started supplying me with materials for the exposure of Sai Baba—books, pamphlets, articles, and defamatory testimonials. I tried to explain to Premanand that there was no point in me trying to write an exposé of Sai Baba's chicanery—people who believed in the powers of the god-man, people like the man who had visited my office in Hawaii, would not be convinced by anything I wrote; and other people, the audience for whom I was writing, already knew that nobody ever really materializes Seiko watches out of thin air by spiritual powers. "My interest," I tried to explain, "is descriptive. I'm more concerned with the aesthetics of magic than with the politics of it." Premanand clearly understood, but as I said the essential words—"I'm not fighting for anything or trying to change anything; I have no cause"—his expression belied a certain pity for me.

"For your book," he smiled sympathetically, pausing to light a cigarette, "I can tell you some stories about priests and swamis who are magicians. The late Pandrimallai Swami, Pig-Hill Swami, made quite a fortune here in Coimbatore with a bell that had no ringer in it. He'd ask people to ring it and, of course, there was no sound. But after they gave him some money for a blessing or prayer, he would show them, his hand upon theirs, that then the bell would miraculously ring. It was, of course, a simple trick—he had a regular bell concealed up his sleeve, in his armpit, that rang when he moved his hand." Premanand laughed, rose from his seat, and went to get a metal bowl that was filled with uncooked rice. He handed me a dagger.

"Go on," he laughed, "stick the knife into the rice and withdraw it." I complied and he asked me to do it again, then again, and again. Finally he took the knife and stabbed it into the rice, repeating the violent gesture several times, and then, as he raised the knife upwards, the bowl of rice rose with it, remained in the air, clinging to the dagger. Premanand laughed as he explained the miracle. "It's so simple, isn't it? Each time the rice is stabbed, it gets packed more tightly, until finally it is packed so tightly that the knife will stick in it. This elementary trick is performed by the priests at the Kalabhairava shrine in the Daksharama Temple. When barren women go to those priests for help, the trick is used to convince them of the priest's magic power. And once the priest has power over the woman's mind, he gets money from her husband through her. Then he arranges for her to have intercourse with the god. It's done in the dark, and the priest also gets money from the man who plays the part of the god. Often the woman will become pregnant after that, since usually the barrenness is due to the husband, who is most likely either impotent or sterile. Sometimes the impotent men themselves go to the priest for a cure, and the priest will do yet another simple trick, something based on the famous Indian Rope Trick. He displays a floppy rope, and after he says some mantras or attaches an amulet to the rope, the rope will become stiff and stand straight up in the air!" Premanand laughed as one laughs over a dirty joke. "All of the street magicians have this same item, the rope encasing the bicycle chain that is limp or stiff depending on how you hold it. Have you seen it?"

"Yes, Tayade gave me a version of it; he manufactures it at his shop in Bombay."

"Yes, it's a common item, easily available from Tayade or from Sam Dalal in Calcutta. These priests order them through the magic catalogues. They show the trick to the impotent man, then sell him the mantra or the amulet. And because impotence is so frequently caused by psychological reasons, mostly lack of confidence, very often the amulet or mantra will actually cure the man! The more money the man pays the priest, the more he will believe in the power of the mantra or the amulet, and the more likely it is that the magic will work."

Premanand took the rice bowl away and returned with a small, white chunk of some chemical. "Camphor," he said, and when he touched a match to it, it flamed. He transferred the ball of fire from one hand to other, smiling happily and assuring me that he was not being burned by it. "You just have to keep it moving." He suddenly handed it to Catherine, and she juggled it back and forth and then tossed it to me, and even though I was not burned by the camphor, I was anxious to get rid of it and quickly passed it back to Premanand, who happily popped it into his mouth. He extinguished the fire by closing his mouth and then gave me what was left of the chunk of camphor. "The mouth," he said cheerfully, "is the best part of the body for tricks with fire. You can control the fire quite easily there, breathing in to increase the flames with oxygen, breathing out to stifle them with carbon dioxide, closing the mouth when the moisture that protects you from being burned is gone."

He made me try it and then announced excitedly, with a radiant smile, "Tomorrow night, firewalking. Tomorrow night I'll make a god-man of you!"

Throughout the town non-Brahmin men were wearing black lungis (while Brahmins wore orange) as a sign that they were observing penances for a period of forty-five days: abstaining from sexual intercourse, from eating meat, drinking alcohol, or sleeping on high beds, all in preparation for a pilgrimage to the shrine of Ayyappa, a South Indian god in whose worship the Shaiva and Vaishnava sects are reconciled: Vishnu had performed a magic trick, taken on the veil of *māyā*, created an illusion, and was seen in female form—Mohini—the Enchanting One; after Shiva made love to her, she gave birth to Ayyappa. Before having a vision of that god, to prove that they had kept their vows of continence and abstinence, devotees would, under the guidance of priests and through the grace and mercy of the deity, walk over burning coals. The bare soles of their feet would not be burned; there would be no pain in that beatitude. The fear they felt before walking would, on the other side of the incendiary path, turn into ecstasy and an affirmation of their faith. Ayyappa would be revitalized, his priests reempowered and paid.

That evening, near where the devout were to walk, Premanand built his fire pit. The coals burned brightly, glowed hot in the Coimbatore night, and dogs, agitated by the loud crowd that had gathered for the spectacle, barked in the darkness. Premanand was all smiles as he scattered salt upon the coals, carefully tapping the blazing embers down. Sparks leapt up with each stamp of the iron.

"You have to make sure the coals are tapped down so that no embers can stick to the feet. As long as nothing sticks, you can't get burned. That's the trick. It's just like when you lick your finger to test an iron for pressing. As long as it doesn't stick you're okay. You won't be burned, don't worry."

"I'd just like to watch," I explained. "I don't think I'll walk tonight. I've got this cold. I'm not really feeling up to it. I think I'll pass."

"No, no, you'll walk," Premanand laughed.

Young men, members of the International Society of Rationalists, waiting in line to step out upon the burning coals, chanted, "No god! No god! No god!" Each one, when coming to the head of the line, illuminated by the fires that lay before him, would announce in Tamil, "I have eaten meat and taken alcohol! I have enjoyed sexual intercourse with my wife and slept on a high bed. I have indulged every wish, and I do not believe in god." And then he would walk, and another man would take his place, shout out the confession and walk, and then another, and then suddenly Catherine was standing there, waving at me, and like Sita, who proved her devotion to Rama by walking through fire, she dashed across the path of flames, over to me, and laughed and urged me on. "It's nothing!" She was joined by the others: "Go on, walk! Go on, do it! No problem! Walk on fire!"

I stood before the coals as before the flames of hell, utterly terrified, and all the more so when I was warned to roll up my pants so that they wouldn't catch fire during my stroll over the inferno. "No god! No god! No god!" they kept chanting. "Shit, they're hot," I said to myself. "I'm going to be burned, badly burned and blistered. It's going to hurt, really hurt." In utter terror and absolute certainty that I was about to be cremated, I imagined headlines in the *Honolulu Advertiser:* "UNIVERSITY OF HAWAII RELIGION PROFESSOR IMMO-LATED IN INDIA TRYING TO PROVE THAT THERE IS NO GOD." Someone behind gave me a shove, but I held my ground. "Mind over matter," I said to myself, but my mind itself screamed back, "Don't walk you fool! If you do, you'll burn your matter." And all my matter was crying out: "If you walk, you're out of your mind."

"No god! No god! No god!" the chanting persisted and then gave way to another incantation: "Walk Dr. Lee! Walk Dr. Lee! Walk! Walk! Walk Dr. Lee! Dr. Lee! Dr. Lee!" Having no choice in the matter, I ran over the coals as fast as I could, and when, on the other side of the fire pit, I felt the exhilaration of confronting my own deep fear, when I realized that my feet were not burned, I let out a great laugh of relief and triumph and returned to the coals to walk once more, a little more slowly, so that I could enjoy it.

Happily, giddily, we walked back to Dayanand's house, laughing and joking. I was happy because I hadn't been burned, and the Rationalists were happy because they had, in their own minds anyway, proved once more that there is no god. While we drank tea and ate sweets in celebration of the evening's triumphs, one of the Rationalists took a needle and thread and sewed limes into his chest and belly. I asked him if it hurt. "No," he said. "Oh maybe it hurts just a little, but I am doing it for a good cause, and so the pain is easy to endure." Several days later, in Cochin, I watched this same young man allow Premanand to insert meat hooks into his back. Ropes connected the hooks to an automobile which he pulled behind him through the town to the exuberant chant of hundreds of Rationalists: "No god! No god! No god!"

On the way to that gathering of Rationalists in Cochin, Dayanand explained that we would stop in Trichur. It was there that Shankar had promised that I would see the Tantric adepts perform miracles at midnight. There I would, with my own eyes, see a priest remove his head, and that head, held by his hands in his lap, would speak to me. I'd see a levitation, the materialization of any object I named, and the transformation of water into milk, wine, or blood. Things would vanish; things would appear. Indra's Net would be cast. "There is only one problem," Shankar had explained apologetically. "To have this night of Tantric magic arranged, you will have to pay 2500 rupees."

There was no temple, no decapitation, no levitation, no materialization, no transformation. The only thing that turned out to be true was that the evening cost me 2500 rupees. That was the price a group of Kerala fakirs known as Thangals charge to come to someone's home and mutilate themselves.

Early in the morning on the day when we were scheduled to leave Coimbatore for Trichur by jeep, there was a furious pounding on my hotel-room door. "MGR has died," the dark and wizened little room servant cried. "No food today. No nothing at all today. No going out on streets. You must stay in the room. And don't turn on any lights at night. Stay in the room always." He looked up and down the hall and then back at me as he whispered, "If you tell me now, I can bring you something secretly. But you must tell me now. Later, nothing."

The death of MGR, the movie-star minister of Tamil Nadu, worshiped as a god in that state, released pent-up energies, angers, and sorrows. The state went mad. There were suicides; it was reported that even children were hanging or burning themselves. Hysterical fits of grief, violence, and frustration gripped and shook the land. Wearing black arm bands and bearing banners with the picture of their Tamil hero, rough, heartbroken men roamed the streets shouting, throwing stones through the windows of any shop that remained open or any home that did not display a black flag or some other makeshift symbol of mourning. There were no trains or planes, no buses, trucks, or cars on the road. Even to ride a bicycle was considered an act of disrespect for the beloved MGR. The rider would be beaten up and his bicycle smashed and mangled.

"How long will this go on?" I asked the servant. "How long will we be stuck in the room?"

"Days for certain. Maybe weeks."

"Then you'd better bring beer and cigarettes, lots of both."

"No, no," he shook his hands in front of my face. "Too dangerous to bring those. I can bring idli and Campa-Cola or Limca."

"You can't get beer or cigarettes?"

"I am not a magician," he said, and it struck me how many people seemed to be saying that to me recently—the doctor in Delhi, an agent at the airlines office where I had tried, because of my cold, to change our reservations, and now the room servant.

That afternoon, despite the rabid throngs of thugs in the street, flocks of hungry spirits enraptured by their misery, Premanand and Dayanand showed up at our door. "How did you get here?" I asked. "I heard no one could drive."

"I'm a magician," Premanand laughed and handed us our black arm bands. "Get ready, we are going to Trichur."

The desk clerk refused to give me the bill. "No. You cannot check out today. I cannot let you leave. I cannot permit you to go out onto the street. Your vehicle will be destroyed. You will definitely be killed." Since Premanand had said I could walk on burning coals without being burned, and I had, I figured that I could go along with him in the jeep if he said we could make it. I said good-bye to the desk clerk and headed for the door. He ran after me with the bill. "Since you cannot be convinced not to go out there," he smiled sadly, "I shall have to pray for you. I shall ask Ayyappa to protect you."

All along the way to Kerala, the home, I was told so many times, of "real Indian magic," there were roadblocks formed of stones and rubble. Dayanand drove slowly up to them, stopped the black jeep, and Premanand fearlessly walked forward each time to speak to the self-appointed ministers of public despair. Each time they let us pass. And on that road that winds its way through paddy fields and palm groves up the slopes of the Western Ghats there were shrines to MGR, fires of grief burning in his honor, and people grouped in sorrow. Men beat drums as they solemnly danced. There was wailing in the air.

At the border of Kerala, where countless trucks were lined up, waiting for the trouble to end before venturing into Tamil Nadu, as day yielded to dusk, the solemn misery of one state gave way to the festive joy of another. There were singing processions of people costumed as angels, as Magi, as Mary and Joseph, and Santa Claus. It was Christmas Eve.

When we arrived at the home of the parents of N. Kumar Kalathil ("Magic Prince" as he called himself), the Thangals were already there. Their grass mats had been arranged on the ground of the courtyard in front of the house. They had waited for us, since I, with my 2500 rupees, was the patron of the hot, mosquito-infested, winter night's ritual performance.

In being introduced to Fakir Muhammad Masthan Thangal, the leader of the group, I was told that he was a master of traditional Indian Cups and Balls. But when I expressed my interest in seeing a performance of his routine, I was scolded. "Cups and Balls is mere conjuring, simple jugglery. Tonight we are here for real magic. Conjuring and magic do not mix."

The fakir stuck his scarred tongue out at me; it looked like the tread of an automobile tire. He pointed to my camera and then to his still protruding tongue. Through the viewfinder of my camera I studied the severe, uncanny face as he proudly displayed his hideously mutilated tongue. His skin had been stigmatized by smallpox, and his right eye, gauzy and unfixed in its gaze, did not match the left. *Click.* He wore a black skullcap, and his shiny, graying hair, much darker and thicker than his beard, curled, unfurled, down to his broad, shawled shoulders. *Click.* He opened his mouth wider, stretched the tongue out farther. *Click.* I look at the photographs now. The expression is scornful. Or is it ironic? Or pious? This could be the face of a saint or a terrorist.

Chanting began the liturgy of pain. A dozen young Thangals played their tambourines as they wailed the haunting doxology: "Allah Allah Allah Allah Allah." Gradually, slowly faster and faster, never losing the rhythm, they cried out, "Allah Allah Allah Allah Allah Allah Allah." Then faster and louder still, "Muhammad Allah Muhammad Allah Muhammad Allah Muhammad Allah Muhammad Allah Muhammad Allah Muhammad Allah Muhammad Allah." And as these young men, his students, sang, swayed, and swooned, Fakir Muhammad Masthan Thangal arranged the implements of the ritual. The knives and daggers, shiny and sharp, were meticulously laid out upon the white cloth with the tongs, the drills, and the bludgeon. He rolled the fresh wicks for the characteristically Hindu lamp that burned with ghee as its fuel. The lamp, the incense, and the mosquito coils were lit. And then the man, his young and strangely handsome little boy leaning against him on the ground, sat waiting for the chant to take effect. He would lead his disciples across a threshold from the ordinary world of pain and pleasure into an extraordinary realm of dark ecstasies and luminous powers.

When I noticed that one of the Thangals, staring at me as he pounded madly on his drum, was missing a thumb, I whispered to Catherine: "Kuttichathan!"

On and on they chanted. The fakir chewed *pān*, looked at his digital watch, lit a bidi, and stroked his son's hair. A youthful amateur magician, a friend of Mr. Kalathil, with a broad and hospitable smile, seated himself next to me. "Usually they recite the Qur'an for several hours before they start the singing. I personally suggested that they leave that part out for your sake. Frankly," he added with an extraordinary cheerfulness, "I wish they would finish the singing and get on to the cutting and piercing."

I asked the young magician to explain the connection between this ritual and magic. "This ritual is magic. It has many mysterious and magical effects. If someone in a certain household is sick, or if they have some grave problem, or if, because of some death or calamity, there is great sorrow in the house, they call these Thangals to perform. So many people in Kerala might do this. Not only

Muslims, but Hindus and Christians as well. Even Jews do it. The Thangals, through their performance, take the pain or misfortune of the household upon themselves. That is what one is paying them to do. After they suffer, the suffering in the home will be no more. That is magic, real magic. And what is real magic? Religion! This ritual is just like Christianity—isn't it? Jesus Christ had some nails put through his hands and feet and then everybody felt better. This is Hinduism too—sadhus and yogis roll around on some bed of nails, hang themselves up on hooks, walk on hot coals, put some needle through their skin or cheek or tongue and then you give them some money and you benefit from it. Basically this is every religion. Every religion has escapegoats, certain holy individuals who suffer so that everybody else can be happy. And these individuals are always magicians. Jesus turned water into wine; Moses turned a stick into a cobra; Buddha performed the Mango Tree Trick; Shankaracharya, right here in Kerala, in a place not far from my own fine home, produced a shower of golden amlaka fruits from above; and Confucius could perform the Chinese Sticks without any gimmick whatsoever. The difference between conjuring and real magic is that the real magician suffers. The conjurer simply imitates, through false means, without suffering, what the real magician actually does. On the stage I can perform a levitation using wires or some other gaff. The real magician actually and empirically rises in the air using no device other than the power he has acquired through the suffering of his penances."

One of the Thangals, a dark old man wearing a plaid lungi and a pure white apron, bright white to vividly show the blood, to display the symbol of pain, death, and the life that pain and death might generate, rose to take the blessings of each of the chanters. They graced his hands with gentle, melancholy kisses. The small man, scarred by years of ritual practice, began to dance, to turn and sway to the strident peal of his faith. "Allah Allah Muhammad Allah . . ." The leader gave him two curved daggers, which he turned, wielded, and waved rhythmically in front of his belly. Closer and closer, as if teasingly, as if torment would be delight, the knives came, and then the first blood, and the syncopated anthem of a painful ecstasy began to swell and pound. Again and again he sliced the skin on his stomach as he danced to the drone. Next the spike. With a mallet he pounded it into his harrowed gut. His knees buckled but his son held him up. The blood-drenched spike was displayed for all to wonder at. Then there was the drill.

The leader stepped forward and, to the persistent strains of the tambourines and chanters, cauterized the old man's wounds with burning incense. He rubbed the cuts with clarified butter. The old man's son, lithe, limber, and inspired, then danced as his father danced, cut and gored himself as his father had done, enduring the anguish that was passed from father to son. He took the blade, stuck out his tongue, and began to slice and gash it. Blood, slowly coagulating as it made its way toward the white apron, dripped down his chin in rivulets to form a crimson network across his muscular breast. Sinuous flesh kept time, bowed, waved, curved, curled, and turned to the swell of the music. Two more daggers, larger and sharper still, lacerated his gut. Faster, deeper, faster, more exquisitely vicious, harder, deeper, deeper—too deep. The leader lunged toward him. The music stopped. The fakir shook the man gently and then held him in his arms. He handed him tenderly over to his father, who wiped the sweat from his face and the blood from his chin, neck, chest, and stomach. The trance had gone too far. The young man's wounds, like his father's, were anointed with the sacred salves and soothing balms, with *vibhūti* and ghee, by the knowing hand of the teacher.

I tried to let the ritual work, to let go of my fever and depression, to let the fakirs take away my illness and remorse, to carry it with them into the tenebrous jungles of Kerala, to bury or burn it there. But I couldn't surrender. The liturgy sickened me all the more.

When the leader started to move, the music joined him, followed him as the other dancers had followed it. He threw off his hat and his hair spread out like the serpentine locks of the madly dancing Shiva. He laughed as he showed the razor blades to us. He found a deep, primordial rhythm to straddle, a dark current to carry him along, and the drummers struggled to keep up with him as he sliced at his chest. Criss-crossed lines over his heart glistened and gave us his blood.

Then the needle. It entered the skin of his arm, crossed over the muscles, and reemerged. Blood oozed out of the punctures. He removed the needle and then did it again. There was more blood. And it was real. The needle was worked, twisted into cheeks, neck, thighs.

Laughing loudly, laughing at pain and gall, at fear and vulnerability, he tossed his head back. A spike was driven up into the roof of his mouth, and another down behind his jawbone so that it emerged, dripping with blood, through his bearded chin. The spike stuck fast in the neck bone.

"You know what is terrible, what is really horrible?" the young magician next to me asked in whispers.

I looked at him. "What? Tell me."

"It is terrible indeed," he smiled good-naturedly, "that you do not have a VCR machine to record this astonishing performance."

The knife sliced through the air above our heads. The Thangal began to slash at his tongue, to really do what the street magicians so often pretended to show.

When the tambourines were being pounded hardest and fastest, when the voices were at their loudest and most plaintive, when the ecstasy was so intense that it seemed to shake the earth, to crack the sky, to be flames from the heart that burned from the throat, the fakir took up the stiletto. He flashed it as the anxious warrior waves his sword before attack, as the assassin brandishes his blade before the kill, and then slowly, ever so slowly, he touched it to the moist ball of his right eye. With yet another terrible laugh and with icy purpose, he delicately pushed the point of the knife into the eye. A translucent liquid bubbled out and dripped down the shining blade, which was then suddenly jammed in and twisted slowly, so slowly. The fakir's hand jerked, and the eyeball, removed from the dark, gaping socket, was visible on the end of the knife.

It was a trick. Premanand explained it later that night in the jeep on the way to Cochin. Years earlier, during a performance of self-mutilation, the fakir, while attempting to pound a spike into his skull, had accidentally put out his right eye. Now, to make the ritual all the more effective, he would, before each performance, insert the eye of a goat or sheep into his own empty eye socket.

In a room above the Kalathil home in which the young Magic Prince kept all of his conjuring equipment, I waited for Fakir Muhammad Masthan Thangal. Entering the crowded studio, he stood in front of the full-length mirror that had been installed for the Prince to practice sleight-of-hand. As he adjusted the eye patch over the empty socket and washed the dried blood from his face, arms, and chest, the fakir stared with his one eye at himself in the mirror. He combed his hair and bushed up his beard, oddly primping like a debutante getting ready for a ball. When he turned, came, and squatted in front of me, I slowly counted out the 2500 rupees, and he recounted it just to make sure.

Premanand helped me interview the fakir, who maintained the same total and enviable sangfroid and nonchalance during the questioning that he displayed throughout the evening, even in his mad dance. He explained that he was fifty-six years old, that he had been trained in the holy art of self-mutilation by a shaik from the Lacadive Islands, and that he was passing on the sacred skill to one of his nine children and to these students. The Thangal lineage, he claimed, could be traced back to the family of Muhammad. His own branch of the line came from Ajmeer.

"Don't ask him too many questions," I was instructed. "He's tired, I think. He's worked enough. He's had a hard day."

I followed the fakir out, descended the stairs back into the courtyard where he had mutilated himself for us. Catherine, waiting at the bottom of the steps, stretched out her arm to show me her watch. It was just moments after midnight. "Merry Christmas," she smiled, and then she laughed. "It's really funny for me as a Catholic to be saying 'Merry Christmas' to a Jew right after watching Muslims torture themselves for a group of Hindus and right before getting into a jeep to drive all night to watch the Rationalists prove that there is no god." She laughed again. "India is wonderful—really full of wonders."

We listened to the address that Premanand, as the convener of the Indian Committee for the Scientific Investigation of Claims of the Paranormal, gave in the great hall before the assembled Rationalists, Atheists, Humanists, and other related groups. Since all of the talks and addresses were in Tamil or Malayalam, Catherine and I, unable to understand them (although the gist was clear), decided to wait outside. We smoked, and through the large, open, but barred windows of the adjoining auditorium where the All-India Weight Lifting Tournament was being held, we watched the final round of the women's division, and witnessed the crowning of a Bengali lady as the "Strongest Woman in India."

We started to follow the young Rationalist from Coimbatore with the hooks in his back as he pulled the automobile through the streets of Cochin, but we were lured away from the chanting procession of Atheists that marched along with him by the sight of a sign for a hotel bar. We did our best in the dark, empty bar to celebrate Christmas.

"New Year's Eve will be better," I promised. "We'll have a real celebration at one of the big hotels in Madras. I know it will be good—I'm feeling better, so much better. Maybe the Thangal ritual cured me, took my cold and blues away. Maybe I'll make a New Year's resolution to give up magic like Doug Henning. Maybe magic is bad for my *sādhana* too. Maybe the resolution for 1988 should be no magic, no tricks, no illusions, no deceptions, no lies."

The New Year's Eve party wasn't so easy to arrange since the government of Tamil Nadu had declared that, out of respect to MGR, there would be no celebrations in the state. People were still committing suicide, rioting, and bombing or breaking the windows of stores and offices that had not closed down to honor the demigod. The newspaper, brimming with panegyrics, read like the chronicle of some ancient Tamil king—his queen and his courtesan were vying for his throne. Since the Russians had, on the grounds that it was too late, refused the state government's request for technical assistance in embalming MGR, he was going to be buried; not burned like an ordinary mortal, but inhumed in an upright position like a holy man on the Marina beach.

"He did so much for the poor," the desk clerk at the Savera Hotel, rocking his head about in a gesture of sorrow, informed me.

"Like what?" I asked.

"Well, for example, whenever he was driven somewhere in his limousine, he would always throw coins out of the window for the poor people. That is just one example. He had a heart of pure gold. That is why we cannot have a celebration. Every Tamil will be in mourning this year."

He looked around, leaned forward, cleared his throat, and then, nervously, spoke in whispers: "Of course, here at the hotel there are many people who have no Tamil blood in their bodies, people like yourselves—people from Japan, Europe, U.S.A., Soviet Union, Australia, also people from North India, Bengalis, Sardarjis, Delhi-*wālās*, Kashmiris, and the like—these people cannot be expected to mourn." Looking around again, he lowered his voice still more: "So, here at the hotel, we are planning a little celebration tonight for foreigners and Indian travelers. But tell no one of it. It will be held in the dining room. We're blacking out the windows so that no one will know of it. If the poor people were to find out, they would certainly bomb the place. We would all be killed—not a good way to begin the new year. Just in case, we're having armed guards. It should be a rollicking good time in any case, although, unfortunately, because of the government decree, it will be impossible to get entertainment from the outside. Usually, for New Year's Eve, we hire a rock-and-roll band, a film singer, sometimes a dancer, or a magician. One year we had an internationally famous belly dancer. She was excellent. Another year we presented the magical extravanganza of the famous Professor Bhagyanath, World's Greatest Magician."

Catherine laughed, looked around, leaned over the desk, and whispered to the desk clerk, "You're in luck tonight. Professor Siegel is a magician! I'm sure he'll perform if you ask him."

The man leaned farther forward still and whispered softly but gleefully: "Great! Everyone loves magic! Happy New Year to you, Professor Siegel! Happy New Year! Here's to a year of magic!"

ON THE STAGE
THEN

Bones and Earth

Scene Seven:

The Skull of Vishvasiddhi

t was the first day of the new year, a year of magic and illusions, spells and omens, death and other mysteries; it was the first day of Chaitra, a season of jasmine, laughing white-and-crimson ashoka blossoming under the magic touch of young women's feet, a time of birth and other mysteries. And Amaruka, the king, celebrated the new year, the transformations of life in this world, with a hunt.

All week the beaters, conscripted from every part of the valley—crying, "Ho! Ho!"—had been forcing the wild goats toward the ravine selected for the royal sport in which war and sacrifice became a game. Vishvasiddhi, as master of Indra's Net, had directed the setting of the nets that kept the goats within the beaters' scope. He was in attendance on every hunting or fishing expedition, for through his mantras and the waving of his peacock feathers, the snares were invested with Indra's magic: "Indra's net is vast, as big as this world, and with Indra's Net—this magic—I enmesh, ensnare, entrap you."

To mark the confluence of beginnings, a banner of white Chinese silk with threads of gold woven into it was raised to wave above the palace. Sky was the ground for the magic cities of cloud. Kites decorated with the images of gods were flown, and to protect himself for the year, the king solemnly placed in his mouth the bitter nim leaf upon which a secret name of Indra had been invisibly written in blessed Ganga water by the sorcerer Bhairavagupta.

They carried Amaruka upon the walnut-wood palanquin, carved with images of gods, along the still-frosted road. Branches of oak and elm, maple and magnolia, silver fir and blue pine gestured messages of persistence, while the purling stream of melted ice whispered the transience of things. That is what the old magician, carried behind the king, heard—the secret murmurs—as he watched the mists roll down from eternally snowy Himalayan peaks to lightly rest on the dark green ridges, softly settle into the dark gray crevices, and rise slowly again into a softer light. Eagles, hawks, and pariah kites circled in these descending, resting, rising mists. The sharp barking and yapping of the yellow dogs, trained by chandalas to track the quarry, their noses never fooled by the tricks of the prey, cracked, cracked and echoed in the awakening valley. But it did not take a dog to smell the rich, smoky urine sprays of the markhor goats that had been driven into the net-fenced canyon.

Waters flowed more swiftly, and pine trees, somehow able to find earth between the massive boulders, began to predominate over the other trees as the hunting party climbed higher and higher into the colder and colder mountains. There was snow in the crevices and gorges, and when the path became too steep, slick, and narrow for the palanquin bearers, the king followed the dogs on foot.

Like great, gnawed bones scattered by pillaging demons, gigantic timber was strewn ominously in the forest. The magician, woolen-shawled, looked back, down, and over the valley, gazed into the obliterating enormity of gaping space. A sudden rustling in the underbrush—a frightened porcupine, shrew, or marten perhaps. But neither the movement nor the scent of it distracted the dogs from the vigorous, spumy smell of the goats. After the long mountain winter, the other animals—the musk deer and wild boar, the black bear and mountain leopard— would be hungry and weak, easy to kill, but not the markhor. They were said to feed on serpents. "They overturn boulders with their horns and unearth the snakes within their liars," the officer of the hunt insisted. "They climb steep cliffs to devour the eggs of eagles. And if there are no eagles' eggs or snakes, neither berries, mushrooms, scorpions, nor any other delicacies, they can survive and thrive by eating stones. I've seen it with my own eyes."

It was exhilaratingly dangerous to hunt the markhor, to be lured into his perilous grounds, to risk slipping into abysses for the sake of killing him. Danger was diversion. There was an exuberant pleasure in the kill and in the boasting that was perfunctory over roasted freshly-slaughtered goat. The meat was never hung to cure. The challenge was always to slay an animal that on the scale proved heavier than the hunter. Thus King Amaruka smiled at the sight of him—the great markhor there, just there, up there, by the stream. The smell of the urine, the bark scraped off the trees, the broken branches, and the feral silences had made his presence felt before the sighting. There. He stood dead still, staring back with bright black eyes, frozen, immobile as the mountain, his winter gray already turning ruddy, his horns curling three full times. Only the flash of the eyes and the steam from the nostrils indicated life in what might have been a statue, a monument to Indra. "That's not a real goat but Indra himself, once again by magic taking on the form of a goat," the chaplain whispered. "Watch out for him—there's lightning in those eyes and thunder in that mouth. He's eaten snakes and eagle eggs, stones and scorpions. He'd eat us too. Watch out—he doesn't want to die."

The whining and growling dogs had been leashed and muzzled with wet hemp ropes, slapped, kicked, shushed, and pulled back. The sky was strangely birdless then, and as if knowing that the nets high atop the rocky ridge above checked escape, the goat stayed still and stared straight into the eyes of Amaruka. There was a fearlessness in the countenance more appropriate to bowman than to prey.

As Amaruka slowly raised the bow, Vishvasiddhi whispered the mantra on the arrow and passed it to the hunter. With the weapon drawn and aimed, slowly, slowly, the king stepped forward, and still the goat stood still, still; and stealing toward him, the king stepped on the pine needles, glistening wet with laces of ice, melting snow, and the hot piss of the goat, slippery wet. And the king slipped: the arrow pierced the earth and the bow fell from the hand that reached for something solid in the air as, stumbling, he tried to catch his balance, but in vain. He fell, groaned, rolled, and lay still. The goat vanished.

The courtiers rushed to their king.

"He's dead!" the chaplain cried in panic. "The king is dead—no breath, no pulse—he's dead!" Hurrying around the fallen tree trunk to kneel by his patron, the old magician placed his head against the chest and his fingers by the nostrils. "*Om aim klīm hrīm śrīm*," he muttered methodically, and then with all his heart invoked Kahneshvari and Kali, Shambara and Indra, Bhairava Shiva and Vasudeva Krishna. "This *māyā*, this magic trick I do, conceals me. Not everyone can see me—the unborn, undying one," he whispered into the ear of the fallen king as he removed the pieces of dried mango leaf, each inscribed with some magic letter, from the amulet around his own neck and sprinkled them on the still, unbreathing chest.

Then, as if by magic, the mouth suddenly gasped, the eyes opened wide, and King Amaruka sat up. Instantly he stood and looked around him at the stunned courtiers who, after a flashing moment of silent incredulity, all at once cried out with the joy of seeing their king returned to life and with the wonder of witnessing such a miracle. They laughed, surprised with the delight of it, cheered with astonishment, and felt no impropriety in clamoring to the side of the king to touch royal resurrected flesh. The chaplain, the officer of the hunt, and Vishvasiddhi embraced him. The magician did it with a wink.

The king said nothing; he smiled just slightly.

Loosening the restlessly clamoring yellow dogs again, the hunters scrambled after them, while Vishvasiddhi and the chaplain remained by their king. As if by the spell enmeshed, ensnared, entrapped in one of Vishvasiddhi's magic nets, the goat was found and beaten to death by the clubs of jubilant courtiers. The officer of the hunt, beheading him with one blow of his sword, let the chandala hold the lota bowl to collect the blood spurting from the severed arteries—a sacred liquor for the sorcerer Bhairavagupta to offer up to Kali. And for the triumphal return to the palace where the celebration would take place, the mammoth head of the goat was mounted on the pole set in the banner hole of the king's litter.

Now the celebration would be not only the ordained ceremonial feast of the conquest of life over death in the birth of the new year, not only the planned rite of celebration of what had been certain victory for the king in the hunt, but now also, unplanned and undivined, it would be a celebration of the resurrection of the king.

The mouth of the goat drooled dark clots of blood and the still-wide, black, staring eyes, not milky with death or gauzy yet, scrutinizing the road to the palace, found the boy in the roadside gathering of dark, shawl-clad forms that watched the royal procession and waved. The monkey on the boy's shoulder shrieked, and "Quiet Vrishakapi," the boy, wearing the winter blanket of a holy man, his hair grown long now, whispered. "It's fine. It's fine. Don't be afraid." Breaking from the others to run alongside one of the dog handlers who was tugged forward by the rope around the neck of a frothy-mouthed yellow hunter, the boy confidently announced himself: "I'm a magician, Indradatta by name. Get word to your king that I, who have performed my magic in courts around the world and have never yet disappointed any king or prince, will delight him with my show. I'll make it worth your while, cut you in on the prize that I'm sure to get."

The dog handler laughed over the brazenness of the child: "Do you do the Rope Trick? I ask because, if you do, I'm certain I can get an audience for you, and the prize will make it worth both our whiles. The king has offered a reward for anyone who can do the trick—it obsesses him."

"I can do it," the boy insisted, and Vrishakapi clapped his small, dark hands together as if to swear that it was true.

The chandala told the officer of the hunt, who told the doorkeeper, who told the chaplain, who arranged the rest and, that night, the young magician, Indragopa, who said Indradatta was his name, was escorted into the open pavilion where a thousand butter lamps illuminated the king, seated still and silent at the far, far end to preside over the festivities.

Smells of night jasmine sprays and bouquets, nocturnal incense and dusky perfumes were stirred into the rich, thick aromas of the procession of foods carried before the king and then set out for the court: roasted fish and birds surrounding the great markhor that had been cooked with ginger, cumin, long pepper, and turmeric, and then decorated with dried fruits. The head of the goat, still impaled, watched over the banquet. There was a table set for Brahmins, heavy with milk puddings, fruit-laced curds, sweet and saffroned rice.

Musicians played music that had never been heard before, and the poets, in turn, sang their magical praises, words that in being sung so perfectly would institute or preserve what they described. The king was Indra in those songs, victorious in battle over Shambara and Vritra. He could fly through the air or dive into the earth, walk through fire or on water. His enemies trembled with fear of him, while their wives trembled too, but with desire. Amaru, the poet and lover, hunter and warrior, patron of scholars and upholder of righteousness, "the dust upon your foot, pollen on a lotus, a magic powder that deludes your enemies, upon the foreheads of those who bow in obeisance to that lotus foot enchants them with your glory."

Indragopa was seated in the back with the acrobats to eat and wait with them until summoned to perform. One of the acrobats, a child funambulist, leaned over and pointed them out to Indragopa—Vishvasiddhi, seated near the king, and Mayeshvari on the women's platform. "They're magicians too. If you want into the court, make friends with them." Over the talk of the acrobats, the music and the laughter, the bantering and boasting of hunters, the babble and gabble, the riddling and word games, the clatter of dishes and jingling of ornaments, he could not hear the whispered stories that were exchanged, the varying accounts of what had taken place that day in the mountains.

"The king fell, struck his head upon a rock, and died. Dead! He was dead, completely dead, and Vishvasiddhi brought him back. That's the greatest magic, to bring back the dead to life, to make whole again what has been rent."

"No, there's no magic like that. No one, no thing, can bring back someone who has died. The fall knocked the king's breath out of him, knocked him unconscious for a time—that's all. He just seemed dead. It was coincidence that he caught his breath and woke up just when the magician spoke the spells and made the signs."

"No, no. It was just a trick—don't you see? They planned it. They had it all worked out. The king pretended to die so that his magician could bring him back to life today so that the celebration of the rebirth of the year would become, more fundamentally, a celebration of his return. That's clever politics, the cunning magic trick of a clever king." That was the opinion of Bhairavagupta, the sorcerer, the *abhicārin*, the king's guru, who had initiated the monarch into the left-hand rites.

"You're saying that because you weren't there. You don't like it that Vishvasiddhi accomplished what you yourself would like to have done. The perceptions of a rival have no more significance than those of a lover." Bhairavagupta's feelings of rivalry were not unfounded. Eight years earlier Vishvasiddhi, then an itinerant magician, had come from Anga and performed for the court. So dazzled were they by the illusions that were presented—endless waters from a bowl, a mango tree that grew before their very eyes, a confounding levitation—that Amaruka invited the wanderer to stay and ornament his court. And he commissioned Vishvasiddhi to keep an eye on Bhairavagupta: "I want you to make sure that his magic is not just conjuring tricks. Does the holy ash that he produces from his palm really manifest from thin air, or is it some sleight of hand? I don't mind being fooled by you because you admit that you're fooling me. But him—I want to trust him. You must tell me if I can."

Mayeshvari, watched by Indragopa, sat on the women's platform next to Surasundari, her closest friend among the sixty-four wives of Amaru. She was

married by the king for her grace and skill with certain toys, and just as Mayeshvari had left a son behind, so she had abandoned her children—twin boys—to
become a queen in Kashmir. "The king hasn't said a word all night," Surasundari
whispered to her friend as she embraced her. "He just stares at us. What's wrong?
Was it the fall? What do you think?"

Mayeshvari did not answer her but, made aware by her that the king was
looking at them, placed her hand upon Surasundari's breast and kissed her; done
in court with just enough abandon to delineate the delicate limits of public
propriety and just enough restraint to promise pleasures remaining to be realized
in private, that always gave a certain pleasure to the king. Indragopa watched them
no less attentively than Amaruka.

The officer in charge of the precious betel from Anga, after having served the
king and his highest ranking officers, kneeled before the women that they might
choose a leaf. Chewing slowly, savoring it, with Surasundari's head resting in her
lap, Mayeshvari watched the boy announced by the doorkeeper: "A magician
requests that he may be permitted to perform before the king." As he took his
place before the raised platform, Vishvasiddhi smiled at him with all the affection
that the old, in certain trades, if they are generous and truly love their discipline,
often feel for young practitioners of their art or craft.

"I understand that the king has offered a reward to any magician who can
perform the Rope Trick," the boy, unruffled by the ruler's expressionlessness,
announced with the confidence he had learned from watching his father play. He
wanted to amaze his mother in ways that Muladeva must once have done. "Send
the treasurers to count out the gold while I, Indradatta, proceed to satisfy royal
curiosity."

Indragopa showed the rope that appeared pliant and normal, stretched it out
straight upon the ground, then, unseen and unguessed by anyone who watched
except Vishvasiddhi and Mayeshvari, he tugged tight the concealed gut cord that
interlocked the kid goat vertebrae around which the rope had been braided, and
then the rope, rigid and stiff, was raised as a pole for the monkey to scale. "You!
Boy! Take this jewel, my offering to Indra," the magician ordered, handing
Vrishakapi the small pouch. "Go on, climb the rope. Up! Higher! Quickly! Climb
into Indra's heaven. Give him my offering; take what he gives you for me and
return at once."

The courtiers and courtesans, everyone except the still and silently observing
king, laughed at the parody of the Rope Trick, laughed all the more when the
monkey refused to obey the boy's playfully angry orders to return: "Come back!
Get down here my son! Come back." Vrishakapi screeched defiantly.

The magician displayed the knife, placed the blade across his leg, slapped his
hand down upon it, drew the blade across the palm grimacing with mock pain,
and then, with a gesture and a scream—"Ho!"—the slice was sent from his hand
to seek the monkey. Vrishakapi slid down the rope and, much to the amusement

of the courtiers, pretended to be dead. The young magician kneeled down by his pet monkey, placed his head against the chest, his fingers by the nostrils, and announced it: "He's dead—no breath, no pulse—my son is dead!"

The monkey remained limp as he was dropped into the wicker basket. Indragopa performed the basket trick, reviving the monkey with magic mango leaves, and was applauded by the court. He bowed first to the king and then to Mayeshvari, who reciprocated with a smile.

"And now the king's magician."

Vishvasiddhi stood where Indragopa had performed. He waved the peacock feathers with a yellow-waxen spotted hand that was still agile and sure in its movements, graceful in the sleights, and full of magic. The stains upon his neck and temples from the blue-black dye with which he tried to hide his gray hair and beard lent the countenance at once a melancholy and a trace of mirth that was enhanced by the shimmering highlights that played within his eyes. "Make obeisance to the feet of Indra whose name is one with magic, and to the feet of Shambara whose glory was firmly established in illusions. I can make the moon appear on earth or a mountain in the sky. I can conjure fire out of water or water out of fire, earth from thin air or thin air from earth!" The magician recited it with a laugh, then bowed, and stood before the king. As he applied a collyrium to the royal eyes, insisting that it would prompt a magic vision, the courtiers watched with pleasure. Vishvasiddhi waved the wand, muttered the mantras, and then cried out for all to hear: "Tell us, tell us what you see! Describe the illusion."

"I see you," the king answered softly. "And I see the courtiers gathered, the courtesans, the officers, the servants, the uneaten food, the burning lamps. That's the illusion that I see."

Vishvasiddhi abruptly laughed to cover his confusion and embarrassment. The court was uneasy, Bhairavagupta glad. "And the gods? Don't you see Brahma on his lotus or Shiva wearing the crescent moon, Vishnu with his discus, or Indra wielding his net? What do you really see?"

"Nothing," the king calmly replied. And the courtiers laughed but were then stunned to silence at the audacity of the child who, with the monkey on his shoulder, glancing at Mayeshvari, swaggered up to where he had performed.

"The old man's magic has obviously dried up. A younger, fitter, craftier conjurer is needed in this court. I would say that's me. But boasting's easy. So I challenge this old man to match his magic against mine. As in the holy places philosophers enter into debate, as in the great courts poets of the king compete for the title of king of poets, as in the heavens Indra and Shambara contest each other with their magic, so let this old man and me each show our best illusion, just one trick. Then you decide: who is the world's greatest magician?"

To the amusement of all but Vishvasiddhi and the king, the competition was arranged for the next week.

"If I win?" Vishvasiddhi asked.

"I'll be your servant, an assistant for your tricks, or, if that's not a prospect that pleases you, then I'll leave the valley—whatever you wish. And you can have anything you ask of me—even my son, this monkey Vrishakapi."

"And if you win?" the old magician tried to laugh as the courtiers did.

"Then your post belongs to me. I'll be the king's magician. And something else—if I win I want your skull. I want it for my alms bowl." The boy's laughter prompted echoes from Bhairavagupta.

"You mean you'd have me killed?" the incredulous magician asked.

"No, no. I'll take it when you die. You're old and I'm young—I can wait for your death. I can wait, and while I do you'll serve me, be my assistant. I'll have you climb the rope."

Bhairavagupta stopped laughing as he thought about it: "No, no, it's just too good. This is yet another trick. Of course, these magicians stick together, share their secrets, help each other out. The boy's the old man's confederate for sure. They've planned this whole spectacle, this a-bit-too-dramatic illusion. And the king's in on it, I'm sure. It's just a trick."

"It's just a trick," Mandana Mishra, on that same night, said to his wife with a certain certainty. "Do you understand what Shankaracharya has done, his cunning countermove to your challenge? He's in hiding. Don't you see the trick? His disciples have spread the rumor that he has left his body—something no man can do. They've got the gossip spreading—Shankaracharya has entered the body of some dead king with many queens in order to learn the arts of love from them without pollution. When we meet again, he'll claim that he speaks with authority on all matters, that he has some basis for rejecting the pleasures of domestic life. He's no doubt reading Dattaka on love while giving hearsay time to become reality. We need a countertrick, something to expose the truth, if we're to triumph in debate. Help me think of something. Aren't women good at that, at deceiving their deceivers?"

The wife of Mandana Mishra laughed, and far away, Mayeshvari, quietly, quietly smiling, tiptoed into the chambers of the king, crept up on him like the hunter on the goat, closed in upon the man who sat cross-legged on the floor, his breath steady, still, so still, and kneeling behind him, she gently placed her hands over his already closed eyes to whisper, to ask him to try to guess which one of his sixty-four concubines she was. Silence. "Who am I?" she asked again. Again silence, and again she asked, and silence. "Why won't you play?" she asked, feigning sulkiness. "Why won't you try to answer? Are you angry or sad? Did the fall today hurt you? Should I massage or kiss or gently breathe a lover's breath upon these temples? Why won't you play? Who am I? Guess who! Whose fingers touch you now? Whose long, painted nails glide down your neck like this and come to rest, here, and here, like this?" She softly kissed the neck. "Who am I?"

"Bashkali asked Bahva about the nature of the self three times, and the latter remained silent," the king spoke without expression in his voice. "Finally Bahva answered, 'I teach, but you do not listen. Silence is the *ātman.*' I have told you who you really are. Now you—tell me who you think you are."

Mayeshvari laughed, rose, walked around the king and kneeled: "Is it a game? A guessing game?"

"No, it's not game," the king strangely whispered. Silence again. Understanding that he could not expect her to discriminate between the illusion and reality, he hesitated, then spoke again: "Listen carefully and try to understand. I am called Shankaracharya. Some months ago in Kashi, on the banks of the Ganga, I met with the Vedic ritualist and householder Mandana Mishra in debate. His wife, having forced me, through the subtle, cunning, clever application of forensic strategies, to agree that true wisdom must encompass a knowledge of all aspects of life, challenged me with questions about the amatory arts and erotic sciences. By means of magical powers accrued through ascetic practices, I was able to divine the future, to see the death of your King Amaruka, and decided there and then that, unbeknownst to anyone but my closest disciples, I would, again by means of magic prowess, leave the celibate form of the renouncer to enter and animate the body of the king at the very moment of his death and then learn from his sixty-four famous wives, each in turn, all of the arts of love. This is the first of the sixty-four nights that I shall spend here with you, mastering what I need to know without corrupting the chaste body of the abstainer. Then I shall return to answer the challenge of the ritualist's wife, to repeat, but from experience, what I have always taught: that *brahman* alone is real. All else is illusory. Even the ideas of bondage and liberation are false notions conjured up by *māyā*. Tricks. The appearance, transformation, and disappearance of the serpent do not abide in the rope. Beware of the serpent. There is neither death nor birth, neither a rope that binds, nor a soul that is bound, neither a seeker of liberation, nor one who has found it. These are the tricks the mind plays upon the mind. I shall do this, and yet I shall not do this. It is all magic, not really done, but seeming done so that others, enmeshed in the net, will think it done, see it done, and hear that revelation of the truth. By that truth the debate will be won."

The king closed his eyes, was silent for a moment, then opened them and, still without expression, spoke to the amused Mayeshvari again. "Now tell me what part you play in this magic show, this evanescent spectacle. Tell me about the name and form that pass for what you really are. Who are you?"

She laughed, leaned forward in a reverential bow, glanced up seductively, then reclined before him on her side, reaching out to stroke his leg. "Who should I be tonight? A consort for the left-hand ritual of the dark shawl? Do you want to initiate me? Or should I initiate you into my mysteries? Should I be Kali taking on some lovely human form for you? Or should I be some devoted wife reborn— Savitri, Draupadi, Queen Bhanumati? Tell me—do you want to make love to a chaste wife of your own or rape the chaste, unwilling wife of another? Should I sigh with contentment as I yield to my duty, or scream with terror as I am taken by force? Or should I be like you? Yes, I'm a Buddhist nun and in my meditations have come to realize that pain and pleasure, sorrow and joy, renunciation and indulgence, are one and the same. Yes, take me, show me the middle path, make love to me that I may be certain that pleasure is no less a vanity than my renunciation or my virginity. No." She softly laughed. "We've done that. Who should I be? Tell me. Who should I say that I am? Which story should I tell? Which part should I play? What will arouse you most tonight?"

"Tell me the truth," the king said unhesitatingly.

"No, no," she giggled. "That's not what you want—the truth is never arousing. It never stirs the flesh. Illusions are what inspire love—thus our ornaments, our garments, the collyrium that makes the eyes seem to reach all the way to the delicate, jeweled ear. Tell me the lie you want to hear tonight."

The king repeated it: "Tell me the truth."

"The truth," the concubine playfully restrained the laugh. "I see. I understand the game. The truth: my husband is a ritualist, Mandana Mishra by name. I have always loved Shankara more than him, but you were celibate. Thus I challenged you, knowing full well, by the powers of my magic, the secret magic that women share, just what you'd do. So here I am in the body of Mayeshvari who died of love upon hearing of the death of her King Amaru. Thus my trick!" she laughed once more without restraint. "It's done with such perfection. Oh, the wonder of it! Yes, I planned it all. In Kashi, sixty-four days from now, you shall forfeit the debate, disgraced by love like Indra in his lust for Ahalya, like Kichaka in his lust for Draupadi, like Ravana in his lust for Sita. And you will not care. For tonight I shall teach you that love is a higher knowledge and more precious experience than that *brahman* of which you philosophers speak. Tonight I shall love you, defeat you, and in that defeat you'll find an exquisite victory."

It startled the king—the slight sorrow with which he looked at her did not seem sham. "Tell me the truth," he said again. "The truth."

"Oh, I see," she smiled. "That's the game tonight, the love game invented by the king. I'm to pretend that you're a chaste philosopher who has never held a woman in his arms so that you can make love to me, Mayeshvari, for the very first time, to let you know the thrill again of first union, to feel again that intense desire that is marked by fear, full of anxiousness, yes, I know my love—the first time of making love, retrievable only by magic, when ineptitude is forgivable, when each part of the body surprises, and each touch is full of wonder. I know the game. Don't I? To make the truth a lie, the reality a sweet illusion. Is that where you'll find your pleasure? Is that the game? Should I say my real name, reveal my real self to you for the sake of tonight's illusion?"

"Yes, tell the truth."

"I am Mayeshvari, dear Shankara," she giggled, "the daughter of the magician Vaitalaki and courtesan Lilavati. I left my husband, the itinerant magician Muladeva, to become a queen in Kashmir, one of sixty-four beautiful concubines who serve you, Amaruka, the king who once filled the body that is now yours. You had taken me because of my skill in conjuring. I made the ring disappear from your finger, and when, in bewilderment, you asked me where it could be, I held up my hand to show you that it, your own ring, inset with nine gems to appease the nine planets, was here on my finger. Remember?"

She held up her hand to show him that while he had been distracted by her story, she had done the trick again. "Now take the ring," she softly sighed. "Pull it gently, gently from my finger. And now another sleight. Watch carefully. Here, the knot on my girdle, watch it come undone as if by itself, unknotted through the magic powers of desire. And now another trick, the greatest trick of all, the loveliest deception in the three worlds . . ."

The magician Vishvasiddhi, anxiously waiting for Mayeshvari in her room, sticking his finger through the fine ivory bars of the pigeon cage that hung in her window, imitated the pigeon's cry.

"That pigeon," she laughed as she entered. "I have my suspicions about that pigeon. One morning after feeding it, I left the cage door open by mistake and it flew away. I was very dismayed but then delighted when, to my surprise and wonder, it returned just before dusk. I decided to try something, to intentionally let the bird fly off. And once again, and to my utter pleasure, it returned. So, often at dawn, confident that my pigeon will return to me, I open the door to the cage and the pigeon flies away only and always to return for the evening. There's nothing unusual in that perhaps, but just yesterday I noticed a slight, very slight, discoloration on the beak."

The magician looked for it.

"No, you won't see it. That's the point. Sometimes it's there and other times it's not. Do you understand? How would you, as a magician, explain it? There's only one way. There are," she laughed with wide, wonder-filled eyes, "really two pigeons, identical except for the slight discoloration on the beak of one. Do you see? Meeting that first time the one escaped from the cage, they decided to trick me. Because they seemed, one to the other, like images in a mirror, they thought they might perform a little magic trick. They realized that by switching places, in alternation they could both have both the pleasures of freedom and the luxuries that come with captivity. Both are free, and yet both are cared for. That's possible only through the sleight. What do you think?"

"That may be," the magician frowned. "But there's something much more urgent for us to discuss right now. Tell me, how did the king seem to you just now? Tell me, was there anything strange about his behavior?"

"Not in the least," Mayeshvari laughed. "Because his behavior is always strange, there is never anything strange about his strange behavior. Listen, I was teasing about the pigeons . . ."

The magician interrupted her: "Please, I'm very concerned about the king. You know the trick I tried to show the court tonight? Do you know why it failed?

After I painted the magic collyrium upon his eyes, waved my peacock-feather wand, and recited the mantras, he was supposed to say, 'Wonderful! Strange! I see Brahma on his lotus, Shiva wearing the crescent moon in his hair, Vishnu with his bow and discus, Indra with his net, the hosts of gods and celestial nymphs dancing, their anklets jingling! Wonderful! Amazing! Marvelous!' Two days ago I had prompted him, worked out the trick, and he had laughed, 'Bravo, they'll never suspect that I, the king, could be a confederate in a mere trick. They'll never guess. We'll fool them, my friend, we'll fool them all.' "

"Instead of playing a trick on them," Mayeshvari laughed, "he played a trick on you. That's all."

"That's one possibility," the magician responded gravely. "Here's another: something's wrong with him, an injury from the fall today. When I came to him, he was motionless, dead it seemed to me, so much so that I was as startled as any observer that my magic spell worked. Imagining that it was a trick inspired by our plan for the trick at court, I couldn't help but wink to congratulate him on his game. But now, because of what happened tonight, I'm afraid that it's possible that it was no game, not that he really died of course, but that he was truly injured, almost dead, and that it has disturbed his mind, destroyed parts of his memory. I suspect he might be mad."

The courtesan laughed all the more as she shook her head. "It's just like the pigeons. Where does the net of illusions end; where does it begin? My guess is that he's playing a trick on both of us. He knew you'd come to me after I left his bed. He knew that, upset over the failure of your trick, you'd come to ask about his behavior and that I'd tell you what went on between us tonight. It's a fine trick."

"No," the old magician insisted with what seemed a real urgency. "Perhaps it's not just a trick. Perhaps he's mad."

Mayeshvari laughed still more. "You prefer that thought more than the thought that you, the great magician, have been tricked by an amateur. There's another possibility. Perhaps it's real magic." She shook her head, lightly laughed again, yawned, stretched, and told the story that the king had told to her, the story of the holy man who had entered the body of a king to learn of love.

"If that's true, or if you can convince me to believe it," the magician frowned, "if I imagine that there is real magic in the world, that there's a man who can foresee the future, leave his body, fly through the air, and enter another form, then I'm the one who's mad."

It was dawn. The pigeon in the cage ruffled its wings, and Mayeshvari approached the old magician and put her arm tenderly around his shoulders to comfort him. When he closed his eyes to rest in her caress, it occurred to her that their conversation might have been yet another magic trick, an extension of the net, that the old man had played it out, shammed sadness and concern, just so that she would hold him, just so that he might touch her. The courtesan imagined that the old man loved her.

THE SKULL OF VISHVASIDDHI

Unaware that the sun had risen, the disciples of Shankara, sitting cross-legged around the still, lunar-white and waxen body of the cool renouncer in a secret cave near Kashi, meditated upon death and upon their teacher's words: "The household asks after one's health as long as life remains in the flesh; but when breath is gone, the body expired, the wife will fear her beloved's corpse. We enjoy the pleasures of love for the sake of happiness only until disease or age seizes the flesh. So adorn yourselves with rags for the road. Set out upon the path of renunciation. Say: 'I am not, you are not, the world is not. . . .' Then why should you feel any sorrow?" Among them Padmapada feared that there was no magic, that his teacher was truly dead, and that no magic could return the dead to life. He whispered Shankara's words to himself for consolation: "Infatuation for such things as the body, any concern with death, is itself a vast net of death, a hunter's snare."

And in the night to come, much to Surasundari's dismay, King Amaruka of Kashmir spoke those very words to the courtesan as she embraced him.

Vishvasiddhi found Indragopa by the river Vitasta, dangling his feet in the cold waters: "I've been looking everywhere for you. I must speak with you about our contest."

The boy laughed contemptuously. "Look Vrishakapi, the old man's afraid. He's going to try to find out what we're up to, what trick we're going to perform, the magic that transforms his skull into my alms bowl."

"No, that's not it," the old magician insisted with a smile. "On the contrary, I'm going to tell you what trick I am going to do. I'll reveal it all to you."

The young magician shrugged his shoulders and spit red juice into the river, "Why would you do that? Do you think I'd trust a magician? Leave me alone. I'll see you at the contest."

The old man sat down next to Indragopa. "Please, Indradatta, listen to me. Perhaps you can't ever trust a magician not to trick you, but you can always trust a magician to keep a secret. It's our *mantragupta* vow. I'm going to let you in on the secret of my trick. Please. Young magicians must listen to older magicians. That's the way it's always been, the way it must be, or there will be no more magic in the future. Didn't your father teach you that?"

"I have no father," the boy said automatically, and it made the old conjurer lightly laugh. "You have no father, and I have no son; also, you have no son, and I have no father! We need each other; we complete each other. You can't really be a magician without a son, nor can you be one without a father. Thus I think it's right for us to talk. You don't have to trust me. But I do want you to help me. I want your assistance for the illusion that I plan to perform for the contest. Bhairavagupta will be watching me, trying to expose my devices. He'll never expect that you, my rival, are my accomplice."

"Get Mayeshvari to help you."

"No, she can't help. I need you."

Curiosity more than compassion seduced the boy away from his natural reluctance to listen. The old man explained that he was going to perform the Buried Alive illusion, that he would be inhumed in the earth for two months without air, water, or food. "The design for the escape is perfect, absolutely indetectable, but complicated. I'm not so strong, and I need help in the construction of it and the preparation of the site. Of course you're wondering why you should help me. All magicians are confederates of all others. That's our law. But it's more than that—there's something in it for you. The fifty-six days that my trick allows you before it's time for your illusion will give you the time you need to prepare and practice for the magic that I'm going to teach you, an illusion that will establish you as the greatest magician in the world. Yes, I want you to win. I'm old, and it is with such difficulty that I now perform. Besides, I think my king is mad. I want to leave. I want to rest. No more illusions. But there should be some dignity in my retirement. I was humiliated in the court last night by the king and you. You made a fool of me. You disgraced a fellow magician. Make it up to me. Let my last illusion be magnificent and then take my place in the court with honor."

"What trick could you teach me that would be so great as to insure my victory?"

"The greatest trick in the world, the illustrious illusion," the old man laughed—"the Rope Trick. Not your amusing little version, not just parts of it, not a theatrical representation of it. No. The real Rope Trick. I'll teach you the secret of how to cut a man to pieces and put him back together again, to make whole what has been rent, to return the dead to life."

Lured by the bait, the boy entered Indra's net. He rose from the bank to follow the old magician, at first to listen willingly and then, impressed by the deceptive design and cunning mechanics of the escape for Buried Alive, to take part eagerly in the preparations for the illusion. The boy did what needed to be done in the secrecy of night. Although it naturally occurred to him, not without an odd pleasure, that because all of the rigging for the escape was in his hands, he could fix it so that the magician died in the grave and then win the contest by doing the trick himself, he nevertheless followed all of Vishvasiddhi's commands carefully and did not ask about the Rope Trick for several days.

"Do you read?" the teacher asked; "No," the student answered. Vishvasiddhi explained that he had a book, the *Indrajālasūtra*, "a skeleton of magic, the bones of it. . . . The Rope Trick is explained in it. But the secret's not correct. Let's say the book were stolen, lost; that it fell into the wrong hands. If they ignore the warning on the book, which of course they'll do, they'll open it eagerly, with curiosity and even greed, to discover the method for the Rope Trick. The trick will be on them: the boy or monkey, man or woman whom they cut apart will die and will not, by any magic, come back to life. But for you, my son, my dear Indradatta, for you I'll reveal the truth behind the trick. Be patient, my son, and you'll accomplish it."

As they worked, the boy asked the man why he had no son, and Vishvasiddhi told a story: he had been married to a Dom woman, a basket maker, an attendant at the burning grounds, and she had been pregnant eight times—seven boys, one girl. Each infant had been born lifeless. "To see the birth of something dead brings a strange sadness . . ." It was, it seemed to him, as if he impregnated her with death. And the last stillborn child, the girl, took her mother with her.

And as they worked, the man asked the boy why he had no father, and Indragopa told a story: "Long ago in the city of Ujjayini there was born a magician, Muladeva by name, son of Shambaradasa, adept at jugglery, accomplished in all the arts of deception . . ." And finally they were done, ready for Vishvasiddhi to perform. On the eve of the contest, the old magician told the child how the Rope Trick might be done, and he seemed to understand. As a gesture of his trust, the boy told the old man his real name.

A set of platforms had been constructed for the king to witness the magic show. Just below Amaruka's platform, eight of his queens, Mayeshvari and Surasundari among them, posed. There was a platform for the Brahmins, one for the officers of the royal army, and another for visiting dignitaries from the south. Bhairavagupta sat with the chaplain and chief ministers. Guards kept the people back, letting only servants through—they ran back and forth from the site to the palace with food, drink, and betel. Announcing the match, the doorkeeper proclaimed that the challenged magician, Vishvasiddhi, servant of the king, would perform his illusion first.

The old man bowed before the royal retinue. He looked into the eyes of the king, Amaruka, then into the eyes of the child, Indragopa, then into the eyes of the courtesan, Mayeshvari. He waved the peacock-feather wand, shook the damaru, then spoke: "Make obeisance to the feet of Indra whose name is connected with magic, and to the feet of Shambara whose glory was firmly established in illusions. I can make the moon appear on earth or a mountain in the sky. I can conjure fire out of water or water out of fire, earth from thin air or thin air from earth! Of all these illusions, I have chosen one most perfect, a trick not on you, but on Yama, the magic of release from death. I shall be buried alive for two months without air, water, or food. Please, come forward, inspect the grave that has been dug for me by the king's gardener." The gardener was called forward to swear that there was nothing unusual about the hole, as the army officers, the chief of police, Bhairavagupta, the chaplain, and Indragopa, playing his part, had the honor of inspecting it.

Displaying and offering for inspection a large bag of white linen into which the thousand names of the goddess had been sewn in gold, he looked once more at the child and the courtesan and then let the magic proceed following his instructions. Once he was crouched, his hands crossed over his heart, his legs curled up, within the bag, the tailors sewed closed the mouth of it. Then, as it was bound with ropes, the form of the old magician became dead still. As the bundle was lowered into the earth, those gathered close could hear the muffled mantras from within. The gardener began to shovel dirt onto the linen that was embroidered with the holy names. After a thick layer of dirt covered the body, several slabs of stone broad enough to cover the hole were set in place, then stamped down, and over them more earth, moistened and patted down with spades to make the surface of the grave smooth and compact. The courtiers stared at the ground silently. Nothing. The place would have gone unnoticed if the soldiers had not been stationed there to watch and mark it. It was announced that all would return in fifty-six days for the grand exhumation.

A poet commissioned to eulogize the king complained to Bhairavagupta that the magic was without dramatic effect, that it hardly inspired the essential sentiment of wonder. "That the trick takes two months is, I suppose, supposed to make the illusion more spectacular. The time, meant to enhance our amazement into wonder, has the reverse effect. We're bound to lose interest. In fact," he laughed in a mannered way, "I'm bored already."

"We'll see what sentiments there are when they dig the rascal up," Bhairavagupta, who disliked the poet even more than he disdained Vishvasiddhi, mumbled. "Dead or alive, we'll see." It confounded him: there had to be some surprise, some trick beyond the expected one of the magician's survival.

Conserving breath and energy, Vishvasiddhi worked slowly on the escape, the emergence from the earth to take place that night. Buried in dark ground, held by her, Vishvasiddhi, warmly swaddled in silk, then wool, then the holy linen, felt not the fear he feared might slow him but, oddly, a courage, even a delight, that quickened his spirit—every part of him at once caressed, dark, warm. Unimpeded, a pleasure, a feeling from childhood, returned to him the moment he had decided it: that he would set himself upon the path of renunciation. To wander again and forever. For an old magician named Vishvasiddhi to vanish in the infinite depths of earth, die or be transformed, so that a nameless, casteless, ageless renouncer might emerge from her, born, released, delivered into the infinite vistas of the night, was an illusion full of joy and wonder. Rag-clad, he'd wander just as he had done in childhood when, playing the damaru and gourd, he roved with his itinerant father from village to village to perform. Magic! Magic! See our show! Sometimes they'd play cities—Kashi, Pataliputra, Ujjayini—and there and then, buried in the earth, the old man remembered the child following his father through the bazaar, keeping his eyes on the long matted hair so as not to lose him as they made their way through the crowded streets.

As the knots in the ropes were undone and the seams in the bag loosened, the magician pushed slightly with his legs, arms, and neck, and earth yielded. A little more. He found the first bladder; it gave him a bit more air and then, deflated, a bit more room. He dug his fingers into the earth, reached for the cords that had been set by Indragopa and pulled, then softly pushed again, pulled and pushed: another bladder, more air, more space. Earth responded, and he rested to listen for his father's faint, faint, almost silent laughter in the earth and smell the mother there, all around him, holding him within her there and willing to let him go. Odor of earth. He breathed it through the cloth.

THE SKULL OF VISHVASIDDHI

Seed syllables of magic hymns were buried in her like jewels. Mantras were in the earth: "Ample goddess blood-drinker milk-giver." He heard them louder: "Patient protectress full, full of grain seed food memories, wondrous dark nourisher and perfect justice, fire in you water in you air in you." He heard them clearer: "Butter gold death and death in you, enchantments, as if by spells, as I'm in you as sap of trees to come and go, rock and stone and dust in us is yours, in you, coming going coming going, ether, seasons in you for you, bones, rocks the birds that fly through earth, you, the scent in us is yours, yours the deathbirth, the snake and scorpion and worm and egg, buried to vanish and return, magic magic, buried alive, mother mother full of blood womb of wealth, mud marrow, earth bones mother bones, take the rain, hold up your mountains for me as Vishnu spreads you out, spreads you open, spreads desires to fill you let me go spread me let me go, Prithvi, Akshaya, earth spread deliver bear release. . ." The magician was faint and dizzy and could not distinguish the directions: "Mother mother dark endless source of magic." He turned his head to find the breath, another bladder, tugged on the rope again, pulled it in close, and then finally felt the edges of the buried net that gave him bearings in the earth. He rested once again, then gently, slowly, worked the net, worked it pleased with how perfectly Indragopa had rigged it. Now set, another bladder; he tugged hard and it worked—the buried skinsacks of water broke, seeped, sucked into earth, left their space for him and suppleness to burrow in, to find the other bladders, the spaces, finally the hollow, the cave, the long and secret passage that would crumble closed behind him, and then the night. Again the old magician rested.

While Indragopa could picture it, could conjure up the old magician in his mind, squeezing through the earth, he did not know the end. Vishvasiddhi had not revealed the climax of the trick to anyone, had not told the boy that when the grave was opened, he would not be there. Vanished, gone, he would have disappeared into the earth. And neither had the magician told the boy of the fiery, dark blood in his urine and stool, the bloating in his stomach. He had not spoken to him of death. It would have detracted from the effect of his last magic trick: the illusion of deathlessness, liberation from death and birth, freedom from time and space, from fear and from desire.

Again the magician pulled on the net, pushed once more, turned his head from side to side, tugged the cloth from his face, and opened his eyes: the stars were infinite in the mountain night, crystalline-eyed and threaded jewels forming and holding together the filaments of Indra's all-encompassing net, and the magician ached with the immensity of it, ached with the joy of deliverance.

In the morning, at the beginning of the watch, one of guards put his ear against the ground. Nothing. He did it every day, and every day—nothing.

Indragopa was anxious for it to be over, anxious to witness the triumph of the old magician. Another trick: without telling Vishvasiddhi, he had decided that he would forfeit victory, that he would announce to the courtiers gathered at the exhumation that he had no magic as wondrous as that of the royal magician.

Just as the eunuchs always permitted Vishvasiddhi into the harem chambers because of his age, they allowed Indragopa through because of his youth, and Mayeshvari received him with the courtesy that she, as a magician herself, would have extended to any conjurer. It would be customary for each of them to show the other their version of Cups and Balls and then, if both were sufficiently impressed, to exchange a trick or two.

"This man's going to Anga," the boy said as he pointed to the red cloth ball, then slapped the courtesan's golden cup over it. "This man's going to Kashi. And this man—he's staying here in Kashmir."

When Mayeshvari, showing her rendition to the boy, vanished the white silk ball, she laughed her sly laughter: "Gone, gone, completely gone—he's become a Buddha, nowhere to be found, never to return!"

"My turn again," the boy smiled. "This feat will amaze you. I am sure of it. I have the power to reveal both past and future. Let's start with the past."

He held her hand, palm upward, as he revealed the pageant of her transmigration through the great round of existence, sometimes looking into the delicate hand, at other times gazing into the eyes that were filled with lamplight. Through the window, moonlight from the crest in Shiva's hair danced in reflection on the gloss of lac upon her lower lip.

"Your first earthly incarnation was in Veshali thousands of years ago—a mysterious birth indeed. Do you remember? You were discovered by a gardener in a grove, at the foot of a mango tree. He named you Ambapali and raised you. Yes, you grew into a beautiful girl, as brilliant and graceful as you were fair, accomplished in all of the sixty-four arts, gentle and yet strong. All men who so much as saw you wanted to marry you: kings would have been willing to give up their kingdoms, merchants their fortunes, and holy men their vows, for your hand. You, who were proficient in all the arts, learned our art, conjuring, from the magician whose name I bear—Indradatta. Remember? The gardener installed you as a courtesan in the holy city of Kashi, for if you were to be possessed by one man only, rivalry and jealousy between men would certainly arise. There would be wars fought for your sake. So you were to belong to all men. But there was one being for whom you felt a special devotion—Lord Buddha. When you heard that he was to speak nearby, you went, together with your great retinue of exquisite beauties, to see him and, descending from your golden chariot to approach him humbly on foot, you bowed and seated yourself near the enlightened one to listen to his words. After the sermon you invited Lord Buddha and all of his monks to dine at your splendid mansion. This part of the story everyone knows. But what they do not know is that when he came for that dinner, he instructed you, explaining that it was your destiny and your duty to keep the birth of a courtesan for century after century, thirty-four times. You're over halfway there."

THE SKULL OF VISHVASIDDHI

Not believing him of course, but relishing his skill at the magician's patter, she was suitably amused. But when he came to her incarnation as Mayeshvari the magician, her amusement turned into an eerie astonishment. There was, it seemed, no way except by magic, real magic, that he could have known what he knew: that she was the daughter of Vaitalaki and Lilavati, who had married her to one Muladeva of Ujjayini. "I can see him—the matted hair, sharp eyes, and rough smile—squatting, elbows resting on his knees. He's cutting a rope in two, 'Short piece, long piece,' he says, 'father, son.' He wraps the cords around his hand . . ."

"Is there a child with him?" Mayeshvari, ensnared, anxiously interrupted.

"No," the boy answered, his eyes still closed. "He has no son." He played the moment of silence perfectly, as well as his father would have done. "There was a child once—your son—a boy named Indragopa. But he's dead, slain, dismembered, beheaded; a trick that didn't work . . ."

"Stop," Indragopa's mother cried, and the child looked into her eyes to divine the feelings in her heart. But, hiding them, she rose and dismissed the wandering young magician: "Go now. Go."

"Don't you want to hear the rest, the story of your future births? You're only halfway there, halfway to liberation. I have stories of distant lands and strange times. Don't you want to hear them?"

"No, please go."

Sitting by the lake at dawn, looking out over the water and into the mists of luminescent grays that softly fused the boundaries between water, earth, and sky, the boy pulled his limbs into his dark shawl for warmth and held Vrishakapi close to him. The branches of jujube and spindle trees shivered, and freshly burgeoned leaves began to tremble. The boy lay down and, with the monkey in his arms, wept himself to sleep upon the earth.

The first day of the week, fifty-six days after Vishvasiddhi's burial, sixty-four days into the new year, the platforms for the courtiers were once again arranged, and there were bets among the spectators on the magician's skill: alive or dead? The odds were even.

Indragopa, as the challenger formally seated on a tripod by the site, looked for Mayeshvari among the women stationed near the king, and as the doorkeeper announced what everybody knew, the boy scrutinized his mother's face for some hint as to what was buried in the cryptic heart. Nothing.

The gardener did the digging. Concealing the joy he felt over his expectations of seeing the old magician once again, of pleasing him with the surprise of victory, a gift to honor the master, Indragopa shammed detachment. As the slabs of stone were hoisted by guards, Indragopa felt the crowd's suspense; he recognized the mood from when his father lifted up the lid of the wicker basket in which he had so many times been sacrificed—hearts were quickened, mouths silenced, and all was still. The sepulchre was open. The gardener cried out: "He's not there! Just the sack, the white linen sack. He's gone!"

The astonished crowd looked to the sorcerer Bhairavagupta for some explanation. Stunned himself, he hesitated; then suddenly inspired, he smiled—it was perfect. He laughed as he walked toward the child and the empty grave.

"Thus my trick!" he laughed again. "It is done. My trick. A magnificent illusion finally completed and with such perfection. Oh, the wonder of it! But nothing is impossible for one who knows the formulas for the rite, the secret magic called *śāmbarī*." He laughed again. "At last I can explain it! At last! Eight years ago it happened: I uttered the incantations, pronounced the spells, made the offerings, focused all my powers, and conjured up a spirit, a *vidyādhara*, the perfect likeness of a man, an illusion so realistic that you—all of you—imagined him to be formed of flesh and blood. My magic! The power of Bhairavagupta! In order to insure a place at court for him, I had him come as a magician (the part the *vidyādhara*s most like to play) to perform, knowing full well that his heavenly magic would so inspire wonder in our king—no less than it dazzles Indra—that he would be installed here with us. Vishvasiddhi you called him, the name I gave him! This was not an entertainment—no sleights, no props, no tricks. No, this was real magic. Real. By my great magic, I conjured him! I created him!"

The sorcerer turned to the astonished boy and loudly laughed again: "What do you say Indradatta? In your bag of tricks do you have any comparable magic to perform? Or do you concede the contest? Do I win the prize? Who is the greatest magician in the world?"

The stunned and startled boy, confused, not understanding why Vishvasiddhi had not risen from the grave, forfeited victory just as he had planned to do.

The audience, unnerved, broke the silence, rose out of the stillness, turned in turmoil to each other to say something, hear something, anything, to sort it out, to inspect the empty grave, to find some explanation, assurance, something that left the world intact. "It must be true," the chaplain said, "since there's no other way to explain it."

Looking for his mother in the scattering throng of courtiers descending from the platforms, Indragopa's eyes were suddenly turned by the sound of the scream: stepping down from his seat, the king had slipped and fallen.

"He's dead!" the chaplain cried in panic. "The king is dead—no breath, no pulse—he's dead!" Hurrying to his side, Bhairavagupta kneeled down by his patron, placed his head against the chest and his fingers by the nostrils. "*Om aim klīm hrim śrīm*," he muttered methodically and invoked Kahneshvari and Kali, Shambara and Indra, Bhairava Shiva and Vasudeva Krishna. He whispered into the king's ear: "This *māyā*, this magic trick I do, conceals me. Not everyone can see me—the unborn, undying one." He waved his hand about, palm down, produced holy ash from it, and sprinkled it on the king's forehead, his still lips and breast. "The king is dead."

"Do you understand?" the chaplain explained to the chief minister. "These past two months the king has, in reality, been dead, killed by the fall during the new year's hunt, seemingly brought back to life by Vishvasiddhi. Only a *vidyā-*

dhara could have done that. And once that heavenly magician, as conjured up by Bhairavagupta, had departed, the king had to die. Without the magician, there could be no illusion. No earthly magician, not even Bhairavagupta, can retrieve him. No earthly magic, no one, no thing, can truly bring back one who has died."

The body of the king was set upon the pyre for cremation, the last sacrifice.

As if by magic, the mouth suddenly gasped, the eyes opened wide, and the chaste Shankaracharya, in the cave near Kashi, sat up, stood and looked around him at the stunned disciples who, after a flashing moment of silent incredulity, all at once cried out with the joy of seeing their teacher returned to life, and with the wonder of witnessing such a miracle. They laughed, surprised with the delight of it, cheered with the wonder of it, and felt no impropriety in clamoring to the side of the philosopher to touch resurrected flesh. Padmapada and Sureshvara embraced him. The latter did so with a wink, for he suspected that his teacher had not ever really left that body, but that he had, as so many renouncers were capable of doing, simply suspended his breath and pulse. The trick was necessary, a way of teaching without words; words, though capable of directing the mind to the truth, too often obscured that truth, and led to further delusion. Shankaracharya stared silently at each one of them and smiled slightly, and the expression was understood by the chaste disciples as a sign that their teacher would defeat Mandana Mishra in debate. The ritualist would have to admit the ultimately ineluctable truth: *brahman* is real, the world is illusory, and the self, without birth or death, self-luminous, uncontained by flesh, is not different than *brahman.*

With Vrishakapi perched on his shoulder, carrying his basket of tricks in one hand and the damaru in the other, the young magician sat by the side of the road to rest. "It's fine. It's fine. Don't be afraid. We'll go south. Maybe back to Kashi. No, better yet, to Anga. We'll try to find the old magician." The boy smiled. "I want to get even with him for tricking me."

Smoke from the body of King Amaruka of Kashmir rose from the distant pyre, curled into the sky, higher, higher, toward the clouds, and Indragopa's gaze followed it. Dogs were barking. Above the eagles, hawks, and pariah kites that circled in the air, a great bank of softly billowed clouds, a white city, full of spreading caverns, aerial bazaars in which *vidyādhara*s performed ethereal magic, slowly turned into a white range of moving mountains, and a white herd of elephants slowly, softly drifted from it and rose to turn again, turn, settle, and transform again. Slowly the clouds rolled, loomed, a luminous white drifting dome, dark shadows beneath, grays curving into streaks and caverns, forms forming, light and dark the whites, the clouds. Indragopa looked at it. He saw it in the sky—made of cloud, the skull of Vishvasiddhi—and it made him laugh aloud.

He rose, and as Vrishakapi climbed onto his shoulder, he started to move. He played the damaru, Mahadeva's drum, at first slowly and softly, then faster and louder, and as he walked in time to the rhythm of it, he smiled with the pleasure of his confidence that the old magician would watch over him.

Historian's Notebook 3:

Magicians at Court

Magic cities carved from gauzy mountains of mist and light, from the penetrable, supple stone of sky, mind-conjured cities worn by wind, are more enduring than those monuments cut from stone, as persistent as they are pliant, with no substantiality to give way and nothing to be broken. Metamorphic metropolises of cloud, undulous and cumulous, their white temple spires curling, growing with the blowing wind, their white colonnades bending, then ascending into white ways and airy courtyards swelling white against azure-washed, wind-whisked arches, are where Gandharvas dwell—nimble dancers robed with laces of cloud, silent singers with nimbuses gracing white faces of cloud. Magic. The city fashioned by ethereal erosion and soft, slow implosion, drifting from white, white oblivion into blue blue and back to white again, is formed by earthly eyes surveying the penetralia of infinite skies, earthly ears searching deep silences for echoes of thunder and the cries of birds that have been cursed never to descend and blessed to soar forever in the infinite illusions of the heavenly magicians. The diaphanous city of cloud, vanishing and reappearing, ever-changing, unchanging, never-changing, its doors, windows, gates, and hatches opened by wind, beckoning, the same now as then, seen then as now, the source of magic, beckoning.

The ancient magician, scrutinizing the clouds and listening to the wind, pronounced his nephemantic oracles and waved his wand of calcinated bone or peacock feathers to move thunderheads to crack with rain. And, sooner or later, they did. It was all show. Magic: a seeming knowledge—the secret of the net, knowing how to tug it here to cause its movement there; a seeming energy—secured through austerities, piety, and faith in seeming; a seeming power—divined then divining, brandished by gods, flaunted by demons, and imitated by human beings in forests or in the courts of kings. Once there was magic: it is necessarily rooted in the past; the net must be fixed upon a distant hook. The power of magic, a trick itself, is always brought here and now from another time and space, a mysterious then and there; the greater the distance, the more magnificent the power.

The magician invoked Indra for the show. The eyes of the audience that does not imagine itself an audience are directed upwards: clouds, taking on shape after shape on the magic stage of sky, play the ministers of the protean lord of magicians, who "appears again and again in form after form, transforming his forms, performing his magic" (*Rgveda* 3.53.8). "Indra took on many forms by means of magic tricks" (*Jaiminīya Upaniṣad* 1.44).

Indra's magic was ecstatic and truculent—a weapon to slay demons of darkness and drought or liberate torrents of rain and gushing rivers from dungeon-dark clouds and tower-bright mountain glaciers. Lightning was his magic wand and thunder his magic word. And the magician on the stage or street now, with his gimmicked lota bowl, his wand and drum, gesture and utterance, knowing it or not, reiterates that primal magic spectacle.

"When the serpent Vritra flashed his fangs at you," the hieratic magician recited for Indra, "you became the hair of a horse" (*Rgveda* 1.32.12). In such sidereal battles the vanishing act was the defense; then the bewildered, wonder-weakened enemy was attacked with the net and ensnared. "Indra's net is vast, as big as this world, and with 'Indra's Net'—this magic—I enmesh, entrap, those people with darkness" (*Atharvaveda* 8.8.5–8). Casting his net, weaving a spell, utilizing the magic, Indra tricks his enemies into their destruction. The more one struggles to get out of the net—to figure out a magic trick—the more one is tangled and caught fast. Suspended between heaven and earth, with the four directions as the poles that support it, the net was envisioned by the magician who served the warrior chieftain. He chanted the magic hymn to Indra to insure the victory represented by the magic net. The warriors of the *Mahābhārata* carried mimetic nets consecrated to Indra: *indrajāla* was a divine weapon wielded by men. And still the people who approach Naseeb to buy rings or amulets from him after his performances often confess to do so in order to beguile an enemy: the boss at work, a competitor in business, some *bhūt*, or someone they think is doing *jādū* against them. The customers want to believe that Naseeb's magic is Tantric, a tradition in which adepts were believed to attain the prowess to accomplish six codified acts: attraction, subjugation, immobilization, eradication, pacification, and liquidation—a list that confirms the bellicose impulses behind the patronage of magicians.

The battlegrounds of gods and demons are inevitably depicted as stages upon which magic spectacles are performed: the sons of Ravana "were invincible warriors—all skilled in magic, all able to levitate and fly through the air" (*Rāmāyaṇa* 6.69.11). As with military camouflage, they were able to make themselves vanish and then reappear, to multiply themselves, or freeze others in a trance. Indrajit, Ravana's magician son, like Sorcar on the BBC, like every Indian stage magician today who can afford the apparatus, performed the Sawing-a-Lady-in-Half routine: "He performed a magic trick, created the illusion of Sita" (6.81.5), and with the enemy army of Rama surrounding him, he then appeared to slice her in two with his sword.

MAGICIANS AT COURT

The *Ṛgvidhāna,* in explaining how a certain hymn in the *Ṛgveda* (10.177) might be used to dispel such illusions, to ward off or counteract another's magic, differentiates two kinds of effective magic, two modes of *māyā—indrajāla* and *śāmbarī:* the magic of Indra and that of his archenemy, Shambara, a *dasya,* a demon of the clouds (4.23.1–2). In an Indian context, the categories white and black, right and left, high and low distinguish not the dynamics of the magic, but its function—apotropaic or goetic. Demons, ever eager to be imagined, can be kept at bay or conjured up.

The ancient mythologies, encrusted with and imbedded in psychologies, endure: in Sorcar Junior's film, *Gili Gili Gay,* twin magicians are pitted against each other in a battle that recapitulates the struggle of Indra and Shambara, Rama and Ravana. Histrionic magic reenacts a hieratic magic that purported to represent a heavenly, mythological magic. Myth invests the performance with power and meaning: in a park in Delhi in 1987, Chand Baba, without fire, cooked rice in a cloth that he had spread out over his lap, just as two Asuras in ancient myth cooked their rice without a visible fire, using the energy of magic (*Jaiminīya Brāhmaṇa* 3.168).

Indian magicians now and then, on the street and on the stage, have continued to invoke the names of the prototypical magicians—Indra, the wielder of the net of illusion, and Shambara, the spinner of the web of delusion. Constructing a magic castle in the sky, Shambara conjured up three demons from his bag of tricks—Snake, Rope, and Straw Mat—to guard the fortress while he slept. Because they were not real, without fear, desire, or a will to live, they were invincible (*Yogavaśiṣṭha* 4.25–34). There is a vulnerability outside the magic show, within it illusions of victory. Magic does not create the illusion, but illusion the magic. In defeating that demon of magic, Vishnu, in keeping with the conventions of the show, assimilated the potency of his magic. In later texts Vishnu supplants Indra as the divine prototype of the magician; in the *Mahābhārata* he is called Mahamayadhara, Bearer of the Great Magic.

Elsewhere others slay Shambara: once upon a time the fiendish magician kidnapped the infant Pradyumna and brought him to his wife, Mayavati, Lady Magic, charging her with his upbringing. Charmed by Pradyumna's beauty, she revealed the secrets of conjuring and sorcery to him and tutored him in the illusionary arts. Among the magicians of Shadipur today, the notion persists that, while females are never to perform magic in public after puberty, it is the woman, the mother, who is the Mayavati, who is to teach magic to the infant magicians. Just as the adolescent now ultimately challenges his father, first in play in the magic circle and then, in time, by leaving his father and setting out on his own, so the adolescent Pradyumna challenged Shambara to a battle, pitting the magic of the son against the magic of the father. The son inevitably wins. Krishna explained the victory: Mayavati, actually Pradyumna's wife in a previous incarnation, used her magic to bewitch the demon and cause him to kidnap the very child who would destroy him. Magic was as sexual as it was martial. The magician is tricked by magic, erotic or aggressive; gods and demons are as eager to be deceived as human beings (*Viṣṇu Purāṇa* 5.27).

The magician in ancient India, under royal patronage, was a priest functionally distinguished from other priests in his role, not of propitiating deities with praise and sacrifice but of dispelling the inauspiciousness accrued by mistakes in sacrifice or counteracting the efficient sacrifices of rival chieftains; the magician recited deadly spells and cast curses, performed exorcisms and divinations, effected cures for snakebite, poisoning, and diseases; with magic words and gestures, he chased away wild animals or birds of ill omen, brought the rains and good crops, and won over the hearts of desired women for his patron. The show was spectacular. The magician was indispensable to the king: *indrajāla* and *māyā* were codified as crucial arts and ancillary sciences within the larger science of politics and the more expansive art of kingship (*Matsya Purāṇa* 222.2–3). Governments, then as now, utilized all the appurtenances of magic—magic words and scepter-wands, sleights and misdirection, hidden wires and hatches, confederates and stooges—to create their great illusions. Governments, now as then, use magicians in campaigns: "Magician S. Chakrabarti performed in support of the Bharatiya Janata Party candidates. In one item he took several strips of paper on which the word *durnīti* [bad government] was written, burnt them, and from the ashes produced a lotus [the BJP electoral symbol]" (*Dainik Deś*, 7 November 1989).

The earthly relationship between king and magician was energized and validated by mythological and legendary antecedents. To abduct Sita and destroy Rama, the demon king Ravana supplicated the ascetic Maricha, "master of the workings of magic" (*Rāmāyaṇa* 3.36.16), who then, in the service of his ruler, used magic to transform his form: "The magician has cunningly conjured up this magical form, this illusion of a deer, no more real than the Gandharvas' cities of cloud" (*Rāmāyaṇa* 3.43.7).

As the demon sovereign Ravana commissioned Maricha, so historical monarchs and princes sought the services of magicians and itinerant conjurers who, in turn, solicited the deliverance from the streets that royal patronage promised. A magician named Chankuna, a wandering conjurer from the land of the Tuhkharas, having demonstrated his ability to spontaneously produce gold coins from thin air (a basic sleight for any magician) was taken into the court of King Lalitaditya Muktapida of Kashmir (c. fifth century C.E.). While leading his army south to what is now the Punjab, the king stopped at a river over which there was no bridge. "When the king asked his ministers for a means of crossing the river, Chankuna, standing on the bank, threw a charm, a magic gem, into the deep waters and at once those waters parted through the magician's power and the king crossed to the other shore. Chankuna drew out the charm by means of another charm and the waters returned" (*Rājataraṅgiṇī* [twelfth century] 4.249–251).

When the king asked his magician for one of the charms, Chankuna replied that they only worked when in his possession. But when the king persisted, pleaded, and promised to give the magician anything he wanted for a magic jewel, the conjurer, doing then as Naseeb does now, playing out the scam that I've witnessed again and again, conceded with seeming reluctance. He gave several magic stones to the king in return for a gold image of the Buddha which, he claimed with seeming piety, he wished to install in the shrine wherein he worshipped. And one can be certain that the king had no more or less success performing miracles with those stones than Naseeb's anxious customers have had with their magic rings from Chandni Chowk.

Magic could be practical accomplishment, effective ritual, or courtly entertainment; the three functions were linked. At the celebration of the royal consecration in the court of Yudhishthira in the *Mahābhārata*, a set of magical illusions are used to trick Duryodhana: lifting up his robes to cross what seemed to be a pond in the court but was really solid, Duryodhana was fooled, and thus made foolish, by magic; then walking over an illusion of solid ground, he suddenly found himself dunked in water, and the servants roared with laughter as they gave him dry, clean clothes; the courtiers laughed as well when Duryodhana, trying to go out the door, bumped his head on the solid wall that looked like air and then shrank away from the space that looked like a barrier (*Mahābhārata* 2.43.1–10).

In royal courts magic rites were conjuring acts, shows within a show within a show. The empirical world is itself a show, as Vashishtha explains to Rama in the *Yogavasiṣṭha*: "The world is an enchanted city, spread out by the magic of that escamoteur who is the mind" (3.104.1). Within that vast, pervasive illusion, a spectacle is conjured up; a king takes his throne amidst an assembly of generals, ministers, and counselors: "Accompanied by the music of lutes, beautiful singers serenaded them and lovely servant girls fanned their ruler with yak-tail whisks. Learned scholars recited the sacred myths from the ancient texts, and the court poets sang the praises of their king" (3.104.20–25). Into that court a magician arrogantly swaggered, waving the peacock-feather wand that is the emblem and prop of the conjurer's craft. Inviting the king to witness a magic trick, he began to spin the magic wand around and around, and as a man led a horse into the court, the king fell into a deep hypnotic trance, where he remained spellbound, enveloped in the magical illusion, for several hours. When the king finally emerged from the trance and told of his adventures, the magician suddenly disappeared. The courtiers reasoned that he could not have been an ordinary magician since he did not ask for money for his show—it was divine magic, the real magic that is ever imitated by dissembling conjurers (3.109.23–29).

Earthly conjurers did versions of tricks attributed to divine magicians. So the magicians in the palace of Bhima, king of Vidarbha, were angered when their own magic show was made to seem amateurish by the appearance of Indra, who performed various entertaining transformations for the court (*Naiṣadhacarita*

14.70). Divine = real; earthly = unreal. One passes for the other. Real magic pretends to be earthly conjuring; cunning sleights pretend to be hierophanies; illusions are hypostasized. The pleasure and terror of magic is that one never knows what's what, what's who, who's what, or who's who. "One day while I was playing dice with my wife," Prince Naravahanadatta recounts in the *Bṛhatkathāślokasaṃgraha* of Budhasvamin (eighth or ninth century), "a magician appeared before me—the man was dressed as a woman—he carried peacock feathers and a skull, and on his neck there was a garland as beautiful as if it had been woven out of rainbows" (19.2–3). The magician in human guise was not human but a *vidyādhara*, one of those attendants upon Shiva who are masters of the science of magic and deception, illusion and sleights of the spirit quicker than the eye. The performer on the stage plays the part of a *vidyādhara* playing the part of man playing the part of *vidyādhara* playing . . . ; it's an intricate net of illusions with no way out.

In the *Vikramacarita* (c. eleventh century), a series of stories that are told by various statuettes to the legendary King Bhoja, a wandering magician who appears in the court of King Vikrama and offers to give a performance of the jugglers' art does a version of the Rope Trick without the rope. Explaining that he, as a servant of Indra, patron deity of magicians, must ascend into heaven to battle demons there, he announces that since Vikrama is renowned for his respect for other men's wives, he would like permission to leave his wife under the guardianship of the king. That granted, the magician disappears, and sounds of battle are heard in the court. Parts of the magician's body begin to fall to the floor of the assembly hall. Then, despite the protests of the king and courtiers, the magician's wife performs the pious rite of self-immolation for her husband. But after her body has been consumed by the flames, the magician suddenly appears in the court again, whole and well, and asks where his wife is. He explains that he has come to take her to heaven to celebrate his victory in celestial battle. The astonished king doesn't know what to say. After that suspenseful, difficult moment that all magicians play for, the resurrected magician laughs: "I'm only a conjurer! What you've just witnessed is no more than a magic trick!" And with all the pleasure of the wonder that is inspired by displays of magic, the king gives the magician "tons of gold and pounds of pearls, one hundred horses and fifty elephants, not to mention one hundred courtesans skilled in all the arts." In the metrical recension of the text, the king recites an aphorism: "Through cleverness in the art of magic and conjuring, the false gives the impression of being true" (114–15).

It was most likely on account of this collection of stories (attributed by Sorcar Senior to Kalidasa) that the figure of King Bhoja became closely associated with magic: Raja Bhoj was a name that inevitably came up among Indian magicians of the present in connection with the magic of the past. For Naseeb it refers to a magician in the court of Akbar; Lal identified him as a stage magician in the early part of this century; The Incredible Mayadhar, among others, explained that he was a magician in the court of Vikramaditya, "along with the great Kalidas, one of the famous nine jewels adorning the court. Believe me, please." And in connection with Raja Bhoj, there is the frequent mention of a Queen Bhanumati (sometimes said to be Bhoja's wife, sometimes his daughter and the wife of Vikramaditya), a magician in her own right: in Bengal, magic is called *Bhanumati-khel*—her game or hobby. The importance of these stories for the modern stage magicians is their potential to illustrate to the government of India that magic, as an art that was previously, in more glorious days, patronized, should once again be subsidized or at least exempted from the entertainment tax.

The despondent prince Rajavahana, in the *Daśakumāracarita* of Dandin (eighth century), was encountered by an itinerant magician, a Brahmin adept in *indrajāla* named Vidyeshvara, a conjurer who traveled from place to place to earn his livelihood entertaining royal audiences. Discovering that Rajavahana's melancholy was caused by being kept apart from his beloved, the princess of Malwa, the magician proposed to use his magic to serve the prince: "By means of the art of magic, I shall beguile the king of Malwa and arrange the marriage between you and his daughter." Vidyeshvara planned his show, arranged to make stooges of the ladies-in-waiting and then, the next day, appeared at the royal palace to announce his trade. Eager to be entertained with a magic show, the king invited the conjurer into the court for a command performance.

Just as it happens now, the drums were played, the peacock feathers waved, and the audience-distracting snakes ("spewing poison and illuminating the palace with the splendor of the jewels in their hoods") were set out. And as the modern magician performs the illusory dismemberment—sawing a lady in half on the stage, decapitating a volunteer on the street—the Brahmin magician did the same, and the patter for the trick was provided by the mythology of Vishnu in his descent as the Man-Lion: the tyrannical demon Hiranyakashipu, assured by Brahma that he could be killed neither during the day nor during the night, neither by man nor beast, neither indoors nor outdoors, neither on earth nor in heaven, confidently proclaimed his dominion over the three worlds. His son, however, refusing to recognize his father's authority, expressed his fealty to Vishnu. "Where is Vishnu?" the demon-king called out in anger; "Everywhere!" his son answered with pious conviction. "In this pillar?" asked Hiranyakashipu and when "Yes, yes" was the reply, he struck the pillar with his staff. Vishnu, the protean trickster, assuming the bodily form of a man with the head of a lion, burst from the pillar; and there, in the pillared doorway to the palace (neither indoors nor outdoors), and then, at dusk (neither day nor night), the Man Lion (neither man nor beast) lifted the demon onto his lap (neither on the earth nor in heaven) and dismembered him.

Acting out the drama, creating an earthly illusion of the mythological illusion, performing a courtly version of the celestial trick, the magician dazzled the king.

The particular patter for the illusion belied the connection between doing a trick on someone and doing a trick for them; having accomplished the latter, the conjurer proceeded to do the former under the pretext of doing the latter once more. That's the trick. "And now for the grand finale of my magic show," Vidyeshvara announced to the king of Malwa: "I'd like to do a trick that will bring blessings with it—I'll conjure up a marriage scene, marry a handsome prince to a beautiful princess who will, through the power of my magic, look exactly like your very own daughter!" Anxious to see it done, the curious king permitted the magician to apply collyrium to his eyes, a balm which the trickster said would enable the king to see the marvelous illusion. The king's daughter, cued by confederates in the harem, entered with Prince Rajavahana, and "everyone watched the spectacle, the performance of the marriage rite, in utter astonishment and wonder as if they were watching a magic show." The reality was perceived as an illusion, a reversal of magic's expected accomplishment wherein an illusion is perceived as a reality. Rewarding the magician for creating such a vivid illusion with a great sum of money, the king retired to his apartment, the lovers to the nuptial bed, and the itinerant magician went happily on his way (*Daśakumāracarita* 1).

Just as sorcerers, Vedic and Tantric magicians alike, were consulted in erotic matters, petitioned for love charms, spells, or potions, commissioned by men to subject women to their will or vice versa; just as magic was commonly understood as a real force that could inspire, intensify, or terminate sexual desire and love; so the magician as entertainer, at least as he is depicted in Sanskrit literature, was frequently called upon to use his skill, Mayadevi's powers, in the service of love.

In the *Ratnāvalī* of Harsha (seventh century), the magician Sarvasiddhi, waving his peacock feathers, appeared in the royal court before the hero-king, who had professed the pleasure he took in magic. "Make obeisance to the feet of Indra whose name is connected with conjuring, and to the feet of Shambara whose glory was firmly established in illusions," (4.7) the magician recited; then he asked the king what illusion he would like to witness: "the moon on earth? a mountain in the sky? fire in water? darkness at noon?" (4.8). The magician conjured up a scene: Brahma on his lotus, Shiva wearing the crescent moon in his hair, Vishnu with his bow, sword, mace, and discus, Indra on his elephant, the hosts of gods and celestial nymphs dancing, their anklets jingling. "Wonderful! Strange!" the king cried out, "Amazing! Marvelous!" The court jester laughed: "Hey, Mr. Magician, you son of a whore, if you want to please the king it's no use showing him all the gods and nymphs—instead, show him Sagarika instead!" (prose after 4.11). Sagarika, the king's beloved, had, unbeknownst to the king, been imprisoned in the palace by her older rival, the first queen. Just as the magician announced that he had another trick to perform for the courtiers, the show was suddenly interrupted by shouting—a fire had broken out in the palace. Fearful that she would be held responsible for the death of Sagarika, the queen confessed that the girl was confined within. The king rescued his beloved, and the flames were immediately extinguished. The palace had not been on fire after all—it was all an illusion, a trick to unite the lovers. "Our magician, that son of a whore," the jester laughed, "said you'd be seeing one more trick!" (prose after 4.19).

Similarly in the *Karpūramañjarī* of Rajashekhara (tenth century), a Tantric magician, Bhairavananda, unites separated lovers with a trick. Offering the magician a seat, the king asked him to do something "amazing," and when the magician boasted that there was nothing that he could not do ("I can bring the moon down to earth, make the chariot of the sun stop in the middle of the sky, make you see Yakshas, demigods, Siddhas, and Shiva's troops. . ." [1.25]), the court jester asked him to conjure up the lovely Karpuramanjari. The stage directions suggest the performance of a theatrical trick: as the magician dances around, the heroine appears "with a quick toss of the curtain." "Ah! Ha! Ha! Amazing! Amazing!" the king exclaims, and, immediately impassioned, he describes what he, his queen, the jester, the magician, and the audience see: a ravishingly beautiful girl, half-dressed as if unexpectedly transferred from her home to the court in the midst of her bath.

The queen suggests that the conjured girl stay in the court for a fortnight, after which the magician can use his magic powers to transport her back home. But, overcome by jealousy over the obvious passion her husband feels for the lovely maiden, the queen, as in the *Ratnāvalī*, imprisons the heroine within the palace. There is a secret passage leading from the prison room to the palace garden upon which the hero and heroine rely throughout the play for their trysts; the theme is magic—the trickeries and sweet deceptions of lovers. When Karpuramanjari appears in the garden, then in the prison room, then outside in the garden again, then back within her cell (as she runs back and forth through the secret passage), the jealous queen attributes the apparent transportation of the girl through walls to the magical powers of Bhairavananda.

There is, the itinerant magician confides to the queen, a girl named Ghanasaramanjari from the land of the Latas, the daughter of King Chandasena, who, according to a consensus of astrologers, is destined to become the wife of an emperor. The queen consents to the magician's plot of arranging a political second marriage between her husband and that girl so that the king can become an emperor. The magic trick: instantly transporting that girl from the land of Latas. How it's done: *yantru-tantru-jālajāla-mantru*, she's already there— Ghanasaramanjari is but another name of Karpuramanjari. The wedding is performed. The magician has tricked both the queen and the audience of the play into thinking that he is tricking the king, when he is tricking the queen. It's a trick that it's a trick—the real trick being that it's no trick.

Various scenes in these plays imply that conjuring procedures and magical special effects were used in theatrical productions. In his discussion of dramatic scenes informed with the sentiment of fury, the *raudra-rasa*, the dramaturgist

Bharata (c. second century C.E.) recommends that "they should be performed by using such magic tricks as decapitation or cutting off the limbs, or by showing the firing of missiles by means of special effects" (*Nāṭyaśāstra* 6.65).

Although the plays and other literary accounts (such as the *Ākhyānakamaṇikośa* of Acharya Nemichandra, 30.105–6) suggest that the Indian magician was always essentially itinerant, that he went from court to court announcing himself and offering to perform, modern Indian stage magicians insist that their historical counterparts were—like poets, dancers, and musicians—important functionaries in the traditional court. Though the ancient magician was primarily an entertainer, his amusements conferred both metaphysical and epistemological insights upon their witnesses. Professor Bhagyanath, speaking of Tenali Raman as a "court magician to the king of Kerala," told a story: "There was a terrible drought in Kerala, and so the king asked his magician if he was capable of making it rain. 'I can do anything you wish,' he said, and so the ruler commanded him to bring a storm. Immediately there was lightning and thunder and then a great downpour; it rained so hard that the rivers rose, and there was a flood. When the waters inundated the palace, the king, standing on the roof, was ready to leap into the torrent. The magician stopped him; it had all been an illusion. That is all a magician can do. He cannot alter reality, only our perception of reality."

Just as Tenali Raman, the archetypal joker-trickster in South Indian folk traditions, is transformed into a magician-trickster by South Indian magicians, so Raja Birbal, the joker-trickster of the north, is said by many stage magicians to have been a conjurer, the Hindu royal magician in the court of Akbar.

Once upon a time, while shaving Akbar, a devious Muslim barber, commissioned by vengeful Muslim courtiers, Birbal's rivals, to trick the trickster, asked the great Moghul if he wondered how his father, Humayan, was faring in heaven. The barber assured Akbar that there was a way of finding out: "You could send a man up there. I know a magician who frequently transports messengers to heaven and brings them back alive. He'd be happy to send an ambassador to heaven for you. It should be a wise and witty man. You could send Birbal. No one is wiser or wittier than he." Delighted with the idea, Akbar gave the barber and the Muslim magician permission to proceed. Thanking Akbar for the honor of being chosen for such an important mission, Birbal requested some time to prepare for the long journey. During the granted time period, Birbal dug a secret passage leading from his house to the place where the pyre was to be assembled. On the day of his departure for heaven, as he mounted the pyre, Birbal asked that extra straw and kindling be placed over him to make the fire burn brighter and hotter. As soon as the fire was set, Birbal slipped into the secret passage and crawled happily home. The Muslim courtiers thought that they had tricked Akbar and Birbal, until, some time later, Birbal arrived back in the court. "Your father is doing very well," the Hindu court magician said to the ruler, "there is only one thing that displeases him—it's absolutely impossible to get a good shave up there.

All the good barbers must be in hell. Your father has only one request. He asked me to tell you to send the royal barber up there as soon as possible." Akbar carried out Humayan's request at once.

The Incredible Mayadhar gave the magical commentary on the well-known fable. "Thus Birbal made popular the Buried Alive trick that was so common in India until the government outlawed it. A vanishing act—every magician does it. I have my version of it based on the story of Birbal in my own show. It's wonderful and astonishing. I use the smoke screen also. The clever employment of the secret passage is something we all do in our stage shows for so many items, believe me please. Secret passages, secret compartments, escapes from fire and flame—these are our stock and trade. And inspiration for the clever usage of these devices we owe to Birbal, World's Greatest Magician of Moghul times."

Although it is certainly unlikely that the real Birbal was a conjurer, there were indeed, as Jahangir's recollections of his father's court attest, performances of magic to entertain the emperor Akbar. The shows were metaphors, perceived or not, for the context in which they were performed: the Moghul court was a world of intrigues and deceptions, of serious tricks, a network of confederates and stooges, a staged show. Magical performances were merely plays within plays within plays, illusions staged within a larger illusion. And of all the great Moghuls to be fascinated and compelled by magic, it was Jahangir himself, the zealous drunkard and sentimental paranoiac, who especially patronized the conjurer's craft. The child in the despot can be heard throughout his self-aggrandizing memoirs: "At the period of which I am about to speak there were to be found in the province of Bengal performers in sleight of hand, or jugglers (Bauzigurs [bājīgars]), of such unrivaled skill in their art that I have thought of a few instances of their extraordinary dexterity not unworthy of a place in this memorial. On one occasion in particular, there came to my court seven of these men, who confidently boasted that they were capable of producing effects so strange as far to surpass the scope of human understanding; and most certainly when they proceeded to their operations, they exhibited in their performances things of so extraordinary a nature, as without the actual demonstration the world would not have conceived possible; such indeed as cannot but be considered among the most surprising circumstances of the age in which we live" (Tūzuk-i-Jahāngīrī). Jahangir lists twenty-eight tricks: the Mango Tree Trick, Levitation, and Cut-and-Restored Person, as already described, as well as displays of ventriloquy (without moving their lips, the seven magicians sang a song in perfect unison) and exhibitions of acrobatics and fireworks. Displaying a cloth in which he had been dressed, one of the magicians produced from under it "a resplendent mirror, by the radiance of which a light so powerful was produced, as to have illuminated the hemisphere to an incredible distance round."

Another conjurer, after exhibiting a bird cage in which two nightingales were singing, rotated the cage, and the birds became parrots; another turn, and another kind of bird began to sing, and then another, on and on, in a wonderful display of avian metamorphoses. Other magical transformations included the presentation of kaleidoscopic carpet which, when turned over, had a different pattern on the other side; turned over again, the first pattern was changed, and with each turn there was an entirely new design. "All is change," the philosophers say; the magicians show.

The Bengali conjurers dug an enormous hole for Jahangir, filled it with water, covered it with a sheet, uncovered it and, *gilli-gilli-gilli*, the water was frozen so solid that an elephant was able to walk across it. They covered it again, removed the sheet and, *yantru-tantru-jālajāla-mantru*, the water and ice had vanished, and the emperor looked into the empty ditch.

The Bengalis set up two empty tents facing each other, and when delighted members of the royal audience named particular animals, those very animals would dash forward, one from each of the tents, to fight each other. "Ostriches!" one noble cried and was dazzled by the magical battle of those exotic birds. The magicians possessed a sack that was open at both ends: when they passed a melon through it, it emerged as a cucumber, which, when passed back through the bag, became a bunch of grapes, which then became an apple. Anything might become anything else. A protean essence informs the world with constant fluctuation. Not only birds and fruit, but words and feelings, were transformed. After showing the Moghul a volume of the poetical works of Saadi, they put the manuscript into a bag that had been examined, and when they removed it, the verses of Saadi had become the poetry of Hafiz.

Or at least that's what the emperor thought he saw, and he was so impressed with what he imagined the panoply of magic had been that he conferred a lavish donation upon the magicians: "In truth we may have bestowed upon these performances the character of trick or juggle, but they very evidently partake of the nature of something beyond the exertion of human energy; at all events, such performances were executed with inimitable skill, and if there were in the execution of any thing of facility, what should prevent their accomplishment by any man of ordinary capacity? I have heard it stated that the art has been called Semnanian (perhaps *asmaunian*, 'celestial'), and I am informed that it is also known and practiced to considerable extent among the nations of Europe. It may be said, indeed, that there exists in some men a peculiar and essential faculty which enables them to accomplish things far beyond the ordinary scope of human exertion, such as frequently to baffle the utmost subtlety of the understanding to penetrate." The talent, it must have occurred to the ruler, would be profitable if only it could be applied in the political domain, if only the magic wand might be a scepter, the magic words a royal proclamation.

Magicians had no place in the austere court of the zealously pious Aurangzeb, the stern upholder of Muslim law who banished singers and musicians, and even historians, from his court. The fun and games, the illusions and deceptions, were over. Islam did not mix with magic, neither with the entertainment nor with the religious practices that the amusement imitated: "Whoever goes to a magician and asks about mysteries and believes what he says, verily is displeased with Muhammad and his religion. . . . As ye have put faith in Islam, believe not in magic" (Islamic scripture as cited by Ja'far Sharif, *Qānūn-i-Islām*). Repeatedly, contemporary Hindu stage magicians blamed that last of the great Moghuls for the fall of magic, the degradation of a once fine art and aristocratic divertisse-ment. "It was only with the English," the old stage magician in Calcutta told me, "that there was, once again, some patronage for our art, the essence of all arts, our Bhanumati-*khel*."

A certain Captain Campbell, returning to England from the colony in 1814, brought a troupe of Indian magicians with him and installed them in Pall Mall, where they demonstrated native juggling, acrobatics, yogic postures, conjuring, and sleight of hand for an audience that was curious about the quaint customs and strange manners of India. "Coming forward and seating himself on the ground in his white dress and tightened turban," the essayist William Hazlitt commented, upon seeing one such performance, "the chief of the Indian Jugglers begins with tossing up two brass balls, which is what any of us could do, and concludes with keeping up four at the same time, which is what none of us could do to save our lives, nor if we were to take our whole lives to do it in. Is it then a trifling power we see at work, or is it not something next to miraculous?" ("Indian Jugglers," *Table Talk*).

The success of the Oriental sideshow inspired other entrepreneurs to import more Indian magicians to England. During the intermission of performances of Dickens's *Nicholas Nickleby* at the Hull Royal Theater on 26 December 1838, a Mr. Ramo Samee, who had first come to England with Captain Campbell, now on his own and billed as "The Celebrated East Indian," presented the mysteries of India for the amusement of the British public. Dickens, an accomplished magician in his own right, who frequently performed at parties for friends, in one of his various conjuring routines called himself Rhia Rhama Rhoos after Khia Khan Khruse, an Indian magician who had been imported along with Ramo Samee years earlier.

Ramo Samee entertained the British at London's Garrick Theatre nightly with the Colored Sands Trick, Cups and Balls, and by swallowing a handful of colored beads and a horse-tail hair—when he then pulled the hair out of his mouth, the beads were neatly strung upon it. When Khia Khan Khruse (who later did the colored beads trick as Fifty-Sewing-Needles) did not appear one night in the Ramo Samee show, rumors spread that he had died while swallowing a sword or that he had been killed on stage trying to catch a bullet in his mouth. "In 1814 some clever Indian jugglers performed in London. . . . One of their feats was the gun trick, in which one of the performers pretended to catch between his teeth a leaden bullet fired from a pistol. . . . [In Dublin] the pistol, actually loaded with

BONES AND EARTH

powder and ball was, by inadvertence, substituted for the weapon prepared for the trick. The bullet crashed through the head of the unfortunate conjuror, who, to the surprise and horror of all present, fell dead upon the stage" (Frost, *Lives of the Conjurors*).

Such stories, true or not, were good publicity. Khia Khan Khruse, quite alive but having broken off from Ramo Samee to work on his own as the Chief of the Indian Jugglers, demonstrated, as attested by posters for his revue, yogic *āsana*s ("some of the most surprising Evolutions, Serpentine Postures &c. ever beheld"), juggling, sword swallowing, and a variety of such items as the linking rings and the swallowing of sewing needles that are retrieved on a thread, tricks that are still done in India and which have become, through an Indian influence that Western magicians do not often admit, conventional in European and American stage magic.

To see an Indian magic show was to get a glimpse into the mysterious core of Indian culture; exotic Indian performances became the rage. Mooty Moodaya, a magician from Madras, took his fashionable London magic show on tour to

FIGURE 9. *Ramo Samee.* From the John Mulholland Collection; courtesy of the Supreme Magic Company.

Southampton and other English towns in 1840. It seems to have been for the sake of recruitment into the British army that the government sponsored such events.

No distinction was made between performances of conjuring and displays of religious austerities or yogic feats—Indian religion was conjuring through and through. In February of 1897 the *Strand Magazine* of London featured an article on a yogi named Bava Lachman Das, who had been brought to England and installed at the Westminster Aquarium, where people came in droves to be amused by the sight of him standing on one leg with his other leg curled around his neck. And they were no less amazed by him than they were by the tiger sharks, electric eels, and warm-water wahoos.

A Mr. A. N. Dutt, sent by his parents from Calcutta to study medicine in Edinburgh, unbeknownst to his family, adopted the name Ram Bhuj and, dropping out of college to travel to the United States with a dance company, capitalized on Western stereotypes of Indian religious practices by billing himself as the Mysterious Hindoo Fakir and performing both Indian tricks and Indianized versions of Western ones. With the funds earned by the success of his "Mysteries of the East" revue, he returned to England at the beginning of this century to form his own company, change his name to Linga Singh, and stage elaborate Indian extravaganzas: against backdrops that conjured up Himalayan ashrams and Hindu temples, nautch girls seductively danced, yogis sat cross-legged in holy trance, defanged cobras were charmed, and gelded elephants took a bow. There were cremations and reincarnations under the direction of Linga Singh, the turbaned magician who sat on stage beneath a great Indian parasol as the maharaja of magic. He fooled his audience as well as he tricked his parents—they thought that the money he sent home had been earned by healing the sick in Edinburgh.

Wilkie Collins' atmospheric detective novel, *The Moonstone*, is evidence that, by the mid-nineteenth century, some Indian magicians in England had taken to the streets and were performing door-to-door, as was the custom in India: "Going round to the terrace, I found three mahogany-coloured Indians, in white linen frocks and trousers, looking up at the house. The Indians, as I saw on looking closer, had small hand-drums slung in front of them. . . . I judged the fellows to be strolling conjurors. . . . One of the three, who spoke English, and who exhibited, I must own, the most elegant manners, presently informed me that my judgement was right. He requested permission to show his tricks in the presence of the lady of the house." A character in the novel explains the magical abilities of the foreigners as "simply a development of the romantic side of the Indian character."

While Indian magicians were performing in Europe, Western magicians—including Chang and the Great Virgil, Nicola and Horace Goldin, Harry Kellar and Howard Thurston—were performing in India, staging private shows for Indian maharajas and British dignitaries alike. Magicians were de rigeur at any really important festivity in India, and Westerners, reputedly more technically polished than Indians, became the new Indian stage magicians. Returning home, those Western magicians, inevitably mounting Indian revues or at least adding a few Indian items to their own repertoires, would invariably announce that they had studied magic with the spiritual adepts of India, land of magic and mystery. Howard Thurston attributed many things, including his youthful appearance (actually attained through repeated plastic surgery), to secrets he had learned from "a Yogi in India."

At the end of the nineteenth century, the magician Samri S. Baldwin returned from India with his wife ("Mrs. Kittie, the Rosicrucian Somnomist") to announce that "by means and methods which I cannot now explain, I became a member and finally a high priest of several secret societies. I was given the oriental title signifying 'The White Mahatma' " *(Secrets of Mahatma Land Explained).* Claiming to have learned methods of mesmerism from the fakirs of India that were entirely unknown in the West, Baldwin, like other Western magicians of the period, advertised himself as all the more amazing and wonderful for his travels to India. On the other hand, and also like the other magicians who had visited and performed in India, he affirmed the fundamental superiority of the white magician over the Indian: "For my gratification a number of the highest class Fakeers had been especially engaged to produce their most marvelous work before me." Thoroughly unimpressed with Indian magic and conjuring, Baldwin,

FIGURE 10. *Kar-mi.* Reprinted from William Doerflinger's *The Magic Catalogue* (New York, 1977); courtesy of William Doerflinger.

asking an interpreter to tell the magicians that he was "much disappointed with so paltry a performance," rose up and did a show of his own. "I immediately stepped to within four or five feet of him and commenced waving my hands in the air. Then suddenly clapping them together, I commanded that he and his assistants be struck with lightning. Suddenly, to his inexplicable horror, the kummerband and breechclout, which are pretty well all the clothes these fellows wear, burst into a blaze, and he and his assistants were enveloped in flames." The terrified Indian magicians tore off their clothes. "There they stood, nude as the day they came into the world, half dazed, more frightened than hurt, staring at each other, rubbing their arms and bodies where they had been uncomfortably hot, and wondering how it all happened. The English guests and spectators of the affair were screaming with laughter. . . . The clothing of the Hindoos was replaced for a few rupees and the present of another five or ten rupees thoroughly healed their wounded feelings and sent them away delighted to spread all over the country a report of my great power." It is a parable of nineteenth-century imperialism: the larger social, political, and economic encounter between England and India seems epitomized in the stories of the British magicians in India—the viceroys and governors of India, in their ceremonial regalia, bedizened with medals, were performing a grand magic show, full of illusions, juggling, and sleights.

Just as Indian officials learned British modes of government, so Indian magicians assimilated Western methods of magic. In nineteenth-century Delhi there was a Professor Agni who, dressed in the tuxedo that became the uniform of Indian stage magicians until Sorcar, advertised himself as available both for parties and for instruction in the art of both Indian and Western conjuring.

In India the great magic was Western; in the West the great magic was Indian—and Westerners had a monopoly on both. Indian stage performers in India were depicted in pathetic terms. "During his performance," Elbiquet explained to English readers at the beginning of this century, the magician "never fails to remind his European audience over and over again that he is performing 'English' tricks. . . . His presentations are wanting in attraction, because he is unable to add to them that essential 'finish' which they would receive in the hands of the performer he endeavours to imitate" (*Supplementary Magic*).

Satyajit Ray, in a story about two magicians—a stage illusionist and a street conjurer—contraposes theatrical magic, which he considers purely Western, with the "*pure magie de l'Inde,*" that pristine Indic magic in which the months and years of practicing sleight of hand become "*une pratique yoguique.*" Indian magic, for Indians conscious of a heritage threatened or lost, enacts religious ideals: "*La meilleure magie du monde repose sur ces facultés. Il ne s'agit pas du tout d'artifices mais de sadhana, de sincérité, de concentration*" ("*Les deux magiciens*").

Sorcar made magic Indian again and retrieved mysteries from the past. Claiming to be the descendant of one of the seven Bengali magicians who had performed for Jahangir, he created an illusion, conjured up the ancient court to offer modern audiences in both India and the West glimpses of that "wonder that was India."

"Now this is that *sabhā* of old," Professor Bhagyanath (whose own revue—the sets, the costumes, and the magic—is modeled on Sorcar's "Indrajal" spectacular), told me with a melancholy smile on the last day of 1987 in Madras at the Savera Hotel, suggesting that, for magicians at least, the royal court of traditional India had become—whether through deterioration or evolution—the Western-style "five-star hotel."

When I had asked if I could get some mouth-coils from him for my proposed New Year's Eve magic show in the hotel restaurant, he had insisted on bringing them himself, so that he could advise me on my routine and patter. We sat by the pool near the modern metallic statue of Shiva and Parvati that decorated the dry fountain which workmen were trying to repair so that once again the Ganges would seem to gush from Shiva's top-knot and descend with blessings over the divine couple. Abba, the Swedish rock group, their rendition of "Mama Mia" coming over the loudspeakers, were the poets replacing those who once sang for the court; the French girls, known at times to remove the tops of their bikinis by the pool, were the favored courtesans; hotel staff members were the counselors and scribes. Over the centuries, through Hindu, Muslim, English, and now Indian democratic rule, the servants alone had changed hardly at all. The nobles now were businessmen, and magicians entertained them at meetings of the Rotary or Lion's Club, at birthday parties or weddings, and occasionally at a hotel cabaret staged for some managerial convention. The king, the blessed MGR, Tamil Nadu's movie-star chief minister, was dead: the city was in mourning while his wife and mistress, rivals like the queen and beloved in both the *Ratnāvalī* and the *Karpūramañjarī*, were pitted against each other for succession.

"I'm going to tell the audience that I came to India to see the old Indian Rope Trick and that, after much travel, I found an old magician who could do it and taught the trick to me," I said to Professor Bhagyanath. "Then I'll show them what he showed me. 'Imagine this is the boy, the old man's chela' I'll say as I hold up a forced jack of hearts. I'll levitate it, float the card the usual way—I've got some Finn Jon thread—then I'll grab the card, have someone sign it, tear it up, and keep a piece, put the rest in a paper bag, say the mantras, and produce the restored, signed jack from the bag."

The old magician thought I should omit the Indian allusions, that, since I was an American, the audience would prefer Western patter: "Something about Merlin or Houdini. Their idea will be that Western magic, like Western technology, is better than Indian magic. That's what things have come to in India. It's a sorry state. That's why we, the greatest of Indian stage magicians, the artists of illusion, must wait for opportunities to work in Muscat or the Emirates, in Moscow or Las

Vegas. The Indian court survives only outside India, or in our dreams, or there, up in the clouds."

Finishing his tea, Professor Bhagyanath rose, smiled, and handed me the mouth-coils with a warning: "If you tell them this was an item in ancient India, which it surely was, they won't appreciate it. They'll think it's a cheap trick. If you tell them it's something Seigfried and Roy do in Las Vegas, they'll be dazzled, amazed, and overcome with wonder."

Above us the clouds, those magic cities of Gandharvas, hung in the sky as if by invisible threads from heaven, suspended from celestial courts where, for the wonder and delight of mythic kings, throngs of magicians with their skulls and peacock feathers play: Shambara and Indra, Maricha and Indrajit, Chankuna and Bhairavananda, Sarvasiddhi and Vidyeshvara, Raja Bhoj and Queen Bhanumati, Tenali Raman and Birbal, Ramo Samee and Khia Khan Khruse, seven magicians from Bengal and P. C. Sorcar Senior, their descendants there if nowhere else.

Standing before the mirror in the bathroom of my hotel room to rehearse several of my tricks for the evening show, to get my angles right, I practiced my patter: "Ladies and Gentleman, I'm not really a magician, but a professor at the University of Hawaii in America. My field is Sanskrit and ancient Indian traditions. I came to India in hopes of seeing the famous Indian Rope Trick and finding out how it was done. I've traveled to Bombay and Delhi, north to Bengal and south to Kerala, in search of Indian magic. Finally in Kashmir, high in the Himalayas, in a remote village, I discovered an old man with a long white beard who called himself Vishvasiddhi. The villagers told rumors about him: some said that through the power of his magic, he had lived for over a thousand years; others claimed that he was a *vidyādhara*, a celestial magician whose human form was but an illusion. I don't know for sure who or what he was. At times I even wonder if he exists or existed at all. Did he cast a magic spell to inspire me and the mountain villagers to see what did not, in reality, exist at all? He did, I believe and would swear it's true, demonstrate the Rope Trick for me: after a young boy climbed a rope into the sky, the magician followed him and cut him into pieces; then, descending and placing the parts of the dismembered body into a wicker basket, Vishvasiddhi restored the child to life. When I asked him to teach me magic, to become my *jādū-guru*, he said that since I had studied Sanskrit, he would give a manuscript to me, an ancient book, full of secrets. I learned how to perform the illusion that I am going to show you now from that manuscript, which was entitled *Indrajālasūtra*."

Scene Eight:
Indrajālasūtra:

A Skeleton of Magic

Midnight. The ring-ringing of the telephone awoke the traveler just enough for him to reach into the darkness from the bed and from the dream in which, as in a magic show, anything was possible: "Professor M. T. Bannerji is here to see you," the voice that came from the desk downstairs in the guest house crackled as if from the other side of the world. "He explains that it is a matter of utter most importance. I join him in his hopes that he has not disturbed you."

"Jesus Christ!" the traveler said out loud as he sat up, turned on the light, and looked at the clock. "What on earth could he want?"

The foreigner pulled on his trousers to the sound of the pounding on the door which, like the tattoo of the damaru, announced the magician. The door opened, like the curtain raised, revealing the gaping gaze and smile of the odd man in the theatrical top hat. The men stared into each other's faces, inexplicably transfixed for an instant that persisted awkwardly; the moment contained much more than itself. The uneasy silence was dispelled by excited exclamations: "Wonderful! Wonderful that you are here!" With what almost seemed a genuine joy, the performer muttered it again as he bounded through the doorway past the foreigner and spun around, his gaze surveying the room. "Wonderful for both of us: for me on account of the pleasurable honor and honorable pleasure of seeing you before your departure from my glorious land, and for you on account of the supreme surprise that I have humbly brought for you. Wonderful in the magical sense, yes, full of wonder. Oh, the world is all magic! You remember me, of course," he said, restraining the inflection in his voice from transforming statement into question, as he took off his top hat with a flourish, then snapped his tricky fingers to produce a lit Gold Flake cigarette from thin air. "Certainly I do not look quite the same with no hair. More like the great Buddh or great Shankaracharya than the great Professor M. T. Bannerji. I was compelled by hallowed tradition, you see, to shave my hair and moustache for the *śraddha*s. Perhaps you are aware of it—my famous and fabulous father died recently. It is our ancient custom, this hair-shaving business. Yes, Professor M. T. Bannerji, World's Greatest Magician, the illustrious illusionist, has taken his last bow and exited this magic show of a world, leaving his magic wand to me, no small responsibility, I can assure you."

The bald magician relaxed his smile and let a silence be. Seeming to echo requiems, the uncomfortable hush beckoned polite words from the foreigner: "I'm sorry."

"No, no, don't say 'I'm sorry' unless, of course, it really was your fault," the magician laughed almost wildly. "Though our previous tête-à-tête was brief, it was more significant for me than you can imagine. I have never forgotten you at all, ever wondering what you have been doing—not only what, but how, why, and where even. Curious to know if your book on Indian magic and conjuring is completed, I have remained ever anxious to read it, not only the parts about myself, but, in all modesty, the other parts as well. Oh your book! Listen: having, since our last meeting, been to America, especially Las Vegas, I am writing my own book about my own peregrinations. Wonderful! Do you understand? Is it not amazing? Here I am, an Indian writing about magic through his travels in America; and here you are, an American writing about magic through your travels in India. Just as I am in your book, you are in mine. Amazing! Here we are, like twin brothers, or more magically speaking, two figures, each on one side of a magic mirror. On one side of the glass is India, on the other America—two realities, each unreal to the other, from which you and I, each one of us a magician, stand looking at the other. Each is the other in reverse. Uncanny and boggling! Astonishing and thoroughly wonderful. Thus my happiness in seeing you. I hope you were not sleeping or in any other way indisposed."

"I was resting," the traveler said, trying to restrain the inflection in his voice from transforming statement into complaint. "I've got to leave for the airport at half-past three. Three and a half hours. I've ordered a taxi. I was resting up for the flight. But have a seat. Let me wash up and I'll be with you in a moment."

"Do you realize how wonderful this is?" the magician continued as if he had either not heard or not understood the foreigner's words. Snapping his fingers once for another cigarette, he snapped them again to produce a match box. "No! You could not fathom what is surely more than serendipity! If my father had not died when he did, I would not be in Delhi right now—please be confident that I shall tell you that whole story in toto—and if the Ramada Inn, where I wished to stay, had not been fully occupied, and if the taxi driver had not taken me to the Ambassador Hotel, which I can hardly afford, and if the Dasaprakash restaurant in that hotel had not been open, then I would not have been recognized by a waiter there who is an amateur magician, and then I would not be here right now. By what seemed sheer chance, but was surely motivated by some deep reason beyond that which can be comprehended by mere mortal man, let alone by me, he asked if I was familiar with you, and 'Yes,' I said, 'yes, the great professor of

America,' and he told me that you sometimes eat at that place and discuss magic with him. All of this culminates in this moment of our reunion. And this is not to mention even everything else that has happened in the waiter's life, in your life, and in my life, these intertwined existences, and our past lives too. Everything has led up to this moment, converged here and now; and, as I always try to remind myself, everything happens for a purpose. But let us get to my point. When the waiter informed me that you were leaving India tonight, I finished my meal as quickly as was humanly possible, risking even indigestion for our sakes, dashed up to my room to fetch my treasure, my surprise and boon to you and, posthaste, came here as soon as I could."

Holding up the newspaper-wrapped package before the traveler's eyes, the magician smiled with all his heart. Again the foreigner diffidently offered his midnight visitor a seat and excused himself.

"Take your time, my brother. I'll telephone for the peon to bring tea. No, why wake him? And paltry tea would not be appropriate for a celebration of our momentous meeting, nor for my bon voyage to you. If champagne were available I would have brought it. That Johnnie Walker there on the desk—perhaps it would be most appropriate and felicitous for us to have a drop or two together."

Nodding his assent, the traveler went into the bathroom. When he emerged, the magician, seated by the coffee table upon which lay the package, the top hat, and a teacup full of scotch, offered some of the whiskey to the foreigner: "Johnnie Walker, world's greatest scotch. Had I known you would be offering me Johnnie Walker, I would have worn my red top hat, just like that one on Johnnie's head. As a dazzling entertainer, necessarily conscious of my wonderful appearance, I'm wearing a hat at all times until my hair grows out again. Black seemed suitable for mourning. But I have a red top hat too, for I am, in all modesty, a man of many hats: turbans and topis, fezes and derbies, chefs' toques, dunces' caps, and kings' crowns, mortar boards, berets, and beanies, a pith helmet and a royal English busby. . . . No, no, I *had* all those hats, and more, chapeaus galore! I *had* a red top hat. But no longer. That is the problem! Let me explain. I was in America, performing my spectacular Indrajal Extravaganza in Las Vegas, capital of American magic, teaching the mysteries of Indian magic to Seigfried and Roy, not to mention the beautiful-buttocked Miss Melinda and a certain Mr. Chuckles; and while I was gone, not for my own sake or prestige by any means, but to spread the glory of Indian magic, do you know, or can you imagine, what happened? Please have a sip of scotch and brace yourself. My troupe mutinied! Yes, a certain and damnable Bhutnath Dey, my Judas, sold everything out from under me—my hats, costumes, sets, and props to some theatrical rental company, my tents to a circus, and, most heinous of all, my apparati. Oh my god! Do you know the fate of my priceless magical equipment? That *rākṣasa* donated it all to the Congress Party. That is why I am here in Delhi, to try to obtain what is rightfully my own. But a case against the Congress Party is a battle both arduous and costly to be sure.

Now, why, you must inevitably be asking yourself, would he give all that magic to a political party? It was so that they would hire him to use that equipment, for now he is claiming to be a magician, amateurishly and mawkishly performing and desecrating the magnificent magic that he gleaned from watching me. He goes around the country, from village to village, and town to town, multiplying rupee notes, producing bags of grain, and the like, announcing that all these things will be done if only the people will vote Congress Party. Please, have a scotch with me."

"I still have a few things to pack," the foreigner demurred, "and the taxi will be here soon. It's a pleasure to see you again, but I'm leaving in a couple of hours."

The magician forced the traveler's scotch upon the traveler. "This hat was not in my wardrobe, or it too would be gone. This was my father's hat," he frowned with what seemed a genuine sadness and put the hat on, then took it off again and handed it to his host. "Inspect it. It is so beautifully constructed, the load for the rabbit undetectable even at close range. I have not used rabbits so often, but mostly doves, actually pigeons. Do you believe it?—I can fit five pigeons into the hat and wear it without anybody knowing it. But let me get to a point please. The top hat is not all my father, Professor M. T. Bannerji, the World's Greatest Magician, *escamoteur extraodinaire*, bequeathed me, his only heir and solo survivor. No, no, mine is all that belonged to him in this world of illusion, not very much to be sure, save our humble Calcutta home and its contents. Not a grand place by any means, because we were always on the road, always traveling, traveling in our tents to ever enchant the people of all India. All India was our home. But in that small house, known throughout Calcutta as the House of Maya, there was my father's library, and among the many books—magical and dramaturgical, poetical and Indological, historical and scientific even—were many, many Sanskrit texts of pertinence to magic: *Rgveda* and *Atharva* too, *Purāṇam*s and *Tantram*s, *Rāmāyaṇam*s galore, works by Amaru and Shankaracharya to name but a few. As a great scholar, my beloved father took time out from many professional and social obligations to do scientific research on the ancient texts of Indian magic. It was not for himself, but for India—it was his dream to redeem the Indian magician of today by excavating from the cultural ruins around us the glory of earlier epochs and pristine periods. Do I not owe it to him, my father, and her, India, my mother, to help promote and materialize that dazzling dream? But never mind my own humble concerns! It is for you that I am here. Though we are both professors in a titular way, you are a great scholar, well versed in the blessed Sanskrit language, while I am but a humble entertainer. Thus I have come to you. In my father's precious library was this book."

Beginning by unwrapping the package with ceremonious care, the magician, like an anxious groom undressing his bride, was unable in the end to restrain his excitement; he tore the cord with his teeth and frantically stripped away the last layers of newspaper. "This book, this mine of mysteries, the *Indrajālasūtra* of Vishvasiddhi the Great!"

He flipped the pages to show that they were empty, laughed, and, with a *gilli-gilli-gilli,* thumbed over them again to show that they were full of words, line after line of Devanagari script. "Just like the modern Magic Album Trick, and the book is so old, proof, I would imagine, that it was the great Vishvasiddhi who invented the gimmick in question, and now popular, over one thousand years ago."

Despite the impoliteness of it, the American professor could not restrain his objection: "The book doesn't look that old. It's about thirty years old, maybe forty, fifty at the most."

Loudly laughing, the Indian magician hastily refilled his teacup with scotch and handed the manuscript to the traveler. "The *copy* of the book is, as you, so perceptively noting the obvious, say, just over forty years old, just like us, but the text itself is over one thousand years old. A text recopied—a transmigrating soul in a new body. Who can say that we are not ourselves that old? Over one thousand years! That is how long it has been in our family, passed down from Vishvasiddhi to my father himself, who copied the ancient palm leaves onto these sheets of paper because the leaves were disintegrating due to the detrimental Calcutta climes. Those palm leaves, I assure you, as I was assured by my own father, were cut short and long, gimmicked just as the copy is rigged. You cannot write your study of magic without this book. While I cling to it for sentimental reasons, you need it for greater things, for the sake of your important research. Thus I am willing to put sentiment behind me and sell it to you. Please do not misunderstand me; it breaks my heart to use this crass word—*sell*—this ugly, vulgar, Kali Yug word. But, you must understand the current plight of one who, through no fault of his own, but on account of the evil machinations of one Bhutnath Dey, Ravan to all that is like Ram in me, has been reduced to penury. The tables will turn; justice always wins out; everything happens for a purpose. That is why I am in Delhi, consulting with lawyers, barristers, prosecutors, and the like, to bring a suit against Bhutnath Dey, and to regain my magical apparati from the Congress Party. Let us drink to a victory that is not just mine, but that of justice itself, not to mention India, and magic to boot."

"Professor Bannerji, you must understand that just because I am an American does not mean that I am rich. On the contrary, I really don't have very much money. I'm afraid it won't be possible for me to buy your book."

Running his fingertips over the stubble on his pate, the magician grimaced. "Professor, you must understand the wonderful nature of the item in question. This book is a treasure, its financial value inestimable. I, not to mention you, could sell it at the famous Southeby's in London for some astonishing sum. But you must further understand why I turn to you. There are many secrets in this book that must not go beyond our International Brotherhood of Magicians, a fraternity established and preserved by secrecy. This book must not fall into the wrong hands, and your hands are the right hands, I assure you. Even your left hand is the right hand! You will glean from the text all that you need to know for the book which will no doubt bring in wonderful revenues and royalties. You will, furthermore, do a service for Indian magicians by making our ancient feats known while not revealing our secrets. You are the only hope of myself, my father, all Indian magicians, and India herself: a man who knows Sanskrit, who is in a position to make his voice heard through publication, and one who can be trusted by magicians. You and you alone, to the best of my knowledge, are qualified to purchase this manuscript from me.

"If money is worrisome to you, let me assure you that I have an additional proposition: once I have won my lawsuits and am again performing, dazzling the world, and earning a livelihood, I will purchase the manuscript back from you for twice what you have paid me for it. Thus you may consider the *Indrajālasūtra* collateral on a loan and an investment to boot. I will, furthermore, make you a major stockholder, regent, and dean in the university I am planning to establish and build: Indrajala University, B.A., M.A., M.Sc. and Ph.D. to be given in all of the magical arts and sciences. Professor M. T. Bannerji is, in all modesty, a man of many dreams! Young, aspiring magicians, rich or poor, will come from all over India, even from all over the world, to learn our magic! Sanskrit will be required, so that our students can master the eternal Vedic texts on magic. You yourself will give illuminating lectures on the history of Indian magic and conjuring, on the philosophy of magic, the psychology of amazement, and the aesthetics of wonder. Our graduates will be encourgaged to use magic to transform the world, creating magnificent illusions to return India to her glory as the home of magic, miracles, and mystery. I have already found my first student, a young boy here in Delhi, in Shadipur Depot, a lad named Kabir, son of one Ibrahim Pasha, a magician through and through, the very age of my own son. I want to help him, to teach him, as if he were my very own son. Once he, adept at the magic he has learned since infancy on the streets, is taught the secrets known to us, the artistes of the stage, he will be great, the world's greatest magician of the future. The money you give me for the book will go to this, my dream, will go to save young children like Kabir from the gutters. You are investing in him, in youth, in India, in magic, in illusion."

"Please, Professor Bannerji, I really can't. Have another drink, and then I must start to get ready; the taxi will be here soon."

The magician laughed. "You don't understand. This is the work of Vishvasiddhi, world's greatest magician of the past. Have you discussed him at length in your book? No? You haven't? What! To write a book about magic and not include Vishvasiddhi would be like trying to write a book about philosophy without including the great Shankaracharya. Thus you must, for your very own sake, let me tell you the story of the great Vishvasiddhi, author of the *Indrajālasūtra*."

A SKELETON OF MAGIC

Realizing that there was no way out of it, that at least he would be saved by a ring of the telephone announcing the arrival of his taxi, the foreigner finally took up the teacup of scotch and listened to the story.

Once upon a time, and I swear that every word of this is true—the magician began—there was a pious Brahmin in Banaras, Varanasi, Kashi, City of Illumination, holiest of Indian cities, and this Brahmin, Jayantaswami by name, an Atharvan priest with hereditary expertise in Vedic magic, had a dream in which Indra, seated upon his great white elephant, lightning bolt in one hand, his net of illusion held by the other, his flesh dotted with eyes, appeared. "You are a pious man," Indra said. "My servant through and through. For while others have ignored me, making offerings to the modern gods—Shiva, Krishna, Kali, and the like—you have remained true to me. And thus for you I have a boon. Name your wish, anything at all, and it shall be conjured up and granted."

There was only one thing that this Brahmin wanted, what every man must finally crave: a son, male issue to perpetuate his existence and materialize his dreams, a son who, when the father dies, will perform the *śraddhas*, that *sapiṇḍi-karaṇa* magic that unites a father's flesh with the bodies of his ancestors to preserve his being for all eternity. Indra promised it, and the Brahmin woke up, emerged from his dream rejoicing with gratitude for the promise of a son who, like himself, would be a great magician, protected and empowered by Indra. Jayantaswami feasted Brahmins, gave them lavish gifts, and made offerings no less wonderful to Indra.

And when the Brahmin's wife became pregnant, Jayantaswami rejoiced for the fetus in her womb, the germ that was charged with the energy of Indra. Performing magical *saṃskāras* for the birth of a son, he exulted unceasingly with tears of joy and thanksgiving in his eyes.

But then one night, shortly before the birth of the magician, our Brahmin had another dream. Once again Indra was conjured up: slowly, slowly the god lifted up the net, stretching it out with both hands, and as Jayantaswami looked through the net at the face of the deity, he saw the terrible transformation, heard the hideous laughter, as Indra turned before his very eyes into the demon Shambara: "By my magic I can assume myriad forms, that of a god or that of a man, the body of Indra or of some poor magician on the street."

The nightmare of Shambara was as full of horror and dread as the dream of Indra had been of joy and promise. The Brahmin trembled in his sleep under the gruesome gaze of demonic eyes that were burning coals, under the grotesque growl of the voice: "You will have a son, a magician whom you will deliver up to me, so that under my inspiration, he will be the master of the magic called *śāmbarī*. Empowered by Indra, endowed with the god's own *śakti*, this magician will help me, will be my secret weapon, the confederate in the magic trick I use to overpower Indra, to take the Indraloka and become ruler of all magic, master of all illusions. After the baby is born, protect him, guard him; and then, after you have performed the rite of first feeding, once the child is weaned, I shall come, and you will present me with him. If not, if there is any hesitation, I'll send you to hell, cut off your head with my magic sword, and impale that head on a white-hot stake planted in the putrid dung that is the earth of hell. Your eyes will watch as the rest of your body is slowly tortured, cut apart and put back together, again and again, healed to be tormented, cut and restored, cut and restored. You'll not be able to cry out, for I will have cut out your tongue. If, however, you cooperate by giving me the infant magician, then, I swear, by my magic, you'll have another child, a good Brahmin boy, studious and obedient to his mother and father, a son to perform the *śraddhas* for you after your death, so that you may live on in the heaven of the fathers."

The Brahmin, awaking from the ominous dream trembling in a bed that was wet with the sweat of anxiety, tears of terror, even urine released by the panic of it all, was afraid to tell his wife the reason for it. Unable to sleep or eat (the certain sign of something very wrong in a Brahmin), he made urgent offerings to Indra, recited the Vedic hymns to that god, begged, pleaded, beseeched Indra to appear and advise him. But the god would not come. His dreamlessness was itself a Naraka hell, more and more anguishing each day. ["I need another sip of scotch for this."]

Soon the cursed child was born, and where normally there would have been great festivity, the father only trembled all the more with fear and sorrow for the infant who was born under the sign of Shani, your Saturn—a dreadful nativity indeed. A vulture is Saturn's vehicle, his color black. Once Saturn looked at the child of Parvati, and the mere glance of the planet decapitated that baby boy, Ganesh. The head of that infant was, by magic, replaced with that of an elephant. You know what we say?—"He who is born under the sign of Shani, malefic of the malefics, will suffer all of his life—his sons and his wife will be destroyed."

Jayantaswami made supplicatory offerings to the elephant-headed god and propitiatory offerings to Saturn. He called for the divinators because, though he himself was versed in that magic, he could not practice it on his own child. The magicians read the lines on the baby's little hands and feet, felt the bumps on his head, and studied the astrological charts. One of them closed his eyes: "I see the man, Vishvasiddhi, a magician, but not like us. No, I see him cutting off the head of a child, dismembering that child, putting him back together, and cutting him apart again. I see the death of seven sons."

Jayantaswami sent them away and wept with sorrow and still did not have the heart to tell his wife the cause of his misery.

One day, just six months later, just after the baby's first feeding on solid food, the *saṃskāra* we call *annaprāśana*, the Brahmin was returning home from the shrine of Indra, walking through the streets of Kashi when, on a certain street corner, he came upon a crowd of people that had gathered around a street magician. Jayantaswami watched the magician, his eyes burning like coals, order a boy to stand in a basket. When the conjurer called that child Shambaradasa, the name made the Brahmin tremble. Placing the basket top on the boy's head, the street magician pushed on it, and the boy settled into the container, out of the sight of the crowd. Tipping the basket to and fro, turning it around and around, the performer assured his audience that there were no escape hatches. When he pierced the basket with the first sword, Jayantaswami shuddered at the sound of little Shambaradasa's scream. Five swords penetrated the basket, and the earth was stained with blood. "I've killed my son," the magician moaned. "I have no son. I no longer have a son. You can't be a magician without a son. I need a son." And the Brahmin Jayantaswami felt that the magician, the gleaming sword in his hand, his dark body smeared with ashes, his long hair matted, was gazing directly into his eyes and speaking right into his ear. His own heart seemed impaled with the five swords.

Rushing to his home where his wife was preparing the meal, Jayantaswami grabbed up his infant son and, while his wife protested—"Come back! Come back"—ran back to the site of the magic show. The magician and his son had disappeared.

In panic asking everyone, "Where are the magicians? Where are they?" he retraced their steps through the *galīs* of Kashi, down to the river, up to the red-light district, back through the town, and back down to the ghats. The baby in his arms was crying as he haggled with the ferryboat-*wālā* who finally rowed him across the Ganga to the camp on the inauspicious shore, where Jayantaswami handed over his infant son to the startled conjurer and ran away in shame and sadness.

Those low-caste performers from Bengal (Anga in those days) laughed at the stupidity of the Brahmin, and the mother of young Shambaradasa took the baby Vishvasiddhi in her arms to hold him close to her and laughed. The father laughed too, saying, "He'll be a fine magician, perhaps the world's greatest magician."

Thus it was, and I swear to you that all of this is true, that Vishvasiddhi was raised by a troupe of itinerant street magicians; and of that life, of what his childhood as a wandering conjurer was like, all of that you know from your research, for the life of the low-caste street performer has not changed one iota in the thousand years that have elapsed. Vishvasiddhi's childhood was no different than the childhood of that Kabir, the Madari boy of Shadipur Depot. In the way that ether permeates the other four elements that form all things material, so there is an ethereal magician, a *vidyādhara*, a spirit of magic, who pervades all of us who do magic. We merely play out the moments of his long, long life. We are his many births, his countless incarnations, and his carnal fluctuations. ["Let us have a few more drops of scotch and drink to the ethereal magician and his eternal tricks."]

Then as now, the Bengali magicians followed the monsoon, pursued the path of the dark clouds in order to arrive in the villages just after the rains, a time of magic with the early rice, the water lilies, and the migratory birds suddenly appearing out of nowhere; a time when people, having been kept within their homes by the seasonal storms, would come out and into the streets anxious for some diversion. Traveling with that band of magicians throughout India—Bengal, Kerala, Kashmir, and Tamil Nadu, north, south, east, and west, to the sacred cities of India, Puri, Mathura, Banaras, and Kanchi—young Vishvasiddhi learned many things. He mastered our standard tricks: Hindu Wands, Leaden Balls from Mouth, Cups and Balls, Mango Tree, Bunder Boat, Cut-and-Restored Turban, Egg Bag, Diving Duck, Levitation, Jumping Egg, and all the like. And the Basket Trick, yes, that trick was his specialty as a boy—getting into that basket, dodging the swords, being sacrificed and reborn. And that trick plays an important part in the life of Vishvasiddhi; for, you see, when he was a young man he met a Dom woman named Lakshmibai, a dark-skinned basket weaver who had the specialty, learned from her mother, of making the baskets shaped just right for the Basket Trick, and magic baskets with hidden loads and compartments for conjurers.

Vishvasiddhi married that basket woman, and she traveled with him, serving him obediently. In those days, you must understand, love was a matter of obedience and reverence, not like modern love which, if we fall into it, is nothing but a magic show, all illusion and deception, all seeming and sleights, all patter and performance. "I'll love you forever," one lover says to the other, and they believe it even while knowing that it is not humanly possible. Love is a perfect example of how desperate, anxious, and needful we are to be deceived.

Vishvasiddhi was, of course, anxious for a son—no less anxious than his real father, that Brahmin Jayantaswami, had been for a son to carry on his life for him and continue all that he had done, and finally to perform the *śraddha*s, that *sapiṇḍi-karaṇa* magic that unites the father with his ancestors for all eternity. A magician must have a son, a boy to be sacrificed, slain, and reborn for him in the basket. But each time Vishvasiddhi's wife became pregnant—seven times, each time a son—the baby died at birth.

Our magician, a man of keen insight and Brahminic intelligence, surmised the reason for it, suspected that he must have been born on a Saturday, under the sign of Shani, the sullen planet of misfortune; for he noticed it, even when he was just a small boy, just three or four years old, performing with the older child, Shambaradasa. He noticed that whenever they did their magic, whether in Kashmir or Kerala, Ujjayini or Pataliputra, in every crowd that gathered around them there was a man, that same man, a fellow following them, that black figure in the black robes, limping in the shadows. Vishvasiddhi knew it—it was the regent of Shani, Kruralochana, the evil-eyed one, the dark, accursed figure, ally of Shambara, a tormentor of souls.

Perhaps, though we can never know for sure, it was a desire to escape that specter of misfortune that prompted Vishvasiddhi to leave the troupe, to renounce conjuring. Or perhaps it was some concern for truth. The magician's problem was that, for some strange reason, he did not enjoy deceiving people, lying, swindling, tricking. Oh, he had a talent for it—all of us do, and that is what separates us from the animals—but he did not savor it then.

Whatever the real reason, Vishvasiddhi stopped performing, but, knowing no other way of life save that of the wanderer, he continued to follow the storm clouds. Surviving only on the bit of money they earned from selling Lakshmibai's baskets, the weave of which was so perfect that the baskets could hold water, they rambled through the land. They would often camp with holy men, roving renouncers, Buddhist monks, Kapalikas, and sannyasis, and among them there were sorcerers, magicians who claimed to have real powers, that real magic that our conjuring imitates. And in one of these camps, Vishvasiddhi met a certain Tantra man, a skull-carrying sadhu who swore that he could teach the Brahmin real spells and conjurations. So with his wife, the Dom woman, as his ritual consort, Vishvasiddhi was initiated into the diabolical cult of Bhairava and Kali. The magic you see on the streets today—all that tongue-cutting, decapitation, limes bleeding, skulls bursting into flames—all that simulates the authentic magic of our ancient Tantric cults.

At midnight on certain days of the month, Vishvasiddhi and Lakshmibai would assemble with other initiates for liturgical orgies, drinking whiskey and smoking bhang, eating meat and garlic, and performing sexual yoga. There were dark pleasures, bizarre ecstasies, holy debaucheries. And why, you might ask, did Vishvasiddhi indulge in these practices? It was to obtain magic powers, authentic energies of a substantial sorcery, so that he might overcome the terrible Kruralochana. So that he might rid his life of the evil and gloomy influence of Saturn, he learned to mutter the mantras, construct the mandalas, and make the mudras—all of the methods of attraction and subjugation, immobilization and eradication. Of course he thought it was possible: Dasharatha, that father of Lord Ram, helped Indra slay the demon of magic, Shambara; and that same Dasharatha, prompted by Vashishtha, after performing austerities, entered into arduous battle with Shani and averted the course of that planet. That is great magic, to change the path of a planet, to alter destiny.

Lakshmibai became pregnant once more, and to save the child, Vishvasiddhi practiced the severest austerities, cast the strongest spells, conjured up all the powers he had mastered in the cremation grounds. But the infant, this time a little girl, just like the seven boys, died at birth. And this time, the dark, beautiful mother, Lakshmibai, the lovely weaver of magic baskets, died with their child. Gently, so gently, Vishvasiddhi placed his head against her breast, resting his fingertips tenderly under her nostrils. *"Oṃ aiṃ klīṃ hrīṃ śrīṃ,"* he muttered methodically and then with all his aching heart invoked Kahneshvari and Kali, Shambara and Indra, Bhairava Shiva and Vasudeva Krishna. "This *māyā,* this magic trick I do, conceals me. Not everyone can see me—the unborn, undying one," he whispered into her ear, weeping, knowing that it was to no avail; weeping as he removed the pieces of dried mango leaf, each inscribed with a magic syllable, from the tarnished copper amulet around his neck and sprinkled them on the still, unbreathing breast of his wife. Weeping, weeping with all his soul, he pleaded for her to come back to him. He summoned all the powers of the Tantras and waved the peacock feather over her eyes. Nothing. She was dead. And nothing, nothing, you must realize, can bring back one who has died. Magic provides us with the illusion that such things are possible. Because of death all of us want to be deceived. All of us believe what we want to believe about death and, whatever we believe, it is wrong. The illusion is inescapable.

Bitter over his powerlessness to bring his wife back, Vishvasiddhi renounced the Tantras, abjured sorcery, and returned to the only way of life he knew, that of the itinerant conjurer, now endeavoring to expose false holy men, those Sai Babas of previous times who used conjuring tricks to hoodwink people so vulnerable on account of their natural hopes, fears, and longings. The magician realized that just to entertain is the highest possible thing, the purest pursuit, that philosophy, religion, art, commerce, everything that engages man is, at the very best, nothing more than entertainment, a pleasant diversion from a void that, if you are not distracted, sucks you into it, devours and eradicates you. *Gilli-gilli*-gone! ["Have another sip of scotch."]

Yes, Vishvasiddhi, resigned once more to be a traveling entertainer, a wandering conjurer just like the ones you see today, all the better with the patter for his experiences of Vedic and Tantric magic, traveled from place to place, and because of his great skill, he often had audiences with kings. And thus it was that he ended up in the court of one King Amaruka of Kashmir. And it was there that Vishvasiddhi took a disciple, a boy named Indragopa.

In his old age, stricken with the ailments that come with time, he resolved to become a sannyasi, to renounce this world, abandon everything, and take to the road. But, consummate entertainer that he was, he wanted to end his career as a magician with a beautiful bang, something spectacular. He performed what he thought was his last trick—the famous Buried Alive illusion—for the courtiers of Amaruka, and instead of being exhumed fully alive as expected, he disappeared into the earth, just as Sita did, never to be seen in Kashmir again. Wonderful. Perhaps that's how I shall end my own career.

The boy, his disciple, knowing that something was up, went searching for the old sannyasi, who was wandering around India, living on alms, contemplating the meaninglessness of all things we hold meaningful. The sannyasi is precisely he who sees through illusions, through all tricks, all magic; he is the man for whom nothing is surprising, who feels no wonder. Thus his liberation from this world.

The old man, progressively becoming sicker and sicker, weaker and weaker, in his ceaseless wanderings, finally came to a village in my own Bengal, a place called Shittal, where until only few years ago, magicians and acrobats, bear and monkey trainers, bards, snake charmers, puppeteers and the like, camped. And those among them, old, tired, or whatever, who wanted either to take a break from the itinerant life or to retire from it, would stay in Shittal village. And each group had a leader, and Shambaradasa was the chief of the magicians.

When the old sannyasi arrived in Shittal village, entered it as sannyasis do, loincloth clad, flesh anointed with ashes, hair hoary with age and matted, "There he is!" the boy Indragopa called out in astonishment. "He's alive! He has come to us! There he is! Come quickly, Grandfather." The child who imagined himself beyond amazement was amazed and moved. And Shambaradasa too, limping with age, hobbling after the boy, was astounded, struck with wonder to the quick: there he was, the boy from many years ago, that orphaned child with whom Shambaradasa had been raised, with whom he had performed as a child, the boy grown old, and Shambaradasa, his hands together in the gesture of greeting and tears streaming down his face, whispered, "Brother."

Taking the sannyasi to his tent, he insisted that he must stay, "You're home now, Vishvasiddhi."

"I have no home," the old man smiled. "I am a renouncer. I am no longer Vishvasiddhi. I have no name. I am no one."

"Have the *sraddha*s been performed for you?" Shambaradasa asked, and "No," the old magician had to admit. And Shambaradasa said, "Then you're still alive. You may have renounced the world, but the world has not yet let go of you. Please stay. We'll take care of you now just as we took care of you then, when, as an infant, you were left with us." And the boy Indragopa, laughing, then weeping, then laughing all the more, repeated Shambaradasa's words and pleaded with the old man to stay.

Tired as he was, the old magician fell asleep in the tent of Shambaradasa, and all of the other performers who were camped or settled in Shittal village, sticking their heads into the tent to see the curious old sannyasi, asked about him. "He's Vishvasiddhi, the world's greatest magician." And they wanted to see the wonderful magic of the master.

When the old man finally woke up, his head resting in Shambaradasa's lap, he was asked: "Will you perform some magic, just one trick, so the magicians here can learn from you, see the perfect magician, behold your magic and be inspired by your skills, the poetry of your hands and eyes."

"I don't perform magic any longer: I'm a renouncer; I'm no longer a magician. I have nothing up my sleeves—in fact," he laughed, "I have no sleeves," Vishvasiddhi insisted. But, as you know, once magic is in your blood, you can't be free of it. You can't give up performing, not for the life of you. Even when you are sleeping, you do magic in your dreams. It is so of me. Thus I believe old Vishvasiddhi would have done the trick even without the pleading of Shambaradasa and Indragopa.

What magic do you think he did? What trick would be the greatest one of all, the accomplishment of a lifetime, the only trick left for him to do? Of course, it's so obvious. He would, for his very last show, topping even his Buried Alive, perform the greatest trick in the world, the illustrious illusion—the Indian Rope Trick!—in the open air and fully surrounded!

Indragopa assumed that the old man would have him climb the rope. But no, he did a different version, the Rope Trick with a twist. After invoking Indra and Shambara, the old man, in the center of the circle of magicians that had gathered around him, threw the rope into the air, a very, very long rope that rose higher and higher, very, very high, so high that one could not, I swear it's true, see the end of it. Then, to the utter amazement of the magicians, Vishvasiddhi placed his own hands upon the rope, took a breath, a bit of *prāṇāyāma*, smiled, then lifted his old, decrepit body up, up, began to climb the rope; up, up, up he went, higher and higher still. And the mouths of Shambaradasa, Indragopa, and all of the magicians, even the little monkey Vrishakapi, were hanging open, their heads tilted back as they watched the old magician climb higher and higher still, until he was out of the range of their vision, gone, gone, completely gone, vanished into the clouds. And then—more amazing still—the rope that hung from the heavens seemed to be pulled upwards, reeled in by the magician so far, far above them. And the rope, like the magician, disappeared.

They were struck utterly dumb with wonder by the miraculous assumption of the magician. The only thing that he left behind was this book, our *Indrajālasūtra*.

The magicians waited and waited until nightfall, but still the old man did not reappear. Indragopa gazed deep into the sky, the sidereal backdrop for Vishvasiddhi's last spectacle, looked into the heavens, and scrutinized the stars and planets. He knew what had happened. He felt it. He understood. Vishvasiddhi had climbed all the way up, right into the heavens, beyond the sky, beyond the spheres of Venus, Jupiter, and Mars, all the way up to the sphere of Saturn, where he confronted that malefic Shani, the planet that had cursed his life, taken his wife and children from him.

"Let me show you a little trick," the old magician said with a laugh, and the dark regent of the planet nodded in assent. "Here I have a begging bowl. And here, some spheres: a red ball—Mangala, the planet Mars; a blue ball—Budh, the planet Mercury; a white ball—Shukra, the planet Venus; and here, my friend, this black ball—this is you yourself, the planet Saturn."

And then our magician did his Cups and Balls routine, that basic trick all street magicians learn from childhood, the simple close-up sleight, and that trick terrified the planet. He saw himself, that black ball, turned into one of pure gold—Brihaspati, the Guru, he who is as benefic as Shani is malefic—and the planet Saturn trembled. And then, *ek, do, tīn*, the gold sphere was vanished.

"The size of the ball does not affect the trick. Do you want to see it done life-size, on full scale? Shall I make you disappear?" the magician laughed, and

Saturn quaked with fear. Do you understand? Simple conjuring, simple sleight of hand, was able to accomplish what the great Vedic and Tantric magic was helpless to do. Saturn pleaded for mercy: "What do you want of me?"

"Take a less malefic course," old Vishvasiddhi smiled. "Do not torment the hearts of men. Life is hard enough as it is."

And since that time those of us born on Saturdays have had somewhat less terrible lives than those in olden times, for Vishvasiddhi—I swear it's true—altered the course of the planet, smoothed out the orbit to make our heavens more gentle.

Once again the old magician threw the rope into the air, once again climbed up it, higher and higher, a hundred leagues, pulled himself into the sphere of the Seven Sages; and then he did the trick again, tossed up the rope, climbed up again, past Dhruva, the pole star, all the way into the Mahar Loka, the sphere of the saints, where he remains, performing magic there, delighting Bhrigu and the other saints with his sweet illusions.

"And that, my brother, was the last time the great Indian Rope Trick was ever performed. The secret of it is with Vishvasiddhi, World's Greatest Magician, in the realm of the saints. And all that is left of him is this book, the *Indrajālasūtra*, the wonderful text that I am now giving you the opportunity to make your own."

The magician, smiling very happily and proudly, a bit drunkenly and a bit sadly, placed the top hat on his shaven head and held out the book to the traveler, who would not touch it.

"Thank you, Professor Bannerji, but I really can't buy it. Please, it's very late now. I must get ready."

"I don't think you comprehend the importance of the book, Professor," the magician said with a sudden desperation that verged on anger. "You don't understand. The success—dare I say the 'truth?'—of your book depends on this book. It is the skeleton key for opening the lock on Indian magic. Let me finish the story. I swear it's true. Indragopa took to the road performing the tricks that he had learned from Vishvasiddhi, from his father, one Muladeva, a scurrilous fellow (but that's another story), and from his grandfather, Shambaradasa. The street magicians of India today, those who have converted to Islam, illiterate as they are, descend from that boy. But what of stage magicians, the great illusionists? There is a lineage unknown by many. A group of magicians from Bengal, from Shittal village to be precise, performed marvelous tricks for the Moghul emperor Jahangir. Where did they learn those tricks? From the *Indrajālasūtra* of Vishvasiddhi, the book that remained with Shambaradasa only to be passed by him to his sons, to their sons, to their sons. And it is from those magicians, the Bengali sons of Shambaradasa, that I myself descend and have come to inherit the book. The book! The magic book! Professor, you must buy the book. That is all there is to it. One thousand dollars."

"I can't. I'm sorry, I really can't," the traveler, taken aback by the audacity of the price, insisted once again. "Excuse me, Professor Bannerji, but it's after three o'clock. My taxi will be here at any moment. I really must get ready."

The magician looked wistfully at the empty bottle of Johnnie Walker and then into his empty teacup. "On the stage," he sadly sighed, "I would be able to refill it, to replenish it again and again. But in life, that is more difficult." He sighed once more. "Okay, okay, because we are friends, because we are both magicians, five hundred dollars."

Bannerji snapped his fingers to produce another cigarette, laughed, and then thumbed the pages to show the effect of the Magic Album once more—the words disappeared, reappeared, disappeared. "The book is a skeleton of magic, the bones of it. It has four sections, or *adhyāya*s, one for each of the elements: fire, air, water, and earth. Ether, the fifth element, permeates the other four. It deals with close-up magic, that magic of the Indian street conjurers, and illusionism, the magic of the court, the stage, the theater."

"It's after three o'clock," the foreigner said with real urgency.

"Yes, yes, time flies, as philosophers East and West have duly noted," the magician laughed. "We are born, and before we know it, *gilli-gilli-gilli*, we are dead. Oh melancholy morphometasis . . . I mean metamorphosis. A baby turns into a boy, who turns into a man like you and me, and then we are transformed into something old that is changed into a corpse. Fire is the magician that turns the flesh to ashes. Is there something else to us, some soul, spirit, self, breath, essence, or whatever? If so, it vanishes. Where? I don't know. That magic is cruel. Unlike the tricks that we do, that illusion is unresolved."

The traveler started to speak, but the magician interrupted his interruption: "When I returned triumphantly from Las Vegas, U.S.A., and arrived at the House of Maya, my poor father was sitting there, all alone in the house except for the Muslim sword swallower, Suleiman Yusuf Shah, the only member of our troupe not to abandon the sinking ship of our magic; and he, my illustrious father, was dressed in his maharaja garb. The jewel in his turban was sparkling like a real diamond, and the old man was fanning a deck of cards with unbelievable sureness. He did not even say hello to me, but only, 'Watch this my son!' He fanned the cards to show me the blue backs of them, then closed them, fanned the fronts to show me they were normal cards, then closed the deck, fanned it again, and all the backs were red. He smiled happily and tears fell from his eyes."

Bannerji laughed piteously. The foreigner, waiting for another break in the story so that he might once again announce the hour, started to speak, but the magician was too quick for him: "My father died in those clothes, the raiment of a maharaja. He was a magician to the end. What does that mean? What is a magician and what is magic? Some people say that magic is an art, and thus it has a certain importance. But I believe that magic is not really an art, not important in any way. I have learned this the hard way. The magician—let's face a truth—is a trivial man. And yet—let us not be hopeless—in its own way, magic is the purest of all the arts because it is so purely for its own sake, so unimportant, so unnecessary, so profoundly trivial that it is profound. Do you understand? There is a certain dignity to the magician's essential absurdity. But at this point I must add that just as the triviality of the magician and his magic is profound, so this profundity is really rather trivial. Is it that I am getting drunk, or does this make sense to you? When you take magic seriously, think that it is important, you realize that it isn't serious, significant, or important in any way; but when you dismiss it, think it's trivial, then it hovers, lingers there, and you know that you are missing something, that it is the greatest of all pursuits because, in its insignificance, it represents all other significant pursuits. The god, the priest, the lover, the artist, the doctor, the lawyer, the businessman, all of these people, try to perform magic, to create illusions. Can you deny it? This philosophical basis of magic, this explanation of magic as a representation of all other activities, is fully covered in the *Indrajālasūtra*. Because we are brothers, I will sell it to you for one thousand rupees, not dollars, but measly rupees."

"I'm sorry, no. Please, I really do need to get ready."

"I understand. You're not a rich man. Okay, five hundred rupees. Let's settle it. Then no more talk of such things. Please, I am a desperate man." The magician was trembling. "Please, all of this is humiliating to me. Please, you must help me. Please."

"Look, Bannerji, I really have to finish packing. My taxi will be here at any moment."

Bannerji smiled his electrifying stage smile. "Packing! I am an expert on packing. One of the basic skills of the magician is being able to fit many large things into small places. I'll help you."

The exasperated traveler rose, went to the closet, and began to put the last few things into his bag. Watching him, noticing his agitation, Bannerji tried to comfort him: "You know, as bereaved as I am over the demise of my great father, death puts things in perspective. After the death of one who is close to you, you realize that packing, getting to the airport on time, all of our little appointments, worries, and the like, are really meaningless. They are illusions. The great Shankaracharya explained all this over a thousand years ago." Bannerji suddenly stopped. Seeing the baseball jacket with the patch on it—"International Brotherhood of Magicians"—removed from the closet and tossed on the bed, the magician could not help himself: "Because you are not a rich man, I have a proposition for you, although I must be crazy for doing such a thing. I'll give you the *Indrajālasūtra* of Vishvasiddhi, a manuscript that has been in my family for over one thousand years, a text full of the very darkest and deepest secrets of Indian magic, in exchange for that jacket. How can you say no?"

Imagining that it was his only way to get rid of Bannerji, the traveler accepted the deal, and the magician put the jacket on. While the foreigner put the manuscript, together with his own papers, journal, and notebooks, into his bag, the performer stood before the mirror, modeling his baseball jacket, smiling his magnoelectrific smile, gazing his electromagnific gaze, and tipping his top hat.

The traveler telephoned the desk: "It's three-thirty. Are you sure the taxi is coming? Please, check on it. I can't be late."

"Sit down," Bannerji insisted with intractable cheerfulness. "Your taxi will come, and I will keep you company until it does. It is for me, in all honesty, as much as it is for you—I want the honor of waving good-bye to you. That will give me sadness and yet happiness as well." He snapped his fingers to produce a cigarette for himself and one for the traveler.

"Do you know the sleight? With the simplest sleights one can do the most profound tricks. I must tell you about my greatest trick, performed by me as part of my *śraddha* for my father."

"Please, Professor Bannerji."

"No, no. Please let me tell you this. You are anxious, worried about your taxi. This will help you get your mind off that until it comes. Worrying and pacing about will not bring it any sooner. Please, listen. This is important. Do you know about the *sapiṇḍī-karaṇa*, that 'making *sapiṇḍa*' that we do for our *śraddhas*? Listen, the son, me in this case, M. T. Bannerji, performed this illusion twelve days after the death of my father, also M. T. Bannerji. On a banana leaf one *piṇḍa* is placed. On another banana leaf three *piṇḍas*—you know *piṇḍas*, rice balls. The three represents another great M. T. Bannerji—my grandfather, my father's grandfather, and my grandfather's grandfather. Do you know what I am supposed to do? In the presence of a Brahmin, dearly paid I might add, and in the presence of the family, of which I had none, I might add, although the Muslim Suleiman Yusuf Shah was, out of his reverence for the great M. T. Bannerji, in solemn and pious attendance. I was supposed to divide the *piṇḍa* representing my father into three pieces, and that is exactly what I did. Then I was supposed to squeeze each of the pieces of my father into one of the three other *piṇḍas*, to unite the body of my father with the bodies of our ancestors. Do you understand? Listen to what I did, damn scurrilous as it may have been. I was looking at those *piṇḍas*, and it was so much like a magic trick! It was as if those banana leaves were magician's mats—I couldn't help myself. I must show you!" With an excited laugh, the magician jumped up and bolted into the bathroom only to instantly reappear with a long streamer of toilet paper. "Toilet paper! This is what the West has given to India. I'll have to use it for the *piṇḍas*." Working frantically, he tore the paper into tiny shreds and rolled the pieces into four small balls. Turning over the teacup from which he had been drinking the scotch, he laughed with haunting exuberance: "Okay, imagine you are that Brahmin, watch me. Here, I divide this *piṇḍa*, my dear father, into three pieces; I divide him as he, when I was a child, seemed to cut me into pieces in his Zig-Zag Boy routine. Now watch—I take one piece of my father and roll it together with this, my grandfather, and I put it here, under this teacup, the *pitṛ-loka*, land of the manes. Okay, now I mix another part of my father with my father's father's father and put it under the cup. Now what remains of my father's body is mixed together with my father's father's father's father's body, and it too is placed under the cup. So how many balls are in the heaven of the fathers? Three?" He laughed and lifted the cup to show a single large, lumpy ball of toilet paper. "In death they have become one!" And he laughed as once more he lowered the cup over his ancestors.

"My father, M. T. Bannerji, now surely Heaven's Greatest Magician, was most certainly laughing there, wherever that is, behind whatever curtain, in whatever concealment." And the magician joined his father in that laughter, pointed at the cup, lifted it again, and it was empty. Nothing. The ancestors had disappeared. And tears of sorrow, compounded by drunkenness, rolled down the magician's cheeks: "There will be no *piṇḍa*s for me, you see, no magical immortality—my wife, you see, has taken my son away. I'll have no one to perform the rite, to do the trick for me. In the early days, I used to cut her in half with an electric saw on the stage. Now she has cut me in half. And half has been taken away. What am I to do? A magician must have a son. Maybe the boy, that little Kabir, maybe he'll do the magic for me."

The doleful, drunkenly sentimental patter was interrupted by the knock on the door that heralded the arrival of the taxi, finally delivering the foreigner from the seemingly endless show of M. T. Bannerji. As he followed the foreigner who followed the boy who carried the suitcase down the hallway, down the stairs, to the desk, and out into the night, the magician kept talking: "That Brahmin practically went crazy, seeing those balls of rice become one and then vanish. Because he thought some real magic was taking place, he started muttering mantras to protect himself. Religion and magic!"

Realizing that the traveler was about to climb through the open door into the taxi, Bannerji suddenly fell silent and gazed searchingly into the foreigner's eyes.

"Good-bye, Professor Bannerji."

"On behalf of the Brotherhood of Indian Magicians, those of yesteryear as well as those of today, I bid you a safe journey and Godspeed, with the hopes that through some magic, our paths, illusory as they ultimately are, may cross again." The magician ceremoniously tipped his magic top hat to the foreigner: "Please take my card and write to me often."

As the taxi pulled away from the guesthouse for Indira Gandhi International Airport, the traveler turned to look through the window in the back of the cab and saw the staggering silhouette of the tottering magician in the American baseball jacket. The satiny finish of the top hat that might have concealed a flock of doves shimmered in the moonlight. His arms, like those of a tightrope walker trying to keep his balance, were extended from his sides as he walked forward. The foreigner looked down at his card: "Professor M. T. Bannerji, World's Greatest Magician, Last of the Maharajas of Indrajal. Poste Restante, Calcutta GPO, India." He looked up and back again. The magician had disappeared.

The taxi disappeared from Bannerji's sight. He rubbed his eyes, laughed for no particular reason that he knew, and weaved his way down the Mathura Road in what he hoped was the direction back to the Ambassador Hotel on Sujan Singh Road. Across the street there was a fire burning, and perhaps because it brought back the image of his father's funeral fire, he headed toward it, drawn to it as if by his love for his father. A small, dark cluster of pariahs were gathered around the flames, and the firelight danced in their glassy eyes. Raggedly draped in a contaminated blanket, one of the homeless beggars coughed as he stretched out his hand toward Bannerji. Clicking on his magnificent smile, the face he wore upon the stage, the Bengali magician showed an empty hand, snapped his fingers and, *gilli-gilli-gilli*, produced a rupee coin. Without any sign of amazement, trembling only with fear, the beggar reached out beseechingly for it, and the others, like crows and jackals around the dead, crowded in. "Connoisseurs, I see," Bannerji laughed, snapped his fingers again, and produced a Gold Flake cigarette, and another dark-blanketed beggar, his terror muted, grabbed it.

"Gentlemen," the magician said with a bow, "welcome to the Indrajal Extravaganza of Professor M. T. Bannerji, World's Greatest Magician, descendent of the great Vishvasiddhi, author of the *Indrajālasūtra.* Here and now, I shall perform my great magic for your pleasure and enlightenment." As he spoke, misdirecting them with his patter, he removed the flash paper that was always kept ready in the band of his watch. "Make obeisance to the feet of Indra, whose name is one with magic, and to the feet of Shambara, whose glory was firmly established in illusions. I can make the moon appear on earth or a mountain in the sky. I can conjure fire out of water or water out of fire, earth from thin air or thin air from earth." The magician flicked unseen the flash paper into the fire and instantly there was the burst of light, the curling billow of bright white smoke, and in terror the beggars disappeared into the darkness.

"Damn them," Bannerji muttered to himself, turned, and staggered on. "These bloodies have no culture! Must wonder be a luxury?" He snapped his fingers to produce another cigarette for himself, snapped them again only to realize he had no matches. Laughing with surprise, he dropped the cigarette and swayed and stumbled forward once more.

"I must help these people. I must help them." The thought echoed in his heart and made him tremble. "Yes, I must help them." He hesitated. "That's it! That's why I have had all of these problems. Of course! Everything has a purpose! Everything has led up to this. Why did I not realize it sooner? Why did I not see that I, Professor M. T. Bannerji, World's Greatest Magician, have a mission? Of course! In my very own Calcutta, with my magic, I shall serve the poorest of the poor, the wretched, the sick, the homeless. When they see me escape from a galvanized iron can filled with water and secured with locks, it will be a promise that, if I can do that, then they can escape from their dark worlds too. Hope will be my gift to them. When they see me dismember a child and put him back together again, it will be a promise that they too have some hope of putting their own shattered flesh or spirit together. When I perform my Waters of India and

Magic Rice Bowl, they will no longer fear starvation. I shall fill their impoverished world with delight, yes, inspire them with the sense of wonder that is deliverance from all that is bleak and gloomy, yes! I will be the Mother Teresa of magic! Yes, I shall emancipate them from reality, teach them the infinite joys of illusion, redeem their hearts with wonder."

The world was spinning, tilting this way and that, and the magician, overwhelmed with joy, drunkenness, and fatigue, could hardly keep his balance. He zigzagged across the empty street, faltered, pitched, and lurched into the park, near the zoo, near the Purana Qila, where the Yamuna once flowed, where the Pandavas once camped, where seven Bengali magicians once performed for Jahangir. He stumbled toward the pipal tree near the little mosque, stretched out his arms to it as a baby does to signal a mama or papa to catch and hold him. The tree bumped his head, knocked off the magical top hat, and when the magician reached for it, he fell, rolled over, and lay on his back. Through the branches of the tree and the smoky night sky, the infinite stars seemed to be the jewels holding together the threads of Indra's Net.

The magician closed his eyes and began: "And now, ladies and gentleman, my great levitation trick, done in the open air, fully surrounded, without prop or gimmick. *Ek, do, tīn. Gilli-gilli-gilli.* Watch me! Please watch me!" He felt himself slowly begin to rise from the ground, just an inch or so, and then he settled back on earth, bouncing just slightly. "Fly Bannerji, fly up, high up, fly as high as you can!" he cried out and sensed his body respond, float up, rise several feet in the air. He felt as light as if his flesh were made of cloud. "Yes, fly! Fly higher!" he urged and felt the restraints of gravity and of all else that was grave fall away like loosened shackles in an escape trick. "*Śābāś!*" he whispered—"*Śābāś* and bravo!"—as he hovered in the air, smiling with the boundless joy of lightness and of a freedom that seemed infinite. And there, in midair, he fell asleep, deep, deep asleep, and dreamed a dream in which, as in a magic show or story, anything was possible.

Historian's Notebook 4:

Field Notes on Magic
(Fragments)

5/29/87 (Bombay)
Anything can happen. That's the pleasure of magic and the terror of it.

6/6/87 (Delhi)
In the park, near the Purana Qila, the magician performed the Diving Duck routine, the Chinese Sticks (which they call *Hindu Wands*), the Indian Basket Trick, and other conventional tricks, including a decapitation—he claimed that Kali wanted his son's head. The performance recapitulated the Vedic sacrifice in which the head of the Prajapati he-goat replaces the head of a human victim. But it recapitulated something more universal, more timeless, as well. The infanticidal impulse, perhaps dormant in every father, with its correspondent fear, perhaps latent in every son, was presented in the trick just as in the ancient rite. The myth in which Shiva beheads his son, Ganesha, was reenacted. A sinister fantasy was played out. What was the appeal of that? Why did everyone pay the magician (conjurer or priest) for doing that? Did he diffuse or in any way resolve their anxieties? Our dread? Looking out at the performance, the members of the audience, I suspect, saw into themselves. Ourselves. Myself. I was the magician. I was the child. That was the trick.

6/7/87 (Delhi)
Descriptions of magic are of no interest whatsoever. What is astonishing to see is dull on the page. The amazement is not that it was done, that I read or hear about it, but that I witness it "with my own eyes, in person." The more vividly it is described, the more essentially it remains description—my trick, my illusion, not theirs.

6/8/87 (Delhi)
How a trick is done is always its least compelling dimension. "Such quibbles are just as harmlessly deceptive as the juggler's cups and pebbles in which it is the very trickery that pleases me. But show me how the trick is done, and I have lost

my interest therein" (Seneca). People who think they want to know how a trick is accomplished, if told, are disappointed (if not threatened) by the inevitable simplicity of the method. *Why*, not *how*, is what is of interest, is what is most secret, is what I cannot quite figure out.

6/9/87 (Delhi)

Again the decapitation (once of a child magician, a little girl named Salma; once of a young man, a member of the audience who, I am assured, is not a confederate but an innocent, nameless passerby); again the unnerving enactment of the figurative idiom of "losing one's head," again and again: the spectators, beheaded no less than the victim, the sacrifice, deprived of reason, control, all that orders and makes sense of the world, pay, they imagine, so that the victim's head will be restored; but it is really to get their own heads back, to retrieve what they feel they've lost; they, we, I purchase order, sanity, sense, redemption from the horror of the metaphor.

6/10/87 (Delhi)

Seeing is not, contrary to the cliché, believing. What, after witnessing magic, after thinking about it and performing it, constitutes belief?

6/11/87 (Delhi)

The child, the magician's son, slumped over in the dirt, was blindfolded with a filthy rag so that he could see what was going on amidst an audience that, by the light of day, was in the dark. Magic prompts a contemplation of paradoxes, the paradoxes of paradoxes, the paradoxes of paradoxes of paradoxes . . . until we're back at the beginning again and ready to start all over.

6/12/87 (Delhi)

The magic show is a world with its own laws, its own distinctive qualities of time and forms of space. And, conversely, the world is a magic show: "Reality is everywhere full of magic," Rama cries out: "It stuns the senses and makes me close my eyes; one sentiment—that of wonder—reverberates through my being" (Mahadeva's *Adbhutadarpaṇa [The Mirror of Wonder]* 4.8). "Know that this world is like the wondrous magic show of a magician, the wielder of Indra's Net," the Buddha, in his effort to convert his half-brother Nanda, warns: "If you want out of the net of sorrow, cut through the net of delusion" (Ashvaghosha's *Saundarananda* 5.45).

6/13/87 (Delhi)

Magic is most clearly understood not when looked at technically, in terms of method, but when contemplated aesthetically, in terms of appeal and function. A trick or conglomerate of tricks, or, as in the case of the Rope Trick, a memory or story of a trick that is thought to have been done has meaning only as a dramatic performance: each trick is a scene in an audience-observed play with a plot and characters, with a theme and an overall sentiment (the *adbhuta-rasa*, the sentiment of wonder) enhanced by subsidiary sentiments (usually comedy, *hāsya*, followed by the macabre, *bībhatsa*). In the act of magic, props become symbolic objects manipulated by the conventionally costumed, stock (even allegorical) characters who interact in archetypal ways which have at once universal and culturally specific associations and significances. The associations—psychological, social, and cosmological—give the power to the drama. And that power, or the experience of it, is the final meaning of the trick.

6/14/87 (Delhi)

The street magicians, when their paths cross, show each other their versions of Cups and Balls and speak in their private, secret language; I meet some university professors, and in a language no less esoteric, we speak about what we're working on. There is a pleasure in fulfilling expectations.

6/16/87 (Delhi)

In a magic show one is expected to do something unexpected.

6/17/87 (Delhi)

"I'm writing a book on magic," I explain, and I'm asked, "Real magic?" By *real magic*, people mean miracles, thaumaturgical acts, and supernatural powers. "No," I answer: "Conjuring tricks, not real magic." *Real magic*, in other words, refers to the magic that is not real, while the magic that is real, that can actually be done, is *not real magic*.

6/18/87 (Delhi)

What is expected in a book or lecture on Indian magic and conjuring by a professor? "The Psychology of Amazement, Aesthetics of Wonder, and Soteriology of Awe." That's what was planned. I carry the notes with me, the first pages of something that, before I arrived here, seemed important. Despite myself, I still can't throw them away:

> Amazement (*vismaya*) is, within the rhetorical taxonomies of early Indian aestheticians, one of eight fundamental emotions which abide innately and universally within the human heart, eight basic affections out of a combination of which all other feelings are formed: amazement, love, courage, sadness, merriment, anger, fear, and disgust. The effects of these emotional experiences, these internal responses to the external world, whether pleasant or unpleasant, wonderful or terrible, pleasurable or painful, when represented in art—on the stage or in a literary text—could be, according to traditional aesthetic theory, transformed or enhanced to precipitate a

purely pleasurable experience, that of an aesthetic sentiment, a *rasa*, in the heart of a spectator or reader. The emotion, or *bhāva*, the psychological experience, is the foundation of the artistic sentiment, the *rasa*, the aesthetic experience. The human emotion of being amazed, astonished, or surprised can be dramatically enhanced into the aesthetic sentiment of wonder, the *adbhuta-rasa*. "The *adbhuta-rasa*," in the words of Bharata (the legendary author of the *Nāṭyaśāstra* [c. second century C.E.], the seminal Indian text on the theatrical arts), "with *vismaya* (amazement or astonishment) as its stable state (its essence, the emotion upon which it is based), arises on account of the following causes: visions of divine beings and acquisitions of desired wishes, going to a temple in a grove or seeing a divine chariot, a divine assembly hall, a magic show (*māyā*), a conjuring act (*indrajāla*), and so forth. It should be acted out with the following affects: staring with the eyes open wide, having goosebumps, shedding tears, sweating, being thrilled, yelling 'Bravo!' continuous gift giving, loudly shouting 'Haha!' twiddling the fingers, trembling, and the like. Its transitory states include: paralysis, tears, perspiration, stammering, goosebumps, paroxysms, bustling, torpor, passing out, and so forth" (after 6.74).

Abhinavagupta, the eleventh-century Kashmiri scholiast, glosses *māyā* (the word I have translated as "magic show") more specifically as "causing transformations of the bodily form"—the repeated trick of gods and demons in the *Purāṇa*s, the adoption of disguises through the power of *māyā* as accrued through performances of austerities. Such metamorphic magic is distinguished from creational magic by his explanation of *indra-jāla*, the general term for magical practices, rather arbitrarily as "making things which don't exist appear" by means of such things as mantras, potions, and other magical devices.

It's misdirection, the stuff that grant applications are made of. It's so easy to be complex, learned, pedantic; so difficult to speak simply, naturally, truthfully.

6/19/87 (Delhi)

If, as Robert-Houdin is said to have said, a conjurer is an actor playing the part of a magician, then a professor might be an actor playing the part of a scholar: I take the part, play a scholar who, to learn about magic, plays the part of a conjurer who plays the part of a magician whose first trick must be to make a professor disappear . . .

6/30/87 (Calcutta)

The mind, by seeking to normalize what it perceives, to make sense and resolve, is deceived, easily and constantly misdirected, and willing to be so for the sake of equilibrium. Our need for order deludes us. I realize this not only at the magic show but while walking down Chowringhee. We dare not see what is really going on.

FIELD NOTES ON MAGIC

7/1/87 (Calcutta)

I thumb a copy of a magazine that has been left in my room and tear out a cartoon. Magic can be a metaphor for anything.

FIGURE 11. *Politicians Try the Mango Tree Trick.* Cartoon by Shankar reprinted from *The Illustrated Weekly of India* (Bombay, 1987); courtesy of *The Illustrated Weekly of India* and the estate of the late Shankar Pillai.

7/2/87 (Calcutta)

Indian rhetoric and aesthetics form an elaborate system of classifications and categorizations, a system of correspondences and subcorrespondences which, as a system of correspondences, is the basis of a magic . . . verbal illusions, semantic palmings and passes, false shuffles and cuts . . .

7/3/87 (Calcutta)

Metaphors are rhetorical conjuring sleights, magically transforming one thing into another, linguistic gaffs to make things appear from nowhere, to make things vanish . . .

7/4/87 (Delhi)

Mind reading, a standard trick of the magician, is in no way different than text reading, a standard trick of the professor.

7/5/87 (Calcutta)

The production of rabbits—from a hat, box, or whatever empty space—has become a kind of symbol for magic in general. The stage magicians' programs here inevitably utilize the icon. It's on every magician's calling card in India. It's everywhere. Why? In India the rabbit is associated with the moon. Perhaps the conjuring trick can be understood as a reenactment of the lunar show, the magic of waxing and waning. We are pleased because the show suggests to us, on a subliminal level, that there are human beings among us who have some control over the larger forces. The conjurer does as a trick what the ancient magician actually endeavored to accomplish—to make it rain, to fertilize the earth, by controlling the moon, the receptacle of soma. The inevitable failure of the latter's efforts marked the predestined birth and evolution of conjuring as entertainment. What couldn't be accomplished empirically, in nature, by the magician-priest could be accomplished aesthetically, psychologically, by the magician-entertainer. The rabbit also, of course, suggests fertility; and witnessing a mastery of that unruly sexual power is no less reassuring.

But Sorcar laughed at me when I spoke like this today: "You're wrong," he said with the same confidence he displays on stage. "Entirely wrong. Rabbits are used because they look larger than they are. They fit nicely into a small load, and they expand when they are removed from it. So too with pigeons, doves, and guinea pigs. That's all there is to it." I became shamelessly professorial: "Sure, but that doesn't contradict my point. At the B. N. Sarkar show in Delhi I noticed that when the magician produced a dove or pigeon, there was, or was supposed to be, a certain awe. But the production of a duck prompted laughter. The same trick had a different aesthetic effect. The object, onstage, has associations—it means something. Every prop in the magic show becomes a symbol tying various realms of experience together. The doves or the tigers, removed from nature where they just are what they are, become, as soon as they appear on the stage, more than what they are—they are complex symbols with individual, cultural, and universal associations. The woman who is cut in half is a woman who stands for other women and represents something about women; the water poured from the lota bowl. . . ." My interpretations of magic, I realize by the expression on Sorcar's face, are to magicians just what my magic tricks are to the academics I know—meaningless, but amusing.

7/6/87 (Calcutta)

"When a singer is great we say, 'Your song was full of magic'; when a dancer is great we say, 'Your dance was magical.' . . . Art aspires to magic. Magic is the essence of all the arts, the highest art, pure art, art's ultimate accomplishment" (P. C. Sorcar Junior). He is unconsciously reiterating the theories of certain traditional Indian aestheticians who made the sentiment of wonder primary and inherent in every successful work of art, an enhancement to any sentiment, the source of the transporting power of every sentiment. Ramachandra and Gunachandra, students of the Jain scholiast Hemachandra, explain that, whatever the dominant aesthetic sentiment, a play ought to end with the acquisition of something (the lover his beloved, the warrior victory over his enemy) and that such a moment should be marked by and informed with a sense of wonder: the *adbhuta-rasa* should act as a secondary *rasa* to enhance any primary mood. The audience should marvel at the conquest of the enemy, should be amazed by the union of lover and beloved. That climactic acquisition should involve something "extraordinary," something more or less impossible in real life (*Nātyadarpaṇa* 1–15). The play should, in other words, be magical. Vishvanatha Kaviraja (fourteenth century), furthermore, in the *Sāhityadarpaṇa*, cites the scholiast Dharmadatta (thirteenth century): "*camatkāra* (poetic delight, poetic astonishment [onomatapoetic for the smacking of one's lips in pleasurable surprise as over a magic trick]) is the essence of *rasa;* thus the *adbhuta-rasa*, in every case, is inherently the chief ingredient of that [magical] poetic-delight (*camatkāra*)." Vishvanatha further comments that Narayana, his great-grandfather, also made *adbhuta* the basis of all *rasa*s and explains that "*camatkāra*—a late synonym for *vismaya* (surprise)—has the form of an expansion of the mind" (commentary following 3.2). My greatest pleasure in India, the lip-smacking astonishment-delight of studying magic here, is in witnessing the past—ancient ideas and feelings, seminal rites and myths—surface in the present, in person, fully surrounded, and before my very eyes.

7/7/87 (Calcutta)

Rasa theory elucidates the pleasure experienced in a magic show: surprise or astonishment, the emotion in the world, may be either pleasurable or unpleasurable; but wonder, the sentiment in and of the magic show is, to the degree that the magic show is successful, only pleasurable; the show, made up of tricks, is itself a trick, a real illusion that depicts an illusory reality, a world in which even the most terrible terrors are a source of pleasurable pleasure.

12/6/87 (Delhi)

Anything can happen. That's the pleasure of India and the terror of it.

12/7/87 (Delhi)

"At any and every moment many things are happening. This happens here, and that happens there. Almost all of the things that are happening are, let's be both realistic and honest for a moment, unrelated to each other. All of life, all that happens, I believe, is coincidental. But people hate coincidence; they want everything to be connected. That is why people love magic, believe me. Magic indicates connections that aren't really there. The telephone rings, the curtain is ruffled by the wind, a dog barks, I set down my glass on the table. . . . The magician merely has the ability to encourage his audience to perceive two or more of these unrelated events as connected in some way. And then the magician takes credit for it" (The Incredible Mayadhar).

12/8/87 (Delhi)

A French woman in the bar at the Imperial Hotel, certain that she was a Hindu in a past life because she feels at home in India (*"Je suis heureuse de respirer l'odeur de l'Inde, le parfum d'une magie ancienne ...'*), is thrilled to discover that I am writing a book about Indian magic and wants to know what magic I've learned. Producing a deck of cards, I perform Paul Curry's Out of This World (a trick I learned from my father as a child, in my opinion the most wonderful card trick there is, so simply accomplished and yet so miraculous to behold). "This is not a trick" is the patter that sets up the trick: "It's an experiment in ESP." Setting out a red card and a black card and handing the deck to her, I explain: "Hold the cards in your hand, face down—don't look at the faces. Place them one at a time, all of them, in any order you want, face down, in a row on either the red card or the black card and then we'll see how many, using your intuition, you get right. I won't touch the cards. Do you understand? Place it here if you think it's red, here if you think it's black." Slowly, feeling each of the cards with her fingertips, her eyes half closed, she begins: *"Rouge ... rouge ... noir ... non! rouge, oui, c'est certainement rouge ... noir ... noir ..."* She's going so slowly that I have to interrupt: "Faster. Don't think about it. Just use your intuition." When it's all over, reminding her that I have not touched the cards, that she has made her choices freely and spontaneously, I turn over the columns, and all the reds are together, and all the blacks are together. Utterly unsurprised, she smiles, *"Mais oui, je suis psychique ..."* She's taking the credit for *my* trick! I try to explain that it's just a trick, that it always works that way, that no matter who sets down the cards, all of the reds always end up in the red pile, and all of the blacks always end up in the black pile. When she recalls that I had said it wasn't a trick, I explain that that was part of the trick. It isn't a trick; it is a trick. Which statement is true, which truth a lie, which lie a truth? Where does patter begin and end? Pick a statement, any statement. Still unsurprised, still smiling, she nods and says she understands. How can you understand?—it's an amazing trick, completely baffling, utterly incomprehensible. Her explanation is that I, knowing the order of the cards, used the power of my mind (a power I've gained from studying Indian magic) to control her mind, to telepathically prompt her where to place the cards. I insist that no one can do that, that no one has such power, but she refuses to believe it—of course people have such power, *"surtout en Inde."* The idea that there are no such supernatural powers is as threatening to her as the idea that there are is threatening to me. "If I could control your mind, I'd use that power to other ends." She senses a sexual innuendo (or am I misreading her mind, the way in which her mind is misreading my mind?). "If I had the power to control your mind, I'd use that power to convince you that no one has the power to control your mind."

FIELD NOTES ON MAGIC

12/9/87 (Delhi)

Naseeb won't let me go with him to Ghaziabad to find the farmer who does the Rope Trick. Is it because I've admitted that I'm not really a magician, but a professor writing about magic? A deceit for the sake of trust, followed by an honest confession for the sake of trust ... what, for the sake of trust or deceit, comes next? It is ironic, with an irony that informs this whole project, that today, while he is in Ghaziabad, perhaps seeing a version of the Rope Trick, I'm in my room reading a version of it:

> The object of the exhibition [of the Rope Trick] is to reveal to the specta-
> tors an unknown and mysterious world: the sacred world of magic and
> religion to which only the initiated have access. The images and dramatic
> themes employed, notably the ascent to Heaven by means of a rope, the
> disappearance and initiatory dismemberment of the aspirant, not only il-
> lustrate the occult power of the magicians, but reveal also a deeper level
> of reality, inaccessible to the profane; they illustrate in fact the initiatory
> death and resurrection, the possibility of transcending "this world" and
> disappearing on to a "transcendental" plane. The images released by the
> rope-trick are capable of producing both an attachment to an invisible,
> secret and "transcendental" reality and doubts as to the reality of the fa-
> miliar and "immediate" world. From this point of view, the rope-trick—
> like all other displays of magic—has a positive cultural value, for it stimu-
> lates the imagination and reflection, one acting upon the other, by the
> questions and problems that it raises and, ultimately, by putting the prob-
> lem of the "true" reality of the World (Mircea Eliade, *The Two and the
> One*).

Would Eliade's illusion amuse Naseeb?

12/10/87 (Delhi)

It is possible, using the techniques of conjuring, to simulate any impossibility. Possible impossibilities (magic tricks) most popularly, in India and universally, serve individual and collective consciousness, neurosis and culture: I know your thoughts (limits of human intimacy overcome); I know the future (limits imposed by time overcome); disappearance, materialization, transformation, or transposi-tion (limits imposed by space overcome). Death, that which imposes the limits and stimulates the desire to overcome them, is the theme of magic, the source of the art of illusion. Each little conjuring trick is a desperate defiance of the primacy and ultimacy of annihilation.

12/11/87 (Delhi)

Magic has been a theological metaphor here since the beginning: God is a magician; the magician is a god. Rudra-Shiva is the lord, owner, holder, and wielder of *māyā*, the net in which we're trapped, nature herself (*Śvetāśvatara Upaniṣad* 3.1, 4.10). God, in the *Bhagavadgītā* (4.6), announces that he comes into being through magic: "This world is my divine magic, hard to figure out . . ." (7.14). Commenting on the verse, Ramanuja explains that God is appropriately envisioned as a magician (*māyāvin*), tricking the world, staging a cosmic version of the street magic performance during which the magician, by his devices, creates not a reality but an idea or illusion of a reality, a meaningless image that is thought to have meaning, significance, palpability. As a magician, God is not affected or defiled by his activities in the world "since they're just manifestations of his *māyā*, like the tricks performed by a juggler" (*Bhāgavata Purāṇa* 12.10.30). Throughout the traditional philosophical literature, *māyā*—magic and this world—is explained with the metaphor of the "illusion of a snake created by a conjurer." The audience may jump back in fear, but the magician is at ease: the *māyā* of the deity has no more power over that deity than "the tricks of the juggler have on the juggler who performs them" (*Tripurārahasya [Jñānakhaṇḍa]*). Tarbell's observation in his textbook on magic could epitomize the theology: "The less mystery there is to the magician in a trick, the more mystery it will have for the audience" (*Tarbell Course in Magic*). One of the tricks of the magician who is God is the creation of an illusion of a human form. Shiva often performs the item, takes on the guise of a wandering mendicant. "It's a good idea to show hospitality to these sadhus," I'm told, "just in case one of them turns out to be God." Naseeb just might be Shiva: "This is Mahadeo's drum," he announces as he plays the Lord's damaru, and then he decapitates his son.

12/12/87 (Delhi)

Magic is a metaphysical and epistemological metaphor in the literature of Vedanta: in a magic show I am amazed, attached by that astonishment, entrapped in the magician's net. Freedom is knowledge: once I'm aware of the secret workings of the tricks, though I still see what others see, I can, at the same time, see through what others see. I am not moved, amazed, enchanted any more. Caught in a net, the harder I squirm and struggle to escape, the more entangled I become; caught in the world, the harder I vie to know, the more entangled in my ignorance I become.

12/13/87 (Delhi)

Like *māyā* in the epistemology and metaphysics of Vedanta, "Indra's Net" in Mahayana Buddhist speculations provided a metaphor for phenomenal existence: a cosmic net hung by a divine magician, stretching out boundlessly in every direction, the crisscrossed cords of it held together by shimmering jewels, each reflecting the others, reflecting the whole, an infinite network of illusions.

FIELD NOTES ON MAGIC

Tricks can be, according to Bharata, a cause of laughter (*Nāṭyaśāstra*, prose after 6.45). Laughter releases the tension that the trick instills, the uneasiness precipitated by not understanding how something has occurred. Naseeb uses the comic sentiment to enhance the overall sentiment of wonder. But surprise, the basis of that sentiment, can inspire fear no less than mirth, and Naseeb, manipulating the connections between them, moves from the latter to the former. Evoking the sentiments of terror and disgust, like an ancient poet, he uses them, just as he uses comedy, to further enhance a sentiment of wonder in which emotional oppositions and intellectual contradictions are reconciled. In the moment of wonder, perceptual and cognitive assumptions are challenged, and yet there is, at the same time, an uncanny reassurance; there is relief from the burdens of sense and logic, the pressures of intellection and cognition. The pleasure of magic is a disconcerting, mysterious pleasure.

Magic and medicine: it's not enough to look at the two endeavors and their practitioners in evolutionary terms; to see, as others have done, magic as primitive medicine, as the Vedic antecedent of medicine; to view the sorcerer as the ancient predecessor of the physician. The physician attempts to conquer disease; the magician strives to appease it. Magic personifies disease and then propitiates that personification. My doctor has prescribed an antibiotic to kill whatever is causing my fever; the ancient magician would have made an offering (the holy *kuṣṭha* plant, the sacred remains of sacrifices, and a gruel made from parched grains) through my mouth to Takman, Fever, the being who was originally born when Agni, the god who is fire, in the form of lightning, penetrated the waters of the earth (*Atharvaveda* 1.25). The doctor advised me to go south; the magician would have commanded Takman to take the journey: "Go, Fever, away, far away. . . . Take your brother, Consumption, and your sister, Coughing . . . and go to foreign places, down south. And bon voyage!" (*Atharvaveda* 5.22). Someone is pyrexic: the priest binds a striped frog with blue and red threads to the patient's bed; the water with which the sick person is washed drips onto the frog, and the fever is transferred from the patient to the animal (*Atharvaveda* 7.116; *Kauśikisūtra* 32.17)—the magician knows the secret connections between fevers and frogs, red and blue, water and health, the connections others do not see. The conjurer, the actor who plays the part of a magician, in the theater or on the street, also understands connections differently than the uninitiated: when I see red liquid come from a child's mouth, and I connect it with a wound, with blood, with the knife, and the piece of flesh that the man holds in his hands, the connections horrify me and trap me in the net of his magic. But if I know the trick, I connect the red liquid with something sweet, and the piece of flesh with a butchered goat in the market, and I'm amused, not horrified, not tricked. I'm outside the net looking in. The secret of any magic trick is simply knowing what is connected and what is not. That's what I'm after—hidden connections.

12/17/87 (Madras)

Yellow *(pīta)* is the color ascribed, in the elaborate classificatory system of the rhetoricians, to the sentiment of wonder, and I wonder why and begin to conjecture. The adjective is probably from the Vedic verb $\sqrt{p\bar{i}}$, "to swell, overflow, increase, grow." That action, as observed in nature, is essentially and fundamentally magical. My associations change directions, follow the pun to *pīta* (from $\sqrt{p\bar{a}}$, "drunk"). As the drinker drinks the drink, both become drunk. The drunken apprehension of the world is the magical one. . . . I suddenly realize that I'm being tricked by the words; what I've learned is always eager to deceive me.

12/18/87 (Coimbatore)

[*Initial assumption:*] Hindu magicians saw women in half (and then restore them to life), levitate women (and then bring them back to earth), make women their victims, imperiling and then redeeming them; Muslim magicians mutilate, decapitate, and then heal boys, levitate boys (and then bring them back to earth). The magic show is a sexual allegory: the lover is a magician; the beloved a passive victim; the act of lovemaking a beguilement, a display of power that redefines the culturally conventional relationship between subject and object: man and woman in Hindu poetry, man and boy in the erotic lyrics of Islam. That it makes sense makes me suspicious: in the magic show we are beguiled by our tendency to make sense of what is presented to us; in India the more I see, learn, and think, the more I see that what I saw was not real, learn that what I learned was false, think that what I thought was wrong.

12/19/87 (Coimbatore)

[*Shifts in focus, assuming new assumptions:*] The distinction should not be made between Hindu and Muslim, but between stage and street, between a bourgeois version of a once-aristocratic performance and a peasant, folk exhibition that has a historical constancy and once inspired the courtly show; the distinction should not be made between heterosexuality and homosexuality, woman and boy—the boy is but a safe, surrogate woman. It makes more sense, and that's all the more suspicious. Again the shifting of assumptions and presumptions that begins to make things clear, the realization that the mind is a sly trickster, a cunning conjurer, a natural magician (*the* magician according to the *Yogavasiṣṭha* 3.104.1).

12/20/87 (Coimbatore)

The magic show is about men, masculinity, a male power that is preserved through lineage, father-to-son, father-to-son across the generations of Man.

Women are important only to the degree that they generate, perpetuate, and, above all, decorate that lineage, that magic show. "Women," Naseeb shouts, "women and children go away, leave the circle." It is not for them to watch and not for them to do: theirs is but to connect the men, the fathers and sons, the seniors and juniors. They are not visible in the streets, and on the stage they are only assistants holding props, or they are themselves props, cheerfully surrendering victims in a sacrifice. "The simple fact that I am the wife of a magician gives me a pride and joy. . . . Gents will be talking and talking throughout day and night. We ladies will be discussing about our husband's showmanship, patter and pitfalls. . . . Any magic function, a dinner meeting or a conference, becomes colourful and charming only if and when ladies are present. It is only us who enthuse and encourage our husbands to be a good magician. . . . Magic is the key to popularity and success. It would indeed be a thrilling experience to be the wife of a magician who delights in creating mysteries to entertain people to forget their worries" ("I am Proud to Be the Wife of a Magician," by Mrs. Grace Durai, happy wife of The Great Appadurai, in *The Magic Wand*, August 1981).

12/21/87 (Coimbatore)

It would be too disturbing for women to perform magic, to put on a public display that required men to openly take pleasure in being fooled, deceived, or tricked by women. The female magician is a witch or sorceress, dangerous and demonic, to be caught, exposed, and punished—placed in a box or basket. The man, however, the hero of the magic show no less than the hero of India's amorous literature, is all the more charming for his deceits—he can be a rogue, a liar, a cheat, a trickster (erotically like Krishna, martially like Rama). The man is a hero to the degree that he is a magician, that he can perform magic or see through it (whether with a woman in love or a man in battle). The power of magic, the essentially female *māyā-śakti* (whether it is exercised politically, fiscally, religiously, sexually, aesthetically . . .), is *pāramparīna*, conserved by being handed down from father to son, maharaja to *yuvarāja*, sage to disciple, magician senior to magician junior (within clearly-defined families within clearly-defined hereditary professions within clearly-defined castes). The more time I spend with the magicians, Hindu and Muslim, on the stage and on the street, the more I am aware that magic serves lineage more than lineage serves magic. The effect of the trick is the attainment of immortality. How it's done: to the degree that a man identifies with his father, he is mortal; to the degree that he identifies with his son, he is immortal; he must do the former in order to do the latter, must realize his mortality in order to believe in his immortality.

12/22/87 (Coimbatore)

So often magic frightens in order to demonstrate that there is nothing to be afraid of: that's one of the many lies of magic that constitute whatever truth it has to offer.

12/25/87 (Cochin)

Last night the Thangals: a ritual of self-mutilation in which the soul is represented as an innocent bystander watching carnal torments. Tongue cutting. A knife on the tip of my tongue. The tongue: sensitive, wet, tasting, speaking, kissing, licking, savoring, feeling, tonguing, sliced, slashed, slit, scored. Mother tongue. Father tongue. Tongue-tied. Tongue-in-cheek. Tongue-in-check. Tongue twisters. Tongue-galls/Thangals. Forked tongue. The organ of enjoyment and communication made the receptor of pain. Mutilated, mute-elated. Silenced, sigh-lanced. Connection with the street magicians? Cf. Kali-*pūjā* in Gujarat, Sinhala Buddhist rituals. See Apastamba's *Dharmasūtra* 2.27.14. N. B. Jihvaka ("Madam Tongueless"), female demon. See Gananath Obeysekere—he thinks (I think?) it's somehow menarcheal: through scarification of the tongue, the man imitates, and thereby incorporates, the power of the woman who naturally, through menstruation, cleanses herself of accumulated pollution. Castration (is that why father Thangal teaches it to Thangal son? Is that why Naseeb does it to Ayasan?) and then menstruation. Cunt-envy? But then the tongue is restored or healed. The initiation is complete: the performer is a man again, first inferior to (more polluted than), then equal to (as polluted as), and then superior to (unpolluted by) the woman ... I looked up to see the fakir drilling a hole in his skull. ... We partake of his accomplishment through our payment for it. Thangal liturgy and the Indian streets (whether we consider the acts of the magicians or the terrorists) demonstrate simply that human beings take pleasure in pain, some in the crucifixion of others, some in the crucifixion of themselves. I keep thinking of Naseeb and Ayasan: the boy, apparently hypnotized, lay on the ground among the smoldering, bleeding limes, the undulating cobras, and the monkey skull. Upon command he extended his tongue. As Abraham approached Isaac, with knife in hand, Naseeb sidled up to his child. Cutting off the tip of his tongue, that magician circled before his audience, wiggling the blood-covered morsel of purplish flesh in his fingers. And more blood gushed in clots from the boy's mouth. "If each of you gives me two rupees I shall restore his tongue. If not, my son will never speak again. He will never sing, he will never pray." And the members of the crowd, with sympathy, fear, or guilt, reached deeply and desperately into their pockets and purses to find the money and redeem the boy.

12/27/87 (Cochin)

Illusions, as escapes from the discomforts of reality, are obviously comforting; but, inevitably, the fugitive feels uncomfortable with the illusion, with the essential loneliness of all illusions, and then reality is understood as comforting simply because there are so many other people there to give solace for what is so discomforting about it.

FIELD NOTES ON MAGIC

12/29/87 (Madras)

Deception is different than betrayal. The magician must accomplish deception without betrayal: the false holy man, the false lover, the false politician betray; the magician merely deceives. And he does so for our pleasure.

5/29/88 (Bombay)

Anything can happen. That's the pleasure of being alive and the terror of it.

6/2/88 (Delhi)

Dinner party with friends: "Do a trick for the children," I'm asked, but they want it for themselves—the children are merely the excuse, a presence that authorizes the illusion, permits the norms of childhood to prevail for adults, and sanctions the regression. Magic is a return to childhood (or, more precisely, what we imagine childhood to have been), and the gratification of the magic show is the pleasure of regression. "Okay," I say, "do you have a deck of cards?" The child anxiously pleads, "Tell me how to do it!" The parent playfully chides, "Magicians can't tell how it's done." During the magic show, children are trying to be adults (capable of figuring it out), and at the same time, adults are trying to be children (capable of feeling wonderment). "Sanctions the regression": we reinstate a child's state of mind, rediscover a world in which our participation (our words and actions, fears and desires) modifies reality. As incontrovertible laws are controverted before our very eyes, the amazement of that carries with it the pleasure of a relief from the burden of reality for the adult; for the child, struggling with an obligation to master an understanding of how things work and why, the amazement must be tinged with fear, a sense of perceptual and cognitive incapacities. "Tell me how to do it!" While for children the satisfaction of magic is in knowing how it's done, for adults the pleasure is in not knowing how it's done. After dinner I show the little girl how to do the card trick, and she performs it for her father. They laugh together with the pleasure of the experience of the momentary transposition of roles, an intellectual resupination. "Teach me another one," she insists, not "show me another."

As a child myself I wanted to have a magic set but did not like to go to magic shows. There was something scary about magicians, something all the more creepy if concealed with clown makeup or jokes. "Women and children leave!" Naseeb shouts in India, and in Hollywood, wanting to take my son to the Magic Castle, I'm told on the telephone that children are not allowed "except on Sundays, when we have a special children's matinee." It's too hard to misdirect children, or (like the French woman at the Imperial Hotel) they take credit for the trick—you knew the card they picked because they picked the right card; or you knew because you're an adult, and children know that adults know things that children don't know, while adults imagine that children know things that adults don't know, that children have access to a world of magic—thus Ayasan can read minds because he is a child. He has a power that we have lost, the shadowy innocence we conjure up and project onto the child lost somewhere in the darkness within ourselves.

6/25/88 (Srinagar)

Magic reveals how wrongly we remember what we have seen, discloses the way in which memory is the bearing and nursing mother of illusion. Memory is the magician's assistant, confederate, and shill. Hearing the description of a trick I've done, I'm amazed at what is described, at the way in which memory has tricked the spectator far more audaciously than I. Moves that seemed unimportant (inevitably the things that were crucial to doing the trick) are forgotten, while other things, never done, are remembered to fill in the spaces, to make sense of what has occurred. In the telling, the trick becomes more miraculous. Is that operative here, in my journals and notebooks? The harder I try to remember what has happened, to reconstruct it from the notes and make sense of it, the more likely I am to change it, to create an illusion out of whatever the reality might have been. Fiction is more honest.

6/26/88 (Srinagar)

The magician's patter is rhetoric in the truest sense of the word—language functioning to persuade, language creating illusions with the status of realities . . .

6/27/88 (Srinagar)

By creating an illusion of either a reality that we want to dismiss as an illusion or of an illusion that we want to believe might be a reality, the magician modulates the reality of reality for us, a modulation necessary for the trick to be amusing or for existence to be endurable. The magician on the street corner or in the theater is, in this role, a personification of a universal faculty of consciousness: consciousness would not be possible without tricks.

6/28/88 (Srinagar)

Illusions are full of pleasure, delusions of terror, a delusion (*moha*) being but an illusion (*māyā*) taken too seriously; once again the line between pleasure and terror is fine, perhaps an illusion if not a delusion.

6/30/88 (Srinagar)

Lies are exonerated the moment they become ironies: the magic show is informed with ironies—ethical and aesthetic ironies, epistemological and psychological ironies, physical and metaphysical ironies.

7/1/88 (Srinagar)

My right hand is closed into a fist after making a gesture with my left hand, and I point a finger of my left hand at my right hand: I lie without uttering a word (and at the same time, because I have not said anything, I have not lied); my spectators believe with their eyes what they would not believe with their ears. Surprised, but not surprised to be surprised, when the right hand opens and is empty, the coin apparently vanished, the eyes, those trusted witnesses, cannot help but look to the left hand, giving the right hand the opportunity to prepare for the next deception, the next step in the construction of the larger illusion.

7/2/88 (Srinagar)

Secrecy. Shhhhh. Joining the International Brotherhood of Magicians (so that I could, through that society, more easily make contact with magicians), I was obliged to sign an oath that I did not take seriously: "I pledge not to expose the modus operandi of any magical effect." In order to learn what I might wish to reveal, I had to promise not to reveal it. When Naseeb heard that I had performed his decapitation on Cheryl for the guests on the houseboat, he was concerned that perhaps his student had not done it well enough, not acted it out with enough terror, and that I had thus given away the ancient secret. Magic's methods are sacred: the sacrality is established by secrecy, the secrecy by a supposed sacrality, which is established in turn by a supposed antiquity. Before showing us how the trick was done (I would never have guessed it was so easy, so easy that it made it difficult to understand), Naseeb had rather solemnly told me never to tell it and certainly not to reveal it in my book on magic, this book. But the ethics of magic are paradoxical, full of ironies and loopholes. Should I tell? He both revealed the trick and insisted on the secrecy, I believe, to intensify my sense of the importance of what I was being shown and told. I could do the same, for the same ends. He certainly lied to me and could hardly have imagined that I would not lie to him.

7/4/88 (Srinagar)

HASHISH. Naseeb gives me a huge chunk of hashish as a good-bye gift, a souvenir, he says, to take back for magicians in America. When I try to explain that I can't take hashish through customs, he laughingly insists that he'll help me, that magicians know how to use secret compartments, and again he shows me a photograph of the falcons that he smuggled into Pakistan. Whenever I turn down the smoke (because it's too early in the morning, because I'm trying to write something, whatever the reason), he chides me—I'll never learn magic unless I smoke hashish with him. Hashish, he says, and magic go hand and hand. Hashish affirms the fact that people enjoy temporary visions of the world through distorted senses, suspensions of sanity, being disarmed of the logic that orders the world, relieved of the burden of orientation. The street magicians are inevitably *ḥashshāshīn*, hashish-smokers literally, and figuratively "assassins"—members of a secret, heterodox order of Muslim warriors—they are epistemological terrorists, assassinating by decapitation. *N.B.* Rashid ad-Din Sinan, the twelfth-century *ḥashshāsh*-conjurer whose repertoire of tricks included holding a conversation with a trunkless head (see Guyard *"Un grand Maître des Assassins"*).

7/13/88 (Srinagar)

Reality is the most convincing illusion, truth the most powerful deceit. A desire to know the truth is nothing more than a conscious manifestation or expression of an unconscious need to be deceived.

7/14/88 (Srinagar)

Lying in bed this morning I have a memory, a memory remembered for the first time in a long, long time: I followed by father. I kept my eye on the dark green jacket so as not to lose him in the crowd on Hollywood Boulevard as we made our way toward the Hollywood Magic Shop, where he bought the Amazing Finger Chopper for me, a little guillotine that would cut a cigarette or carrot stick in half, but seemed to go right through my finger without causing me the slightest pain or harm. It was on that day, I realize right now, that I began to work on this book.

7/22/88 (Delhi)

"You're leaving India tonight on airplane, and tomorrow you'll be in Honolulu. Simple! Is it? Or is it amazing? A few hundred years ago if someone did that, it would have been magic—wouldn't it?—either a trick or real magic. Believe me, please, the magic of the past inevitably becomes the not-magic of today. The extraordinary becomes ordinary. Or does it? Perhaps it is still extraordinary, perhaps it is still magic. Is it magic or not that you can fly to Honolulu? It depends on how you look at it, doesn't it? How do you look at it?" (The Incredible Mayadhar). Magic and wonder in a state of degradation, the extraordinary necessarily, essentially, becoming increasingly more and more ordinary; the ultimacy of entropy, the inert uniformity that is, despite the efforts of the magician, the end.

7/22/88 (Delhi)

"You have to decide for once and for all whether you are a magician or a professor. The two callings are not compatible, believe me. When I began as a magician, my wife suggested that I myself take the title of professor, calling myself Professor Mayadhar. So many magicians call themselves professor, like your friends Professors Shankar and Bhagyanath, like the famed Professors Jam, Pepper, and Mingus; but I, believe me please, refused because I believe a professor must show the truth, whereas a magician must show the illusion. The professor must be credible; the magician incredible—thus my own name choice. Which one, my darling man, are you interested in—the truth or the illusion? Which one do you want to be—credible or incredible?" (The Incredible Mayadhar).

The Coda

Words and Ether

"**I**'m a magician."

"Why did you previously state that you were a professor?" the officer for United States Customs in Honolulu, standing over the pile of belongings that she had emptied from my bag, continued her interrogation.

"Well, I am a professor. I mean that's my profession, but I'm a magician too—that's why I have all this stuff. It's magic equipment."

As the customs official examined the balls of cloth and brass cups, the gimmicked Himber Wallet and Egg Bag, the packets of colored sand and carefully wrapped lengths of Invisible Thread, the Okito Coin Box and the Pen of Perfumes, I tried to make sense of it for her: "I'm a professor in the Religion Department at the University of Hawaii. I'm writing a book on magic and conjuring in India. In order to be able to make contact with magicians there, I've had to learn to perform a bit of magic . . ."

"What's this for?" she interrupted, and I was surprised at how unsurprised she was to witness the floppy rope become stiff and stand erect in my impromptu performance, fully surrounded beneath the bright fluorescent lights, of the famous Indian Rope Trick.

"And this? What's this?"

"Blood. Magician's Blood. Fake blood. It's for a trick. You fill this needle with it. Here, let me show you the effect," I said, eager to demonstrate my willingness to reveal everything to her, to establish my credibility and convince her that nothing was being cached or concealed, as I produced the thick packet of photographs that Cheryl had taken from my inside coat pocket, and quickly thumbed through them to find and exhibit the one of Naseeb performing the Needle-through-Arm illusion on me in Vasant Vihar.

"The photographs please," she said glassily as she reached for them: "Hand me the photographs." Slowly surveying the pictures of the stage and street magicians, scrupulously inspecting each one, she set certain ones aside: Me, smiling with a needle in my arm; Naseeb kissing the ring on my finger; Ayasan on my lap, me hugging him; Cheryl hugging him; a monkey skull amidst a pile of bones next to a collection of strange rings and amulets; Naseeb and I, laughing and smoking, a chillum in my hand; Ayasan lying on the ground, his eyes rolled back in their sockets, blood gushing from his mouth, Naseeb behind him holding a blood-stained knife in one hand and a tongue in the other; Constable Kushi Ram menacing Naseeb with a lathi; the Thangal slicing his breast with the razors, driving a spike into his head, sticking out his scarred tongue; an eyeball impaled on a knife . . .

"It looks like you've had quite a trip," she said ominously and then coolly instructed her attentive assistant to call for the supervisor.

"Don't you understand? These are tricks, magic tricks," I anxiously insisted, feeling that the harder I tried to be honest, the more it seemed that I was lying, that I was hiding something, trying to fool them. My belongings smelled of subterfuge, deception, and tricks.

"Are you aware of President and Mrs. Reagan's anti-child-pornography campaign?" she asked.

"What?"

"There are some questionable photographs here," she said with an expressionless patience, a dreadful and officious calm, as, in the way a magician spreads a deck of cards, she splayed the stack of photographs that she had freely selected out of the larger pack: Salma, naked to the waist, a knife through her neck, blood drenching her chest; a naked little boy, a three-year-old Qalandar posing with his bear and incidentally twiddling the end of his penis with his grimy fingers; four more children, Maslets, child magicians in Shadipur, all naked; also naked a four-year-old snake charmer's daughter playing with a cobra . . .

"Aren't President and Mrs. Reagan aware that all children in the Third World are naked when it's 114 degrees out?" I said with an urgency that made me seem all the more guilty of some deceit or crime. I was defensive and trembling. My mouth was dry.

My interrogator stood some feet away whispering to her supervisor as, nodding, his lips purposefully pursed, he inspected the incriminating photographs that she had uncovered. He came toward me: "I understand that there's some confusion as to your profession. It's important to state the facts clearly, not to conceal anything, not to distort the truth in any way. You say you're a magician. Is that correct?"

With an irritation that was tempered by fear, I tried to untangle things once more: "I'm a professor of religion at the University of Hawaii. I've been in India doing research for a book about magic. With support from the Social Science Research Council, the American Institute of Indian Studies, and the University here, I'm currently working on a history of Indian magic and an anthropological study of contemporary Indian magicians." After a month of trying not to sound professorial, I was now trying to play the part convincingly: "See, here's my typewriter. This is a Sanskrit text, the *Ratnāvalī* of Harshavardhana. Here are my field notes—see: 'Historian's Notebook.' These documentary photographs are of the magicians I've been studying. This is magic equipment . . ."

As I spoke, he went through the pile of clothes before him, pushed aside a pair of underwear with the pencil he had removed from his pocket so that he could inspect one of my notebooks, and like a magician performing the Magic Album routine, he thumbed it from back to front, from front to back, stopping here and there to randomly read a line or two from this page or that: "Did you write this, Professor?"

"Yes, those are my field notes on magic."

"And this? You wrote this?"

He turned the notebook around with his finger marking the paragraph in question: "HASHISH. Naseeb gives me a huge chunk of hashish as a good-bye gift, a souvenir, he says, to take back for magicians in America. When I try to explain that you can't take hashish through customs into America, he laughingly insists that he'll help me, that magicians know how to use secret compartments, and again he shows me a photograph of the falcons that he smuggled into Pakistan . . ."

My sudden silence, as I read what I had written, seemed like a confession of heinous crimes.

"Did you bring the hashish, just a little bit of it maybe?"

"No," I insisted, and I kept trying to remind myself that since I had done nothing wrong and was concealing nothing, I had nothing to be afraid of; but everything I knew about magic told me that I would be judged as guilty as I seemed—I was afraid that I seemed to be hiding something and that fear made me seem to be hiding something. I tried to hide the fear and the fear of the fear as well.

"If you could come along this way please," the customs officer said with deadpan cordiality, and I was led to a small room, where I was instructed to undress.

"Turn around," he ordered: "Lift up your arms. What did you say you teach? Do you have tenure?"

Two more uniformed customs agents joined us. While one of them asked me to lift up my testicles, the other, after checking for secret compartments in the heels of my shoes, was inspecting my clothes—looking up the sleeves of my coat and shirt, examining the hems, scrutinizing the lining, searching the pockets. "What's this?" he asked, holding up my Jimmy Yoshida thumb-tip.

"It's a gimmick used by magicians. I'll show you," I said, feeling that if I could demonstrate my skill as a magician, show them that I could trick them, it would convince them that I was not trying to trick them. I asked for a cigarette.

"No smoking," was the solemn answer.

"No, no, I won't light it. Just let me have a cigarette out of the pack in my coat pocket. It's for the magic trick."

WORDS AND ETHER

After passing me a Benson and Hedges Deluxe International, the three customs officers warily watched me as I stood before them, as completely naked as the children of Shadipur except for Naseeb's ring on my right hand and a Jimmy Yoshida thumb-tip on my left thumb, trembling with fear and anger, overwhelmed with fatigue and exasperation, ready to perform the vanish that I had done so many times as Naseeb's confederate. "Watch, watch carefully," I instructed them as I placed the cigarette in my half-closed right hand. "Keep your eye on the magic ring." And making the magic gestures with my left hand, I could not help but laugh out loud as, for the very last time, I intoned the magic words:

Oṃ!
Gilli-gilli-gilli!
Yantru-mantru-jālajāla-tantru!

Bibliography

TEXTS CITED

(texts with authors unknown are listed by title)

Abraham, Thomas. "The Sorcar Magic." *Frontline*, 18 April 1987, 50–75.

Abū al-Fazl ibn Mubārak. *'Āīn-i-Akharī.* 2d ed. Translated by H. Blochmann. Edited by D. C. Phillott. Calcutta: Asiatic Society of Bengal, 1927.

Andrews, Val. *Goodnight Mr. Dante.* Alcester, England: Goodliffe. 1978.

Āpastamba. *Dharmasūtra.* Edited with the commentary of Haradatta Miśra by A. Chinnaswami Shastri and A. Ramanath Shastri. Kashi Sanskrit Series, no. 93. Varanasi: Jai Krishna Das Haridas Gupta, 1932.

Asaṅga. *Bodhisattvabhūmi.* Edited by Unrai Wogihara. Tokyo: 1930–36.

Aśvaghoṣa. *Saundarananda.* Edited with an English translation by E. H. Johnston. Indian reprint of the 1928 Lahore edition. Delhi: Motilal Banarsidass, 1975.

Atharvaveda. Edited with the *Gopatha Brāhmaṇa* by Sūryakānta. Kāśī Saṃskṛta Granthamālā, no. 166. Varanasi: Chowkhamba Sanskrit Office, 1964.

Ayling, Will. *Oriental Conjuring and Magic* (from an index by S. H. Sharpe). Devon, England: Supreme Magic Company, 1981.

Baldwin, Samri S. *Secrets of Mahatma Land Explained.* Brooklyn: T. J. Dyson, 1895.

Bernier, François. *Travels in the Mogul Empire A.D. 1656–1668.* Revised and edited from the translation of Irving Brock by Archibald Constable. London: Oxford University Press, 1891.

Bertram, Charles. *A Magician in Many Lands.* London: George Routledge and Sons, 1911.

Bhagavadgītā. Edited with the commentary of Śaṅkarācārya by Dinkar Vishnu Gokhale. Pune: Oriental Book Agency, 1950.

Bhāgavata-Purāṇa. Edited with the commentary of Gaṅgāsahāya by Pāṇḍeya Rāmateja Śāstrī. Varanasi: Pandita-Pustakalaya, 1965.

BIBLIOGRAPHY

Bharatamuni. *Nāṭyaśāstra*. Edited with the commentary of Abhinavagupta *(Abhinavabhāratī)* by Pandit Śivadatta and Kāśīnāth Pāṇḍuraṅg Parab. Kavyamala Sanskrit Series, no. 42. Bombay: Nirnaya-Sagara Press, 1894.

_____. Edited by M. Ramakrishna Kavi et al. 4 vols. Gaekwad Oriental Series, nos. 36, 68, 124, 145. Baroda: Oriental Institute, 1926–64.

Bhāsa. *Avimāraka*. In *Bhāsanāṭakacakra*, edited by C. R. Devadhar. Poona Oriental Series, no. 54. Pune: Oriental Book Agency, 1962.

Bhavabhūti. *Mahāvīracarita*. Edited by Anundoram Borooah. Gauhati: Assam Publication Board, 1969.

Branson, Lionel H. *Indian Conjuring*. London: George Routledge and Sons, n.d. [1922].

Budhasvāmin. *Bṛhatkathāślokasaṃgraha*. Edited with an English translation by Ram Prakash Poddar. Prācyabhāratī Series, no. 21. Varanasi: Tara Printing Works, 1986.

Chiu T'ang shu (The Old T'ang History). Compiled by a commission under the direction of Liu Hsu and submitted to the throne on 12 July 945. Shanghai: Chung-hua shu-chu, 1975.

Claflin, Edward, in collaboration with Jeff Sheridan. *Street Magic: An Illustrated History of Wandering Magicians and Their Conjuring Arts*. Garden City, N.Y.: Doubleday, 1977.

Collins, Wilkie. *The Moonstone* [1868]. Harmondsworth, England: Penguin Books, 1966.

Crooke, William. *Castes and Tribes of the North Western Provinces and Oudh*. 4 vols. Calcutta: Office of the Superintendant of Government Printing, 1896.

Daṇḍin. *Daśakumāracarita*. 7th ed. Edited with four commentaries by Nārāyaṇa Balakṛṣṇa Godabole. Bombay: Nirnaya-Sagara Press, 1913.

Dare, Paul. *Magie blanche et magie noire aux Indes*. Paris: Payot, 1947.

Das, Harihar. *The Norris Embassy to Aurangzeb (1669–1702)*. Calcutta: Firma K. L. Mukhopadhyay, 1959.

Dīgha Nikāya. Edited by T. W. Rhys Davids and J. E. Carpenter. 3 vols. London: Pali Text Society, 1890–1911.

Dubois, Abbé J. A. *Hindu Manners, Customs and Ceremonies*. Translated from French by Henry K. Beauchamp. 3d ed. Oxford: The Clarendon Press, 1928.

Dunninger. *Dunninger's Complete Encyclopedia of Magic*. New York: Lyle Stuart, 1967.

Durai, Grace. "I Am Proud to Be the Wife of a Magician." *The Magic Wand*. Hat 12, Dove 8 (August 1981): 13–14.

Elbiquet. *Supplementary Magic*. London: George Routledge and Sons, 1913.

Éliade, Mircea. *The Two and the One*. Translated by J. M. Cohen. New York: Harper and Row, 1965.

———. *Patañjali et le Yoga*. "Maîtres Spirituels" collection, no. 27. Paris: Seuil, 1969.

Elliot, Robert Henry. *The Myth of the Mystic East*. London: William Blackwood, 1935.

Filliozat, Jean. "Limites de pouvoirs humains dans l'Inde." In *Limites de L'Humain, Etudes Carmelitaines*. Paris: Desclée de Brouwer, 1953.

Fischer, Ottokar. *Illustrated Magic*. Translated and edited by J. B. Mussey and Fulton Oursler from *Das Wunderbuch der Zauberkunst* (Vienna, 1929). New York: Macmillan, 1931.

Frost, Thomas. *The Lives of the Conjurers*. London: Tinsley Brothers, 1876.

Fryer, John. *A New Account of East India and Persia, 1672–1681*. London: Chiswell, 1698. Indian reprint. Delhi: Periodical Experts Book Agency, 1985.

Gauḍapāda. *Kārikā* on the *Māṇḍūkya Upaniṣad* with the *bhāṣya* of Saṅkara. Anonymously edited. Gorakhpur: Gita Press, 1967–68.

Gibson, Walter B. *Secrets of Magic: Ancient and Modern*. New York: Grosset and Dunlap, 1967.

Guyard, S. "Un grand Maître des Assassins." *Journal Asiatique*. Paris, 1877.

Hamilton, Lord Frederic. *Here, There and Everywhere*. London: Hodder and Stoughton, 1921.

Harṣavardhana. *Ratnāvalī*. 3d ed. Edited with an English translation by M. R. Kale. Bombay: Booksellers' Publishing Co., 1964.

Hazlitt, William. "The Indian Jugglers." In *Table Talk, or Original Essays*. London: J. M. Dent and Sons, 1908.

Hockley, William Browne. *Panduranga Hari, or Memoires of a Hindu*. London: H. S. King, 1873.

Ibn Battūta. *Voyages*. 3 vols. French translation from the Arabic by C. Defremery and B. R. Sanguinetti, (1858). Paris: François Maspero, 1982.

Indrajālavidyāsaṃgraha. Edited by Jīvānanda Vidyāsāgara Bhaṭṭācārya. Calcutta: V. V. Mukharji, 1915.

Jacolliot, L. *Occult Science in India and Among the Ancients*. Translated from French by Willard L. Felt. New York: John H. Lovell, 1884.

Ja'far Sharif. *Islam in India or Qānūn-I-Islām*. Composed and translated by G. A. Herklots. Edited by William Crooke. Oxford: Oxford University Press, 1921.

Jahangir. *Tūzuk-i-Jahāngīrī*. Translated by David Price as *Autobiographical Memoirs of the Emperor Jahangueir* (London, 1829). Calcutta: Editions Indian, 1972.

Jaiminīya Brāhmaṇa. Edited by Raghu Vira and Lokesh Chandra. Sarasvati Vihara Series, no. 31. Nagpur, 1954.

James, Stewart, ed. *Abbott's Encyclopedia of Rope Tricks*. Colon, Mich.: Abbott's Magic Novelty Co, n.d.

BIBLIOGRAPHY

Jātakas. Edited by V. Fausböll. 6 vols. London: Pali Text Society, 1877–1896.

Kabir. *The Bījak of Kabir*. Translated by Linda Hess and Shukdev Singh. San Francisco: North Point Press, 1983.

Kalhaṇa. *Rājataraṅgiṇī*. Edited by Vishva Bandhu. Part 1 (*Taraṅgas* 1–7). Woolner Indological Series, no. 5. Hoshiapur: Vishvaranand Vedic Research Institute, 1963.

Kauśikasūtra. Edited by Maurice Bloomfield. New Haven, Conn.: American Oriental Society, 1890.

Kellar, Harry. *A Magician's Tour Up and Down and Round About the Earth: Being the Life and Adventures of the American Nostradamus, Harry Kellar*. Edited by "his faithful familiar, 'Satan Junior.'" Chicago: R. R. Donnelley, 1886.

——. "High Caste Indian Magic." *The North American Review* 56, no. 3 (1893).

Kipling, Rudyard. *Rudyard Kipling's Verse*. Garden City, N.Y.: Doubleday, Doran, 1942.

Lāl Rām Nāth, ed. *Talismāt Nātak Kalān*. Amritsar: Indian Book Agency, n.d.

McGill, Ormond. *The Mysticism and Magic of India*. London: Thomas Yoseloff, 1977.

Mahābhārata. Edited by Vishnu S. Sukthankar et al. 21 vols. Pune: Bhandarkar Oriental Research Institute, 1933–1960.

Mahādeva. *Adbhutadarpaṇa*. Kavyamala Sanskrit Series, no. 55. Bombay: Nirnaya-Sagara Press, 1896.

Mahāvaṃsa. The Great Chronicle of Ceylon. Translated into English by Wilhelm Geiger. Colombo: Ceylon Government Information Department, 1950.

Mammaṭa. *Kāvyaprakāśa*. Vol. 1. Edited with the commentary of Śrīvidyācakravartin and an English translation (*The Poetic Light*) by R. C. Dwivedi. Delhi: Motilal Banarsidass, 1967.

Maskelyne, Nevil. *Maskelyne on the Performance of Magic*. New York: Dover Books, 1976.

Matsya Purāṇa. Ānandāśrama Sanskrit Series, no. 54. Pune: Ānandāśrama Press, 1907.

Mulholland, John. "The Great Rope Trick Mystery." *This Week*, 6 April 1958.

Mundy, Peter. *The Travels of Peter Mundy in Europe and Asia, 1608–1667*. Edited by Sir Richard Carnac Temple. 6 vols. London: The Hakluyt Society, 1914.

Murphet, Howard. *Sai Baba, Man of Miracles*. York Beach, Maine: Samuel Weiser, 1973.

Murray. "The Indian Rope Trick." *Goldston's Magical Quarterly* 1, no. 1 (Summer 1934):21.

Nemicandra. *Ākhyānakamaṇikośa*. With the commentary of Ācārya Amaradeva. Prakrit Text Society: Varanasi, 1962.

Norris. See Das, Harihar.

Obeyesekere, Gananath. *Medusa's Hair.* Chicago: The University of Chicago Press, 1981.

Oman, John Campbell. *The Mystics, Ascetics and Saints of India.* London: T. Fisher Unwin, 1903.

Ovington, John. *A Voyage to Suratt in the year 1689.* London: Oxford University Press, 1929.

Padma Purāṇa. Ānandāśrama Sanskrit Series, no. 131. Pune: Ānandāśrama Press, 1893.

Patañjali. *Yogasūtra.* Edited and translated by J. Ballantyne. Reprint. Calcutta: Susil Gupta, 1963.

Pelsaert, Francisco. *Remonstrantie* [1626]. Translated by W. H. Moreland and P. Geyl as *Jahanghir's India* (1925). Delhi: Idarah-I Adabiyat, 1972.

Premanand, B. *Lure of Miracles.* Podanur: Premanand, 1976.

Rājaśekhara. *Karpūramañjarī.* Edited by Sten Konow with an English translation by Charles Rockwell Lanman. Harvard Oriental Series, no. 4. Cambridge: Harvard University Press, 1901.

Rāmacandra/Guṇacandra. *Nāṭyadarpaṇa.* 2 vols. Edited by G. K. Sugandekar and L. B. Gandhi. Gaekwad Oriental Series. Baroda: Oriental Institute, 1929.

Rāmāyaṇa of Vālmīki. Critically edited by J. M. Mehta. Baroda: Oriental Insititute, 1960–75.

Ray, Satyajit. "Les deux magiciens." In *Autres nouvelles du Bengale.* Translated from Bengali into French by Michèle Mercier. Paris: Presses de la Renaissance, 1989, 55–69.

Ṛgveda. Edited with the commentary of Sāyaṇa by F. Max Muller. Indian Edition. Chowkhamba Sanskrit Series, no. 99. Varanasi: Chowkhamba Sanskrit Office, 1966.

Robert-Houdin, Jean Eugène. *Confidences d'un prestidigitateur.* Paris: Librairie nouvelle, 1859.

Rose, H. A. "Magic (Indian)." In *Encyclopædia of Religion and Ethics.* Edited by James Hastings. New York: Charles Scribner's Sons, 1922, 8:289–294.

Russell, R. V. and Hiralal. *The Tribes and Castes of the Central Provinces.* 4 vols. London: Macmillan, 1916.

Śaṅkara. *Śāradātilaka.* Edited with an English translation by Fabrizia Baldissera. Bhandarkar Oriental Series, no. 14. Pune: Bhandarkar Oriental Research Institute, 1980.

Śaṅkarācārya. *Vivekacūḍāmaṇi.* In *Śrīśaṅkaragranthāvali.* 10 vols. Srirangam: Vani-Vilasa Press, 1952–1960, 10:1–100.

_____. *Bhāṣya* on the *Māṇḍūkya Upaniṣad.* Anonymously edited. Gorakhpur: Gita Press, 1967–8.

Śatapatha Brāhmaṇa. 2d ed. Chowkhamba Sanskrit Series, no. 96. Varanasi: Chowkhamba Sanskrit Office, 1964.

Śaunaka. *Ṛgvidhāna.* Edited by R. Meyer. Berlin, 1897.

Somadevabhaṭṭa. *Kathāsaritsāgara.* Edited by Pandit Durgāprasād and Kāśīnāth Paṇḍuraṅg Parab. 3d ed. Bombay: Nirnaya-Sagara Press, 1915.

Sorcar, P. C. *Sorcar on Magic.* Calcutta: Indrajal Publications, 1960.

———. *History of Magic.* Calcutta: Indrajal Publications, 1970.

———. *TW's GM, The Great Sorcar.* Calcutta: The All India Magic Circle, n.d.

Śrīharṣa. *Naiṣadhacarita.* Edited by Nārāyaṇa Rāma Ācarya. Bombay: Nirnaya-Sagara Press, 1952.

Śvetāśvatara Upaniṣad. Vol. 1 of *Eighteen Principle Upaniṣads.* Edited by V. P. Limaye and R. D. Vadekar. Pune: Vaidika Samsodhana Mandala, 1958.

Tarbell, Harland. *Tarbell Course in Magic.* 7 vols. New York: Tannen Magic, 1941–72.

Tavernier, Jean-Baptiste. *Travels in India.* 2d ed. 2 vols. Translated by V. Ball. Edited by William Crooke. New Delhi: Oriental Books Reprint Corp., 1977.

Tripurārahasya (Jñānakhaṇḍa). Translated by A. U. Vasavada. Chowkhamba Sanskrit Studies, no. 50. Varanasi: Chowkhamba Sanskrit Office, 1965.

Trivedi, Shikha. "The Great Magician." *The Illustrated Weekly of India,* 3 August 1986, 6–16.

Vaid-Fera, Minnie. "On the Trail of the Godmen." *Imprint* 27, no. 7 (October 1987): 59–66.

Vātsyāyana. *Kāmasūtra.* Edited with the commentary of Yaśodhara by M. P. Durgāprasād. Bombay: Nirnaya-Sagara Press, 1900.

Vikramacarita (Siṃhāsanadvātriṃśikā). Edited in four recensions, with an English translation by Franklin Edgerton. Harvard Oriental Series, vols. 26–27. Cambridge: Harvard University Press, 1926.

Viṣṇu Purāṇa. Edited with the commentary of Śrīdhara. Calcutta: Vangavasi Steam Machine Press, 1887.

Viśvanātha Kavirāja. *Sāhityadarpaṇa.* 4th ed. Edited with the commentary of Rāmacaraṇa Tarkavāgīśa Bhattācārya by Gurunath Vidyanidhi and Dhirendranath Bhaṭṭacharya. Calcutta: Sanskrit Book Depot, 1971.

Wright, Arthur F. "Fo-t'u-teng: A Biography." *Harvard Journal of Asian Studies* 11(December 1948): 321–71.

Yeats-Brown, Francis. *The Lives of a Bengal Lancer.* New York: Viking Press, 1930.

Yogavāsiṣṭha. 3d ed. Edited by V. L. S. Pansikar and revised by N. R. Acharya. Bombay: Nirnaya-Sagara Press, 1937.

Yva, Yvon. *Les Fakirs et leurs secrets.* Paris: Gallimard (L'Air du Temps 178), 1963.

Zürcher, E. *The Buddhist Conquest of China.* Sinica Leidensia, Institutum Sinologicum Lugduno-Batavum, vol. 11. Leiden, Holland: Brill, 1972.

BIBLIOGRAPHY

OTHER TEXTS

The following works, although not cited, are relevant to the study of Indian magic and conjuring.

Travel: John Booth, *Wonders of Magic* (Los Alamitos, California: Ridgeway Press, .1986); H. J. Burlingame, *Around the World with a Magician and a Juggler* (Chicago: Clyde, 1891); J. W. Holden, *A Wizard's Wanderings from China to Peru* (London: Dean, 1886); John A. Keel, *Jadoo* (New York: Julian Messner, 1957); H. S. Lynn, *The Adventures of a Strange Man* (London: published by the author, 1873); G. Normanton, *Wandering Around the World* (London: Mortimer Ltd., 1923).

History and Analysis: Milbourne Christopher, *The Illustrated History of Magic* (New York: Thomas Y. Crowell, 1973), and *Panorama of Magic* (New York: Dover, 1962); Edwin A. Dawes, *The Great Illusionists* (Secaucus, N.J.: Chartwell Books, 1979), and "The Indian Jugglers and Their Tricks" (*Magic Circular*, April/May 1977, and June/July 1977); Henry Ridgley Evans, *History of Conjuring and Magic* (Kenton, Ohio: International Brotherhood of Magicians, 1928); V. Farelli, "A Chronological History of Cups and Balls," in *John Ramsay's Routine with Cups and Balls* (London: Armstrong, 1948); Teun Goudriaan, *Maya Divine and Human* (Delhi: Motilal Banarsidass, 1978); Victor Henry, *La magie dans l'Inde antique* (Paris: Editions Ernest Leroux, 1904); M. Hermanns, *Die religiös-magische Weltangschuang der Primitivstämme Indiens* (Wiesbaden: 1966); J. H. Hunt, "Indian Fakirs" (*St. Bartholomew's Hospital Journal* [Oct-Nov-Dec 1934]); Adolf Jacoby, "Zum Zerstückelungs und Wiederbelebungswunder der indischen Fakire" (*Archiv für Religionswissenschaft* [Leipzig] 17 [1914]: 455–75); C. Jacques, "Le monde du sorcier en Inde" (Le monde du sorcier, Sources Orientales 7 [Paris: 1966]); Andrew Lang, "Indian Conjuring" (*The Wizard* 8, no. 21 [May 1907]:331); Alfred Lehmann, "Einige Bemerkungen zu indischen Gaukler-Kunststücken" (*Jarbuch des Museum für Völkerkunde zu Leipzig* 11 [1952]:46–63); Wendy Doniger O'Flaherty, *Dreams, Illusion, and Other Realities* (Chicago: The University of Chicago Press, 1984); Benjamin Robinson, "Indian Magic" (*The Linking Ring* 62, no. 12 [1982]:41–44); Richard Schmidt, *Fakire und Fakirtum im alten und modernen Indien* (Berlin: Verlag von Hermann Barsdorf, 1908); A. V. Subramanian, *The Aesthetics of Wonder: New Findings in Sanskrit Alaṇkāraśāstra* (Delhi: Motilal Banarsidass, 1988); Robert van Gulik, "The Mango Trick in China" (*Transactions of the Asiatic Society of Japan*, 3, no. 3 [1954]: 117–75); Heinrich Zimmer, *Maya, der indische Mythos* (Stuttgart-Berlin: 1936).

Performance: Dai Dexter, *The Feats of Karma* (London: East London Magical Supplies, 1960); Eddie Joseph, *The Hindu Cups and Balls* (New York: Max

BIBLIOGRAPHY

Andrews, 1956), and *Magic and Mysteries of India* (Colon, Mich.: Abbott's Magic Novelty Co., 1941); Joseph Ovette, *Miraculous Hindu Feats* (Oakland, Calif.: Lloyd E. Jones, 1947).

Fiction: Jonathan Fast, *Golden Fire: A Novel of Ancient India* (New York: Arbor House, 1986); Fanny Penny, *The Malabar Magician* (London: Chatto and Windus, 1912); Satyajit Ray, *Fatik et le jongleur de Calcutta* (translated from Bengali into French by France Bhattacharya [Paris: Bourdas, 1981]).

Illustrations

453

ILLUSTRATIONS

Acknowledgments

The great delight of working on this book has been in meeting the many magicians who were willing to talk to me about magic, teach me tricks, and let me come behind the scenes: Abdul Alafrez in Paris, Neil Boisen and Jimmy Yoshida in Hawaii, John Booth in Los Angeles, Patrick Lindley in England, Magic Slim and his Amazing Albino Frog in Chicago; Tayade and Bharucha in Bombay, Premanand and Dayanand in Coimbatore, Professor Bhagyanath and P. K. Ilango in Madras, K. Lal, P. C. Sorcar Junior, and Shyamal Kumar in Calcutta, The Great Mayadhar and the consumately generous Professor Shankar and Shankar Junior in Delhi. Above all, I am grateful to Naseeb and Ayasan Shah and the magicians of Shadipur Depot.

Catherine Cornille, Liz Cuny, Edward Dimock, Jr., Richard Gombrich, Nicholas Murray, Ramdas Lamb, Graham Parkes, Shalini Reys, Alexis Sanderson, Burton Stein, Cheryl Wicker-Siegel, my parents, and my sons—all in different ways—helped me with this enterprise.

I am indebted to the following individuals, publishers, and institutions for permission to reproduce the images that illustrate this book: P. C. Sorcar Junior, William Doerflinger, the Supreme Magic Company, *The Illustrated Weekly of India*, the India Office Library, and Dover Publications.

I would not have been able to conduct research in India if it had not been for the support of the American Institute of Indian Studies; further study was assisted by grants from the Joint Committee on South Asia of the Social Science Research Council and the American Council of Learned Societies, with funds provided by the National Endowment for the Humanities and the Ford Foundation. The University of Hawaii and the Department of Religion of that institution have also been generous in their sponsorship of my work—a Fujio Matsuda scholarship enabled me to finish this project and begin another. In 1988–89 a fellowship from the John Simon Guggenheim Foundation allowed me to write about Indian magic in Paris.